The **Rough Guid**

Devon & Cornwall

written and researched by

Robert Andrews

Contents

Devon and Cornwall on a plate colour section following p.112

The Sea, The Sea... colour section following p.272

◀◀ St Michael's Mount, Penzance ◀

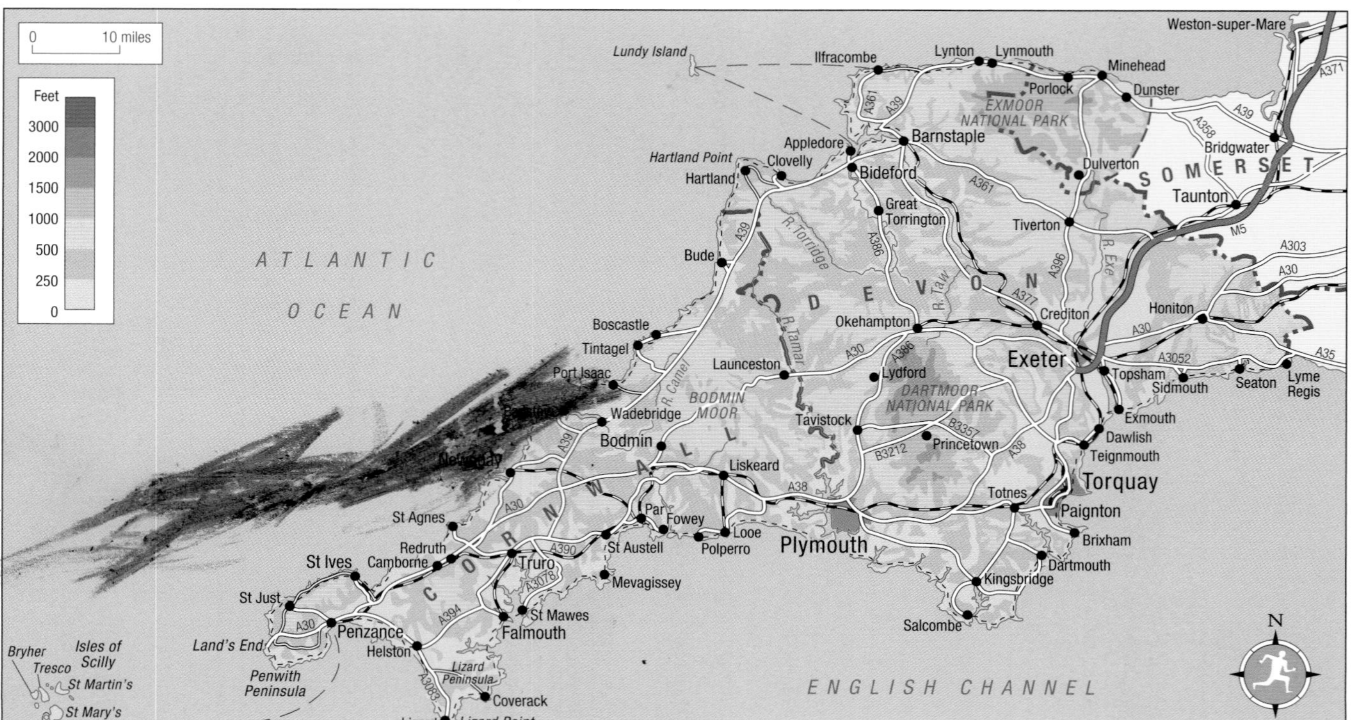
0 10 miles
Feet
3000
2000
1500
1000
500
250
0
ATLANTIC OCEAN
ENGLISH CHANNEL
N
Lundy Island
Weston-super-Mare
Ilfracombe
Lynton
Lynmouth
Minehead
Porlock
Dunster
EXMOOR NATIONAL PARK
Barnstaple
Appledore
Bideford
Bridgwater
SOMERSET
Dulverton
Taunton
Hartland Point
Clovelly
Hartland
Great Torrington
Tiverton
R. Torridge
R. Taw
R. Exe
DEVON
Bude
Okehampton
Crediton
Honiton
Exeter
Topsham
Sidmouth
Seaton
Lyme Regis
Exmouth
Dawlish
Teignmouth
Torquay
Paignton
Brixham
Dartmouth
Totnes
Kingsbridge
Salcombe
Boscastle
Tintagel
Port Isaac
R. Tamar
R. Camel
Launceston
Lydford
DARTMOOR NATIONAL PARK
Princetown
Tavistock
BODMIN MOOR
Wadebridge
Bodmin
Liskeard
Plymouth
CORNWALL
Par
Fowey
Looe
Polperro
St Austell
Mevagissey
St Agnes
Redruth
Camborne
Truro
St Mawes
Falmouth
St Ives
St Just
Penzance
Helston
Land's End
Penwith Peninsula
Lizard Peninsula
Coverack
Lizard
Lizard Point
Isles of Scilly
Bryher
Tresco
St Martin's
St Mary's
A371
A39
A358
A361
A386
A396
A377
A303
A30
A35
A3052
M5
A38
B3357
B3212
A390
A3078
A394
A3083

Introduction to

Devon & Cornwall

Pointing away from England into the Atlantic, the dangling limb of land holding Britain's westernmost counties of Devon and Cornwall has long wielded a powerful attraction for holiday-makers – not to mention second-homers, retirees, artists, writers and anyone keen on rugged landscape and ever-changing coastal scenery. The two counties have a markedly different look and feel: Devon's rolling swards of pasture, narrow lanes and picturesque thatched cottages are a striking contrast to the craggy charms of Cornwall, imbued with a strong sense of Celtic culture. The essential elements, however, are shared: first and foremost of which is the sea – a constant theme and the strongest lure of the place – whether experienced as a restless force raging against rocks and reefs, or as a more serene presence, bathed in rich colours more readily associated with sultry Mediterranean shores.

You're never very far from the coast in Devon and Cornwall, where the panoramic sequence of miniature ports, placid estuaries, embattled cliffs and sequestered bays are linked by one of the region's greatest assets, the **South West Coast Path**, stretching from the seaboard of Exmoor to the Dorset border. Most visitors are primarily drawn to the magnificent **beaches** strewn along the deeply indented coast, ranging from grand sweeps of sand confronting ranks of surfer-friendly rollers to intimate creeks and coves away from the crowds. The **resorts** catering to the armies of beach fans

Fact file

- With an **area** of 2,591 square miles and a **population** of nearly 1,110,000, Devon is almost twice the size of Cornwall, which has an area of 1,376 square miles and a population of a little over half a million.
- The chief administrative **centres** are Exeter in Devon and Truro in Cornwall. Politically, the counties are solidly Conservative and Liberal Democrat in complexion.
- Devon and Cornwall attract more **tourists** than any other area in Britain after London, with each receiving around 5 million visitors per year.
- **Agriculture** suffered long-term damage from the foot-and-mouth epidemic of 2001, but the region still has roughly twice the national average of workers in the fields of agriculture, hunting, forestry and fishing.
- Cornwall had an unemployment rate of 2.6 percent in 2009, in Devon, it was around 2.4 percent – below the national average in both cases. However, the average gross pay in both counties is also below the national average.

▲ The Jubilee Pool, Penzance

that inundate the South West every summer also come in all shapes and sizes, from former fishing villages to full-blown tourist towns offering every facility, and from sedate Victorian watering-holes to spartan beaches backed by caravan parks and hot-dog stalls. It is this sheer diversity which accounts for the region's enduring popularity, and which has made it the destination of travellers since the Napoleonic Wars forced the English to look closer to home for their annual break.

Inland, the peninsula offers a complete contrast with the dramatic wildernesses of Exmoor, Dartmoor and Bodmin Moor, whose appeal extends to outdoor activity enthusiasts as well as to wildlife watchers. Alongside these barren tracts, Devon and Cornwall also boast supreme specimens of English rural life – unsung hamlets off the beaten track, where clustered cottages and brilliant flower displays perfectly complement the lush meadows and tidy dells surrounding them. But even these idyllic places can be invaded and spoiled in high season, and therein lies the rub: the millions of tourists who descend on the M5 motorway every summer are both the economic lifeblood of the West Country and the biggest threat to its beauty and integrity.

Though **tourism** represents a godsend for the local economy at a time when both farming and fishing are in the doldrums, its seasonal nature and fluctuating trends leave many without much backup. Moreover, the demand for second homes and inflated prices have meant that many locals are literally priced out, and you'll find hotels and B&Bs managed and staffed by people with every kind of accent except the local one. The pressures of the holiday industry have also given some places an artificial veneer, apparent in a few of Devon's cosily gentrified villages and Cornwall's quainter fishing ports, where the nostalgia is underpinned by a sharp commercial sense. On the plus side, the South West's popularity has meant that zealous care is taken to preserve some of the prettiest sections of coast and countryside in a more or less "natural" condition, limiting intrusive development and thoughtless exploitation.

Adventure counties

If you're looking for a piece of the action, Devon and Cornwall have it all. The tracts of rugged wilderness inland combine with miles of cliffy coastline and beaches to make the region the destination of choice for adventure enthusiasts of every kind. The region's moors are ideal for **caving, climbing** and **kayaking,** while out to sea, **sailing** and **diving** appeal to beginners and experts alike. New options appear every year, and the popular staples of **riding, hiking, surfing** and **swimming** have been augmented by **coasteering, kitesurfing** and **zipwiring,** among numerous other pursuits. You can rent bikes, surf equipment and canoes, join a guided walk or pony trek, and hone your survival skills. **Adventure centres** scattered throughout the region cater to action addicts, offering day, weekend or week-long sessions. Once the bug bites, you'll be coming back for more.

Where to go

Where you go in Devon and Cornwall will depend on your primary interest. If **beaches** are the priority, you can pick just about any stretch of coast with a guarantee of finding a patch of sand or rocks to swim from. As a rule, the cliffier northern littoral has fewer beaches, though some of these are first choice for surfers, notably at Woolacombe and Croyde in Devon and, in Cornwall, those around Bude, Padstow and Newquay. Devon's most popular seaside towns are on the more

5 best lodgings

Burgh Island Hotel, Bigbury (South Devon) p.121

Mount Tavy Cottage, Tavistock (Dartmoor) p.148

Rocks Hotel, Woolacombe (North Devon) p.204

Tresanton Hotel, St Mawes (South Cornwall) p.245

Troytown Farm campsite, St Agnes (Isles of Scilly) p.312

Literary Cornwall

Cornwall's far-flung position on an extremity of the mainland has attracted and inspired a disparate bunch of writers and poets. **Thomas Hardy**, who as a young architect worked near Boscastle (see p.343), set his novel *A Pair of Blue Eyes* (1873) there, while **Sir Arthur Quiller-Couch**, born in Bodmin, set numerous works in "Troy Town" – actually the river port of Fowey, where he lived from 1892 to 1944. Fowey is also associated with **Daphne du Maurier**, whose "Cornish" works include *Jamaica Inn* (1936), *Rebecca* (1938) and *Frenchman's Creek* (1941). Further west, **Virginia Woolf** spent her summers in St Ives as a child, taking inspiration from Godrevy lighthouse for her novel *To the Lighthouse* (1927) – though she transferred the setting to the Hebrides – while **D.H. Lawrence** moved to nearby Zennor in 1915, where he completed *Women in Love* and dreamed of setting up a writers' colony. The poets **John Betjeman** and **Charles Causley** also had strong Cornish connections – the former spent his childhood around Daymer Bay where he is buried, while the latter was born, lived and is buried in Launceston. More recently, the novelists **Winston Graham** and **Derek Tangye** relied on Cornish settings for, respectively, the "Poldark" series (also televised) and the Minack Chronicles. For a selection of books relating to the region, see p.387.

sheltered southeast-facing coast, where there is superb swimming to the north and south of Torquay, capital of the self-styled "English Riviera". Elsewhere in Devon, you'll find less coming and going around the classic resorts of the East Devon coast, where the predominantly shingle shores are backed by eroded sandstone-red cliffs and interspersed with classic old resorts such as Sidmouth. In Cornwall, crowds home in on St Austell Bay and around Falmouth, but the beaches are more inviting at the western end of the region, where the twin prongs of the Lizard and Penwith peninsulas are liberally studded with small sheltered bays such as Porthcurno and Kynance Cove, as well as more extensive surfing beaches such as Sennen Cove and Poldhu. All, however, pale into insignificance when compared with the dazzling white-sand strands found in abundance on the Isles of Scilly, where the sea can take on a tropical brilliance, though the water temperatures are decidedly chilly.

Likewise, hikers need only head for the nearest coast to find some of the best **walking** in Britain. Circling the entire peninsula, the coast path allows endless opportunities for long-distance or shorter jaunts, and links up with other routes such as the **Tarka Trail**, around **Barnstaple** and **Bideford** in North Devon, and the **Camel Trail**, which weaves inland from the coast at **Padstow** to **Bodmin Moor**. Unsurprisingly, it is the moors that hold the greatest range of paths and bridleways, and of these **Dartmoor** has the densest concentration, though the walks and rides on smaller, more cultivated **Exmoor** should not be discounted.

The pleasures of Devon and Cornwall are not confined to the great outdoors, however. History and culture can be soaked up at the region's main centres, not least at **Exeter**, which features stunning medieval architecture and a first-rate museum. Devon's leading part in England's maritime history is in evidence here and at **Plymouth**, which has preserved its medieval core around the old harbour despite severe bomb damage during World War II. On a smaller scale, the nautical tradition is perpetuated in such estuary ports as **Dartmouth**, **Salcombe** and **Fowey** on the south coast, all favourite anchorages of yachting folk.

The West Country's past is also evident in the numerous ruins scattered throughout the peninsula. These range from the primitive hut circles and Iron Age remains on the moors and even on the remote **Isles of Scilly**, to the various castles of diverse eras – fragmentary but dramatic, as at **Tintagel**, fabled home of King Arthur on the north Cornish coast, or immaculately preserved, such as at **St Mawes** and **Pendennis Castle** in South Cornwall. The region's former wealth, derived above all from mining and wool, is reflected in a rich assortment of stately homes, usually tucked out of sight in splendid countryside, as at **Hartland Abbey**, in North Devon, and **Lanhydrock**, on the edge of Bodmin Moor. The endowments of landowners and merchants helped to fund some of Devon's most striking examples of ecclesiastical architecture, as at **Crediton**, in mid-Devon, while Cornwall's myriad **Methodist chapels** are testament to the markedly different style of popular religion proselytized by John Wesley in the eighteenth century. **Truro**'s twentieth-century cathedral – a bold neo-Gothic statement that has divided local opinion – has, literally, raised the profile of Cornwall's county town.

The region's modernity is well evident a few miles west at **St Ives**, whose branch of the Tate celebrates the various schools of art that colonized the area in the twentieth century. Other flagship

5 best walks

Coast path: Start Point–Bolt Tail (South Devon) pp.116–120
Hike to Hound Tor (Dartmoor) p.136
Circular walk: Allerford–Selworthy Beacon (Exmoor) p.181
Hike to Rough Tor and Brown Willy (Bodmin Moor) p.362
Coast path: St Ives–Land's End (Penwith Peninsula) pp.279–287

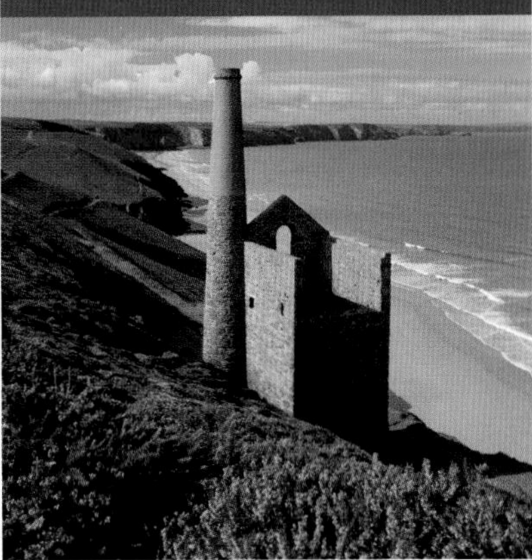
▲ Tin mine, St Agnes, Cornwall

attractions in the region highlight the diversity of the natural environment with an accent on conservation, most famously the ambitious **Eden Project** near St Austell, a clay pit converted into an immense complex of conservatories, marrying technology with ecology on an eye-popping scale.

For many people, however, the magic of Devon and Cornwall lies in the multitude of **remote villages** dotted along the coast, often sandwiched between rocky headlands, where a few fishing vessels still operate and timeless tranquillity sets the tone. There are any number of well-known examples – **Boscastle** and **Port Isaac**, on Cornwall's northern coast, or **Beer** and **Brixham** in South Devon – but the best ones are usually serendipitous discoveries. At the same time, many places have succumbed to their own myth and turned into synthesized versions of the perfect coastal hamlet, as is the case at **Clovelly** in North Devon and **Polperro** in South Cornwall. Drop in on these places when the crowds have gone, however, and you'll find their authentic charm shining through.

5 best gardens

Bicton Park (East Devon) p.79
Lost Gardens of Heligan (South Cornwall) p.238
Rosemoor (North Devon) p.211
Trellisick Garden (South Cornwall) p.246
Tresco Abbey Gardens (Isles of Scilly) p.306

When to go

With the highest average year-round temperatures in Britain, Devon and Cornwall make a viable destination in all seasons. This makes an even more compelling case for avoiding the peak summer months, if at all possible, when your visit will coincide with that of crowds of other holiday-makers. Admittedly, the sea is at its warmest and the possibility of rain at its lowest in July and August, but given the unpredictability of the English climate in any season, it's worth missing the hassle of this period, which sees congested roads and paths, packed beaches and reduced availability for all forms of accommodation. The school holiday period – from late July to early September – is the busiest time, when hotels and guesthouses may raise their room rates and insist on minimum stays of two, three or even seven nights. Other busy periods include the **Easter** holiday and, to a lesser extent, around Christmas and New Year. Individual places can get very busy when a local festival is under way (see pp.33–35). At other times, weekends see most movement, and Saturday in particular – "changeover day" for the weekly renters – is traditionally the worst day for traffic.

On the other hand, don't expect to enjoy all that the peninsula has to offer in the middle of **winter**. Wet weather can ruin any outdoor pursuit, and in the case of walking can be downright risky. This is particularly true on the coast and on the moors, where mists and blinding rain can descend amazingly quickly – note that the moors attract more **rainfall** than other areas: Dartmoor, for example, gets nearly twice as much annually as Torbay, just fifteen miles away. Moreover, attractions, including stately homes, often close during the winter months, and many B&Bs and hotels are also shut between October and Easter, as well as most campsites. Public transport services, too, are severely curtailed. All the same, you can find good weather in winter, when you'll have many places pretty much to yourself, and when experienced surfers appreciate the bigger swells; if you're in the Isles of Scilly, you'll be well placed for the flower harvest – the best time to appreciate the scale of this local industry.

▲ Clovelly

Spring sees the famous plants and shrubs of the peninsula's south coast at their most spectacular, while the turning of the colours in **autumn** is also a visual feast, especially on the moors. However, you'll have to guard against the strong winds which can still blow fairly cold, and only the hardiest will risk swimming in the sea. On balance, the ideal would be to plan your visit between May and late July, before the schools' summer break, or between September and October, when everything is open, but you won't find yourself spending too much of your holiday in a queue.

Average monthly temperatures and rainfall

	Jan	Feb	Mar	Apr	May	Jun	Jul	Aug	Sep	Oct	Nov	Dec
Plymouth												
Max/min (ºF)	47/39	47/38	50/40	54/43	59/47	64/52	66/55	67/55	64/53	58/49	52/44	49/41
Max/min (ºC)	8/4	8/3	10/4	12/6	15/8	18/11	19/13	19/13	18/12	14/9	11/7	9/5
Rainfall (mm)	98	73	68	53	63	53	70	75	78	90	113	108
Newquay												
Max/min (ºF)	47/39	47/38	50/40	53/42	58/47	62/51	66/56	66/56	63/52	58/48	52/43	49/41
Max/min (ºC)	9/4	9/3	10/5	12/5	14/8	17/11	19/13	19/13	17/11	14/9	11/6	9/5
Rainfall (mm)	120	87	81	62	58	65	56	73	90	108	121	121

17 things not to miss

It's not possible to see everything that Devon and Cornwall have to offer in one trip – and we don't suggest you try. What follows is a selective and subjective taste of the region's highlights: outstanding natural features, outdoor activities, festivals, museums, history and beautiful architecture. They're arranged in five colour-coded categories to help you find the very best things to see, do and experience. All entries have a page reference to take you straight into the Guide, where you can find out more.

01 **Isles of Scilly** Page **297** • Although often subject to ferocious Atlantic storms, these isolated islands enjoy above-average sunshine and temperatures, and offer the ultimate getaway.

02 Surfing Page **40** • Some of the country's most alluring surfing strands are arrayed along the north coast and western tip of the peninsula, usually at their best in winter.

03 Exeter Cathedral Page **55** • With its imposing carved west front and immense vaulted ceiling, the cathedral is the region's greatest medieval monument.

04 Fresh seafood Page **31** • Experience the freshest fish cooked in the tastiest ways from a range of eateries a stone's throw from the sea.

05 Beaches of North Cornwall Page **317** • The numerous and varied patches of sand on the North Cornwall coast are wilder and less sheltered than others on the peninsula, but generally more scenic.

06 Walking on the coast path Page **177** • Britain's longest waymarked footpath, the South West Coast Path, is the best way to explore Devon and Cornwall's ever-changing seaboard.

07 Sidmouth Folk Week Page **81** • Folk, roots and other esoteric sounds feature at this good-natured gathering in East Devon's most elegant resort.

08 St Enodoc Page **338** • Deep tranquillity envelops the tiny chapel where poet John Betjeman lies buried, within view of Daymer Bay.

09 Fowey Page **229** • A scenic setting, inspiring walks and great pubs make this Cornish harbour town an agreeable place to linger.

10 Tate St Ives Page **290** • An essential stop for art lovers and anyone else intrigued by the various art colonies established in this seaside town in the last century.

11 Gig-racing Page **302** • A local passion in Cornwall, boat racing in the open sea is one of the highlights of the summer season.

12 Minack Theatre Page **278** • Perched on a cliff-top, this mini-amphitheatre hewn out of the rock makes a memorable venue for drama and music productions.

13 Lanhydrock Page **357** • This stately home on the edge of Bodmin Moor ranks among the region's grandest, not least for its relics of Victorian domestic life and the stunning grounds.

14 St Neot Church Page **364** • Fifteenth-century church on the southern edge of Bodmin Moor, rich in historical detail and boasting fine stained glass.

16 Cornish pasties Page **32** • Follow local advice (or tips in the Guide) to track down the best pasty in town, an essential element of any sojourn in Cornwall.

15 Eden Project Page **233** • The hype, for once, is justified – Eden is everything it's cracked up to be, and well worth a visit. Come early to avoid the crowds.

17 Hiking on Dartmoor Page **125** • Solitude and untrammelled nature are the biggest lures for walkers on southern England's greatest expanse of wilderness.

Basics

Basics

Getting there

Getting to Devon and Cornwall is easily accomplished along one of the main westward-bound road and rail routes. By road, most use the M5 motorway, which swoops south from Birmingham and connects with the M4 from London at Bristol. The M5 terminates at Exeter, from where roads radiate out to different parts of Devon and further west. The A30 offers a slower route from London and Salisbury, extending via Exeter all the way to Land's End. Exeter is also the junction of the two main rail lines – from Salisbury, and from London, the Midlands and Bristol – and is the hub of a network of bus routes throughout Devon. Bus and train travellers from Scotland or Wales might need to change at Birmingham or Bristol. For all rail and bus timetable information, consult Traveline (ⓣ0871/200 2233, ⓦwww.traveline.info).

By bus

National Express buses connect Devon and Cornwall with London, Bristol, Birmingham, Manchester (and Manchester Airport), Newcastle, Sheffield, Southampton and other major centres. Standard ticket prices for all National Express services are slightly reduced if you buy at least seven days in advance, and are subject to a minor increase if you travel on Fridays or, in July and August, on Saturdays, or between December 15 and January 4. Certain services qualify for "fun fares", available online only and as cheap as £5 for specific journeys with advance booking – the earlier you book, the cheaper.

From **London's Victoria Coach Station**, there are ten daily departures to Exeter (4–5hr; £42–48 return); some services carry on to Torquay, Paignton and Totnes. A separate service leaves seven times daily from London Victoria to Plymouth (5hr 30min; £44–52.50 return), with some coaches continuing to St Austell (4 daily; from London around 7hr; £48–57 return), Truro (4 daily; from London 7–8hr; £53–62 return) and Penzance (5 daily; from London 8–9hr; £53–62 return). Ilfracombe, Barnstaple, Bude, Bodmin, Newquay, Falmouth and St Ives are connected by less frequent daily services from London.

From Birmingham, there are up to five buses daily to Exeter (4–5hr; £43–55 return); four daily to Plymouth (5–6hr; £54–69 return); two daily to Penzance (8hr 30min–9hr; £65–79 return), and one daily to Truro (7hr 30min; £65–79 return).

From Bristol, there are five daily buses to Exeter (around 2hr; £19–24 return); four daily to Plymouth (around 3hr; £34–44 return); two daily to Penzance (around 6hr 30min; £49–61 return) and one daily to Truro (5hr 10min; £46–59 return).

Megabus also operates a once-daily bus service westwards from **London's Victoria Coach Station**, stopping at Exeter, Plymouth, Newquay, Redruth and Penzance, and with journey-times similar to those of National Express. Tickets are cheapest when bought in advance, starting as low as £5 for Exeter.

Between June and mid-October, surf enthusiasts and others travelling from London to Newquay can take advantage of the **Big Friday Surf Bus** (ⓣ020/8960 2471, ⓦwww.bigfriday.com) leaving Hammersmith on Friday evening and returning to London on Sunday evening (£69 return).

By train

The cost of tickets varies according to how far ahead you book and the restrictions imposed. There are three types of ticket on UK trains: Advance (limited availability; book up to twelve weeks in advance and before midnight of the previous day, with specified date and time of travel), Off-peak (ie weekday trains not departing from London before 9.30am or between 4.40pm and 6.30pm) and Anytime (completely

Six steps to a better kind of travel

At Rough Guides we are passionately committed to travel. We feel strongly that only through travelling do we truly come to understand the world we live in and the people we share it with – plus tourism has brought a great deal of **benefit** to developing economies around the world over the last few decades. But the extraordinary growth in tourism has also damaged some places irreparably, and of course **climate change** is exacerbated by most forms of transport, especially flying. This means that now more than ever it's important to **travel thoughtfully** and **responsibly**, with respect for the cultures you're visiting – not only to derive the most benefit from your trip but also to preserve the best bits of the planet for everyone to enjoy. At Rough Guides we feel there are six main areas in which you can make a difference:

- Consider what you're contributing to the **local economy**, and how much the services you use do the same, whether it's through employing local workers and guides or sourcing locally grown produce and local services.
- Consider the **environment** on holiday as well as at home. Water is scarce in many developing destinations, and the biodiversity of local flora and fauna can be adversely affected by tourism. Try to patronize businesses that take account of this.
- Travel with a purpose, not just to tick off experiences. Consider **spending longer** in a place, and getting to know it and its people.
- Give thought to how often you **fly**. Try to avoid short hops by air and more harmful night flights.
- Consider **alternatives to flying**, travelling instead by bus, train, boat and even by bike or on foot where possible.
- Make your trips "**climate neutral**" via a reputable carbon offset scheme. All Rough Guide flights are offset, and every year we donate money to a variety of charities devoted to combating the effects of climate change.

open and unrestricted). It may be cheaper to buy two singles online instead of a return, especially for tickets well in advance.

From **London Paddington**, First Great Western run all trains to Exeter, Plymouth and Penzance, with roughly one departure hourly. Journey time to **Exeter St David's** is two to three and a half hours, and standard-class tickets cost around £34–60 for an Advance return, £65 for an Off-peak return and £199 for an Anytime return. Services from London to **Plymouth**, taking 3–4hr, cost £32–70 for an Advance, £72 for Off-peak, £230 for Anytime (all return fares). You can reach **Penzance** from London Paddington in five or six hours, with Advance return tickets costing £33–80, Off-peak returns £83, and Anytime returns £239; advance single tickets can be as low as £13.50.

From **London Waterloo**, South West Trains take slightly longer – around three and a quarter hours – to reach Exeter, running via Salisbury (where you may need to change) and Honiton in East Devon, but are cheaper: £27–62 for an Advance return, £58 for an Off-peak return, £113 for an Anytime return. Advance one-way tickets can be as low as £12. **Megatrain** uses South West Trains for its discounted service to Exeter, running just once or twice daily (not Sun); tickets, best booked online, cost as little as £15 one way according to availability.

CrossCountry operates train services from Birmingham New Street Station to Exeter in around two and a half hours, charging £33–92 for an Advance return, £71 for an Off-peak return, £123 for an Anytime return. From Birmingham, Cross-Country also runs services to Plymouth in around three hours forty minutes, with Advance tickets costing £39–127, Off-peak £94, and Anytime £169 (all return fares). To Penzance, trains take about five hours forty minutes; Advance return tickets cost £49–177, Off-peak returns £118, and Anytime returns are £210.

From Paddington, **bikes** are carried free on First Great Western trains, but reservations are essential between 7–10am and 3–7pm, and are advised in any case due to restricted availability. From Waterloo, South West Trains carry bikes for free but only allow two to six bikes per train and they need booking at least 24 hours ahead. Bikes cannot be carried with a Megatrain ticket. On services from Birmingham, CrossCountry doesn't charge a fee but can only carry two bikes making advance reservations highly recommended. For information on taking bikes on trains within Devon and Cornwall, see p.23.

By car

Although drivers from **Salisbury** may be on the A30 or the faster A303 (which branches off the London–Southampton M3), the most direct route into Devon and Cornwall by car is along the **M5** motorway, which runs to Exeter from Birmingham, and links with the M4 from London outside Bristol. You can calculate around ninety minutes' driving between Bristol and Exeter, depending on the volume of traffic. Bank holiday weekends and high summer see intense traffic, particularly on the M5 around Bristol. Saturday is "changeover day", when holiday-makers on weekly rentals clog up the roads in and around the region, and should be avoided if possible. You can get up-to-date **information** on bottlenecks and other possible delays from the **AA** (Ⓣ0906/888 4322, or 84322 from mobile phones, Ⓦwww.theaa.com) and **RAC** (Ⓣ0900/344 4999 or 64644 from mobile phones, Ⓦwww.rac.co.uk); calls cost around 60p per minute. Both organizations also provide a route-planning service. It's also worth tuning in to local radio stations for traffic news – frequencies are posted up at the side of major roads (and see p.43).

If you want to reduce fuel costs, you might consider joining one of two nationwide **liftshare** schemes, which put members in touch with others travelling the same way. Contact National CarShare (Ⓣ0871/871 8880, Ⓦwww.nationalcarshare.co.uk) or visit the Liftshare website (Ⓦwww.liftshare.org).

Ferries and flights

Travellers from France and Spain can cross over to Plymouth by **ferry** with Brittany Ferries (Ⓣ0871/244 0744, Ⓦwww.brittany-ferries.co.uk) from Roscoff in Brittany (5–12 weekly; 6–8hr) and Santander in Spain (1 weekly; 20hr).

Exeter, Plymouth and Newquay have the region's main airports for anyone intending to **fly** to the South West. There are scheduled flights **to Exeter International Airport** (Ⓣ01392/367433, Ⓦwww.exeter-airport.co.uk) from Leeds-Bradford, Manchester, Newcastle and Norwich in England; Aberdeen, Edinburgh and Glasgow in Scotland; Jersey and Guernsey in the Channel Islands; Belfast and Dublin in Ireland, and various European airports in Austria, France, Germany, the Netherlands and Spain; all are run by Flybe (Ⓣ0871/700 2000, Ⓦwww.flybe.com).

Air Southwest (Ⓣ0870/241 8202, Ⓦwww.airsouthwest.com) operates frequent flights **to Plymouth City Airport** (Ⓣ01752/204090, Ⓦwww.plymouthairport.com) from Bristol, Cork (Ireland), Glasgow, Jersey, Leeds-Bradford, London City, London Gatwick, Manchester and Newcastle. Air Southwest also operates regular flights **to Newquay Airport** (Ⓣ01637/860600, Ⓦwww.newquaycornwallairport.com) from Bristol, Cork, Dublin, Glasgow, Leeds-Bradford, London City, London Gatwick, Manchester and Newcastle; Ryanair (Ⓦwww.ryanair.com) flies to Newquay from London Stansted; bmibaby (Ⓣ0905/828 2828, Ⓦwww.bmibaby.com) from Birmingham and Manchester; Flybe (see above) from Edinburgh, Isle of Man and London Gatwick, and Jet2.com (Ⓣ0871/226 1737, Ⓦwww.Jet2.com) also flies from Belfast and Leeds-Bradford. Most Newquay flights are summer-only.

Fares vary greatly, according to specific dates and how far in advance you book; for example, a one-way flight from London to Newquay can cost £30–160, flight-time around one hour. Consult the websites for the right numbers if calling the airlines from abroad.

Transport operators and information

Cornwall Public Transport Information ⓣ0300/123 4222, ⓦwww.cornwallpublictransport.info. Cornwall County Council's public transport information service.
CrossCountry ⓣ0844/811 0124, ⓦwww.crosscountrytrains.co.uk.
Devonbus ⓣ01392/382800, ⓦwww.devon.gov.uk/buses. Devon County Council's public transport information service.
First ⓣ0845/600 1420, ⓦwww.firstgroup.com/ukbus/southwest/devon. For First bus schedules throughout the region.
First Great Western ⓣ0845/700 0125, ⓦwww.firstgreatwestern.co.uk. For First train schedules and to purchase tickets.
Megabus/Megatrain ⓣ0900/160 0900, ⓦwww.megabus.com.
National Express ⓣ0871/781 8181, ⓦwww.nationalexpress.com.
National Rail Enquiries ⓣ0845/748 4950, ⓦwww.nationalrail.co.uk. For all train timetables, information on passes and ticket purchase.
South West Trains ⓣ0845/600 0650, ⓦwww.southwesttrains.co.uk.
Stagecoach ⓣ01392/427711, ⓦwww.stagecoachbus.com/southwest. For Stagecoach bus services in the region.
Traveline ⓣ0871/200 2233, ⓦwww.traveline.info.
Western Greyhound ⓣ01637/871871, ⓦwww.westerngreyhound.com. For Western Greyhound bus services in North Cornwall.

Getting around

While your own vehicle can seem like a cumbersome burden in Devon and Cornwall's towns and villages, which are prone to traffic snarl-ups, a car does provide the freedom to explore more remote parts of the region and avoids being at the mercy of sporadic public transport timetables, which can be woefully limited in some of the most attractive areas of the region. There are viable alternatives to cars both for longer and shorter journeys, however, not least the various walking and cycling routes that traverse the peninsula. Additionally, you may need to make use of a sketchy network of ferries; there's also the option of flying to the Isles of Scilly or Lundy. Although general points are covered below, you'll find detailed listings of transport schedules and frequencies at the end of each chapter in the Guide. Comprehensive transport timetables for the region are listed in booklets available free from tourist offices and travel shops. For local and national rail, bus and National Express timetable information, consult Traveline (ⓣ0871/200 2233, ⓦwww.traveline.info).

By train

The **train network** in Devon and Cornwall is a mere shadow of the system that covered the region in Victorian times. The main spine survives today, running from Exeter through Plymouth, Bodmin and Truro to Penzance, and this provides a quick and efficient way to travel through the peninsula. With rare exceptions (such as Bodmin Parkway), stations are centrally located. A few **branch lines** remain, too, providing unique opportunities to see some of the region's most scenic parts; all are operated by First Great Western. From Exeter, a frequent service runs the brief distance south alongside the Exe estuary to Exmouth, while **Tarka Line** trains run northwest to Barnstaple, making a handy link to mid- and North Devon. From Plymouth, the **Tamar Valley Line** runs north to Gunnislake, close to a cluster of sights as well as to Dartmoor. In Cornwall, the **Looe Valley Line** links

Liskeard, on the main line, with Looe, on the south coast, while from Par in St Austell Bay, a branch line goes northwest to Newquay. The **Maritime Line** runs between Truro and Falmouth, and the St Ives Bay Line constitutes one of the most beautiful West Country tracks, running from St Erth (the last stop on the main line before Penzance) along the Hayle estuary to St Ives. The website Ⓦwww.greatscenicrailways.com includes timetables for six of these branch lines.

There are a few restored **private lines** running in summer and school holidays, too, chiefly the **Paignton & Dartmouth Steam Railway** (see p.106), tracing the Dart estuary from Torbay to Kingswear, which is connected by ferry to Dartmouth, and the **South Devon Railway** (see p.112) between Totnes and Buckfastleigh on the edge of Dartmoor. They're touristy but fun, and provide useful links in the transport network.

Although they're not valid on the private lines, **rail passes** are a worthwhile investment if you're going to make regular use of the trains. Covering Devon, Cornwall and places east as far as Gloucester, Bath and Salisbury, a **Freedom of the South West Rover** allows three days' travel in seven at a cost of £70, or eight days' travel in fifteen at £95, while a **Freedom of Devon and Cornwall Rover** is £40 for three days' travel in seven, £60 for eight days' in fifteen. A **Devon Day Ranger** is valid for one day's travel throughout Devon and costs £10; a **Devon Evening Ranger** for use after 6.30pm costs £5. A **Ride Cornwall Ranger** allows one day's travel on trains as well as most buses in Cornwall and costs £10 for adults, £24 for a family (up to two adults and three children). A **Branch Line Ranger** is good for a day's travel on one of the peninsula's branch lines (£3.30–7.50). A further discount on all these passes is given for holders of a Young Person's, Senior or Disabled Railcard. The passes, which are generally not valid for weekday travel before 9am, can be obtained from any staffed train station.

Bikes can be carried for free on all trains, though as availability is usually limited to just two spaces, reservations at least 24 hours beforehand are recommended.

By bus

While National Express provides a long-distance service linking the main centres of Devon and Cornwall, the chief companies running **bus services** in Devon are Stagecoach and First, and in Cornwall, First and Western Greyhound (mainly in North Cornwall). Most villages in the region are covered at least once daily, though others, for example on the moors or on remote sections of coast, may be visited just once or twice weekly, or on school days only.

Day-return **tickets** are cheaper than two singles, and family tickets for up to two adults and three children are also discounted. If you're going to be using buses extensively, you might want to consider buying a **pass**: an Explorer ticket covering travel on the complete Stagecoach South West network for one day (£6.50) or a Megarider Gold covering all Stagecoach South West services for a week (£22); there are also cheaper versions covering local areas. The FirstDay Southwest ticket covering travel on First buses throughout Devon and Cornwall during one day costs £6.70 for off-peak travel, while versions covering just Devon or Cornwall cost £6.50 each. FirstWeek tickets allow a week's travel on First buses in either Devon or Cornwall for £31, and FirstMonth covers both counties for a month for £86. There are also local versions of the day and week passes available for North Devon, Dartmouth, Tavistock, Plymouth and Penzance. Day Rover tickets are also available for travel on Western Greyhound services (£7), and can be used on Stagecoach Devon and Hookways services. The Ride Cornwall Ranger (see above) also covers bus and train travel. You can buy all the passes listed here at some travel agents and tourist offices, and on board the bus. Note, too, that students can use their NUS cards to travel at the children's price.

By car

Though a **car** is often the fastest way to get around Devon and Cornwall, the nature of the region's roads and the level of summer traffic mean that you may often get entangled in irritating hold-ups. The peninsula's three **main roads** – the A39, running along the north coast; the A30, which cuts through the middle as far as Land's End; and the A38, which takes the southern route through Plymouth, joining the A30 near Bodmin – can get seriously clogged in holiday season, with caravans and camper vans adding to the congestion. As soon as you leave the main roads, you'll often find yourself in narrow, winding country lanes, flanked by high hedges and with minimal visibility, often used by farm vehicles and where a low speed is unavoidable. Other rural hazards include horses and riders, straying sheep and ponies, and hunt followers on the moors.

If you're driving, you'll often find that the best policy is to deposit your vehicle at the first available car park whenever you reach a destination – negotiating convoluted one-way systems while trying to map-read can be a nightmare and parking spaces on streets are few and far between. **Car parks**, though, are relatively cheap; most are pay-and-display, so a small cache of change is a useful item to have to hand.

Car rental companies are distributed throughout the region; a selection of them are detailed in the Guide. The companies listed here have branches in Exeter, Plymouth, Newquay, Falmouth and Penzance. Prices start at around £120 per week. Alternatively, consider renting a **camper van**, a more expensive option but you'll save money on accommodation. Local operators include O'Connors Campers (Ⓣ01837/659599, Ⓦwww.oconnorscampers.co.uk), South West Camper Hire (Ⓣ01392/811931, Ⓦwww.swcamperhire.com) and Classic Campervan Hire (Ⓣ0800/970 9147, Ⓦwww.classiccampervanhire.co.uk); prices range from £350–700 per week.

Telephone numbers for **taxis** are provided for the major centres. Contact BioTravel (Ⓦwww.biotravel.co.uk) for eco-friendly **biodiesel** taxis and minibus hire in the Newquay area.

National car rental companies

Avis Main office Ⓣ0844/581 0147; Exeter office Ⓣ0844/544 6015, Ⓦwww.avis.co.uk.
Europcar Exeter office Ⓣ01392/363520, Ⓦwww.europcar.co.uk.
Hertz Main office Ⓣ0870/844 8844; Exeter office Ⓣ0870/850 7196, Ⓦwww.hertz.co.uk.
Holiday Autos Ⓣ0871/472 5229, Ⓦwww.holidayautos.co.uk.
Thrifty Main office Ⓣ01494/751500; Exeter office Ⓣ01392/207207, Ⓦwww.thrifty.co.uk.

By bike

A significant stretch of the **National Cycle Network** links Bristol and Bath with Land's End in Cornwall, making biking through the region a particularly attractive possibility. Known as the **West Country Way**, the Bristol–Padstow route connects and overlaps with the **Cornish Way**, which runs between Bude and Land's End. Parts of the West Country Way run along the **Tarka Trail** in North Devon, and the **Camel Trail**, which runs between Bodmin Moor and the Camel estuary at Padstow, two first-class walking and cycling routes. The West Country Way also connects with the **Devon Coast to Coast** route, running across the peninsula between Ilfracombe and Plymouth (much of it on disused railway lines and along the western flank of Dartmoor) and the **Cornwall Coast to Coast** route between Portreath and Devoran. Other **cycleways** have been developed on the **Mineral Tramways** in Cornwall's mining country (see p.321) and the **Clay Trails** around St Austell and the Eden Project (see p.235).

For more information on the West Country and Cornish Ways, and on the entire National Cycle Network, contact **Sustrans** (Ⓣ0845/113 0065, Ⓦwww.sustrans.org.uk). See Ⓦwww.devon.gov.uk/cycling and www.visitcornwall.com for cycling in the region, including information on rental, routes and accommodation along the way. Bike **rental outlets** are found throughout the region, especially around the main trails. A selection are included in the Guide; expect to pay around £15 per day including helmet; a deposit and proof of identity are usually required.

See p.23 for information on carrying bikes on trains in Devon and Cornwall.

By boat

With its long coastline and profusion of rivers, the Southwest peninsula has a number of **ferry** services, which can save long detours by road or on foot, and often link up with train routes. Some are equipped just for foot-passengers and bicycles, for example the Exe estuary crossing between **Exmouth** and **Starcross** (see p.76) and the tourist service between **Fowey** and **Mevagissey** (see p.229); others transport cars, such as the **Dartmouth–Kingswear** crossing (see p.113), and the **King Harry Ferry** on the Roseland Peninsula (see p.246). A network of passenger ferries links **Truro**, **Falmouth** and **St Mawes** in and around the Carrick Roads estuary (details at ⓣ01872/861914, ⓦwww.falriverlinks.co.uk).

Between around Easter and October, there's a regular boat service **to the Isles of Scilly** (see Chapter 10) from Penzance operated by Isles of Scilly Travel (ⓣ0845/710 5555, ⓦwww.islesofscilly-travel.co.uk), and **to Lundy Island** (see p.218) from Ilfracombe and Bideford by Lundy Island Ferries (ⓣ01271/863636, ⓦwww.lundyisland.co.uk).

On foot

Britain's longest national trail, the **South West Coast Path** tracks the peninsula's coast all the way round from Minehead in Somerset to Poole in Dorset, and offers an unrivalled way to experience coast and sea. The path was conceived in the 1940s, but it is only in the last thirty years that – barring a few significant gaps – the full 630-mile route has been open, much of it on land owned by the National Trust, and all of it well signposted with the acorn symbol shared by all national trails. Local shops stock **maps** of the route (the 1:25,000 *Explorer* series is the most useful) and there are several guides giving detailed directions, including a series of four describing different stretches of the path which include Ordnance Survey maps; simply called *South West Coast Path*, they're published by Aurum Press (ⓣ020/7284 7160, ⓦwww.aurumpress.co.uk), and are also obtainable from Amazon (ⓦwww.amazon.co.uk). Walkers should get a reliable local **weather** check from a nearby tourist office before setting out each day, and carry waterproofs and rations; solid footwear is important, since even the gentlest coastal sections cross uneven ground.

Consult the official website, ⓦwww.southwestcoastpath.com, for general information and updates on the route; various other websites offer route descriptions and news updates, for example ⓦwww.explorethesouthwestcoastpath.co.uk. The **South West Coast Path Association** (ⓣ01752/896237, ⓦwww.swcp.org.uk) publishes an annual guide to the route, costing £10.50 including postage; though lacking much detail in its descriptions and maps, it's more up to date than other guides, and includes practical information such as **tide tables** (these can also be bought from local tourist offices, newsagents, souvenir shops and bookstores for around £1). The South Devon stretch in particular needs careful timing, as there are six ferries to negotiate and one ford to cross between Plymouth and Exmouth. **Accommodation**, which is relatively plentiful along the way, should also be booked ahead. Even campsites can fill up, though campers have the flexibility of asking farmers for permission to pitch in a corner of a field.

The South West Coast Path also touches on other long-distance paths in the region, including the **Saints' Way**, linking Cornwall's coasts between Padstow and Fowey, and the **Two Moors Way**, which connects Exmoor and Dartmoor between Lynmouth and Ivybridge. Local tourist offices have route maps of both, and you can write to the Two Moors Way Association (63 Higher

Devon and Cornwall mileage chart

	Exeter	Penzance	Plymouth	Torquay	Truro
Exeter	–	120	42	23	94
Penzance	120	–	78	102	26
Plymouth	42	78	–	24	52
Torquay	23	102	24	–	76
Truro	94	26	52	76	–

Coombe Drive, Teignmouth TQ14 9NL; Ⓦwww.twomoorsway.org.uk) for an accommodation list (£1.50 including postage) or the official guide (£4.99 including postage), which is also available from local tourist offices.

Tours

Taking a **tour** allows you to see and learn a lot quickly with minimum effort. Most are conducted in minibuses by guides who possess an expert knowledge of the area and mix personal experience with history and context. Some of the best focus on individual **themes**, such as the archeology of Penwith, Arthurian links in Cornwall and wildlife on the moors, giving you a deeper insight into one particular area, and a new angle on the region as a whole. Specialist tours tend to change frequently, but local tourist offices can update you on what's currently on offer.

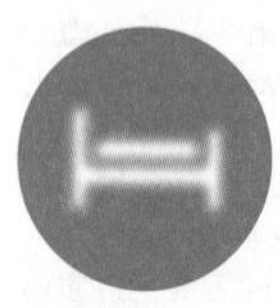

Accommodation

You'll find a fantastic range of accommodation to suit every pocket and taste throughout the region. Nonetheless, rooms can be scarce in high season. At peak periods – Christmas/New Year, Easter, public holidays and all school holidays (particularly the six-week summer break from late July to early Sept) – you should always book ahead. Many establishments will insist on a minimum three-day or week-long stay at peak periods. Single rooms can be hard to come by at any time of year. If you're economizing, hostels, university rooms, campsites and camping barns are all options. Local tourist offices will sometimes make bookings in hotels and B&Bs over the phone, for which a deposit (normally ten percent) is charged and later deducted from your bill. Tourist offices are usually abreast of vacancies, and when offices are closed, a list of nearby possibilities may be pinned up on the door. There are also several dedicated websites listing all kinds of accommodation with the option of booking online (see p.44). Note that smoking is banned in all hotels and B&Bs, though it may be allowed in the garden.

Hotels and B&Bs

Most ubiquitous of the accommodation options in the West Country are **B&Bs**, often quite modest private homes with a couple of rooms available. On the whole these offer more personal service than more expensive places; owners are usually friendly and informative, and will often give you a fairer picture of a place than the tourist office can. As a rule, B&Bs (also known as guesthouses) are cheapest where they're remotely located; some of the best deals are on rural farms, where prices can be as little as £20 per person; more commonly, prices start at around £25 per person in double or twin rooms, with singles paying a supplement. Rooms at this price usually have tea- and coffee-making facilities and a TV, though for en-suite bathrooms you'll usually pay a few pounds more – and even then these may amount to little more than a cupboard with a toilet and shower. Rooms with shared facilities (often described as "standard" rooms) will sometimes have a sink.

There's a great uniformity of style in B&Bs; most are decked out in either functional or chintzy furnishings and offer identical breakfasts of juice, toast, cereals, a fry-up ("Full English Breakfast") and tea or coffee. Amenities are generally minimal, though some have guest lounges and gardens, and some provide evening meals. Breaking the

Accommodation price codes

Throughout this book, hotel and B&B accommodation is coded on a scale of ❶ to ❾, the code indicating the **lowest price** you can expect to pay per night for a double room in high season. The prices indicated by the codes are as follows:

❶ **£39 and under** (very basic accommodation with shared bathroom facilities)

❷ **£40–49** (expect small, plainly furnished rooms with shared bathrooms)

❸ **£50–59** (nothing fancy, but usually perfectly adequate accommodation, sometimes with private bathrooms)

❹ **£60–69** (for this price you should get decent rooms, private facilities and a good location)

❺ **£70–89** (comfortable en-suite accommodation, usually with parking space and dining facilities)

❻ **£90–109** (rooms with views, superior service and all the trimmings)

❼ **£110–149** (spacious rooms with elegant furnishings, quality food and plenty of extras)

❽ **£150–199** (in the luxury class: hotels in this category may have grounds with swimming pools and other sports, health and cosmetic services)

❾ **£200 and over** (the sky's the limit – and you might even get a helipad!)

mould, the region has seen an increase in upmarket "**boutique**" **B&Bs**, where guests can expect all the comforts and style of a chic hotel but in a more intimate, informal setting. In most places, you're expected to vacate your room by 10 or 11am for cleaning whether or not you're staying a second night.

Hotels in Devon and Cornwall come in all shapes and sizes. Many are little more than B&Bs with fire doors, some are dismally furnished and tawdry, while others are the acme of comfort, character and class. On the whole, though, you can expect at least a bar, restaurant and parking space; some places offer a pool, gym or games room at correspondingly higher prices. Designer-led **boutique hotels** can be found in seaside or rural locations, often marketed at urbanites on weekend breaks (and therefore often booked up at weekends). The best ones are listed in the Guide. Some more upmarket retreats offer **spa breaks** and various therapy and **beauty treatments** for some serious pampering – contact tourist offices for details of local establishments. Foodies and weekend-breakers will also be interested in the growing number of "**restaurants with rooms**" in the region – essentially quality restaurants which have two or three guest rooms available. These are usually of a high standard with prices to match, but staying over lets you off a late-night drive at the end of a meal, and you're virtually guaranteed a top-notch breakfast!

Tariffs in hotels and B&Bs reflect the level of comfort, their location and the season. Within the same establishment, rooms with panoramic views or four-poster beds generally cost more, while most hotels and some B&Bs increase their rates in summer. Hotels in particular often dispense with fixed tariffs altogether, and quote rates according to availability and demand. Low-season, midweek and last-minute bookings can be especially good value. Most hotels and B&Bs additionally offer discounts for stays of two or more nights, or "special breaks" – usually referring to packages including meals – and in B&Bs and smaller hotels these can often be negotiated. In any case, the combined dinner, bed and breakfast rates offered by numerous hotels and some B&Bs can work out to be an excellent deal. In some places, particularly in rural areas or on the Isles of Scilly, half- or full-board is obligatory, especially in summer. All hotels and pubs, and an increasing number of B&Bs, accept **credit cards** – we've noted in the Guide all establishments that don't.

Hostels and bunkhouses

There are 22 official **YHA youth hostels** in the area covered by this Guide, and we've listed them all at the relevant places in the text. Outside the cities, many close during the winter months but may open for groups with advance booking. Even in season (from around Easter to Sept), it's always advisable to call ahead to check opening and availability – they are often booked up weeks in advance, particularly in summer and at weekends, with groups sometimes booking an entire hostel. You'll find the majority of the hostels clean, and many are well equipped with laundries, internet access and bike rental; most have canteens and/or **self-catering** facilities. On the minus side, most places still operate a curfew and are closed during the day.

Sleeping arrangements are pretty similar in all hostels: **dormitories** rarely have more than eight bunk beds, most are en suite and there are usually twin and family rooms available. Expect to pay around £18 for a dorm bed, less in winter, or a little more per person for a double; bed linen is free, but towels are not provided. Membership of the **Youth Hostel Association** is required to stay in their hostels; this costs £15.95 per year (£9.95 for under-26s) with good-value family rates; contact the YHA (Ⓣ01629/592700, Ⓦwww.yha.org.uk), or join online or at one of the hostels. Most members of hostelling associations in other countries have automatic membership of the YHA. **Non-members** can stay at hostels by buying temporary membership, costing £3 per person per night (£1.50 for under-18s).

While YHA hostels may often be located in highly scenic spots, **accessibility** can be a problem when they are hidden away in remote rural settings that are difficult, if not impossible, to reach by public transport. Most of the **independent hostels**, on the other hand, are conveniently located in the centres of towns and villages, and they usually stay open all year. They have a less institutional atmosphere, but may offer as good a range of facilities – kitchen, laundry, internet access and bike rental – as you'll find in the YHA hostels. On the downside, they can sometimes be scruffy, and you might not be comfortable with the fact that dorms are sometimes mixed-sex. **Prices** are usually lower than those at YHA hostels, with discounts negotiable for longer stays, and linen is usually supplied for an extra £1 or so per stay. The website Ⓦwww.independenthostelguide.co.uk and publication *Independent Hostel Guide*, available for £4.95 (plus £1 post and packing) from Backpackers Press, Speedwell House, Upperwood, Matlock Bath, Derbyshire DE4 3PE (Ⓣ01629/580427), contain selective listings of independent hostels, and the backpackers' website Ⓦwww.backpaxmag.com and magazine *Backpax*, published three times a year and usually available from the hostels themselves, in tourist spots or on subscription (£6), have news on hostels in the West Country, as well as tours, employment opportunities, surf and other activities. The US-based site, Ⓦwww.hostels.com, also has information on and reviews of hostels worldwide, including Devon and Cornwall, and allows you to book online.

Often located on remote moorland, **bunkhouses** make useful bases for outdoor pursuits. Some are run by the YHA, others are annexed to pubs or campsites, and they can range from basic dorms with cooking and bathroom facilities to swish, fully equipped and well-heated rooms. Most will provide bed linen, but check. Always call ahead, as they're often used by groups.

Self-catering

Self-catering holiday properties can be a cheaper alternative to hotels and B&Bs, while others are chic and luxurious, with prices at the top of the scale. There are literally thousands of properties on offer, ranging from flats by the sea to rustic barn conversions, though many of the best are booked a year in advance. **Prices** can range from £200 to over £1500 a week, according to size and season, and usually include bed linen and towels. In high season, most are rented by the week only – Saturday to Saturday – though some operate more flexible rental periods, and three-night breaks are often available.

The companies listed below will send out **brochures** with photos and full details of individual properties; the info is generally available on the website as well. Local tourist offices, newspapers and notice boards are also worth consulting. For something a little different you might consider renting a **yurt** for a week; a number of places offer these

fully insulated and equipped Mongolian-style tents accommodating two to four people, for example Yurtworks (ⓣ01208/850670, ⓦwww.yurtworks.co.uk), on Bodmin Moor, and Plan-it Earth (ⓣ01736/810660, ⓦwww.plan-itearth.org.uk), near Penzance.

Holiday property agencies

Beach Retreats ⓣ01637/861005, ⓦwww.beachretreats.co.uk. Upmarket and contemporary holiday homes close to North Cornwall beaches.

Breakwater Holidays ⓣ01288/352338, ⓦwww.breakwater-holidays.co.uk. Specializes in quality contemporary holiday accommodation in North Cornwall.

Cartwheel Holidays ⓣ01392/877842, ⓦwww.cartwheel.org.uk. Directory of farmhouse and other rural breaks throughout the region.

Classic Cottages ⓣ01326/555555, ⓦwww.classic.co.uk. Country properties throughout the West Country.

Coast and Country Cottages ⓣ01548/843773 (bookings), ⓦwww.coastandcountry.co.uk. Holiday lodgings in Devon's South Hams district, from barn conversions to waterside apartments.

Cornish Cottage Holidays ⓣ01326/573808, ⓦwww.cornishcottageholidays.co.uk. Thatched cottages and seaside nooks galore.

Cornish Farm Holidays ⓣ0845/602 8843, ⓦwww.cornish-farms.co.uk. Farm properties to rent and B&B on farms across Cornwall.

Cornish Traditional Cottages ⓣ01208/821666, ⓦwww.corncott.com. Self-catering properties throughout the county.

Devon Farms ⓣ0870/225 0079, ⓦwww.devonfarms.co.uk. Self-catering accommodation and B&B on farms throughout Devon.

Forest Holidays ⓣ0845/130 8225, ⓦwww.forestholidays.co.uk. Modern woodland cabins near Liskeard.

Helpful Holidays ⓣ01647/433593, ⓦwww.helpfulholidays.com. Dartmoor-based company, offering everything from apartments to manor houses throughout the West Country.

Hoseasons Holidays ⓣ01502/502588, ⓦwww.hoseasons.co.uk. Self-catering properties available country-wide, in country lodges, cottages and caravans on holiday parks.

Mullion Cottages ⓣ01326/240333, ⓦwww.mullioncottages.com. Properties on the Lizard peninsula.

National Trust Holiday Cottages ⓣ0844/800 2070, ⓦwww.nationaltrustcottages.co.uk. More than 150 National Trust lodgings are available in the West Country.

Unique Home Stays ⓣ01637/881942, ⓦwww.uniquehomestays.com. High-end accommodation in luxury holiday homes – especially good for house parties or groups – as well as in boutique hotels and B&Bs, for three nights or a week.

Campsites and camping barns

Camping is popular throughout Devon and Cornwall, and you'll find sites in most coastal areas and inland. Many are mega-parks dominated by caravans and motorhomes, but the ones we've recommended in the Guide are mainly smaller-scale and tent-friendly. Most are closed in the winter months (usually Oct–May) though smaller sites attached to farms or pubs often stay open – always ring first, however. Busier sites sometimes require a minimum two-night stay at peak weekends. The website ⓦwww.ukcampsite.co.uk is useful for locating sites, allowing you to narrow your search to specific requirements, and also has up-to-date reviews. **Prices** vary from £5–10 for pitches in farmers' fields to £25 per pitch for the best-equipped places, which may have a pool, nightclub and on-site store. Some YHA hostels (Penzance, Land's End, Coverack and Okehampton, in the region) also offer camping facilities, charging half the adult dormitory price, or around £10 per person. Campers can use all the hostel's other facilities, including the kitchen (if one is available). Always book ahead, as camping places are restricted. Other campsites also fill up quickly in high season.

Another popular option on or around Dartmoor and Exmoor is **camping barns**, usually rudimentary but weather-tight bunkhouses fitted with showers, toilets and often with basic self-catering facilities. Costing from around £6 per night, most are run by, or associated with, the YHA (see p.28), which can supply a full list (also on the YHA website); you don't need to be a YHA member to stay in a camping barn. Bed linen and blankets are usually available, but most people just roll out their sleeping bag and bed-mat. Camping barns are often rented out to groups, so always call first. Places in YHA-affiliated barns can be booked by phoning ⓣ01629/592700; for others, call the numbers printed in the Guide.

By and large, **camping rough**, or **"wild camping",** is not so easy. Most land is privately owned and on most of the rest – for instance on parkland or National Trust property – it's illegal, though it's always worth asking around, as some easy-going farmers will provide a pitch. Expect a hostile reception if you camp without asking. On Dartmoor, you are allowed to camp out for a maximum of two nights as long as you're out of sight of houses and at least 100m away from roads, away from reservoirs and archeological sites, and not on farmland or on certain commons, as specified on the website Ⓦwww.dartmoor-npa.gov.uk, where you can download a useful map showing all camping options (also available as a leaflet). Open fires are forbidden, but you can use stoves, taking due care especially after a spell of dry weather. Free camping is not allowed on the other moors unless permission by landowners is granted first, and overnight camping in any of the region's car parks is also prohibited.

Food and drink

The foodie revolution that has swept Britain in the last few years has found particularly fertile ground in the West Country. Eating out in Devon and Cornwall has improved immeasurably as a result, and it's now possible to find a wide range of quality restaurants – several of them Michelin-starred – serving adventurous Modern-British cuisine, and often specializing in seafood. Alongside these are more modest places offering traditional local fare and pub food aplenty, while staples such as the Cornish pasty are a permanent feature of the culinary landscape. Despite the peninsula's reputation for quality seafood, however, don't always expect perfect fish and chips to munch along the quayside – there is as much junk food about as you would expect to find in any English holiday region.

Even the smallest villages of Devon and Cornwall may have surprisingly sophisticated **restaurants**, while the larger towns will have the gamut of Indian, Thai, Chinese and Italian places. What really marks out the menus of Devon and Cornwall, however, is the **fish**, ranging from the salmon caught in the rivers of Exmoor and Dartmoor to the freshest seafood from the local ports. Despite drastic reductions in the catches and restrictive quotas, the region's fishing industry is still relatively strong, and good seafood restaurants abound, not least in the Cornish port of Padstow, where TV chef Rick Stein has carved an empire that draws food fans from far and wide. Restaurants aren't the only places to sample the freshest seafood, though – crab sandwiches are sold in many pubs and make an excellent light lunch.

The speciality **meat** found in most of Devon and Cornwall's restaurants is lamb, cooked all ways, while Exmoor and Dartmoor are renowned for grouse and other game. Though they may not rise above a nut roast, **vegetarian** dishes are almost always available. **Delicatessens** selling local produce and **wholefood shops** can be found in remote villages as well as in the towns. **Farmers' markets** are always a good source of the best local produce, setting up in many towns and villages once or twice monthly (for dates and places, see Ⓦwww.farmersmarkets.net).

Regional specialities

Though some have claimed Cornwall's greatest export has been the **Cornish pasty**, the form has been so adulterated and debased that much of what is sold under the name fails to live up to the genuine article. Pasties were originally made as a full meal-in-one for miners to take underground, with vegetables at one end and jam at the other. The crimped edge ensured that they didn't need to wash their hands, and was not eaten. At home, each member of the family would have their own tastes catered for and marked with initials in the corner of their pasty.

If you're in search of a good pasty, forget about the stodgy lumps stuffed with gristle and mince that you'll see in chill cabinets, and head for the local baker's. Ideally, the pasty should have a rich, short or flaky pastry, neatly crimped on the rounded edge and filled with steak, turnip and potato – and dripping with gravy. You can also find a wide range of **non-traditional fillings** in some delis.

Other local specialities include **star gazy pie** (also known as starry gazy pie), a fish pie with the heads and tails of the fish, traditionally pilchards or mackerel, sticking out of the pastry. Tradition has it that this originated after a local fisherman returned from a fierce storm with seven types of fish, which were then cooked in a pie with their heads sticking out for easy identification. In Devon, you may come across **cobbler**, a baked meat dish with a scone topping, and you'll also find casseroles of pork or rabbit cooked in cider.

Sweet dishes include fruity **Cornish heavy cake** and **saffron cake**, a loaf baked with currants and saffron – though, these days, genuine saffron is rarely used (and when it is, it's probably been imported). Everywhere in the West Country, from quaint tearooms to farmhouses and cafés, you'll be tempted by **cream teas**: fluffy scones thickly spread with strawberry jam and clotted cream. The best advice is to surrender to the temptation at least once. The region's **ice cream** is equally prized – we've mentioned the best places to sample it in the Guide. Lastly, it's also worth looking out for local cheeses, most famously **Cornish Yarg** – mild, creamy and wrapped in nettles or wild garlic leaves.

Drinking

Devon and Cornwall boast some of the snuggest **pubs** in the land, often of the thatched and inglenook variety, and equipped with old slate floors, beamed ceilings and maritime paraphernalia. Most pubs are open all day from 11am until 11pm (10.30pm on Sun), and many offer food – Sunday lunches can be exceptionally good deals at £5–10. The region is dominated by the St Austell brewery, responsible for superlative **beers** such as Tinners, Tribute and Admiral's Ale. Truro-based Skinner's is the leading local independent, though there are shining examples of smaller operations, notably the *Blue Anchor* pub at Helston (p.259), where renowned Spingo bitter is brewed on the premises.

You'll occasionally come across **meaderies** in the South West – usually bawdy, faux-medieval halls that serve meals alongside the various types of mead (an alcoholic drink made from fermented honey) on offer, which can be surprisingly strong with a corresponding effect on the customers. They're pretty tacky places, but are relatively cheap and can be a good laugh.

In Cornwall, where it's common to see **cider** advertised in farm shops, you might also look out for home-made **scrumpy,** which weighs in at around 8 percent alcohol by volume.

Look out, too, for local **wines** such as Sharpham, from around Totnes, or Camel Valley, near Bodmin. If you're interested in wines and wine-making, you can tour either of these vineyards, (see p.112 & p.358). Note that some restaurants allow you to bring your own bottle of whatever alcohol you fancy ("BYOB").

See the *Devon and Cornwall on a plate* colour section for more on the food, wine and beer of the region.

Festivals and events

The demands of the tourist industry combine with authentic local traditions to ensure a full programme of annual festivals and events, especially over the summer. As nearly every village stages an annual event of some sort, and carnivals surface year-round, it would be impossible to detail them all. The main events listed below are arranged according to the week in which they occur, as most are fixed to weekends or specific days; contact the local tourist office or see festival websites for precise dates.

Unsurprisingly, given the region's long seaboard, a large proportion of events in Devon and Cornwall focus on the sea. The smartest of these are the various **regattas** which take place throughout the summer; larger ones, such as at Dartmouth and Fowey, get jam-packed. A peculiarity of Cornwall is **gig races** – rowing-boat races held in the summer between teams from different West Cornwall villages or from different islands in the Isles of Scilly. Foodies might take more interest in the **Newlyn Fish Festival** on August bank holiday (see p.275) and Falmouth's **Oyster Festival** in mid-October (see p.251); in both cases the quaysides have all sorts of seafood on display, cookery demonstrations and Celtic entertainment.

Other festivals are firmly tied to the land, especially those with an element of fertility ritual such as Padstow's May Day **Obby Oss** celebration (see box, p.335), when a weird and wonderful hobbyhorse in a circular hooped skirt prances its way through the town, and Helston's **Flora Day** (see box, p.258), which has smartly turned out couples dancing to the tune of the *Flora Dance* (Furry Dance), taking place on May 8. Dance features strongly in both events, as it does in many other Cornish festivities such as the midsummer **Golowan Festival** in Penzance (see p.271), a week-long community celebration with pagan elements, featuring fireworks and cultural events. You're most likely to come into contact with Cornish – or at least Celtic – heritage at the **Lowender Peran** festival (see p.325) held at Perranporth over five days in mid-October.

For a winter festival, you'd be hard-pressed to beat the **Tar Barrels** ceremony at Ottery St Mary in early November (see box, p.89), when people rush through the narrow streets with flaming barrels on their shoulders.

Probably the most famous of the West Country's **arts festivals** is the **Dartington International Music Festival** (see p.112),

Public and bank holidays

January 1
Good Friday (late March or early April)
Easter Monday (as above)
First Monday in May
Last Monday in May
Last Monday in August
December 25
December 26
(Note that if Jan 1 or Dec 25 or 26 falls on a Saturday or Sunday, the next weekday becomes a public holiday.)

from late July to late August, where you might take in three concerts a night ranging from classical to contemporary jazz and world in the antique setting of Dartington Hall. Fowey's **Daphne du Maurier Festival** in May includes plenty of walks, concerts, workshops and exhibitions as well as talks by literati and others, while the **St Ives September Festival** (see p.293) has an eclectic brief, with the emphasis on music.

The biggest and best known of the region's **folk-music festivals** is **Sidmouth Folk Week** (see box, p.81), which attracts a diverse audience in early August. The four-day **Wadebridge Folk Festival** takes place towards the end of the month (see p.337) in North Cornwall, while nearby **St Endellion** hosts two **classical music festivals**, for a week at Easter and around ten days in July/August (see p.340).

Lastly, many towns and villages pull out all the stops when it comes to **Christmas** illuminations – those at Mousehole (see p.276), near Penzance, are especially awesome.

For the main events, see the **websites** ⓦwww.visitdevon.co.uk and ⓦwww.feastoffestivals.co.uk.

A festival calendar

March/Easter

Vibraphonic Exeter, most of month. Live music, mainly urban, jazz and blues.
Festival of Spring Gardens (Cornwall) from mid-March to May Various venues.
Easter Festival St Endellion (North Cornwall), Easter. A week of classical music concerts.

April

Exeter Festival of Food and Drink Second week. The South West's premier food and drink jamboree, held over a weekend.

May

Daphne du Maurier Festival Fowey (South Cornwall). Literature, talks and walks.
Exmouth Festival Exmouth, (East Devon), fourth week. Eight days of concerts, dance, poetry, sand sculptures and workshops.
Gala Week Budleigh Salterton (East Devon). Mainly family-orientated events, including dog shows and a barbecue.
Flora Day Helston (West Cornwall), May 8 or Sat. Ancient fertility dance through town.
Isles of Scilly World Pilot Gig Championships First week.
English National Surfing Championships Watergate Bay (North Cornwall), first week.
Obby Oss Padstow (North Cornwall), early May. May Day shenanigans.
Re-enactment of the Battle of Stamford Hill Bude (North Cornwall), second/third week.

June

Exeter Summer Festival All month. Music, comedy, and more.
Golowan Festival Penzance (West Cornwall), third week. Week-long cultural binge.
Royal Cornwall Show Wadebridge (North Cornwall), second week. Agricultural show with folk dancing, military bands, flower displays and much more.
Salcombe Festival Salcombe (South Devon). Sailing displays, races, folk and jazz bands, barbecues and a street party.
St Ives Regatta St Ives (West Cornwall), third week. Boat races at all levels.
Tavistock Steam Fair Tavistock (Dartmoor), first week. Vintage and classic cars alongside steam rollers and traction engines.

July

Ale Tasting and Bread Weighing Ashburton (Dartmoor), third week. Medieval fair with procession.
Budleigh Salterton Festival Budleigh Salterton (East Devon), last week. Classical concerts over nine days.
Dartington International Music Festival Dartington (South Devon), last week. A month of concerts, mainly classical, but also world, folk and jazz.
Dartington Literature Festival Dartington (South Devon), second week. "Ways with Words", one of the UK's top literary gatherings, lasting ten days.
Honiton Fair and Hot Penny Ceremony Honiton (East Devon), last week. The town's annual fair traditionally kicks off with catching heated pennies.
Launceston Agricultural Show Launceston (Bodmin Moor), third week. Livestock and the floral arts.
Padstow Carnival Padstow (North Cornwall), last week. Numerous events, stalls and family entertainment.
Plymouth Regatta Fourth week. A week of sailing in and around Plymouth Sound.
Port Eliot Festival St Germans (South Cornwall), last week. Literature, music and comedy over a weekend on the Rame peninsula.

St Endellion Summer Festival St Endellion (North Cornwall), last week. Classical concerts over twelve days.
Stithians Show Stithians (North Cornwall), second week. One of the biggest agricultural shows in the west, including music, food and crafts.

August

Beer Regatta Week Beer (East Devon), second week. Competitions and street entertainment.
Boardmasters Festival Newquay (North Cornwall), first/second week. Five days of surf and live music on Fistral Beach and Watergate Bay.
Bude Carnival Week Bude (North Cornwall), third week. Competitions by day, followed by an evening procession.
Bude Jazz Festival Bude (North Cornwall), fourth week.
Dartmouth Royal Regatta Dartmouth (South Devon), fourth week. Races and displays in the Dart estuary over three days.
Falmouth Carnival Falmouth, (South Cornwall), first/second week.
Falmouth Regatta Week Falmouth (South Cornwall), second week. A rival to Cowes, this features displays of maritime prowess and, on shore, entertainments and fireworks.
Fowey Royal Regatta Fowey (South Cornwall), third week. Races, air displays, carnival floats and fireworks.
Newlyn Fish Festival Newlyn (West Cornwall), fourth week. Seafood galore, to eat and watch in culinary demonstrations.
Newquay Summer Finale Newquay (North Cornwall), fourth week. Free entertainment, dance workshops and food and drink stalls, over a weekend.
Paignton Regatta Paignton (South Devon), second week. Air displays and fireworks, as well as boating events.
Re-enactment of the Battle of Camlann Tintagel (North Cornwall), first week.
Sidmouth Folk Week Sidmouth, (East Devon), first week. One of the country's top folk festivals.
Torbay Royal Regatta Torbay (South Devon), fourth week. Six days of sailing and shore-based events.
Wadebridge Folk Festival Wadebridge (North Cornwall), fourth week.

September

Agatha Christie Festival Torbay (South Devon), third week. A week of Christie-related events.
Ladies' County Gig Championships Newquay (North Cornwall), second week.
Men's County Gig Championships Newquay (North Cornwall), fourth week.
St Ives September Festival St Ives (West Cornwall), second week. Top-ranking arts festivals, with music, theatre, literature and exhibitions.
Widecombe Fair Widecombe-in-the-Moor (Dartmoor), second week. Famed Dartmoor fair, now grown to include agricultural displays and competitions.

October

Beer Rhythm and Blues Festival Beer (East Devon), second week.
Boscastle Food, Arts and Crafts Festival Boscastle (North Cornwall), first week.
Exmouth Carnival Exmouth (East Devon), second week. Floats and family fun, with illuminated costumed procession.
Goose Fair Tavistock (Dartmoor), second week. Traditional gathering, with stalls and family amusements.
Lowender Peran Perranporth (North Cornwall), third week. A celebration of Celtic culture, with music and dance to the fore.

November

Exeter Autumn Festival First week. Two weeks of entertainment: mainly music, dance and theatre.
Tar Barrel Rolling Ottery St Mary (East Devon), Nov 5. Featuring flaming barrels in a local tradition taking place on Bonfire Night.

December

Tom Bawcock's Eve Mousehole (West Cornwall), Dec 23. Featuring choirs and the consumption of star gazy pie.

Outdoor activities

There's plenty of scope for experiencing the outdoor life in Devon and Cornwall, from hiking to mountain biking, and from caving to kayaking. The biggest draw for visitors is the coastline, chiefly for its beaches, which number among Britain's finest – if the water is too cold for total immersion, you can still experience the waves on board a boat. But the range of outdoor pursuits extends far beyond the obvious pastimes. See the websites ⓦwww.itsadventuresouthwest.co.uk, www.adventure-devon.co.uk and www.adventure-cornwall.co.uk for online listings of the full gamut of activities and extreme sports.

Beach life

The West Country's biggest asset for visitors is its hundreds of miles of **coastline**, most of it more or less unspoilt and studded with many of Britain's cleanest **beaches** and bathing waters. The prestigious **Blue Flag**, awarded to beaches on the basis of various criteria including facilities and environmental standards as well as water quality, was in 2009 awarded to the beaches at Blackpool Sands, Dawlish Warren, Torbay's Meadfoot, Oddicombe, Preston, Breakwater and Broadsands, Challaborough and Bigbury-on-Sea (all in South Devon); Tunnels Beach, Woolacombe Sand and Westward Ho! (North Devon); Gyllyngvase (South Cornwall); St Ives' Porthmeor and Porthminster, Sennen Cove, Marazion and Carbis Bay (West Cornwall), and Porthtowan and Polzeath (North Cornwall). You can check the latest results at ⓦwww.blueflag.org. Focusing on water quality alone, the **Marine Conservation Society** recommends many more than these – over half of the total number of beaches listed in the region – which have achieved 100 percent compliance with the EU Mandatory Standard: the full list can be downloaded from the website ⓦwww.goodbeachguide.co.uk.

The shores are certainly not free of problems, however, with various forms of **pollution** affecting a number of beaches; untreated sewage is still discharged close to the shore in some places and is washed back onto the sands. Both the local water companies have put considerable investment programmes in place to deal with the continuing scandalous condition of some coastal stretches, but they're still regularly criticized by groups such as Surfers Against Sewage (ⓦwww.sas.org.uk).

Remember that the **currents** around the peninsula are powerful and can quickly pull you out to sea; it's best not to swim alone or too far out. Between June and September, the most popular beaches are under lifeguard surveillance and a system of **flags** is in operation: a red flag indicates danger and means that the beach is closed for swimming and surfing; the zone between two red-and-yellow flags designates an area safe for swimming, belly-, boogie- and body-boarding, while the area between black-and-white chequered flags is reserved for surfing, wave skis, canoes and windsurfing. An orange windsock signifies high winds, when it is inadvisable to go out on inflatables.

Note that all beaches around the Devon and Cornwall coasts – including the Isles of Scilly – are subject to **tides**, which dramatically transform the appearance of the seashore. Low tide can leave you feeling like you're sitting in a bath after the water has run out, while sudden high tides can pose a significant risk by cutting off your return from a rock or strip of sand. Take local advice, see the website ⓦeasytide.ukho.gov.uk or buy tide times booklets (usually less than £1) from tourist offices or newsagents.

Most beaches are closed to **dogs** from Easter to early October; however, a map, showing beaches open throughout the year, may be obtained from the leaflet *Beach Guide for Dog Owners*, available from tourist information centres, or see ⓦwww.thecornishcoast.co.uk.

Biking

Touring Devon and Cornwall **by bike** makes an efficient, eco-friendly and relaxing way to discover the hidden corners of the peninsula. As well as the various cycleways (see p.24 for an overview of the region's main **cycling routes**), there are numerous opportunities for off-road biking, particularly on the moors, for which you should be fully equipped with waterproofs, maps and liquids – as with hiking, preparation is paramount, not least with regard to bad weather.

The website Ⓦwww.ukmountainbiker.com is an invaluable resource for cycling in the region, including routes and stores. Bike **rental outlets** are listed in the Guide for all the major centres and the main trails. See p.23 for information on taking bikes onto trains.

Caving and climbing

The granite landscape of the West Country's moors are ideal for **caving** and rock **climbing**, neither of which should be undertaken without expert guidance or adequate equipment. There are scores of activity centres in the region catering for caving and climbing enthusiasts, offering day, weekend or week-long courses, for example Essential Adventure (Ⓣ01395/200522, Ⓦwww.essential-adventure.co.uk) and Isca Outdoor, which also provides bunkhouse accommodation on Dartmoor (Ⓣ01392/494053, Ⓦwww.iscaoutdoor.co.uk). Contact local tourist offices for a full list.

Coasteering

North Devon and North and West Cornwall offer some of the UK's best areas for **coasteering**, the adrenaline-fuelled sport of negotiating sea cliffs and rocky stretches of coast by all means possible. Half-days and longer sessions can be booked from specialist agencies – contact the local tourist office for which ones. EBO Adventure leads sessions from centres near Barnstaple and Newquay (Ⓣ0800/781 6861, Ⓦwww.coasteering.org), Essential Adventure does the same from Exmouth (Ⓣ01395/200522, Ⓦwww.essential-adventure.co.uk).

Diving

With some of the clearest waters around the UK, Devon and Cornwall offer a wealth of **scuba diving** and **snorkelling** possibilities. Dive sites are scattered around the coasts, with those around West Cornwall and the Isles of Scilly especially rich in opportunities for poking around shipwrecks and reefs.

Numerous places offer **tuition** and equipment hire (usually around £15 for a couple of hours' taster) – make sure that instructors have the appropriate PADI qualifications. The British Subaqua Club (Ⓣ0151/350 6200, Ⓦwww.divingcornwall.com) lists approved schools and instructors, as well as information on local dive sites and services.

Fishing

The **rivers** of Dartmoor and Exmoor are much prized for their fishing opportunities, well stocked with wild brown trout, sea trout and the occasional salmon. Always enquire about **licences**: many local **clubs** offer temporary membership allowing you to use their streams and rivers (around £15 for a day). The website Ⓦwww.fishingnet.com has details of fishing venues, fisheries and angling clubs in the region. For **fishing in lakes**, you can also go to one of the four sites in Devon and Cornwall managed by the South West Lakes Trust (Ⓣ01566/771930, Ⓦwww.swlakestrust.org.uk).

Sea-angling is another popular activity, and in summer you'll find numerous outfits advertising two- or three-hour excursions for bass, mackerel or even shark – Looe, in Cornwall, is the region's **shark-fishing** centre (see p.226). See Ⓦcornwallfishing.com for Cornish coastal fishing.

Hiking

In addition to the **long-distance footpaths** crossing the region, detailed on pp.25–26, the South West also boasts a multiplicity of shorter **hiking routes**, most notably the network of tracks over Exmoor, Dartmoor and Bodmin Moor, and around the region's river estuaries. The excursions outlined in the Guide present a cross section of the kinds of walks you can find, with terrains ranging from bare moorland to wooded valley. These are more general descriptions than specific route guides, however, and the walks should not be undertaken without a proper 1:25,000 or 1:50,000 map (see p.42) and a compass. Ask at local tourist offices for leaflets – either free or costing around £1 each – detailing circular routes, which take in places of interest. If you're not on a circular route, you'll probably have to rely on public transport to get you home at the end; on the moors, **bus routes** often link up with walking routes and the local timetables even suggest walks with good directions. Coastal transport routes lend themselves to spurts of hiking on the South West Coast Path, too, with frequent intersections of path and bus route. The websites Ⓦwww.trailsfromthetrack.com and www.railaletrail.com detail walks that can be accessed from the peninsula's branch rail lines, indicating pubs en route.

All walks should be approached with forward planning and suitable **equipment**. Supportive, waterproof hiking boots are ideal – moorland is particularly uneven terrain – and you should carry a waterproof jacket and hood, a warm, dry change of clothing on wet days and around two litres of water per person on a hot day. For longer hikes, something to eat is also essential. You might also consider using a **luggage-transfer** service, for example Luggage Transfers South West (Ⓣ0800/043 7927, Ⓦwww.luggagetransfers.co.uk), covering the coast path in North and West Cornwall. Take advice on the **weather** (local tourist offices, local press, radio and TV and the website Ⓦwww.metoffice.gov.uk/weather/uk/sw are useful sources of information): bad conditions can set in fast, and fogs are a particular hazard on the coast and moors. **GPS receivers** can be a useful back up to a map; more advanced models display location details superimposed on Ordnance Survey maps.

If you're inexperienced, consider joining one of the regular **organized walks** on Exmoor and Dartmoor and along the coast. These may be of varying length and difficulty: contact local tourist offices and moorland visitor centres for details.

Kayaking and canoeing

The rivers and seas around the Southwest peninsula offer ample scope for **kayaking and canoeing**, whether drifting lazily along a meandering stream or battling against rapids or surf in white-knuckle escapades. **Inland**, the rivers Exe and Barle on Exmoor, Dart on

Health hazards for hikers

Apart from hiking injuries, the main hazards facing walkers in the West Country (as elsewhere in the UK) are snakes, ticks and overexposure to sun. **Sunburn** can be avoided by using some form of headwear and sunblocks. Among the resident snakes, **adders** (or vipers) are the only dangerous species: distinguished by a zigzag stripe along its back, the adder is rare to encounter, and bites are uncommon. If you should be unlucky enough to be bitten, it is extremely unlikely to be fatal, though you should seek medical attention as soon as possible.

Ticks are an irritation in many areas of Britain and may cause Lyme disease if left untreated. They occur in wooded areas and where there is thick vegetation, for instance bracken; the creatures are brushed (or fall) onto your exposed skin, where they burrow in to suck your blood. They are small, the bites are painless, and victims are often unaware they have been bitten. If you find one, the best advice is to go to a doctor to have the tick removed. If you do decide to remove a tick yourself, don't apply any oil or lotion or squeeze it; the correct method is to twist it gently anti clockwise using tweezers, cleansing the area thoroughly with antiseptic afterwards. Always keep the extracted tick to show to a medical authority. The best prevention is to avoid exposing skin while walking, but note that pets are more prone to catch ticks than humans, and can easily pass them on to humans.

A further possible hazard is **toxocara**, a small parasite carried in the faeces of some animals (especially dogs) – it can cause blindness and is therefore something to be aware of in areas frequented by dogs, for example picnic areas where children might play.

Dartmoor and Fowey in South Cornwall are all favourite venues for taking up the paddle, and you'll find operators – mainly active in the winter months – in and around Dulverton, Princetown and Fowey. The waters here can get very fierce and expertise is required; the local tourist offices can inform you of qualified instructors. For a calmer experience, the four sites in Devon and Cornwall managed by the South West Lakes Trust (ⓣ01566/771930, ⓦwww.swlakestrust.org.uk) offer canoeing and kayaking **on lakes**. For a single kayak, expect to pay around £15 for two hours' hire, £25 for a day.

On the coast, **sea-** and **surf-kayaking** are increasingly popular; you can opt for more sheltered spots around, for example, Exmouth, St Austell Bay and Falmouth, or brave the waves from typical surfing beaches on the northern coast, such as Polzeath and Bude. Some outfits offer sea-kayaking trips to Lundy Island. Surf-kayakers should observe the same safety procedures as surfers, and always allow others plenty of space.

Canoe England has details of approved centres (ⓣ0845/370 9500, ⓦwww.canoe-england.org.uk).

Specialist operators and activity holidays

Adventureline Walking Holidays ⓣ01209/820847, ⓦwww.adventureline.co.uk. Accommodation and guided walking packages enabling you to explore Dartmoor, the Cornish coast and the Isles of Scilly on foot.

Big Friday ⓣ020/8960 2471, ⓦwww.bigfriday.com. Weekend surf packages in Newquay, including travel from London, accommodation and tuition. Also women-only weekends.

Classic Sailing ⓣ01872/580022, ⓦwww.classic-sailing.co.uk. Sailing holidays around St Mawes and the Isles of Scilly, from luxury to more hands-on.

Contours Walking Holidays ⓣ01768/480451, ⓦwww.contours.co.uk. Self-guided hikes on the Tarka Trail, Dartmoor Way, Saints' Way, Two Moors Way and Coast Path, with accommodation and transport arranged.

Dartmoor Llama Walks ⓣ01364/631481, ⓦwww.dartmoorllamawalks.co.uk. Moorland walks accompanied by luggage-carrying llamas.

Elemental Tours ⓣ01736/811200, ⓦwww.elementaltours.co.uk. Wildlife-watching on land and sea, based in West Cornwall. Accommodation arranged.

Encounter Cornwall ⓣ01208/871066, ⓦwww.encountercornwall.com. Walking, paddling and pedalling holidays around and between Padstow and Fowey, accompanied or self-guided.

Explore Southwest ⓣ01637/818338, ⓦwww.exploresouthwest.com. Tailor-made activity packages and tours, with accommodation mostly around Newquay.

Footpath Holidays ⓣ01985/840049, ⓦwww.footpath-holidays.com. Guided and self-guided walks on Exmoor and in South Devon and West Cornwall, including at Christmas and New Year.

Global Boarders ⓣ01736/711404, ⓦwww.globalboarders.com. Surfing holidays in Cornwall, with beach transfers and stylish accommodation – good for families.

Let's Go Walking/Biking ⓣ01837/880075, ⓦwww.letsgobiking.com. Escorted and self-guided walking and biking holidays in the West Country, including on Dartmoor and the coast. Luggage transport and accommodation arranged.

Lightfoot Walking Holidays ⓣ01736/850715, ⓦwww.lightfootwalkingholidays.co.uk. Self-guided hikes along the Cornish coast for three days or more, with all luggage, estuary crossings and accommodation taken care of.

Mountain Water Experience ⓣ01548/550675, ⓦwww.mountainwaterexperience.co.uk. Kayaking, caving, coasteering and other adventure pursuits, based in Dartmoor and South Devon.

Riding Holidays Cornwall ⓣ01288/331204, ⓦwww.riding-holidays-cornwall.co.uk. Self-catering accommodation attached to stables at Morwenstow, near Bude, Cornwall, for week-long riding holidays and short breaks.

Shoreline Extreme Sports ⓣ01288/354039, ⓦwww.shorelineactivities.co.uk. Year-round outdoor activities including archery, sea-kayaking and rock climbing, based in Bude, North Cornwall.

Spirit of Adventure ⓣ01822/880277, ⓦwww.spirit-of-adventure.com. Hiking, kayaking and climbing, or a combination of different activities on an adventure weekend, with top-notch bunkhouse accommodation in the heart of Dartmoor.

Square Sail Shipyard ⓣ01726/70241, ⓦwww.square-sail.com. Cruises on square-rigged sailing ships along the Cornish coast, with hands-on experience.

Surfers World ⓣ01271/871224, ⓦwww.surfersworld.co.uk. Surf breaks in North Devon, with B&B, surf cabins or self-catering accommodation in lakeside cottages or apartments with sea views, plus tuition.

Way2Go4 Walking Holidays ⓣ01288/331416, ⓦwww.way2go4.com. Week-long or short-break guided and self-guided walking holidays on the North Devon/Cornwall border, in standard or superior farmhouse accommodation.

West Cornwall Geology Tours ⓣ0788/755 6245, ⓦwww.cornwallgeology.co.uk. Walks that offer insights into the geology of the area, taking in coastal sites and the mining heritage. Accommodation can be arranged.

West Country Walks ⓣ01271/883131, ⓦwww.westcountrywalks.co.uk. Self-guided walks in North Devon and Exmoor with accommodation and transport provided. Downloaded routes for self-guided hiking and cycling are for sale from the website.

YHA Okehampton ⓣ0845/371 9651, ⓦwww.yha.org.uk. The YHA's adventure centre at Okehampton offers a range of activity holidays for individuals and families, including biking, climbing and pony-trekking.

Riding

Dartmoor and Exmoor are particularly ideal for **riding**. Stables can be found in some of the most scenic parts of the moor, as well as in coastal areas, and are detailed in the Guide, or contact the specialist operations listed here. Expect to pay about £20 per hour for riding or tuition. Check the directory of riding schools and trekking centres at the website ⓦwww.bhs.org.uk.

Sailing

The sight of sailors messing around in boats in every port in Devon and Cornwall is an inspiration for anyone yearning to try their hand at **sailing**. Richly endowed with inlets, estuaries and creeks, the peninsula is ideal for first-timers and old salts alike. The more sheltered south coast offers the best conditions: Teignmouth, Dartmouth, Salcombe and Plymouth in Devon, and Fowey and Falmouth in Cornwall.

A residential course is the best option for **tuition**, with a range of specialist schools listed by the Royal Yachting Association (ⓣ0845/345 0400, ⓦwww.rya.org.uk). For the slightly less daunting experience of sailing on **lakes**, contact the South West Lakes Trust (ⓣ01566/771930, ⓦwww.swlakestrust.org.uk), which offers a range of watersports including sailing at four sites in Devon and Cornwall.

Surfing

The north coast of Devon and Cornwall has some of the country's most outstanding **surfing beaches**, which, thanks to wet suits, are used year-round by surf enthusiasts. The most popular areas are Woolacombe Bay and Croyde Bay in Devon, and the areas around Bude and Newquay, and the beaches at Polzeath, Constantine Bay, Porthtowan, Perranporth, Portreath and Sennen Cove in Cornwall. In summer, you'll find plenty of kiosks on the beaches renting out **surf equipment** – boards and wet suits, each about £10 per full day (plus a deposit); details of dedicated watersports equipment-rental outlets are given in the Guide. **Surfing courses** are also readily available, with two- to- three-hour lessons costing about £30, private tuition £40–60 for two hours or so, including all equipment. The British Surfing Association (ⓣ01637/876474, ⓦwww.britsurf.co.uk) has a list of approved surfing schools in the South West that are open all year.

Updated reports on **surf conditions** and forecasts are available at ⓦwww.getaforecast.com and magicseaweed.com. You can check surf conditions on live webcams here and at the links listed at ⓦwww.southwestsurf.info, which has numerous other links to surf-related websites as well as information on local beaches and breaks.

Windsurfing and kitesurfing

While **windsurfing** has ebbed in popularity in recent years, it's still practised all over the South West, especially in sheltered spots such as the Exe estuary, Plymouth Sound and the Carrick Roads estuary. Basic tuition in a group starts from £15 per hour, and you'll pay around the same to rent equipment by the hour. The Royal Yachting Association (ⓣ0845/345 0400, ⓦwww.rya.org.uk) lists schools in the area, while the South West Lakes Trust (ⓣ01566/771930, ⓦwww.swlakestrust.org.uk) offers windsurfing among other watersports at four inland sites in Devon and Cornwall.

Kitesurfing, on the other hand, attracts increasing interest among extreme sports fans on the peninsula's beaches. Equipment can be rented and tuition given at various activity centres, such as Cornwall's Extreme Academy, on Watergate Bay (ⓣ01637/860543, ⓦwww.watergatebay.co.uk). The British Kitesurfing Association (ⓣ01305/813555, ⓦwww.britishkitesurfingassociation.co.uk) has a list of recognized schools and suitable beaches.

Travel essentials

Costs

If you're watching your budget – hostelling or camping and buying some of your own food in shops and markets – you can get by on as little as £25–50 a day, but a more realistic average daily budget is £50–100, including B&B accommodation and some travel costs, while on £100–150 a day you'll be living pretty comfortably: staying in a decent hotel and dining out every night.

Many of the most treasured sites in Devon and Cornwall – from castles, abbeys and great houses to tracts of protected landscape – come under the control of the private **National Trust** (Ⓦwww.nationaltrust.org.uk) or the state-run **English Heritage** (Ⓦwww.english-heritage.org.uk), whose properties are denoted in the Guide with "NT" or "EH". Both these organizations charge an entry fee for the majority of their historic sites, and these can be quite high, especially for the more grandiose National Trust estates. Note that there are reduced entry rates for anyone arriving at NT properties by cycle or on public transport.

If you think you'll be visiting more than half a dozen places owned by the National Trust or more than a dozen owned by English Heritage, it's worth taking out annual **membership** (around £50, or £22 for anyone aged 13–25 for NT; £44, or £33 for students for EH), which allows free entry to the organizations' respective properties. Many **stately homes**, however, remain in the hands of the landed gentry, who tend to charge in the region of £6 for admission to edited highlights of their domains.

Attractions owned by the local authorities, generally charge lower admission charges; municipal art galleries and museums, for example, are usually free. Although Exeter **Cathedral** makes an entry charge, the region's other **churches** are free (but may suggest a voluntary donation and charge a small fee for a photographic permit).

The majority of fee-charging attractions have reductions for senior citizens, the unemployed, full-time students and children under 16, with under-5s being admitted free almost everywhere. The entry charges given in the Guide are the full adult charges.

Emergencies

Dial Ⓣ999 for all **emergencies**, including police, fire, ambulance and coastguard. For non-emergency cases, call Ⓣ0845/277 7444 (24hr) for **police** in Devon and Cornwall, or see Ⓦwww.devon-cornwall.police.uk.

Family travelling

Devon and Cornwall are ideally suited to **family holidays**, with dozens of family-targeted attractions in every area. The great outdoors, of course, is the biggest draw, though options may be limited in bad weather (the website Ⓦwww.101-things-to-do-on-a-rainy-day-in-cornwall.co.uk is a useful resource). Paying attractions can be highly expensive: always ask about **family tickets** (usually for two adults and up to three children), which are especially good value in National Trust and English Heritage sites. You can also save money using family rail passes. Many **accommodation** options, including hostels, offer family rooms.

Health

Although the South West does not present particular **health hazards** that are exclusive to this region of the country, there are some tips that are worth remembering whether or not you are covered by health insurance (see p.42). Remember that the sun can be deceptively strong in the South West, especially (but not only) in the summer months, and ensure that you use a suitable **sunscreen** (sun factor 30+ is recommended). On beaches, the wearing of "jelly shoes" – available at many seaside shops – is a good safeguard against the **weaver fish**, which lurks under the sand at low tide and can cause painful stings from the venomous spines along its dorsal fin. If stung, you should wash the wound in hot water, allowing it to bleed freely, and seek medical attention. For ticks, snakes and **toxocara**, see the box on p.38.

More generally, it's worth packing any prescription medication that you normally take, as well as carrying contact details of your own doctor. Should health issues arise, you can consult **NHS Direct** at ⓣ0845/4647 for most problems, or dial ⓣ999 in an **emergency**. Hospital Accident and Emergency departments are mentioned in the Guide in the relevant chapters.

Insurance

A typical travel insurance policy usually provides cover for the loss of baggage, tickets and – up to a certain limit – cash or cheques, as well as cancellation or curtailment of your journey. Most of them exclude so-called dangerous sports unless an extra premium is paid: in England this can mean most watersports, rock climbing and mountaineering, though probably not activities such as hiking and kayaking.

Internet

Dedicated internet cafés are increasingly rare in the South West. Some tourist offices offer access, as do most public libraries, where you are not charged for your first half-hour online, then around £1.50 per 30 minutes. Note there may be a queue to use the terminals in libraries, which you can avoid by booking. A growing number of bars, cafés, pubs and accommodation options offer **wireless** (wi-fi) connections. We've listed logging-on points throughout the Guide.

Maps

The best general **map** of the South West is the *A–Z Devon Cornwall Visitors' Atlas and Guide*, showing the region at a scale of 2.5 miles to the inch (one mile to the centimetre). Produced by Geographers' A–Z Map Company, and available from most newsagents in the region, it has visitor information and large-scale town plans at the back. *Philip's Street Atlas: Cornwall* reproduces the county at a scale of 1.75 inches to the mile (about a quarter-mile to the centimetre), with towns at 3.5 inches to the mile (about an eighth of a mile to the centimetre). Walkers, however, should get hold of one of the two series published by Ordnance Survey (ⓦwww.ordnancesurvey.co.uk): the 1:50,000 maps of the *Landranger* series, and the more detailed 1:25,000 maps of the *Explorer* series. All the above are on sale at outdoors shops and bookshops in the region, or from dedicated **map outlets** such as Stanfords, whose nearest branch is in Bristol (29 Corn St, Bristol BS1 1HT; ⓣ0117/929 9966, ⓦwww.stanfords.co.uk) and who also offer a mail-order service. It's also worth checking such **websites** as ⓦmaps.google.co.uk, www.multimap.com or www.streetmap.co.uk, which have road maps, town plans and satellite images of the whole area.

The media

Local publications are often an excellent source of up-to-date information and entertainment listings. National TV channels have some local news and current affairs programmes, while radio stations based in Devon and Cornwall are useful for weather and traffic bulletins.

One of the South West's most widely read local **newspapers** is the daily *Western Morning News* (www.thisiswesternmorningnews.co.uk), based in Plymouth and covering most of Devon and Cornwall – a sort of middle-England paper with national as well as local news. The same company (part of Northcliffe Media) publishes the weekly *North Devon Journal*, *Mid-Devon Gazette*, *The Cornishman*, *Cornish Guardian* and *West Briton*, the last three covering respectively Penwith, mid-Cornwall and the Lizard, and East Cornwall; all are strong on local news, events and general tittle-tattle. **Magazines** geared toward the region include the monthly glossies *Inside Cornwall*, *Cornwall Today*, *Devon Life* and *Devon Today* – all of them with articles on food, culture, local issues and other aspects of living in the West Country.

You'll pick up more practical information from **free newspapers**, which relate to specific regions. Look out particularly for the *Exmoor Visitor*, the *Dartmoor Visitor* and *Coastlines and Countryside News* (the latter covering the North Cornwall coast); all have information on walks, wildlife, accommodation and services. For music, theatre, exhibitions and other events, seek out the monthly free **listings magazines** *247* (247magazine.co.uk) and *What's On Southwest* (www.whatsonsouthwest.co.uk) for the latest places and dates. All these publications can be found in tourist offices and in pubs, clubs and hotels.

Providing the usual mix of chat and chart music, **local radio stations** can be useful sources of information on traffic and sea conditions, weather and local events. The BBC's **Radio Cornwall** (95.2 or 103.9FM) and **Radio Devon** (103.4FM) are staid but authoritative, with the accent on local issues; phone-ins tend to feature complaints about the state of the roads and problems with gulls. The main independent stations are **Heart FM** (96.4, 97 or 103FM) and **Palm FM** (105.5FM) in Devon, and, in Cornwall, **Pirate FM** (102–103FM) and **Atlantic FM** (105–107FM), also covering Plymouth; all have national and local news, traffic, weather and surf reports, and a fairly mainstream musical output.

Money

Britain has so far declined to adopt the euro, preferring instead its **pound sterling** (£), divided into 100 pence (p). Coins come in denominations of 1p, 2p, 5p, 10p, 20p, 50p and £1 and £2. Notes are in denominations of £5, £10, £20 and £50.

Cash is easy to come by, with the main **banks** represented in all towns and some larger villages; some smaller villages also have branches with **cash machines** (ATMs) that accept most cards. Many food stores also have cash machines. If you're stuck, ask about cashback facilities in stores and supermarkets. You can rely on **credit cards** for most daily expenditure, though pubs and cafés prefer cash, and the majority of B&Bs will not accept them (they will generally accept **cheques**, however). Relatively few places accept American Express or Diners Club cards.

Opening hours

Opening hours to attractions are given in the Guide, though as these change regularly you might want to check in advance if you're making a long journey to a sight. Many paying attractions stop admitting visitors 45 minutes to an hour before closing. Larger and more important **churches** are almost always open during daylight hours, but you'll often find country churches locked up unless they're particular tourist attractions – most in any case close at 4 or 5pm. **Shops** generally open from 9am to 5.30pm Monday to Saturday, with many bigger stores and supermarkets open on Sunday as well. When all else is closed, you can normally find a garage selling basic items. In summer, food shops in tourist areas often stay open until 10 or 11pm.

Phones

Public telephone kiosks are fairly ubiquitous in towns and villages throughout the South West peninsula, though many do not accept coins. **Mobile phones** are not always to be relied upon – parts of the region are out of range or have only a weak signal – for example, stretches of the north coast of Devon and Cornwall, the Isles of Scilly and the moors.

Shopping

Devon and Cornwall have always attracted artisans and craftspeople keen to merchandise their wares, ranging from candles in Totnes to sword-and-sorcery trinkets in Tintagel. Fishermen's **smocks** are well in evidence throughout Cornwall, and you'll also find a bewildering range of objects fashioned from **serpentine** from the Lizard. It's worth checking out Devon's **pannier markets** – covered bazaars where a motley range of items are sold alongside the foodstuffs – and you'll find other markets in most towns, including **farmers' markets** for local foodstuffs, usually once or twice monthly (see Ⓦwww.farmersmarkets.net).

Tourist information

While **regional tourist boards** (see below) can supply maps and general information, local **tourist offices** have their ears closer to the ground and are better placed for practical information. Fairly ubiquitous, they are always well supplied with reams of information on public transport, local attractions and accommodation, though it's worth noting that much of the material relates only to places which have paid for their entries and listings in the official brochures. All the same, it's worth grabbing whatever accommodation and dining info they have – in summer especially, places fill up quickly and those listed in this Guide may not always be available. Though mostly overworked, staff are knowledgeable and extremely helpful as a rule. **Opening hours** for most tourist offices are Monday to Saturday from 9am to 5pm; in high summer, many are open daily, while in winter some are open at weekends only or else close altogether. Larger offices will change money, some will book accommodation, and many also sell tickets for tours, ferries and National Express buses.

Regional tourist boards

Visit Cornwall Ⓣ01872/322900, Ⓦwww.visitcornwall.com.
Visit Devon Ⓦwww.visitdevon.co.uk.
South West Tourism Ⓣ0870/442 0880, Ⓦwww.visitsouthwest.co.uk.

Travelling with disabilities

Concessionary rates for **travellers with disabilities** are patchy, but one of the better deals is the **Disabled Persons Railcard**, which knocks up to a third off the price of most railway tickets. The card costs £18 and is valid for one year. Call Ⓣ0845/605 0525 or see Ⓦwww.disabledpersons-railcard.co.uk for an application form and the postal address it must be sent to. Good sources of information on UK holiday accommodation are Ⓦwww.accessatlast.com and www.goodaccesscottages.co.uk.

Useful websites

Ⓦwww.bbc.co.uk/devon and www.bbc.co.uk/cornwall Invaluable websites for local news, weather and travel, as well as events, attractions and other information relating to the two counties.
Ⓦwww.chycor.co.uk Mainly useful for all kinds of accommodation in Cornwall.
Ⓦwww.cornwall.gov.uk Official county website, worth exploring for its tourism and transport pages and more.
Ⓦwww.cornwall-online.co.uk and www.devon-online.com Offering a range of accommodation in the region, including farm holidays and weekend breaks, as well as a wealth of information on places, activities and attractions.
Ⓦwww.devon-connect.co.uk Accommodation in Devon, including camping and self-catering.
Ⓦwww.devon.gov.uk Good all-round site covering everything from museums to the economy, environment and transport.
Ⓦwww.eatoutcornwall.com Cornish restaurants, recipes, reviews and food facts, with links.
Ⓦwww.english-heritage.org.uk General information for visiting historic attractions run by English Heritage.
Ⓦwww.lemonrock.com For events, gigs and festivals throughout the region, with links and interactive features.
Ⓦwww.lotstodo.co.uk Useful descriptions of the top Devon attractions, including what's on, kids' favourites and beaches, with links.
Ⓦwww.metoffice.gov.uk/weather/uk/sw Detailed five-day forecasts for the region.
Ⓦwww.nationaltrust.org.uk Background and visiting details for National Trust properties.
Ⓦwww.sugarvine.com/devonandcornwall Restaurants in the region, including news and reviews.
Ⓦwww.thisiscornwall.co.uk and www.thisisdevon.co.uk Websites linked to the *Western Morning News* and other local newspapers, useful for traffic reports, films, classified ads and regional news.

Guide

Guide

1 Exeter and mid-Devon

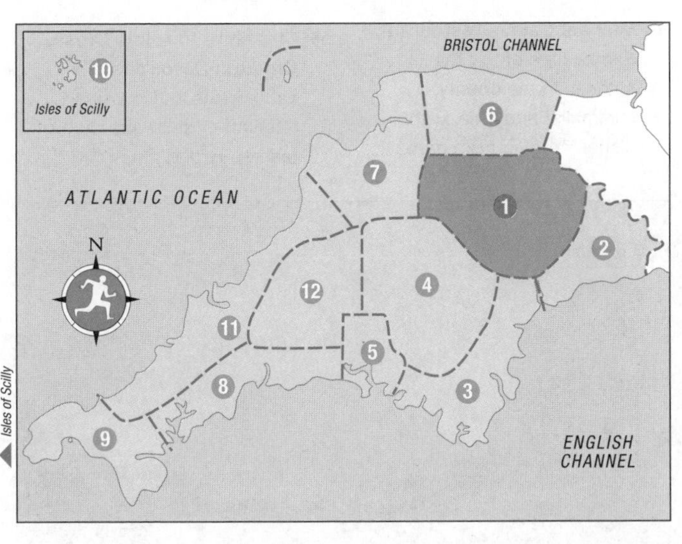

CHAPTER 1 Highlights

* **Exeter Cathedral** One of the country's greatest cathedrals, rich in architectural interest and boasting the longest continuous Gothic ceiling anywhere. See p.55
* **Royal Albert Memorial Museum** A delightfully miscellaneous treasure trove, with informative sections on everything from Devon pottery to Tahitian mourning dress. See p.56
* **Michael Caines restaurant, Exeter** One of the top eateries in the county; minimalist and chic, with dishes ranging from game and seafood to some outstanding puds. See p.59
* **A trip along Exeter Canal and the Exe estuary** Explore the Exeter Canal and River Exe by bike or boat, with pub stops along the way. See p.59
* **Knightshayes Court** This Victorian Gothic house holds striking examples of the work of the medievalist designer William Burges, and also has fine gardens. See p.63
* **Church of the Holy Cross, Crediton** Devon's former cathedral is an imposing fifteenth-century structure of red sandstone. See p.66

▲ Exeter Quay

1

Exeter and mid-Devon

One of Britain's oldest settlements, **Exeter** is also the most vibrant of Devon and Cornwall's cities, and one where you may be tempted to spend more than a day or two. Formerly a crucial pivot in Devon's flourishing wool industry, Exeter has maintained its status as a major commercial centre, one that you're likely to pass through at least once on your West Country travels.

The city's premier sight is also its most visible: rising above the concrete of the modern centre, Exeter's **cathedral** represents the apotheosis of one of the most brilliant periods of English architecture, its intricate web of roof-vaulting unique for its prodigious length. The other unmissable attraction is the dense collection of art and artefacts in the **Royal Albert Memorial Museum** – an excellent overview of the city and county, displaying everything from a menagerie of stuffed animals to the silverware and clocks at which the city excelled. Even without the city's traditional sights, Exeter's range of accommodation, pubs, clubs and restaurants make it a fun place to soak up the more contemporary cultural scene, and an ideal base for visiting other places in this part of Devon

North of Exeter, sandwiched between the rugged moorland to the north and south, mid-Devon has preserved its profoundly rural nature, its valleys and meadows still intensively farmed and dotted with sheep. North of Exeter, the A396 brings you to **Tiverton**, inland Devon's biggest town, brimming with interest and within easy distance of a cluster of grand country houses: **Knightshayes Court**, a showcase for the work of Victorian architect and designer William Burges; **Bickleigh Castle**, with its own Norman chapel and fifteenth-century gatehouse, situated just across the river from the much-photographed village of Bickleigh; and, to the south, **Killerton**, famous for its extensive collection of costumes. Elsewhere in the region, there's little to tempt you to stay in one place, but there are some destinations worth visiting in passing. Northwest of Exeter, **Crediton** is home to one of Devon's grandest churches, well worth a brief detour.

Served by frequent **trains** on the main line to Penzance, and the departure point for branch lines to Barnstaple, Exmouth and, in summer, Okehampton, Exeter is at the centre of the region's transport network. Good bus services link the city to most places in mid-Devon, though your own vehicle would be useful for reaching the area around Tiverton. **Bus** travellers can get a discount by purchasing an Explorer ticket (see Basics, p.23).

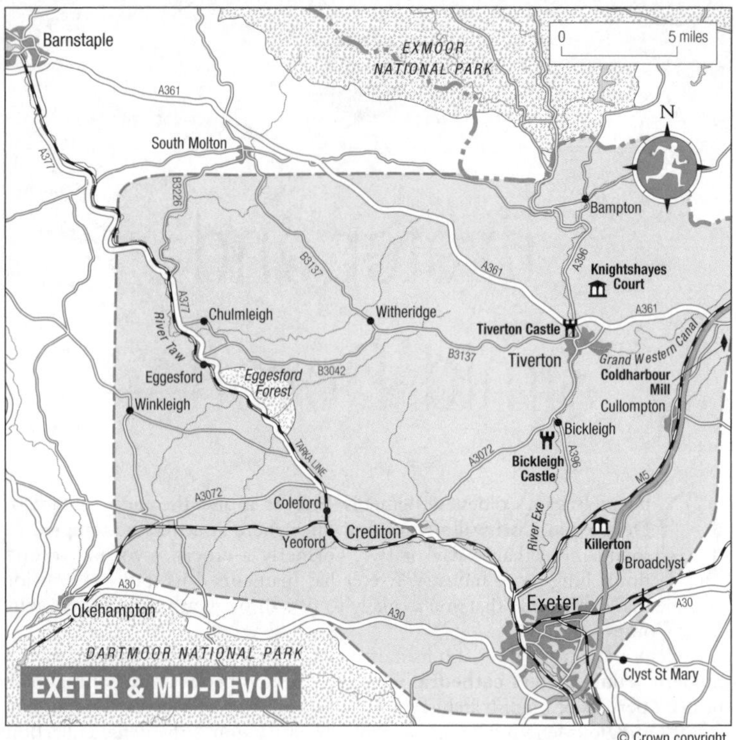

Exeter

A major transport hub and the terminus of the M5 motorway, Devon's county town, **EXETER**, is the first stop on many a tour of the West Country. Despite having much of its ancient centre gutted by World War II bombs, the city retains plenty of its medieval heritage, not least its sturdy **cathedral**, whose flanking Norman towers are Exeter's most recognizable landmark. Other remnants of the old city include a clutch of medieval churches, fashioned – like the sparse remains of the castle and city walls – in the local pinkish-red sandstone, and a fascinating network of subterranean passages. The history and geography of the whole region is covered in the town's fine **museum**, which also has a respected ethnographic section. Away from the centre, the **Quay** is the starting point for canalside walks and bike rides during the day and a lively focus for pubbers and clubbers in the evening.

Some history

Previously a settlement of the Celtic Dumnonii tribe, Exeter was fortified by the **Romans** in around 50–55 AD, and renamed Isca Dumnoniorum – the most westerly outpost of Rome in the British Isles. Little of note has been excavated from this period, however, suggesting that it was primarily a military occupation.

The city was refounded by **Alfred the Great** at the end of the ninth century, and grew to become one of the largest towns in Anglo-Saxon England, profiting from its position on the banks of the River Exe as the major outlet for the inland wool industry. The **Normans** strengthened the old Roman walls, rebuilt the cathedral and expanded the wool trade, which sustained the city until the eighteenth century. Woven in rural Devon, the serge cloth was dyed and finished in Exeter and then exported from the quays on the Exe to France, Spain and the Netherlands. By the first quarter of the sixteenth century, Exeter was one of the largest and richest towns in England – only York, Norwich, Bristol and Newcastle were more important outside London. Although the countess of Devon diverted most of the shipping trade to Topsham by building a weir across the Exe in around 1285, Exeter's role as a major port was restored by the construction of the Quay and the Exeter Ship Canal between 1564 and 1566 – the first canal to be built in England since Roman times.

During the **Civil War**, Exeter – unusually for the West Country – held predominantly Parliamentarian sympathies, but was besieged and taken by the Royalists in 1643, becoming their headquarters in the west and sheltering Charles I's queen. The city fell to a Roundhead army in 1646, which stayed in occupation until the Restoration. Exeter subsequently entered its most prosperous age; the scale of its cloth trade moved the traveller and diarist Celia Fiennes, who visited in 1698, to marvel at the "incredible quantity of [serges] made and sold in the town…The whole town and country is employed for at least twenty miles around in spinning, weaving, dressing and scouring, fulling and drying of the serges. It turns the most money in a week of anything in England." Trade ceased during the **Napoleonic Wars**, and by the time peace was restored, the centre of textile manufacturing had shifted to England's northern industrial towns; Devon's wool industry never regained its former importance.

The severe bombing sustained during **World War II** miraculously spared the cathedral, but the bland reconstruction that followed couldn't make up for the loss of much of the historic centre. In recent times, however, an infusion of energy provided by the university and the tourist trade has prevented Exeter from sliding into provincial decline, and the daily bustle of the modern centre as well as a raft of fashionable new hotels and restaurants testify to its economic wellbeing today.

Arrival and information

Of Exeter's two **train stations**, Exeter Central is smack in the middle of town on Queen Street, while Exeter St David's lies further northwest on Bonhay Road, closer to some of the cheaper B&Bs. Trains on the London Waterloo–Salisbury line stop at both, as do Tarka Line services to Barnstaple (see p.199)

Exeter tours

Free ninety-minute **walking tours** of the city (ⓣ01392/265203, ⓦwww.exeter.gov.uk/guidedtours), conducted by Red Coat guides, take place daily all year, focusing on such themes as "Exeter Old and New" and "Ghosts and Legends". Mostly starting from Cathedral Close, outside the *Royal Clarence Hotel*; some leave from outside the Quay House (on the Quay), tours begin at 10.30am (weekdays only), 11am, 2pm and 7pm (Tues–Fri only) between April and October, and at 11am, 2.30pm and 7pm (Tues only) between November and March.

A377

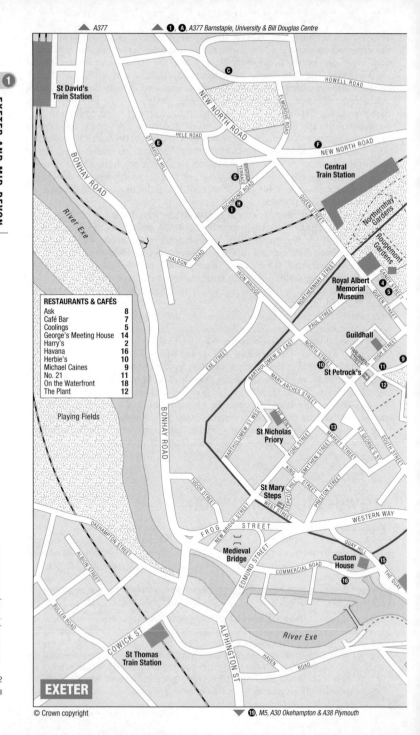

1, A, A377 Barnstaple, University & Bill Douglas Centre

EXETER

St David's Train Station
Central Train Station
Northernhay Gardens
Rougemont Gardens
Royal Albert Memorial Museum
Guildhall
St Petrock's
St Nicholas Priory
St Mary Steps
Medieval Bridge
Custom House
St Thomas Train Station
Playing Fields
River Exe

HOWELL ROAD
NEW NORTH ROAD
ELMGROVE ROAD
HELE ROAD
ST DAVID'S HILL
BONHAY ROAD
BYSTOCK TERRACE
RICHMOND ROAD
QUEEN STREET
HALDON ROAD
IRON BRIDGE
NORTHERNHAY STREET
GANDY STREET
PAUL STREET
NORTH STREET
HIGH STREET
PARLIAMENT STREET
BARTHOLOMEW ST EAST
MARY ARCHES STREET
EXE STREET
BARTHOLOMEW ST WEST
THE MINT
FORE STREET
MARKET STREET
ST GEORGE'S ST
SOUTH STREET
SMYTHEN STREET
KING STREET
STEPCOTE HILL
PRESTON STREET
WEST STREET
TUDOR STREET
NEW BRIDGE STREET
FROG STREET
WESTERN WAY
QUAY HILL
THE QUAY
COMMERCIAL ROAD
EDMUND STREET
OKEHAMPTON STREET
ALBION STREET
BULLER ROAD
COWICK ST
ALPHINGTON ST
HAVEN ROAD

RESTAURANTS & CAFÉS	
Ask	8
Café Bar	7
Coolings	5
George's Meeting House	14
Harry's	2
Havana	16
Herbie's	10
Michael Caines	9
No. 21	11
On the Waterfront	18
The Plant	12

19, M5, A30 Okehampton & A38 Plymouth

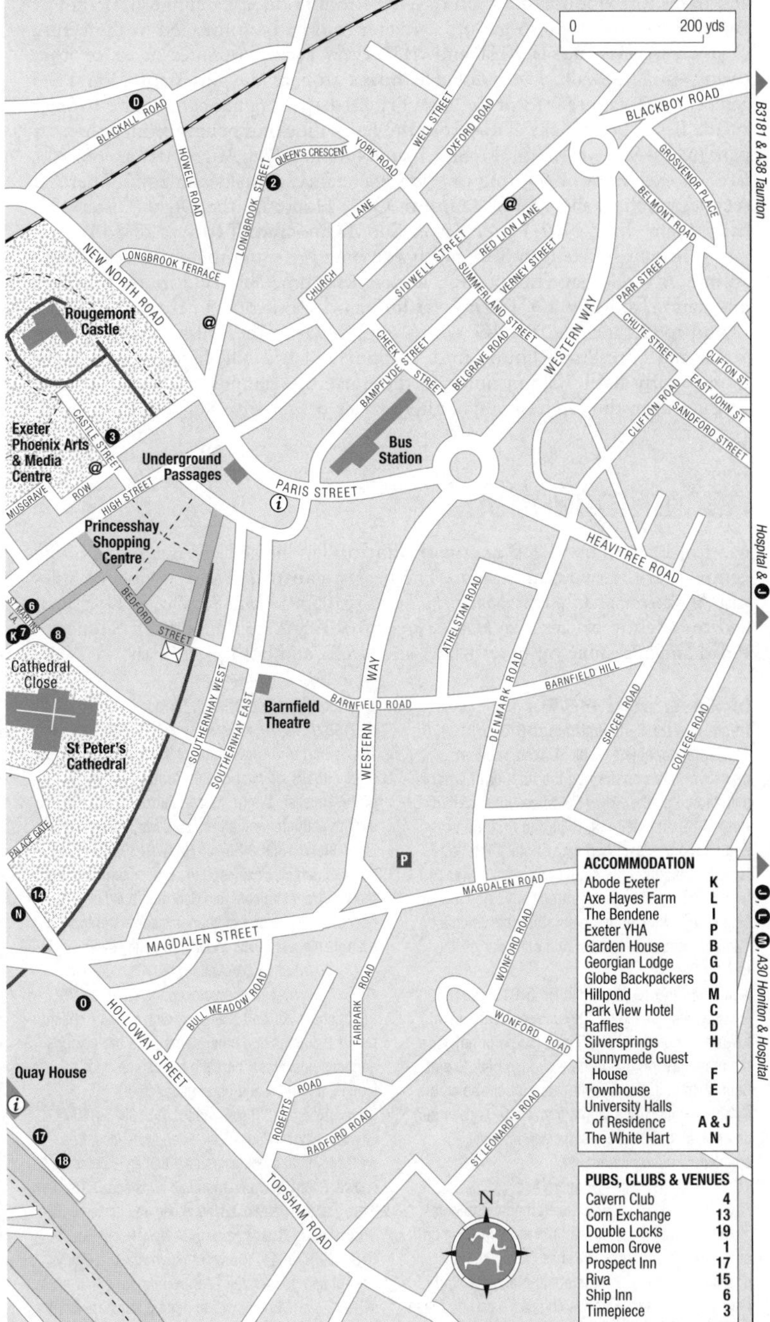
Rougemont Castle
Exeter Phoenix Arts & Media Centre
Underground Passages
Princesshay Shopping Centre
Bus Station
Cathedral Close
St Peter's Cathedral
Barnfield Theatre
Quay House
NEW NORTH ROAD
BLACKALL ROAD
HOWELL ROAD
LONGBROOK STREET
LONGBROOK TERRACE
QUEEN'S CRESCENT
YORK ROAD
WELL STREET
OXFORD ROAD
BLACKBOY ROAD
GROSVENOR PLACE
BELMONT ROAD
CHURCH LANE
SIDWELL STREET
RED LION LANE
SUMMERLAND STREET
VERNEY STREET
WESTERN WAY
PARR STREET
CHUTE STREET
CLIFTON ST
EAST JOHN ST
SANDFORD STREET
CLIFTON ROAD
CHEEK STREET
BAMPFYLDE STREET
BELGRAVE ROAD
CASTLE STREET
MUSGRAVE ROW
HIGH STREET
PARIS STREET
HEAVITREE ROAD
ST MARTINS LA
BEDFORD STREET
ATHELSTAN ROAD
DENMARK ROAD
BARNFIELD HILL
BARNFIELD ROAD
SOUTHERNHAY WEST
SOUTHERNHAY EAST
SPICER ROAD
COLLEGE ROAD
PALACE GATE
MAGDALEN ROAD
MAGDALEN STREET
WONFORD ROAD
HOLLOWAY STREET
BULL MEADOW ROAD
FAIRPARK ROAD
ROBERTS ROAD
RADFORD ROAD
ST LEONARD'S ROAD
TOPSHAM ROAD
0 200 yds
N
B
B3181 & A38 Taunton
Hospital & J
J, L, M, A30 Honiton & Hospital
P, M5, A376 Exmouth, Hospital & Topsham B3182
ACCOMMODATION
Abode Exeter K
Axe Hayes Farm L
The Bendene I
Exeter YHA P
Garden House B
Georgian Lodge G
Globe Backpackers O
Hillpond M
Park View Hotel C
Raffles D
Silversprings H
Sunnymede Guest House F
Townhouse E
University Halls of Residence A & J
The White Hart N
PUBS, CLUBS & VENUES
Cavern Club 4
Corn Exchange 13
Double Locks 19
Lemon Grove 1
Prospect Inn 17
Riva 15
Ship Inn 6
Timepiece 3

and trains to Exmouth, but train travellers from London Paddington, Bristol or Birmingham will have to get off at Exeter St David's, connected to the centre of town by **city buses** #H1 and #H2 every twenty minutes or so, or it's a twenty-minute walk. Long-distance **buses** stop at the bus station on Paris Street, at the eastern end of the new Princesshay shopping centre. The **tourist office** lies at Dix's Field, across from the bus station and behind Princesshay car park (Mon–Sat 9am–5pm, also Sun 10am–4pm in July & Aug; ⓣ01392/665700, ⓦwww.exeter.gov.uk/visiting or www.exeterandessentialdevon.com). There's a second, much smaller visitor centre in Quay House on the Quay (Easter–Oct daily 10am–5pm; Nov–Easter Sat & Sun 11am–4pm; ⓣ01392/271611). The city is best negotiated on foot, but if you envisage using the city buses during an intensive one-day visit, pick up leaflets with timetables and routes from the bus station and buy a £4 "**Day Rider**" all-day bus ticket here or on board. Useful routes include the #G, which goes down to the Quay from the High Street and Fore Street hourly until 3.15pm, and #D, which runs two to four times hourly until 7.30pm north to the university campus and the Northcott Theatre from the High Street; neither service operates on Sunday.

Accommodation

Most of Exeter's best B&B **accommodation** lies in the leafy area north of the centre, near the two train stations. The nearest **campsites** are a couple of miles east of Exeter at Clyst St Mary: *Hillpond* (ⓣ01395/232483; closed Dec–Feb) and the slightly pricier *Axe Hayes Farm* (ⓣ01395/232336), both off Sidmouth Road and accessible on buses #52A and #52B, and both pretty basic.

Hotels and B&Bs

Abode Exeter Cathedral Yard ⓣ01392/319955, ⓦwww.abodehotels.co.uk. A flash, modern makeover has transformed the interior of what is still known as the *Royal Clarence Hotel*, dating from 1769 and claiming to be the first inn in England to be described as a "hotel". With a superb position opposite the cathedral, rates are high; rooms not facing the front have no view at all. Its co-owner – the celebrated chef Michael Caines – has a restaurant and café-bar on the ground floor. ❼

The Bendene 15 Richmond Rd ⓣ01392/213526, ⓦwww.bendene.co.uk. The central location and heated outdoor swimming pool (summer only) are the main lures in this terraced house near Exeter Central station. Rooms with shared bathrooms are small, en suites (one with a four-poster) are larger and pricier, but all are quiet, clean and wi-fi-enabled. Limited parking. ❸

The Garden House 4 Hoopern Ave ⓣ01392/256255, ⓦwww.exeterbedandbreakfast.co.uk. In a quiet cul-de-sac just ten minutes north of the High Street, this B&B has charming and hospitable owners. Rooms are immaculate, and breakfast – offering various choices – can be taken in the lovely garden. ❺

Georgian Lodge 5 Bystock Terrace ⓣ01392/213079, ⓦwww.georgianlodge.com. This is part of a small chain of similar and similarly priced hotels, all near Exeter Central station. Most of the smallish, bright, functional rooms have views over the square, and all are en suite with wi-fi. ❹

Park View Hotel 8 Howell Rd ⓣ01392/271772, ⓦwww.parkviewexeter.co.uk. Equidistant between the two train stations, this Georgian building has peaceful, airy rooms of various sizes – the top room is biggest – and mostly en suite. ❸

Raffles 11 Blackall Rd ⓣ01392/270200, ⓦwww.raffles-exeter.co.uk. Victorian B&B full of character and crammed with military chests, risqué paintings and other items from the owner's antiques business. There's a handsome guests' lounge, a garden and parking space. ❺

Silversprings 12 Richmond Rd ⓣ01392/494040, ⓦwww. silversprings.co.uk. Friendly service, free wi-fi and great breakfasts make this an excellent choice. Rooms have comfortable beds and DVDs, and there's a nice garden. Advance booking advised. ❺

Sunnymede Guest House 24 New North Rd ⓣ01392/273844, ⓦwww.sunnymede.biz. Fairly central and good-value B&B; rooms are either en suite (❸) or with shower and hand basin, and triples and family rooms are also available. ❷

Townhouse 54 St David's Hill ⓣ01392/494994, ⓦwww.townhouseexeter.co.uk. Appealing Edwardian guesthouse, midway between the train stations, with bright, spacious rooms with wi-fi access. Some bathrooms and shower rooms are small. ⑤
The White Hart 66 South St ⓣ01392/279897, ⓦwww.marstonstaverns.co.uk. Centrally located old coaching inn with period trappings. The courtyard and bar are especially atmospheric, but some of the bedrooms are bland. Weekend rates fall into the next price bracket down. ⑤

Hostels and university accommodation

Exeter Youth Hostel 47 Countess Wear Rd ⓣ0845/371 9516, ⓔexeter@yha.org.uk. Country house two miles southeast of the city centre, accessible on minibuses #K and #T from High St or South St, and #57 and #85 from the bus station, as far as the post office on Topsham Rd, from where it's a ten-minute signposted walk. Alternatively, you could do the whole journey on foot along the canal path from the Quay. There's a kitchen, restaurant and internet access. Rooms have 2–8 beds, costing from £16.
Globe Backpackers 71 Holloway St ⓣ01392/215521, ⓦexeterbackpackers.co.uk. Clean and central, with good showers and an upbeat atmosphere. Bunk beds in dorms of 6–10 are from £16.50 each and there's one spacious family room with a four-poster (but shared bathroom) at £42 for two people. Kitchen facilities and wi-fi access are available.
University Halls of Residence ⓣ01392/215566, ⓦwww.exeter.ac.uk/hospitality. Accommodation on the campus – east on Heavitree Rd (slightly more useful for the bus station) or north off New North Rd (better for the trains) – is available in single rooms (£22–27; £35 en suite), or twin rooms (£35–40; £54 en suite) during student vacations over Easter & July to late Sept. Advance booking advisable.

The City

Exeter's sights are easily visited on foot; the furthest from the centre is the Bill Douglas Centre, on the university campus a mile or so north (bus #D). Almost everything else you'll want to see lies between the cathedral and the quayside, from which you can extend your explorations by following the canal and River Exe south.

Exeter Cathedral

In the centre of town, but aloof from the commercial bustle, **St Peter's Cathedral** (Mon–Sat 9.30am–5pm, Sun open for services only; £5; ⓦwww.exeter-cathedral.org.uk) is the logical place to kick off your exploration of the city. Begun around 1114, the structure was thoroughly remodelled between about 1275 and 1369, resulting in one of the country's finest examples of the decorated Gothic building style. Seen from afar, the two massive Norman towers, built, unusually, on the transepts, are the stately building's most distinctive feature; close up, it is the facade's ornate Gothic screen that commands attention, its three tiers of sculpted figures – including the kings Alfred, Athelstan, Canute, William the Conqueror and Richard II – begun around 1360, and now badly eroded. On entering, you're confronted by the longest unbroken Gothic ceiling in the world, an arresting vista of rib-vaulting which has been compared to an avenue of stately trees, the effect heightened by the multiplicity of shafts on each of the stout piers and of mouldings on the arches. The bulbous bosses running along the length of the ceiling are vividly painted – one shows the murder of Thomas à Becket.

High up on the left side, a minstrels' gallery is sculpted with angels playing musical instruments, below which are figures of Edward III and Queen Philippa. The walls of the aisles are densely packed with tombs and memorials that show a range of styles – most eye-catchingly in the right transept, where the fourteenth-century sepulchre of Hugh Courtenay, Earl of Devon, and his wife is carved with graceful swans and a lion. A door from here leads to the **Chapter House**, with a fine wooden ceiling and an array of discordant sculptures from the 1970s. In the left transept, the fifteenth-century **astronomical clock** shows the earth with the moon revolving around it, turning on its own axis to show its phases, and the sun represented by a fleur-de-lys. The minute dial above was added around 1760. **The Choir** is dominated by a spectacularly ugly sixty-foot bishop's throne, built in oak in around 1316, whose intricate canopy is said to be the largest of its kind in Britain. There are some good misericords here, decorated with foliage and grotesque beasts and dating from around 1260; they are thought to be the oldest in the country. However, if you want to see more than the elephant – the only one on public view – you'll need to ask one of the stewards to lift up the seats for you. On the way out of the cathedral, note the simple plaque to R.D. Blackmore, author of *Lorna Doone*.

To make the most of your visit, you can join a **guided tour** (March–Oct: Mon–Fri 11am & 2.30pm, Sat 11am, additional tour 12.30pm July–Sept), and you can soak up the ethereal atmosphere at evensong, which takes place at 5.30pm (Mon, Tues & Thurs–Sat) or 3pm on (Sun). Leaflets available in the cathedral list various other **events** taking place here throughout the year, such as organ and choral recitals, and classical concerts.

Outside, a studious-looking statue of the locally born theologian Richard Hooker surveys the Cathedral Close, a motley mixture of architectural styles from Tudor to Regency, though most display Exeter's trademark red brickwork. One of the finest buildings is the Elizabethan **Mol's Coffee House**, impressively timbered and gabled. Said to be named after a local Italian woman in the sixteenth century, it's now a shoe shop.

The Royal Albert Memorial Museum

After the cathedral, Exeter's most compelling attraction is the excellent **Royal Albert Memorial Museum** (Mon–Sat 10am–5pm; free), located north of the High Street on Queen Street. The collection is due to be closed for a major refit until 2011, but for the present the neo-Gothic building sports a boldly coloured interior with an impressive central staircase. The rich assortment of items exudes a Victorian spirit of wide-ranging curiosity, and the museum has an appropriately labyrinthine layout, with wildly contrasting eras and spheres of interest cheek by jowl. Unless you're here to see specific sights – for which consult the floor-plan at the entrance – you might as well let yourself get lost. Broadly speaking, however (though all will change in the planned restructuring), archeology and local history are on the left as you enter, natural history on the right, while upstairs, the **Rowley Gallery** is devoted to art, next to rooms full of clocks, ceramics, glass-and silverware, and the ethnography rooms.

The archeological section, displaying a mere fraction of more than half a million artefacts stored in the museum, shows finds from the numerous Bronze Age barrows excavated in Devon, including a substantial haul from Hembury, near Honiton – arrowheads, axe-heads and such rudimentary tools as "chippers" and "bashers". Local history begins with the Romans, whose coins and other items from the legionary fortress at Exeter are displayed along with coins from the time of the Saxon, Danish and Norman rulers. The collection is enlivened by imaginative reconstructions of period rooms to illustrate typical building styles from various eras, notably a typical Devon wagon roof from the medieval period, with displays of bench ends carved with Gothic and Renaissance motifs.

Other mock-ups include a heavily panelled room from the period 1550–1660, with a superb wooden overmantel above the fireplace showing the Judgement of Paris, and a room from around 1700 complete with an original plaster ceiling and cornice.

Once you've had your fill of the stuffed kangaroos, polar bears, moose and bison in the **natural history section**, head upstairs to the **art gallery** which, when not devoted to temporary exhibitions, has some good specimens of West Country art – mainly landscapes by local painters alongside work by other artists associated with Devon such as Turner, Reynolds and Opie. The adjoining **clocks and watches room** is filled with the clicking and whirring of an eclectic display of timepieces, from grandfather clocks to stopwatches. Prize exhibits include a "Turret clock" from 1741 – one of the earliest mechanical timepieces to have survived in Britain – and, from the same period, the Exeter Clock, an unbelievably complex mechanism of which only the painted dial – showing days of the week and month, phases of the moon, relative solar time and feast days – and a section of the intricate musical and automaton workings survive from bomb damage in 1941. Next door, the **glass collection** shows elegant examples of flasks and jars going back to the Roman era, as well as silver spoons, for which the West Country was famous, among other examples of the silverware that has been crafted in Exeter from at least the twelfth century. Look out, too, for the case of Martin-ware – pottery by the Martin brothers, who were among the most successful of the so-called "art potters" of the late nineteenth and early twentieth centuries. Their slightly weird works include a two-faced jug and various grotesque jars incorporating birds and other animals.

Backtrack through the art gallery to get to the **World Cultures room**, particularly strong on items from the Pacific, West Africa and the Congo River area; an elaborate priest's garb from the latter is the most eye-catching, with a painted wooden mask and a flamboyant robe made from vegetable fibre and hornbill feathers. The relaxed ground-floor **café** makes the perfect pit stop during or after your museum visit.

The High Street

East of the Royal Albert Memorial Museum, Exeter's pedestrianized High Street has a scattering of older buildings among the usual roster of retail outlets. The city's finest civic building is the fourteenth-century **Guildhall** (Mon–Fri 11am–1pm & 2–4pm, Sat 10.30am–12.30pm; free; may be closed for official functions and every other Sat in winter; call ⓣ01392/265500 to check), marked out by its elegant Renaissance portico (built in the 1590s from Beer stone) and said to be England's oldest municipal building still in regular use. The main attraction is the panelled main chamber, where the city's councillors meet; entered through an impressive oak door, the room has giant portraits of such worthies as George II and General Monck, the Devon-born Civil War veteran, and a fine example of a collar-and-brace timber roof from 1460 to 1470. The brackets supporting the main roof trusses are in the form of bears holding a ragged staff, symbol of the earls of Warwick and possibly carved in honour of "Warwick the Kingmaker", a major player in the Wars of the Roses who visited the city while the roof was being constructed.

Just down from the Guildhall, the impossibly narrow Parliament Street, just 25 inches wide at one end, stands almost opposite **St Petrock's** – one of Exeter's six surviving medieval churches in the central area.

The Underground Passages and Rougemont Castle

Round the corner from the north end of the High Street, 2 Paris St holds the entrance to a network of **underground passages**, first excavated in the fourteenth century. In the 1340s, masons at work on the cathedral were enlisted to improve the water supply intended for the cathedral precincts, laying down new lead pipes and creating conduits for which the vaulted passages visible today formed a kind of maintenance tunnel. The townspeople were entitled to a third of this precious piped water supply, but in the 1420s the city went to the trouble of building its own network, which was later upgraded. The interlinking passages, unusual for their length and good state of preservation, can be explored on a diverting 35-minute **guided tour** (June–Sept & school hols Mon–Sat 10am–5pm, Sun 10.30am–3pm; Oct–May Tues–Fri noon–4.30pm, Sat 10am–5pm; last tours 1hr before closing; no under-5s; £4.90) – the narrow stone corridors, requiring much stooping, are not recommended for the claustrophobic. In summer the tours are often fully booked, while in winter they sometimes don't leave at all if not enough people show up: call ⓣ01392/665887 to check.

At the top of Castle Street, off the High Street, you can see the red-coloured gatehouse of **Rougemont Castle**, the original fortress erected by William the Conqueror soon after his invasion of England. It was later rebuilt and augmented but little else remains today beyond the perimeter of red-stone walls extending from here through Rougemont and Northernhay Gardens.

Fore Street to the Quay

Southwest of the castle, the High Street becomes Fore Street. On the latter's west side, around halfway down, The Mint leads to **St Nicholas Priory** (school hols Mon–Sat 10am–5pm; school term time Sat 10am–5pm; £2.50), originally part of a small Benedictine foundation that became a merchant's home after the Dissolution. The interior has been restored to show how it might have looked in Tudor times, including a splendidly plastered ceiling in the parlour, and there's a collection of replica furniture and textiles on view.

On the other side of Fore Street, King Street leads to cobbled Stepcote Hill, sloping down towards the river. It's difficult to imagine today that this steep and narrow lane was once the main road into Exeter from the west. At the bottom, surrounded by some wobbly timber-framed houses, **St Mary Steps** is another of Exeter's ancient churches, with a fine seventeenth-century clock showing a knight and two red-coated retainers on its tower, and a late Gothic nave. The church is only open for services (currently Thurs 6pm and Sun 9.30am & 6.30pm).

At the bottom of Fore Street, off New Bridge Street, the red ruins of the medieval bridge lie in a small park tucked away from the traffic swirling over the more modern bridges across the River Exe. Walk along the riverbank (or follow Commercial Road) to reach the old port area, **the Quay**; now mostly devoted to leisure activities, the area gets quite busy in the evening, with clubs and pubs attracting punters, but it's worth a wander at any time. Shops and cafés share the space with the smart **Custom House**, built in 1681, its opulence reflecting the former importance of the cloth trade. The fine plaster ceilings within can be seen as part of a free thirty-minute guided tour of the area, taking place on Sundays at 2pm between April and October; there's no need to book, just turn up. The nearby **Quay House** has an information desk and a short video on Exeter's history (free) – see p.54 for opening times. Further along the Quay, a handsomely restored pair of five-storey warehouses, dating from 1835, are prize examples of the industrial architecture of the period, with hatches and winches hanging from their windows. You can cross the Exe via a pedestrian suspension bridge or by the hand-pulled chain **ferry** that shuttles across (Easter–Oct daily 10am–5pm; Nov–Easter Sat & Sun 10am–dusk; 30p).

From the Quay, you can **rent bikes and canoes** (see p.61) to explore the Exeter Canal to Topsham and beyond, or join a **canal trip** (April, May & Sept Sat & Sun; June–Aug daily; £5 round trip) as far as the *Double Locks Inn* (see p.60). The canal, which runs parallel to the river and southwest of it, dates from the sixteenth century, and was the first to use pound locks (vertical guillotine sluice gates). Good pubs along the route provide refreshment.

The Bill Douglas Centre

Exeter's most offbeat attraction is the **Bill Douglas Centre** (Mon–Fri 10am–4pm; closed bank hols; free; Ⓦwww.billdouglas.org), on the university's Streatham Campus to the northwest of the town centre off New North Road (roughly a twenty-minute walk, or take bus #D). The Centre, which is both a public museum and a research facility, explores the development of visual media from the late seventeenth century to the present day. Much of the collection of more than 70,000 artefacts was assembled by Peter Jewell and the great Scottish film-maker Bill Douglas, best known for his epic account of the Tolpuddle Martyrs, *Comrades* (1987), and includes such examples of early moving image forms as magic lanterns, optical toys and the first film cameras, as well as memorabilia, from Hollywood cigarette cards and Disney toys to Chaplin comics and Harry Potter lunchboxes. From the sublime to the hilarious, the exhibition will especially appeal to film buffs, collectors and lovers of kitsch.

Eating and drinking

Exeter's range of **restaurants** offer both lively sophistication and a relaxed vibe. Most pubs also serve food, and the bars and pizzerias around the Quay are especially popular in summer.

Restaurants and cafés

Ask 5 Cathedral Close Ⓣ01392/427127. Pastas and pizzas (£6–9) are the main event at this capacious, child-friendly Italian restaurant – part of a chain – in an atmospheric old building. If there's no space by the large windows overlooking the cathedral, eat in the low-beamed back rooms or on the red-brick veranda.

Café Bar Cathedral Yard Ⓣ01392/223626. Casually modish spot for a coffee or lunch, serving toasties, salads, burgers and pastas in small or large sizes (£8–10), and full meals in the evenings, with good fixed-price menus (£9–14). Live jazz on alternate Fridays (booking advised). Outdoor tables available.

Coolings Gandy St Ⓣ01392/434184. This wine bar is popular for lunchtime soups, salads and burgers (£6–9), and stays open until late for drinking, with a nice cellar bar (Wed, Fri & Sat). The place gets packed out at weekends.

George's Meeting House 10–12 Palace Gate Ⓣ01392/252525. In a converted chapel from 1760, this Wetherspoons pub has a range of bar food (from £3) – including beef and ale pie (£7.50) steaks (£9) – available until 10pm. There's an outdoor garden, and usually a crowd at night.

Harry's 86 Longbrook St Ⓣ01392/202234. Good-value Mexican and Italian staples (£8–10) are on the menu in this converted church, popular with students. Book at weekends.

Havana Kennaway Warehouse, Commercial Rd, The Quay Ⓣ01392/498181. With views over the river, and good fajitas, burgers and steaks on the menu (£8–12), this is a roomy, laid-back place by day, and lively in the evening when there are DJs (Thurs), live salsa bands (Fri & Sat) and comedy (Sun; £6).

Herbie's 15 North St Ⓣ01392/258473. The city's only wholefood restaurant, with fast and friendly service and organic wines and ice cream on the menu. Mains £8–10. Closed all day Sun & Mon eves.

Michael Caines Cathedral Yard Ⓣ01392/223638, Ⓦwww.michaelcaines.com. One of Exeter's – and Devon's – classiest restaurants, where you'll find sophisticated Modern-European cuisine in sleek surroundings. Reasonable fixed-price menus (£14.50 and £19.50) at lunchtime, with main courses in the evening costing around £23, for example sauté John Dory with crushed olive potato and shellfish sauce, or roast Creedy Carver duckling. Closed Sun.

No. 21 Cathedral Yard ⓣ01392/210303. Café-bistro facing the Cathedral and offering daytime coffees, teas and snacks as well as full meals, from fresh pasta to chicken and leek pie and salmon fillet (around £9). Closed eves.

On The Waterfront The Quay ⓣ01392/210590. With a vaulted interior and tables on the quayside, this is a popular eatery with a selection of pizzas, pastas and burgers on the menu, mostly £7–9.

The Plant Cathedral Yard ⓣ01392/428144. This veggie café-deli with outdoor tables near the Cathedral serves scrumptious breakfasts (including Persian baked eggs) for under £5, and such hot lunches as risotto for under £8. It's also good for coffees and teas, with some tasty cakes. All the produce is organic and/or locally produced. Closed eves.

Pubs

Double Locks Canal Banks, Alphington. A pleasant two-and-a-half-mile walk, boat ride or cycle ride along the canal banks from the Quay brings you to this brick-built inn, which has a large food menu, a beer garden and, in summer, barbecues on weekends and live music on Saturdays (3–5pm).

Prospect Inn The Quay. You can eat and drink local ales sitting outside at this seventeenth-century waterside tavern, which was the setting for TV drama *The Onedin Line*. Live bands on Saturday evenings.

Ship Inn St Martin's Lane. Claiming to have once been Francis Drake's local, this pub also serves food (jacket potatoes, baps and French sticks), either in the low-ceilinged bar adorned with knots and clay pipes or, at lunch, in the upstairs room.

Nightlife and entertainment

The **Exeter Phoenix Arts and Media Centre** (ⓣ01392/667080, ⓦwww.exeterphoenix.org.uk), behind the museum off Gandy Street, is the focus of diverse cultural pursuits, including non-mainstream films, plays, concerts and various workshops; there are usually free exhibitions and there's an excellent café-bar with an outdoor terrace (closed Sun eve). Of the town's theatres, the **Northcott Theatre**, on the university campus on Stocker Road (ⓣ01392/493493, ⓦwww.exeternorthcott.co.uk), is the main venue for plays, also offering readings, concerts, dance and opera, while the **Barnfield Theatre**, on Barnfield Road, Southernhay (ⓣ01392/270891, ⓦwww.barnfieldtheatre.co.uk), is the home of Exeter's Little Theatre Company and stages a range of amateur and professional productions.

Over a fortnight in mid-June, the **Exeter Festival** (ⓣ01392/493493, ⓦwww.exeter.gov.uk/festival) takes place at various venues around town, and features jazz, world and classical concerts as well as cabaret. Exeter's "autumn festival", in late October and early November, also has a musical emphasis, as does the **Vibraphonic** festival (ⓦwww.2020vibraphonic.co.uk), held over 18 days in March, with the accent on jazz, world, blues, urban and reggae. For details of all festivals, contact the tourist office or call the festivals and events office on ⓣ01392/265200, ⓦwww.exeter.gov.uk/festival. You'll find details of various other cultural events throughout the year at the tourist office or in the quarterly *Exeter Events* pamphlet; the magazines *247* (ⓦ247magazine.co.uk) and *What's On Southwest* (ⓦwww.whatsonsouthwest.co.uk) also give Exeter plenty of coverage.

Clubs and venues

Cavern Club 83 Queen St/Gandy St ⓣ01392/495370, ⓦwww.cavernclub.co.uk. A great underground venue for live music (mainly punk, electro and indie) and club nights (indie, drum'n'bass, dubstep, etc). Also open for daytime snacks (not Sun).

Corn Exchange Fore St/Market St ⓣ01392/665866. Mainstream venue for regular dance, folk and rock concerts as well as comedy evenings.
Lemon Grove Cornwall House, university campus ⓣ01392/263511, ⓦwww.exeterguild.org/lemon. The university's club – aka the *Lemmy* – is open term time only and hosts a variety of live acts from metal to rap. Tickets and info available from the Exeter Phoenix.

Riva 4 The Quay ⓣ01392/211347, ⓦwww.rivaexeter.co.uk. There's a touch of urban chic at this smart lounge-style club, with clean, minimalist lines, and funk, hip-hop and r 'n' b providing the soundtrack on two dancefloors.
Timepiece Little Castle St ⓣ01392/493096, ⓦwww.timepiecenightclub.co.uk. Formerly a prison and now offering dance mixes (Mon & Sat), Latin (Tues), student nights (Wed), urban (Thurs), indie (Fri) and world (Sun).

Listings

Airport Exeter International Airport (ⓣ01392/367433, ⓦwww.exeter-airport.co.uk) lies 6 miles east of Exeter at Clyst Honiton, off the A30 (buses #56, #56a and #379). Links to Belfast City, Glasgow, Leeds-Bradford, Manchester among other airports (see Travel details, p.68), as well as to European cities such as Alicante, Amsterdam, Dublin, Paris and Salzburg.
Bike and canoe rental Saddles & Paddles at 4 King's Wharf, The Quay (ⓣ01392/424241, ⓦwww.sadpad.com) rents out bikes (£14 per day), kayaks (£9–12 for 2hr) and Canadian canoes (£15 for 2hr). Booking essential.
Car rental Most agencies have offices at the airport, such as Avis (ⓣ0844/544 6015, ⓦwww.avis.co.uk), or in the Marsh Barton Industrial Estate, off Alphington Rd (bus #B), including Enterprise, 20 Marsh Barton Rd (ⓣ0800/230 0218, ⓦwww.enterprise.co.uk); Hertz, 8b Christow Rd, (ⓣ0870/850 7196, ⓦwww.hertz.com), and Thrifty, 12 Marsh Barton Rd (ⓣ01392/207207, ⓦwww.thrifty.co.uk).
Hospital Royal Devon and Exeter Hospital on Barrack Rd (ⓣ01392/411611) has an emergency department.
Internet access *New Horizon* café, 47 Longbrook St (daily 9am–9pm; £3 per hour; ⓣ01392/277523), where you can also nibble on Moroccan snacks; Central Library, Castle St (Mon, Tues, Thurs & Fri 9.30am–7pm, Wed 10am–5pm, Sat 9.30am–4pm, Sun 11am–2.30pm; first 30min free, then £1.50 for 30min; ⓣ01392/384206).
Laundries St David's Laundrette, corner of Richmond Rd and St David's Hill (daily 8am–9pm), also has internet access; Isambard Parade, outside St David's train station (Mon–Sat 8.15am–7.45pm, Sun 10.15–3.45pm).
Left luggage Capital Taxis, on the forecourt of Exeter St David's station, will stash your gear (£1.50 per average-size bag per 24hr).
Markets Outdoor market on Sidwell St, at the top of the High St, where a few stalls sell practical odds and ends daily (except Sun) until 4.30pm. On Thursdays, a Farmers' Market offers fresh local produce at the junction of South and Fore sts 9am–2pm.
Post office Bedford St, Princesshay shopping centre (Mon–Sat 9am–5.30pm).
Taxis A1 Cars, Richmond Rd (ⓣ01392/218888); Capital Taxis, Exeter St David's station (ⓣ01392/433433); Gemini (ⓣ01392/666666); all 24hr.

Mid-Devon

Covering the area between Exeter and Exmoor, mid-Devon is an intensely rural region of deep lanes and high hedgerows, largely free of the tidily thatched appearance of much of the county, and also of much tourism. The few specific sights are scattered. **Tiverton**, upstream of Exeter on the River Exe, is the only town of any significance, and one which, like many of the inland settlements around here, prospered from the local wool industry. The beneficiaries of the trade not only poured their largesse on the town but built some splendid mansions in the locality. Nearest of these is **Knightshayes Court**, which features rich decorative work by the exuberant Victorian Gothic designer, William Burges. Just downriver of the well-preserved village of **Bickleigh**, you can find traces of nine centuries of history at Bickleigh Castle, while **Killerton House** boasts a unique collection of costumes and an unusual bear's hut and ice house in the grounds.

If you're heading to Barnstaple from Exeter, you have the choice of taking the A377 or the Tarka Line (see p.200), the one surviving train service connecting Devon's north and south coasts. Either way, you'll pass through **Crediton**, eight miles northwest of Exeter and the site of one of Devon's most splendid churches – the only reason for stopping here.

General information on the region is available from Tiverton's tourist office or online at Ⓦwww.exeterandessentialdevon.com and www.devonshireheartland.co.uk.

Tiverton and around

At the heart of a rich agricultural region of red soil and lush meadows, **TIVERTON** lies thirteen miles due north of Exeter. The town owes its fortune to textiles, its mills powered by the Exe and Lowman rivers that meet here. The main pedestrianized Fore Street leads westwards down Angel Hill to the Exe Bridge, from where you can see the last remaining textile factory, a prominent landmark that was opened as a cotton mill in 1792 by a lace and textile entrepreneur, John Heathcoat.

The locality's one-time wealth is reflected in the number of churches in town – no fewer than eleven, including what is reckoned to be Devon's finest Georgian church, **St George**, south of Fore Street on St Andrew Street. Constructed partly of Purbeck stone in 1733, it lends a dignified air to the town's centre, the harmonious interior lined with Ionic columns. Further along St Andrew Street, **Tiverton Museum** (Mon–Fri 10.30am–4.30pm, Sat 10am–1pm; closed late Dec & Jan; £4.25; Ⓦwww.tivertonmuseum.org.uk) outlines the background of the town's cloth industry and includes a room belonging to a wool merchant of 1600. It also displays a variety of local items illustrating domestic and social life, from agricultural implements, mantraps and farm wagons to cooking utensils and lace-making machinery from the Heathcoat factory.

Two of the many buildings financed by wealthy wool merchants can be seen on St Peter Street, at the bottom of Fore Street: **Slee's Almshouses**, built in 1613 and fronted by two storeys of wooden galleries, and **St Peter's Church** (usually open daily: mid-May to mid-Sept 9.30am–4.30pm; mid-Sept to mid-May 9.30am–3.30pm), whose south porch has Gothic tracery depicting the Assumption of the Virgin Mary flanked by images of the benefactor and his wife. The church's south chapel, built in 1517, is richly ornamented with a frieze of well-armed ships and accoutrements of the wool trade – bales of wool, ropes and anchors – though the rest of the church is largely Victorian.

A few yards north of St Peter's on Park Hill stands the pinkish sandstone **Tiverton Castle** (Easter–Oct Sun & Thurs and bank hols 2.30–5.30pm; £5; Ⓦwww.tivertoncastle.com), a distinctly unmenacing fortification which traces its origins to 1106. It last saw action when Oliver Cromwell's general

Thomas Fairfax attacked and took it in 1645, and has since slumbered as a family house. The renovated rooms hold seventeenth-century armoury and such items as a "brass monkey" (a cannonball holder) and "morning star" (a spiked holy-water sprinkler). **Guided tours** take place on most Sundays at 2.45pm.

The Grand Western Canal

Just off Canal Hill on the Cullompton road and a mile southeast of the town centre, you could spend a serene hour or two strolling along the **Grand Western Canal**. The waterway was originally conceived as a means of linking the English and Bristol channels, but only the stretch from Taunton to Tiverton was completed (in the early 1800s), and was mainly used by barges carrying coal and limestone. The canal fell into decline following the growth of the railway in the 1840s, but has been restored and now forms the focus of a country park; a leaflet describing walks along the canal banks can be bought at the Tiverton tourist office.

Practicalities

Tiverton's **tourist office** (May–Oct Mon–Fri 9.15am–4.30pm, Sat 9.15am–3.30pm; Nov–April Mon–Fri 9.15am–4pm, Sat 9.15am–3pm; ⓣ01884/255827, ⓦwww.discovertiverton.co.uk), is next to the bus station in Phoenix Lane, just south of Fore Street. The **train station**, Tiverton Parkway, lies six miles west of the town centre, connected by buses #1 (Mon–Sat hourly) and #1B (Sun four times daily).

If you're looking for somewhere **to stay** in the centre, the best bet is *Bridge Guest House*, 23 Angel Hill (ⓣ01884/252804; no credit cards; ④), a modernized red-brick Victorian house with all rooms overlooking a peaceful garden on the banks of the Exe. A mile north of Tiverton on the A396, close to Knightshayes Court (see below), the elegant Georgian *Hartnoll Hotel* at Bolham (ⓣ01884/252777, ⓦwww.hartnollhotel.co.uk; ⑤) is equally tranquil; rooms are spacious and elegantly decorated, and there's a conservatory for breakfasts, and extensive gardens.

Daytime **eating** needs can be satisfied at the *Four and Twenty Blackbirds* café at 43 Gold St, which dishes up inexpensive quiches, omelettes and toasted sandwiches (closed Sun). The *White Ball Inn*, a Wetherspoons pub at 8 Bridge St, serves food all day, or pick up a snack at Tiverton's Pannier **Market** (Tues, Fri & Sat mornings for food), between Fore Street and Newport Street, where there's also a flea market every Monday.

Bikes can be rented for £9.50 per day from Abbotshood Cycle Hire, Abbotshood Farm, opposite the Grand Western Canal car park at Halberton (ⓣ01884/820728 or 07958/916165); they can also deliver bikes to and collect bikes from Tiverton or Tiverton Parkway station.

Knightshayes Court

Off the A396 at Bolham a couple of miles north of Tiverton, **Knightshayes Court** (house: mid-March to Oct daily except Fri 11am–5pm; £7.45; garden: mid-March to Oct daily 11am–4pm; £5.90; NT) is a Victorian Gothic pile partly designed by the flamboyant and idiosyncratic architect William Burges for John Heathcoat Amory (1829–1914), MP for Tiverton and grandson of John Heathcoat (see opposite). Burges' offbeat ideas, however, led to him being replaced in 1874 by J.D. Crace, whose contributions were considerably blander

▲ Knightshayes Court

than his predecessor's. Characteristic of Burges' work are the corbel figures in the hall stairwell, and the hall itself, an imitation of a medieval vaulted hall, holding a bookcase designed by Burges and painted by the Pre-Raphaelites Burne-Jones and Rossetti. The library demonstrates one of Burges' favourite motifs in the jelly-mould-like miniature vaults of the ceiling, which combine with cedar panelling and stencilling, heavily encrusted antique gold wallpaper and the leather and gold spines of the books to give the library a truly sumptuous feel. It's a suitable complement to the magnificent arched red drawing room with its Burges-designed marble chimneypiece, originally from Worcester College, Oxford. Burges' work is also evident in the bedroom, splendidly decorated with wall paintings of more than eighty birds and furnished with a magnificent golden bed. There's no information on display, but there are stewards in every room to answer questions, and guidebooks are on sale at £4.50.

From Tiverton, you can get to Knightshayes Court via bus #398 to Bolham or bus #348 or #349 to Lea Road; from either stop it's nearly a mile walk (uphill). The taxi fare from Tiverton is around £5.

Coldharbour Working Wool Museum

Signposted from junction 27 of the M5 and seven miles east of Tiverton on the B3440, **Coldharbour Working Wool Museum** (April–Oct daily 10am–4pm; Nov–March Mon–Fri 10am–4pm; £4; Ⓦwww.coldharbourmill.org.uk), outside the village of Uffculme, was a fully fledged working mill for two hundred years until its closure in 1981. Now reduced to supplying its shop with wool, the mill provides a fascinating insight into the techniques and machinery of the wool industry in the nineteenth century, when it was the area's major employer. Tours around the site reveal huge flying shuttles and colourful bobbins, all set against the whirring racket of machinery, alongside fine examples of steam engines in the engine house, including a 1867 beam engine and a rare wagon boiler. Contact the mill directly (Ⓣ01884/840960) or consult the website to find out when tours are scheduled, otherwise you can only view the boiler room and the steam engines outside the mill. Beside it, the area around the weir makes a good picnic spot. You can reach the mill from Exeter, Tiverton and Cullompton on buses #1 (not Sun), #1B (on Sun), #92 (not from Tiverton), and #92A (not Sun). #1 and #1B also run from the train station at Tiverton Parkway.

Bickleigh

Four miles south of Tiverton on the A396, the picturesque village of **BICKLEIGH** may suffer from occasional coach-party fatigue, but nevertheless makes an attractive stop, with a well-preserved castle and a five-arched bridge dating from 1630 that spans the tumbling waters of the River Exe. Idyllically sited by the river half a mile west of the village, the sandstone **Bickleigh Castle** – more of a fortified manor house than a castle – has parts dating back to the Norman era, though many of the older sections were destroyed during the Civil War, when the building was a Royalist stronghold. The original gatehouse survives, however, displaying weapons from the armoury and a vigorously carved stone overmantel showing a windmill, a walled city and figures in seventeenth-century dress. The castle now holds pretty designer cottages for rather pricey **accommodation** (Ⓣ01884/855363, Ⓦwww.bickleighcastle.com; ❼). You'll find less expensive rooms plus good views at the superbly sited, timbered and thatched *Fisherman's Cot* (Ⓣ01884/855237, Ⓦwww.marstonsinns.co.uk; ❺), which offers stylish rooms right on the river. You can **eat** here too, with a carvery on Sundays until 6pm serving good-value meat dishes. Further afield, seek out the small, sixteenth-century *Butterleigh Inn* at Butterleigh, three miles east of Bickleigh, which serves excellent-value meals such as steak and ale, fish and game pies, and there's a carvery at Sunday lunch for which booking is advised (Ⓣ01884/855407; no dinner Sun eve).

Bickleigh is connected to Tiverton and Exeter by buses #55, #55A, #55B, #155, and to Tiverton and Crediton by #347. Only services #55 and #55A run on Sundays.

Killerton

Five miles south of Bickleigh and twelve miles south of Tiverton off the B3185, **Killerton** (house: mid-March to late July, Sept & Oct Mon & Wed–Sun 11am–5pm; late July to Aug daily 11am–5pm; early to late Dec daily 2–4pm; garden: daily 10.30am–7pm or dusk; house and garden £7.25, garden only £5.35, reduced in Nov–Feb; NT) is attractively set on a hillside amid a landscaped garden of lawns and herbaceous borders. The elegant eighteenth-century house is most famous for its collection of **costumes**, one of the largest in the South West. Exhibitions on the first floor, drawn from the 18,000 items in store, are changed each year; recent ones include hats, underwear and wedding dresses. On the ground floor, the music room has a grand, swirly fireplace, a rare nineteenth-century quartet table to the right of the organ and fake marble (scagliola) columns. Accessible from the grounds, the laundry, too, is worth looking at, where pride of place goes to the Victorian pull-out floor-to-ceiling drier, and there's a rare example of a box mangle.

At the back of the house a path brings you to the **bear's hut**, a rustic summerhouse named after a pet bear once housed within. The three rooms are variously decorated with fir cones, cobbles, log sections, mullioned windows, stained glass and a floor made from, of all things, the tiny knucklebones of deer. Close to the large and steep rockery nearby, the **ice house**, constructed in 1808, could store up to three years' worth of ice in its twenty-foot-deep brick-lined pit.

Regular **talks and guided walks** take place here between March and October, and **drama productions** are staged in the gardens on August evenings (£12–15) – call ⓣ01392/881345 for details. Killerton has two **tearooms**, but for evening and bar meals, the excellent *Red Lion*, five miles south in the village of Broadclyst, offers good-value pies, steaks and home-made puddings.

Crediton and around

At the precise geographical centre of Devon, **CREDITON** was established as an important settlement and market town in Saxon times, serving as the meeting point of trade routes from Okehampton, Exeter, Tiverton and Barnstaple. The great missionary Saint Boniface, originally called Wynfrith, was born here around 680; he went on to convert the German tribes east of the Rhine whom even the Romans had steered clear of, for which he was later declared patron saint of both Germany and the Netherlands. At his request, a monastery was founded in his home town, which helped to establish Crediton as an important ecclesiastical centre. The monastery's church became Devon's first cathedral in 909, but even after the diocese was transferred to Exeter in 1050, Crediton retained a central role, and by the fifteenth century it was one of Devon's most prosperous wool towns.

In the eighteenth century, however, most of its ancient buildings were destroyed by fire, and the only item of note today is its splendid red collegiate **Church of the Holy Cross** (ⓦwww.creditonparishchurch.org.uk), whose cathedral dimensions and pinnacled central tower lie at the heart of what is now a mere village. It was started at or near the site of the monastery church in the mid-twelfth century, though only the base of the present tower remains from this period. Most of what you see today dates from a reconstruction in the early Perpendicular style between 1410 and 1478, as a result of which, what might have been a gloomy interior is now flooded with the light coming in through two rows of generous windows (including those of the clerestory) – the plain glass here replaced the original stained glass blown out by a landmine in 1942.

The nave arch of the tower is dominated by a gaudy monument erected in 1911 to commemorate local hero General Sir Redvers Buller, mainly remembered now for putting the British army into khaki. At the eastern end of the nave, the dignified Lady Chapel is thought to have provided the model for the eponymous chapel in Exeter Cathedral. The south choir aisle gives access to the Chapter House, dating from around 1300; the lovely old room now displays a collection of local knick-knacks – pieces of seventeenth-century armour, a few musket barrels and the like.

Once you've taken in the church, there's little reason to hang around in Crediton, unless you're looking for refreshments or you're stuck for a bed for the night (see below). A continual flow of traffic unfortunately mars the flavour of the broad main street, and the rest of the town lacks much interest.

Practicalities

Crediton's **train station** is off the A377 Exeter road just south of town, a stop on the Tarka Line between Exeter and Barnstaple. Buses stop in the High Street, with frequent connections to Exeter.

Taw Vale (Ⓣ01363/777879, Ⓦwww.tawvale.co.uk; ④) is the most central **place to stay**, a detached house at the southern end of town very near the train station, offering four rooms with en-suite facilities or (for a bit less) a separate private bathroom; one ground-floor room has its own patio shaded by a healthy grapevine. Breakfast includes home-made jams and marmalades. Otherwise, try the secluded, ivy-clad *Great Park Farm* (Ⓣ01363/772050, Ⓦwww.creditonbandb.co.uk; ③), half a mile west of the train station, signposted along a private road just before the railway line; all four airy rooms have private or en-suite facilities, and there's a spacious garden.

The town offers few good **eating options**. On the High Street, you can dig into cheap bar food at the *General Sir Redvers Buller*, with real ales, a conservatory and a garden. You'll find more character, however, at *The Three Little Pigs* on Parliament Square, a quirky pub and restaurant with everything from stuffed animals to musical instruments and model trains hanging from its walls and ceiling. The food ranges from burgers and pizzas to rump steak at around £8.50 (book at weekends: Ⓣ01363/774587). At 38 High St, Treloar's Delicatessen provides perfect food for picnics – hams, cheeses, pâtés and fruit juices (closed Wed afternoon & Sun). Four miles west of Crediton off the A377, the thatched *New Inn* at Coleford attracts foodies from far and wide; B&B is also available here (Ⓣ01363/84242, Ⓦwww.thenewinncoleford.co.uk; ⑤).

Travel details

Trains

Crediton to: Barnstaple (Mon–Sat hourly, Sun 6 daily; 1hr); Exeter (Mon–Sat hourly, Sun 6 daily; 10–15min).
Exeter to: Barnstaple (Mon–Sat hourly, Sun 6 daily; 1hr 20min–1hr 35min); Crediton (Mon–Sat hourly, Sun 6 daily; 10–15min); London (hourly; 2–3hr); Penzance (hourly; 3hr); Plymouth (hourly; 1hr 5min); Tiverton Parkway (2–3 hourly; 15min).
Tiverton Parkway to: Bristol (1–2 hourly; 50min); Exeter (1–2 hourly; 15–20min); Plymouth (1–2 hourly; 1hr 25min).

Buses

Crediton to: Exeter (Mon–Sat 3 hourly, Sun hourly; 25–30min); Tiverton (Mon–Sat 4 daily; 50min).
Exeter to: Barnstaple (Mon–Sat 15 daily, Sun 2 daily; 1hr 55min–2hr 15min); Bickleigh (Mon–Sat 2–3 hourly, Sun 8 daily; 25–45min); Bude (Mon–Sat 6–7 daily, Sun 2 daily; 1hr 45min–2hr); Crediton (Mon–Sat 2–3 hourly, Sun hourly; 25min); Exeter Airport (hourly; 15–25min); Exmouth (Mon–Sat 3–4 hourly, Sun every 30min; 40min); London (9–11 daily; 4hr 40min); Okehampton (Mon–Sat 1–2 hourly, Sun 2 daily; 40–50min); Plymouth (Mon–Sat hourly, Sun 6 daily; 1hr 35min); Sidmouth (Mon–Sat every 30min, Sun 1–2 hourly; 55min–1hr 25min); Tiverton (Mon–Sat 4 hourly, Sun 13 daily; 40min–1hr 30min); Torquay (Mon–Sat 8–12 daily, Sun 3 daily; 50min); Uffculme (Mon–Sat hourly, Sun 7 daily; 45min–1hr).
Tiverton to: Bickleigh (Mon–Sat 2–3 hourly, Sun 8 daily; 10min); Crediton (Mon–Sat 4–5 daily; 45min); Exeter (Mon–Sat 4 hourly, Sun 12 daily; 35min–1hr 30min); Uffculme (Mon–Sat 1 hourly; Sun 4 daily; 35min).

Flights

(main destinations only; see ⓦwww.exeter-airport.co.uk for full schedules)
Exeter to: Belfast (5–6 weekly; 1hr 15min); Dublin (5–6 weekly; 1hr 15min); Edinburgh (1–2 daily; 1hr 30min); Glasgow (1–2 daily; 1hr 30min); Leeds-Bradford (5 weekly; 1hr 5min); Manchester (Mon–Fri & Sun 1–2 daily; 1hr 5min); Newcastle (1 daily; 1hr 15min); St Mary's, Isles of Scilly (Mon–Sat: mid-March to Oct 3–9 weekly; 1hr).

2

East Devon

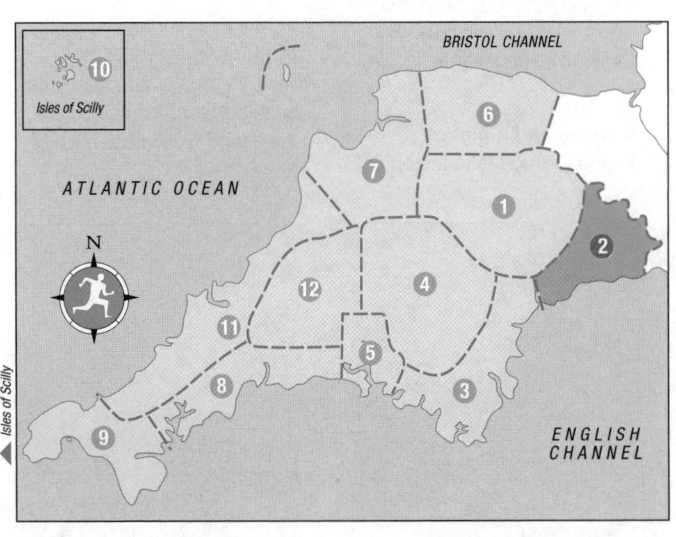

BRISTOL CHANNEL
10
Isles of Scilly
ATLANTIC OCEAN
N
6
7
1
2
12
4
11
5
8
3
9
Isles of Scilly
ENGLISH CHANNEL

CHAPTER 2

Highlights

* **Buzzard Cycle Route** The best way to explore the coast and interior of this rural region, covering eighty miles on a circular route. See p.73

* **A La Ronde** A unique neo-Gothic folly created by two women travellers and crammed with their offbeat souvenirs collected on the Grand Tour. See p.74

* **Sidmouth Folk Week** One of the country's most exuberant folk-music festivals, not least for its seaside setting. See p.81

* **A pause and a pint at Branscombe** Make a stop in this secluded hamlet, home to a fine church, a delightful beach and a great pub, the *Fountain Head*. See p.83

* **The coast path from Sidmouth to Beer** This hilly stretch of coastline takes in the thickly grown Hooken Undercliff, pebble beaches and a stupendous view from chalky Beer Head. See pp.83–85

* **St Mary's Church, Ottery St Mary** A contender for Devon's most glorious church, beautifully sited on a hill; the interior is a visual feast. See p.89

▲ A La Ronde

2

East Devon

Bordered by Dorset to the east and the Exe estuary to the west, **East Devon** is often bypassed by travellers speeding westward, and though the resorts and beaches can still get fairly busy in summer, the region is relatively free of the congestion which afflicts other parts of Devon. While its majestic red cliffs and shingle beaches are popular with young families in August, you can't fail to notice a preponderance of well-heeled retirees and older holiday-makers throughout the area, which is renowned for the strength of its "grey pound", helping to shape its character as a genteel, tranquil oasis of drowsy villages and old-fashioned, Regency-style seaside towns.

Immediately south of **Exeter**, at the head of the Exe estuary, the small port of **Topsham** is closely linked to the county capital, but with a very separate identity that's redolent of its seafaring past. Further south, the Gothic fantasy of **A La Ronde** sits above the estuary; it's one of the most delightful architectural curiosities in the West Country, whose fascinating contents recall the travels of the two eighteenth-century women who designed it. At the mouth of the estuary, **Exmouth** is as busy as things get in this region, a family resort embellished by some elegant Georgian terraces. It's the first of a succession of eighteenth- and nineteenth-century beach resorts strung out along this coast, all of which have been saved from mass tourism by their predominantly stony beaches, even if water quality consistently rates highly. Exmouth makes a good starting point for walks and cycle rides, as there is a pretty group of sedate villages just east of town, clustered around the River Otter. On the coast, **Budleigh Salterton** is the largest of these, with a wide stony seafront and a diverting museum that focuses imaginatively on the human and natural history of the region. You can get a close-up view of rural Devon at the unspoiled village of **East Budleigh**, a couple of miles inland, and at **Otterton**, reachable on a riverside walk from Budleigh. Back on the coast, a mile east of Otterton, the beautifully sited beach at **Ladram Bay** is the biggest crowd-puller hereabouts.

Working east along the coast, **Sidmouth**, the most appealing of East Devon's seaside resorts, is an elegantly aged Regency town with considerable architectural charm. Like Exmouth, it gets pretty lively in summer, not least when the annual **Sidmouth Folk Week** takes over in early August. There are cliff-backed beaches to either side of town, and the coast path provides an ideal way to reach more isolated stony strands, such as **Branscombe**, a secluded hamlet with a monumental church. Further east, **Beer**, though overcrowded in high season, is an immediately likable village with an intriguing network of subterranean caverns to explore. Across the bay, **Seaton** marks the last of the coastal resorts, but lacks Sidmouth's charm

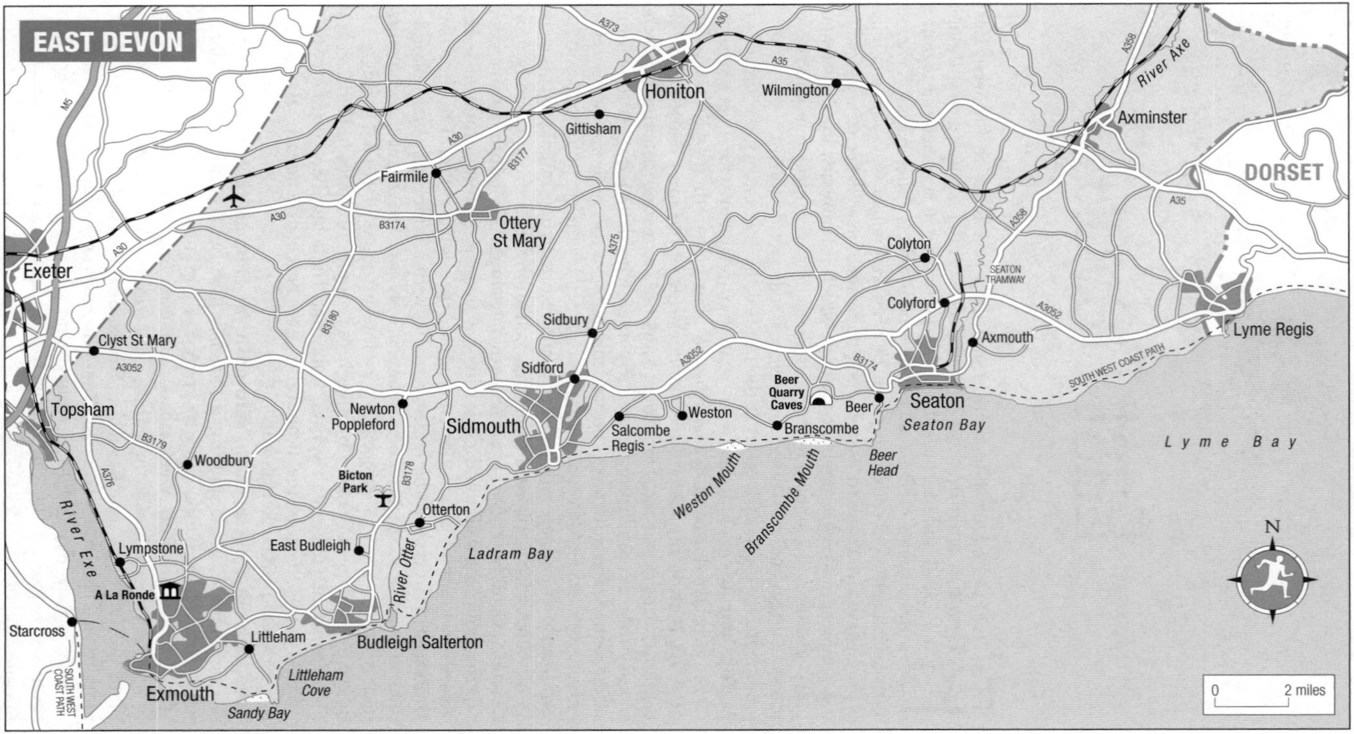

EAST DEVON

Exeter
Topsham
Clyst St Mary
Woodbury
Lympstone
A La Ronde
Exmouth
Starcross
River Exe
Littleham
Budleigh Salterton
Littleham Cove
Sandy Bay
East Budleigh
Bicton Park
Newton Poppleford
Otterton
River Otter
Ladram Bay
Fairmile
Ottery St Mary
Gittisham
Honiton
Sidbury
Sidford
Sidmouth
Salcombe Regis
Weston
Weston Mouth
Branscombe
Branscombe Mouth
Beer Quarry Caves
Beer
Beer Head
Seaton
Seaton Bay
Colyton
Colyford
Seaton Tramway
Axmouth
Wilmington
Axminster
River Axe
DORSET
Lyme Regis
Lyme Bay
South West Coast Path
M5
A30
A373
A35
A358
A375
A3052
A376
B3174
B3177
B3178
B3179
B3180
N
0 2 miles

Inland, the agricultural heartland that has created so much of Devon's wealth has remained more or less unchanged for centuries. The unruffled rural ambience is the main reason for straying away from the sea, but the lace museum at **Honiton** is also quite absorbing, while **Ottery St Mary** has one of Devon's most impressive churches, an expression of the largesse of the local merchants.

It's easy to explore the area via **public transport**, though train routes are limited to the branch line from Exeter St David's to Exmouth – a lovely ride along the Exe estuary – and the less frequent service from Exeter to Honiton. The most useful bus routes from Exeter are #52A, #52B, #X53, #56, #57 and #380; full details are given in the relevant places in the Guide, and at the end of the chapter. Leaflets detailing the eighty-mile circular **Buzzard Cycle Route**, which takes in all the towns mentioned in this chapter, are available from local tourist offices or at bike rental shops. Other useful publications for cyclists include the free *Cycling in East Devon* leaflets, which describe road routes and short cuts.

Topsham and around

South of Exeter, the Exe estuary assumes a broad, marshy appearance along its five-mile length. Frequent buses and trains connect the county capital with **TOPSHAM**, five miles south, though many visitors prefer to arrive via the scenic route, following the Exeter Canal on foot (then the ferry across the River Exe) or by bike from Exeter Quay. Exeter's main port since the middle of the first century, Topsham prospered from the European and later the transatlantic wool trade, and when this faltered at the end of the eighteenth century, the port was sustained by shipbuilding and its subsidiary activities, such as chain- and rope-making, until well into the nineteenth century.

The former warehouses and seventeenth-century merchants' houses along Topsham's central Fore Street and the Strand include good examples of the Dutch-influenced gabled architecture that was introduced by merchants trading with Holland. You can get some lively background on the town's shipbuilding and trading traditions at the **Topsham Museum** at 25 The Strand (April–Oct Mon, Wed, Sat & Sun 2–5pm; free). Arrayed around a seventeenth-century house and former sail loft, exhibits include a model of the town as it was in 1900, a selection of local craftwork and records of families prominent in the serge-cloth trade. Twentieth-century interest is provided in the form of memorabilia relating to the film star Vivien Leigh, sister-in-law of the museum's founder.

Further down the Strand, the sea wall offers good birdwatching at low tide, when there are views across the reedy mud flats – look out for curlews, redshanks and, if you're lucky, the odd avocet. Closer to the centre, at the bottom of the steps behind the church of St Margaret's on Fore Street, boatyards and ships' chandlers line the riverfront. From behind the Antiques Warehouse on the quayside, Stuart Line (Ⓣ01395/222144, Ⓦwww.stuartlinecruises.co.uk) runs hour-long **river cruises** down to Exmouth (May to mid-Oct; £5), departing two or three times a week at different times, depending on the tide; a Round Robin ticket (£7) allows you to take any of the frequent trains back. From nearby Trout's Boatyard, the *Sea Dream* ferries passengers downstream to the waterside *Turf Locks Inn* for a peaceful drink or meal (Easter–Sept; £4.50 return; Ⓣ07778/370582,

Ⓦwww.topshamtoturfferry.co.uk), with several departures daily. In winter, the *Sea Dream* also runs ninety-minute **birdwatching cruises** with commentary in conjunction with the Royal Society for the Protection of Birds (£10) – call the RSPB at Ⓣ01392/432691 for details.

Practicalities

General **information** and background on Topsham is available on the town website, Ⓦwww.topsham.org. There are some good **accommodation** options here, and it's a quieter and more relaxed alternative to lodging in Exeter. First call should be *Broadway House*, 35 High St (Ⓣ01392/873465, Ⓦwww.broadwayhouse.com; ④), a handsome red-brick Georgian house built by an Oporto merchant in 1776, with spacious rooms and good facilities. There's a touch more luxury at the *Globe Hotel* at 34 Fore St (Ⓣ01392/873471, Ⓦwww.globehotel.com; ⑥), a sixteenth-century coaching house opulently furnished with antiques; half-testers (partly canopied beds) and four-posters are available for a small supplement.

There's a good range of smart bistros and **restaurants** in town, from the top-quality *La Petite Maison* at 35 Fore St (Ⓣ01392/873660; closed daytime and Sun & Mon), an elegant bistro offering inventive Anglo-French dishes on fixed-price menus (£29 and £35), to the more casual *Georgian Tea-Room* (closed eves and all Sun & Mon), part of *Broadway House*, where you can enjoy casseroles, seafood, vegetarian dishes (all £6–7) and memorable puddings, as well as coffees and teas, or *The Café*, 76 Fore St (closed eves and Sun), which has all-day breakfasts, bacon baguettes and delicious cakes served in a large room with wooden tables.

Topsham's many **pubs** tend to be stuffed with souvenirs of the town's seafaring tradition, and most have bar food and good local ales. Try the *Lighter Inn*, at the junction of Fore Street and the Strand, which has tables outside by the Exe, or the sixteenth-century *Bridge Inn* on the eastern edge of town, overlooking the muddy River Clyst on Bridge Hill, and claiming to be the only pub ever visited by the Queen in an official capacity – in 1998, when she bought some beer to take back to Philip. Opposite the *Lighter*, *Route 2* has coffees, snacks, home-made ice cream and **bikes for rent** (Ⓣ01392/875085).

A La Ronde

On a hillside overlooking the Exe estuary, resembling something out of a fairy tale, the Gothic folly of **A La Ronde** (mid-March to Oct: Mon–Wed, Sat & Sun 11am–5pm; £6.40; NT) lies four miles south of Topsham and a couple of miles north of Exmouth, along a signposted turn-off from the A376 (a five-minute walk from the bus stop).

An extravagant flight of fancy dating from the 1790s, A La Ronde was the achievement of two cousins, Jane and Mary Parminter, who were inspired by a European Grand Tour to construct this sixteen-sided house – possibly based on the Byzantine basilica of San Vitale in Ravenna – filled with the various mementos of their travels. To these, the Parminters added a number of their own eccentric creations, ranging from concoctions of seaweed and sand to a frieze made of game-bird and chicken feathers. At the top of the house, which has an enclosed octagonal hall at its centre, the gallery and staircase are completely covered in shells; a closed-circuit TV system lets you home in on details.

The Parminter cousins intended that the house should be inherited by their female descendants alone, but fifty years after Mary Parminter's death in 1849, the conditions of her will were broken when the building was inherited by the Reverend Oswald Reichel, the only male owner in the house's history. Reichel's modifications are generally considered to have been an improvement;

dormer windows now admit much-needed natural light and afford superb views westward over the Exe estuary to Haldon Hill and Dawlish Warren.

If you're taken by A La Ronde's unconventional style, it's worth heading a little further up the lane to **Point-in-View** (same hours; free). This tiny Congregational chapel with adjoining almshouses was built in 1811 on the instructions of the Misses Parminter, for "four spinsters over fifty years of age and approved character". The design is as eccentric as A La Ronde's, the minuscule chapel sporting a pyramidal roof with triangular windows, surrounded by the low almshouses and topped by a jaunty weather vane.

Exmouth and around

At the southeastern corner of the Exe estuary, **EXMOUTH** claims to be the oldest seaside resort in Devon and signs of its early gentility are evident in some graceful examples of Georgian architecture. However, there are few surprises in the repertoire of resort attractions, and the town is primarily a holiday base – no more, no less. The place was unmentioned in history books before a Viking raiding party landed on a marauding invasion in 1001, fanning out to burn and pillage as far as Exeter. By 1200 Exmouth was an important port, and it later became a noted smugglers' haunt. From the time of the Napoleonic Wars, the town evolved as a resort and the central core preserves much of the feel of that era, with its terraces rising above lawns, rock pools and two miles of **sandy beach** – a rare thing in East Devon. Together with the stunning views across the estuary and out to sea, the beach is the focus of the town's continuing popularity as a family destination.

Arrival and information

Exmouth's **train and bus stations** sit side by side a few minutes north of the centre of town on The Parade; buses #56 and #57 link the town frequently with Exeter. The **tourist office** is on Alexandra Terrace, which runs alongside Manor Gardens from the bottom of The Beacon to the sea (Easter–Oct Mon–Sat 10am–5pm; Nov–Easter Mon–Sat 10am–2pm; Ⓣ01395/222299, Ⓦwww.exmouth-guide.co.uk). For **windsurfing tuition** and watersports equipment, contact Waterfront Sports, 2 Shelley Court, Exmouth Marina (Ⓣ01395/276599, Ⓦwww.waterfront-sports.co.uk). Tiger Charters (Ⓣ07836/792626, Ⓦwww.tigercharters.co.uk) operate **fishing trips** from the beach.

Accommodation

The most convenient places to stay lie between the train station and the harbour; you'll normally pay a little extra for rooms with sea views.

Barn Hotel Foxholes Hill Ⓣ01395/224411, Ⓦwww.barnhotel.co.uk. Exmouth's top choice, a fifteen-minute walk east of the centre and convenient for the beach and coast path. The Arts and Crafts house is set in its own quiet gardens and built according to a "butterfly" design by Edward Prior, a contemporary of William Morris, with bright, light rooms – the old nurseries on the top floor have great views – and gardens with an outdoor swimming pool. ⑤

Prattshayes Farm Ⓣ01395/276626. A couple of miles east of the centre, this is the town's nearest campsite, on National Trust land a half-mile along Maer Lane from the *Clinton Arms* pub in Littleham (bus #95 or #98). It's a plain but clean, cheap and well-equipped site, and just half a mile from the beach – advance booking is essential for July and August. Closed Oct–March.

Royal Beacon Hotel The Beacon Ⓣ01395/264886, Ⓦwww.royalbeaconhotel.co.uk. This is one of the more stylish options; rooms are spacious and elegantly old-fashioned – it's worth spending £15 extra for those with a sea view (first- and second-floor rooms are best). There's a fine restaurant. 6

Seaforth Hotel 45 Morton Rd ⓣ01395/275252, ⓦwww.seaforthexmouth.co.uk. Among the central options, an easy-going place close to the Esplanade, with shared bathrooms, rooms sleeping up to four and an outdoor smoking area. 3

The Town

Though the seafront is the main event here, most of Exmouth's finer architecture is set back from the coast, concentrated on a hill known as **The Beacon**, which once accommodated such folk as the wives of Nelson and Byron – installed at 6 and 19 The Beacon, respectively. In the western end of town lies the old port, now redeveloped as a luxury marina, though there are still some working fishing boats in evidence, and it's a good place to buy fresh wet fish or to join **boat trips**, including a range of cruises (see box below).

For indoor amusement, the **Exmouth Museum** on Sheppards Row, off Exeter Road and near the bus and train stations (April–Oct Mon, Fri & Sat 10.30am–12.30pm, Tues–Thurs 10.30am–12.30pm & 2.30–4.30pm; £1.50), offers a whirl through local history by means of reconstructions of a Victorian kitchen and a 1930s dining room as well as examples of bobbin lace and children's toys.

Most visitors to Exmouth, however, are drawn to the town's beach, a broad sandy sweep below the Esplanade, backed by a promenade and extending as far as the eastern cliffs. **Swimmers** should pay attention to the red warning flags, as the offshore tides can stir up strong currents. Summer sees a lively hubbub here, with traditional Punch and Judy puppet shows on the beach and kiosks from which wet suits, windsurfing equipment, surf- and body-boards can be rented (alternatively, try Tad Shop, 14a Rolle St ⓣ01395/227007, with another outlet at the Marina at 4 Pier Head). From Phear Park (a right turn from Exeter Road), you can access the level **cycle path** that follows a disused inland railway track to Budleigh Salterton (see opposite); a turn-off from the route along Castle Lane takes you to the village of **Littleham**, where Lady Nelson is buried in the churchyard. The East Devon stretch of the **South West Coast Path** (see Basics, p.25) starts from the cliffs at the eastern end of Exmouth's seafront (keep to the landward side of the café and car park at the far end of the Maer recreation ground, then branch right off Foxholes Hill). It's a very hilly but marvellously panoramic start to this section of the path, which continues for 26 miles to the Dorset border at **Lyme Regis** – leaflets detailing the route are

Boat trips from Exmouth

From Exmouth's marina, Stuart Line (ⓣ01395/222144, ⓦwww.stuartlinecruises.co.uk) operates **cruises** to Topsham (£5), Torbay (£12) and Sidmouth (£10) between June and September, as well as less frequent full-day wildlife coastal cruises (£15); three-hour **birdwatching trips** in the Exe estuary (Nov–March; £9), and river cruises (all year; £5). A Round Robin ticket allows you to cruise up to Topsham and return by train (£7). A separate **water-taxi service** to Dawlish Warren (see p.95) runs between April and early September (ⓣ07970/918418; £4 return), while an hourly ferry service with Exe to Sea Cruises (ⓣ01626/774770 or 07974/772681, ⓦwww.exe2sea.co.uk) crosses the estuary to Starcross – a useful way to get to or from South Devon without passing through Exeter (mid-May to mid-Sept 10.40am–5.40pm, extra crossing at 6.15pm in Aug; April to mid-May and late Sept 10.40am–4.40pm; £4.50 one way/£5 return, bikes £1 each way).

The Jurassic Coast

The 95-mile stretch of the East Devon and Dorset coasts between Exmouth and Studland Bay has been named the **Jurassic Coast** in honour of the long geological record displayed here, Despite the name, some 185 million years are represented, covering the Triassic, Jurassic and Cretaceous periods, together forming the Mesozoic Era. The Dorset section of the coast is the most rewarding area for fossil-hunters, but the East Devon stretch is the oldest, and includes the richest mid-Triassic reptile sites in Britain. The coast is distinguished for its diversity, ranging from the red sandstone of the sea stacks at **Ladram Bay** – the reddish colouring of the cliffs hereabouts is due to the presence of iron – to the white chalk of **Beer Head**, and the areas where landslides have created "**undercliffs**", thickly grown with trees and other vegetation. The best ways to explore the coast are either by sea – **boat trips** are available in summer from all the major resorts – or on foot along the **coast path**. For more information, pick up a free leaflet or the official guide (£4.95) from local tourist offices, or see Ⓦwww.jurassiccoast.com.

available from the tourist office. From the cliff-top, steps lead down to beaches at Orcombe Point and Sandy Bay (the latter is also accessible April–Oct on the hourly #95 bus). From Rodney Point, a zigzag path leads up to the Geoneedle, an obelisk marking the western end of the **Jurassic Coast** (see box above).

Eating and drinking

Exmouth is poorly served with **restaurants** or **pubs**, though the places listed below will fit the bill for most requirements.

Bath House The Esplanade. Pub with tables outside facing onto the sea and serves vast portions of food at rock-bottom prices; the beer is good, and there's darts and pool.

Fountain Café The Beacon. A cheap and friendly spot for a quick lunch, baguette or jacket potato.

Nico's 3 Tower St Ⓣ01395/276734. Expertly prepared Italian standards (£8–10) in a cosy environment. Eves only.

Seafood Restaurant 9 Tower St Ⓣ01395/269459. Exmouth's top choice, close to the tourist office and The Beacon and offering zesty fish soups among other dishes; mains £14–17. Closed eves and all Sun & Mon.

Budleigh Salterton and around

Bounded by red-sandstone cliffs to the west and the pebblestone ridge of the Otter estuary in the east, **BUDLEIGH SALTERTON**, four miles east of Exmouth along the B3178, is the apotheosis of Devon respectability. The motto on its coat of arms, "Beau Sejour" ("Have a good stay"), has been taken to heart by the legions of elderly folk who have settled here, giving the place a slow, somnolent feel. The town takes its name from the salterns, or saltpans, in which monks evaporated sea water during the thirteenth century – long since disappeared. In the twentieth century, Budleigh's whitewashed cottages and houses attracted such figures as Noël Coward and P.G. Wodehouse, and it is the old-fashioned flavour associated with these names that constitutes the principal charm of the place today.

The town's **High Street** is bordered by a fast-flowing stream at its lower end, where it becomes Fore Street, site of the **Fairlynch Museum** (Easter–Sept Mon–Fri & Sun 2–4.30pm; £2), housed in a nineteenth-century *cottage orné*, or ornamental rustic cottage, of which the region holds several examples. Built in 1811 and sporting narrow Gothic windows, the thatched museum holds a fine collection of Victorian and Edwardian costumes and locally made Edwardian dolls, while geological exhibits include examples of radioactive nodules found in local cliffs. There's a diverse array of historical relics in a damp, low-ceilinged "smuggler's cellar", while upstairs you can see beautiful examples of lace, an east Devon speciality, and demonstrations of lace-making take place on most Fridays.

A few steps below the museum, Fore Street ends at Marine Parade and a wide arc of beach where you can still see the wall shown in the iconic *Boyhood of Raleigh*. Painted here by John Millais in 1870, this work depicts a salty dog spinning a yarn to the young Walter Raleigh and his half-brother, Humphrey Gilbert, another sailor-to-be (the picture is now in London's Tate Britain gallery). The Octagon, the house where Millais stayed, stands next to the museum. The great crescent of beach extending to either side from here has little of the seaside paraphernalia to be found in some of Devon's other resorts. If you're tempted to swim, you'll find the pebbles shelving quite steeply into the sea, though the currents are reasonably safe in calm weather. Tree-topped cliffs rise above the shore to the west, below which one of the oldest naturist **beaches** in the country is hidden away. If that's not your scene, you'll find a few tiny, sheltered strips of sand by following the coast path two miles west of Budleigh to Littleham Cove. There's also a **cycle track** between Budleigh and Littleham, following the course of the old railway, and allowing you to bike the whole way between Budleigh and Exmouth's seafront with only a brief stretch on roads.

Tracking Budleigh's beach to the east, you'll come across the windlass and cable still used to haul up small lobster- and crab-fishing boats at the mouth of the River Otter, Otter Point. A small, saltwater **wildlife reserve** and reed bed in the Otter estuary lies on the landward side of the pebble-ridge here. From here, you can follow the River Otter's banks for two miles northeast to **OTTERTON**, a handsomely thatched and timbered village with a broad street and open stream running through the centre. The **Otterton Mill Centre** (daily 10am–5pm; free) is the last working mill on the river, where you can view the flour-milling process. There's an extensive gallery of local art here, a craft centre and a market, while jazz, blues and folk concerts as well as other events are held on most Thursday evenings, for which booking is recommended (call ⓣ01395/568521 or see ⓦwww.ottertonmill.com for details). The bakery provides tasty bread for the excellent **café/restaurant**, where a range of wholesome snacks and full meals are available at lunchtime and on Thursday (concert-goers only), Friday and Saturday evenings. A signposted minor road leads a mile east from Otterton to **Ladram Bay**, a secluded pebbly beach sheltered by woods, beautifully eroded cliffs and red-sandstone stacks. It's a lovely spot for a swim, though somewhat marred by the nearby caravan site, and it gets extremely crowded in summer.

Less than two miles north of Budleigh Salterton on the B3178, **EAST BUDLEIGH** is famed for its connection with Walter Raleigh, whose father was warden at the church of **All Saints**, at the top of the village (daily 8am–dusk). Inside you can see the family's pews (the front two on the left), as well as a collection of superbly carved sixteenth-century bench ends, said to be among the oldest in the country. Entirely secular, they mainly display the arms of local families and emblems representing local trades; others show exotic plants and animals, and one (near the pulpit), depicts the Green Man of May Day celebrations. Raleigh himself was born one and a half miles west in the hamlet of Hayes Barton.

Budleigh Salterton Festival

The **Budleigh Salterton Festival** takes place over nine days in late July and early August, featuring mainly classical concerts in local churches and village halls. Tickets cost around £15 per event – see ⓦwww.budleigh-festival.org.uk or contact the tourist office for a programme and ticket sales.

A mile or so further up the B3178, **Bicton Park** (daily: April–Sept 10am–6pm; Oct–March 10am–5pm; £6.95; ⓦwww.bictongardens.co.uk) is East Devon's showiest garden, famed for its formal arrangement and specialist greenhouses. Spread over some sixty acres, the sweeping lawns, arboretum and exhibition hall displaying bygone items of rural and agricultural life provide plenty of diversion. However, horticulturalists and amateur gardeners alike are most drawn to the immaculate, set-piece gardens, mainly nineteenth-century in origin, though the Italian Garden dates back to the 1730s. The most impressive of the glasshouses is the Palm House, a graceful construction incorporating 18,000 panes of glass, and, built in the 1820s, two decades prior to the Palm House at Kew. Kids will appreciate the adventure playground, maze and miniature train.

Practicalities

Bus #357 connects Exmouth and Budleigh Salterton, as does the #157, which also runs to East Budleigh, Otterton, Bicton Park and Sidmouth. At the bottom of Fore Street, Budleigh's **tourist office** (Easter–Oct Mon–Sat 10am–12.30pm & 1.30–4.30pm; Nov–Easter Mon–Thurs & Sat 10am–1pm, Fri 10am–3pm; ⓣ01395/445275, ⓦwww.visitbudleigh.com) has information on local activities, including walking and birdwatching. The Budleigh Salterton Riding School on Dalditch Lane, Knowle, a couple of miles northwest of the village (ⓣ01395/442035, ⓦwww.devonriding.co.uk; closed Mon), provides **tuition and rides** on Woodbury Common (£22 for one hour, £36 for 2 hours), and also offers holiday cottages.

If you want to **stay** in Budleigh, try *Rosehill Rooms and Cookery*, a boutiquey B&B at 30 West Hill (ⓣ01395/444031, ⓦwww.rosehillroomsandcookery.co.uk; no credit cards; ⑤; closed Jan), a ten-minute walk up the High Street; the plushly refurbished Victorian country house offers spacious rooms with nice bathrooms, as well as cookery courses. Alternatively, there are great views from the airy and well-equipped rooms of the *Long Range Hotel*, 5 Vales Rd, off East Budleigh Road (ⓣ01395/443321, ⓦwww.thelongrangehotel.co.uk; ⑤), where there's a conservatory leading on to a lawned garden. Nearby, on Bear Lane, close to the cycle track to Exmouth and a mile inland, there's a sheltered **campsite**, *Pooh Cottage* (ⓣ01395/442354, ⓦwww.poohcottage.co.uk; closed Nov–March), with a pub nearby.

Among Budleigh's **restaurants**, *Tobias* at 53 High St (ⓣ01395/446644; closed Sun eve and all Mon & Tues) has an elegant, mellow ambience and serves lamb and duck as well as fresh fish dishes for £12–17, followed by some great desserts. On Chapel Street, off the High Street, the *Salterton Arms* has decent pub grub (except Sun eve & Mon), while, for superb home-made **ice cream**, check out the *Creamery*, across from the museum. For a do-it-yourself meal, there's Delytes, 44 High St, a deli with a good line in cheeses, pâtés and sausage rolls. Out of town, on the Sidmouth road, *Otterton Mill* (see opposite) is the place for local organic produce to eat in or take away.

Sidmouth and around

Nestled in the Sid valley six miles northeast of Budleigh Salterton, **SIDMOUTH** is the region's architectural aristocrat. Characterized by its terraces with castellated parapets and Gothic windows, the seaside resort boasts nearly five hundred listed buildings. The majority of these date from the first forty years of the nineteenth century, when Sidmouth became fashionable among the upper classes after the Duke of Kent retired here in 1820; his family, including his daughter, the future Queen Victoria, moved into Woolbrook Glen, now the *Royal Glen Hotel*. What had previously been a very low-key fishing village subsequently enjoyed the fashionable patronage of such figures as the Grand Duchess Hélène of Russia, sister-in-law of the tsar, and the Empress Eugénie, wife of Napoleon III. The town's "silvery, pink and creamy" facades inspired poet and architecture buff John Betjeman to extol "Devon Georgian" as "the simplest, gayest, lightest, creamiest Georgian of all".

Arrival and information

Bus service #357 runs daily between Exmouth, Budleigh Salterton and Sidmouth, while buses #52A and #52B connect Sidmouth with Exeter via the inland A3052. The #899 service (Mon–Sat) links Branscombe with Sidmouth, Beer and Seaton. Sidmouth's **tourist office** (March & April Mon–Thurs 10am–4pm, Fri & Sat 10am–5pm, Sun 10am–1pm; May–July, Sept & Oct Mon–Sat 10am–5pm, Sun 10am–4pm; Aug Mon–Sat 10am–6pm, Sun

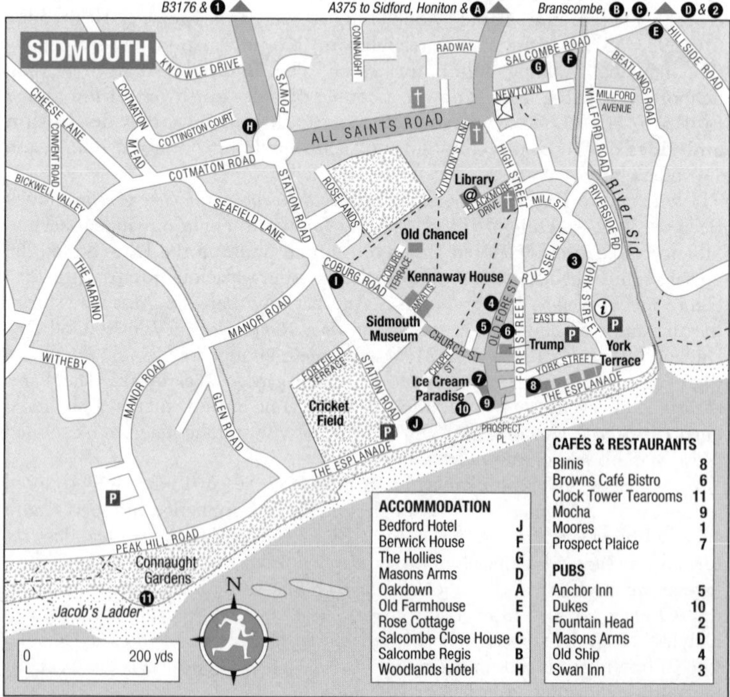

Sidmouth Folk Week

With its diverse range of musicians, excellent setting and eclectic atmosphere, **Sidmouth Folk Week**, taking place at the beginning of August, is widely rated as one of the country's best folk festivals. Around 500 events, including folk and roots acts, workshops and ceilidhs, take place in venues ranging from 1000-seater marquees to pubs and hotels around town, as well as numerous spontaneous sessions and pavement busking. Ticket prices for the whole week are £140 when bought before April, and £160 from April 1, weekend tickets are £56 and £64 respectively and day tickets are £28 and £32. These tickets cover all events except the headline acts at the Ham Marquee, though ticketholders get priority booking for these. Without one of these, you'll pay £8 for each workshop or talk and up to £8 for performances. It's always worth booking early, especially for the main acts. Accommodation is at a premium and also needs to be booked well in advance, even the capacious *Bulverton Campsite* outside Sidmouth (which lays on frequent shuttle buses to the centre). For more details and to book, call ⓣ01395/578627, visit the website ⓦwww.sidmouthfolkweek.co.uk), or call Sidmouth's tourist office (ⓣ01395/516441).

10am–5pm; Nov–Feb Mon–Sat 10am–1.30pm; ⓣ01395/516441, ⓦwww.visitsidmouth.co.uk) is by the car park on Ham Lane, off the eastern end of the Esplanade behind the lifeboat station. It sells pamphlets about the many walks in the area, and the *Blue Plaque Guide* (£2), which documents the town's historic houses. You can rent **bikes** from W.V. Fish, 71 Temple St (Easter–Sept; ⓣ01395/512185), and **internet** access is available at the tourist office or from the library on Blackmore Drive, opposite Somerfield supermarket (Mon & Fri 9.30am–7pm, Tues & Sat 9.30am–1pm, Wed & Thurs 9.30am–5.30pm).

Accommodation

Sidmouth has **accommodation** to suit all pockets; more expensive places lie nearer the sea, while most of the cheaper guesthouses are on or around Salcombe Road and Alexandra Road, about a mile back from the Esplanade and reached from the High Street or on foot on the Byes, running alongside the River Sid. Many places are booked up months ahead for Sidmouth Folk Week. The best **campsites** are east of Sidmouth, along or off the A3052; take any bus for Beer or Seaton.

Hotels and B&Bs

Bedford Hotel The Esplanade ⓣ01395/513047, ⓦwww.bedfordhotelsidmouth.co.uk. On the seafront, and right at the heart of the folk festival (when there are regular late-night sessions in the bar), this Regency hotel has great views from its sea-facing rooms, many of which have balconies. ⑤

Berwick House 4 Albert Terrace, off Salcombe Rd ⓣ01395/513621, ⓦwww.berwick-house.co.uk. Clean and comfortable B&B, with smallish rooms (all en suite) and off-road parking. Guests get free access to Sidmouth's indoor pool. No under-12s. No credit cards. ④

The Hollies Salcombe Rd ⓣ01395/514580, ⓦwww.holliesguesthouse.co.uk. Rooms in this Regency building are an elegant blend of contemporary and traditional, spotlessly maintained and some with DVD players. Watercolours by the owner adorn the walls, and the seafront is less than ten minutes' walk. No credit cards. ④

Masons Arms Branscombe ⓣ01297/680300, ⓦwww.masonsarms.co.uk. Ancient inn a ten-minute walk from the beach. The luxurious rooms boast wooden beams, antique furnishings and designer fabrics, and there's a great bar and restaurant. Gets busy in summer and on holiday weekends. ⑤

The Old Farmhouse Hillside Rd ⓣ01395/ 512284. On the east side of the Sid (accessed from Salcombe Rd), half a mile from the seafront, this building dating from 1569 has oodles of antique atmosphere. All rooms are en suite, and evening meals are available on request. Advance booking essential. No under-12s. No credit cards. Closed Nov–Easter. ⑤

Rose Cottage Coburg Rd ⓣ01395/577179, ⓦwww.rosecottage-sidmouth.co.uk. Family-run B&B with four comfy, tastefully furnished rooms – all en suite or with private bathroom – and a garden with a children's play area. It's 200m from the Esplanade and a beach hut is available for 15 a day. 5

Salcombe Close House Sid Lane ⓣ01395/579067, ⓦwww.salcombeclosehouse.com. Just two airy rooms are available in this B&B, both overlooking a pleasant garden. One room, slightly pricier, is huge. It's a peaceful spot, and though relatively distant from the seafront (a twenty-minute walk), it's a lovely walk into town, along the River Sid. 5

Woodlands Hotel Cotmaton Cross ⓣ01395/ 513120, ⓦwww.woodlands-hotel.com. One of Sidmouth's most stylish hotels, a few minutes' walk up Station Road from the Esplanade, this large *cottage orné* was built in its present form around 1809, but parts date back over 700 years. There are antiques in the bedrooms and the grounds boast a conservatory and gardens. 7

Campsites

Oakdown Weston ⓣ01297/680387, ⓦwww.oakdown.co.uk. Spacious, well-maintained site some four miles east of Sidmouth. Washing facilities are first-class, but there's some road noise from the adjacent A3052. There's a three-night minimum stay during the August bank holiday and seven nights during Folk Week. Closed early Nov to late March.

Salcombe Regis Salcombe Regis ⓣ01395/514303, ⓦwww.salcombe-regis.co.uk. The nearest campsite to Sidmouth – a mile and a half east of town – this lies within view of the sea and a twenty-minute walk from Weston Mouth beach. It's more tent-friendly than *Oakdown*, with level pitches and good general facilities including a shop. A three-night minimum stay is required at Easter, late May and late August, and seven nights during the folk festival. Closed Nov–Easter.

The Town

The strongest echoes of Sidmouth's regal connections survive today along **the Esplanade**, at the end of the shop-lined High Street and its continuation, Fore Street. Most people end up here to promenade among the deckchairs and benches which, in summer, are almost permanently occupied by people contemplating the gravelly beach below. Here and elsewhere in the town, wrought-iron balconies with curved canopies rise above the numerous hanging baskets and lavish flower displays that have helped make Sidmouth a multiple winner of floral awards. Though the town beach makes absorbing viewing, the best area for bathing is west of the centre at **Jacob's Ladder**, a stretch of gently shelving shingle (sandy at low tide) that's backed by crumbly red cliffs and overlooked by lush gardens and a tearoom housed in a clocktower. In summer, Stuart Line (ⓣ01395/222144, ⓦwww.stuartlinecruises.co.uk) operates **coastal cruises**, either to Exmouth, returning by bus (£10), or three-hour round trips along the Jurassic Coast with commentary (£8). Departures are from opposite the *Bedford Hotel* on the Esplanade. Phone or consult the website for times and dates, which vary according to the tides.

Away from the seafront, you can take in Sidmouth's best features on a leisurely amble around Fortfield Terrace, off Station Road, where the dignified white facades with covered blconies are fronted by lawns and flower beds, and York Terrace, on the seafront east of Fore Street. One curiosity on Coburg Terrace (off Church Street, beyond the parish church) is the **Old Chancel**, a private house standing tall and turreted beside the bowling green, made up of parts rescued from a church after this was remodelled in 1860; living quarters were added to the original chancel, which retains its Perpendicular window, resulting in a bizarre Victorian/medieval pastiche.

Church Street also holds the **Sidmouth Museum** in the Sid Vale Heritage Centre (Easter–Oct Mon 1–4pm, Tues–Sat 10am–4pm; £1.50), which has displays of Regency prints, various Victoriana, a comprehensive lace collection (with lace-making demonstrations usually on Thurs afternoons) and illustrations of the complicated geology of East Devon. Between Easter and October, you can get a fuller picture of the town's historical and architectural heritage on the free two-hour **walking tours** which leave from here (Tues for the western side of town, Thurs for the eastern side – both starting at 11am – Wed for the seafront starting at 2pm). Next to the museum, the restored **Kennaway House**, dating from 1805, hosts occasional exhibitions.

Around Sidmouth

Outside Sidmouth, the main attractions are all accessible from the **coast path**, which climbs steeply eastwards up Salcombe Hill, along cliffs that give sanctuary to a range of birdlife. You'll find plenty of places to pause for a swim or a picnic, but the best **beaches** are at **Weston Mouth**, about two and a half miles east of Sidmouth's Esplanade, and **Branscombe Mouth**, a couple of miles further on, where the grassy cliffs and wide, secluded stony shores are managed by the National Trust. You can also reach these beaches on signposted footpaths from the inland hamlets of Weston and Branscombe, themselves accessible on minor roads from Sidmouth.

One of the region's loveliest villages, **Branscombe** is especially worth a wander, with thatched cottages strung along a meandering valley. In a sheltered spot below the road, the surprisingly large twelfth-century church of **St Winifred**, with its prominent Norman tower, has an unusual triple-decker pulpit from the eighteenth century and fragments of medieval wall painting. There are a couple of good pubs nearby (see below), and the thatched *Sea Shanty Tearooms*, once a coal yard, provide welcome refreshment right on the beach at Branscombe Mouth (Easter–Oct).

Eating and drinking

With most of the local hotels serving evening meals, there's not a great choice of **restaurants** in Sidmouth. However, you'll always find somewhere open, and there's a good selection of **pubs** which also offer meals. Ice Cream Paradise has over 25 flavours to accompany a seaside promenade, while Trump, a delicatessen on Fore Street, has enticing picnic ingredients, including pâtés, quiches, chutneys and cakes.

Cafés and restaurants

Blinis corner of Fore and York sts ☎01395/513043. Inexpensive café-bar in a relaxed, modern setting, ideal for breakfasts, snacks and coffees. Daily specials include speciality pies (£8–10). Closed eves and all Sun.

Browns Café Bistro 33 Fore St ☎01395/516724. Reasonably priced and locally sourced dishes are available here, including polenta and grilled seafood. Most mains cost around £14, and there's a good-value early-evening menu. Coffees and snacks are also available during the day, and there's a laid-back lounge area upstairs (normally open summer only). Closed Sun & Mon (except school hols).

Clock Tower Tearooms Connaught Gardens ☎01395/515319. Overlooking Jacob's Ladder beach, this is a great place for seafood dishes, lasagne and local crab, as well as cakes and teas. Closed eves.

Mocha The Esplanade ☎01395/512882. Seafront views and simple but satisfying snacks are offered here; tuck into jacket potatoes, paninis and a seafood platter for under £13. Daytime only, also eves in July & Aug.

Moores High St, Newton Poppleford ☎01395/568100. It's worth the drive out (or bus #52A or #52B) to this village four miles northwest of Sidmouth on the A3052 for fine dining in elegant surroundings. Local lamb and duck and fresh seafood are on the set-price menus (£15 at lunch, £17.50 in the evening but £27.50 Sat eve), and special diets are catered for. Accommodation also available (3–4). Closed Sun eve & Mon.

Prospect Plaice Old Fore St. Straightforward fish, chips and paninis, to eat in or take away.

Pubs

Anchor Inn Old Fore St. Dating from 1350, this has a gnarled feel to it, with dark oak beams and panels. Bar food and a good selection of coffees available.

Dukes The Esplanade. Spacious modern bar with outdoor and conservatory seating. It's always heaving at festival time, when live music and merriment take over.

Fountain Head Branscombe. At the higher, less visited end of the village, this unspoiled fourteenth-century tavern serves superb local beers and ciders and generous portions of food.

Masons Arms Branscombe. Fairly pricey grills and seafood are served at this popular pub and hotel half a mile from Branscombe Mouth. Tables outside and ship's beams, slate floors and open fires within.

Old Ship Old Fore St. Good beers and a range of bar meals, including chargrilled steaks and stir-fries, are offered at this reconditioned old boozer, with a few outdoor tables.

Swan Inn 37 York St. Convivial place with real ales, bar meals and a garden – a fun place during Folk Week.

Beer and around

Seven miles east of Sidmouth, and two miles east of Branscombe, the tiny fishing port of **BEER** is one of the gems of the Devon coast. The allure of the village – whose name has nothing to do with the drink, but is a corruption of the old English word *bearu* meaning small wood – derives largely from its location, huddled in a narrow cove between gleaming white headlands, with a gurgling stream running through its centre.

Arrival and information

By bus Beer is linked with Sidmouth by the #899 (not Sun) and with Exeter by #X53. For local **info**, see Ⓦwww.beer-devon.co.uk.

Accommodation

The availability of **accommodation** can be very restricted in summer, when early booking is strongly advised. **Campers** will find *Beer Head Caravan Park* (Ⓣ01297/21107, Ⓦwww.beer-head.com; closed late Oct to late March) beautifully sited with panoramic views and easily reached along Common Lane, by the *Anchor Inn* at the bottom of Fore Street; caravans are available for weekly rent.

Anchor Inn Fore St Ⓣ01297/20386, Ⓦwww.anchorinn-beer.com. A good choice if you don't mind being in the thick of things. Some rooms have sea views, others costing a little less face the back, and all have private facilities. ❺

Bay View Fore St Ⓣ01297/20489, Ⓦwww.bayviewbeer.com. B&B opposite the *Anchor Inn*, recommended for position and price, with most rooms overlooking the sea. No credit cards. Closed Nov–Easter. ❸

Beer Youth Hostel Bovey Combe Ⓣ0845/371 9502, Ⓔbeer@yha.org.uk. East Devon's only youth hostel is on a hillside half a mile northwest of Beer. Beds in dorms cost from £13.95, and there are family rooms (❹) with shared or private bathrooms. Meals are available, or you can use the kitchen – both kitchen and lounge are accessible by day. To reach the hostel, follow signs for Beer Quarry Caves, turning right about 300m from the end of Fore St.

Dolphin Hotel Fore St Ⓣ01297/20068, Ⓦwww.dolphinhotelbeer.co.uk. Rather more idiosyncratic than Beer's other choices, this has Victorian pictures, posters and fairground mirrors, though bedrooms are rather more staid. ❻

The village and around

Hardly surprisingly, given its picturesque setting, Beer is something of a tourist honeypot, and you probably won't feel like lingering in high summer when the place is bursting at the seams. Free of congestion, however, it still manages to work its charm, with the core of the village seemingly unchanged from the time when it was a smugglers' eyrie; local inlets were used by such characters as Jack

Beer festivities

Beer attracts huge crowds during **Regatta Week**, in mid-August, accompanied by such shenanigans as barrel-rolling at the local football club on Stovar Long Lane, and during the annual **Rhythm and Blues Festival**, over three days in mid-October; local accommodation in both these periods may be hard to come by.

Rattenbury, whose famous exploits were chronicled in his 1837 book *Memoirs of a Smuggler*. Lace-making was a more legitimate local industry, though there is precious little evidence of this left. At the bottom of the main Fore Street, fishing vessels are winched up on Beer's shingle beach, where lines of painted wooden bathing huts are arrayed beneath white cliff walls and there are self-drive **motorboats to rent** (£18 per hour). If you're taking a dip, be aware that the shore shelves steeply under the water.

A mile or so west of the village on the Branscombe road, **Beer Quarry Caves** (daily: Easter–Sept 10am–6pm; Oct 11am–5pm; last tour 1hr before closing; £6; Ⓦ www.beerquarrycaves.fsnet.co.uk) are the main attraction hereabouts. The quarries, which include vast chambers and narrow tunnels, were worked continuously from Roman times until 1900, and the extracted Beer stone has been used in countless Devon churches and houses, not to mention Winchester Cathedral, Westminster Abbey, St Paul's Cathedral and the Tower of London (and you can see a good example of it on Beer's church tower). Its malleability when newly quarried (it hardens on exposure) and smooth texture make it an ideal medium for screens and tracery, for example in the internal masonry of Exeter Cathedral. On the hour-long walking tours, which take in a chapel 200ft underground and the etched signatures of quarrymen going back to the year of Queen Victoria's accession, you can appreciate the enormous scale of the excavations, all the more remarkable when you consider that everything was worked by hand; old mining tools and pieces carved by medieval masons are on display in a small exhibition in the old Roman section. The temperature in the caves is cool even on a warm day, so sweaters are advisable.

Back on the coast, the cliff path, soaring above stony beaches, can be followed on either side of Beer. To the south, the path climbs for a mile up to **Beer Head**, a majestic 426-foot vantage point at the most westerly end of the south coast's chalk white cliffs. From here, you have the choice of sticking to the cliff-top or descending to an area known as **Hooken Undercliff**, the result of a landslip in 1790 and now a thickly grown wilderness that provides sanctuary for birds and other wildlife as well as a means of accessing the beach.

Eating and drinking

For such a small place, Beer is well endowed with **eateries**, including some decent **pubs**, all within a short walk. For takeaway food, you can pick up award-winning pasties, pies and cheeses from Woozies, a **deli** on Fore Street.

Anchor Inn Fore St (see opposite). You can tuck into a choice of food here – from baguettes to fresh fish – in the bar, cliff-top garden or fairly formal restaurant.

Barrel o' Beer Fore St ⓣ 01297/20099. The superior pub food served here includes local delicacies such as Devon oysters, crab and lobster for £10–17. No under-5s. No food Sun eve in winter.

Ducky's Café on the beach. Shaded by parasols, you can get close to the sea here, though the hot and cold snacks are fairly ordinary. Open summer only.

Steamers New Cut, off Fore St ⓣ 01297/22922. The top choice in Beer: light meals by day and there's a wine bar and full restaurant in the evenings, serving such dishes as local scallops and chargrilled rump steaks (£16–20). Closed Sun & Mon.

Seaton and around

Following the coast path eastwards from Beer, a smooth stroll of less than a mile brings you round Seaton Bay to the resort of **SEATON**. With its useful harbour, the town was strategically important to the Romans and subsequently to the Saxons and Danes, who launched inland invasions from this deep inlet. The town's character today stems from its development as a spa and holiday destination after the railway arrived in 1868. It's not a particularly inviting place nowadays: the mile-long pebbly beach backed by a promenade and a large and dominating sea wall, without any of the scenic grandeur of East Devon's other resorts. The biggest attraction is **Seaton Tramway** (Easter–Oct 2–3 hourly 10am–5pm, also some departures in Feb, March, Nov & Dec; up to £8.35 return; ⓣ01297/20375, ⓦwww.tram.co.uk), running from the terminus on Harbour Road, adjacent to the tourist office. The trams, the oldest of which dates back to 1904 and which are mostly open-topped (enclosed versions operate in bad weather), make a stop at the village of Colyford and end their run at Colyton, three miles north of Seaton (a thirty-minute trip). It's touristy, but the ride through the verdant **Axe valley** is pleasant, with opportunities to see flocks of various wading birds.

In Seaton itself, the town's **museum**, on the top floor of the town hall on Fore Street (late May to Oct Mon–Fri 10.30am–12.30pm & 2.15–5pm; free), merits a brief visit. Covering the whole of the lower Axe valley, the displays include an excellent collection of black-and-white photographs of the area, local Roman remains, Victorian costumes and natural history.

Across Seaton Bridge and the Axe estuary, the **Jurassic Coast** (see box, p.77) stretches six hilly miles beyond Axmouth to Lyme Regis in Dorset, a bracing route for walkers with a chance to explore a semi-wild area of undercliffs.

Practicalities

Seaton is served by **buses** #899 from Sidmouth and Beer (not Sun), and #X53 from Exeter and Beer (the #X53 follows the Jurassic Coast eastwards as far as Poole in Dorset). Information on Beer and Seaton can be obtained at Seaton's **tourist office** close to the tram terminus on the Underfleet (Jan & Feb Fri & Sat 11am–2pm; March Mon–Wed, Fri & Sat 10am–2pm; April–June, Sept & Oct Mon–Wed, Fri & Sat 10.30am–3.15pm; July & Aug Mon–Sat 10am–4.45pm; Nov & Dec Mon, Tues, Fri & Sat 11am–2pm; ⓣ01297/21660, ⓦwww.seatontic.com). **Bikes** can be rented from Soanes Cycles, Queen Square, Colyton (ⓣ01297/552308); ask about a local delivery and collection service.

If you want to **stay** in **Seaton**, opt for *Beaumont Guest House* (ⓣ01297/20832, ⓦwww.smoothhound.co.uk; ④), an elegant Victorian B&B at the western end of the Esplanade, with spacious rooms, all sea-facing apart from one on the ground floor, or try *The Bay Tree*, behind the *Beaumont* at 11 Seafield Rd (ⓣ01297/24611, ⓦwww.baytreeguesthouse.co.uk; ④), which has rooms overlooking a public garden. Both have en-suite rooms and neither accepts credit cards.

For a **meal** in Seaton, try *The Terrace Arts Café* (ⓣ01297/20225; closed Mon in winter), on the roundabout at the western end of the Esplanade, which offers moderately priced organic and vegetarian daytime snacks and stays open for evening meals on Friday and Saturday. For the best grub hereabouts, however, you'll need to head to **Axminster**, six miles northeast, where chef and food campaigner Hugh Fearnley-Whittingstall has established the *River Cottage Stores and Canteen* in Trinity Square (ⓣ01297/631862; closed eves Sun & Mon) as a pilgrimage centre for foodies. You can eat snack lunches or fuller evening meals (advance booking essential), all made with local, organic and ethically produced ingredients. Main courses cost £12–20, and a wealth of takeaway goodies are also available.

Honiton

The market town of **HONITON** is the biggest centre in inland East Devon. Once an important coaching stop on the London to Exeter road, with as many as thirty-five coaching inns, it was also famed as the most rotten of the parliamentary "rotten boroughs", when the purchasing of votes was commonplace among the small electorate – a practice stopped by the 1832 Reform Act. A couple of disastrous fires in the eighteenth century destroyed most of the town's medieval fabric, which was replaced with the fine red-brick Regency houses visible today. These are solid evidence of the prosperity enjoyed by the merchants from the local wool industry in the seventeenth and eighteenth centuries, and later from lace (see box, p.88). More recently the town has become an important centre of the antiques trade, accounting for its numerous antiques shops. The best days to visit are Tuesday and Saturday, when there are general **markets** in the broad High Street.

Arrival, information and events

Honiton is most easily reached by public transport on the #52B bus from Sidmouth and Exeter (Mon–Sat only, #379 on summer Sun), #20 from Seaton (Mon–Sat), or by train from Exeter. The local **tourist office** in the Lace Walk car park (March–Oct Mon–Sat 10am–4pm; Nov–March Mon–Sat 10am–2pm; ⓣ01404/43716, ⓦwww.honitontic.org.uk) provides information on walks and cycle routes. The huge **Honiton Agricultural Show** (ⓦwww.honitonshow.co.uk) takes place annually on the first Thursday in August, in the New Showground on the old A30 towards Exeter; a free bus service shuttles punters there from Lace Walk.

Accommodation

Honiton has a paltry choice of **accommodation**, with the cheapest places tucked away at the west end of the High Street. Otherwise, you're best off venturing outside town. The nearest **campsite**, *Putts Corner* (ⓣ01404/42875; closed Nov–March), three miles south of Honiton on the B3174, is for motorhomes and caravans only; for tents, head for *Forest Glade* (ⓣ01404/841381, ⓦwww.forest-glade.co.uk; closed Oct–March), a lovely, well-sheltered site in the Blackdown Hills, six miles northwest of town, accessible from the A373 (call for directions) – it boasts an indoor pool and tennis court.

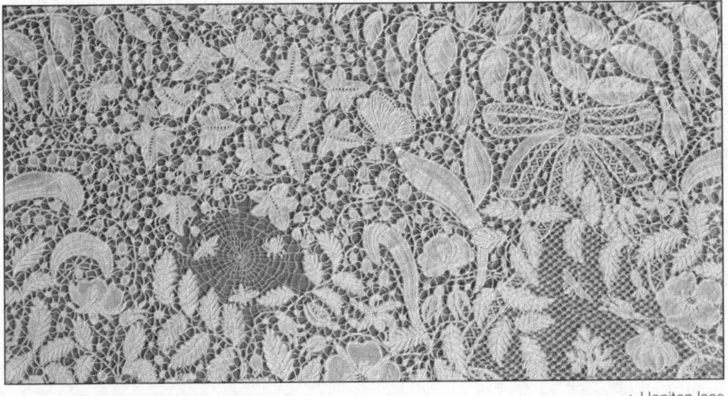

▲ Honiton lace

Honiton lace

Lace has been made in Honiton and the surrounding area for over four hundred years. The industry originated in the sixteenth century when Flemish refugees introduced the craft, and escalated in importance when Parliament forbade the import of foreign-made lace at the end of the seventeenth century. With as much as ten hours needed to produce one square inch, lace was much in demand throughout this period and provided employment for half of the town's population. Merchants paid the lace-makers – mainly women and girls – to work at home, and then either sold the finished product in their shops or sent it on to London and beyond. It was primarily used as costume lace – for collars, cuffs, edgings and wedding veils – and was chosen to embellish Queen Victoria's wedding dress in 1839 (at a cost of £1000); the christening gown made for her eldest son, the future King Edward VII, in 1841, is still used by the Royal Family today.

Although there's been no commercial production since the beginning of the twentieth century, some locals still make lace as a hobby. Samples are available for sale at **Honiton's** Allhallows Museum.

Combe House Hotel Gittisham ⓣ01404/540400, ⓦwww.thishotel.com. Situated a couple of miles southwest of Honiton – a classic Elizabethan manor house beautifully situated within extensive grounds. ⑧

Montgomery's 115 High St ⓣ01404/44667, ⓦwww.montgomeryshotel.com. Plain but comfortable en-suite rooms in the centre of town. Breakfast costs extra. ⑤

Oaklands Exeter Rd ⓣ01404/44282. An unpretentious, good-value and friendly B&B with three rooms (one en suite). No credit cards. ③

Wessington Farm Awliscombe ⓣ01404/549333 or 01404/42280 eves, ⓦwww.eastdevon.com/bedandbreakfast. A couple of miles northwest on the A373, this has two en-suite rooms, a guest lounge, a spacious garden and great views over the Blackdown Hills and the Otter valley. ④

The Town

In the High Street, Honiton's chief attraction is **Allhallows Museum** (Easter–Oct Mon–Fri 9.30am–4.30pm, Sat 9.30am–1pm; £2; ⓦwww.honitonmuseum.co.uk), housed in the oldest building in town, a fourteenth-century chapel later used as a schoolroom and dining hall and now holding three galleries stuffed with examples of the fine lace with which Honiton is synonymous. It's a comprehensive, informative and well-presented collection, displaying examples of Honiton lace from 1630 onwards and the tools of the lace trade and illustrating its history. Sections on other aspects of the town's history will appeal to those immune to the fascinations of lace. Prehistoric artefacts are displayed in the Murch Gallery, including the bones and tusks of the Honiton Hippos, which date back some 100,000 years, and there are absorbing exhibits relating to other local industries such as pottery, cream-making and whetstone-making. Lace-making demonstrations take place daily from June to August.

Eating and drinking

You needn't wander further than Honiton's High Street for a choice of good options for a meal, coffee or drink. If you're looking for evening **entertainment**, the *Orange Tree*, behind *Montgomery's* at 115 High St has live bands on Fridays and DJs on Saturdays.

Boston Tea Party 53 High St. Friendly and relaxed, this place offers tasty snacks, coffees and teas until 6pm, and there's a garden.

The Holt 178 High St. Offers imaginative snacks for lunch and a range of evening meals, including bubble and squeak, game and good vegetarian options at around £13; the flagstoned bar downstairs, serving local Otter ales, gets very crowded in the evenings. Closed Sun & Mon.

Red Cow 43 High St. Quaintly decorated with potties on the ceiling, this pub offers a good range of bar meals (£10–15).

Vine Inn Vine Passage. In an alley four doors down from *Montgomery's* (see opposite), this dispenses real ales and also serves teas, scones and meals and has a small garden.

Ottery St Mary

Five miles southwest of Honiton, **OTTERY ST MARY** sits on the banks of the River Otter in a lovely valley that runs to the sea at Budleigh Salterton (see p.77). The river was eulogized by Samuel Taylor Coleridge ("Dear native brook! Wild streamlet of the West!"), who was born in the locality and whose father was the local vicar from 1760 until 1781. Ottery was also the occasional home of William Makepeace Thackeray, who set his novel *Pendennis* here. The predominantly Georgian town fans out from a medieval central hub, now comprising elegant seventeenth-, eighteenth- and nineteenth-century houses. The street names – Jesu Street, Paternoster Row, Amen Court – evoke its ecclesiastical heritage, and the main reason for visiting today is the church of **St Mary** (open daily 8.30am–6pm except during services), sprawling on a steep hill, Cornhill, overlooking the centre of town, and displaying extravagant dimensions for such a small place. It was the work of Bishop Grandisson of Exeter, who in 1335 bought the existing church, then owned by Rouen Cathedral, and rebuilt it using Exeter Cathedral as his model, copying such features as the idiosyncratic positioning of two towers over the main transept; the weathercock atop one tower is reputed to be the oldest *in situ* in Europe. In the richly decorated interior, your eye is drawn to the magnificent roof bosses and the bright colours of the roof ribs, screens and stonework, the result of a restoration in 1977 hoping to show how the original medieval colours would have looked. The Dorset aisle, added in the early sixteenth century, boasts intricate fan-vaulting and corbel heads showing images of an owl, an elephant and the pagan figure of the Green Man (one of three in the church). Look out, too, for the astronomical clock in the south transept, one of the oldest still in working order, possibly dating from Grandisson's reconstruction.

Practicalities

Ottery St Mary is linked to Exeter by **buses** #60, #60A and #380, to Honiton by #380, and to Sidmouth by #382, all Monday to Saturday only (#379 links

Tar barrelling in Ottery St Mary

If possible, try and time your visit to Ottery St Mary to coincide with Bonfire Night, November 5, when instead of fireworks, the ancient ritual of **tar barrelling** takes place (www.otterytarbarrels.co.uk). The practice is thought to have originated in the seventeenth century with the aim of ridding the streets of the devil. Each pub sponsors a wooden barrel, which is soaked in tar for about three days before the event. The barrels are then set alight and carried on the back through the town until the flames die down. The evening starts with the smallest barrels, with the last and biggest specimen carried around the square at midnight. A huge bonfire is lit at the lower end of town, a funfair adds to the merriment and the drink flows freely, with ambulances at the ready to attend to any of the twenty-thousand-odd crowd who happen to stray into the path of a flaming barrel. The event takes place on the preceding Saturday when November 5 falls on a Sunday. Car parking costs £10.

all four places on summer Sun). The town's **tourist office** is at 10a Broad St, downhill from the church off Silver Street (April to early Nov Mon–Fri 9.30am–5pm, Sat 10am–1pm; early Nov to March Mon–Fri 9.30am–2pm, Sat 10am–1pm; ⓣ01404/813964, ⓦwww.otterytourism.org.uk).

There are some good **accommodation** choices, such as the Georgian *Stafford House* at 5 Cornhill (ⓣ01404/811800; ❹), with three en-suite and wi-fi-enabled rooms – three of them looking towards the church – and a quiet terraced garden to relax in. Alternatively, try *Fluxton Farm* (ⓣ01404/812818, ⓦwww.fluxtonfarm.co.uk; no credit cards; ❸), one and a half miles south of town on the Sidmouth road, a sixteenth-century farmhouse with en-suite rooms looking onto spacious gardens, which hold accommodation for rescued cats, ducks and chickens.

You can **eat** well at the riverside *Tumbling Weir*, Canaan Way, which has a good selection of seafood and game among other choices; accommodation is also available here (ⓣ01404/812752, ⓦwww.tumblingweir-hotel.co.uk; ❺). *Stafford House* (see above) offers evening meals using locally sourced ingredients (closed Mon & Tues), while *Seasons* at 9 Silver St (ⓣ01404/815751; closed Sun & Mon) serves inexpensive lunches and teas with freshly baked cakes and pastries, and there's a garden; evening meals are served on Fridays and Saturdays, with mains costing around £10.

Travel details

Trains

Exmouth to: Exeter (Mon–Sat 2 hourly, Sun hourly; 25min); Topsham (Mon–Sat 2 hourly, Sun hourly; 15min).
Honiton to: Exeter (Mon–Sat hourly, Sun 10 daily; 25–30min); London (Mon–Sat 11 daily, Sun 8 daily; 3hr 10min–3hr 30min); Salisbury (Mon–Sat 14 daily, Sun 10 daily; 1hr 35min).
Topsham to: Exeter (Mon–Sat 2 hourly, Sun hourly; 10min); Exmouth (Mon–Sat 2 hourly, Sun hourly; 15min).

Buses

Beer to: Branscombe (Mon–Sat 3–4 daily; 15min); Exeter (May to late Oct 7–9 daily; 55min); Seaton (Mon–Sat 3–15 daily, also Sun May to late Oct 7–17 daily; 10min); Sidmouth (Mon–Sat 3–6 daily; 30min).
Branscombe to: Beer (Mon–Sat 3–4; 15min); Seaton (Mon–Sat 3–4 daily; 25min); Sidmouth (Mon–Sat 3–4 daily; 20min).
Budleigh Salterton to: Exmouth (Mon–Sat 2 hourly, Sun hourly; 20min); Sidmouth (Mon–Sat hourly, Sun 4 daily; 40min).
Exmouth to: Budleigh Salterton (Mon–Sat 2 hourly, Sun hourly; 20min); Exeter (Mon–Sat 3–4 hourly, Sun 2 hourly; 35–50min); Sidmouth (Mon–Sat hourly, Sun 4 daily; 50min–1hr); Topsham (Mon–Sat 4 hourly, Sun 2 hourly; 20min).
Honiton to: Exeter (1–2 hourly, also Sun late May to late Sept 3 daily; 50min–1hr 30min); Ottery St Mary (Mon–Sat 6–9 daily, also Sun late May to late Sept 3 daily; 20–25min); Seaton (Mon–Sat 4 daily; 40min); Sidmouth (Mon–Sat hourly, also Sun late May to late Sept 3 daily; 35–40min).
Ottery St Mary to: Exeter (Mon–Sat hourly, also Sun late May to late Sept 3 daily; 40min); Honiton (Mon–Sat 6–9 daily, also Sun late May to late Sept 3 daily; 25min); Sidmouth (Mon–Sat 6 daily, also Sun late May to late Sept 3 daily; 25–55min).
Seaton to: Beer (Mon–Sat 3–15 daily, also Sun May to late Oct 7–17 daily; 10min); Branscombe (Mon–Sat 3–4 daily; 25min); Exeter (Mon–Sat 1–2 hourly, Sun 4–11 daily; 1hr–1hr 20min); Honiton (Mon–Sat 4 daily; 45min); Sidmouth (Mon–Sat 1–2 hourly, Sun 4–5 daily; 30–45min).
Sidmouth to: Beer (Mon–Sat 3–6 daily; 25min); Branscombe (Mon–Sat 3–4 daily; 20min); Budleigh Salterton (Mon–Sat hourly, Sun 4 daily; 40min); Exeter (Mon–Sat every 30min, Sun 1–2 hourly; 50min–1hr); Exmouth (Mon–Sat hourly, Sun 4 daily; 1hr); Honiton (Mon–Sat hourly, also Sun late May to late Sept 3 daily; 35min); Ottery St Mary (Mon–Sat 6 daily, also Sun late May to late Sept 3 daily; 25–55min); Seaton (Mon–Sat 1–2 hourly, Sun 4 daily; 30min).
Topsham to: Exeter (Mon–Sat 4 hourly, Sun 2 hourly; 20min); Exmouth (Mon–Sat 4 hourly, Sun 2 hourly; 20min).

South Devon

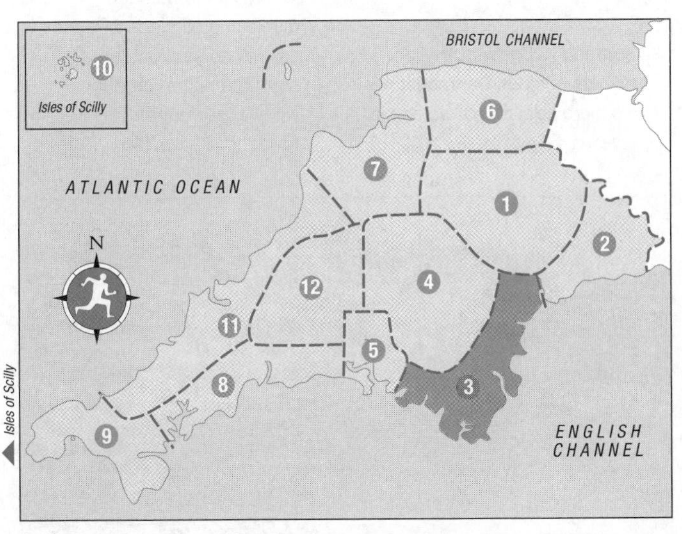

BRISTOL CHANNEL
10
Isles of Scilly
6
7
ATLANTIC OCEAN
1
N
2
12
4
11
5
8
3
Isles of Scilly
9
ENGLISH CHANNEL

CHAPTER 3

Highlights

* **Berry Head, Tor Bay** At the southern end of the "English Riviera", this limestone promontory boasts fortifications from the Napoleonic Wars, a conservation area beloved of birdwatchers and sublime views across the bay. See p.107

* **Totnes** Historic atmosphere with a New Age veneer make this riverside town a compelling stop. See pp.109–113

* **Seafood in Dartmouth** A culinary hotspot, Dartmouth has a superb selection of waterside eateries. See pp.115–116

* **Start Bay** Stretch out on the beaches at Blackpool Sands and Slapton Sands, or explore the wildlife at the Slapton Ley nature reserve. See p.116

* **River trip on the Dart** A mellow way to explore the river, with departures from Totnes and Dartmouth. See p.116

* **Overbeck's Museum and Garden** Delightfully idiosyncratic museum displaying all kinds of curios as well as sections on maritime history and local wildlife, surrounded by lush gardens. See p.119

▲ Dartmouth

3

South Devon

South of Exeter, the wedge of land between **Dartmoor** and the sea is one of Devon's most picturesque areas, a rich agricultural region that backs onto a hugely diverse range of coastal resorts. **Dawlish** and **Teignmouth** have retained a sober, small-scale appeal, while the holiday industry is most intense around **Tor Bay**, a ten-mile stretch curving between the two promontories of Hope's Nose and Berry Head. Torbay is also the collective name for the towns of **Torquay**, **Paignton** and **Brixham**; of these, the first is the standard-bearer, and, with its marina and long seafront offering sparkling views across the bay, is the one which most closely measures up to the "English Riviera" moniker optimistically attached to Torbay.

Inland from the Torbay conurbation, things get much quieter around **Totnes**, a historic riverside town that makes an agreeable base for exploring the whole region. From here you can take boats or buses eight miles downstream to the classic estuary town of **Dartmouth**, a great place to eat fish and explore the rivermouth on foot. There are some enticing beaches hereabouts, particularly those at **Start Bay** to the southwest, where a wildlife reserve and the rocky headland of Start Point deserve lengthy exploration on foot.

The intensely rural region of the **South Hams** extends southwest of the River Dart as far as Plymouth, cut through by a splay of rivers flowing off **Dartmoor**. At the mouth of the **Kingsbridge** estuary, the attractive sailing resort of **Salcombe** makes the best base for trips around the estuary and the dramatic coast on either side of it. To the west, the coast path gives access to some choice beaches dotted around **Bigbury Bay**.

Trains from Exeter to Plymouth run down the coast as far as Teignmouth before striking inland for Totnes – to get to Torbay, you may have to change at Newton Abbot. For the hinterland and points south and west along the coast, you can rely on a network of **buses** from Torquay and Totnes, and the latter is also linked to Dartmouth by **river ferries**. Between mid-April and October, travellers between East Devon and South Devon can make use of the Starcross Ferry, which links Starcross, on the western side of the Exe estuary, with Exmouth (foot passengers only); see p.76 for details.

Check the **website** Ⓦwww.visitsouthdevon.co.uk for information on everything from walks to events, accommodation and beaches. If you're coast-walking or planning to spend time on the beach, you may find it useful to know the local **tide times**, for which call the nearest tourist office or see Ⓦhttp://easytide.ukho.gov.uk.

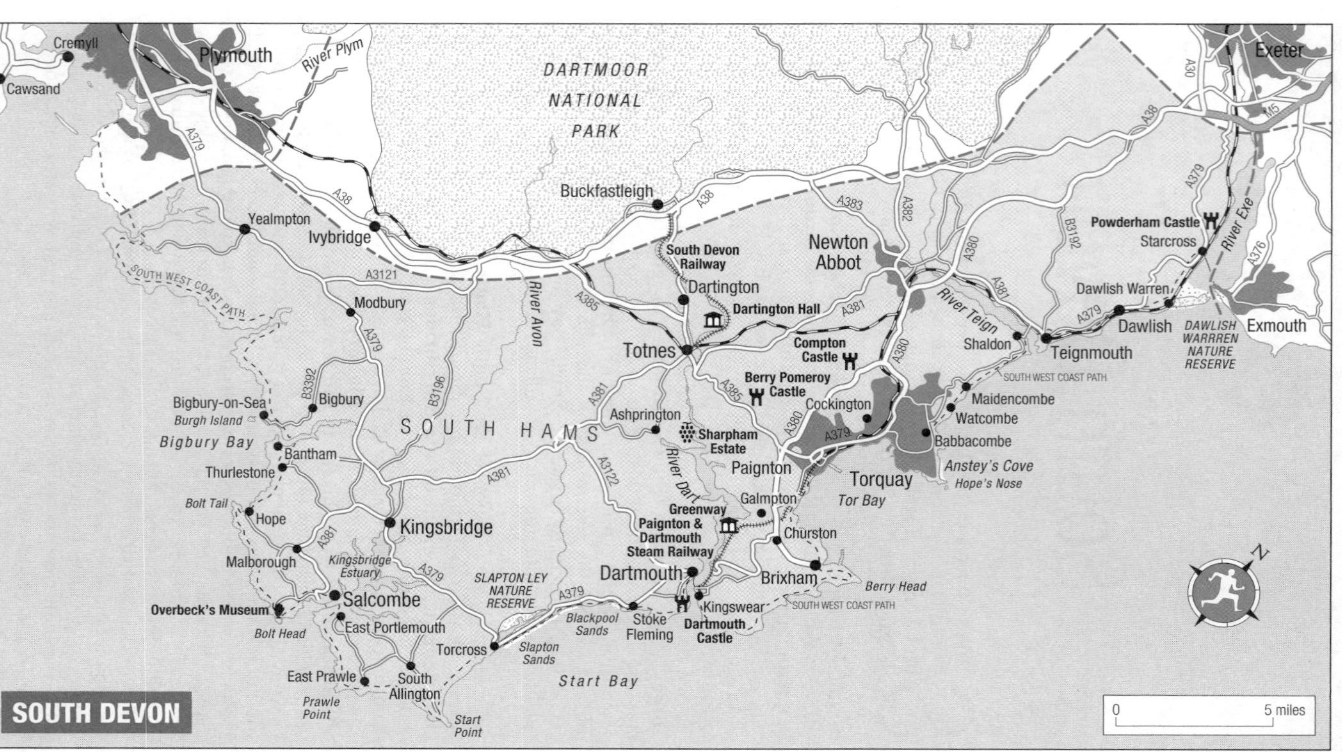

© Crown copyright

Dawlish, Teignmouth and Torbay

South of Exeter, train passengers are afforded good estuary views, while road users following the A379 touch the shore only at the small village of Starcross and, south of the estuary mouth, at **Dawlish**, a modest resort of Regency and Victorian buildings with a low-key appeal; most of the interest for beach buffs and naturalists, however, lies north of town at **Dawlish Warren**, on the mouth of the Exe estuary. Four miles south, the river port of **Teignmouth** provides a livelier take on seaside atmosphere.

Making the most of the bay's sheltered climate and exuberant vegetation, **Torbay** is the main tourist mecca in these parts, and accordingly holds the thickest concentration of accommodation. Despite the occasional Mediterranean echo, the area has a quintessentially English feel, dotted with golf courses and pervaded by a blend of traditional gentility and knockabout seaside atmosphere. The jewel in the tiara, **Torquay** has the strongest echoes of some balmier southern shore, even without the endless strings of fairy lights which are *de rigueur* hereabouts, and has recently been lent a dynamic edge by its full-on club culture. **Paignton**, on the other hand, has been assigned the role of a rather bland family resort, while **Brixham** is a genuine fishing port enlivened by arcades and fish and chip shops. The best beaches are found at the northern end of Tor Bay, notably the cliff-backed strands at **Anstey's Cove** and **Babbacombe**.

With centrally located stations, both Dawlish and Teignmouth are served by **trains** on the main London–Penzance line – one of the West Country's loveliest stretches of rail, with views over the Exe estuary (and frequently subject to spray during rough weather) – while a branch line from Newton Abbot runs down to Torquay and Paignton. Frequent #2 **buses** connect Exeter with Dawlish, Dawlish Warren and Teignmouth, while #32T links Teignmouth with Torquay, #X46 runs between Exeter, Torquay and Paignton, and #12 is the main link between Torquay, Paignton and Brixham.

Dawlish and around

Small and sedate **DAWLISH**, a couple of miles south of the Exe estuary, is a typical Devon seaside resort that was favoured by nineteenth-century holiday-makers, but today pales in comparison to the flashier resorts further south. The sand and shingle town beach runs alongside a granite railway viaduct built by Brunel, and though the passing trains contribute occasional excitement, you'll find more seclusion at the broader, cliff-backed beach at **Coryton Cove**, a few minutes' walk south.

The best bathing, however, is around the mouth of the Exe estuary, where dune-backed sands slope gently down to the sea at **DAWLISH WARREN**. Caravan parks have colonized large portions of the area, but you need walk only a few hundred yards north or south to find a little more solitude. To the north, a sandy spit jutting into the estuary holds the **Dawlish Warren National Nature Reserve**, harbouring a range of wildfowl and wading birds as well as a huge variety of flowering plants, mosses, liverworts and lichens (see Contexts, p.379).

You can get some background at the **interpretation centre** (April–Sept daily 10.30am–1pm & 2–5pm; Oct–March Sat & Sun 10.30am–1pm & 2–5pm or dusk), but the best way to take it all in is by joining a two- to three-hour **guided walk** (£3.50) conducted by the reserve's rangers. These usually take place once or twice a month; to check days and times, consult the list at the visitor centre, call ⓣ01626/863980 or see ⓦwww.teignbridge.gov.uk. Autumn and winter see the greatest numbers of birds, which can be observed from hides. In summer (April–Oct), you have to negotiate a sometimes noisy and intrusive fairground/amusements arcade to access the reserve, though the tranquillity of the estuary location soon reasserts itself.

Three miles north of Dawlish Warren off the A379, drivers from Exeter will have passed **Powderham Castle**, a pleasing mélange of Gothic, Georgian and Victorian which is home to the eighteenth earl of Devon (Mon–Fri & Sun: April it to mid-July, Sept & Oct 11am–4.30pm; mid-July to Aug 11am–5.30pm; £8.95; ⓦwww.powderham.co.uk). Enhanced by colourful anecdotes, the hour-long guided tours point out Baroque bookcases, portraits by Joshua Reynolds, an eighteenth-century music room designed by James Wyatt and a restored Victorian kitchen, and the grounds offer walks and a deer park.

Practicalities

Dawlish has a **tourist office** in the gardens behind the viaduct (Easter–Nov Mon–Sat 10am–5pm, plus July–Sept Sun 10am–4pm; Nov–Easter Fri & Sat 10am–1.30pm & 2–4pm; ⓣ01626/215665, ⓦwww.visitsouthdevon.co.uk). If you choose to **stay**, head for *Lammas Park House*, a Georgian building 300m from the seafront at 3 Priory Rd (ⓣ01626/888064, ⓦwww.lammasparkhouse.co.uk; ❹), where there are three airy and elegant rooms with superb views over town and sea, and top-notch dinners are available for £15–19. Campers should head for *Leadstone Camping*, in a sheltered spot half a mile from the sea at Dawlish Warren (ⓣ01626/864411, ⓦwww.leadstonecamping.co.uk; mid-June to early Sept).

Teignmouth and Shaldon

At the mouth of the River Teign three miles down the coast from Dawlish, **TEIGNMOUTH** (pronounced "Tinmuth") is a larger, more graceful affair. On the seafront, to either side of the pier that once segregated male and female bathers, the narrow, unexceptional bathing beach is backed by **the Den**, a tidy swathe of lawns and flower beds interspersed with tennis courts, bowling greens and miniature golf courses. Overlooking the gardens are some of the town's most elegant Georgian and Victorian villas, several dating from Teignmouth's evolution as one of Devon's first seaside resorts at the end of the eighteenth century. Until that time, the town was primarily concerned with the export of granite – transported downriver from Dartmoor – from its port in the estuary just south of the Den. There's still a thriving harbour here, and this estuary side of town is the most interesting part, with a clutter of boats moored in the river and fishing vessels hauled up onto the pebbly Back Beach. The water here is too oily to invite taking a dip, and fast currents make swimming around the estuary mouth risky, but Teignmouth's main **beach** is safe enough.

From Back Beach, you can cross the estuary via a **passenger ferry** (£1.30), which operates daily from 8am or, between November and Easter, 9am on weekdays, 10am at weekends, with the last service posted on a board at the departure point (usually around dusk). If you're driving, take the road bridge further upstream. On the opposite bank, **SHALDON** is a daintier and more sequestered version of Teignmouth, sheltered under the Ness headland, and often bypassed by the seasonal crowds. The tidy network of lanes off the Strand and Middle Street invites a brief wander, while the steep slopes of the **Ness** (reached from Marine Parade) offer fine estuary views. Below the promontory, you can reach a cliff-backed strip of sand via a tunnel bored through the rock by a local landowner in the early nineteenth century – the beach is cut off at high tide. On **Wednesdays** between late May and mid-September, trinkets and food are sold at stalls on the green by locals in eighteenth-century garb, commemorating an attack at the hands of the French in 1785, and there are free evening entertainments. **Teignmouth Jazz Festival** (Ⓦwww.teignmouthjazz.org) takes place over a long weekend in mid-November, with trad, swing and contemporary bands playing in pubs and clubs.

Practicalities

Teignmouth's **tourist office** is behind the pier at the Den (Easter–Oct Mon–Sat 10am–5pm, plus late July to early Sept Sun 10am–4pm; Nov–Easter Mon–Sat 10am–1.30pm & 2–4pm; Ⓣ01626/215666, Ⓦwww.visitsouthdevon.co.uk). Good **accommodation** choices in Teignmouth include *Seaway Guest House*, 27 Northumberland Place (Ⓣ01626/879024, Ⓦwww.seawayteignmouth.co.uk; ❷), with spacious, en-suite and wi-fi-enabled rooms – one with a four-poster bed – centrally located, near the seafront and just a few steps from the river, and the much posher *Thomas Luny House* on Teign Street, near Back Beach (Ⓣ01626/772976, Ⓦwww.thomas-luny-house.co.uk; no under-12s; ❻), a Regency villa that was the home of a renowned local artist; it's beautifully furnished, with books and flowers in the rooms, and has an enclosed garden; rates include afternoon tea and home-made cake, early-morning tea and a newspaper. The nearest **campsite** to Teignmouth is the *Coast View Holiday Park*, half a mile outside Shaldon on the main A379 south (Ⓣ01626/872392, Ⓦwww.coastview.co.uk; closed Nov–Easter), where chalets, caravans and a clubhouse and pool are available.

For **food and drink**, Teignmouth's alleys conceal atmospheric old pubs such as the *Ship Inn* on Queen Street, a great spot for a sundowner, and the nearby *New Quay Inn*, on New Quay Street. Both overlook the harbour and serve good food, and the *New Quay* has live music at weekends. The best eatery in town is *The Owl and the Pussycat*, 3 Teign St (Ⓣ01626/775321, Ⓦwww.theowlandpussycat.co.uk), open for morning coffees and lunches ranging from paninis to local mussels (£5–7), and in the evening for its Modern-British dishes (£14–20) or the "Tunisian Feast" offered on the last Sunday of the month. The restaurant places a high emphasis on animal welfare, and there's a garden for fine weather. In Shaldon, the *Ferryboat Inn* on the Strand provides estuary views and excellent liquid or solid sustenance, including daily garden barbecues in summer; there's live music every Friday evening and Sunday afternoon.

Torquay and around

Five miles south of the Teign estuary mouth, **TORQUAY** owes much of its appeal to its combination of hills and extensive palm-planted seafront from which views take in the whole of Tor Bay. The sheltered location and comparatively clement weather were factors in its elevation from a group of fishermen's cottages to an important naval base during the Napoleonic Wars, and Napoleon himself was a visitor – though without setting foot on land – when he was held

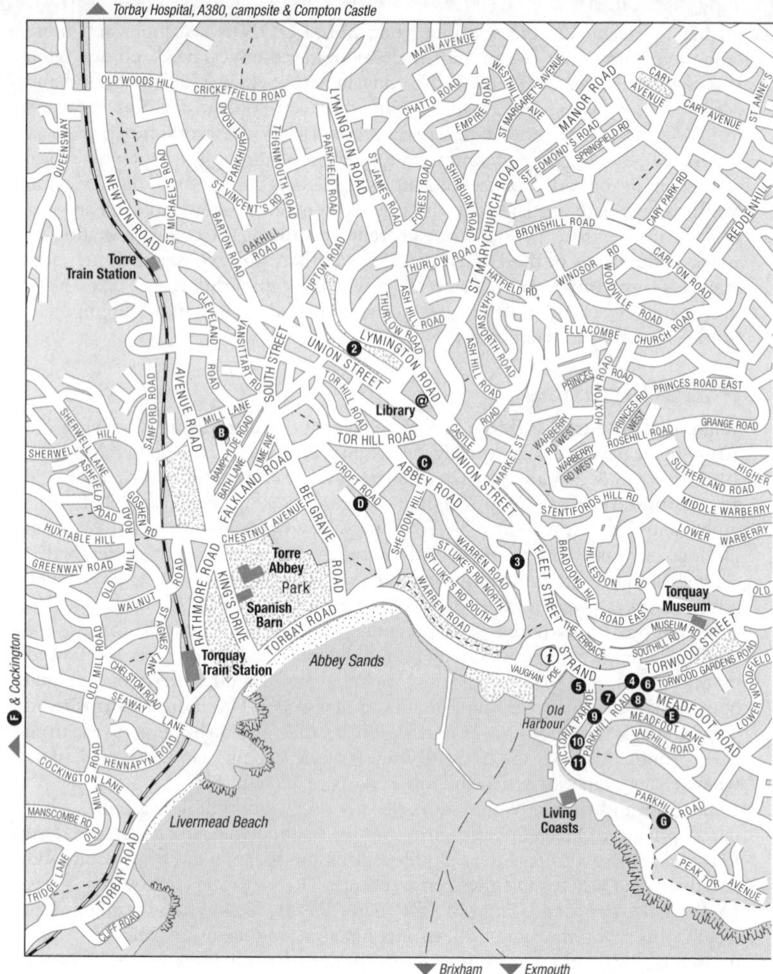

for seven weeks aboard the HMS *Bellerophon* in Tor Bay following his defeat at Waterloo. Torquay then became a fashionable haven for invalids – among them the consumptive Elizabeth Barrett Browning, who lived here 1838–41 – a process accelerated by the extension of the railway from Newton Abbot in 1848. More recently the town has been associated with crime writer **Agatha Christie** (see box, p.102) and the fictional TV hotelier Basil Fawlty, whose anachronistic attitudes reflect Torquay's forced adaptation to mass tourism. The *Gleneagles Hotel*, the inspiration for *Fawlty Towers*, is still going strong.

The Mediterranean myth as promoted by the tourist bosses doesn't stretch very far today, and evaporates altogether on a Friday or Saturday night when the town centre swarms with drink-sodden revellers. Away from the seafront, however, Torquay has a subtler appeal. The hilly residential areas reveal creamy villas on quietly elegant streets, with greenery and sea views all around, and the town also offers two of South Devon's top museums, one located within Torbay's most

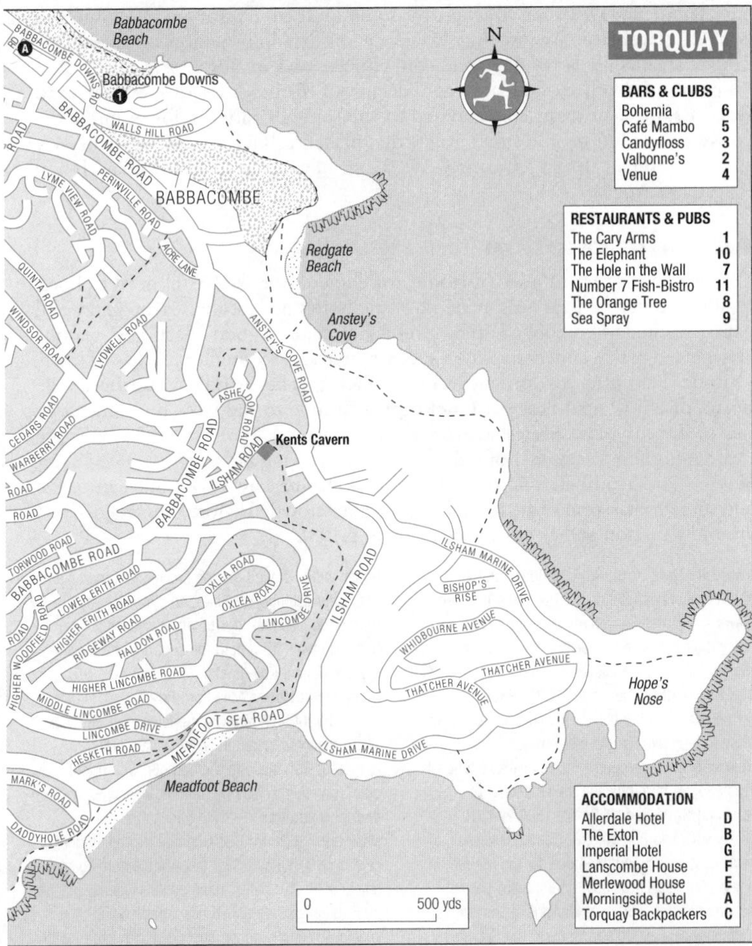

noteworthy historical building, **Torre Abbey Mansion**. Activity enthusiasts will find the full range of **waterskiing, surfing and sailing** facilities at nearby coves and beaches, many of which are accessible via pleasant coastal walks.

Arrival and information

Torquay's main **train station** lies a mile west of the centre on Rathmore Road, while another stop, Torre station, lies a mile further north at the top of Avenue Road. Most **buses** stop at the Old Harbour, including the #X46 bus between Exeter and Torquay, the #X80 for Totnes and Plymouth, and the frequent #12 service linking Torquay with Paignton, Brixham and Newton Abbot. The **tourist office** is also at the Old Harbour, on Vaughan Parade (June–Sept Mon–Sat 9.30am–5pm, Sun 10am–4pm; Oct–May Mon–Sat 9.30am–5pm; ⓣ01803/211211), and can provide the full gamut of maps, accommodation and transport listings as well as piles of information on local attractions and entertainments. Discount vouchers for some local attractions are also dispensed here. The **website** Ⓦwww.englishriviera.co.uk has information on the whole Torbay area, while Ⓦwww.torquay.com concentrates on Torquay.

The tourist office has dates and details of Torbay's various **events and festivals**, most of them concentrated in the summer months, for example the concerts, exhibitions and street events that make up Riviera Live between May and September, Torbay Carnival Week in July/August, and Torbay Royal Regatta in August.

Accommodation

Torquay has dozens of **accommodation** choices, but you'll still need to book in advance during peak season. Most of the hotels nearest the sea are glitzy and expensive, and often booked up by groups, but there's a good selection of reasonably priced places concentrated on specific streets in the higher reaches of town. Outside the centre, you can stay nearer the best beaches at **Babbacombe**, a mile north, or enjoy rural peace at **Cockington**, a mile to the west, both linked by bus to Torquay. The nearest **campsite** is *Widdicombe Farm*, an adults-only site near Compton accessed from the A380 Torbay ring road (Ⓣ01803/558325, Ⓦwww.widdicombefarm.co.uk; closed mid-Oct to Easter); facilities are clean and there's a bar/restaurant, though it gets quite crowded. More sites are grouped around Paignton and Brixham see p.106 & p.108).

Allerdale Hotel Croft Rd Ⓣ01803/292667, Ⓦwww.allerdalehotel.co.uk. The place to come for views and stately surroundings, with a long, lawned garden sloping below it and all en-suite rooms. Meals cost £25. Snooker and free wi-fi. ④

The Exton 12 Bridge Rd Ⓣ01803/293561, Ⓦwww.extonhotel.co.uk. Small, clean and quiet hotel, very close to Belgrave Rd and a ten-minute walk from the train station. Three-course meals available for £16. Free pick-up from bus and train stations. ④

Imperial Hotel Parkhill Rd Ⓣ01803/294301, Ⓦwww.barcelo-hotels.co.uk. One of Devon's swankiest hotels, and the model for the *Majestic* in Agatha Christie's novels, this sumptuous palace dating from the 1860s has lashings of aristocratic trimmings and period atmosphere. *The Regatta* restaurant makes a grand setting for a formal and fairly expensive meal, while there's a more relaxed bar area for snacks or a great cream tea; both offer panoramic views over the bay. Sea-facing guest rooms may cost considerably more than inward-facing ones. There's also a health club with tennis and squash courts, pools, sauna and solarium. ⑥–⑦

Lanscombe House Cockington Ⓣ01803/606938, Ⓦwww.lanscombehouse.co.uk. A couple of miles west of Torquay in the extremely quaint (and touristy) village of Cockington, this solid old country house with a walled garden has elegant rooms and period furnishings. It's linked to the centre by frequent buses March–Oct, otherwise it's a half-mile walk from both the seafront and the train station. Closed Nov–Easter. ④

Merlewood House Meadford Rd Ⓣ01803/200951, Ⓦwww.merlewoodhouse.co.uk. Well-preserved Victorian Gothic villa offering upmarket B&B close to the harbour, with bright, quiet rooms, delicious breakfasts, in-house therapies and free wi-fi. No under-12s. ④

Morningside Hotel Babbacombe Downs, Babbacombe Ⓣ01803/327025, Ⓦwww.themorningsidehotel.co.uk. This out-of-town option is ideally placed for Babbacombe Beach. It has a garden and spacious rooms – some (costing slightly more) with views over the bay – and there are frequent bus connections to the centre (see p.104). ④

Torquay Backpackers 119 Abbey Rd Ⓣ01803/299924, Ⓦwww.torquaybackpackers.co.uk. One of Devon's best independent hostels, providing cheap and friendly accommodation in a central location. Dorm beds are £14 a night and a double with shared bathroom is available for £30 (prices drop in winter). Washing, cooking and internet facilities are on hand, and it's a ten-minute walk from the station.

The Town

Torquay is liveliest around the **Old Harbour**, where the quayside shops and cafés attract a melee of idling crowds during the day and on summer evenings. The marina here is packed with pleasure craft, and stalls advertising **boat trips** (weather permitting), for example to Paignton and Brixham (£3.50) or Dartmouth and the Dart River (£12–15). Fishing and wildlife trips and evening cruises are also advertised (£7–15). On the southern edge of the Old Harbour, on Beacon Quay, **Living Coasts** (daily: summer 10am–6pm; winter 10am–dusk; £8.35; Ⓦwww.livingcoasts.org.uk) focuses on the coastlines of the world, with reconstructed beaches, cliff faces and an estuary, as well as underwater viewing areas and a huge meshed aviary. You can see such aquatic birds as avocets, redshanks, puffins, penguins, gulls and terns, and there is even an exhibition dedicated to *Rattus rattus*, the black rat that, in addition to spreading bubonic plagues, has devastated ground-nesting sea bird colonies around the world (they are held at least partly responsible for wiping out the dodo). The kiddies' favourites are the South America fur seals, to be seen cavorting in the seal pool. Feeding times are once or twice an hour, and there's a strong educational element. Finish your visit off with refreshments at the waterside **café**, if only for the views of Tor Bay (there's also a restaurant open for Sun lunch, worth booking at ⓣ01803/202499). Ask about discounted joint tickets if you're also visiting Paignton Zoo.

To the west of the Old Harbour, limestone cliffs sprinkled with white high-rise hotels and apartment blocks separate the harbour area from Torquay's broad main beach, **Abbey Sands**, extending below the main promenade. Good for chucking a frisbee about, but too busy in summer for serious relaxation, the gently sloping beach gets completely covered at high tide. It takes its name from **Torre Abbey**, founded in 1196 and the chief power in these parts until it was razed by Henry VIII in 1539. Tucked out of sight above Abbey Sands, behind the ornamental gardens, only the gatehouse, tithe barn, chapter house and tower have survived of the Abbey, and now form part of the seventeenth- and eighteenth-century construction that today holds one of Devon's finest galleries (daily: March–Oct 10am–6pm; Nov, Dec, & Feb 10am–5pm; last entry 1hr before closing; £5.75; Ⓦwww.torre-abbey.org.uk). The collection includes silver, glass, sculpture and minutely detailed marine paintings by, among others, the Teignmouth artist Thomas Luny. Other highlights include a series of Pre-Raphaelite window designs by Edward Burne-Jones, proof copies of William Blake's haunting illustrations for the Book of Job and a small but eclectic choice of twentieth-century art – a refreshing modern interlude among all the antiques. Outside the main building, you can admire the square, crenellated gatehouse and the handsome brick **Spanish Barn** just beyond, named after the 397 Spanish prisoners captured from one of the Armada warships and imprisoned here in July 1588. On the north side of the house are scattered remains of the abbey and cloisters, and the sultry Palm and Cactus houses, which provide welcome heat and shelter in bad weather.

In contrast to the finery of Abbey Mansion, **Torquay Museum**, a few minutes uphill from the harbour at 529 Babbacombe Rd (Mon–Sat 10am–5pm, also Sun mid-July to Sept 1.30–5pm; £4.50; Ⓦwww.torquaymuseum.org) contains a more down-to-earth but no less absorbing miscellany of objects relating to the area. The collection includes displays on everything from natural history and prehistory in the Time Ark gallery – where exhibits include a Victorian model of Noah's Ark – to life during World War II. On the second floor, one of the museum's most popular sections is the **Agatha Christie Gallery**, which explores the life and achievements of the crime writer (see box, p.102), from the earliest photos of the young Agatha Miller with sister Madge, dog and "Nursie", to her writing career, represented by manuscripts, book covers and other items connected to TV and film adaptations, and there's even her fur coat. Non-Christie fans shouldn't be put off though as the exhibition

The Christie connection

There are constant reminders of **Agatha Christie** (1890–1976) in South Devon, as the provincial life of the upper classes here was so often depicted in her murder mysteries. Born and raised in Torquay, she married Colonel Archie Christie in 1914, divorced him in 1928 and subsequently married the distinguished archeologist Max Mallowan, with whom she pursued an interest in Mesopotamia and its finds, making frequent visits there. She was inspired to write crime stories after making a bet with her sister Madge as to who could write the best mystery tale, so discovering a talent for ingeniously – and eventually formulaically – plotted murder yarns which usually featured one of her principal sleuths, **Hercule Poirot** or **Miss Marple**.

Christie's formidable output – she once described herself as "a sausage machine, a perfect sausage machine" – relied on rather predictable scenarios and cardboard-thin characters, but this hasn't dented her success. To date, her 78 crime novels have sold more than a billion copies in English alone, with as many again sold in translation and many filmed, notably **Murder on the Orient Express** (1934, filmed 1974) and **Death on the Nile** (1937, filmed 1978). Her play **The Mousetrap** opened in 1952 and is still going strong, making it the world's longest-running continuous theatre production.

In 1938 she purchased and rebuilt **Greenway**, a solid country residence overlooking the Dart which became the setting for several of her stories and is now run by the National Trust (see p.116). Fans should also seek out **Torquay Museum** (p.101), where a separate gallery is devoted to the author's life and work. Torbay's tourist offices dole out a free pamphlet which details all the local Christie connections, including a walking trail with a "murder mystery" to solve along the way. They can also supply details of Torbay's **Agatha Christie Festival**, with talks, walks, film screenings, theatre performances and a tea dance taking place over a week in mid-September.

provides an absorbing retrospective of upper-class Torquay in the twentieth century, as well as illustrating what happens when English parochialism takes up the art of murder and achieves worldwide celebrity.

Further up Babbacombe Road, about a mile from the harbour (take bus #32), turn right onto Ilsham Road to find the entrance to **Kents Cavern** (daily: April–June & Sept–Oct 10.30am–4pm; July & Aug 10am–4.30pm; Nov, Dec and mid-Jan to March tours at 11am, 12.30pm, 2pm and 3.30pm; £8.50; Ⓦ www.kents-cavern.co.uk), a cave system excavated in the nineteenth century and showing signs of human habitation stretching back 450,000 years. It's a good wet-weather, child-friendly attraction with showy audiovisual effects and an underground exhibition filling in some of the history.

Around Torquay

A mile west of Abbey Mansion, Torbay suddenly turns deeply rural at the showcase village of **COCKINGTON**. Though frequently overrun by crowds of strolling tourists, it's worth a brief stop if you can stomach the chocolate-box imagery, the result of an over-zealous preservation programme dating from the 1930s. There's more than a whiff of artifice, but the core of the original Saxon village can still be discerned, and the only completely "modern" building you'll see is the *Drum Inn*, concocted by Edwin Lutyens in 1934 in traditional thatched style as part of a much larger development project which never materialized.

The main crowd-puller is **Cockington Court**, whose picturesquely landscaped grounds lie uphill to the left from the crossroads at the centre of the village. This much remodelled house now holds a complex of craft studios and souvenir shops, and there's a glass-blowing workshop and an organic garden in the grounds; you're free to wander round. More interestingly, a grassy mound next to the house holds the parish church of **St George and St Mary**, a good-looking thirteenth- to fourteenth-century red-sandstone construction whose interior has a triple barrel-vaulted ceiling and a Renaissance pulpit, though the intricate wooden screen is recent. The surrounding parkland filled with woodland walks and lakes makes ideal picnicking country. There's also a café in the main building, or you can have a full meal at the *Drum Inn*. The village has a good accommodation choice (see p.100) – an option you might consider in order to see the village at its best, once the coach parties are gone. To reach Cockington, follow Cockington Lane, a signposted right-hand turn-off from Torbay Road just south of the train station, which follows a stream for just under a mile through woods and meadows; the bus stop is on Torbay Road. Bus #62 (or marked "Cockington") plies to the village every 30 minutes or so between March and October (Mon–Fri, also Sat April–Sept) from Torquay's seafront (opposite the *Torbay Hotel*).

Three miles west of Torquay, signposted off the A380 near Marldon (but difficult to reach without your own transport), it's worth the excursion to **Compton Castle** (April–Oct Mon, Wed & Thurs 11am–5pm; £4.20; NT), home to the seafaring Gilbert family – related to Sir Walter Raleigh – for the last six centuries. Buttressed and battlemented, its dramatic exterior has proved a favourite with film-makers (*Sense and Sensibility* was shot here), while the more modest interior includes Elizabethan portraits in the reconstructed Great Hall and a vast fireplace in the old kitchen.

Many of Tor Bay's finest **beaches** are accessible via boats departing from the Old Harbour (see p.100), and some are also accessible on foot from here. If you're walking, follow the footpath signposted to the right from Parkhill Road (itself just southeast of the marina) round the coast and through Daddyhole Plain, a large grassy chasm in the cliff caused by a landslide that's locally attributed to the devil ("Daddy"). Path and road converge on the sea wall at **Meadfoot Beach**, traditionally the more "select" of Torquay's beaches, where Agatha Christie bathed in her youth. The pebble-and-sand strip, most of which is covered at high tide, is backed by a road with cafés and shops where you can rent **boats** and pedalos; waterskiing, diving and windsurfing lessons are available, as well as equipment rental.

Continuing east, the coast path winds to the end of Hope's Nose, the northern point of Tor Bay, and connects with Marine Drive for a while before heading north to **Anstey's Cove**, a tiny, sheltered, shingle-and-rock beach offering good bathing – though you may be jostling for elbow-room in summer. Another half mile along, the coast path brings you to **Babbacombe Beach**, a long sand-and-shingle expanse where there's a pub, the *Cary Arms*, and an outdoor beachside café selling drinks, bacon baps and the like. The shallow bay provides ideal conditions for **diving**, and you can rent equipment and arrange courses at Divers Down, 139 Babbacombe Rd (Ⓣ01803/327111, Ⓦwww.diversdown.co.uk), open daily in summer. The car park near the *Cary Arms* was once the site of a beach house, The Glen, where Miss Emma Keys, a local resident, was murdered in 1884, for which John "Babbacombe" Lee was convicted. After three attempts to hang him, he was released in 1907 having served a life sentence. The "man they could not hang" was immortalized in various books and by Fairport Convention's ballad "Babbacombe Lee" in 1971.

A few minutes' walk north round the bay brings you to **Oddicombe Beach**, an arc of sand and stone where floats, pedalos and motorboats are available for rent, as well as deckchairs and free changing cabins. Northwards, you can press on a mile or two to the more secluded sand-and-shingle beaches and cliff-backed coves at **Watcombe** and **Maidencombe**, both also accessible on bus route #32T from the centre of Torquay. If you don't want to continue north from Oddicombe Beach, you can ascend 240ft of cliff face on a cliff railway from here (Easter–Sept; £1.50 single, £1.75 return; last departure, alerted by a bell, at 5pm Easter–May, 5.30pm June–Sept) to the village of **BABBACOMBE**. Now really a suburb of Torquay (to which it's linked by bus #32T), it's a peaceful place with lofty views over the sea, and a choice of hotels (see p.100) and tea-gardens.

Eating, drinking and nightlife

Sandwiched between a plethora of fast-food outlets, Torquay's **restaurants** can reach heights of excellence, with an emphasis on fresh seafood brought in from nearby Brixham. Many of the town's **pubs** can also be relied upon for a decent feed, though some get quite boisterous at weekends. Torquay's **nightlife** draws in punters from far and wide, with some of the hottest and rowdiest **clubs** in Devon. For live gigs and other evening pursuits, consult one of the free events mags, for example the bimonthly *That's Entertainment* or the monthly *What's On Southwest* (Ⓦ www.whatsonsouthwest.co.uk).

Restaurants and pubs

The Cary Arms Babbacombe Beach, Babbacombe Ⓣ 01803/327110. Away from the hullaballoo of Torquay's centre, this gastropub and hotel has beamed ceilings, stone walls, books and board games. Soak up great views across the bay while enjoying a range of moderately priced meals including a recommended lobster salad and, in summer, barbecues and pizzas from the outdoor pizza oven. Most dishes cost £8–16, and local ales are on offer.

The Elephant 3–4 Beacon Terrace Ⓣ 01803/200044. Choose between more casual surroundings in the ground-floor brasserie or the formal restaurant upstairs (evenings only), with its harbour views. The food is superlative at both, though pricey: fixed-price menus downstairs are £23 for two courses, £27.50 for three (at lunch £16.50 and £20), while upstairs they are £35 and £45 respectively. Closed Sun & Mon.

The Hole in the Wall 6 Park Lane Ⓣ 01803/200755. Reputedly the town's oldest pub, this was Irish playwright Sean O'Casey's local when he lived in Torquay. There's a bar menu and a separate restaurant (worth booking) where you can dine on delicious mussels, duck breast or pork tenderloin (£12–18). There are a couple of benches on flower-festooned flagstones outside, and live music Tues, Thurs & Sun.

Number 7 Fish-Bistro Beacon Terrace Ⓣ 01803/295055. The place to come for great seafood, overlooking the harbour. Choose whatever's in season, from king scallops to baked monkfish (around £16 for mains). Closed lunchtimes Sun–Tues, also Sun eve June & Oct, all Sun & Mon Nov–May.

The Orange Tree 14 Parkhill Rd Ⓣ 01803/213936. British/European contemporary cuisine is offered at this elegant, rather formal place. The menu features well-presented game, poultry and other meat dishes (mostly £14–18), and there are also seafood and vegetarian choices. Desserts include a delicious coconut and lime cheesecake. Closed daytime & all Sun.

Sea Spray 8 Victoria Parade Ⓣ 01803/293734. Overlooking the harbour, this smart but unpretentious restaurant offers everything from pies and pastas (upto £10) to fillets of Brixham plaice (£14), available all day.

Bars and clubs

Bohemia 41 Torwood St Ⓣ 01803/292079, Ⓦ www.bohemianightclub.com. Popular venue for house, indie and r'n'b in two rooms, with big-name and resident DJs. Open Fri & Sat (sometimes until 5am), also Sun in summer.

Café Mambo 7 The Strand Ⓣ 01803/291112, Ⓦ www.cafemambo.co.uk.The three floors include a balcony giving a nice view of the harbour and, at the top, *Club Mambo* with something happening on most evenings, from Metal Mondays to cheese, r'n'b and dance on Sat. Thai food available daily.

Candyfloss Rock Rd, off Abbey Rd Ⓣ 01803/292279, Ⓦ www.candyfloss-club-torquay.co.uk. Long-established gay club with two dance-floors, a smoking area and a pool table. Open Thurs–Sat eves.

Valbonne's 161 Higher Union St Ⓣ 01803/290458, Ⓦ www.thevalbonne.co.uk. Anthems and chart music predominate here, one of Torquay's most popular clubs. Open Thurs–Sat.

Venue 13 Torwood St Ⓣ 01803/213903, Ⓦ www.venueclubbing.co.uk. Torquay's largest club on three floors has mainstream urban, commercial and house tracks for a young crowd. Open Fri–Sun.

Listings

Bike rental Simply the Bike, 100 Belgrave Rd ⓣ01803/200024. £16 per day.
Bus information Stagecoach ⓣ01803/664500, ⓦwww.stagecoachbus.com/southwest; Traveline 0871/200 2233, ⓦwww.traveline.org.uk.
Car rental Thrifty is located in the train station ⓣ01803/294786, ⓦwww.thrifty.co.uk; local operators include Practical Car and Van Hire, 114 St Mary Church Rd ⓣ01803/323323, ⓦwww.practical.co.uk.
Hospital Torbay Hospital, Lawes Bridge (off Newton Rd), has an Accident and Emergency department ⓣ01803/614567.
Internet Torquay Library, Lymington Rd, open Mon, Wed & Fri 9.30am–7pm, Tues 9.30am–5pm, Thurs 9.30am–1pm, Sat 9.30am–4pm (free first hour, then £1.50 per hr). Near the harbour on Fleet St, *Le Munch Box* has a room upstairs with four terminals, available Mon–Sat 9.30am–5pm (£1 per 20min).
Police South St ⓣ0845/277 7444.
Taxis Babbacombe Cabs ⓣ01803/690100; First Price ⓣ01803/322322; Torquay and Paignton Taxis ⓣ01803/213213.

Paignton

Three miles south of Torquay, and not so much a sister-resort as a poor relation, **PAIGNTON** lacks the gloss – and the pretensions – of its neighbour. Its beach, pier, arcades and other seaside amusements identify it as a family resort, though it is somewhat spoiled by the torrents of traffic flowing through. From **the Esplanade**, a couple of hundred yards east of the main shopping centre, lawns back on to the rather uninspiring, level pink sands of the main town beach. At its southern end, a small harbour nestles in the lee of the aptly named **Redcliffe headland**, quite a lively spot in summer with restaurants and boat tours, while to the south, the wide, shell-specked **Goodrington Sands** are the best spot for a paddle or a dip, backed by a low sea wall and a long strip of park.

A mile inland on Totnes Road, **Paignton Zoo** (daily: summer 10am–6pm; winter 10am–4.30pm or dusk if earlier; last entry 1hr before closing; £12.35; ⓦwww.paigntonzoo.org.uk) is the town's most famous attraction, its 75 acres divided into savannah, forest, wetland, tropical forest and desert zones, all with hands-on displays. There's plenty to take in and the various habitats are imaginatively presented with an emphasis on ecology and conservation; the hot and humid **Crocodile Swamp** holds crocs from Cuba and the Nile, as well as boa constrictors and pythons, while the **Wetland** zone has a series of lakes and a large walk-through aviary, and the **Forest** zone features endangered Asiatic lions and Sumatran tigers. Ask about discounted joint tickets if you're also visiting Torquay's Living Coasts exhibition.

Paignton's other main attraction, **Oldway Mansion** (Mon–Sat 9am–5pm, plus June–Sept Sun 9am–4pm; free), lies half a mile west of the town beach off Torquay Road, surrounded by lush parkland. Built by the US sewing-machine tycoon Isaac Merritt Singer (1811–75), it's mostly occupied by council offices today, but owes much of its gaudily Neoclassical appearance to a 1904 restoration by Isaac's son Paris. He lived here with his mistress, the American dancer Isadora Duncan (1878–1927), who was famously strangled when her scarf tangled in the wheels of the car she was driving (the 1969 biopic *Isadora*, starring Vanessa Redgrave, was filmed here). The house is surrounded by an Italian garden and – overlooked by two hilarious stone sphinxes with the heads of society ladies – a croquet lawn, which you are free to explore, though the round, red-brick rotunda to one side, once holding a swimming pool, is not accessible. Indeed, the only trace of past glory on view inside – and the main reason to visit – is the mansion's eye-poppingly sumptuous marble stairway, modelled on one at the palace of Versailles. It's dominated by a reproduction of a painting by Jacques-Louis David, showing Napoleon's coronation of Josephine at Notre Dame, said to be the largest replica of an oil painting in the world.

Just off the staircase, the small exhibition of early Singer sewing machines is worth a glance, displayed alongside a grandfather clock cleverly modelled on Paignton's parish church, and photos and other mementos of the house's history, including photos of Isadora Duncan. You can sip tea and munch pasties, toasties and quiches at the tearoom here (Mon–Sat 9.30am–4.30pm, but may close some Sat), with outdoor seating in fine weather.

Paignton is the northern terminus of the **Paignton & Dartmouth Steam Railway** (daily late May to Sept, plus most days April to late May & Oct and some dates in Dec; £9 return, bikes free; ⓣ01803/555872, ⓦwww.pdsr.co.uk), which runs from the main Queen's Park train station near the harbour to Kingswear (see p.116). The accent is on Victorian nostalgia, with railway personnel in period uniforms, but even without the trappings it's a nice way to view the countryside, the line connecting with Goodrington Sands before veering inland and trundling alongside the Dart estuary. You could make a day of it by buying a combined ticket to include the **Kingswear–Dartmouth ferry** (£11 return), or a Round Robin ticket, which additionally covers the river trip up the Dart to Totnes, and the bus from there back to Paignton (£17.50).

Practicalities

Paignton's **bus and train stations** are next to each other off Sands Road, five minutes west of the harbour. On the Esplanade, the **tourist office** is next to the Apollo cinema (June–Sept Mon–Sat 9.30am–5.30pm Sun 10am–4pm; Oct–May Mon–Sat 9.30am–1pm & 2–5pm; ⓣ01803/211211, ⓦwww.englishriviera.co.uk). There's a **bike rental** shop, Cycle Hire, at 20 Dartmouth Rd (ⓣ01803/521068; £5 for 24hr). You can log on to the **internet** at Puffin Computers, close to the station at 4a Totnes Rd (Mon–Fri 9.30am–6pm, Sat 10.30am–3pm; 80p per 15min).

Much of Paignton's budget **accommodation** suffers from both traffic noise and an excess of chintz and frills. Refreshingly free of either is *Trentham Guest House* at 6 Norman Rd (ⓣ01803/557704, ⓦwww.trenthamguesthouse.co.uk; ❷), a couple of minutes' walk from the seafront off Polsham Road and offering a pick-up from the stations. Nearer Paignton's centre at 2 Kernou Rd, the crisply contemporary *Cosmopolitan* (ⓣ01803/523118, ⓦwww.paignton-cosmopolitan.com; no under-18s; ❹) has neutrally coloured, en-suite rooms with wi-fi access. Guests get discounted rates from the bike hire also available here. The heights above Paignton hold most of Torbay's **campsites**, though none of them remains open all year for tents; *Beverley Park*, Goodrington Road (ⓣ01803/843887, ⓦwww.beverley-holidays.co.uk), one of the best equipped with pool, sports facilities and restaurant, and with panoramic views over the bay, stays open year-round for caravans and motorhomes (April–Oct for tents). Alternative sites lie outside Torquay (see p.100) and Brixham (p.108).

Paignton has few **restaurants** that rise above the mediocre, though at the *Harbour Light*, on the harbourside, you can enjoy fresh seafood within view of the boats (mains £11–16) and a three-course Sunday lunch costs £13 (ⓣ01803/666500; May–Oct closed daytime Mon–Sat, Nov–April closed all Mon–Fri). Among the **pubs**, the spacious *Spinning Wheel Inn*, at the bottom of Kernou Road, serves food all day (dishes around £7) and offers a good-value Sunday carvery (£6). In the evening it features nightly **live music** and has a late licence.

Brixham

From Paignton, it's about five miles round the bay to **BRIXHAM**, the smallest of the Torbay trio. (In summer, you can also get here on a motor launch leaving every fifteen to twenty minutes from Torquay harbour.) Fishing has always been Brixham's lifeblood; at the beginning of the nineteenth century, it was the major fish market in the West Country, and it still supplies restaurants as far away as London. Among the trawlers moored up on the quayside is a full-size reconstruction of the **Golden Hind** (daily: March–Oct 10am–4pm, with longer opening in summer; £3.50; Ⓦwww.goldenhind.co.uk), the surprisingly small vessel in which Francis Drake circumnavigated the world in 1577–80, and on board which he was knighted by Elizabeth I on his triumphant return – the ship has no connection with the port, however. Below decks you can see the extremely cramped surgeon's and carpenter's cabins, and the only slightly grander captain's quarters.

From the quayside, steep lanes and stairways thread up to the older centre around Fore Street, where the bus from Torquay pulls in. At the top of Fore Street, the **Brixham Heritage Museum**, housed in the old police station on New Road (Easter–Oct Tues–Fri 10am–4pm, Sat 10am–1pm, may also open late Feb to Easter Mon–Fri 10am–1pm; £2; Ⓦwww.brixhamheritage.org.uk), provides an entertaining and instructive review of the town's maritime past, with displays of sail-making, tools and navigation aids. There are also items of the area's social and domestic history, as well as some background on the Reverend Henry Francis Lyte (1793–1847), the first incumbent of the church of All Saints in nearby Church Street and the author of the famous hymn *Abide with Me*. The tune rings out from the church's carillon each day at midday and 8pm.

From the harbour, it's a thirty-minute walk east to the promontory of **Berry Head**, along a path winding up from the *Berry Head House Hotel*. Fortifications built during the Napoleonic Wars are still standing on this southern limit of Tor Bay, which is now a conservation area attracting colonies of nesting seabirds and affording fabulous views across the bay. In summer, you can explore the coastline hereabouts on various **boat tours** leaving from Brixham's harbour (£10–15), or make the 30-minute crossing to Torquay, departing roughly every hour (£3.50).

Practicalities

Brixham's **tourist office** (June–Sept Mon–Sat 9.30am–5.30pm Sun 10am–4pm; Oct–May Mon–Fri 9.30am–1pm & 2–5pm, Sat 9.30am–1pm & 2–4pm; Ⓣ01803/211211, Ⓦwww.englishriviera.co.uk) is on the quayside. The best **accommodation** choices overlook the harbour along King Street: try the *Harbour View Hotel* at no. 65 (Ⓣ01803/853052, Ⓦwww.harbourviewbrixhambandb.co.uk; ❹), where all rooms have bathrooms but can be small, or the *Quayside Hotel*, two doors down (Ⓣ01803/855751, Ⓦwww.quaysidehotel.co.uk; ❻), with larger and classier rooms, plus two bars and a restaurant, and live folk on the first Thursday of the month. Away from the seafront, there's *Brookside* at 160 New Rd (Ⓣ01803/858858, Ⓦwww.brooksidebrixham.co.uk; no under-16s; ❹), a bungalow with a more contemporary style and organic breakfasts. All three places offer wi-fi.

The *River Dart Youth Hostel* (ⓣ0845/371 9531, ⓔriverdart@yha.org.uk; from £13.95) lies four miles away outside the village of **Galmpton**, on the banks of the Dart; there's a café but no self-catering (except for groups). Bus #12 (every 10–15min), and the Paignton & Dartmouth Steam Railway (see p.106), which passes right through the hostel's grounds, takes you as far as Churston Bridge, from where it's a two-mile walk – call ahead to check opening. The nearest **campsites** are *Centry Touring* (ⓣ01803/856389), a no-frills site half a mile east of Brixham and close to Berry Head Country Park, and the better-equipped *Upton Manor Farm*, St Mary's Road (ⓣ01803/882384, ⓦwww.uptonmanorfarm.co.uk; no single-sex groups), a mile south of town; both are a few minutes' walk from the sandy beach at St Mary's Bay and the coast path, and both are closed roughly mid-October to Easter.

As for **eating**, Brixham offers fish and more fish, from the harbourside stalls selling cockles, whelks and crab sticks to *The Poopdeck* at 14 The Quay (ⓣ01803/858681; closed all Mon Oct–June & lunchtime Tues–Fri), a great seafood restaurant where a plate of grilled local fish costs £14.50 and a hot shellfish platter is £22 – book early for a table overlooking the harbour. Among the **pubs**, head for the *Blue Anchor* on Fore Street, which has coal fires, low beams and live music at weekends. *The Vigilance* on Bolton Street (at the top of Fore St) has maritime items adorning its walls and cheap eats all day.

Totnes, Dartmouth and the South Hams

Known as the **South Hams**, the area between the Dart and Plym estuaries holds some of Devon's comeliest villages and most striking coastline. The chief towns of the region are all on rivers: **Dartmouth**, the most touristy but still unspoiled, with a strong maritime tradition; **Totnes**, further up the Dart and lately a centre for therapists and crystal-gazers; and **Salcombe**, near the mouth of the Kingsbridge estuary, a pretty, steep and narrow-laned sailors' resort. Dartmouth and Totnes in particular have preserved numerous relics of their medieval past – for example the slate-hung facades for which this part of South Devon is known – which help to draw the tourists, though there is nothing like the same full-on holiday atmosphere of the Torbay area.

Outside the towns, the South Hams is a hilly patchwork of fields. The area enjoys a sheltered, **mild climate** (a "hamme" is a sheltered place in Old English) which encourages subtropical plants as well as the vines that produce the famous Sharpham wine. But the real beauty resides in the rocky and ever-changing sixty miles of **coastline**, making for highly scenic but occasionally exhausting walking country, particularly west of Salcombe; **tourist offices** can equip you with leaflets on walks and cycling on off-road routes. Totnes is the best centre for **train connections** – it's on the main Exeter–Plymouth rail line – while Totnes, Dartmouth and Kingsbridge have **bus services** to all other South Hams villages.

Totnes and around

Five miles inland of Torbay, **TOTNES** has an ancient pedigree, its period of greatest prosperity having occurred in the sixteenth century, when this inland port on the west bank of the River Dart exported cloth to France and brought back wine. Some evocative structures from that era remain, but Totnes has mellowed into a residential market town today, its warehouses converted into gentrified flats. The arcaded High Street, secretive flowery lanes, Norman castle and preserved steam railway have attracted some tourist overflow from nearby

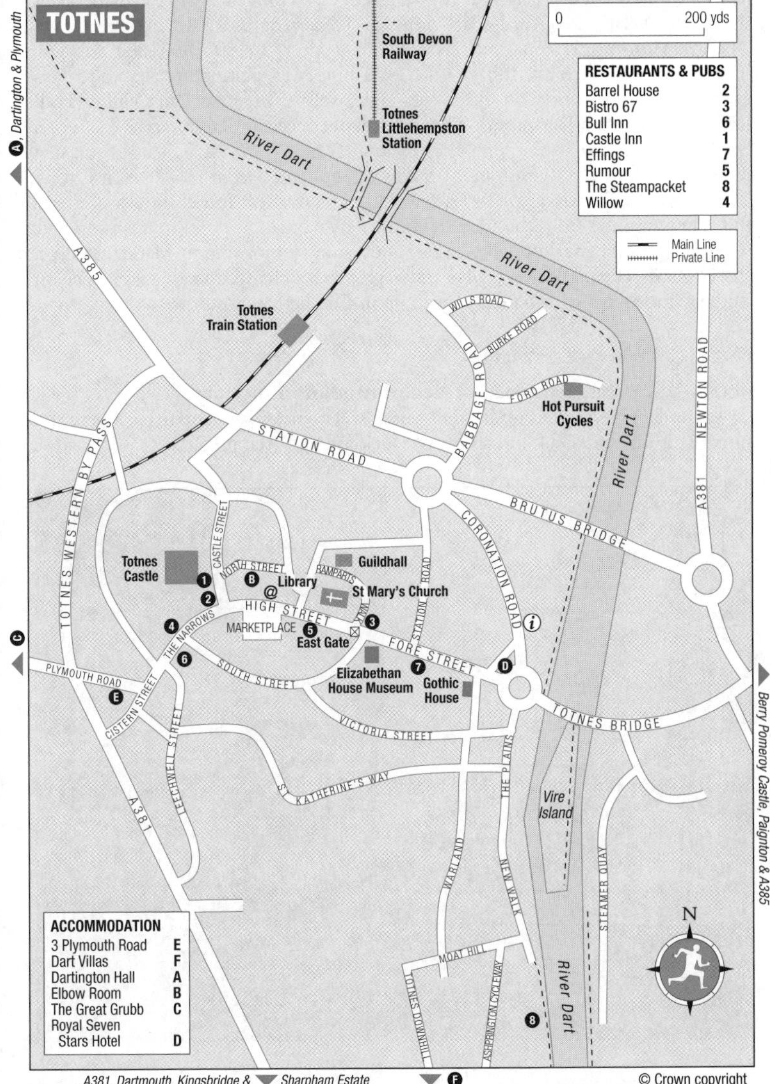

Torbay, but so far its allure has survived more or less intact – enough, anyway, to attract the New Age candles-and-crafts crowd in recent years, accounting for the town's numerous vegetarian and wholefood cafés.

Arrival and information

Totnes is served by regular **trains** on the Exeter–Plymouth line, which stop at the station on Station Road, at the end of Castle Street, by trains from Buckfastleigh on the South Devon Railway (see p.112) which stop at Totnes Littlehempston Station, and by frequent **buses** #X80, #X81, #88 and #100 (summer only) from Paignton and #X80, #X81 and #111 from Torquay. The **tourist office** is in the Town Mill, off The Plains at the bottom of Fore Street, near Morrisons supermarket car park (April–Oct Mon–Fri 9.30am–5pm, Sat 10am–4pm; Nov–March Mon–Fri 10am–4pm, Sat 10am–1pm; ⓣ01803/863168, ⓦwww.totnesinformation.co.uk). It has a small local-history exhibition upstairs, and hikers can pick up information on the sixteen-mile, well-waymarked **Dart Valley Trail** linking Totnes with Dartmouth. There's **internet** access in the library at 27a High St (Mon & Wed 9.30am–5pm, Tues & Fri 9.30am–7pm, Sat 9.30am–1pm; first 30min free, then £1.50 for 30min). **Bikes** can be rented from Hot Pursuit Cycles, 26 The Stables, Ford Rd (ⓣ01803/865174; £15 a day), on Totnes Industrial Estate, just a few minutes from the train station, where advice on good routes is offered. There's a general **market** every Friday and Saturday morning in Marketplace, off the High Street, and between May and September a charity market takes place on Tuesday mornings with traders togged up in Elizabethan costumes.

Accommodation

Totnes has a scattered range of **accommodation**, not always easy to track down, and often booked up in high summer. The nearest **campsite** is five miles northwest on the A384, just south of Buckfastleigh (see p.139).

▲ Totnes

3 Plymouth Road ⓣ01803/866917, ⓦwww.mlfen.freeserve.co.uk. Friendly, good-value B&B close to the centre. There are three smallish rooms, one of them en suite, and a small roof terrace. 3

Dart Villas 3 Dart Villas, Totnes Down Hill ⓣ01803/865895, ⓦwww.dartvillasbb.co.uk. Tastefully furnished Georgian B&B with hilltop views, a ten-minute walk from The Plains. Breakfasts are organic and vegetarian. Treatments, therapies and internet available. 4

Dartington Hall Dartington ⓣ01803/847100, ⓦwww.dartingtonhall.com. Arranged around the Fourteenth-century courtyard of Dartington Hall, two miles north of Totnes, rooms here range from standards with shared bathrooms to en-suite doubles (6). Breakfast and meals are served in the *White Hart* bar. Accommodation is not available during the summer school and festivals (including most of July & Aug). 4

Elbow Room North St ⓣ01803/863480, ⓦwww.theelbowroomtotnes.co.uk. A good central choice opposite the castle car park, this 200-year-old converted cottage and cider press has two quiet, tastefully furnished rooms, both en suite. No credit cards. 4

The Great Grubb Fallowfields, Plymouth Rd ⓣ01803/849071, ⓦwww.thegreatgrubb.co.uk. Leather sofas, restful colours, healthy breakfasts and a patio are the main appeal of this friendly B&B, where work by local artists is displayed in the rooms. wi-fi-enabled. 4

Royal Seven Stars Hotel The Plains ⓣ01803/862125, ⓦwww.royalsevenstars.co.uk. Seventeenth-century coaching inn with old-fashioned comforts but contemporary bedrooms with free wi-fi. 6

The Town

Totnes centres on the long main street that starts off as Fore Street and becomes High Street at the white, castellated **East Gate**, a heavily retouched medieval arch. A number of eye-catching old buildings line both streets, for example the mustard-yellow, late eighteenth-century **Gothic House** on Fore Street; 16 High St, a house built by pilchard merchant Nicholas Ball, whose initials are carved outside (his wealth, inherited by his widow, was eventually bequeathed by her second husband, Thomas Bodley, to found Oxford's Bodleian Library); and 28 High St, overhung by curious grotesque masks. Many of the structures are Elizabethan in origin, with later facades added, often with a handsome covering of slate tiles.The **Elizabethan House Museum** at 70 Fore St (mid-March to Oct Mon–Fri 10.30am–5pm; £2) is one of the best preserved of these. Packed with an entertaining assortment of domestic objects and furniture that reveals how wealthy clothiers lived at the peak of Totnes's success, the four-storey building also holds a room devoted to local mathematician **Charles Babbage** (1791–1871), whose "analytical engine", programmed by punched cards, was the forerunner of the computer (he was assisted by Lord Byron's daughter, Ada, countess of Lovelace).

Beneath East Gate, **Ramparts Walk** trails east along the old town walls, curling round the fifteenth-century church of St Mary, where an exquisitely carved stone rood screen stretches the full width of the red-sandstone building. Behind the church, the colonnaded eleventh-century **Guildhall** (Mon–Fri: April–June, Sept & Oct 11am–3pm; July & Aug 10.30am–4pm; £1), originally the refectory and kitchen of a Benedictine priory, now houses the town's Council Chamber, which you can see together with the former jail cells and the courtroom, and a table used by Oliver Cromwell in 1634.

At the top of the High Street, Castle Street leads to **Totnes Castle** (daily: April–June & Sept 10am–5pm; July & Aug 10am–6pm; Oct 10am–4pm; £3; EH), the town's oldest monument. It's a classic Norman structure of the motte and bailey design, with a simple crenellated keep atop a grassy mound reached along a winding path. Not much else remains other than this shell, but it's a panoramic spot, offering wide views of the town and Dart valley.

Totnes presents a very different face at river level, around **Totnes Bridge**, at the bottom of Fore Street. At the highest navigable point on the River Dart for seagoing vessels, the quaysides here see various comings and goings, including, between April and October, regular departures of **river cruises** to Dartmouth from Steamer Quay (Ⓣ01803/834488, Ⓦwww.riverlink.co.uk; £8 one way, £10 return). Half a mile north of Totnes Bridge, a riverside walk leads to the station of the **South Devon Railway**, from where steam trains depart four to eight times daily for a thirty-minute ride to Buckfastleigh (see p.138), on the edge of Dartmoor. The service operates between Easter and October (and also on specific dates in winter: call Ⓣ0845/345 1466 or check Ⓦwww.southdevonrailway.org for details) and costs around £10 return. You'll pass some glorious scenery, and there's a stop at **Staverton**, where there's an inn and access to the riverside path.

Around Totnes

A couple of miles north out of Totnes, both rail and footpath pass near the estate of **Dartington Hall** (Ⓣ01803/847070, Ⓦwww.dartington.org/arts), an arts and education centre set up in 1925 by US millionairess Dorothy Elmhirst and her husband. The #165 bus connects the estate with Totnes (not Sun), the last one back leaving at around 6pm, or catch the daily #X80 Torquay–Plymouth bus, which stops at Shinner's Bridge, about a mile west of Dartington Hall. You can walk through the sculpture-strewn gardens, which contain an immaculately kept tiltyard and terraces, at any time and – when it's not in use – visit the fourteenth-century Great Hall, originally built for Richard II's half-brother John Holand and rescued from dereliction by the Elmhirsts. As well as the constant programmes of films, plays, concerts, dance and workshops, an **annual literature festival** takes place here in mid-July, featuring big-name writers, and there is a **summer festival** of mainly classical music from late July through to late August. Signposted near the Hall, the **Cider Press Centre** (open daily) retails Dartington Crystal and an assortment of upmarket crafts as well as edible goodies from the farm shop, and there are meals available from *Cranks*, the sole surviving branch of the 1970s wholefood restaurant chain.

Three miles east of Totnes off the A385, amid deep woods, **Berry Pomeroy Castle** (daily: April–June & Sept 10am–5pm; July & Aug 10am–6pm; Oct 10am–4pm; £4.20; EH) is one of Devon's most romantic ruins, a fifteenth-century fortress converted into an Elizabethan mansion by the powerful Seymour family, but never completed and abandoned by 1700. You can enter the gatehouse, walk along the few intact walls – affording great views – and listen on the supplied audioguide to tales of the ghosts said to dwell here. Bus #111 between Totnes and Torquay stops nearby (Sun in summer only).

A couple of miles downriver of Totnes, some of the country's finest wines are produced at **Sharpham Estate** (March–Christmas Mon–Sat 10am–5pm, also June–Sept Sun 10am–5pm; Ⓦwww.sharpham.com), which you can explore on trails, self-guided walks (£5) or two-hour guided tours (May to mid-Sept Wed at 3.30pm; £10, no booking required), with tasting and shopping opportunities aplenty. The estate lies a mile outside the village of Ashprington, signposted from the A381 Kingsbridge road.

Eating and drinking

You don't need to stray off the Fore Street/High Street axis to find a good range of **eating** options, all fairly laid-back. There are several decent **pubs** in town in addition to the *Steampacket* listed below: the lively *Castle Inn* on Fore Street and the *Bull Inn* at the top of the High Street both have a warm atmosphere, bar meals and local ales. At **Dartington**, you can replenish yourself at the *Roundhouse* café-bar or the atmospheric *White Hart* bar/restaurant.

Devon and Cornwall on a plate

Put it down to fashion, to self-pampering, to fabulous locations, or – more likely – to the availability of the freshest locally sourced ingredients, but the renaissance of restaurant culture in the UK has had a significant impact on Devon and Cornwall. No longer the preserve of the cream tea and pasty – though these two institutions are still alive and well in the West Country – many of the region's restaurants now offer lip-smackingly delicious meat and seafood dishes, either enjoyably simple or adventurously prepared and boldly presented. From stylish beachside bistros to secluded rural gastropubs, the venues alone are enough to inspire a serious exploration of the counties' epicurean delights.

Newlyn crabs ▲

Traditional Cornish cream tea ▼

Fresh from the sea

With so many miles of coastline and an abundance of fresh fish, it's natural that **seafood** should feature on menus throughout the peninsula, from lobster at sophisticated restaurants to crabs and whelks sold from quayside stalls. Among the local star chefs, the best-known, **Rick Stein**, has built his reputation on seafood: people flock from far and wide to sample his creations in his home town of Padstow, ranging from fish and chips to the fanciest culinary concoctions. Nearly a quarter of the country's **oysters** are produced in oyster beds in the Helford and Fal rivers while, inland, **salmon** and **trout** from the rivers of Exmoor and Dartmoor are prized. In general, what's on offer depends entirely on the catch – a guarantee that it'll be fresh and local.

Local specialities

Although **seafood** may not be strictly a local speciality, local chefs have excelled in ways of preparing this great resource from locally fished waters. Away from the coasts, local **lamb** and **venison** are celebrated meat dishes, while the region's dairy herds are responsible for the creamiest **cream teas** and **ice cream** to be found anywhere in Britain. Cornwall has also contributed an impressive list of artisan **cheeses** (such as nettle-wrapped Yarg cheese) and **star gazy** pie, but nothing to match the ubiquity of its famous and variously filled **pasties**, sometimes cited as the original convenience food, three million of which are produced in the county every week. These were the traditional tin-miner's lunch – to avoid ingesting the arsenic that miners had on their fingers, they would eat the fillings and discard the pastry, though nowadays a pasty's very much an all-in-one meal.

West Country wines

As the English **wine boom** has gathered pace, winemakers have reaped the benefits of the soil conditions and mild climate of the Southwest peninsula – most of whose vineyards lie on an almost identical latitude with the Moselle Valley – making the region one of Britain's top producers. Devon currently has about thirty vineyards, many planted in the last few years; the area around Exeter and the Exe Valley is a particular hotspot, home to **Kenton**, **Sharpham** and **Yearlstone** vineyards, among others. Cornwall has a smaller number – perhaps due to the sea air – the most outstanding of which is **Camel Valley**, near Bodmin. Others include **Lambourne**, from the Roseland Peninsula, and **Bosue** near St Austell. These all produce red, white, rosé and sparkling wines, though the majority of the medal-winners tend to be crisply dry still or sparkling whites. Look out too for some delicious **fruit wines**, such as the plum wine made at Polmassick – it's mixed with local Pinot Noir grapes and best drunk chilled as a dessert wine. Most vineyards are open to the public, for tours and sales, and wines can be sampled at such events as Devon Wine Week in late May (Ⓦwww.devonwineweek.co.uk).

▲ Camel Valley vineyard

▼ Devon's Otter Ale

Real ale and cider, Devon and Cornwall style

You don't have to be a beer bore to want to spend time on the pub trail in Devon and Cornwall. The best of the boozers (listed in the Guide) have the winning formula of traditional ambience, quiet conviviality and authentic local ales. Devon in particular is an area to seek out locally brewed alcoholic

Porthminster Beach Café ▲

Fifteen Cornwall, Watergate Bay ▼

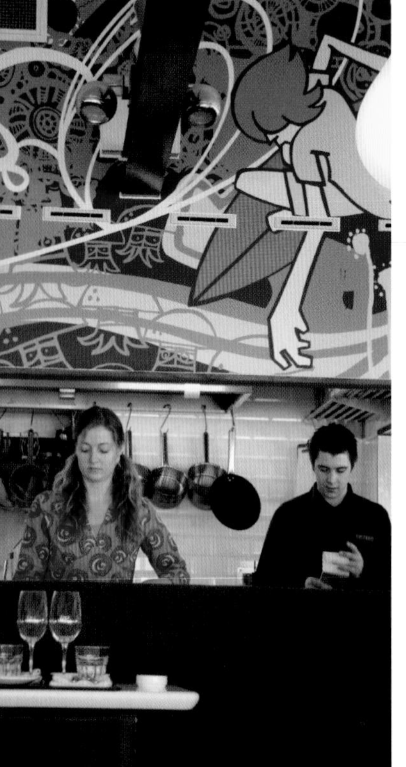

still cider some of its drier variants being termed as scrumpy; and here and there you'll come across mead (made from fermented honey). But the chief enticement is the **beer**: Branscombe Vale, Exe Valley, Dartmoor, O'Hanlon's. Otter and Teignworthy ales in Devon, Ales of Scilly, St Austell, Sharp's, Skinners and **Tinners** in Cornwall, to name just a few breweries, and the choice of real ales (beers that have been allowed to ferment naturally in the cask, and are served by handpumps or straight from the cask) has mushroomed in recent years. Among the **pubs** worth going out of your way for, in Devon try the *Peter Tavy Inn*, Peter Tavy, on the edge of Dartmoor (p.17) and the *Royal Oak* in Winsford, Exmoor (p.191); in Cornwall, you should seek out the *Blisland Inn*, Blisland, on Bodmin Moor (p.359), and the *Blue Anchor* in Helston (p.259), the most famous of the region's **microbreweries** – brewing their own cask-conditioned beer on the premises.

Ten restaurants worth a detour

- **Moores**, Newton Poppleford (see p.83)
- **River Cottage Canteen**, Axminster (see p.86)
- **Gidleigh Park**, Dartmoor (see p.145)
- **The New Angel**, Dartmouth (see p.115)
- **Restaurant Nathan Outlaw**, Fowey (see p.231)
- **Alba**, St Ives (see p.293)
- **Porthminster Beach Café**, St Ives (see p.293)
- **Fifteen Cornwall**, Watergate Bay (see p.331)
- **Seafood Restaurant**, Padstow (see p.337)
- **No. 6**, Padstow (see p.336)

Barrel House 58–59 High St ☎01803/863000. A café at street level, and upstairs a lounge in a former ballroom with chandeliers and cinema seats, where you can eat salads, paninis and burgers (£7–9), or just come for a cup of tea and a slice of cake or drop by for a beer. Regular events, from poetry readings to ska gigs. Closed Mon–Wed eves.

Bistro 67 67 Fore St ☎01803/862604. Arty café /restaurant with wooden floor and tables, offering breakfasts, lunches, teas and a range of meals from crêpes and hot bacon salad to vegetable or chicken satay and Goan tiger prawns (all £6–10). Soups and hot baguettes also available. Closed Sun eve.

Effings 50 Fore St ☎01803/863435. They really care about food at this small (five-table) deli-café, where dishes range from Farmhouse Indulgence (roast beef, gammon and cheddar) to Italian antipasti and Spanish snacks, all around £9 or £12 (for "light" or "main"). If it's booked up, take your pick from the tasty takeaway items. No credit cards. Closed eves & all Sun.

Rumour 30 High St ☎01803/864682. With a buzzy atmosphere, this is good for coffees, snacks or globally inspired full meals, for example Thai green curry or make-your-own pizzas (from £6.50). Most mains are around £15. Closed Sun lunch.

The Steampacket St Peter's Quay ☎01803/863880. Riverside inn with a conservatory and patio. Good-value, well-prepared traditional meals (£8–15) and real ales are served. There's live acoustic music on Tues eve, and Sun lunches are worth booking.

Willow 87 High St ☎01803/862605. Vegetarian and vegan food and organic wines are offered here, with an Indian menu on Wed night and live music on Fri night (booking advised). The courtyard's good for lunches and teas. Main courses average at £8. No credit cards. Closed Sun, also Mon, Tues & Thurs eves.

Dartmouth

Seven miles downstream of Totnes and a mile in from the sea, **DARTMOUTH** has thrived since the Normans recognized the potential of this deep-water port for trading with their home country. The maritime connection is still strong today: fishing and freight are among the town's main activities, and officers are still trained at the imposing red-brick **Royal Naval College**, majestically sited on a hill behind the port.

Arrival and information

Dartmouth is connected to Totnes and Torquay by bus #111 (not Sun Oct–May). Dartmouth's **tourist office** is opposite the car park just off the quayside, north of Duke Street (Easter–Oct Mon–Sat 9.30am–5pm, Sun 10am–2pm; Nov–Easter Mon–Sat 9.30am–4.30pm; ☎01803/834224, Ⓦwww.discoverdartmouth.com). Ask here about the town's biggest event, **Dartmouth Royal Regatta** (Ⓦwww.dartmouthregatta.co.uk), taking place over three days around the last weekend of August. The river races, air displays and fireworks attract huge crowds, making accommodation scarce during this period.

You can log onto the **internet** in the library in the Flavel arts centre, near the tourist office on Flavel Place (Mon & Thurs 9.30am–7pm, Tues & Fri 9.30am–5pm, Sat 9.30am–1pm; first 30min free, then £1.50 for 30min). The

Dartmouth ferries

Travellers between Torbay and Dartmouth can save time and a long detour through Totnes by using the frequent **ferries** crossing the Dart, either the **Higher Ferry** linking with the A379 (£1 single, £3.50 for cars with passengers) or the **Lower Ferry** from Kingswear via the minor B3205 (£1 single, £3.20 for cars with passengers). Service is continuous from 7am (8.10am on Sun) to around 10.45pm.

For the Dartmouth Castle ferry, see p.115.

Flavel (Ⓣ01803/839530, Ⓦwww.theflavel.org.uk) is also good for films, music, dance and art.

Accommodation

Accommodation in Dartmouth is generally expensive; some of the best choices lie at the top of steep hills, all the better to appreciate the exquisite views over the river. If you prefer to avoid the uphill trudge, you'll find a good range lower down too, for example in and around Victoria Road (the continuation of Duke St). There's a convenient **campsite** just outside town on the A3122, opposite Sainsbury's supermarket, *Little Cotton* (Ⓣ01803/832558, Ⓦwww.littlecotton.co.uk), with spacious, modern and clean facilities, though if you want to be near Blackpool Sands, head for *Leonards Cove* (Ⓣ01803/770206, Ⓦwww.leonardscove.co.uk), three miles south of town near Stoke Fleming and Leonards Cove. Both are closed between November and mid-March, though *Leonards Cove* has self-catering lodges and bungalows available for rent all year.

Alf Resco Lower St Ⓣ01803/835880, Ⓦwww.cafealfresco.co.uk. Great central choice above a café, with river views from the two beautifully furnished en-suite rooms at the top (one a bunkroom). There's also a self-catering flat. No credit cards. ③

Avondale 5 Vicarage Hill Ⓣ01803/835831, Ⓦwww.avondaledartmouth.co.uk. Friendly, spacious and elegantly furnished place, with terrific views over the town and river. Free wi-fi. No credit cards. ④

Browns 27–29 Victoria Rd Ⓣ01803/832572, Ⓦwww.brownshoteldartmouth.co.uk. Small, up-to-the-minute hotel, with stylish rooms, contemporary paintings and a spruce feel. Good Mediterranean dishes are served in the bar and restaurant. Two-night minimum stay at weekends. ④

Res Nova Inn Ⓣ0777/062 8967, Ⓦwww.resnova.co.uk. For something completely different, you might consider this barge moored in mid-river. Cabins are cramped but comfy with shared bathroom, and there's also a single berth. Guests are ferried to and from town by arrangement. No kids. Closed Sun & Mon. ④–④

Royal Castle Hotel The Quay Ⓣ01803/833033, Ⓦwww.royalcastle.co.uk. Right in the heart of things, this ancient hotel combines contemporary decor with a plush, antique atmosphere. Rooms have river views or surround a courtyard. ⑧

The Town

Tightly packed on the River Dart's western bank, and rising steeply above it, Dartmouth enjoys a wonderful setting unspoiled by the excessive traffic that mars many other South Devon towns. A number of lopsided but well-preserved old buildings add to the congenial atmosphere – the timber-framed **Butterwalk**, just behind the enclosed boat basin at the bottom of Duke Street, the town's central thoroughfare, is one of the most askew. Overhanging the street on eleven granite columns, the four-storey construction, richly decorated with wood carvings, was built in the seventeenth century for a local merchant. It now holds shops and the small **Dartmouth Museum** (Mon–Sat: April–Oct 10am–4pm; Nov–March noon–3pm; £1.50), mainly devoted to maritime curios. The highlight is the King's Room, with its original wood panelling and plaster ceiling, and displays of model sailing ships alongside delicate ivory models of Chinese craft and a man-of-war constructed from bone by French prisoners. There's a richly decorated room devoted to William Cumming (1860–1919), a local self-educated polymath, while mementos of Thomas Newcomen (1663–1729), "Ironmonger of Dartmouth" and inventor of the world's first successful steam piston, can be seen in the Holdsworth Room. Used to pump water out of mines, Newcomen's creation was an essential aid to Devon's miners, and was a forerunner of James Watt's steam engine. An original Newcomen engine is on view in **The Engine House**, annexed to Dartmouth's tourist office in gardens backing onto the quayside (same hours as tourist office; free, but donation requested); you can see the great rocking beam in action.

Across Duke Street, the fourteenth-century **St Saviour's** Church was rebuilt in the 1630s, when timberwork from the captured flagship of the Spanish Armada was incorporated in the gallery. There's a finely carved fifteenth-century stone pulpit and wooden screen and, on a door leaning up inside the south porch, some superb medieval ironwork depicting the elongated lions of Edward I and the tree of life, remounted here at the time of the rebuilding. Behind St Saviour's, Higher Street holds several notable buildings: the tottering, timber-framed *Cherub Inn*, dating from 1380, and, at no. 3–5, the larger and more ornate **Tudor House**, a handsome grey-beamed building with oriel windows, whose facade dates (despite its name) from 1635. Equally impressive, on the parallel Lower Street (at no. 28), is timber-framed **Agincourt House**, built by a merchant after the battle for which it is named, then restored in the seventeenth century and again in the twentieth.

Lower Street leads down to Bayard's Cove, a short cobbled quay lined with well-restored eighteenth-century houses, where the Pilgrim Fathers put to shore en route to the New World. A twenty-minute walk south of here along the river takes you to **Dartmouth Castle** (April–June & Sept daily 10am–5pm; July & Aug daily 10am–6pm; Oct daily 10am–4pm; Nov–March Sat & Sun 10am–4pm; £4.20; EH), one of two fortifications on opposite sides of the estuary (the other is Kingswear Castle) built at the end of the fifteenth century. The larger and more complete of the two, Dartmouth Castle was the first in England to be constructed specifically to withstand artillery, but was never tested in action and consequently remains in an excellent state of preservation. Various examples of weaponry are on display, and panels explain the castle's historical function. If you don't relish the return walk, you can take a ferry back to town, departing from the creek below the castle (Easter–Oct; £2).

Eating and drinking

Dartmouth has acquired a certain renown for its **restaurants**, of which the town has a prolific number, including some good fast-food and snack stops. In the best places, fish is top choice, but it doesn't come cheap. If you're in town on a Tuesday or Friday morning, you might find some takeaway bites from the general **market** that fills Market Square, just north of Duke Street.

Café Alf Resco Lower St. Popular but still laid-back spot for breakfasts, coffees and light lunches (until 2pm) for £5–7. There are outdoor tables, and internet access is available on a laptop or using your own via wi-fi. No credit cards.

Crab Shell 1 Raleigh St. Tucked away in an alley between Fairfax Place and the riverfront, this tiny shop (which closes at 2.30pm) dispenses generously stuffed fresh crab sandwiches amongst other items to take away for under £5. No credit cards. Closed Dec–Easter.

The Dolphin Market Square ⓣ01803/833835. Traditional-looking gastropub with well-prepared bar meals and a seafood restaurant upstairs, where the menu includes scallops, plaice and poached salmon (around £10). Closed eves Sun & Mon.

New Angel 2 South Embankment ⓣ01803/839425, ⓦwww.thenewangel.co.uk. Michelin-starred restaurant run by celebrity chef John Burton Race, with an open kitchen on the ground floor and more intimate dining upstairs, where there are splendid river views. The tone is refreshingly informal and prices are not too high (set dinners cost £25–30). Dishes are French- and Mediterranean-influenced, using local ingredients, for example poached lobster in a basil sauce. Closed Sun eve, all Mon & Tues lunch.

Res Nova Inn ⓣ0777/062 8967. As well as offering accommodation, this boat moored in mid-river serves delicious seafood suppers (including fresh lobster kept in baskets on the side of the hull), alongside roasts and bangers and mash. You can eat breakfast here, lunch on soup and sandwiches, book a candlelit dinner for two in the wheelhouse (at no extra cost), or just drop in for a late-night drink. Most main courses cost £9–15. Call to be picked up from the quayside. Closed Sun eve, all Mon & Tues lunch, in winter open just Thurs–Sat eves & Sun lunch.

Spice Bazaar Anzac St ⓣ01803/832224. Mouth-watering Indian-fusion cuisine in a cool, modern space next to St Saviour's Church. Main dishes cost £9–15, and you can order set-price lunches for under £10.

Around Dartmouth

Beyond Dartmouth Castle, it's a thirty-minute walk round the estuary mouth to **Start Bay**, home to the best swimming in these parts; it's also reachable by road via the A379 from Dartmouth. Three or four miles south of town and a 45-minute walk from the castle, past the pretty hilltop village of Stoke Fleming, **Blackpool Sands** is easily the most popular of the bay's beaches, an unspoilt cove flanked by steep, wooded cliffs. There's a car park among other facilities here, and excellent **refreshments** at the *Venus Café* (closed Nov–Easter), which features organic and local ingredients in its meals that span everything from breakfasts to barbies. It's normally open until 5pm, but stays open for evening **meals** July to mid-September (except Tues, also Sun & Mon in Sept), worth booking at ⓣ01803/712648.

Beyond here, road and coast path descend to another good but much less sheltered swimming spot, **Slapton Sands** – three miles of shingle used during World War II by US navy and infantry divisions for rehearsing the D-day landings. Behind the beach, the lagoon of the Slapton Ley **nature reserve** (unrestricted access; free) supports herons, terns, widgeon and – rarest of all – great crested grebes. The only development is at **Torcross** on the lagoon's southern end, where there's a handful of B&Bs and restaurants, and a memorial to the 639 US servicemen killed when German E-boats succeeded in breaching the coastal defences here in 1944; alongside is a Sherman tank that sank in 1944 and was recovered forty years later, its black and oily appearance giving the impression that it has only just been dredged up from the mud.

From Torcross, which is connected with Dartmouth, Kingsbridge and Plymouth by the #93 bus, coastwalkers can continue south down to Start Point, from where the coast path snakes west to **Prawle Point** (see p.119), Devon's southernmost headland.

Other excursions from Dartmouth can be made by river. There are regular ferry crossings to **KINGSWEAR**, terminus of the **Paignton & Dartmouth Steam Railway** (see p.106), either via the Lower Ferry, which departs from below Lower Street, or, less than a mile upriver, off North Embankment, the Higher Ferry (see p.113 for details). The village itself has little of interest beyond its pubs, but you can follow the path south along the estuary past the remains of **Kingswear Castle** (now holiday homes) to the World War II gun battery at the estuary mouth.

The **River Dart** itself can be explored on the regular **cruises to Totnes** operated by River Link (April–Oct; 1hr 15min; £8 one way, £10 return; ⓣ01803/834488, ⓦwww.riverlink.co.uk), bookable at kiosks on Dartmouth's quay. It makes a relaxed way to view the deep creeks and the various houses on the slopes above, among them the Royal Naval College. To get a closer look at one of these, however, **Greenway** (March to mid-July & Sept to late Oct Wed–Sun 10.30am–5pm; mid-July to Aug Tues–Sun 10.30am–5pm; £7.45; NT), you'll have to join a separate excursion, also run by River Link and Greenway Quay Cruises (ⓣ0845/489 0418, ⓦwww.greenwayferry.co.uk; £7.50 return). At the top of a daunting 800-metre ascent from Greenway Quay, the house is famous as the birthplace of Walter Raleigh's three seafaring half-brothers, the Gilberts, and was later rebuilt for Agatha Christie as a holiday home (see box, p.102). Now with a predominantly 1950s flavour, the house displays the diverse collections of archeology, china and silver that Christie and her archeologist husband acquired, as well as a few photos and letters relating to the author. The panoramic woodland gardens hold rich growths of camellias and magnolias among other shrubs, with terrific estuary views. There's also a gallery showing local art, and two cafés.

Note that, although it is possible to come here by car along the extremely narrow local lanes, parking places are few and must always be booked in advance by phone or on the National Trust website (Ⓣ01803/842382, Ⓦwww.nationaltrust.org.uk). It's far more fun anyway to arrive by boat, which involves a stop at the very quaint village of **Dittisham**, on the west bank of the Dart. Non-drivers will also get discounted entry to Greenway. For walkers, both Greenway and Dittisham are on the Dart Valley Trail.

Kingsbridge

The "capital" of the South Hams region, **KINGSBRIDGE**, is easily accessible by hourly buses from Dartmouth or Totnes, and is the hub of local services to the South Hams villages. Fine Tudor and Georgian buildings distinguish this busy market town at the top of the Kingsbridge estuary, especially along steep Fore Street. Near the top of the street, the colonnaded **Shambles** is largely Elizabethan on the ground floor, its granite pillars supporting an upper floor added at the end of the eighteenth century, while the **Kingsbridge Cookworthy Museum** at no. 108 is housed in a seventeenth-century grammar school (April–Sept Mon–Sat 10.30am–5pm; Oct Mon–Sat 10.30am–4pm; £2.20), where you can immerse yourself in local history and rural culture, with nearly 10,000 photos from 1870 onwards, and there are changing exhibitions. Next to the Shambles, the town hall hosts various **markets**: a flea market on Mondays (May–Oct), country produce on Wednesdays and crafts on Fridays (Easter to Christmas), and there are also regular markets on the Quay.

Practicalities

Kingsbridge tourist office, right by the Quay, has information on the whole region (Easter–Sept Mon–Sat 9am–5.30pm, Sun 10am–4pm; Oct–Easter Mon–Sat 9am–5pm; Ⓣ01548/853195, Ⓦwww.kingsbridgeinfo.co.uk). As for **accommodation** hereabouts, try the excellent *Old School House*, Church Street (Ⓣ01548/857678, Ⓦwww.1osh.co.uk; no credit cards; ❹), in the centre of town, where there's one large en-suite room overlooking a garden on the ground floor. South of town, seek out *Park Farm* (Ⓣ01548/852103, Ⓦwww.parkfarmbythewater.co.uk; no credit cards; ❹), which enjoys marvellous estuary views from its en-suite rooms, and has a plant-filled conservatory, wi-fi access and a two-night minimum stay. To reach it, follow Rope Walk – near the tourist office – for about a mile.

For a **snack** or an excellent selection of takeaway items, make a beeline for *Red Earth*, a café and deli at 1 Duke St, at the bottom of Fore Street (closed eves & Sun); for a drink or meal in a mellow environment, cross Fore Street to the *Seven Stars* **pub** on Mill Street, where you'll find good ales, locally sourced food, outdoor seating and free wi-fi.

Salcombe

Five miles downriver of Kingsbridge, and reachable by ferry, Devon's southernmost resort, **SALCOMBE**, occupies a superb location almost at the mouth of the estuary, reachable on a summer ferry from Kingsbridge. Although there is still some fishing activity here, the town's steep and narrow lanes are mobbed with holiday-makers in summer, while amateur sailors are drawn to the place at any time, accounting for the myriad small craft strewn across the deep, clear waters of the estuary and the boat yards along its banks. The entrance to the harbour is overlooked by the ruined **Fort Charles**, a Civil War relic that injects a touch of romance amid the villas and hotels.

There's enough to amuse in simply strolling up the main Fore Street, at the bottom of the town, or wandering among the mix of pink, green and white cottages interspersed with ships' chandlers that overlook the estuary's calm waters. On Market Street, off the north end of Fore Street, you can bone up on boating and local history at the **Salcombe Maritime Museum** (April–Oct 10.30am–12.30pm & 2.30–4.30pm; £1.50). Small but jam-packed with nautical mementos, including gold coins and other items retrieved from the seabed, the museum has copious amounts of information about local wrecks as well as paintings of the brigantines, barques and schooners that set sail from Salcombe's harbour. A working model boat illustrates various sailing manoeuvres, which you can try out at first hand.

If you're inspired by the museum, or if you just want to explore the estuary and coasts, ask at the quays below Fore Street about **boat trips** and fishing excursions. Whitestrand Boat Hire (Ⓣ01548/844475) on Whitestrand Quay arranges cruises and fishing trips and will **rent** out canoes and motorboats. You can also rent boats or pick up the basics of **sailing** at ICC Salcombe, based on a converted ferry in the estuary and with an office at 28 Island St (Ⓣ01548/531176, Ⓦwww.icc-salcombe.co.uk).

Practicalities

The hourly #606 **bus** connects Kingsbridge with Salcombe (#X64 on Sun, but with only two departures). **Salcombe's tourist office** is above the museum on Market Street (April to mid-July, Sept & Oct daily 10am–5pm; mid-July to Aug Mon–Sat 9am–6pm, Sun 10am–5pm; Nov–March Mon–Sat 10am–3pm; Ⓣ01548/843927, Ⓦwww.salcombeinformation.co.uk). Access the **internet** in the library on Cliff Road (Mon & Fri 3–6pm, Wed & Thurs 9.30am–12.30pm, Sat 10am–noon; first 30min free, then £1.50 for 30min).

Salcombe has fewer choices than Kingsbridge and most are more expensive. You'll get wonderful estuary views, however, from *Rocarno* on Grenville Road (Ⓣ01548/842732, Ⓦwww.rocarno.co.uk; no credit cards; ❸), with all rooms en suite. Further out, try *Beadon Farmhouse* (Ⓣ01548/843020, Ⓦwww.salcombe bandb.co.uk; no under-12s; no credit cards; ❹), a cream-coloured Victorian building on the edge of town (a 15-minute walk from the centre) with neat, chintz-free en-suite rooms and great rural views – self-catering is also available here. Local **campsites** include the basic *Alston Farm* (Ⓣ01548/561260, Ⓦwww .alstoncampsite.co.uk), one and a half miles northwest of town and signposted off the A381 just north of Malborough. At Rew Cross, a mile southwest of Salcombe and about the same distance from South Sands beach (see opposite) and Soar Mill Cove, the panoramic *Higher Rew* (Ⓣ01548/842681, Ⓦwww.higherrew .co.uk) is much better equipped but less sheltered; a three-night minimum stay is required in high season. Both places are closed November–March.

Whether you're hankering for fish or happy with a burger, Salcombe's **restaurants** should satisfy. Always book for evening meals in high season, or be prepared to queue.

Restaurants

Captain Flints 82 Fore St ⓣ01548/842646. You'll find a casual, family-friendly atmosphere and moderate prices at this eatery specializing in salads, steaks, pastas and pizzas (£8–10). Closed Oct–Easter.

Catch 55 Fore St ⓣ01548/842646. This small, smart Italian restaurant serves pastas and pizzas (£7–10) and grills (£16–18), and also has pizzas to take away. Closed daytime.

Dusters Bistro 51 Fore St ⓣ01548/842634. Bright and friendly, this place is open during the day for coffees and light lunches and is popular in the evenings for its seafood dishes, for example grilled cod fillet (£14–18), though the menu also includes such dishes as baked Brie tart. Live jazz on Sun Easter–Sept. Closed Nov to mid-Feb.

Oyster Shack 11–13 Island St ⓣ01548/843596. Modern seafood restaurant with a great waterside deck for alfresco dining. Lobster, tiger prawns and crab are regulars on the menu, as well as oysters prepared in various ways. Most main courses cost £12–19. Booking essential. Closed daytime & Oct to mid-March.

Winking Prawn North Sands ⓣ01548/842326. Right on the beach, this makes an alluring stop for a cappuccino, baguette or ice cream by day, or a steak or chargrilled chicken in the evening (around £15). It's worth arriving early for the best tables in the garden. Closed Sun–Wed eves late Oct to Easter.

Around Salcombe

The coastline around Salcombe offers some superb **walking**. From Ferry Steps, accessible from Fore Street, or in winter from Whitestrand Quay, a regular (weather permitting) **passenger ferry** (Easter–Oct 8am–7pm, until 7.30pm at weekends, continuous service; Oct–Easter 8am–5.30pm, until 6pm at weekends, every 30min; £1.30) crosses the narrow estuary channel to **East Portlemouth**. From here you can follow the coast path past the craggily photogenic **Gammon Point** to Devon's most southerly tip, **Prawle Point**, about five miles' walk in all; if you want a circular walk to this stretch of coast, **East Prawle** is a useful starting point, with several routes linking the village to the cliff-tops.

There's an estuary beach at East Portlemouth, but if it's **swimming** you're after, you should stick to the estuary's western bank and head south of Salcombe to **North Sands**, a small sandy strip adjacent to Fort Charles, or follow the coast down to the more extensive **South Sands**, about a mile's pleasant stroll south of Salcombe's centre; between Easter and October you can also get here on the **South Sands ferry** (£2.90), sailing from Whitestrand Quay every thirty minutes between about 9.45am and 5.30pm (6pm in July & Aug). Both beaches, and the adjacent Splat Cove, are scenic, sheltered and have fine sand, making them popular in summer. There are shops, cafés and pubs on hand, and **kayaking**, **windsurfing** and **sailing** sessions are available. From here, it's a ten-minute uphill walk to Sharpitor and Overbeck's Museum (see below).

Sharpitor to Bolt Tail

A couple of miles south of Salcombe, along the western side of the estuary, an elegant Edwardian house in the hamlet of **SHARPITOR** holds the excellent **Overbeck's Museum and Garden** (museum mid-March to June & early Sept to Oct Mon–Wed, Sat & Sun 11am–5pm; July to early Sept daily 11am–5pm; garden mid-Feb to mid-March daily 11am–5pm; mid-March to Oct as museum; Nov to mid-Feb Mon–Fri 11am–5pm £6.40, or £3.50 garden only Nov to mid-March; NT). The one-time home of Otto Overbeck, a research chemist and eccentric inventor, it's mainly dedicated to natural and local history, but also displays such curios as a polyphon – a nineteenth-century jukebox – and a "rejuvenating machine". This, like many of the artefacts, was created by Overbeck, who believed that everyone could live to the age of 350. The museum building has wonderful estuary views and is surrounded by a luxuriant **subtropical garden** (mid-Feb to Oct daily 11am–5pm or dusk; early Feb & Nov–Jan Mon–Fri 11am–5pm or dusk; same ticket), where plants range from Japanese banana to flax. You can reach Sharpitor on (very) minor roads signposted from Salcombe, or preferably on foot from South Sands beach (see above).

Bolt Head, a mile south of Sharpitor, marks the western end of the Kingsbridge estuary, and the start of a magnificent, moderately challenging six-mile, three-hour hike to the massive cliffs of **Bolt Tail**. Along the way, you'll see shags, cormorants and other marine birds swooping above the ragged coast, and wild thyme and sea thrift underfoot.

Thurlestone and Bigbury-on-Sea

West of Bolt Tail, **Bigbury Bay** is dotted with sandy beaches offering first-class, sheltered swimming. The nearest, **Hope Cove**, is nestled in the lee of Bolt Tail, and holds the tiny hamlets of **Inner Hope**, backed by fishermen's cottages and pubs, and **Outer Hope** to the north, surrounded by cliffs and with a slipway serving as a small harbour. The infrequent #162 bus (not Sun) connects Hope Cove with Kingsbridge and, two miles further up the coast, with **THURLESTONE**, a thoroughly thatched village of pink-washed cottages. Backed by rolling farmland and a sprawling golf course, **Thurlestone Sands** is highly rated for its water quality and for surfing. At its southern end, you can explore the rock pools around the spectacular arched rock to which the village owes its name, which means "holed rock" in Old English. A mile or so further west is **Bantham Sands**, the most popular surfing beach hereabouts, at the mouth of the Avon (pronounced "Awn") estuary. Walkers can cross the estuary easily enough at low tide, and at high tide in summer can use the ferry between the hamlets of Bantham (a mile upstream) and Cockleridge. Drivers will have to take the long way round, making a left turn off the A379.

On the opposite side of the Avon is another popular family beach at **BIGBURY-ON-SEA**. Though the village is modern and brash, the level sands and sheltered waters are great for sunbathing and swimming, and visual interest is provided by **Burgh Island**, a few yards out to sea, dominated by the grand Art Deco *Burgh Island Hotel*. You can walk to this tiny islet at low tide, or, which is more fun, jump on the high-rise tractor-like vehicle (£2; last ride around 11pm) that operates when the tide is in. There's public access to most of the green and rocky promontory, whose shores are lined with low cliffs, and there's a nice old pub (see below). **Surfing** equipment and tuition is supplied by Discovery Surf School (Ⓣ0781/363 9622; Ⓦwww.discoverysurf.com), open here daily in summer (weekends only Nov–Easter). Board hire is £10 for 2 hours, wet suits are £5 for 2 hours.

Practicalities

The **tourist offices** in Salcombe (see p.118) and Kingsbridge (see p.117) have information on the region. **Public transport** is practically nonexistent to smaller places outside these two towns. **Accommodation** options are almost as scarce, and prices can be high, but they include some excellent choices, such as the rural, mansion-like *South Allington House* (Ⓣ01548/511272; Ⓦwww.southallingtonhouse.co.uk; no under-4s; no credit cards; ④), three miles east of East Portlemouth and a couple of miles north of Prawle Point, with quiet and comfortable rooms and self-catering accommodation also available; guests can play tennis or croquet in the extensive gardens. **Bigbury-on-Sea** has the small and stylish *Henley Hotel* (Ⓣ01548/810240, Ⓦwww.thehenleyhotel.co.uk; closed mid-Oct to mid-March; no under-12s; ⑦) on Folly Hill, which enjoys great views of the Avon estuary and Burgh Island and offers amazing food, while the *Burgh Island Hotel* (Ⓣ01548/810514, Ⓦwww.burghisland.com; ⑧) is a dazzling display of Art Deco finery, with a stained-glass dome and sumptuous furnishings – Agatha Christie's *Evil Under the Sun* was filmed here in 2001. Book well ahead to stay in one of the huge themed suites. At the opposite extreme, there's an idyllically situated **youth hostel** on the upper floor of Overbeck's Museum in Sharpitor (Ⓣ0845/371 9341, Ⓔsalcombe@yha.org.uk; call to check opening), where dorm beds cost from £16 and there's a kitchen and restaurant. **Campers** should stay in one of the sites around Salcombe (see p.118) or head for *Pennymoor*, some five miles north of Bigbury and two miles east of Modbury, a level, grassy field with spotless facilities and caravans to rent (Ⓣ01548/830452, Ⓦwww.pennymoor-camping.co.uk; closed Nov to mid-March).

Right above the beach at **Bigbury**, the *Venus Café* can supply you with daytime **refreshments** including organic burgers, chicken drumsticks and breaded oysters, all under £7. Otherwise, the area's **pubs** are the best choice for inexpensive meals: at Thurlestone's *Village Inn*, dishes include sausages, pork medallions and seafood (£10–15), and there are real ales on tap. Just below the *Burgh Island Hotel*, the weathered old *Pilchard Inn* offers rolls, pies and full meals cooked in the *Burgh Island Hotel*'s kitchen. Right above the beach at Bigbury-on-Sea, the *Venus Café* has organic snacks.

Travel details

Trains

Dawlish to: Exeter (1–3 hourly; 15–30min); Newton Abbot (1–3 hourly; 12min); Teignmouth (1–3 hourly; 5min); Torquay (hourly; 25min).
Newton Abbot to: Dawlish (1–3 hourly; 12min); Exeter (2–4 hourly; 20–40min); Paignton (1–2 hourly; 15–20min); Plymouth (1–3 hourly; 45min); Teignmouth (1–3 hourly; 10min); Torquay (1–2 hourly; 10min); Totnes (1–3 hourly; 15min).
Paignton to: Exeter (1–2 hourly; 50min–1hr); Newton Abbot (1–2 hourly; 15–20min); Torquay (1–2 hourly; 5min).
Teignmouth to: Dawlish (1–3 hourly; 5min); Exeter (1–3 hourly; 15–30min); Newton Abbot (2–3 hourly; 8min); Torquay (1–2 hourly; 20min).
Torquay to: Dawlish (1–2 hourly; 25–30min); Exeter (1–2 hourly; 45min); Newton Abbot (1–3 hourly; 10min); Paignton (1–2 hourly; 5min); Teignmouth (1–2 hourly; 20min).
Totnes to: Exeter (2 hourly; 30–40min); Newton Abbot (1–3 hourly; 12min); Plymouth (1–3 hourly; 30min).

Buses

Brixham to: Kingswear (1–2 hourly; 15–25min); Paignton (every 10–15min; 25min); Torquay (every 10–15min; 50min).
Dartmouth to: Kingsbridge (Mon–Sat hourly, Sun 4 daily; 1hr); Plymouth (Mon–Sat 8–9 daily, Sun 4 daily; 2hr 15min); Torcross (Mon–Sat hourly, Sun 4 daily; 30min); Torquay (Mon–Sat hourly, Sun in summer 4 daily; 1hr 20min–1hr 40min); Totnes (Mon–Sat hourly, Sun in summer 6 daily; 50min).
Kingsbridge to: Dartmouth (Mon–Sat hourly, Sun 4 daily; 1hr); Salcombe (Mon–Sat hourly, Sun 2 daily; 20–25min); Totnes (Mon–Sat hourly, Sun 2 daily; 40–55min).
Kingswear to: Brixham (1–2 hourly; 20min).

Paignton to: Brixham (every 10–15min; 20min); Torquay (every 10–15min; 20–25min); Totnes (Mon–Sat 3–4 hourly, Sun hourly; 20–30min).
Salcombe to: Kingsbridge (Mon–Sat hourly, Sun 2 daily; 20–25min).
Torquay to Brixham (every 10–15min; 45min); Dartmouth (Mon–Sat hourly, Sun in summer 3 daily; 1hr 30min–1hr 45min); Exeter (Mon–Sat hourly, Sun 3 daily; 1hr); Paignton (every 10–15min; 25min); Plymouth (Mon–Sat hourly, Sun 6 daily; 1hr 50min); Totnes (Mon–Sat 3 hourly, Sun 7–10 daily; 40–55min).
Totnes to: Dartmouth (Mon–Sat hourly, Sun in summer 6 daily; 45min); Kingsbridge (Mon–Sat hourly, Sun 2 daily; 40min); Paignton (Mon–Sat 3–4 hourly, Sun hourly; 20–30min); Plymouth (Mon–Sat hourly, Sun 6 daily; 55min–1hr 10min); Torquay (Mon–Sat 3 hourly, Sun 7–10 daily; 40–55min).

Dartmoor

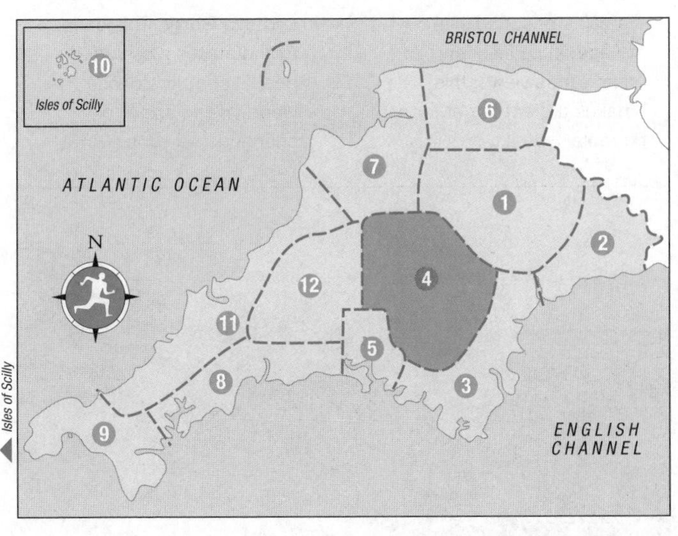
BRISTOL CHANNEL
10
Isles of Scilly
6
7
ATLANTIC OCEAN
1
N
2
12
4
11
5
8
3
Isles of Scilly
9
ENGLISH CHANNEL

CHAPTER 4 Highlights

* **Walking on Dartmoor** The best reason for coming here – it's easy to lose sight of civilization in this remote and surprisingly varied granite landscape. See pp.125–126

* **Wistman's Wood** Ancient, tangled wood in the heart of the moor, but an easy destination for a walk and a picnic. See p.130

* **Hound Tor** With the remains of a medieval village on its flank and marvellous views, this makes a great target for a ramble. See p.136

* **A meal at Gidleigh Park** Treat yourself to a memorable dinner – or a considerably less expensive lunch – at this Michelin-starred restaurant, run by super-chef Michael Caines and reckoned to be one of the best in the country. See p.145

* **Castle Drogo** A neo-medieval extravagance that has an undeniable impact in this lush corner of the moor. See p.145

* **Lydford Gorge** This deep ravine makes a secluded beauty spot, the dense woods rising above a churning river. See p.149

▲ Dartmoor hikers

Dartmoor

The longer one stays here the more does the spirit of the moor sink into one's soul, its vastness, and also its grim charm. When you are once out upon its bosom you have left all traces of modern England behind you, but on the other hand you are conscious everywhere of the homes and the work of the prehistoric people... If you were to see a skin-clad, hairy man... fitting a flint-tipped arrow on to the string of his bow, you would feel that his presence there was more natural than your own.

Arthur Conan Doyle, *The Hound of the Baskervilles*

Covering the sweep of country between Exeter and Plymouth, **DARTMOOR** is southern England's greatest expanse of wilderness, some 365 square miles of raw granite, barren bogland, grassland, deep-wooded and heather-strewn moor. Things weren't always so desolate though, as testified by numerous remnants of scattered prehistoric settlements, and the ruined relics of nineteenth-century quarrying and tin-mining industries. Today, desultory flocks of sheep and groups of ponies are virtually the only living creatures you'll see wandering over the central regions of the National Park, with solitary birds – buzzards, kestrels, pipits, stonechats and wagtails – wheeling and hovering high above.

For many, the emptiest parts of Dartmoor are the most appealing, uncrossed by roads and miles from the nearest villages. These are mainly in the northern and southern reaches, appearing as bare tracts on the map, and characterized by tumbling streams and high tors chiselled by the elements. The specific attractions are mostly concentrated on the periphery of the National Park, though the central east–west belt has both villages with accommodation and some famous beauty spots, making viable starting points for walks into the core of Dartmoor.

The original **Dartmoor Forest** – a royal hunting zone in Saxon times – has largely disappeared, with only about eleven percent of the moor nowadays defined as woodland. Since the fourteenth century, the area has been owned by the Duchy of Cornwall, but public access is almost unlimited today, provided certain guidelines are followed: parking overnight in unauthorized places is prohibited; vehicles are not allowed further than fifteen yards from any road; and, though "wild camping" is permitted out of sight of houses and roads, fires are strictly forbidden. Parts of the moor are designated as firing ranges by the military (see box), and should be avoided at specific times.

Walking is the main reason to be on the moor. Ranging from short and simple jaunts to more challenging treks over long, isolated stretches of rugged uplands, a thick web of trails crisscross what many regard as the country's most inspiring wilderness. Much of it is open access, with the granite tors providing invaluable landmarks; a compass is advisable. Broadly speaking, the gentler contours of the southern moor provide less strenuous rambles, while the harsher northern tracts require more skill and stamina. Seasoned hikers might also link up with some of the longer-distance walks, for example the **Dartmoor Way**, **Tarka Trail**, **Templer Way** and the **Two Moors Way**. Of these, the Dartmoor Way offers the most comprehensive experience of Dartmoor itself – the ninety-mile, unwaymarked circular route takes in Tavistock, Okehampton, Chagford, Moretonhampstead, Bovey Tracey, Ashburton, Buckfastleigh, Holne and Princetown, interspersed with acres of bare moorland, agricultural land and diverse woodland. We've outlined some simple hikes in this chapter, but detailed itineraries are widely available, from specific Dartmoor walking guides (see Contexts, p.390) to pamphlets and other publications on sale at tourist offices; see Ⓦwww.devon.gov.uk for information on all the above walks. **Guided walks** take place all year; an extensive programme of options, varying from two (£3) to six hours (£8), is listed in the *Visitor Guide*'s *What's On* supplement, at information points in

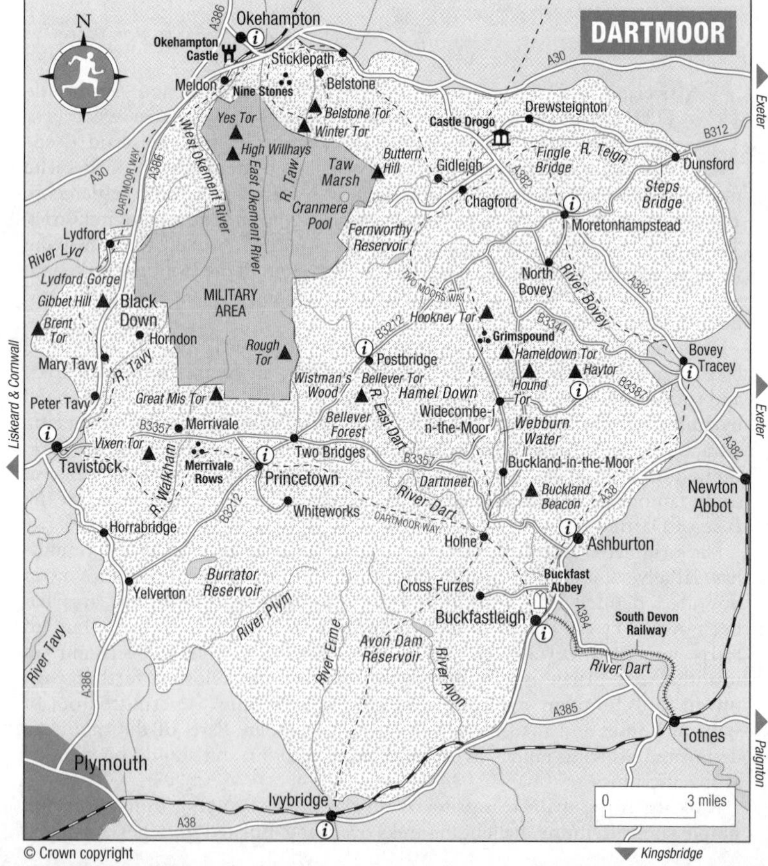

© Crown copyright

Useful Dartmoor websites

Ⓦ**www.dartmoor.co.uk** Independent site with events, attractions, accommodation and pubs.

Ⓦ**www.dartmoor-npa.gov.uk** Official National Park website, with pages of info on accommodation, wildlife, walking and general background.

Ⓦ**www.dartmooraccommodation.co.uk** Links to all kinds of accommodation on the moor, including self-catering, as well as to some food outlets.

Ⓦ**www.discoverdartmoor.com** Website of the Dartmoor Tourist Association, good for accommodation, news and background, with a useful arrangement by town and village.

Ⓦ**www.dartmoorsociety.com** History, culture and other aspects of Dartmoor, including local campaigns.

smaller villages, and on the website Ⓦwww.dartmoor-npa.gov.uk, where you can access maps of start points. Some walks are free if you produce a bus ticket, and most don't require booking; for those that do, and for further information, call Ⓣ01822/890414. Devon Wildlife Trust (Ⓣ01392/279244, Ⓦwww.devonwildlifetrust.org) and the Royal Society for the Protection of Birds (Ⓣ01392/432691, Ⓦwww.rspb.org.uk) also organize guided walks – call or log onto the websites for details. And if you want to go solo, and participate in a Dartmoor institution that has seen a phenomenal growth in recent years, tourist offices can provide information on **letterboxing** (see box, p.150). See Basics, p.38, for a summary of some of the health hazards to be aware of while walking on the moor.

Although some walks are signposted or waymarked with painted stones, map-reading abilities are a prerequisite for all but the shortest of strolls, and a good deal of experience is essential for longer distances – search parties seeking hikers gone astray are not uncommon. The single-sheet, double-sided 1:25,000 Ordnance Survey *Explorer* map OL28 is an impressively detailed piece of mapping, giving copious information down to field boundaries. Another fine way to experience Dartmoor is on **horseback**; several stables are dotted over the moor, and we've mentioned the best in the text. (For biking on Dartmoor, see box, p.128.)

Dartmoor has a fairly good range of **accommodation**, from classy country hotels to rudimentary campsites, mostly concentrated in and around the towns of Okehampton and Tavistock, and larger villages such as Princetown and Chagford. As availability can be extremely restricted in high season, it's always advisable to book ahead, particularly at weekends or in high season. Walkers especially may be interested in the **camping barns** scattered across the moor, offering bunks, toilet facilities, camping grounds and sometimes cooking equipment – again, always book ahead, by calling the barns directly at the numbers supplied in this chapter, or by contacting the **reservations office** of the YHA, which administers most of them (Ⓣ01629/592700, Ⓔcampingbarns@yha.org.uk).

General and practical information relating to Dartmoor is available at Princetown's helpful **High Moorland Visitor Centre** (see p.130), or at tourist information offices in the towns and larger villages. See box above for useful websites.

Getting around

Unless you're using the **steam trains** connecting Buckfastleigh with Totnes (see p.109), or Okehampton's seasonal Sunday rail link with Exeter (p.140), you'll have to rely on a rather sketchy **bus network** for public transport

Dartmoor by bike

Cyclists are well served on Dartmoor, with several dedicated cycle routes, including the **Granite Way**, an eleven-mile cycle- and walkway from Okehampton to Lydford, part of the National Cycle Network's Route 27. Pick up a leaflet on this and other leaflets outlining routes and regulations from tourist offices. **Books** for cyclists include *Dartmoor and Surrounding Area for Cyclists* (£12.95) and *Dartmoor Mountain Bike Routes* (£6.99), on sale at tourist offices and local bookshops.

The free **Dartmoor Freewheeler** service, a minibus that carries cyclists and their bikes on a trailer on four routes onto the moor, was recently suspended, but may be revived: see Ⓦwww.dartmoor-npa.gov.uk for the latest news.

within Dartmoor. The summer-only Transmoor Link (#82), operating at weekends between Exeter and Plymouth, stops at Moretonhampstead, Postbridge, Two Bridges and Princetown (plus places in between), and runs five times daily at weekends between late May and late September (Sun) or late October (Sat). Also from Exeter, the regular #173 (not Sun) runs to Castle Drogo, Chagford and Moretonhampstead, on the northeast side of the moor. Okehampton is served by #X9 and #X90 between Exeter and Bude; #510 between Exeter and Newquay; #179 from Chagford and Moretonhampstead (not Sun); #187 from Tavistock (summer Sun only); #274 and #279 (summer Sun only), from Castle Drogo, Moretonhampstead and Widecombe-in-the-Moor, and #118, running from Tavistock to Okehampton via Lydford (not Sun). Bus #98 connects Princetown with Tavistock five or six times daily (not Sun), and #83, #84 and #86 run up to four times hourly from Tavistock to Plymouth. There are two further limited services that may be useful: the #270, connecting Bovey Tracey, Haytor, Widecombe, Ashburton and Buckfastleigh with Totnes and Newton Abbot, and the #272, connecting Tavistock, Princetown, Two Bridges, Dartmeet, Ashburton and Widecombe (both on Sun only between late May and late Sept). The summer-only Haytor Hoppa circular bus links Bovey Tracey, Haytor, Widecombe and Manaton, with four journeys each Saturday. Apart from these, there's little except once-weekly runs to remote villages.

There are also a couple of **train services**, one, along an old goods line, linking Okehampton with Exeter via Yeoford in about 1 hour 45 minutes on Sundays between late May and late September (for info call Ⓣ01837/55667), while the Tamar Valley Line runs 5–9 times daily all year along the Tamar River between Plymouth and Gunnislake, five miles southwest of Tavistock, just over the Cornish side of the river. The **Sunday Rover ticket** (£6.50), available from late May to late September on Sundays and national holidays, covers all transport on the moor including the Exeter–Okehampton, Tarka Line and Tamar Valley rail lines, and gives you reduced-price entry to several Dartmoor attractions. For all timetables, contact Traveline (Ⓣ0871/200 2233, Ⓦwww.traveline.org.uk). DevonBus (Ⓣ01392/382800 Mon–Fri 9am–5pm, Ⓦwww.devon.gov.uk/buses) does not issue timetable information, but can advise on passes and publications.

The **speed limit** throughout Dartmoor is 40mph, and drivers should beware of ponies, sheep and other livestock straying onto the roads, particularly in early autumn, when they find it the warmest place to be. If you hit an animal, or come across an injured one on the road, contact the police on Ⓣ0845/277 7444.

The central moor

Running diagonally across the moor, the B3212 and B3357 provide easy access to central Dartmoor and, accordingly, the area attracts plenty of visitors. Many are drawn by some of the region's most famous beauty spots, including tumbling brooks and ancient forest, and you would do well to see these places outside the peak periods, when you can still find a degree of isolation. Inevitably, most of the tourist comings and goings are focused on **Princetown**, a strictly functional place that's home to the National Park's main **information centre**. You're unlikely to want to spend much time in Princetown, but what this dull collection of buildings lacks in beauty is amply compensated for by the epic splendour of the surrounding country, accessible on paths or from points within a short drive. The main priority, however, is to get away from the roads. From **Two Bridges**, three miles northeast and the meeting point of two rivers, you can venture forth into **Wistman's Wood**, a hoary survival of the old forest that once covered much of the moor. Further up the B3212, **Postbridge** holds one of Dartmoor's picturesque clapper bridges, and marks the start of a superb riverside route which winds south from here through **Bellever Forest** to where the East and West Dart rivers combine at **Dartmeet** – also reachable via the B3357 from Two Bridges.

Princetown

PRINCETOWN owes its growth to the presence of **Dartmoor Prison**, whose grim spirit seeps into the place; some of the drab granite buildings – like the parish church of St Michael (now closed) – were even built by French and American inmates at the beginning of the nineteenth century. The somewhat oppressed air of the village, not improved by the tall TV mast towering above it on North Hessary Tor, does not invite much lingering, though you'll find most of the facilities you'll need along the main Tavistock Street, which heads northwest from the Square (site of the main tourist office and the intersection with the B3212). Half a mile up Tavistock Street from here, Dartmoor Prison was just one of the schemes instigated by **Thomas Tyrwhitt**, appointed auditor for the Duchy of Cornwall in 1786 and responsible more than anyone for developing the moor's central territory. After the failure of his grandiose project for turning this part of the moor into a cereal-growing prairie, he began work on the prison in 1806, and two years later it was home to 2500 captured French soldiers, and later still to American prisoners from the 1812 war. The prison brought unprecedented commercial activity to this empty heart of the moor,

Military Ranges on Dartmoor

The main restriction on access to Dartmoor is in the Ministry of Defence **firing ranges** that, much to the irritation of locals and visitors alike, take up significant portions of the northern moor, an area that contains Dartmoor's highest tors and some of its most famous beauty spots. The ranges are marked by red-and-white posts; when firing is in progress, red flags by day or red lights at night signify that entry is forbidden. As a general rule, assume that if no warning flags are flying by 9am between April and September, or by 10am from October to March, there is to be no firing on that day. August is usually a firing-free month. Firing-range **schedules** are posted in the National Park's free annual *Visitor Guide* (available from visitor centres in the moor's major towns and villages) and other local newspapers, on BBC Radio Devon, on village notice boards, in some pubs and post offices and in tourist offices; alternatively, call ⓣ0800/458 4868 or check on ⓦwww.dartmoor-ranges.co.uk.

and the weekly market held within its confines attracted traders from throughout the region. After closure in 1816, the prison reopened in 1850 to take the overload from other British jails; it later held conscientious objectors from World War I and, in 1921, IRA prisoners. Nowadays it houses about 600 inmates and remains one of the country's most unpopular penal institutions, long designated a punishment prison for "difficult" and "awkward" prisoners. It has witnessed several riots over the years – one major "mutiny" in 1932 reduced it to ruins, while a more recent riot in 1990 led to extensive refurbishment, though prison conditions continue to be criticized in official reports.

You can learn much more about life inside, view escape tools and see a mock-up of a cell at the **Dartmoor Prison Museum**, 150m from the main prison gate on Tavistock Road (daily 9.30am–12.30pm & 1.30–4.30pm; closes 4pm Fri & Sun; last entry 45min before closing; £2.50; ⓦwww.dartmoor-prison.co.uk). It's probably not what you came to Dartmoor for, but it's a thought-provoking diversion when weather conditions preclude outdoor pursuits.

Practicalities

Reams of information on the whole moor are available at the main **High Moorland Visitor Centre** on the village's central green (daily: Easter–Oct 10am–5pm; Nov–Easter 10am–4pm; closed for one week in early March; ⓣ01822/890414, ⓦwww.dartmoor-npa.gov.uk).

Princetown itself is well provided with inexpensive **accommodation**, though much of it is fairly drab. Best choice among the **B&Bs** is *Duchy House* on Tavistock Road (ⓣ01822/890552, ⓔduchyhouse@aol.com; closed Nov; ❸), 200m from the centre, offering traditionally furnished rooms – one with its own bathroom – and a guests' lounge. The two **pubs** in the Square also offer B&B: the slate-hung *Plume of Feathers*, which claims to be the oldest building in town, dating from 1795, has bright, pine-furnished rooms, one en suite (ⓣ01822/890240, ⓦwww.theplumeoffeathers.co.uk; ❹), while the next-door *Railway Inn*, run by the *Plume*, has five basic, pastel and floral rooms, one of them en suite but priced the same as the other rooms (❹). The *Plume of Feathers* also has two **bunkhouses** with two, four or ten beds per room (£10–12; book well ahead), as well as a **campsite**. There's another bunkhouse two doors down from the *Plume*, above the *Fox Tor Café* on Two Bridges Road (ⓣ01822/890238, ⓦwww.foxtorcafe.co.uk; £9.50), with three rooms holding four beds in each, and self-catering facilities.

For **meals**, both the above pubs provide staple bar food, while the *Railway Inn* has regular **live music**. During the day, the *Fox Tor Café* provides breakfasts all day, snacks and teas.

Internet access is available at Princetown's library in Claremont House, Tavistock Road (Mon 9am–1.30pm & 2.30–5pm, Wed 9.30am–1.30pm, Fri 2.30–5pm, Sat 9.30am–1pm).

Two Bridges

A couple of miles northeast of Princetown, at the intersection of the B3212 and the B3357, **TWO BRIDGES** represents Dartmoor's centre point. Only one of its bridges now remains, a five-span clapper which crosses the **River Cowsic** (the other originally crossed the West Dart), and there's little else here now other than a **hotel**, useful for rest and refreshment before or after a wander in the vicinity. The favourite excursion is to head for the misshapen dwarf oaks of **Wistman's Wood**, little more than a mile north via a footpath running parallel to the West Dart from the small car park opposite the *Two Bridges Hotel*. Cluttered with lichen-covered boulders and a dense undergrowth of ferns, it's an evocative relic of the original **Dartmoor Forest**. The gnarled old trees once lay on the "lych way" – a route for transporting the dead to **Lydford** (see p.149), where all inhabitants of Dartmoor Forest were buried until 1260 – and the woods are reputed to have once been the site of druidic gatherings, a story unsupported by any evidence but which feels quite plausible in this solitary spot.

The *Two Bridges Hotel* (Ⓣ01822/890581, Ⓦwww.twobridges.co.uk; ❼), in sixty acres of private land beside the West Dart River, makes a luxurious place to **stay**, with its leather sofas and four-poster beds, and you can sample the locally brewed Jail Ale in the bar. A couple of miles northeast of here, set back from the B3212 Postbridge road and surrounded by moorland, *The Cherrybrook* (Ⓣ01822/880260, Ⓦwww.thecherrybrook.co.uk; ❺) offers an updated farmhouse ambience, comfy rooms and a rated restaurant that's open to nonresidents: a four-course meal made with local produce costs £29.50. Alternatively, another half-mile or so further north, signposted off the B3212, *Powder Mills*, housed in part of an old gunpowder factory, offers first-class **bunkhouse** accommodation (Ⓣ01822/880369, Ⓦwww.spirit-of-adventure.com; £14) and can arrange activity holidays.

Along the East Dart: Postbridge to Dartmeet

Three miles northeast of Two Bridges, the largest and best preserved of Dartmoor's **clapper bridges** crosses the East Dart River at **POSTBRIDGE**, an otherwise nondescript hamlet to which it gives its name. First used by tin-miners and farmers in medieval times, these simple structures consist of huge slabs of granite supported by piers of the same material. This one, standing tall over the water close to the main road bridge, makes a good starting point for walks up and down the East Dart. Northward, along a riverside path on the eastern side of the road bridge (turn immediately left into the field), you can hike as far as **Fernworthy Reservoir** (three and a half miles), which is surrounded by woodland and lies in the midst of a number of stone circles and stone rows. South of Postbridge, you can take an easier option by following the broad track (turn left at the cattle-grid by the Bellever turning) through **Bellever Forest** to the open moor beyond. This dense working forest, planted with sitka spruce, Japanese larch and other conifers, has provoked the ire of many conservationists over the years, as do all plantations of non-indigenous trees on Dartmoor. However, as the true native trees of these parts – the dwarf oak and mountain ash – are few and far between nowadays, the woodland at least provides some variety from the otherwise bare landscape, and is inhabited by deer, as well as tree pipits and nightjars in the newer parts, and buzzards, sparrowhawks, dippers, ravens and tawny owls in the most mature sections; crossbills and siskins also breed here. Waymarked circular routes loop through the forest, starting from a forestry car park by the river (about a mile south of Postbridge, on the Bellever road); one finger-posted path brings you up to the open moorland around **Bellever Tor** (443m; map ref SX644764), from which there are outstanding views in all directions.

Beyond Bellever Forest, four miles south of Postbridge, the East and West Dart rivers merge at **Dartmeet** after tortuous journeys from their remote sources. A place of rocky shallows and the full range of river-crossings – stepping stones over the **West Dart**, a humpback bridge and the remains of a clapper bridge over the **East Dart** – this beauty spot is a magnet for crowds, but the valley is memorably lush and you don't need to walk far to leave the car park and ice-cream vans behind.

Practicalities

Postbridge has a useful **tourist office** in the main car park near the bridge (Easter–Oct daily 10am–5pm; Nov and Dec Sat & Sun 10am–4pm; ⓣ01822/880272).

There are a number of alternatives for those wanting to **stay** in the area. *Beechwood House*, near the church (ⓣ01822/880332, ⓦwww.beechwood-dartmoor.co.uk; ④), a friendly, cottagey place with granite walls and fireplaces, offers rooms with shared or private bathrooms, and evening meals, while *Lydgate House Hotel*, signposted off the B3212 half a mile southwest of Postbridge (ⓣ01822/880209, ⓦwww.lydgatehouse.co.uk; no under-14s; ⑥), has plush, Victorian-style rooms, easy access to Bellever Forest, and a complimentary cream tea. Signposted a mile south of Postbridge, Bellever **youth hostel** (ⓣ0845/371 9622, ⓔbellever@yha.org.uk; £12–18, reduced for anyone not arriving by car) supplies a welcoming log fire, meals and a wealth of information on the moor. Bus #98 from Tavistock and Princetown makes a couple of stops in Bellever daily (not Sun), otherwise the nearest bus stop is at Postbridge, a stop for Transmoor Link bus #82. Half a mile down the road to Widecombe from Postbridge, and also reachable on the #82 bus, *Runnage Farm* (ⓣ01822/880222, ⓦwww.runnagecampingbarns.co.uk) offers a **camping barn** (£7.50) and a **bunkhouse** (£12), both with a minimum two-night stay at weekends, and **camping** is also possible in a meadow next to a stream.

For **meals**, try the *East Dart Hotel* a nineteenth-century coaching inn just up from the Postbridge car park, serving soups, pies and puddings, and there's a Sunday carvery.

The eastern and southeastern moor

Though more populous than other parts of Dartmoor, the eastern and southeastern sections of the moor contain some of its most scenic terrain. Peripheral towns such as **Bovey Tracey** have most of the accommodation, but it's the country west of here that holds most interest, in the shape of walking routes and specific sights – not least the various **prehistoric remains** dotted around

Dartmoor ponies

There have been ponies on Dartmoor since the **Bronze Age**: small of stature, strong and hardy, they were traditionally used as working and pack animals, and at the end of the nineteenth century supplied the **coal mines** of Somerset and South Wales. With the decline of mining, and the fall in demand for **horsemeat** for which the ponies were also prized, numbers have dwindled from thirty thousand at the end of World War I to fewer than three thousand today. Of those remaining, few survive of the original hardy stock, as much cross-breeding has taken place over the years. Contrary to popular belief, Dartmoor ponies are not wild, merely unbroken; all have an owner and sport a brand, cut or tag to indicate who they belong to. During the "**drifts**" – roundups that take place each September and October – the ponies are herded into yards, grouped according to ownership and, in some cases, sold on.

As they can bite and kick, you should steer clear of the ponies, and above all don't feed them – it encourages them to approach traffic, and is against the law. For more information, see ⓦwww.dartmoorponytrust.com and ⓦwww.dartmoor-npa.gov.uk, the National Park site.

(many of them accessible by road). You may also come across the relics of old tin workings – once a common sight hereabouts.

High up in the heart of eastern Dartmoor, **Widecombe-in-the-Moor** has immense charm, its tall, granite church tower set against a magnificent backdrop of high moorland. The village also makes a great base for **hikes** around two of the moor's most popular attractions: the wind-whittled rockpile of **Haytor**, and **Grimspound**, a well-preserved Bronze Age settlement. South, the equally picturesque villages of **Buckland-in-the-Moor** and **Holne** make good stops for a pint, but you'll have to press on three or four miles east to **Ashburton** for a better choice of **accommodation**. Further south, **Buckfastleigh** also has a range of B&Bs, convenient for the main attraction hereabouts, **Buckfast Abbey**.

Ashburton and Buckfastleigh are connected by hourly #X38 and #88 **buses**; Buckfastleigh is also the terminus of the **South Devon Railway**, which runs steam trains down to Totnes (see p.109).

Bovey Tracey

Despite the surrounding steep wooded valleys, **BOVEY TRACEY** (pronounced "Buvvy"), built at a crossing over the **River Bovey** on the eastern edge of the moor, has an open, spacious feel. Drifting lazily through, the stream contributes to the town's leisurely air, and its capacious teashops make this a favourite stop-off point for coach parties in summer. For entertainment on a wet day, you could do worse than head for the **House of Marbles** (Mon–Sat 9am–5pm, Sun 10am–5pm; free), a shop off the roundabout on Pottery Road where gigantic glass marbles whizz down convoluted tracks and you can view the machine that made the world's biggest marble; **glass-blowing** demonstrations also take place daily.

Most of the **pubs** and **shops** are concentrated along Fore Street, which leads up from the **tourist office**, a wooden chalet on Station Road (mid-March to Oct daily 10am–4pm; Nov to mid-March Tues 11am–1pm, Fri 1–3pm, Sat 9.30am–1.30pm, Sun 10am–noon; ⓣ01626/832047). A little further up and adjoining the river, the *Riverside Inn* was where Oliver Cromwell surprised Royalist troops at the time of the Battle of Bovey Heath in 1645; it now has comfortably modernized rooms (ⓣ01626/832293, ⓦwww.riversideinnbtracey.co.uk; ❺). Housed in the stone mill next to the *Riverside*, the *Devon Guild of Craftsmen* has a range of enticing craftwork for sale and also offers inexpensive **meals** cooked with cider and other local ingredients – farm cider is also served at the welcoming *King of Prussia Inn* at the top of Fore Street.

On Saturdays between June and October, the **Haytor Hoppa** stops at Bovey Tracey's Union Square, running four times a day on a circular route that takes in Haytor and Widecombe-in-the-Moor (see below); day tickets cost £2.

Widecombe-in-the-Moor and Haytor

Six miles west of Bovey Tracey on the B3387, in a hollow amid high, granite-strewn ridges, **WIDECOMBE-IN-THE-MOOR** is a candidate for most-visited Dartmoor village. Its church of **St Pancras**, dubbed the "cathedral of the moor", provides a famous local landmark, its lofty pinnacled tower dwarfing the fourteenth-century nave whose spacious interior boasts a barrel roof with vigorously carved and painted roof bosses depicting a green man, a pelican and, above the communion rail, rabbits – the emblem of the tinners who funded the building.

The village's other claim to fame is as the inspiration for the traditional song, *Widdicombe Fair* (see box below), a celebration of the event which has been held in the village since at least the nineteenth century. **Widecombe Fair** still takes place annually in a field outside the village on the second Tuesday of September – rather commercialized now, but still fun, with vintage tractors, tug-of-war, bale-rolling and sheep-shearing. Tickets cost £7; see Ⓦwww.widecombefair.com for details.

About two and a half miles east of Widecombe and reached along the B3387 (itself paralleled for part of the way by a footpath), the dramatic and much-frequented **Haytor** (454m; map ref SX757770) makes an excellent vantage point over the open moor, the views south sometimes extending as far as the coast. The granite quarries here were worked in the nineteenth century, providing stone for the British Museum and the 1831 version of London Bridge, which now resides in Arizona after being purchased by a US tycoon. On summer Saturdays, you can also reach Haytor on the Haytor Hoppa (see p.128).

Walkers from Widecombe-in-the-Moor to Grimspound (see opposite) should take the Natsworthy road past the *Old Inn*, turning left at the playing fields (signposted Grimspound) and following the track across open moorland at the top. The long uphill climb is rewarded by a superb panorama.

Practicalities

There's a **park information centre** (Easter–Oct daily 10am–5pm; Nov–Easter weekends 10am–4pm; Ⓣ01364/661520) in the lower car park at Haytor, while the **website** Ⓦwww.widecombe-in-the-moor.com has local information for Widecombe.

You'll find a good range of inexpensive **accommodation** within and around the village. A few steps down from the *Old Inn* and set in a lovely garden, *The Old Rectory* (Ⓣ01364/621231, Ⓔrachel.belgrave@care4free.net; closed Nov–March; no credit cards; ❸) has spacious rooms packed with character, one en suite, two others sharing a bathroom with a whirlpool bath and a view. Signposted next to *The Old Rectory*, *Manor Cottage* (Ⓣ01364/621218; no credit cards; ❸) has a double/twin bedroom in a converted barn with private facilities, and two rooms with shared bathroom; there's an inglenook fireplace in the dining room and a nice garden. Half a mile south, *Higher Venton Farm* (Ⓣ01364/621235; no credit cards; ❸) is a peaceful thatched longhouse close to a couple of good pubs. Nearby, alongside the East Webburn River one and a half miles south of Widecombe, *Cockingford Farm* is a highly scenic **campsite**, though facilities are basic (Ⓣ01364/621258; closed mid-Nov to mid-March).

Widecombe's social hub, the fourteenth-century *Old Inn*, attracts the crowds for its pub grub, but the small, secluded and unspoilt *Rugglestone Inn*, signposted just south of the village, is quieter and serves up very reasonably priced meals such as hot salted brisket in a roll and lamb and chicken hot-pots. For a fry-up or a **cream tea**, relax in a blue Lloyd loom chair at the capacious, if touristy,

Widdicombe Fair (traditional song)

The popular ballad, published in 1880, relates the journey of Uncle Tom Cobbleigh and companions to the annual fair.

Tom Pearse, Tom Pearse, lend me your grey mare,
All along, down along, out along, lee.
For I want for to go to Widdicombe Fair,
Wi' Bill Brewer, Jan Stewer, Peter Gurney,
Peter Davey, Dan'l Whiddon, Harry Hawk,
Old Uncle Tom Cobbleigh and all.
Old Uncle Tom Cobbleigh and all.

Hut circles, stone rows and cairns on Dartmoor

Any glance at a map of Dartmoor will reveal a wealth of remains from the Bronze and Iron Ages, taking a variety of forms. You're likely to chance upon one or more of these prehistoric fragments on even the shortest of walks or rides across the moor, though they may be hard to distinguish from the general rubble of exposed granite. Among the most arresting – and most numerous – items are the five thousand or so **hut circles** that pepper the landscape. Some are freestanding, others in groups, enclosed by circular stone walls or by the walls of fields. What remains is not easy to see: mostly you're looking for scant remains of the granite bases of the huts; the walls would once have supported timbers leaning in to a central post, the conical roof covered with gorse, heather or reed. Many of the structures were probably used only seasonally by shepherds and farmers bringing their livestock to the higher grounds in summer, while others may have been permanent homes; some sites show evidence of corn-grinding, spinning and cheese-making and, occasionally, pits dug in the ground as ovens. One of the biggest concentrations of hut circles can be found on **Buttern Hill**, northwest of the hamlet of Gidleigh (two miles west of Chagford), but those at **Grimspound** (see below) are in far better condition.

Often found in proximity to hut circles, some seventy-five **stone rows** are known to exist on Dartmoor (over half of the total number in England). No one knows what purpose was served by these uneven lines of rock, often in the remotest areas, and ranging from 32m to 3.4km in length. You can find double and triple rows, as well as circular arrangements ("stone circles"). Long treks over rough terrain are required to visit the most striking examples, but those at **Merrivale** (see p.151) are more accessible, close to a main road.

Around 1500 **cairns**, or mounds of rough stones used as landmarks and monuments, have been found on Dartmoor, mostly 3000–5000 years old. Often dramatically placed on tors and ridges, many mark the burial places of Bronze Age men and women, though most have been pillaged over the centuries, leaving behind an untidy heap of grey rocks around a hole, at the bottom of which the slabs of a cist (a stone burial chamber) may sometimes be seen.

Aside from these, **menhirs** (standing stones), **barrows** (burial chambers), **hillforts**, **stone ramparts**, **defensive ditches** and **reaves** (earth-covered field boundaries) can all be encountered on the moor, though you will often need a knowledgeable guide to identify them.

Café on the Green, with tables on a shady patio; as the name suggests, it's right on the village green.

Just outside the village, **Shilstone Rocks Stud and Riding Centre** (Ⓣ01364/621281, Ⓦwww.dartmoorstables.com) offers **horseriding** at all levels; to get there, take the turning opposite the *Old Inn*, with the church on the left – the stables are at the first junction on the left.

Grimspound and Hound Tor

North of Widecombe-in-the-Moor, a four-mile hike on marked tracks across Hamel Down (or a three-mile drive along the minor road connecting the village with the B3212) takes you to **Hameldown Tor**, on whose flank lies the Bronze Age village of **Grimspound** (map ref SX701809). If you're travelling by car, the unsignposted site lies about 1.5 miles south of the junction with the B3212: heading north from Widecombe, look out for five granite steps leading off on the right soon after the entrance to Headland Warren Farm – you can park in a small lay-by opposite. A brisk ten-minute upward walk brings you to a rough granite track on the left ascending to **Hookney Tor**,

The Hound of the Baskervilles – Dartmoor's greatest yarn

When **Arthur Conan Doyle** published his new Sherlock Holmes story, *The Hound of the Baskervilles*, in 1901, there was a public frenzy to obtain a copy. Fiction's most famous detective was resurrected, eight years after Conan Doyle – hoping to concentrate on more serious works – had killed him off by having him fall to his death at the Reichenbach Falls. The detective's demise had sparked off something approaching national mourning, with reports of clerks going to work wearing black armbands, and Conan Doyle himself received sackfuls of letters of complaint. The fact that the new adventure was said to predate Holmes's death did not lessen public enthusiasm. In fact, at its conception, the detective had not even featured in the tale: Holmes was drafted in to fill the leading role and solve the mystery as the story took shape.

The tale has diverse roots. The inspiration for it came from Bertram Fletcher Robinson, a young journalist and author, who related a legend from the Dartmoor countryside where he had been brought up, in which a phantom dog – "Black Shuck", a terrifying creature, big as a calf, and with eyes that bled fire – was said to haunt the moors; anyone unfortunate enough to meet this apparition was sure to die.

At Robinson's invitation, Conan Doyle travelled to Dartmoor, the two men staying in Princetown's *Duchy Hotel* (now refurbished as the **Visitor Centre**), where much of the book was written. From here they roamed the moor, guided by Harry Baskerville, Robinson's coachman, and taking in such locations as the Bronze Age site at **Grimspound** – described by Robinson as "one of the loneliest spots in Great Britain" – and **Fox Tor Mire**, setting of the tale's climax, where it is known as Great Grimpen Mire. There are few actual Dartmoor place-names mentioned in the story (though **Fernworthy**, **Princetown** and **Bellever Tor** all feature), but enthusiasts have filled in some of the gaps in locating the various places described, for example Grimpen, thought to be Postbridge.

As for the Hound itself, Dartmoor has no shortage of folklore relating to creatures that might fit the bill. Many of these myths centre on the mysterious **Dewer**, a huntsman who terrorizes the local countryside accompanied by a pack of savage, red-eyed hounds, variously referred to as "Whist Hounds", "Wish Hounds", "Yeath Hounds", or "Heath Hounds", and usually associated with **Wistman's Wood** (see p.130), where the hounds live during daylight hours. Anyone attempting to follow the Whist Hounds across the moors will meet his death by plunging over a cliff, known as the **Dewerstone**, on Dartmoor's southern tip, to the supernatural accompaniment of thunder, lightning, sinister laughter and mournful baying.

whose fortress-like rock formations offer stunning views over Grimspound and for miles beyond. To the right, you'll soon see the extensive stone periphery of the village. Inhabited some three thousand years ago, when Dartmoor was fully forested and enjoyed a considerably warmer climate than it does today, it is the most complete example of the moor's prehistoric settlements, with its comparative remoteness helping to protect it from plundering. A stone wall up to nine feet thick surrounds the foundations of 24 circular huts scattered within the four-acre enclosure, several of which have raised bed-places, and you can see how the villagers ensured a constant water supply by enclosing part of a stream with a wall.

Grimspound is thought to have been the model for the prehistoric settlement in which **Sherlock Holmes** camped out in *The Hound of the Baskervilles*. It is also claimed that the original inspiration for Conan Doyle's tale was **Hound Tor** (415m; map ref SX743790), a crumbly outcrop three miles to the southeast, halfway between Widecombe and Manaton. According to local legend, phantom hounds were sighted racing across the moor here to hurl themselves on the tomb of a hated squire after his death in 1677. Just southeast of the tor, you can see the remains of a medieval village, now no more than a collection of low walls – with entrances and fireplaces in evidence – enclosing patches of grass, lapped on all sides by a sea of bracken.

If you're looking for somewhere to **stay** on this remote moorland tract, the only choice is an old farmhouse converted into a **camping barn** at Great Houndtor, less than half a mile northeast of **Hound Tor** towards Manaton (Ⓣ01629/592700; £6). It's basic, but has loads of atmosphere and a stash of wood for the open fire. A mile and a half west of Grimspound on the B3212, the isolated *Warren House Inn* offers warm, firelit comfort (the fire has been kept burning for over 150 years), and good, inexpensive **food**: local sausages, cheese and home-made pies. By road, turn left when you get onto the B3212 from the Grimspound road.

Buckland-in-the-Moor and Holne

BUCKLAND-IN-THE-MOOR, a couple of miles south of Widecombe, is one of the prettiest of the cluster of moorstone-and-thatch hamlets on this eastern side of Dartmoor. Though surrounded by open country, the scattered village lies enveloped within thick woods in the winding **Webburn valley**. At its western end, the restored fourteenth-century church of **St Peter** is the main point of interest, with a medieval rood screen painted on both sides and a good Norman font – the clock on its castellated tower has "MY DEAR MOTHER" replacing the numbers on its face. It was a gift to the parish from the local lord of the manor William Whitley in 1939, who had earlier been responsible for inscribing two slabs of granite with the Ten Commandments on top of **Buckland Beacon**, a mile east of the hamlet on the Ashburton road, in celebration of the rejection of the new Prayer Book in 1928. They're still there today, and the view from this high point is rated as one of Dartmoor's best.

From the village, the Webburn Water River trails south to join the Dart after a mile and a half, accompanied for part of the way by the road. Another mile or so south, the village of **HOLNE** is also enclosed on three sides by wooded valleys. The vicarage here was the birthplace of **Charles Kingsley**, author of such Devon-based tales as *Westward Ho!*, who is commemorated by a window in the village church. In the churchyard, you'll also see a whimsical epitaph on the grave of **Edward Collins**, landlord of the next-door *Church House Inn* until 1780. This timbered old pub was built several hundred years before that, and is said to have accommodated Oliver Cromwell; today it offers up-to-date **accommodation** and good meals and ales (Ⓣ01364/631208, Ⓦwww.churchhouseinn-holne.co.uk; ⑤). Near the inn, look out for *The Stone Barn*, a **camping barn** with good facilities including a cooker and woodburner, backing onto a small camping field (Ⓣ01364/631544; £5). It's right on the route of the **Two Moors Way** (see box, p.146).

Ashburton

Thankfully bypassed by the A38 and three miles east of Holne, **ASHBURTON**, a pleasing ensemble of slate-hung buildings with projecting first storeys and oriel windows, preserves an unpretentious but well-to-do air. One of Dartmoor's four **Stannary towns**, where tin was brought to be assayed and taxed, it was also an important centre of the wool trade during the Middle Ages, when nine cloth mills were at work. There's a more leisurely feel to the place these days, inviting a stroll among the antique shops, cafés and stores. The oldest buildings here reflect Ashburton's former mercantile wealth, most strikingly the fifteenth-century parish church of **St Andrew**, a few yards from the centre along West Street, marked out by its lofty tower and sporting a typical Devon barrel (or cradle) roof with fine bosses. Turning left from West Street onto Lawrence Lane brings you to the fourteenth-century **St Lawrence Chapel** (May–Sept Tues & Thurs–Sat 2–4.30pm, may close late June to early July; free). Originally the private chapel of a former bishop of Exeter, it became a school before the Reformation, and remained such until 1938. Relics of the school are on show today, but more impressive is the delicate pendant plasterwork around the walls, placed here when the chapel was largely rebuilt around 1740. It is also the meeting place of the **Court Leet**, a judicial court of Saxon origin, where the Portreeve – the local market official and representative of the monarch (now an honorary position) – is still sworn in, along with his entourage of ale tasters, bread weighers, pig drovers and tree inspectors, on the fourth Tuesday in November each year.

Ashburton's town hall on North Street is the main venue for the **Ashburton Blues Festival**, taking place over the last weekend in late May (Ⓦwww.ashburtonbluesfestival.com).

Practicalities

Part of the town hall, Ashburton's **tourist office** (Mon–Sat 9.30am–4.30pm; closes 1pm Sat Sept–March; Ⓣ01364/653426, Ⓦwww.ashburton.org) has information on the moor and on **accommodation**, of which the town has a fair selection. Top choice is the Georgian *Roborough House*, 85 East St (Ⓣ01364/654614, Ⓦwww.roboroughhouse.co.uk; no credit cards; ❺), where there are three stylish and spacious rooms (one with a small patio courtyard), all with bathrooms, DVD players and wi-fi access; children can play on the slides in the garden. *Agaric*, a restaurant at 30 North St (Ⓣ01364/654478, Ⓦwww.agaricrestaurant.co.uk; ❼), has five stylish rooms in a separate building with plants, books and quirky decor. A much plainer and cheaper choice is the friendly *Old Coffee House*, 27–29 West St (Ⓣ01364/652539, Ⓦwww.theoldcoffeehouse.co.uk; no credit cards; ❸), which offers four en-suite rooms. *Parkers Farm Holiday Park* at Higher Mead Farm, a couple of miles northeast of town, provides pitches for **camping** (Ⓣ01364/654869, Ⓦwww.parkersfarm.co.uk), and also has caravans, chalets and cottages available for weekly rental.

For a **meal**, try the modish *Café Green Ginger*, 26 East St (daytime only), which serves breakfasts, snack lunches, coffees and cakes – you can sit in the conservatory, in the walled garden or in front of the fire – or *Moorish*, a café/restaurant at 11 West St (Ⓣ01364/654011; closed Sun & Mon) with good tapas and three-course meals for under £20. For more sophisticated fare, there's the informal but elegant *Agaric* (see above; closed Sat lunch and all Sun, Mon & Tues), where a light lunch costs under £15 and main courses on the evening menu, which might include venison and roast breast of duck, are £17–19.

Buckfastleigh and Buckfast Abbey

Given its somewhat subdued air, it's hard to believe that **BUCKFASTLEIGH**, three miles southwest of Ashburton on the A38, was once Devon's most important wool-manufacturing town, and a major staging post between Plymouth and Exeter. You'll find useful facilities here, but little to detain you other than a surprisingly engaging nostalgia-fest in the form of the **Valiant Soldier** on Fore Street (Easter & mid-April to Oct Wed–Sat 12.30–4.30pm; £3.50; Ⓦwww.valiantsoldier.org.uk). Having called last orders for good in the 1960s, the pub remained untouched until its recent sympathetic restoration, which has retained all the bric-a-brac of a working-man's taproom during the 1940s and 1950s, when a pint of mild cost 1s 4d.

Most of the tourist traffic, however, converges a mile north of Buckfastleigh, where the River Dart weaves through a wooded green valley to enter the grounds of **Buckfast Abbey** (church Mon–Thurs & Sat 9am–6pm, Fri 10am–6pm, Sun noon–6pm; grounds daily: 9am–6pm; free; Ⓦwww.buckfast.org.uk), reachable on the hourly bus #88 from Buckfastleigh (not Sun). This imposing modern monastic complex occupies the site of an abbey that was founded in the eleventh century by King Canute, abandoned two hundred years later, refounded, and finally dissolved by Henry VIII. The present buildings were the work of a handful of French Benedictine monks who, in 1932, consecrated the new abbey, built in a traditional Anglo-Norman style that followed the design of the Cistercian building razed in 1535. It's a pretty clinical exercise, which doesn't invite much lingering, though there are good examples of the monks' renowned proficiency in the art of stained-glass windows. The vivid slabs of red, blue and yellow glass in the chapel and the huge corona of lights in front of the high altar are at their best in daylight, though for atmosphere, come to the candlelit compline here at 8.40pm.

Stained-glass production helps to keep the community funded, along with the honey, handicrafts and tonic wine on sale here – a flourishing trade which has inspired locals to dub the place "Fastbuck". An exhibition outside the abbey church takes you through the process of making the stained glass, and also explains the abbey's history by way of information boards, and glass cases containing life-size dummies of young monks taking a pause from their building labours. In the grounds, re-created Physic, Sensory and Lavender gardens make for a peaceful wander.

In summer, restored steam trains of the **South Devon Railway** (late March to Oct daily; check for winter schedule; Ⓣ0845/345 1466, Ⓦwww.southdevonrailway.org) offer a scenic way to view the Dart valley south of here. The trains leave from Buckfastleigh station, a mile east of town, on their journey alongside the River Dart as far as Littlehempston station outside Totnes (30min; return ticket around £10). At Easter and May–September, a free vintage bus transports ticketholders from Buckfast Abbey and the town centre to the station (Tues–Thurs but daily during school hols).

Practicalities

Buckfastleigh's **tourist office** is situated at the Valiant Soldier (Easter & mid-April to Oct Wed–Sat 12.30–4.30pm; Ⓣ01364/644522) and offers **internet access**. There are only two **accommodation** options in the town centre, both inns: the basic *King's Arms Hotel* at 15 Fore St (Ⓣ01364/642341; ❸), which has one double en-suite room and two rooms sharing a big bathroom, and the slightly more upmarket *Globe Inn*, 123 Plymouth Rd (Ⓣ01364/642223, Ⓦwww.globeinnbuckfastleigh.co.uk; ❸–❹), which has five en-suite rooms; both have lively bars below. Better choices cluster around the abbey: on Buckfast Road, most of the bedrooms in the eighteenth-century *Abbey Inn* (Ⓣ01364/642343; ❺) face the River Dart, while *Dartbridge Manor* (Ⓣ01364/643575; no credit cards; ❸), a few yards further down, over the roundabout on Dartbridge Road, has sofas, paintings, antiques and two en-suite rooms, and also offers free salmon fishing. There's a rare open-all-year **campsite** a couple of miles south of town on Colston Road: *Beara Farm* (Ⓣ01364/642234), a scenic site on the banks of the Dart, but pretty basic, with no hook-ups. It's calm and peaceful most of the time, though steam trains of the South Devon Railway pass close by.

For inexpensive daytime **eating**, try the *Singing Kettle*, 54 Fore St (closed Sun & Mon; no credit cards), where you'll find a good selection of vegetarian food and puddings among the other home-made items on the menu. On Plymouth

Road, the continuation of Fore Street, the *White Hart* is renowned for its lunchtime pies and evening specials; big flagstones and a log fire contribute to the congenial air. The *Abbey Inn* (see p.139) has a terrace right on the river for a bar snack, and a moderately priced restaurant for something more substantial such as venison casserole for around £10.

The northern and northeastern moor

Although huge swathes of Dartmoor's northern reaches are often off-limits due to military shenanigans, there is a wealth of rugged grandeur here that's well worth seeking out. Few roads cut into the wildest parts, though plenty of tracks radiate out from the biggest town, **Okehampton**, itself a good place to hole up when bad weather sets in, with an absorbing **museum**. There's another cluster of villages and sights in the northeastern section of the moor, where the main centres are **Moretonhampstead** and **Chagford**, both of which have good accommodation choices. North of the A382, near Drewsteignton, **Castle Drogo** is one of the last English houses planned on the grand scale, and its extensive grounds give access to some excellent walks along the Teign, taking in picturesque **Fingle Bridge**.

While Okehampton enjoys good **public transport** connections with Exeter and points west, there are only a couple of bus links daily on the #179 service linking Okehampton with Chagford and Moretonhampstead, slightly more on bus #173 from Exeter to Castle Drogo, Chagford and Moretonhampstead. Neither service operates on Sunday.

Okehampton

The main centre on Dartmoor's northern fringes, straddling the two branches of the River Okement that merge here, **OKEHAMPTON** was dependent on the wool trade in medieval times, and also benefited from its position on one of the principal routes to Exeter, now the A30. A few good-looking old buildings survive from this period, though today Okehampton shows little evidence of either the grace or the pretensions that typify many of Devon's other wool towns.

Arrival and information

Okehampton is well connected by **bus** with Exeter (#X9, #X90 and #510), and is also a stop on a once-daily National Express **coach** route running between London and Launceston, Bodmin and Newquay (summer only). Between late May and late September, an old goods line provides the town with a useful **rail connection** to the Tarka Line and Exeter via Yeoford (check for times at Ⓣ01837/55164, Ⓦwww.dartmoor-railway.co.uk). Okehampton's **station** is a fifteen-minute walk up Station Road from Fore Street. The **tourist office** (April–Oct Mon–Sat 10am–5pm; Nov–March Mon, Fri & Sat 10.30am–4.30pm; Ⓣ01837/53020, Ⓦwww.okehamptondevon.co.uk) is near the museum and the *White Hart* on West Street.

Bike rental is available from the youth hostel adjacent to the station (Ⓣ01837/53916), otherwise head out to Devon Cycle Hire, at Sourton Down, about a mile southwest of Meldon off the A386 and on the Granite Way cycle-route (Ⓣ01837/861141, Ⓦwww.devoncyclehire.co.uk; call first Oct–Easter). For **riding** on the moor, contact Skaigh Riding Stables (mid-April to Sept; Ⓣ01837/840917, Ⓦwww.skaighstables.co.uk) or Eastlake

(Ⓣ01837/52513, Ⓦwww.eastlakeridingstables.co.uk), both east of town in the Belstone/Sticklepath area.

Accommodation

Okehampton has a good range of **accommodation**, the cheaper places situated away from the centre. Both campsites listed below are next to pubs, and are within a short walk of stops on any Tavistock-bound bus.

Hotels and B&Bs

Fountain Hotel East St Ⓣ01837/53900. In the centre of town, this riverside coaching inn has six smallish rooms, including a family room, all clean and en suite. ❺

Meadowlea 65 Station Rd Ⓣ01837/53200, Ⓦwww.meadowleaguesthouse.co.uk. This basic B&B lies a short walk south of the centre, below the train station. The seven rooms are mostly en suite and there's wi-fi access and cycle storage. ❸

Upcott House Upcott Hill Ⓣ01837/53743, Ⓦwww.upcotthouse.com. Half a mile north of Okehampton's centre, this Edwardian B&B was once a boarding school. It has amiable hosts, a spacious garden and smallish, old-fashioned rooms – some sharing bathrooms – with floral motifs aplenty. No credit cards. ❸

White Hart Hotel Fore St Ⓣ01837/52730, Ⓦwww.thewhitehart-hotel.com. Dead central, next to the tourist office and museum, this place offers traditionally furnished rooms (some with four-posters), decent food and all the atmosphere you'd expect of a seventeenth-century coaching inn. ❺

Campsites and hostel

Betty Cottles Inn Graddon Cross Ⓣ01837/55339, Ⓦwww.bettycottles.co.uk. Two miles southwest of town on the B3260, Okehampton's nearest campsite is clean, flat and shady. The inn also offers B&B (❹) and a bunkhouse (£12.50).

Bundu Sourton Down Ⓣ01837/861611, Ⓦwww.bundu.co.uk. Four miles southwest of Okehampton off the A386, this small, relaxed site has clean facilities but suffers from some traffic noise. It's on the edge of the moor, right on the Granite Way.

Okehampton Youth Hostel Klondyke Rd Ⓣ0845/371 9651, Ⓦwww.adventureokehampton.com. This converted goods shed at the station has bunks (from £14) in two-, four- and six-bed rooms, many en suite, and also camping pitches. A range of outdoor activities is offered, including rock climbing, pony-trekking, sailing and cycling (the hostel is on the Granite Way and rents bikes).

The Town

For the most part an unexceptional working town, Okehampton preserves few vestiges of its long past, though the prominent fifteenth-century granite tower of the chapel of **St James** survives, at the east end of Fore Street. Along with its continuation, West Street, Fore Street forms the town's main thoroughfare, lined with **shops and banks**. Across from the seventeenth-century town hall, a granite archway leads off West Street to the **Museum of Dartmoor Life** (Easter–Oct Mon–Fri 10.15am–4.30pm, Sat 10.15am–3.30pm; Nov to mid-Dec Mon–Sat 11am–3pm; £3.50 Ⓦwww.museumofdartmoorlife.eclipse.co.uk), an excellent overview of habitation on the moor since earliest times. Laid out over three floors, the imaginatively presented collection features motley items of antique agricultural equipment alongside everything from a 1922 Morris Cowley farm pick-up to a pump made to keep newly dug graves dry. Upstairs is devoted to the various industries of the moor – notably tin-streaming, mining and quarrying – and the railway, though the serried ranks of domestic bric-a-brac on the top floor command more attention; look out for such curiosities as the "slipper bath".

Loftily perched above the West Okement River, a mile southwest of the centre, **Okehampton Castle** (daily: April–June & Sept 10am–5pm; July & Aug 10am–6pm; £3.30; EH) is the shattered hulk of a stronghold laid waste by Henry VIII; its ruins include a gatehouse, Norman keep and the remains of the Great Hall, buttery and kitchens. No shot was ever fired in anger from the granite and shale walls, and during the Civil War both Royalists and Roundheads found themselves

A walk around Dartmoor's northern tors

This varied seven-mile, three-hour **circular walk** from **Okehampton** skirts the east of the MoD's Okehampton range, brings you within view of the highest points on the moor and then plunges into the recesses of the **East Okement River**, before rounding **Belstone Common** and returning north to Okehampton via the village of **Belstone.** It's not overly arduous, though there are steep stretches along a variety of terrain, for which a compass and the 1:25,000 *Explorer* OL28 map are essential.

From Okehampton, follow signs for Ball Hill and the East Okement valley from the Mill Street car park south of the centre (at the end of George St). Past Okehampton College, the track quickly meets up with the East Okement River and passes under the graceful arches of the **Fatherford Viaduct**, which carries the Exeter–Okehampton railway. South of here, the signposted path threads through the East Okement valley, which slopes for about a mile through **Halstock Wood**, above and alongside the East Okement River, with weathered boulders and lovely cascades along the way. Cross the river at **Chapel Ford** (map ref SX607935) using either the ford, stepping stones or footbridge; it's a picturesque spot for a picnic.

Once you've crossed, walk up the eastern bank of the East Okement for 500m before following the path through an opening in the hedge and leaving the valley to head towards **Winter Tor** (map ref SX609915), just over a mile due south of the ford. At the tor, carry on up to the top of the ridge, from where a splendid panorama unfolds, with Dartmoor's highest peaks of **Yes Tor** (619m) and **High Willhays** (621m) visible about three miles southwest. To the east the great bowl of **Taw Marsh** can be seen.

Follow the rock-strewn ridge northeastwards to the pinnacles of **Belstone Common**. Between Higher Tor and Belstone Tor, you'll pass **Irishman's Wall**, the vestige of an attempt to enclose part of the moor against the wishes of the locals, who waited until the wall was nearly complete before gathering to push the structure down. Carry on heading north, descending sharply towards the **Nine Stones** cairn circle (map ref SX615928), 700m below Belstone Tor. This Bronze Age burial ground was popularly held to be the petrified remains of nine maidens turned to stone for dancing on Sunday (there are in fact twelve stones). Some 250m north, a track leads northeast to the village of **Belstone**, half a mile away, where the Dartmoor Way temporarily merges with the Tarka Trail. From Belstone's post office, follow the road signed "Okehampton Indirect" in a northwesterly direction; either follow this route (part of the Dartmoor Way) along a minor road and through fields right back to town, or, after about half a mile, turn left just beyond the private **Cleave House** onto a track which descends to Chapel Ford on the East Okement River and your outward-bound route, returning along the riverbank to Okehampton.

garrisoned here at different times. Free audioguides provide plenty of background on the site, and from the castle, woodland walks and riverside picnic tables invite a gentle exploration of what was once the deer park of the earls of Devon.

Four miles east of Okehampton at Sticklepath (bus #X9, #179 or #510, on Sun #X9, #274 or #279), **Finch Foundry** (mid-March to Oct Mon & Wed–Sun 11am–5pm; £4.50; NT) is a water-powered Victorian forge that once produced agricultural machinery and hand tools. The foundry is still in working order, and there are regular demonstrations.

There are numerous **walking** possibilities from Okehampton (see box above). One way of getting onto the moor quickly is by means of a brief stretch of the **Dartmoor Railway** (Ⓣ01837/55164, Ⓦwww.dartmoorrailway.co.uk) from Okehampton station to **Meldon**, a couple of miles southwest of town. The ten-minute ride operates 7–9 times daily at weekends between June and late September (£4 day return, or £3 with Dartmoor Sunday Rover). Meldon station is close to the **Dartmoor Way**, and is also on the **Granite Way** cycle-route between Okehampton and Lydford (see p.149), which parallels the rail route as far as Meldon, then continues over the disused railway viaduct – offering superb views over the moors – and along the old train line.

Eating

Okehampton has a fairly mediocre selection of **cafés and restaurants**, with one or two exceptions worth seeking out.

Restaurants

J Street Diner Fairplace Terrace. Tucked away behind the museum and at the end of the shopping arcade, this US-style 1950s diner is a cheap retreat for all-day breakfasts, burgers and nachos, all under £6. Closed eves & Mon.

Panache Red Lion Yard. In the shopping precinct off West St, this café/restaurant has rattan chairs and a few outdoor tables. As well as teas and coffees, inexpensive lunches are served, including panini and salads. Closed eves & Sun.

The Pickled Walnut 25 Fore St ⓣ01837/54242, ⓦwww.thepickledwalnut.co.uk. This red-tiled, candlelit basement hidden behind St James Chapel makes a great spot for a snack or full meal; at lunchtime, order a sandwich, omelette or jacket potato, while the eclectic evening menu might include salmon fillet and local rump steak (£12–16). Closed all Sun & Mon and eves Tues–Thurs.

White Hart Hotel Fore St ⓣ01837/52730. A range of food is available at this central inn, from its two bars, a pizzeria (open Wed–Sat; booking advised) and the slightly more formal *Courtenay* restaurant.

Moretonhampstead

At the intersection of the B3312 and the A382, which cuts across the north-eastern wedge of the moor, **MORETONHAMPSTEAD** is an essentially unspoilt market town that makes an attractive entry point from Exeter – and, incidentally, shares with Woolfardisworthy (near Bideford) the honour of having the longest single-word place-name in England. Apart from its arcaded stone almshouses in Cross Street, dated 1637, the town is not particularly noteworthy architecturally. It does, however, have a range of facilities that make it a useful base for stocking up or staying overnight.

Practicalities

The #359 is the most useful **bus** from Exeter (not Sun), or #82 on weekends in summer, while the #173 **bus** (not Sun) takes a more circuitous route between Exeter, Chagford and Moretonhampstead. The #178 links Moretonhampstead with Bovey Tracey and Newton Abbot (not Sun), and #274 and #279 (summer Sun only) serve Okehampton, Castle Drogo, Moretonhampstead and Widecombe-in-the-Moor. Local information is handled by a small **tourist office** at 11 The Square (Easter–Oct daily 9.30am–5pm; Nov–Easter Fri–Sun 10am–5pm; ⓣ01647/440043, ⓦwww.moretonhampstead.com).

Moretonhampstead's good choice of **accommodation** includes, in the heart of the village, the *White Hart*, The Square (ⓣ01647/440043, ⓦwww.whitehartdartmoor.co.uk; ❼), a stylish spot for a getaway break, with elegant, richly coloured and fully equipped bedrooms and a smart brasserie. At the western edge of the town, there's the friendly *Old Post House*, 18 Court St (ⓣ01647/440900, ⓦwww.theoldposthouse.com; no credit cards; ❸), where walkers are welcomed and the spacious, top-floor family room enjoys moorland views. At 33 Court St, the large, white Victorian *Cookshayes* (ⓣ01647/440374, ⓦwww.cookshayes.co.uk; ❸) is furnished in an old-fashioned country-hotel style and offers packed lunches and full evening meals; most rooms are en suite. Moretonhampstead also has a first-rate, independent **hostel**, *Sparrowhawk*

Backpackers, centrally located at 45 Ford St (Ⓣ01647/440318, Ⓦwww.sparrowhawkbackpackers.co.uk), with a dormitory (£15) and large kitchen in a converted stone stable, and a double/family room in the main house (❶–❷). Showers are solar-heated and there's a spacious yard for sitting and eating in summer. A camping kit can be rented for "wild camping" on the moor. The nearest **campsites** are north of Chagford (see below).

For inexpensive daytime **eating**, try the beamed *Gateway Tearoom* at 17 The Square, with home-made cakes and clotted cream to take away, or the less genteel *Central Stores* café at 11 The Square, with all-day breakfasts, hot snacks and freshly baked cakes and pastries. If you're staying locally, the *White Horse Inn* at 7 The Square offers a relaxing ambience for an evening **drink** and has occasional music nights. Further afield, you can find food, drink and atmosphere at the *Ring of Bells*, a thatched and beamed medieval tavern at **North Bovey,** a mile and a half southwest, or the *Royal Oak*, four miles northeast of Moretonhampstead in **Dunsford**, on the boundary of the National Park, with great views over Dunsford and the Teign valley from its large garden; B&B is also available here (❹).

Chagford

Moretonhampstead has a historic rivalry with neighbouring **CHAGFORD**, a Stannary town that also enjoyed prosperity from the local wool industry. Standing on a hillside above the River Teign, the village has a pointy "pepperpot" **market house** from 1862 at its centre, said to have been modelled on the Abbot's Kitchen at Glastonbury. On one side, the fine, mainly fifteenth-century church of **St Michael the Archangel** is surrounded by thatched-roofed houses, pubs and hotels. The church's sanctuary has an inscription dedicated to Mary Whiddon, a member of a powerful local family who was shot and killed outside the church following her marriage on 11 October 1641 – apparently the victim of a jealous suitor (the tale may have been the inspiration for R.D. Blackmore's classic romance *Lorna Doone*). In front of the church, next door to the *Three Crowns*, the sixteenth-century **Endecott House** is claimed to be the birthplace of John Endecott, a Pilgrim Father who was governor of the Massachusetts Bay Colony 1649–1665. Apart from the church, the main attraction in town is an open-air **swimming pool** located a ten-minute walk north on the minor road to Sandy Park (May–Sept daily 2–5.45pm; £3.20); it's fed from the nearby River Teign.

Chagford is accessible on **bus** #173 from Exeter and the even less frequent #179 from Okehampton; both routes include occasional connections with Moretonhampstead but neither runs on Sunday. There are good **accommodation** options in the village, including *The Globe* (Ⓣ01647/433485, Ⓦwww.globeinnchagford.co.uk; ❺), an inn facing the church with friendly management and spacious, modern rooms – sensitive sleepers who may be bothered by the hourly tolling of the church clock should avoid front-facing ones. There are a couple of quieter alternatives nearby: the sixteenth-century *Cyprian's Cot*, 47 New St (Ⓣ01647/432256, Ⓦwww.cyprianscot.co.uk; no credit cards; ❸), a cosy cottage where you can warm your bones at the inglenook fireplace and breakfast in the garden in fine weather, and *Farleigh Cottage*, Lower Street (Ⓣ01647/432600, Ⓦwww.farleighcottage.co.uk; no credit cards; ❸), offering home-made cakes and separate self-catering accommodation.

Campers have two excellent choices, both north of Chagford: *Woodland Springs*, Venton, Drewsteignton (Ⓣ01647/231695, Ⓦwww.woodlandsprings.co.uk), a quiet, adults-only site a couple of miles north as the crow flies, but longer by road (B3206 to the A382, then two miles northwest) – it's on the #179 bus route – and *Barley Meadow*, Crockernwell (Ⓣ01647/281629,

Ⓦwww.barleymeadow.com; closed Nov to mid-March), a sheltered spot with good facilities off the A30, a steep mile from the excellent *Drewe Arms* and 200m from the Two Moors Way. Both places are convenient for Castle Drogo and Fingle Bridge.

All of Chagford's **pubs** offer good meals at moderate prices. Just below the Square, *The Courtyard Café* has pies, salads, samosas, organic fruit and wholefoods, which you can eat in the small yard (closed Sun). There's also a highly rated **restaurant**, *22 Mill Street* (Ⓣ01647/432244, Ⓦwww.22millstreetrestaurant.co.uk; closed Sun–Tues), which concentrates on top-quality Modern-European cuisine, for example seared scallops, while more local dishes include Dartmoor lamb and Exmoor venison; set-price lunchtime menus cost £15 or £20, dinners are around £40 per person. There are also two luxury rooms available (❻).

Although beyond most people's budget, the moor's most celebrated restaurant – and one of the best in the country – lies a couple of miles west of Chagford at **Gidleigh Park** (Ⓣ01647/432367, Ⓦwww.gidleigh.com), a top-notch hotel set in 45 acres of riverside and woodland gardens, where doubles start at around £310 a night. The French-inspired restaurant, which has garnered two Michelin stars, is run by celebrity chef Michael Caines (who also co-owns Exeter's *Royal Clarence Hotel*), and offers three-course dinner menus for £95, or slightly more expensive eight-course tasting menus; set lunches are a little more affordable at £33 for two courses, £41 for three.

Castle Drogo and Fingle Bridge

Three miles north of Chagford, the twentieth-century granite extravaganza of **Castle Drogo** (castle: mid-Feb to late Feb daily 11am–4pm; early March and late Nov to mid-Dec Sat & Sun 11am–4pm; mid-March to Oct daily 11am–5pm; grounds: mid-Feb to late Feb and late Dec to early Jan daily 10.30am–4.30pm; early March, early Nov to mid-Dec and early to late Jan Sat & Sun 10.30am–4.30pm; mid-March to Oct daily 10.30am–5.30pm; £7.45, or £4.77 in winter, grounds only £4.77, or £2.19 in winter; NT) occupies a stupendous site above the Teign gorge. It was built by grocery

▲ Castle Drogo

magnate Julius Drewe who, having retired at the age of 33, unearthed a link that suggested his descent from a Norman baron (Drogo); he therefore set about creating a castle befitting his pedigree. Begun in 1910 to a design by Sir Edwin Lutyens, the original project was never completed (the money ran out in 1930), but the result is still an unsurpassed synthesis of medieval and modern elements. With six-foot-thick walls in the main complex, the rooms are cold and austere (130 electric fires were installed to heat the place), with bare unplastered walls. The living rooms are furnished for the most part with tapestries and other items bought wholesale from a bankrupt Spanish financier. Look out for the forerunner of Subbuteo in the library and the chic 1930s fashions hung on a rail in the bedroom upstairs. Immaculately clipped yew hedges surround the huge circular **croquet lawn** (you can rent mallets and balls if you fancy a game) and recur throughout the sunken garden, shrubbery and herbaceous border. Below the terraced gardens, paths lead down to where the River Teign burrows through the gorge, surrounded both by coppiced oakwoods – where you might spot the odd fallow deer – and bare heath, making a nice contrast for a prolonged amble.

Buses #173 between Exeter and Moretonhampstead (Mon–Sat) and #274 and #279 between Okehampton and Moretonhampstead (Sun May–Sept) stop here. Tickets are discounted for anyone arriving on public transport or by bike.

From the eastern end of the grounds, follow **Hunter's Path**, higher up, or **Fisherman's Path**, by the riverside (both well signposted) to one of Dartmoor's most noted beauty spots, **Fingle Bridge**, a little over a mile east. This simple granite structure over the Teign, with buttresses recessed for packhorses to pass, lies in the midst of woodland that's carpeted with

The Two Moors Way and the Coast to Coast Walk

The major walking route linking North and South Devon, the **Two Moors Way** stretches for roughly a hundred miles between Ivybridge on Dartmoor's southern edge to Lynmouth (see p.184) on Exmoor's coast. The southern end of the walk links with the Erme–Plym Trail between Ivybridge and Plymouth (13 miles) and a two-mile stretch between Plymouth and Wembury to form the **Coast to Coast Walk** from Wembury to Lynmouth (116 miles). The walking is good: much of the Dartmoor section follows a disused tramway, then switches to the **Abbot's Way**, the ancient track between Buckfast and Tavistock abbeys, before passing through Holne (usually regarded as the first overnight stop), Widecombe-in-the-Moor, Chagford and Castle Drogo. There are also link paths to other routes, for example the **Tarka Trail**, the **Templer Way** (a granite tramway from Haytor to Teignmouth) and the **Exe Valley Way**.

The best **maps** to use are 1:25,000 Ordnance Survey *Explorer* maps nos. OL28, 113, 114, a very small section of 127, and OL9; no. 20 covers the Erme–Plym Trail. If you want to walk all or part of the Two Moors Way, you should first consult the website of the **Two Moors Way Association** (Ⓦwww.twomoorsway.org.uk), which has plenty of information. The Association can provide a list of accommodation including information about a packhorse service for luggage-carrying along the route (£1.50) and with the official guide to the route (£4.99). The two best guides, both titled *The Two Moors Way*, by John Macadam and James Roberts respectively, are currently out of print, but a Devon County Council publication, *The Two Moors Way and Devon's Coast to Coast* (£4.99), is readily available, and you can also pick up leaflets on the Erme–Plym Trail from local tourist offices. The **tourist office** at Ivybridge (Mon–Fri 9am–5pm, Sat 9am–1pm; Ⓣ01752/897035, Ⓦwww.visitsouthdevon.co.uk), situated at the start of the Two Moors Way next to the River Erme on Leonard's Road, can also supply plentiful information on the route and accommodation options.

daffodils and bluebells in spring and is a haven for birdlife all year round. Walking westwards along the riverbank path from the bridge, you might have the luck to spot a kingfisher or any of the three types of woodpecker that frequent these shaded green pools in which trout, salmon and even otters frolic. At the bridge, the *Fingle Bridge Inn* is a handy spot for a drink on its terrace fronting the river, though its pricey restaurant is not recommended. **Licences to fish** for salmon, brown trout and sea trout are issued here (£12.50–20 for a day).

Tavistock and the western moor

More rugged and less picturesque than its other sections, Dartmoor's western side is also less permeated by tourism. With few obvious attractions in the neighbourhood, the moorland here has an emptier and more desolate tone. The only significant centre is **Tavistock**, an unspoilt, well-heeled market town on the A386 Plymouth–Okehampton road, which holds a good range of **accommodation**. There are some first-rate walks to be made from here – south to Double Waters or northwards to forbidding **Brent Tor** and **Gibbet Hill**. You could also explore these tracts from **Lydford**, a quiet place six miles north with a couple of excellent pubs and a small castle. The hamlet stands at one end of the deep **Lydford Gorge**, a gushing torrent enclosed by thick woodlands. East of Tavistock, the B3357 leads after four miles to **Merrivale**, site of the **Merrivale Rows**, two long, stone rows that form part of one of the moor's finest prehistoric sites.

The most useful **bus routes** are #83, #84 and #86, travelling between Plymouth and Tavistock, and #118, between Tavistock and Okehampton via Lydford.

Tavistock and around

On the western extremity of the moor, but just ten miles north of Plymouth, **TAVISTOCK** has its own very separate identity, partly the result of having been the seat of the most powerful abbey in the West Country during the Middle Ages. After the abbey's dissolution by Henry VIII, the town continued to prosper as a tin and wool centre, but it owes its distinctive Victorian appearance to the building boom that followed the discovery of copper deposits in the vicinity in 1844.

Arrival and information

Tavistock's well-stocked **tourist office** is housed in the town hall on Bedford Square (April–Oct Mon–Sat 9.30am–5pm, daily in school hols; Nov–March Mon, Tues, Fri & Sat 10am–4.30pm; ⓣ01822/612938). You can access the **internet** at *Bob's East End Café*, at the back of the Pannier Market (closed Sun & Mon). **Bikes** can be rented from Tavistock Cycles, Paddons Row, Brook Street (ⓣ01822/617630), and Dartmoor Cycle Hire, 6 Atlas House, West Devon Business Park, next to Morrisons supermarket (ⓣ01822/618178).

Accommodation

Tavistock has a good range of **accommodation** options. The best nearby **campsite** is *Harford Bridge Holiday Park* (ⓣ01822/810349, ⓦwww.harfordbridge.co.uk), on the Peter Tavy road just off the A386 north of town; it's on the banks of the Tavy and a mile from the *Peter Tavy Inn* (see p.149). Alternatively, try

Tavistock Camping and Caravanning Club at Higher Longford (Ⓣ01822/618672, Ⓦwww.campingandcaravanningclub.co.uk), two miles east of Tavistock on the B3357 and reachable on buses #98 (not Sun) and #272 (Sun late May to late Sept); self-catering cottages are also available.

Browns 80 West St Ⓣ01822/618686, Ⓦwww.brownsdevon.co.uk. A smart choice in the centre of town (off Bedford Square), this cream-and-brown-liveried boutique hotel offers swish and plush accommodation without a hint of stuffiness. Embossed French radiators, Delabole slate floors and Egyptian cotton bedding set the tone, and a well on the premises provides bottled water. 7

Horn of Plenty Gulworthy Ⓣ01822/832528, Ⓦwww.thehornofplenty.co.uk. For a rural splurge, you can't fault this luxury retreat signposted at Gulworthy Cross, three miles west of Tavistock off the A390. Rooms are richly furnished with antiques, service is impeccable yet without airs, and there's a top-notch restaurant, a stunning garden and panoramic views over the Tamar valley. 7

Mount Tavy Cottage Ⓣ01822/614253, Ⓦwww.mounttavy.co.uk. About half a mile east of Tavistock off the B3357 Princetown road, this 250-year-old building enjoys a beautiful setting with a lake and a lush garden roamed by chickens and guinea fowl. Rooms have pristine white bed linen and freestanding baths. Breakfasts are organic and dinner can be prearranged – taken on a pier on the lake. Self-catering accommodation also available. 4

Westward 15 Plymouth Rd, Ⓣ01822/612094, Ⓦwww.westward-tavistock.co.uk. A five minute-walk south of Bedford Square, this Victorian B&B with a lush rear garden has three elegant rooms, two en suite and a single with a bathroom on the next floor. 4

The Town

The granite, cobbled and crenellated **Bedford Square** serves as the centre of the town, and is reckoned to be one of the country's finest examples of Victorian ensemble building. To one side, **St Eustachius**, the parish church, has a longer heritage, dating from the fourteenth century, though restored in the 1840s. Inside, you can see a stained-glass window designed by William Morris's studio to the left of the altar, and a couple of grandiose memorials to local worthies from the fifteenth and sixteenth centuries. On the opposite side of the square, behind the imposing Victorian town hall, the bustling **Pannier Market** has been a Friday fixture since 1105, though the present-day market buildings are nineteenth-century. On other days, craftwork, antiques and collectables are traded, making for an interesting wander (the market is closed Sun & Mon). Stalls spill out from the main building, and you can usually pick up some bargains among the offerings from farmers or the Women's Institute. Tavistock is also associated with another of Dartmoor's markets, **Goose Fair**, a sprawl of stalls that take over Plymouth Road, southwest of the square, on the second Wednesday of October. You may well see some geese among the motley wares on sale, and a funfair sets up for the occasion.

Eating and entertainment

Tavistock has numerous good **eating** choices in town, and a couple of exceptional choices a short distance outside. In the evening, check out **The Wharf theatre and arts centre** (Ⓣ01822/611166, Ⓦwww.tavistockwharf.com), adjacent to the canal, which puts on year-round films and entertainment varying from Chinese opera to Abba tributes.

Browns 80 West St Ⓣ01822/618686. This smart hotel has a brasserie for snacks or full meals (£7–12) and a more formal restaurant (set menus £15 and £20 at lunch, £35 and £40 at dinner).

Horn of Plenty Gulworthy Ⓣ01822/832528. Enjoy gourmet dining at this foodie shrine, where ingredients are locally sourced – some from the chef's organic garden. Set-price lunches are £26.50 and dinners are £47, except on Monday when there's a restricted "Pot Luck" menu costing £28.

Monterey Jacks 15 West St Ⓣ01822/612145. This Wild West-style restaurant incorporated into the more traditional *Cornish Arms* pub offers burgers, grills and Mexican specials for £6–16.

Peter Tavy Inn Peter Tavy ⓣ01822/810348. Classic gastropub in a village three miles northeast of Tavistock. Alongside the real ales, there are ploughman's lunches with six different types of local cheese. Hot meals include such brilliantly cooked dishes as minted lamb and orange casserole, grey mullet, and vegetable crumble. You'll pay around £9 for a hot dish at lunchtime, £10–15 in the evening.

Steps West St ⓣ01822/614280. Pastas, pizzas and such dishes as beef cobbler pie (£7) and grilled lamb chops (£8.50) can be ordered at this smart-casual place. Closed Sun & Mon.

Excursions from Tavistock

Plymouth Road runs parallel to the **River Tavy** and, between them, to the **Tavistock Canal**, built in the early eighteenth century to carry copper ore to **Morwellham Quay** (see p.169), five miles away. Richly bordered with pampas grass, the towpath now provides a lovely stroll of up to one and a half miles before it disappears underground. Another fine walk is along the **viaduct** that bestrides the town to the north (walk north from Bedford Square, passing under the viaduct, then turn right at Kilworthy Road to gain access). It once carried a train track and now affords marvellous views over town and moor.

More ambitious excursions starting from Tavistock will bring you onto moorland. North of town, a four-mile lane wanders up to **Brent Tor** (344m; map ref SX471804), dominating Dartmoor's western fringes. Access to its conical summit is easiest along a path that gently ascends through the gorse that covers its southwestern side, and leads to the small church of **St Michael** at the top. A dark, granite structure with a squat tower, surrounded by a scattering of gravestones, the church surveys a lonely scene. Bleak, treeless moorland extends in every direction, wrapped in silence that's occasionally pierced by the shrill cries of stonechats and wheatears. You'll see **Gibbet Hill** (353m; map ref SX503811) looming over **Black Down** a couple of miles eastwards; it's said to be where criminals were left to die in cages during the Middle Ages.

The tourist office can provide a pack for **Drake's Trail**, a cycling and walking network between Tavistock and Plymouth that forms part of Route 27 of the National Cycle Network.

Lydford

Six miles north of Tavistock, **LYDFORD** has an unassuming appearance that gives little hint of its eventful history as a Saxon outpost against the Celts, and one of Alfred the Great's four principal settlements in Devon, founded for defence against the Danes. Traces of the Saxon fortifications – an earth rampart – can still be seen on either side of the main road at the northeastern end of the village, but the Saxon castle was completely destroyed by the Danes in 997. The best-preserved monument is the sturdy but small-scale **Lydford Castle** (unrestricted access; free), a square Norman keep that, until 1800, was used as a prison for offenders against the Stannary, or Tinners' Law, with the Stannary Court on the first floor. The justice administered from here had a fearsome reputation throughout Dartmoor, as described by a local poet in the seventeenth century: "I oft have heard of Lydford Law/How in the morn they hang and draw/And sit in judgement after."

The chief attraction here, though, is **Lydford Gorge** (mid-Feb daily 11am–3.30pm; mid-March to early Oct daily 10am–5pm; early to late Oct daily 10am–4pm; early Nov to late Dec Sat & Sun 11am–3.30pm; £5.27; NT); the main entrance is a five-minute walk downhill from the village. Overgrown

Dartmoor's letterboxes

The pursuit of **letterboxing** – a sort of treasure hunt with a rubber stamp as the prize – originated on Dartmoor in 1854 when hardy walkers started a tradition of leaving their calling cards in a jar at **Cranmere Pool** near the head of the West Okement River, then one of the most inaccessible points on the northern moor. In 1937, a stone "letterbox" was erected over the spot, and the practice was adopted at other tors. The "letterboxes" gradually multiplied, and today, there are around 4000 of them. Each contains the rubber stamp and inkpad that are the key elements of this early form of orienteering. The popularity of letterboxing has much to do with the fact that it needs no organization or set starting point, though organized walks with a competitive bent also take place occasionally: **tourist offices** can provide trail leaflets and schedules for forthcoming events, and see Ⓦdartmoorletterboxing.org or www.letterboxingondartmoor.co.uk.

with thick woods, the one-and-a-half-mile gorge – said to be the deepest gorge in the South West – was once the hide-out of a large family of outlaws, the Gubbins, who terrorized the neighbourhood and stole sheep from Dartmoor farms in the seventeenth century. Its very seclusion makes it an idyllic place to visit, alive with butterflies, spotted woodpeckers, dippers, herons and clouds of insects – though you'll usually be sharing it with plenty of other visitors. A circular walk starts off high above the River Lyd, dropping down to the hundred-foot **White Lady Waterfall**, and returning along the opposite bank to the foaming whirlpools of the **Devil's Cauldron**, near the main entrance. The full course would take you roughly two hours at a leisurely pace, but there's a separate entrance at the south end of the gorge if you want to visit only the waterfall. In winter months (between Nov and March), when the river can flood, only the waterfall and top part of the gorge are open to the public, with a reduced ticket price.

Practicalities

Lydford is served from Tavistock by buses #118 (not Sun in winter) and #187 (Sun in summer), both also connecting to Okehampton. The **website** Ⓦwww.lydford.co.uk has useful **info** on accommodation, attractions and local history, Back in the village and right next to the castle, the picturesque sixteenth-century *Castle Inn* offers low-ceilinged, oak-beamed **rooms** (Ⓣ01822/820241, Ⓦwww.castleinnlydford.co.uk; ❹), though you'll find more luxury at the grand *Lydford Country House* (Ⓣ01822/820347, Ⓦwww.lydfordcountryhouse.co.uk; ❺), at the eastern end of the village, 300m from the A386 turning. The former home of Victorian painter William Widgery, it has extensive gardens, an Italian restaurant (closed lunch & all Tues) and self-catering accommodation, as well as comfortable rooms, and also offers bike hire – the Granite Way runs alongside.

You can have a **drink** and get something to **eat** in the *Castle Inn*'s firelit bar, where wild boar burgers feature alongside curries and game – but the best choice hereabouts is the *Dartmoor Inn* (Ⓣ01822/820221; closed Sun eve & Mon lunch, also Mon eve in winter), on the A386 opposite the Lydford turning, which serves bar meals for under £10 as well as set-price meals (£15–£20) of delicious, Mediterranean-inspired dishes for which booking is essential.

Horseriding in the area is on offer at Cholwell Farm (Ⓣ01822/810526), near the village of Mary Tavy, about six miles north of Tavistock off the A386; tuition and all equipment are provided.

Merrivale

The River Walkham crosses the B3357 five miles east of Tavistock at **MERRIVALE**, a hamlet which amounts to little more than the large *Dartmoor Inn*, where you can get basic meals and refreshments. At 1000ft, Merrivale commands views extending – on a very clear day – as far as the Eddystone Lighthouse in Plymouth Sound.

The spot's main claim to fame, however, is its proximity to one of Dartmoor's most spectacular prehistoric sites, the **Merrivale Rows**, an easy half-mile walk west and just a few yards from the B3357 (map ref SX553746); to reach the unsigned site, walk in a southeasterly direction (towards the antenna on North Hessary Tor) from the first parking space east of the *Dartmoor Inn* on the B3357. This double row of upright stones, dating from any time between 2500 BC and 750 BC, form a stately procession for 850ft across the bare landscape. Probably connected with ancient burial rites, the rows are known locally as "Potato Market" or "Plague Market" in memory of the time when provisions for plague-stricken Tavistock were deposited here. Halfway along the southern row, a stone circle surrounds a cairn over a cremation pit; blocking stones, *kistvaens* (rough granite box tombs) and hut circles complete the complex.

Various tracks from here offer a choice of rewarding **hikes**, for instance along the western slopes of the Walkham valley, where the pinnacle of **Vixen Tor** (320m; map ref SX542742), a mile southwest of Merrivale's stone rows, crouches inscrutably above the barren moor like a sphinx – from some angles resembling an old woman's head or a humped animal. (Note that access to the Tor itself is currently not possible while a right-to-roam issue is being disputed, though a public footpath runs close by.) A mile and a half northeast of Merrivale, **Great Mis Tor** (539m; map ref SX562770) affords more inspiring views and has a distinctive rock basin, **Mistor Pan**, also known as the "Devil's Frying Pan". However, as this lies on the edge of a firing area, you'll need to check on accessibility. The #98 (not Sun) and summer-only #272 (Sun) **buses** connect Merrivale with Tavistock and Princetown, just three miles northwest (see p.129).

Travel details

Trains

Okehampton to: Yeoford, for Exeter (late May to late Sept Sun 5 daily; 45min).

Buses

Ashburton to: Bovey Tracey (Sun late May to late Sept 4 daily; 50min); Buckfastleigh (Mon–Sat 2 hourly, Sun every 2hr; 5–10min); Widecombe-in-the-Moor (Sun late May to late Sept 3 daily; 20min).
Bovey Tracey to: Ashburton (Sun late May to late Sept 4 daily; 40–50min); Moretonhampstead (Mon–Sat 2 daily, Sun late May to late Sept 5 daily; 20–25min).
Buckfastleigh to: Ashburton (Mon–Sat 2 hourly, Sun every 2hr; 5–10min).
Chagford to: Moretonhampstead (Mon–Sat 2 daily; 15min).
Lydford to: Okehampton (5–6 daily; 20min); Tavistock (Mon–Sat hourly, Sun 2–8 daily; 25min).
Moretonhampstead to: Bovey Tracey (Mon–Sat 2 daily, late May to late Sept Sun 5 daily; 20–25min); Chagford (Mon–Sat 2 daily; 15min); Okehampton (Mon–Sat 2 daily, late May to late Sept Sun 4 daily; 35min–1hr); Postbridge (Sat June–Oct 5 daily, Sun late May to late Sept 5 daily; 20–25min); Princetown (Sat June–Oct 5 daily, Sun late May to late Sept 5 daily; 30–40min); Widecombe-in-the-Moor (late May to late Sept Sun 3 daily; 40min).
Okehampton to: Lydford (7–10 daily; 20min); Moretonhampstead (Mon–Sat 2 daily, late May to

late Sept Sun 4 daily; 30–55min); Tavistock (Mon–Sat every 2hr, Sun 2–7 daily; 50–55min).
Postbridge to: Moretonhampstead (Sat June–Oct 5 daily, Sun late May to late Sept 5 daily; 20–30min); Princetown (Mon–Fri 2 daily, Sat 2–7 daily, Sun late May to late Sept 5 daily; 15min).
Princetown to: Merrivale (Mon–Sat 6 daily, late May to late Sept also Sun 4 daily; 5min); Moretonhampstead (Sat June–Oct 5 daily, Sun late May to late Sept 5 daily; 30–45min); Postbridge (Mon–Fri 2 daily, Sat 2–7 daily, Sun late May to late Sept 5 daily; 10–15min); Tavistock (Mon–Sat 6 daily, late May to late Sept Sun 4 daily; 25min); Widecombe-in-the-Moor (late May to late Sept Sun 3 daily; 55min).
Tavistock to: Lydford (Mon–Sat every 2hr, Sun 2–8 daily; 25min); Merrivale (Mon–Sat 5–8 daily, late May to late Sept also Sun 4 daily; 20min); Okehampton (Mon–Sat every 2hr, Sun 2–7 daily; 50min); Plymouth (Mon–Sat 3–4 hourly, Sun hourly; 55min); Princetown (Mon–Sat 6 daily, also late May to late Sept also Sun 4 daily; 25min).
Widecombe-in-the-Moor to: Ashburton (Sun late May to late Sept 4 daily; 20min); Moretonhampstead (late May to late Sept Sun 3 daily; 40min); Princetown (late May to late Sept Sun 3 daily; 55min).

Plymouth and around

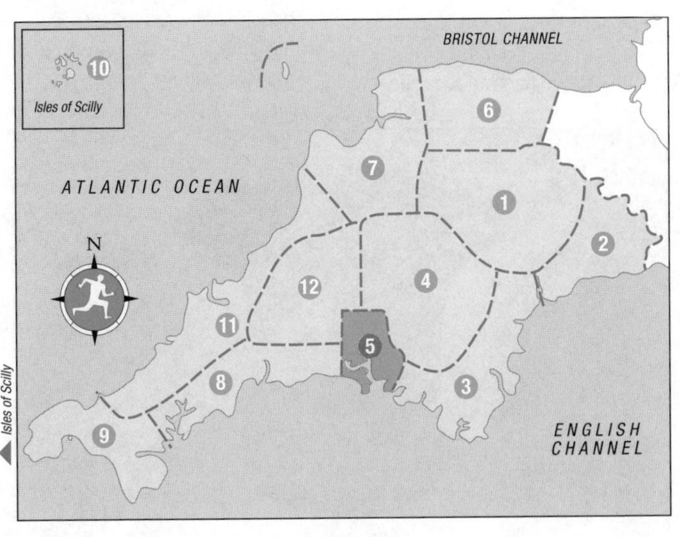

CHAPTER 5 Highlights

* **View from Plymouth Hoe** This historical grassy esplanade offers a stupendous panorama over Plymouth Sound and the city. See p.159

* **National Marine Aquarium** A variety of aquatic environments are imaginatively re-created in one of Europe's top aquariums, right on Sutton Harbour. See p.161

* **Mount Edgcumbe** Just a boat ride from the city, the house and landscaped gardens lie within an expanse of country park, with woodlands and stunning coastal walks all around. See p.165

* **Saltram House** This perfectly proportioned mansion east of Plymouth makes a grand setting for paintings by Joshua Reynolds and interiors by Robert Adam. See p.167

* **Cotehele** Fascinating Tudor house filled with tapestries, furniture and weaponry, in a glorious setting. See p.169

▲ Saltram

Plymouth and around

As the largest city in Devon and Cornwall, **Plymouth** has a very different feel to anywhere else in the region. There could be no greater contrast to the snug villages nearby in the South Hams, or the miles of wilderness in Dartmoor, than the city's urban sprawl or the immensity of Plymouth Sound, with its docks and naval base. Nonetheless, Plymouth is an essential component of Devon's seafaring identity, and the city's maritime traditions are most obvious when you're gazing down onto the Sound from historic Plymouth Hoe. While much of modern Plymouth is off-puttingly ugly, the Barbican and Sutton Harbour are as compact and unspoiled as any of the West Country's medieval quarters, and the city's National Marine Aquarium holds one of the country's finest marine collections.

Moreover, Plymouth serves as a lively base for day-trips to the handful of attractions that surround the city. The nearest of these is the wooded **Rame promontory** across the Sound, where formal gardens give onto a wild coastline at **Mount Edgcumbe**, and **Cawsand** and **Kingsand** preserve their villagey character; all three places are within easy distance of the only decent swimming spot hereabouts, **Whitsand Bay**. Further out lie a ring of elegant country houses; most dazzling of which is **Saltram House**, an aristocratic pile to the east of the city containing a wealth of work by Robert Adam and Joshua Reynolds. If you find the overstated decor here indigestible, you may get more out of two Tudor mansions north of Plymouth – **Buckland Abbey**, former home of the mariners Drake and Grenville, and **Cotehele**, a rich repository of tapestries, embroideries and sixteenth-century furnishings. On a very different note, the nearby open-air museum of industrial archeology at **Morwellham Quay** provides a fascinating insight into the history of this nineteenth-century copper-shipping port on the **River Tamar**.

Plymouth

Though dominated by mediocre architecture and beset with heavy traffic along the main roads slicing ruthlessly through its residential and shopping neighbourhoods, **PLYMOUTH** has gone to great lengths to preserve its surviving older buildings and revitalize its modern centre. To an extent, the efforts have paid off, and the city is worth a visit for its appealing historic core

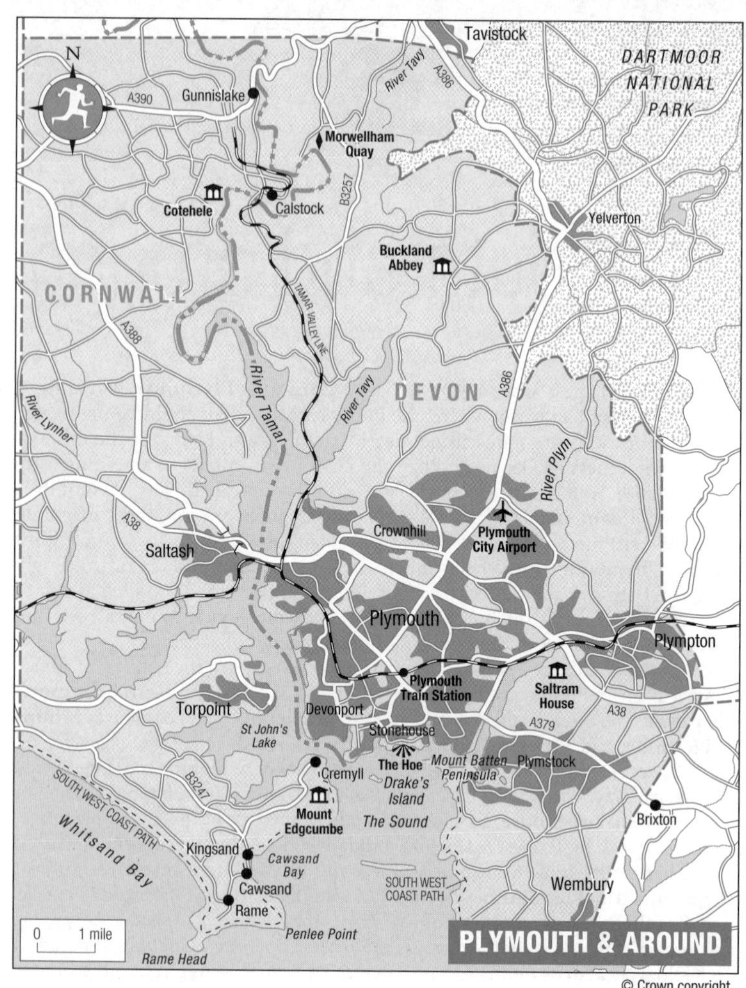

and some absorbing newer attractions, not to mention its supremely panoramic location. With your back to the dreary terraces of housing sprawling across the hills, the vista over **Plymouth Sound** – the basin of calm water at the mouth of the combined Plym, Tavy and Tamar estuaries – is indeed glorious, best appreciated from the high grassy expanse of **Plymouth Hoe**, itself largely unchanged since Drake played his famous game of bowls here prior to taking on the Spanish Armada. The best-preserved remnants of the medieval town lie in a compact area within a short walk of the Hoe, down by **Sutton Harbour** and around the Elizabethan warehouses and inns of the adjacent **Barbican** area, now the focus of the nightlife scene with a gamut of bars and restaurants. Across from the Barbican, the **National Marine Aquarium** is Plymouth's premier draw, housing a diverse aquatic population in imaginatively recreated watery habitats.

Some history

Plymouth grew from the "littel fishe towne" of Sutton, a site at the mouth of the **River Plym** owned by the monks of **Plympton Priory**. The growing importance of its sheltered deep-water anchorage during the **Hundred Years' War** against France led to the amalgamation of Sutton – freed from monastic rule in 1439 – with other settlements in the estuary, and the town, under its present name, became the first in England to receive a charter by Act of Parliament. Plymouth also prospered as a result of the silting up of the River Plym upstream, making the port an important outlet for wool shipments; its wealth in Tudor times is attested by the grand houses surviving from that era in and around the city. Alongside its natural attributes, the town owed its leading role as a **naval base** to the fact that it was home to such great mariners as **Hawkins** and **Drake**. The royal fleet was stationed here during the wars against Spain, and it was from here that Drake sailed to defeat the Spanish Armada in 1588. Raleigh and Grenville launched their failed attempts to colonize Virginia from Plymouth, and 32 years later Sutton Harbour was the last embarkation point of the **Pilgrim Fathers**, whose New Plymouth colony became the nucleus of the English settlement of North America.

Plymouth sided with the Parliamentarians during the **Civil War**, consequently enduring a two-year siege by Royalist troops, and after the Restoration Charles II prudently commanded the **Royal Citadel** to be built to safeguard against future anti-Royalist eruptions. The construction of the **Royal Naval Dockyard** at the end of the seventeenth century, in what's now the Devonport area, ensured the city's continuing importance. Cook and Darwin both sailed from Plymouth in later eras of discovery, and the town's prestige was further enhanced by the building of the **Royal Albert Bridge** in 1859, spanning the Tamar at Saltash to connect Devon with Cornwall by rail – the last engineering feat of Isambard Kingdom Brunel. Plymouth's Victorian street-plan was obliterated by heavy bombing during **World War II**, but the subsequent rebuilding has gone some way to restoring the city centre, while leaving some areas distinctly down-at-heel. Modern-day Plymouth retains its links with the sea: the naval presence is still strong, and the **Devonport dockyards** continue to be a bulwark of the local economy.

Arrival and information

Easily reached by road or rail from Exeter, Plymouth has good **public transport** connections with all the major centres of the West Country, and to the towns and villages of Cornwall's southern coast. The **train station** is a mile north of the Hoe off Saltash Road, connected to Royal Parade by bus #20 (every 30min) or, by walking out of the station area, by numerous other services including #16, #29 and #43. From Royal Parade, bus #25 goes to Sutton Harbour, the Hoe and the Citadel every ten minutes (twice hourly on Sun), or it's a brief walk. The **bus station** on Bretonside, just over St Andrew's Cross from Royal Parade, is much more central, and has left-luggage lockers (£2–3; maximum 24hr). Drivers will find parking difficult, as car parks fill quickly; however, **park and ride schemes** operate between Monday and Saturday from Coypool, to the east of the city off the A38 and B3416 near the Marsh Mills roundabout; Milehouse, near the Plymouth Argyle football ground, just north of the train station on the A386 (no Sat service when matches are on), and The George, further north on the A386 Tavistock road. You might also consider parking at Ivybridge, Liskeard or Gunnislake train stations, from which there are frequent rail and bus services. If you're planning on using public transport frequently, invest in a FirstDay South West pass (£6.70–7.50), valid for travel all day on services operated by First (Ⓣ0845/600 1420, Ⓦwww.firstgroup.com), and available on board the bus or from the bus station. Alternatively, a Day Rider ticket allows for unlimited travel just in the city on City Buses; it costs £3.20 and is available from the bus driver.

The main **tourist office** is just off Sutton Harbour at Plymouth Mayflower, 3–5 The Barbican (April–Oct Mon–Sat 9am–5pm, Sun 10am–4pm; Nov–March Mon–Fri 9am–5pm, Sat 10am–4pm; Ⓣ01752/306330, Ⓦwww.plymouth.gov.uk). There's a small interactive exhibition here summarizing the history of the city (£2).

Accommodation

Befitting its size, Plymouth has a wide range of **accommodation**, though the many conventions and events taking place here year-round mean that rooms can still be scarce. If you want to be near the sights, your best choice is the row of **B&Bs** edging the Hoe on Citadel Road, but if you prefer to stay close to the **train station**, you won't be more than a short bus ride or twenty-minute walk from the Hoe and Barbican areas in any case. The nearest **campsite** is the well-equipped *Riverside Caravan Park*, Longbridge Road (Ⓣ01752/344122, Ⓦwww.riversidecaravanpark.com), just north of the Marsh Mills roundabout and close to the Coast to Coast cycle route. There's an alternative, much more basic site at *Venn Farm*, Brixton, 5 miles east of town on the A379 (Ⓣ01752/880378, Ⓦwww.vennfarm.co.uk; closed Nov–Feb). B&B and self-catering are also available here.

Acorns and Lawns 171 Citadel Rd Ⓣ01752/229474, Ⓦwww.plymouthhoeguesthouse.co.uk. One of a terrace of competitively priced B&Bs close to Plymouth Hoe and the Barbican, offering modern, chintz-free, en-suite rooms, two with views over the Hoe. Free wi-fi. No one-night bookings May–Sept. No credit cards. ④

The Beeches 177 Citadel Rd Ⓣ01752/266475, Ⓦwww.beechesplymouth.moonfruit.com. A good choice on this row, close to the Hoe and Barbican. All the fresh and clean rooms are en suite except for two singles, and some have views over the Hoe. Free wi-fi. ③

Bowling Green Hotel 9–10 Osborne Place, Lockyer St Ⓣ01752/209090, Ⓦwww.thebowlinggreenplymouth.com. Smart and friendly Georgian lodging, with bright, uncluttered en-suite rooms overlooking the Hoe and comfy beds. There's a plush conservatory and free wi-fi. ④

Brittany Guest House 28 Athenaeum St Ⓣ01752/262247, Ⓦwww.brittanyguesthouse.co.uk. This quiet B&B with modern rooms offers good value, and there are room-only rates if you want to skip the excellent breakfasts (which include a good vegetarian option). Guests have use of a private car park (a bonus around here). Free wi-fi. No under-5s. ②

Dudley Hotel 42 Sutherland Rd Ⓣ01752/668322, Ⓦwww.dudley-hotel.com. Clean and welcoming place convenient for the train station (some rooms suffer from train noise), offering spacious rooms with modern furnishings. Tasty breakfasts and free wi-fi are added inducements. ④

Georgian House Hotel 49–51 Citadel Rd Ⓣ01752/661950, Ⓦwww.georgianhouseplymouth.mfbiz.com. This friendly establishment run by a Greek family makes an excellent choice on this strip, with en-suite rooms on three floors and a bar and restaurant (Thurs–Sat eves only) that serves Greek dishes. ③

Plymouth University Gibbon St Ⓣ01752/588599, Ⓦwww.plymouth.ac.uk/holidayaccommodation. Cheap, clean and functional student accommodation ten minutes' walk from the Barbican is available during summer vacation (late June to early Sept). Singles are £21–28, en-suite doubles £49, all with internet access. Breakfast is not provided, but there's a shared kitchen that can be used at any time. ②

Plymouth Backpackers 172 Citadel Rd Ⓣ01752/225158, Ⓦwww.plymouthbackpackers.co.uk. This central hostel has a relaxed atmosphere, a kitchen and a small courtyard. Dorm beds cost £15–16, and there are four simple double rooms with shared bathrooms. Can be grungy. ②

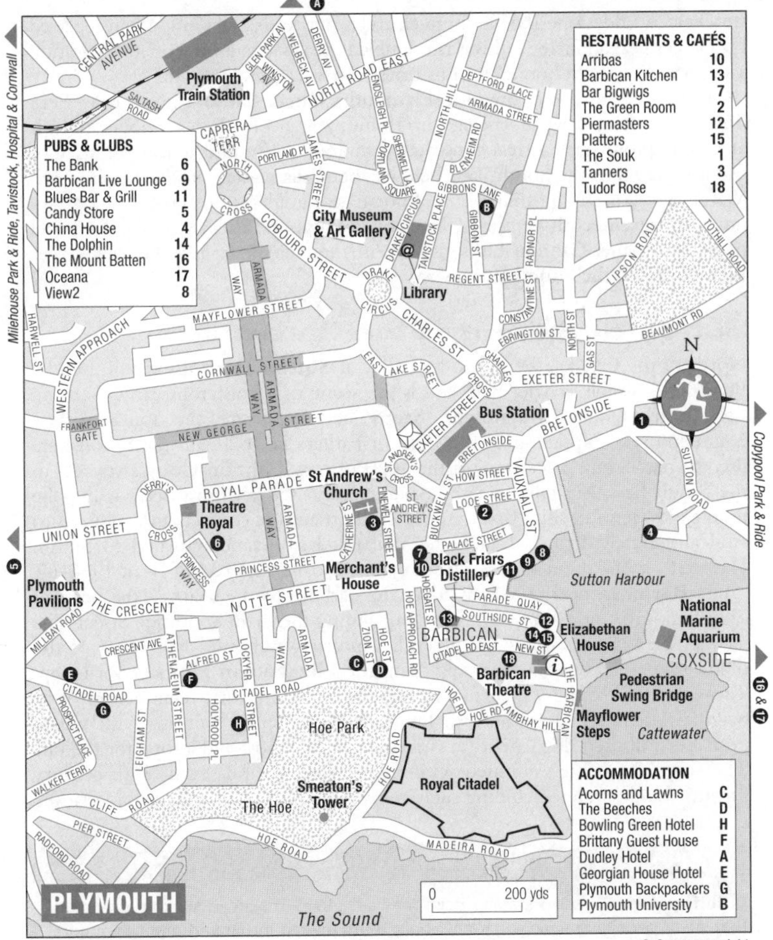

© Crown copyright

The City

A broad grassy esplanade studded with reminders of the city's great events, **Plymouth Hoe** is a stirring spot to start a tour of the city. Resplendent in fair weather, the Hoe (from the Saxon "high place") can also attract some pretty ferocious winds, making it an unappealing prospect in wintry conditions. The seaward views, however, are glorious, taking in **Drake's Island** in the centre of the Sound, previously a fortification, then a prison. Approaching from the city centre, you'll pass a distinctive tall, white naval cenotaph and smaller monuments to the defeat of the Spanish Armada and to the airmen who defended the city during the wartime blitz, alongside a rather portly statue of Sir Francis Drake gazing grandly out to sea. Appropriately, there's a bowling green back from the brow of the Hoe.

In front of the war memorials, the red-and-white striped **Smeaton's Tower** (Tues–Sat: April–Sept 10am–noon & 1–4.30pm, closes 4pm Sat; Oct–March 10am–noon & 1–3pm; £2) was originally erected as a lighthouse on the treacherous Eddystone Rocks, fourteen miles out to sea, in 1759. When replaced by a larger beacon in 1882, it was reassembled here, where it now offers the loftiest view over Plymouth Sound from its lantern room, around 90ft high.

On the seafront east of the Hoe, Plymouth's **Royal Citadel** (tours May–Sept Tues & Thurs at 2.30pm, lasting 1hr 15min; £4, £3 for EH members; EH), is an uncompromising fortress constructed in 1666 to intimidate the populace of the only town in the South West held by the Parliamentarians during the Civil War; it is still partly in military use. Informative guided tours take in the grassy ramparts, seventeenth-century Governor's House and the 1845 Royal Chapel of St Katherine. Cannon buffs will be in their element, and the views over Plymouth and the Sound are superb.

Sutton Harbour and the Barbican

North of the Citadel, the old town's quay at **Sutton Harbour** is still used by Plymouth's sizable trawler fleet and is the scene of a boisterous early-morning **fish market**. The **Mayflower Steps** here, opposite the tourist office, commemorate the sailing of the Pilgrim Fathers in 1620; an inscription here lists the names and professions of the 102 Puritans. **Captain Cook's** voyages to the South Seas, Australia and the Antarctic also set sail from here, as did the nineteenth-century ships that transported thousands of convicts and colonists to Australia; finally, Francis Chichester embarked from and returned to Sutton Harbour on his round-the-world solo jaunt aboard *Gipsy Moth IV* in 1966–67.

The **Barbican** district, which edges the harbour to the south, is the heart of old Plymouth, with shops and restaurants lining the main Southside Street. The parallel New Street holds seventeenth-century warehouses and some of the oldest residential buildings, among them the **Elizabethan House** (April–Sept Tues–Sat 10am–5pm; £2), a former captain's dwelling that retains most of its original architectural features, including a lovely spiral staircase with what's probably a disused ship's mast for the central newel post and a rope for the rail. The three floors are crammed with fine sixteenth- and seventeenth-century furniture and textiles, including such items as a child's chair and a geometrically

Boat trips from Sutton Harbour

Sutton Harbour is the starting point for boat trips – mostly in summer only, and weather permitting – ranging from 1-hour **tours** around the **Sound and Devonport naval dockyard** (£6–7) to a four-and-a-half-hour **cruise** up the Tamar to the Cornish village of **Calstock** (£9.50 return; see p.170). Call Sound Cruising (Ⓣ01752/408590, Ⓦwww.soundcruising.com) or Tamar Cruising (Ⓣ01752/822105, Ⓦwww.tamarcruising.com) for details of sailings from the Barbican, or Plymouth Hoe Cruises (Ⓣ0797/120 8381, Ⓦwww.plymouthhoecruises.co.uk) for departures from Pebbleside Steps, Hoe Road. For **fishing trips** out to sea, contact Fish 'n' Trips (Ⓣ07971/208381, Ⓦwww.fishntrips.co.uk): a two-and-a-half-hour mackerel-fishing expedition costs £15, or you can join a four-hour deep-sea expedition for £24.

Between May and September, the **Mayflower Steps** are the embarkation point for the **Cawsand Ferry** (Ⓣ0783/393 6863, Ⓦwww.cawsandferry.com), which crosses the Sound to the village of **Cawsand** (see p.166) in Cornwall, departing at 10.30am, noon, 2.30pm and 4pm (£4 one way; 30min), and the Mount Edgcumbe Connection to Cremyll Quay and **Mount Edgcumbe** (see p.165) departing at 11am, 12.30pm, 2pm and 3.30pm, operated by Tamar Cruising (£9.50, including entry to Mount Edgcumbe House). For both services, check first at the Steps or the tourist office if conditions are unsettled.

Plymouth Gin

Even without the naval and *Mayflower* connections, the name of Plymouth is familiar worldwide on account of the popularity of **Plymouth Gin**. Soon after **Coates & Co** opened a distillery in the heart of the city's Barbican quarter in 1793, Plymouth Gin began to be exported all over the world. **Royal Navy ships** took the spirit on board before setting sail and, in the 1930s, it became the most widely distributed gin in the world. Protected by the equivalent of an *appellation contrôlée* (in other words, it must be made in Plymouth), it owes its flavour to its "magnificent seven botanicals" and soft Dartmoor water, and comes in varying strengths, ranging from 100 percent proof (57 percent abv), the version that was supplied to the Navy, who mixed it with Angostura bitters to make pink gin, or "pinkers" (said to be capable of curing everything from indigestion to depression), to the less daunting 41.2 percent abv version. The milder version has a richer, more citrusy flavour than London gins, containing less juniper and other bitter botanicals, and makes a pukka **dry martini** or **G&T**. Mixed with cranberry juice, pink grapefruit juice and sloe gin, it also makes a very acceptable Arkansas Breeze. Fans of Plymouth Gin are said to include **Winston Churchill**, **Franklin D. Roosevelt** and **Bill Clinton**. A 70cl bottle of classic Plymouth Gin or sloe gin currently costs around £16 at the **Black Friars Distillery** on Southside Street, where you can learn more about the history of gin and the distilling process (see below).

patterned spice cabinet in the dining room. The attic bedrooms hold a pair of grand beds, an oak-carved canopied tester and a Brittany box bed with sliding door, decorated with winged cherubs.

Near the top of Southside Street, you can tour **Black Friars Distillery** (Mon–Sat 10.30am–4.30pm, Sun 11.30am–4.30pm; last admission 1hr before closing; £6; ⓣ01752/665292, ⓦwww.plymouthgin.com), which has been producing the excellent **Plymouth Gin** since 1793. Dating from 1431, the buildings originally housed a monastery and, following the Dissolution, later became a prison and a refuge for French Huguenot refugees; in 1620 the Pilgrim Fathers gathered here before embarking on the *Mayflower*. **Guided tours** start with an educational presentation covering the history of gin, the Barbican area and the building itself. You can view the gin-making process and sample the finished product, which is for sale in various incarnations in the on-site shop. The tickets entitle you to a discounted gin and tonic in *The Refectory* cocktail bar.

The National Marine Aquarium

Cross the footbridge by the Mayflower Steps over Sutton Harbour to reach the grand **National Marine Aquarium** (daily: April–Sept 10am–6pm; Oct–March 10am–5pm; last admission 1hr before closing; £11 ⓦwww.national-aquarium.co.uk), whose three tanks include Britain's deepest. Note that buying a ticket in advance from the tourist office or online will save waiting in line; all tickets allow re-entry for one day.

Exhibits are on three levels, arranged according to habitat; visitors proceed from shallows to river estuary, shore and shallow sea, descending to coral seas and the shark theatre. The most popular exhibits are the sea horses, the colourful reefs and the sharks, of various species and sizes, though some of the smaller tanks hold equally compelling exhibits – the anemones, for example. It is impossible to label the various, often beautiful and bizarre creatures in the curved tanks, so it's worth seeking guidance from the helpful attendants on hand to identify the fish – look out for the extraordinary frog fish waving its tentacles and the stately diamond-like lookdown jacks. At the top of the building, **Explorocean** highlights the

▲ National Marine Aquarium

technological aspects of oceanography, alongside a child-friendly exhibition of the ecological role of the sea and the effects of climate change. **Talks and presentations** take place throughout the day and **feeding-times** are particularly worth catching, usually accompanied by short talks (the sharks are fed on Mon, Wed & Fri at around 2pm) and there are daily dives; there's usually something going on – a talk, dive or feed – every 30 minutes (call ⓣ01752/600301 for details). The excellent *Ocean View Café* on the second floor overlooks Sutton Harbour.

Merchant's House Museum and St Andrew's

Across Notte Street from the top of Southside Street, the handsome timber-framed **Merchant's House Museum** at 33 St Andrew's St (April–Sept Tues–Sat 10am–5pm; £2) dates back to 1608 when it accommodated William Parker, a merchant, privateer, mayor of Plymouth and probably the master of the *Mary Rose*, which victualled Francis Drake's fleet when it sailed against the Armada. Preserving its original architecture, the house now holds an engrossing collection of relics from Plymouth's past. Each of the three floors follows a historical theme: the Victorian schoolroom can be quickly passed through, but the photographs documenting the wartime blitz are enlightening, and the reconstructed prewar pharmacy on the third floor, resplendent with variously coloured bottles, invites a linger, and you can also see the old Barbican ducking stool, used to punish alleged miscreants.

Behind the museum, off Royal Parade, the city's chief place of worship is **St Andrew's** (Mon–Fri 9am–4pm, Sat 9am–1pm, Sun open for services only; ⓦwww.standrewschurch.org.uk), a reconstruction of the original fifteenth-century building that was almost completely destroyed by a bomb in 1941. Occupying the role of the Anglican cathedral which Plymouth (strangely) never had, the church has always been at the heart of the city's life: local boy William

Bligh, of *Mutiny on the Bounty* fame, was baptized here, and the entrails of the navigator Martin Frobisher are buried within, as are those of Admiral Blake, the Parliamentarian who died as his ship entered Plymouth after destroying a Spanish treasure fleet off Tenerife in 1657. However, the real draw is the set of six **stained-glass windows** installed in 1958 and designed by John Piper (responsible for the more famous stained glass in Coventry Cathedral). Luridly coloured in deep reds and blues, and incorporating symbols from the scriptures – the central east window shows the elements air, earth, fire and water – the windows were a radical departure from the norm, raising plenty of hackles among traditionalists.

City Museum and Art Gallery

To the north of St Andrew's Cross at Drake Circus, the **City Museum and Art Gallery** (Tues–Fri 10am–5.30pm, Sat 10am–5pm; free; Ⓦwww.plymouthmuseum.gov.uk) is an engaging collection that's well worth an hour or two, especially for its paintings and changing exhibitions. The **Art Gallery** has a particularly good collection of modern British paintings which form the basis of rotating exhibitions, including works by artists of the Newlyn and St Ives schools such as Stanhope Forbes, Peter Lanyon, Patrick Heron, Bryan Pearce and Alfred Wallis. Prominent local artists such as Joshua Reynolds, James Northcote and Benjamin Haydon are also represented, and there's a wall dedicated to the work of **Beryl Cook** (1926–2008), the modern artist most associated with Plymouth, including works depicting local scenes such as *Beach at Looe* and *Lockyer Street Tavern*. Among the items in the permanent museum displays, the fine eighteenth-century Plymouth porcelain in the **China Connection** room is worth seeking out, while **Plymouth: Port and Place**, on the ground floor, is an interactive review of Plymouth's past from prehistory to recent times, with a plethora of model ships, photos and film.

Eating and drinking

Plymouth is well served with **eating** and **drinking** establishments, of which you'll find an eclectic range in and around the Barbican quarter.

Restaurants and cafés

Arribas 58 Notte St ⓣ01752/603303. Mexican diner with a lively atmosphere, offering fajitas and burritos (£11–15) as well as steaks, pizzas and seafood. There's a tequila and cocktail lounge upstairs open on Fri & Sat eves.

Barbican Kitchen 60 Southside St ⓣ01752/604448. In an attic of the Black Friars Distillery, this offshoot of the posh and prestigious *Tanners* (see below) is a much more relaxed affair with moderate prices. Dishes include baguettes, salads, beer-battered fish and chips (£9.25), burgers (£9.50–11.50) and steaks (£13–15.50).

Bar Bigwigs 15 St Andrew's St ⓣ0780/710 4457. Mellow bar/restaurant that makes a great spot for lunch or supper, with dishes ranging from crab salad (£9) and fajitas (£7.50–10.25) to fish pie (£10.50), and live music every other Fri.

The Green Room 38 Looe St ⓣ01752/206114, Ⓦwww.plymouthac.org.uk. Part of Plymouth Arts Centre, this quiet café/restaurant is convenient for anyone coming for the exhibitions, films and performances. Open until 8.30pm for snacks and such dishes as red lentil curry (£7.25). Closed Sun & Mon.

Piermasters 33 Southside St ⓣ01752/229345. Plain but elegant restaurant that's supplied straight from the nearby harbour. Evening dining can be expensive, with dishes such as grilled turbot fillet costing around £22, but there's a five-course dinner menu for £36, and there are great lunchtime deals (£10–12 for 2–3 courses). Closed Sun.

Platters 12 The Barbican ⓣ01752/227262. Popular, down-to-earth place where diners are surrounded by plaster relief illustrating the life of a guppy fish. The food (mainly seafood) is not bad either, from fish and chips (£9) to lemon calamari (£17), and service is brisk.

The Souk Sutton Harbour ⓣ01752/221111. Modern Moroccan restaurant, richly coloured and adorned with textiles, serving mezes including falafel, tabbouleh and calamari (£4.50 each) and tagines (£12). The tangy orange cake makes a great pudding, and sheeshas are on hand for a fruity smoke. The £8 lunch menu is a bargain. Closed Sun & all Mon.

Tanners Prysten House, Finewell St ⓣ01752/252001. Set in what is reputed to be Plymouth's oldest building, this place blends antique flagstones, New Age painted walls and a semi-formal atmosphere. The Mediterranean-meets-the-West-Country dishes are served on set-price menus ranging from £17.50 for a two-course lunch to £39 for a three-course dinner and £48 for a six-course tasting menu. Booking essential. Closed Sun & Mon.

Tudor Rose 36 New St. Traditional English tearoom and restaurant, where you can tuck into such inexpensive snacks as cottage pies (£7–9), with a garden open in summer. Daytime only. Closed Mon in winter.

Bars and pubs

The Bank Old George St. Rarely for central Plymouth pubs, this one has plenty of character and is popular with theatre-goers. Originally designed as a bank, its two bars retain their opulent mahogany ambience, and there's a garden and occasional live music (Thurs). Baguettes, baked potatoes and excellent steaks are on offer.

China House Coxside. An ex-porcelain factory, this spacious place has stone walls, beams, flagstone floors and roaring fires in winter. Booth-like partitions help to separate the crowd. Real ales and meals are dispensed.

The Dolphin 14 The Barbican. Unpretentious, old-time fishermen's pub, full of personality, with a mixed clientele and Tribute and Bass ales straight from the barrel. Local artist Beryl Cook set some of her works here.

The Mount Batten Lawrence Rd, Mount Batten. Reachable by water taxi from the Mayflower Steps, this large pub and hotel with wrought-iron pillars and great harbour views has a good choice of drinks and bar meals. Gets busy, especially for the Sunday carvery at lunchtime.

Nightlife and entertainment

Nightlife in Plymouth, from theatre-going to clubbing, gets fairly lively all year round. The monthly free listings magazines *247* (ⓦwww.247magazine.co.uk) and *What's On Southwest* (ⓦwww.whatsonsouthwest.co.uk) are worth consulting for up-to-date entertainment information, including concerts and films.

Venues and clubs

Barbican Live Lounge 11 The Parade, Sutton Harbour ⓣ01752/672127, ⓦwww.barbicanlivelounge.com. You can hear a range of live music in this long, arched space, which gets very busy after 11pm. Open Wed–Sun.

Barbican Theatre Castle St ⓣ01752/267131, ⓦwww.barbicantheatre.co.uk. Next to the tourist office off Sutton Harbour, you can see dance and experimental performances here, as well as comedy, jazz and world music.

Blues Bar & Grill 8 The Parade, Sutton Harbour ⓣ01752/257345, ⓦwww.bluesbarandgrill.com. Live blues music is played here Tues–Sat, which you can enjoy while munching on burgers and downing drinks.

Candy Store 101 Union St ⓣ01752/601616, ⓦwww.candystore.co.uk. Ibiza anthems, r'n'b, hip-hop and dancehall are the menu on Wed, Fri & Sat.

Oceana Barbican Leisure Park, Coxside ⓣ0845/293 2864, ⓦwww.oceanaclubs.com/plymouth. Glitzy complex big on fancy dress and foam parties. Dance anthems, r 'n' b and chart sounds predominate.

Plymouth Pavilions Millbay Rd ⓣ0845/146 1460, ⓦwww.plymouthpavilions.com. The major regional venue for pop, rock, classical concerts and comedy.

Theatre Royal Royal Parade ⓣ01752/267222, ⓦwww.theatreroyal.com. Mainstream plays, opera, ballet and musicals are staged throughout the year. The Drum is also here, a more intimate venue for drama and musicals.

View2 With an alfresco terrace on Sutton Harbour, this bar/restaurant has a great location, DJs playing Latin and funk sounds, and comedy on Wed; they also serve pastas and sizzling pizzas.

Listings

Airport Plymouth City Airport lies 4 miles north of the city at Crownhill, off the A386 (℡01752/204090, ⓦwww.plymouthairport.com). Buses stop at Derriford Roundabout, a 10-minute walk; a taxi to or from the centre costs around £7.50, a fifteen-minute ride. Frequent flights to and from London, Manchester, Glasgow and Ireland (see Travel Details, p.170).
Bike rental Plymouth Cycle Scene, on the roundabout at Mutley Plain ℡01752/257701. Bikes are available Easter–Oct for around £12 per day.
Buses For local bus information, call City Buses ℡0845/077 2223, ⓦwww.plymouthcitybus.co.uk or First ℡0845/600 1420, ⓦwww.firstgroup.com. For routes further afield, call Traveline at ℡0871/200 2233, ⓦwww.traveline.org.uk.
Car rental Avis, 20 Commercial Rd, Coxside ℡0844/544 6090 and at airport ℡0844/544 6024, ⓦwww.avis.co.uk; Enterprise, 8 The Octagon, off Union St ℡01752/601000, ⓦwww.enterprise.co.uk; Thrifty, Sutton Rd, Coxside ℡01752/207207. All are closed on Sun.
Hospital Derriford Hospital, Derriford Rd, Crownhill ℡0845/155 8155, four miles north of the centre, has a 24hr Emergency Department.
Internet You can log on at the central library off Drake Circus (Mon–Fri 9am–7pm, Sat 9am–5pm; ℡01752/305923; free).
Post office St Andrew's Cross (Mon–Sat 9am–5.30pm).
Taxis There are ranks at the train station, as well as at Raleigh St (off Derry's Cross) and the Barbican. You can also call Plymouth Taxis ℡01752/606060 or Taxifast ℡01752/222222.

Around Plymouth

The various sights around Plymouth provide a welcome antidote to the urban bustle, and all are within an hour's journey of the city. At **Mount Edgcumbe**, accessible by ferry from Plymouth, woods and meadows lie within easy reach of some fabulous sand beaches, and you can stroll to to the villages of **Cawsand** and **Kingsand**, once notorious smuggling bases. Just east of Plymouth, the aristocratic opulence of **Saltram House** offers contrasting refinement, the ornate Georgian mansion stuffed with fine art and furniture. There's a cluster of attractions a few miles further out to the north of the city, in the **Tavy and Tamar valleys**. On the edge of Dartmoor, Drake's old residence at **Buckland Abbey** has more of the flavour of a museum than a historic home, and displays items relating to the sea dog. A few miles northwest of here, **Morwellham Quay** was once the country's greatest copper port; it now throngs with coach parties but is well worth seeing nonetheless for its riverside works and mine shafts. Nearby, the tastefully preserved **Cotehele** abounds with treasures and curiosities redolent of the Tudor era.

From Plymouth, **public transport** connections can be tricky: for Buckland, Cotehele and Morwellham Quay, you'll need to change buses at Tavistock (see p.147) or else take a train on the **Tamar Valley Line** from Plymouth and either board a bus at Gunnislake or Calstock stations, or walk the last stretch: details are given below. There's also a summer **ferry service** from Plymouth to Calstock (see p.160).

Mount Edgcumbe and around

Situated on the Cornish side of Plymouth Sound and visible from the Hoe, **Mount Edgcumbe** is a winning combination of Tudor house, landscaped gardens and acres of beautiful rolling parkland alongside the sea, with access to coastal paths. Though the **house** (April–Sept Mon–Thurs & Sun 11am–4.30pm; £6;

Ⓦwww.mountedgcumbe.gov.uk) is a reconstruction of the Tudor original that was gutted by incendiary bombs in 1941, the predominant note inside is eighteenth-century, with authentic Regency furniture in the elegantly restored rooms. Paintings (including works by Joshua Reynolds), sixteenth-century tapestries and items of Plymouth porcelain hold mild appeal, but the real interest lies in the enticing **park** (unrestricted access; free), which includes immaculate gardens divided into French, Italian and English sections – the first two a blaze of flower beds adorned with classical statuary, the last an acre of sweeping lawn shaded by exotic trees. In the Amphitheatre – a series of ponds in a valley garden overlooking Plymouth Sound – some of the thousand-odd species and varieties of camellias cultivated in the grounds can be seen from January onwards. The park covers the whole eastern side of the **Rame peninsula**, which juts into the estuary to the southwest of Plymouth. It holds a section of the **South West Coast Path** (see box, p.177), which you can join at the quayside at Cremyll, on the peninsula's northeastern tip. Whether following the coast path or roaming at random within the park, you'll come across some singularly beautiful spots, the landscaped wooded walks making the best of the estuary and sea views. A memorable way of taking it all in is by taking a 6-mile circular hike that's almost entirely coastal, following the coast path from Cremyll Ferry to Kingsand, then heading inland via a combination of lanes and paths past Maker church and before joining the north side of the peninsula where you continue near the water's edge back to the ferry.

The best way to reach Mount Edgcumbe is on the **Mount Edgcumbe Connection**, a passenger ferry to Cremyll leaving four times daily in summer from Mayflower Steps (£9.50 including entry to Mount Edgcumbe House; see above), or on the **Cremyll Ferry**, every 30 minutes all year from Admiral's Hard (£1.50), a small mooring in the Stonehouse district of the city (reachable on bus #34 from Royal Parade once or twice hourly). Both are operated by Tamar Cruising (see p.160). **By car** from Plymouth, you'll have to use the Torpoint **chain ferry** (every 10min; £1) from Devonport (well signposted) to Torpoint and drive around the peninsula, but it's a lengthy route.

Walkers also have the option of taking the ferry to **CAWSAND**, an old smugglers' haunt a couple of hours' pleasant hike from the house. A direct motor launch, the **Cawsand Ferry** (see p.160) sets off from the Mayflower Steps – weather permitting – four times daily between Easter and September, returning thirty minutes later. Cawsand's narrow lanes of colour-washed and red-stone cottages descend to a quay and beaches in a protected bay. Until 1830, the Devon–Cornwall border divided the village from **KINGSAND**, its slightly smaller twin village just a few minutes' walk north up the coast and marked by its Institute clocktower right on the sea.

There is access to Mount Edgcumbe Park from the northern end of Kingsand, and from either village walkers can follow the coast path south around the peninsula for sweeping views of Plymouth Sound and the open sea from the headlands of **Penlee Point** and **Rame Head**. Both villages lie just a mile east of the extensive sands of **Whitsand Bay**, the best **bathing beach** in the area, accessible from paths snaking down from the cliffs and from the B3247. With the wind blowing from the southwest, the four miles of flat sands here get long ranks of rollers, but as the currents can be strong, swimmers should take care not to go too far out.

Practicalities

General information on Mount Edgcumbe, Cawsand and Kingsand can be accessed at Ⓦwww.crabpot.co.uk. Staff at Kingsand's **post office** located in a shop, Shipshape (summer daily 9am–6pm, winter Mon & Wed–Fri

9am–5.30pm, Tues 9am–1pm, Sat 9am–12.30pm; ⓣ01752/822288), can also fill you in on **accommodation** in the twin villages. Kingsand's *Halfway House Inn* on Fore Street (ⓣ01752/822279, ⓦwww.halfwayinn.biz; ⑤) is one good possibility, decorated in Victorian style with quietly elegant rooms and a big central fireplace. In Cawsand, the large plate-glass windows of the *Cawsand Bay Hotel* on the Bound (ⓣ01752/822425, ⓦwww.thecawsandbay hotel.co.uk; ⑥) face right on to the sea. For meals, the *Halfway House Inn* does a good line in fresh fish (in the bar or the small restaurant, where it's best to book), and the *Cross Keys Inn* on the Square, Cawsand, makes an unpretentious stop for pub grub.

Saltram House

Three miles east of Plymouth, just south of the A38, the grand, white, eighteenth-century **Saltram House** (house: mid-March to Oct Mon–Thurs, Sat & Sun noon–4.30pm; garden: mid-March to Oct daily 11am–5pm; Nov to mid-March Mon–Thurs, Sat and Sun 11am–4pm; last admission 45min before closing; house and garden £8.25, garden only £4.10; NT) is Devon's largest country house, and attracts quite a scrum of visitors. If you're a fan of Neoclassical exuberance, you'll be in your element, and even if you're not, there are individual features here which will appeal. Staff are present in most rooms to answer specific questions about the items on display, alternatively a guidebook **costs** £5.

The original Tudor building received its dramatic Georgian makeover at the hands of the Parker family, local bigwigs who numbered **Joshua Reynolds** among their acquaintances. Born nearby in Plympton and a master at the local grammar school, Reynolds was a regular guest at the hunting, shooting and gambling parties held here, and left several works scattered around the house, including fourteen portraits of the family. Saltram's showpiece, however, is the **double-cube Saloon** designed by Robert Adam, supposed to be the perfect embodiment of a classically proportioned room of the era. A fussy but exquisitely furnished room dripping with gilt and plaster, it's an eye-popping sight, set off by a huge Axminster carpet especially woven in 1770. This and other rooms here featured in the 1995 film of *Sense and Sensibility*, in which the house served as Norland Park in Jane Austen's novel.

Other high points include works by the eighteenth-century Swiss portraitist **Angelica Kauffman** – one a likeness of her friend and mentor Reynolds – in the staircase hall, where you'll also see George Stubbs' *The Fall of Titan*. The first floor is rich in chinoiserie – wallpaper, mirror paintings and Chinese Chippendale – and there is much Chippendale furniture elsewhere too. You have to exit the house to visit the **Great Kitchen**, where the chopping block has been so worn down as to resemble a saddle. The scale of entertaining can be judged by the hundreds of items of copperware on display here, alongside such curiosities as glass cockroach-catchers, which would be filled with beer to entice the offenders.

Saltram's **landscaped park** provides a breather from this riot of interior design, with garden follies and lovely riverside walks, though it's partially marred by the proximity of the road. You can reach Saltram on the hourly #22 bus (not Sun) from Royal Parade to Merafield Road, from where it's a fifteen-minute signposted walk.

Buckland Abbey

Eight miles north of Plymouth via the A386, **Buckland Abbey** (mid-Feb to mid-March & early Nov to mid-Dec Fri–Sun 11am–4pm; mid-March to June, Sept & Oct Mon–Wed & Fri–Sun 10.30am–5.30pm; July & Aug daily 10.30am–5.30pm; last admission 45min before closing; house & grounds £7.40; grounds only £3.80, free in winter; NT) stands right on the edge of Dartmoor (see Chapter 4) close to the **River Tavy**. In the thirteenth century, this was the most westerly of England's **Cistercian abbeys**, and was converted after its dissolution to a private home by the privateer Richard Grenville (a cousin of Walter Raleigh), from whom the estate was acquired by **Francis Drake** in 1581. Though it remained Drake's home until his death, the house – a stone Tudor construction with an ungainly central tower – reveals few traces of his residence, as he spent most of his retirement years plundering on the Spanish main. There are, however, numerous maps, portraits and mementos of his buccaneering exploits on show, most famous of which is **Drake's Drum**, said to beat a supernatural warning of impending danger to the country.

The house displays various other relics of the Elizabethan seafaring era, though most eye-catching are the architectural embellishments in the oak-panelled **Great Hall**, dated 1576 but previously the nave of the abbey. One end of the room sports a frieze of holly and box interspersed with allegorical scenes, musicians and sheila-na-gigs (women in less than decorous poses), and there's fine ornamental plasterwork on the ceiling.

Sir Francis Drake

Born around 1540 near Tavistock (see p.147), **Francis Drake** began his seafaring career at the age of 13, working in the domestic coastal trade before taking part in the first English **slaving expeditions** between Africa and the West Indies, led by his Plymouth kinsman John Hawkins. Later Drake was active in the secret war against Spain, raiding and looting merchant ships in actions unofficially sanctioned by Elizabeth I. In 1572 he became the first Englishman to sight the Pacific, and soon afterwards, on board the *Golden Hind*, became the first one to circumnavigate the world, for which he received a knighthood on his return in 1580. The following year Drake was made **mayor of Plymouth**, settling in Buckland Abbey (see above), but was back in action before long – in 1587 he "singed the king of Spain's beard" by entering Cadiz harbour and destroying 33 vessels that were to have formed part of Philip II's Spanish Armada. When the replacement invasion fleet appeared in the English Channel in 1588, Drake – along with Raleigh, Hawkins and Frobisher – played a leading role in wrecking it. The legend that he took his time in finishing a game of bowls on the Hoe before setting sail is most probably due to the fact that he was conversant with the tides and could gauge his time. The following year he set off on an unsuccessful expedition to help the Portuguese against Spain, but otherwise most of the next decade was spent in relative inactivity in Plymouth, Exeter and London. Finally, in 1596 Drake left with Hawkins for a raid on **Panama**, a venture that cost the lives of both captains.

Though Drake has come to personify the Elizabethan Age's swashbuckling expansionism and patriotism, England's naval triumphs were as much the result of John Hawkins' humbler work in building and maintaining a new generation of warships as they were of the skill and bravery of their captains. Drake was simply the most flamboyant of a generation of reckless and brilliant mariners who broke the Spanish hegemony on the high seas, so laying the foundations for England's later imperialist pursuits.

To get to Buckland by **bus**, take the #83, #84 or #86 towards Tavistock from Plymouth's bus station, changing at Yelverton to the hourly #55 minibus (not Sun); on Sunday there's a direct service between Plymouth's Royal Parade and Buckland Abbey on bus #48.

Morwellham Quay

Three miles northwest of Buckland Abbey, and ten miles north of Plymouth via the A386 and the B3257, the sleepy, narrow river at **Morwellham Quay** (daily: Easter–Oct 10am–5.30pm; Nov–Easter 10am–4.30pm; free, attractions £8.50; Ⓦwww.morwellham-quay.co.uk) makes it difficult to believe that this was once a hive of activity at the heart of Devon's mining industry. Morwellham first came to prominence as a port in the twelfth century, when tin, silver, lead ore and arsenic (a by-product of the mines) were exported. Its main commodity, however, was **copper**, used in Tudor times for cannons and throughout the Napoleonic Wars for the copper-bottoming of sailing ships. During the reign of Queen Victoria, it was the country's greatest copper port, and in the early and middle years of the nineteenth century, when the River Tamar outdid the Mersey for the number of its ships, it was said there was enough arsenic piled up on the quays to poison the world. Today, the site has been sensitively restored to its 1860s glory as a working quay, equipped with warehouses, lime kilns and a giant water wheel, and there are enough diversions to provide a good half-day's entertainment.

Though a fixture on coach- and school-party itineraries, the site has largely escaped falling into terminal tackiness: the costumed attendants are down to earth and knowledgeable, and a big-screen video provides informative background. The entry ticket includes a **tramway ride** into the copper mine, and visits to the **mining museum** and a "gypsy camp", though most are content with wandering around the quay and overhead tramways, and poking around in the cottages and blacksmith's and cooper's workshops, where there are daily demonstrations and lots of hands-on activities. Other attractions include a ketch restored to its 1909 appearance, and a wildlife area with birdwatching hides.

From Plymouth, getting to the site by **public transport** is a two-stage process: from the bus station at Bretonside, take services #83, #84 or #86 to Tavistock, where you change onto the #87 or #87A (not Sun) to Morwellham.

Cotehele

Nestled in the wooded and exotically planted **Tamar Valley**, two miles west of Morwellham and ten miles northwest of Plymouth, **Cotehele House** (house: mid-March to Oct Mon–Thurs, Sat & Sun 11am–4.30pm; mill: mid-March to Sept daily 11–5pm; Oct daily 11–4.30pm; garden: daily 10am–dusk; £8.30 for all three, or £5 garden and mill only; NT) is one of the best-preserved and least altered medieval houses in the country. Built largely between 1485 and 1539, it remained in the Edgcumbe family for six hundred years, though their residence at Mount Edgcumbe (see p.165) from the end of the seventeenth century meant that Cotehele remained mostly unmodified, preserving its tranquil Tudor character. **Exhibits** – chiefly a fascinating collection of needlework, tapestries, weaponry and vigorously carved seventeenth-century furniture – are arranged in an interlinked group of granite, slate and sandstone buildings around three courtyards. It's best to visit on a bright day, if you can, as there's no electricity indoors a fact which has aided the remarkable state of preservation of the many textiles.

Each of the rooms displays something that grabs the eye. The fine arch-braced **Hall**, with its bare lime-ash floor, has a rare set of folding, mid-eighteenth-century chairs, still with their original leather, while the **Old Dining Room**, hung with Flemish tapestries, leads to the chapel in which you can see the earliest domestic clock in England, dating from 1485 and still in its original position. The rooms on the first and second floor are embroiderers' heaven: Jacobean floral crewelwork in the white bedroom; delicate seventeenth-century bed hangings, stumpwork and an eighteenth-century bedspread in the south room; gros point in **King Charles's Room**, and Victorian patchwork in **Queen Anne's Room**. Don't miss the grenade-like Victorian glass fire-extinguishers on the lower landing and, on the upper, the carved Welsh bed-head from 1532, replete with a hunting and hawking frieze and a scaly angel expelling Adam and Eve from the Garden of Eden. The **grounds** are densely wooded and full of surprises. A mile-long walk brings you to the working **water mill** on the Tamar, and nearby **workshops** display tools belonging to blacksmiths, carpenters and other craftsmen connected to the mill.

Practicalities

To get to Cotehele by **public transport**, you can take the scenic **Tamar Valley Line train** from Plymouth to Calstock, from where you can either walk the one and a half miles to the house (a pleasant stroll through woods) or catch one of the frequent **ferries** from Calstock to Cotehele's quay (Easter to late Sept; £3 single, £4 return; ⓣ01822/833331, ⓦwww.calstockferry.co.uk). There are also **river cruises** to Calstock from Plymouth operated by Sound Cruising and Tamar Cruising (see p.160 for details of both). By **bus**, services #83, #84 and #86 run from Plymouth's bus station to Tavistock, where you can change onto the #79 or #X79 (not Sun) to get to Calstock; the same service also runs past Gunnislake train station. On Sundays from late May to late September, a Dartmoor **Sunday Rover Ticket** (£6.50) will cover you for the Plymouth–Calstock train or bus journey. By road, you have to negotiate the narrow but well-signposted lanes leading off the A390 to Cotehele.

On Cotehele Quay, the cosy *Edgcumbe Arms* provides **refreshment** in the form of teas and inexpensive meals.

Travel details

Planes

Plymouth to: Bristol (1–2 daily; 35min); Cork, Ireland (3–4 weekly; 1hr 40min); Dublin, Ireland (3–4 weekly; 1hr 45min); Glasgow (6–7 weekly; 2hr 25min); London City (1–2 daily; 1hr 10min); London Gatwick (4 daily; 1hr 45min); Manchester (Mon–Fri 1 daily; 2hr); Newcastle (4–7 weekly; 1hr 35min–2hr 10min).

Trains

Plymouth to: Bristol (1–2 hourly; 2hr); Calstock (5–9 daily; 35min); Exeter (1–2 hourly; 1hr); Gunnislake (5–9 daily; 45min); London (hourly; 3hr–4hr); Penzance (hourly; 2hr); St Austell (hourly; 50min–1hr).

Buses

Plymouth to: Exeter (1–2 hourly; 1hr–1hr 30min); Kingsbridge (Mon–Sat hourly, Sun 4 daily, Sun 4 daily; 1hr); Tavistock (Mon–Sat every 15min, Sun hourly; 50min–1hr); Yelverton (Mon–Sat every 15min, Sun 1–2 hourly; 30–40min).

6

Exmoor

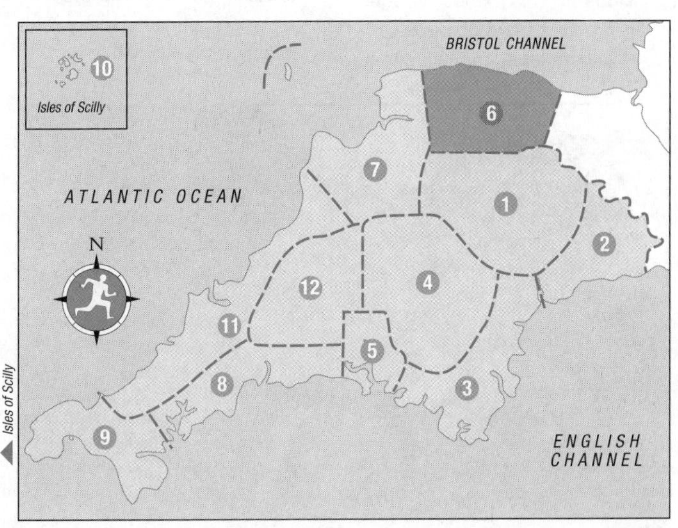

BRISTOL CHANNEL
Isles of Scilly
10
ATLANTIC OCEAN
N
6
7
1
2
4
12
11
5
8
3
9
Isles of Scilly
ENGLISH CHANNEL

CHAPTER 6 Highlights

* **Riding on the moor** Experience the moor at an amble, trot or canter – a memorably exhilarating way to spend half a day. See p.175

* **Coastwalking** The hogback cliffs at Exmoor's northern edge can be tough going, but the ever-changing views more than compensate. See p.177

* **Dunster** This Exmoor village is a near-perfect composition – with its tapering main street, medieval yarn market and the romantic backdrop of Dunster Castle. See pp.178–180

* **Lynton and Lynmouth** These sister towns, separated by a steep cliff, make an excellent base for moor and coastal expeditions. See p.182

* **Tarr Steps** One of the moor's famed beauty spots, where a clapper bridge crosses the Barle and there are scenic strolls in every direction. See p.189

▲ Riding on Exmoor

6

Exmoor

A high, bare plateau sliced by wooded combes and splashing streams, Exmoor presents a very different aspect to Dartmoor, the South West's other National Park. Though it boasts tracts of wilderness every bit as forbidding, Exmoor is smaller, with greater expanses of farmland breaking up the heath, and owes its distinctiveness mainly to the proximity of the sea, from which mists and rainstorms descend with alarming speed. Exmoor's geographical unity ignores county boundaries, meaning that though most of it lies outside Devon in the county of Somerset, we've included most of the park in this chapter. The Brendon Hills, east of the A396, are officially part of the National Park, but this area is quite distinct from Exmoor and so is not covered.

Though most of the park is privately owned – including about ten percent held by the National Trust – there's good access through a dense network of footpaths and bridleways as well as numerous access areas where you can wander at will. Exmoor's coastal section is the most easily accessible part for visitors, with the A39, which runs parallel to the sea, providing an easy link to the alluring small towns and villages around here. On the eastern edge of the moor, the traditional seaside resort of **Minehead** is the biggest centre, but the town's main appeal is its range of accommodation, which makes it a useful base for excursions onto the moor, and its proximity to the well-preserved medieval village of **Dunster** with its impressive castle. Minehead also marks the start of the **South West Coast Path**, which offers the best way to get acquainted with Exmoor's seaboard, including Britain's highest cliffs.

Working west along the coast, a string of coastal villages including **Porlock**, **Lynmouth**, **Lynton** and **Oare** make up part of what's known as "**Doone Country**", an indeterminate area that includes some of Exmoor's wildest tracts, and which is now inextricably tied to R.D. Blackmore's tale, *Lorna Doone*. Surprisingly soon after its publication in 1869, this romantic melodrama, based on the outlaw clans inhabiting these parts in the seventeenth century, established itself as part of Exmoor's mythology, and remains so today despite the fact that the book is not as widely read as it once was.

Inland Exmoor lacks any main road running through it, though you'll almost certainly make use of the B3223, B3224 and B3358, which traverse the moor in an east–west direction and which provide access to some of the best walking country. (Drivers, incidentally, should beware of sheep and ponies straying over Exmoor's roads, including the relatively fast coastal A39; after dark you may even find sheep lying down on the tarmac.) Basing yourself at **Dulverton**, on the moor's southern edge and site of the park's main information office, or at **Exford**, at the centre of the moor, you'll be well placed for some of the choicest areas, including such celebrated beauty spots as **Tarr**

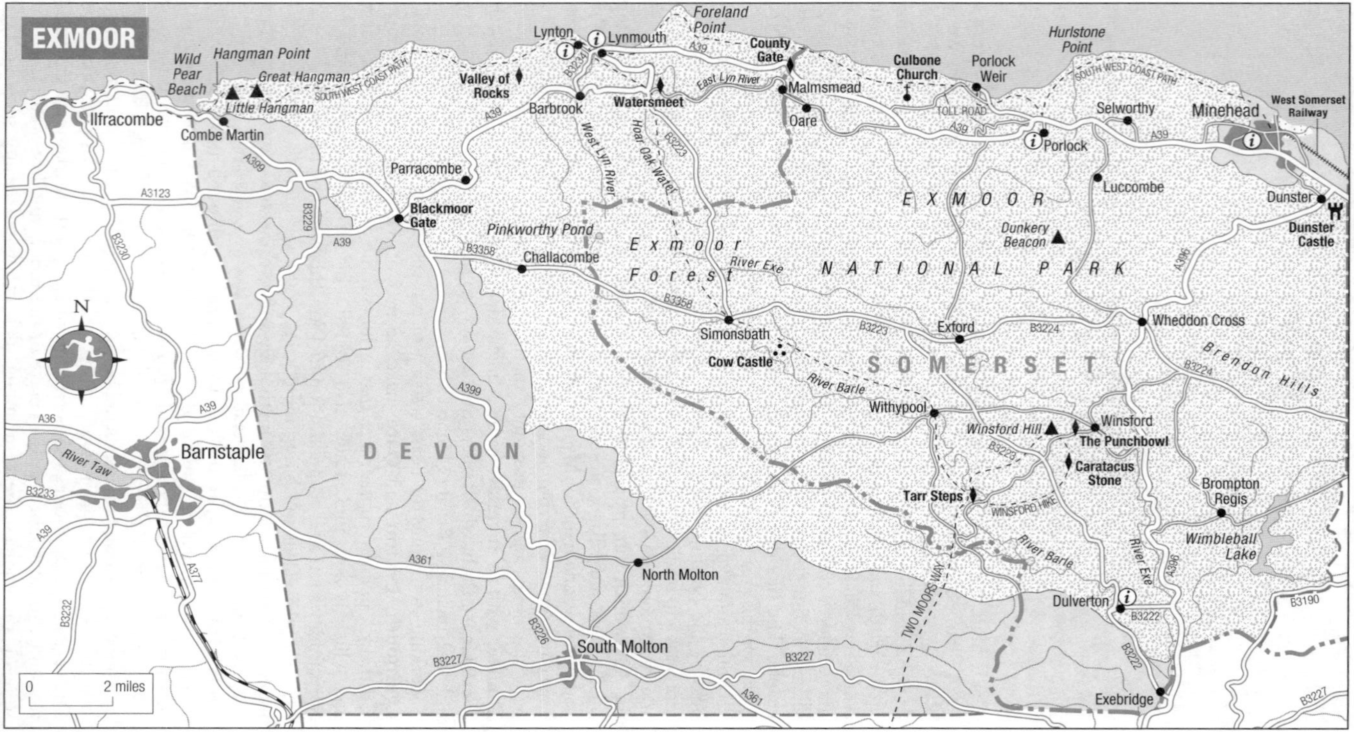

EXMOOR

Wild Pear Beach
Hangman Point
Great Hangman
Little Hangman
SOUTH WEST COAST PATH
Ilfracombe
Combe Martin
Valley of Rocks
Lynton
Lynmouth
Barbrook
Watersmeet
Foreland Point
County Gate
East Lyn River
Malmsmead
Oare
Culbone Church
Porlock Weir
TOLL ROAD
Hurlstone Point
Selworthy
Porlock
Minehead
West Somerset Railway
Luccombe
Dunster
Dunster Castle
Taunton
Parracombe
Blackmoor Gate
West Lyn River
Hoar Oak Water
Pinkworthy Pond
Challacombe
Exmoor Forest
River Exe
EXMOOR NATIONAL PARK
Dunkery Beacon
Simonsbath
Exford
Wheddon Cross
Cow Castle
SOMERSET
Brendan Hills
River Barle
Withypool
Winsford Hill
Winsford
The Punchbowl
Caratacus Stone
Tarr Steps
WINSFORD HIKE
Brompton Regis
Wimbleball Lake
TWO MOORS WAY
River Exe
Dulverton
Exebridge
N
Barnstaple
River Taw
DEVON
North Molton
South Molton
A39
A3123
A399
B3229
B3230
B3358
B3234
B3223
B3224
A396
A36
B3233
A377
A361
A399
B3232
B3226
B3227
B3222
B3190
0 2 miles

Steps and the moor's highest point of **Dunkery Beacon**. Though these rank among the most popular destinations, you'll generally find yourself alone on the moor, except at weekends, when groups of hikers, photographers and hunting and shooting folk descend (incidentally taking up much of the region's accommodation). Be aware that winter, especially, is the time when you'll run into the **organized hunts** for which Exmoor is notorious – at least until the law on hunting with dogs is tightened.

Walking is the most popular recreation activity on the moor. You can pick up good, simple route cards of "Golden Walks" (£1) from Visitor Centres, while the National Park Authority has a full programme of **guided walks** (see box, p.188) for all abilities. See Basics, p.38, for possible hazards walkers may encounter. Stables scattered across the moor provide opportunities for **riding** – we've mentioned the best stables. Despite some serious-looking hills, there are also diverse **cycling** possibilities: see Ⓦwww.activeexmoor.com for details of the 60-mile on-road **Exmoor Cycle Route**. Biketrail Cycle Hire, based at Fremington, near Barnstaple (Ⓣ01271/372586 or 0778/813 3738, Ⓦwww.biketrail.co.uk), rents out bikes and provides a delivery and collection service with free route maps. For more on guided walks, Land Rover safaris and adventure sports on Exmoor, see p.188.

Getting around

Apart from the steam and diesel trains of the **West Somerset Railway** (Ⓣ01643/704996, Ⓦwww.west-somerset-railway.co.uk), which, between late March and early November (plus some dates in Feb & Dec), ply between Bishops Lydeard (with bus connections to the nearby main-line station at Taunton), Dunster and Minehead, **public transport** around Exmoor is limited to a sketchy **bus** network. Connections between Exmoor's coastal centres are fairly regular, but services to small inland villages are sporadic at best. Many lines run in the summer only; all services are greatly reduced in the winter months, and few buses run on Sundays at any time. Service **#398** between Minehead, Dunster, Wheddon Cross, Dulverton and Tiverton runs throughout the year (not Sun). Two useful but limited seasonal services are the **#400** "Exmoor Explorer" vintage bus, which is open-top in fine weather and loops between Minehead, Dunster, Wheddon Cross, Exford and Porlock

Useful Exmoor websites

Ⓦ**www.activeexmoor.com** Useful resource for activities generally, from mountain biking to fly-fishing, as well as events, accommodation, and food and drink.

Ⓦ**everythingexmoor.org.uk** Wide-ranging directory and encyclopedia on all things Exmoor, from adders to youth hostels – though not always up to date.

Ⓦ**www.exmoor.com** Accommodation, attractions, food, drink and events, with links.

Ⓦ**www.exmoor-accommodation.co.uk** Efficient directory of all types of accommodation, including campsites and self-catering, with info on activities and attractions.

Ⓦ**www.exmoorevents.co.uk** Listings for all events from fun runs to country fairs.

Ⓦ**www.exmoor-nationalpark.gov.uk** Official National Park site; reliable and comprehensive.

Ⓦ**www.visit-exmoor.co.uk** Official tourist website, useful for attractions, events and accommodation.

Ⓦ**www.whatsonexmoor.com** General info for such interests as gardens and fishing, plus links for accommodation, weather forecasts, activities and attractions.

(twice daily on Sat & Sun between Easter and late Sept), and **#401**, which connects Dulverton, Tarr Steps, Winsford, Exford, Simonsbath, Watersmeet and Lynmouth (twice daily on Wed & Sun between late July and late Sept). There are also a few once- or twice-weekly community buses connecting Dulverton, Minehead and Lynton. On the coast, the (usually) open-top "Exmoor Coastlink" **#300** connects Lynmouth with Porlock and Minehead daily all year, and with Combe Martin and Ilfracombe daily in summer (late May to late Sept), weekends only in winter, while the **#39** runs hourly between Minehead and Porlock (not Sun).

You can flag down a **bus** anywhere in the national park, providing it is safe for it to stop. If you're planning to use bus services on Exmoor, it's worth checking routes beforehand, as services can be withdrawn or changed, depending on annual local transport budgets. Consider buying a money-saving all-day FirstDay South West pass (£6.70–7.50), valid for travel on services operated by First (Ⓣ01823/272033, Ⓦwww.firstgroup.com), which can be bought on board the buses or from tourist offices. The other main bus company in these parts is Quantock Motor Services (Ⓣ01823/251140, Ⓦwww.quantockmotorservices.co.uk). Traveline (Ⓣ0871/200 2233, Ⓦwww.traveline.org.uk) has full schedules for the whole region.

The Exmoor coast

The thirty-odd miles between Minehead and Combe Martin form Britain's highest section of **coastline**, with cliffs rising to 318m/1043ft. With gentle upper slopes, the hogbacked hills still make for some fairly strenuous hiking if you're following the **South West Coast Path**, and long stretches of woodland add variety to an already diverse landscape. The narrow, stony strips of beach here don't compare with those in other parts of the West Country, but the **sea** is still the central attraction, with an ever-changing shoreline and constant views across the Bristol Channel to the Welsh coast. Tracking the coast, the A39 frequently affords sublime sea views, especially between Porlock and Lynmouth.

Minehead, Somerset's chief resort, lacks much atmosphere but is useful for its accommodation, transport links and proximity to both moor and the medieval wool-town of **Dunster**, a typically genteel and quaint Somerset village crowned by a flamboyant castle, and an appealing place to stay. **Porlock** has a stronger flavour of Exmoor and also makes an attractive base for excursions to places such as **Culbone Church**, deeply hidden in the woods west of the village, and around the Doone Country south of Oare and Malmsmead. West of Foreland Point, there are more terrific walks to be enjoyed from **Lynton** and **Lynmouth** – sibling villages which occupy a niche in the cliff wall with woodland and moorland on all sides. Two of the easiest excursions present Exmoor's most contrasting faces: west to the dramatic **Valley of Rocks** and inland to **Watersmeet**, where two of the moor's rivers merge. Nine miles west, **Combe Martin** marks the edge of the moor and the end of one of the toughest sections of the coastal walk.

Minehead

If you're travelling from the east, **MINEHEAD** may be your first stop on an exploration of Exmoor. This traditional family resort has little in common with the high, windswept moorland, but is useful for its range of shops, services and accommodation. Chiefly characterized by its jaunty promenade and wide sandy beach, **the town** also preserves some residue of its older character, notably in the well-to-do area of **Higher Town** on North Hill, which holds thatched and colourwashed cottages some delightful and offers splendid views across the Bristol Channel. Steep lanes link the quarter with **Quay Town**, the harbour area at Minehead's western end, where a few fishing vessels still operate. If you're here for the **South West Coast Path** (see box below), head down to Quay Street: a brown sign points the way about 100m beyond the harbour.

Practicalities

A terminus for the West Somerset Railway, Minehead's **station** lies at the south end of the Esplanade. The **tourist office** is nearby on the seafront on Warren Road (March–June, Sept & Oct Mon–Sat 10am–5pm; July & Aug Mon–Sat 10am–6pm, Sun 10am–2pm; Nov–Feb 10am–3pm; ⓣ01643/702624, ⓦwww.visit-exmoor.co.uk). You can **rent bikes** from Pompy's, behind the station on Mart Road (ⓣ01643/704077; mountain bikes £14 per day), and access the **internet** at PC Webshop on Tregonwell Road, off the Avenue (Mon–Fri 9am–5pm).

Although Dunster (see below) makes a more appealing overnight stop, Minehead's **accommodation** is generally less expensive. *Kildare Lodge* on Townsend Road (ⓣ01643/702009, ⓦwww.thekildarelodgehotel.co.uk; ⑤) has more character than most: a reconstructed Tudor inn designed by a pupil of Edwin Lutyens and strongly influenced by him, it has a courtyard, garden and comfortable "period" rooms. Attractively located overlooking a tidy public garden midway between the sea and the centre, the friendly *Baytree*, 29 Blenheim Rd (ⓣ01643/703374, ⓔderekcole@onetel.com; closed Nov–March;

The South West Coast Path

Britain's longest National Trail, the **South West Coast Path** begins its journey at Minehead, where a signpost points the way to Poole, Dorset, 630 miles away. Some degree of planning is essential for any walk of more than half an hour or so along the path, and nowhere more so than on Exmoor's coast, where the weather can change abruptly and you can be exposed to driving rain, not to mention disorienting mists. Make a reliable **weather** check before departing by calling the tourist office nearest to the area you're walking in, and carry waterproofs and rations; solid footwear is important, and a compass and good maps are essential – once you've strayed onto the high, featureless moors, one blasted heath looks very similar to another. **Accommodation** needs to be considered too: don't expect to arrive late in the day and find a bed – even campsites can fill to capacity.

The relevant Ordnance Survey **maps** can be found at most village shops en route; for Exmoor you'll need the all-in-one *Explorer* map OL9 (1:25,000) or the *Landranger* maps 180 and 181 (1:50,000). Many local newsagents, bookshops and tourist offices also stock books or pamphlets containing route plans and details of local flora and fauna. Aurum Press and the South West Coast Path Association both publish walking **guides** to the route – for more on these, see Basics, p.25.

no credit cards; ③) is cheaper, offering spacious rooms with private bathrooms, including a family suite – the science fiction author Arthur C. Clarke was born a few doors along at no. 13. By the old harbour and convenient for the start of the coast path, there's the *Old Ship Aground*, a pub on Quay Street with fairly basic en-suite rooms (ⓣ01643/702087; ④).

The local **youth hostel** lies midway between Minehead and Dunster, signposted from the village of Alcombe and pleasantly situated in a secluded combe on the edge of Exmoor (ⓣ0845/371 9033, ⓔminehead@yha.org.uk; from £11.95). Bus #28 from Minehead, Dunster and Taunton stops a mile away at Alcombe. You can **camp** near the coast path at the *Camping and Caravanning Club Site* (ⓣ01643/704138; closed Nov–March), a mile northwest of Minehead's centre, above Higher Town on North Hill. The car-less can save the uphill hike by taking a taxi from the rank on the Parade, near the main bus stop.

Minehead is crammed with **places to eat**, most very mediocre. However, you could do a lot worse than an evening at the *Queen's Head*, on Holloway Street, off the Parade and near the tourist office, a free house with a range of ales and inexpensive menu selections, as well as darts and pool. Drinks and bar meals can also be had at *The Old Ship Aground*. For ploughman's lunches, quiches and pasties, or coffees and cream teas, head up the road to *The Quayside Tearooms*, on Quay Street near the harbour. Also on Quay Street, the *Old Harbour House* offers a range of evening meals and Sunday lunch (ⓣ01643/705917; closed Sun eve & Mon eve; no credit cards;); mains cost £12–16, and there are set-price menus.

Dunster

Three miles southeast of Minehead, **DUNSTER** was an important cloth centre that reached its peak of wealth in the sixteenth century. The well-preserved village's handsome, broad High Street is dominated by the towers and turrets of **Dunster Castle** (castle: mid-March to Oct Mon–Wed & Fri–Sun 11am–5pm; grounds: mid-March to Oct daily 10am–5pm; Nov to mid-March daily 11am–4pm; house and grounds: £7.80, grounds only £4.30; NT). The site was once a Saxon frontier post against the Celts and was rebuilt by the Normans, but almost nothing of these earlier constructions survived the thorough pasting the building received during the Civil War. Inherited by Lady Elizabeth Luttrell in 1376, the property remained in her family for six hundred years until the National Trust took over in the 1970s. It owes its present castellated appearance to a drastic remodelling it received around 1870, though this itself was little more than a veneer on what remains essentially a stately home, predominantly Jacobean within.

Dating back to 1420 and flanked by a pair of squat towers that formed part of the Norman construction, the formidable battlemented **gatehouse** smacks of authenticity, while beyond here, the irregular design of the main building reflects the various changes it has undergone over the years. The highlights of the interior are all seventeenth-century: most obvious is the grand oak and elm **staircase**, magnificently carved with hunting scenes – a recurrent theme throughout the house. Alongside the stags' heads, numerous portraits of the Luttrells gaze across the rooms, including one showing the sixteenth-century John Luttrell wading Triton-like across the Firth of Forth. Much of the furniture and artwork is sixteenth- or seventeenth-century, such as the odd "thrown" chairs of ash, pear-wood and oak in the Inner Hall, and the rare **gilt-leather hangings** in the upstairs Gallery, which vividly depict the story of Antony and Cleopatra. Outside, it's well worth a stroll round the sheltered terraced **gardens**, where oranges and lemons have been growing since 1700 (including what is claimed to be Britain's oldest lemon tree), and there's a renowned collection of strawberry trees. Mimosas and palm trees contribute a subtropical ambience, and picturesque paths lead down to the River Avill. In summer, drama productions and other events are staged in the castle or grounds: for details, call ⓣ01643/821314.

Below the northern gateway of the castle, Dunster village makes a pleasant place for a wander before or after a tour of the house. In the High Street, the octagonal **Yarn Market**, dating from 1609, is the most evocative of a handful of relics of the village's wool-making heyday, its hefty oak rafters in the cone-shaped roof rising above a bare space. From the southern end of the High Street, it's just a few steps to one of the area's finest churches, **St George's**, on the corner of Church Street. Originally a Norman priory church, it has a fine bossed wagon-roof and a magnificent rood screen from about 1500, said to be the longest in the country. Among the tombs of various Luttrells, look out for a group at the top of the south aisle which includes the alabaster floor slab inscribed to Elizabeth Luttrell, from 1493. The sloping chest here is thought to be unique, and was probably used by the Benedictine monks of the priory in the fifteenth century. Behind the church, the sixteenth-century **Tithe Barn** stands opposite a circular dovecote from the same period, kept by the monks – the only people allowed to keep doves as they damaged farmers' crops.

A few yards beyond St George's on West Street, turn down Mill Lane to reach the three-hundred-year-old **Dunster Water Mill** (April–Oct daily 11am–4.45pm; £3.25; NT, though members must pay entry fees), still used commercially for milling the grain which goes to make the flour and muesli sold in the shop. There isn't a great deal to see or do here once you've absorbed the mysteries of milling and viewed the small array of agricultural tools, but the riverside café and garden make a good spot for refreshment. A path along the Avill from the mill soon brings you to **Gallox Bridge**, a quaint packhorse bridge from the eighteenth century surrounded by woods.

Sprouting out of the woods at the northern end of Dunster's High Street, the hilltop **Conygar Tower** is a folly dating from 1776, worth the brief ascent from the Steep for the excellent views. There are also longer walks from here, for which you can get route maps from the tourist office: **Grabbist Hill**, a mile or so west from the village via a path that starts near the school opposite St George's, or eastwards for about a mile to the sandy and rocky **Dunster Beach** – not great for swimming but with a long foreshore that makes an appealing spot for a picnic.

Practicalities

Although Dunster is a stop on the West Somerset Railway, its **station** is inconveniently located a mile north of the village, near Dunster Beach; from Minehead, you're better off using the frequent **buses** #28 and #398 (not Sun).

For **information on Exmoor** generally, seek out the **Exmoor Visitor Centre** (April–Oct daily 10am–5pm, also weekends in Dec & March 11am–3pm; ⓣ01643/821835, ⓦwww.exmoor-nationalpark.gov.uk), by the main car park at the top of Dunster Steep (follow the High Street round to the north), which also houses a free exhibition focusing on the peculiarities of the moor, with hands-on activities and background on the local wool and timber industries and conservation issues. You can also pick up information here on **guided walks** on the moor, and a leaflet for a self-guided walk around the village. **Information on Dunster** is also available at ⓦwww.visitdunster.co.uk.

As for **accommodation**, try *No. 7*, 7 West St (ⓣ01643/821064, ⓦwww.no7weststreet.co.uk; ④), a seventeenth-century cottage offering beamed, en-suite rooms with brass bedsteads, gourmet dinners, and, for hikers, hampers and a drop-off/pick-up service. Alternatively, opt for the *Yarn Market Hotel*, 25–33 High St, Dunster ⓣ01643/821425, ⓦwww.yarnmarkethotel.co.uk; ⑥), a traditional, family-run hotel with attractive rooms – some with four-posters – overlooking the Yarn Market, spacious bathrooms and a restaurant.

Among the twee tearooms **in Dunster**, you'll find quality **eating** at *Reeves*, 20 High St (ⓣ01643/821414; closed Sun eve & Mon, also lunch in winter), a chic restaurant with woody decor, specializing in Modern-British cuisine, and there's a garden; most mains cost £13–19. Alternatively, you can get bar snacks or full meals at the atmospheric *Luttrell Arms*, right by the Yarn Market on the High Street.

Porlock and around

The real enticement of **PORLOCK**, six miles west of Minehead, is its extraordinary position in a deep hollow, cupped on three sides by Exmoor's hogbacked hills. The thatch-and-cob houses and dripping charm of the village's long High Street, with its succession of hotels, cafés, antique shops and stores selling outdoor gear, have led to invasions of tourists. Some are also drawn by the place's literary links: according to Coleridge's own less than reliable testimony, it was a "man from Porlock" who broke the opium trance in which he was composing *Kubla Khan*, while the High Street's ancient *Ship Inn* prides itself on featuring prominently in the Exmoor romance *Lorna Doone* and, in real life, having sheltered the poet Robert Southey, who staggered in rain-soaked from a ramble on Exmoor, and wrote a sonnet here ("Porlock, thy verdant vale so fair to sight..."). Porlock is one end of the **Coleridge Way**, a 36-mile route that takes in a good stretch of the Quantock and Brendon Hills and Exmoor from Coleridge's former home in Nether Stowey. A free leaflet describing the walk is available at the tourist office.

Arrival, information and accommodation

Bus #39 connects Minehead with Porlock and Porlock Weir (not Sun). Porlock's helpful **tourist office** is at West End, at the western end of the High Street (April–Oct Mon–Sat 10am–5pm, Sun 10am–1pm; Nov–March Tues–Fri 10.30am–1pm, Sat 10am–2pm; ⓣ01643/863150, ⓦwww.porlock.co.uk). At the other end of the High Street, you can **rent bikes** from Porlock Cycle Hire (daily 9am–5pm, reduced hours in winter; ⓣ01643/862535), which offers delivery and collection of bikes. Escorted **pony treks** (not Sat) are offered at *Burrowhayes Farm* campsite (see below).

Accommodation

Porlock has some excellent **accommodation** choices, mostly on or around the High Street – though this gets very busy in high season. To escape the crush, head for Porlock Weir (see below). There's a small, central **campsite**, *Sparkhayes Farm* (ⓣ01643/862470), signposted off the High Street near the *Lorna Doone Hotel*, and a better-equipped, more rural site a mile or so southeast at West Luccombe, off the A39, *Burrowhayes Farm* (ⓣ01643/862463, ⓦwww.burrowhayes.co.uk; closed Nov to mid-March).

A walk near Porlock

East of Porlock, the much-photographed double-arched packhorse bridge at **Allerford** makes a starting point for a varied 5-mile circuit. A path leads northwest through the Allerford Plantation and later emerges into the open before reaching **Hurlstone Point**. From there, the coast path climbs southeast onto the rolling moor reaching its highest point at Selworthy Beacon (308m), with a huge view across to Wales and far inland. From there, a choice of tracks leads down into a wooded combe and into the National Trust-owned village of **Selworthy**, a parade of whitewashed thatched cottages, and a church with a notable barrel-vaulted ceiling; at the bottom of the village, a track leads west back down to Allerford.

Andrew's on the Weir Porlock Weir ⓣ01643/863300, ⓦwww.andrewsontheweir.co.uk). This "restaurant with rooms" offers luxurious but unfussy bedrooms with magnificent sea views. The food is renowned, but neither meals nor accommodation are available on Monday and Tuesday. Closed late Dec to late Jan. ⑥

The Gables Doverhay ⓣ01643/863432, ⓦwww.thegablesporlock.co.uk. Classically thatched seventeenth-century cottage near Porlock's museum, with restful rooms, including a family suite, all with bathrooms. A self-catering cottage is also available. No credit cards. ④

Glen Lodge Hawkcombe ⓣ01643/863371, ⓦwww.glenlodge.net. Away from the High St, up Parson's St, you'll find perfect seclusion plus comfort and character at this beautifully furnished Victorian country house. There are distant sea views from the rooms, access to the moor right behind, wi-fi and healthy breakfasts. No credit cards. ⑤

Lorna Doone Hotel High St ⓣ01643/862404, ⓦwww.lornadoonehotel.co.uk. Conspicuously sited on the main drag, this old lodge offers three sizes of rooms, all clean, comfortable and en suite. ②

Sparkhayes Farmhouse Sparkhayes Lane ⓣ01643/862765. Handsome, centrally located seventeenth-century lodging offering tastefully furnished rooms with en-suite facilities, and there's a guests' sitting room. No credit cards. Usually closed Nov–Easter. ③

Local attractions

Porlock's main appeal is its atmosphere and charm, but it does have a specific attraction at the eastern end of the High Street in the form of the **Doverhay Manor Museum** (Easter & May–Oct Mon–Fri 10am–1pm & 2–5pm, Sat 10am–noon & 2.30–4.30pm; free), housed in a fifteenth-century cottage. A couple of cramped rooms show traditional domestic and agricultural tools of Exmoor – including a mantrap – together with some material on the local wildlife and a few photos and portraits, though the most impressive items here are the building's beautiful mullioned window and huge fireplace on the ground floor.

Outside the village, it's worth a brief sortie two miles west along reclaimed marshland to the tiny harbour of **PORLOCK WEIR**, whose sleepy air gives little inkling of its former role as a hard-working port trafficking with Wales. With its thatched cottages and lovely stony foreshore, it's a peaceful, atmospheric spot, giving onto a bay that enjoys the mildest climate on Exmoor. A rambling old pub and a classy restaurant (see p.182) share prime position. Nearby, the **Field Centre** provides everything you might want to know about the natural history of the area (contact Porlock's tourist office for opening details), illustrated by pictures and panels showing the local fauna and flora. An easy two-mile stroll west from Porlock Weir along the South West Coast Path brings you to **Culbone Church** (always open), a tiny church – claimed to be the country's smallest – sheltered within woods once inhabited by charcoal burners.

West of Porlock, the A39 climbs over 400m in less than three miles – cyclists and drivers might prefer either of the gentler and more scenic **toll roads** to the direct uphill trawl, one from Porlock (a right turn off the A39, after the *Ship Inn*; cars £2.50, bikes £1), the other narrower and rougher-going from Porlock Weir (cars £1, bikes free), both passing mainly through woods. Just before the Devon–Somerset border at **County Gate**, the hamlet of **OARE** has another minuscule church, famous in the annals of Lorna Doonery as being the scene of the heroine's marriage, and where she was shot. R.D. Blackmore's grandfather was rector here, and it's likely that the author derived much of the inspiration for his border tale from the local stories told to him on his visits. Accordingly, the surrounding area, particularly Badgworthy Water and the valleys of Lank Combe and Hoccombe Combe, identified as the heart of "**Doone Country**", is rich with echoes of Blackmore's fictional Doone Valley. If you want to explore further, head three-quarters of a mile west to the hamlet of **Malmsmead**, from where you can follow the Badgworthy Water river upstream; Porlock's tourist office can supply a detailed route. **Riding** and **guided walks** in Doone Country as well as camping and self-catering accommodation are offered at Doone Valley Riding Stables, Cloud Farm (ⓣ01598/741234, ⓦwww.doonevalleyholidays.co.uk); turn right at Oare's church and follow the road for about a mile until you come to the clearly marked turning on the left.

Eating and drinking

Porlock's High Street and Porlock Weir have a handful of excellent **eating** options for snacks or complete meals, including some congenial **pubs**. The Big Cheese, on the High Street, is the place for quality picnic ingredients.

Andrew's on the Weir (see p.181), Porlock Weir, Top-notch contemporary cuisine using local ingredients. Lunch and early-evening menus are particularly good value, otherwise main courses cost £15–20. Closed Mon, & Tues, also late Dec to late Jan.

Lorna Doone High St. Known for its Thai curries, among other more domestic dishes (mostly £10–12), and the small bar has real ales. Book for evening meals.

Ship Inn High St. Real ales, bar billiards, darts, skittles and occasional folk evenings are the draw in this old tavern, and the food's not bad either, with main dishes around £10.

Ship Inn Porlock Weir. Crab sandwiches are a lunchtime favourite in this oak-beamed pub, which has a range of other bar food and outdoor tables idyllically sited by the harbour.

Whortleberry Tearoom High St. Drop in to this place for soups and other daytime snacks, and don't miss out on its speciality whortleberry jam, thickly spread on scones and tea-cakes. Closed Mon & Tues.

Lynton and Lynmouth

On the Devon side of the county line nine miles along the coast from Porlock, the Victorian resort of **LYNTON** perches above a lofty gorge with dramatic views over the sea and its sister resort of **LYNMOUTH**, down at sea level. Encircled by cliffs, both places were pretty isolated for most of their history, but struck lucky during the Napoleonic Wars when frustrated Grand Tourists unable to visit their usual continental haunts discovered a domestic piece of Swiss landscape here. Coleridge and Hazlitt trudged over to Lynton from the Quantocks, but the greatest spur to the villages' popularity was the 1869 publication of *Lorna Doone*, which led to swarms of literary tourists in search of the book's famous settings. Most of the present-day visitors are similarly attracted by the natural beauty of the place, while the existence of a number of walks radiating out from here onto Exmoor and along the coast are a major bonus.

Arrival and information

The area's main **tourist office** is in Lynton's town hall on Lee Road (Easter–Oct Mon–Sat 9.30am–5.30pm, Sun 10am–4pm; Nov–Easter Mon–Sat 10am–4pm, Sun 10am–2pm; ⓣ0845/660 3232, ⓦlynton-lynmouth-tourism.co.uk), which also offers **internet access** (£1 for 15min). You'll find a **post office** and a **bank** nearby on Lee Road. Lynmouth has a **National Park Visitor Centre** opposite *Shelley's Hotel* in the Lyndale car park (March Sat & Sun 10am–3.30pm; Easter–Oct daily 10am–1.15pm & 1.45–5pm; ⓣ01598/752509, ⓦwww.exmoor-nationalpark.gov.uk). The office may also be open at weekends and during school holidays in winter.

Accommodation

There is no lack of **hotels and B&Bs** in either of the two villages, with prices usually higher in Lynmouth. You can **camp** next to the West Lyn River at *Sunny Lyn*, Lynbridge (ⓣ01598/753384, ⓦwww.caravandevon.co.uk; closed Nov to early March), halfway between Lynton and Barbrook off the B3234; it's a lovely site, but small so booking is essential. There's an on-site shop and café (closed in low season), and the excellent *Bridge Inn* right next-door.

Riverside Cottage Riverside Rd, Lynmouth ⓣ01598/752390, ⓦwww.riversidecottage.co.uk. Central choice above a busy teashop. The en-suite rooms enjoy river views, and some – costing extra – have balconies (most rooms are in the ⑤ category). ④

Rock House Hotel Harbourside, Lynmouth ⓣ01598/753508, ⓦwww.rock-house.co.uk. Splendidly sited at the harbour entrance, this has smart but smallish rooms, some with four-posters. The pub, restaurant and garden here are popular, so don't expect seclusion. ⑥

Seaview Villa 6 Summerhouse Path, off Watersmeet Rd, Lynmouth ⓣ01598/753460, ⓦwww.seaviewvilla.co.uk. Posh pampering is the main draw at this secluded boutique B&B in a Georgian building that blends contemporary and antique furnishings. Elegant rooms have wi-fi, DVDs and stirring views, and beauty treatments and Exmoor safaris are on offer, as well as sophisticated meals. ⑦

Shelley's Hotel Lynmouth ⓣ01598/753219, ⓦwww.shelleyshotel.co.uk. Smart lodging adjacent to the Glen Lyn Gorge with bright, clean rooms and great views. The owners are friendly, and you can stay in the room supposed to have been occupied by the poet – he apparently left without paying his bill. ⑥

St Vincent Hotel Castle Hill, Lynton ⓣ01598/752244, ⓦwww.st-vincent-hotel.co.uk. Centrally located next to the museum, this whitewashed Georgian house has spacious, tastefully furnished bedrooms, a garden and a great restaurant (see p.185). Closed Nov–Easter. ⑤

Tregonwell 1 Tors Rd, Lynmouth ⓣ01598/753369, ⓦwww.thecaptainshouseinlynmouth.co.uk. Back from the sea and away from the tourist hubbub, this Victorian B&B has a great position overlooking the East Lyn, and period decor. There's a tranquil tea garden in the front. ③

The Turret 33 Lee Rd, Lynton ⓣ01598/753284, ⓦwww.turrethotel.co.uk. One of a row of guest-houses, this friendly, Victorian B&B was built by the same engineer who built the cliff railway. All six spacious rooms are en suite – including the turreted room at the top – or have private facilities. No under-14s. ③

Lynton

Lynton's imposing **town hall** on Lee Road epitomizes the Victorian-Edwardian accent of the village. It was the gift of publisher George Newnes, who also donated the nearby **cliff railway** (mid-Feb to March & early Oct to early Nov daily 10am–5pm; April to mid-June & mid-Sept to early Oct daily 10am–6pm; mid-June to late July & early Sept daily 10am–7pm; late July & Aug 10am–9pm; £2.85 return), which connects Lynton with Lynmouth, 150m below. The device is an ingenious hydraulic system, its two carriages counterbalanced by water tanks which fill up at the top, descend, and empty their load at the bottom. A short distance away, opposite the school on Market Street, one of the oldest

Walks from Lynton and Lynmouth

The major year-round attraction in these parts is **walking**, not only along the coast path but inland. Most trails are waymarked, and you can pick up walkers' maps of the routes from the tourist office or Park Visitor Centre. One of the most popular walks is about two miles eastward, either along the banks of the River Lyn or high up above the valley along the Two Moors Way to Watersmeet (see p.186), itself the starting-place for myriad trails; from Lynmouth, the path starts from the Lyndale car park opposite *Shelley's Hotel*. An easy expedition takes you west out of Lynton along the North Walk, a mile-long path leading to the **Valley of Rocks**, a steeply curved heathland dominated by rugged rock formations. The poet Robert Southey summed up the raw splendour he found here when he described it as "the very bones and skeleton of the earth, rock reeling upon rock, stone piled upon stone, a huge terrific mass". At the far end of the valley, herds of wild goats range free as they have done here for centuries; a short climb up Hollerday Hill yields a terrific view over the whole area.

Lynmouth is the best starting point for coastal walks eastwards, including to the lighthouse at **Foreland Point**, a little over two miles away, via a fine, sheltered shingle beach at the foot of Countisbury Hill – one of a number of tiny coves that are easily accessible on either side of the estuary – while the route west towards Combe Martin (see p.186) traces some of Devon's most majestic and unspoiled coastline.

Further west, the *Hunter's Inn* snuggles in a deep, wooded valley from where you can head north to **Heddon's Mouth Cleave** to join the coast path, which crosses the River Heddon a short way inland. Either direction is amply rewarding for views. Eastwards it contours halfway up the coastal slopes to Woody Bay, where you can climb up and return on a parallel path that wiggles its way round a higher contour. Westwards you can head to Trentishoe Down and the summit of **Holdstone Hill** for a breezy all-round view.

houses in the village – probably early eighteenth-century – holds the **Lyn and Exmoor Museum** (Easter–Oct Mon–Fri 10am–4pm, Sun 2–5pm; £1), holding a motley selection of relics from the locality; the ground floor has a reconstructed Exmoor kitchen from around 1800, and there are displays of history, geology and wildlife upstairs.

Lynmouth

Directly below Lynton, **LYNMOUTH** lies at the junction and estuary of the East and West Lyn rivers, in a spot described by Gainsborough as "the most delightful place for a landscape painter this country can boast". Shelley spent his honeymoon here (see box opposite) – two different houses claim to have been the Shelleys' love-nest – and R.D. Blackmore, author of *Lorna Doone*, stayed in **Mars Hill**, the oldest part of the town, whose creeper-covered cottages are framed by the cliffs behind the Esplanade.

Lynmouth's peace was shattered in August 1952 when nine inches of rain fell onto Exmoor in 24 hours and the village was almost washed away by **flood-waters** raging down the valley. Huge landslips carried hundreds of trees into the rivers, all the bridges in the area were swept away, houses were demolished and 34 people lost their lives. Since the disaster, rumours have circulated regarding one possible cause of the inundation, in particular that secret tests were then being carried out by the Ministry of Defence in the Exmoor area, which involved sending pilots to "seed" clouds with dry ice to make them rain. The story has been denied by the MoD, but the suspicions remain. There are numerous reminders of the tragedy around Lynmouth, the most vivid being the boulders and other rocky debris still strewn about the **Glen Lyn Gorge** (Easter–Oct & school holidays daily 10am to 1hr before dusk; £4), a steep wooded valley through which the destructive torrent took its course. Entered from the main road at the back of the village, the gorge has a deeply tranquil air that makes it difficult to imagine the fury of that stormy night. The walks and waterfalls upstream make ideal picnic-spots, and there are also displays on the uses and dangers of water-power, including a small hydroelectric plant which provides electricity for the local community.

You can ask at the gorge about **boat trips** from Lynmouth harbour with Exmoor Coast Boat Cruises (April–September; ⓣ01598/753207), under the same management as Glen Lyn Gorge. The hour-long excursion to Woody Bay and back allows you to view the abundant birdlife on the cliffs between April and September, and mackerel-fishing trips are also offered (both £10).

Eating and drinking

Lynton has the better choice of **restaurants**. Among local **pubs**, check out *The Crown* on Market Street, Lynton, a former coaching inn that's still at the heart of local life, with real ales, bar snacks, stir fries and other diverse dishes (£8–13), as well as occasional live music.

Esplanade Fish Bar The Esplanade, Lynmouth. Fresh fish and chips, to eat in or take away. Smoothies, cappuccinos and ice creams also available.

The Greenhouse Lee Rd, Lynton ⓣ01598/753358. Large, informal eatery offering everything from teas and coffees to hot crab baguettes and lamb's liver at varying prices.

The Kensington Tea Room 1 Castle Hill, Lynton ⓣ01598/753972. Breakfasts, teas, lunchtime snacks and Sunday roasts are served at this congenial eatery. Stays open for simple evening meals Thurs–Sat in summer. Closed Mon Sept–June.

On the Steps Church Steps, Lynton ⓣ01598/753614. Fresh seafood is the main choice at this upmarket restaurant, including lobster from Lundy, but there are also locally sourced free-range and organic meat dishes, mostly costing £15–20. Closed lunchtime.

Rising Sun Harbourside, Lynmouth ⓣ01598/753223. Atmospheric pub and restaurant serving classic English dishes of lamb, duck and seafood (£10–15) as well as vegetarian options. Gets crowded.

Rock House Hotel Harbourside, Lynmouth ⓣ01598/753508. By the harbour, this has a tea garden, snacks at the bar and meals in its restaurant, where seafood and Exmoor lamb are the specialities (£13–16). Closed Mon–Wed & Sun Oct–Easter.

St Vincent Hotel Castle Hill, Lynton ⓣ01598/752244. The top restaurant in the area is cottage-like, elegant and quite pricey, where such dishes as *escargots* and Bouillabaisse reflect the Belgian roots of its co-owner and chef. Set-price menus are £24 (two courses) and £27 (three courses). Eves only. Closed Mon & Tues, and all Nov–Easter.

Shelley in Lynmouth

In the summer of 1812, Percy Bysshe Shelley, aged twenty, stopped in Lynmouth in the company of his 16-year-old bride Harriet Westbrook, Harriet's sister Eliza, and Dan Healy, their Irish servant. This, Shelley decided, would be the place to establish the commune of freethinking radicals that he had long contemplated. Although this vision never materialized, Shelley used his nine-week stay – in what is now *Shelley's Hotel* (see p.183) – to work on his polemical poem *Queen Mab* and to compose his seditious manifesto, or *Declaration of Rights*, which declared, among other things, that "titles are tinsel, power a corrupter, glory a bubble, and excessive wealth a libel on its possessor". Copies of the *Declaration* were attached to balloons, inserted into bottles launched from Lynmouth's harbour and distributed in nearby Barnstaple (for which Healy was arrested and imprisoned). Now under observation, Shelley and his entourage took flight soon after, hiring a boatman to ferry them to Wales, where the poet continued to work on *Queen Mab*.

Watersmeet and around

The East Lyn River is joined by Hoar Oak Water one and a half miles east and inland of Lynton and Lynmouth at **Watersmeet**, one of Exmoor's most celebrated beauty spots. Try to avoid visiting in peak season or at weekends to see this thickly wooded location at its best. Even without other visitors present, the tranquillity can be utterly transformed after a bout of rain, when the rivers become roaring torrents and the water that is usually crystal-clear is stained brown with moorland peat. Drivers can leave vehicles at a car park (around £1 per hour) off the A39, and follow the path down through oak woods to the two slender bridges where the rivers merge. On the far side of the bridges, the only building in sight is **Watersmeet House** (daily: March & Oct 10.30am–4.30pm; April & May 10.30am–5pm; June–Sept 10.30am–5.30pm; free), an old fishing lodge now owned by the National Trust, which operates a shop and restaurant in summer. There's a pleasant veranda where you can consume teas, salads and soups, and a small exhibition of photos of the 1952 Lynmouth floods in the back.

Watersmeet is surrounded by signposted **paths**, many of which were established as donkey tracks when the local charcoal and tanning industries flourished in the nineteenth century. One short route from the bridge takes you south up Hoar Oak Water to **Hillsford Bridge**, the confluence of Hoar Oak and Farley Water, while the Fisherman's Path leads east along the East Lyn River, climbing and swooping through the woods above one of the river's most dramatic stretches. Another marked route strikes off from the Fisherman's Path after only a few hundred metres, zigzagging steeply uphill to meet the A39, about a mile north of Watersmeet and 100m east of the *Sandpiper Inn*. Opposite the pub, a path leads a quarter-mile north to meet the coast path and gives access to **Butter Hill** which, at over 300m, affords stunning views of Lynton, Lynmouth and the North Devon coast. You can pick up pamphlets with full details about all the various routes at Watersmeet House.

Combe Martin

At the western edge of Exmoor's seaboard, **COMBE MARTIN** has little of the spirit of the moor but has some diversions that merit an hour or two of your time. Sheltered in a fertile valley, the village is famous for its prodigiously long and straggling main street, which follows the combe for about a mile down to the seafront, and holds the unusual *Pack o' Cards Inn*, supposed to have been built by a gambler in the eighteenth century with his winnings from a card game. Originally possessing 52 windows (some were later boarded up), it has four storeys – decreasing in size as they get higher – each with thirteen doors, and chimneys sprouting from every corner; it's now a hotel (see below).

Near the seafront on Cross Street, displays at the **Combe Martin Museum** (Daily: Easter–Oct 10.30am–5.30pm; Nov–Easter 10.30am–1pm; £2.75) illustrate local silver-mining, lime-quarrying, agriculture, horticulture and maritime history.

Follow the High Street down to reach Combe Martin's **beach**, a good swimming spot which is sandy at low tide, with rock pools and secluded coves on either side. A spectacular stretch of coast extends east of Combe Martin, notably round Wild Pear Beach to Little Hangman and Hangman Point, part of the **Hangman Hills**. The waymarked path – a section of both the South

West Coast Path and the Tarka Trail – is signposted off the north end of the car park behind the *Foc's'le Inn*. It's a gruelling route, involving a two-mile uphill slog, with no refreshments to hand, to the great gorse-covered headland of **Great Hangman** – at 318m/1043ft, the highest point on the South West Coast Path. The payback is the incredible panorama, occasionally taking in glimpses of the Gower peninsula in Wales. From here you can retrace your steps back or complete a circle by veering inland round Girt Farm and west down Knap Down Lane to Combe Martin, the whole well-marked circuit adding up to about six miles.

You can find out more details on this route and others at the **tourist office** next to the museum on Cross Street (Easter–June daily 10am–2pm; July–Oct daily 10am–5pm; Nov–Easter Mon–Sat 10.30am–12.30pm; ⓣ01271/883319, ⓦwww.visitcombemartin.co.uk). As for **accommodation**, the *Pack o' Cards Inn* (ⓣ01271/882300, ⓦwww.packocards.co.uk; ④) has more conventional rooms than its appearance might suggest – some with four-posters – and there's a large riverside garden. Nearer the sea, the best place to stay is *Saffron House* on King Street (ⓣ01271/883521, ⓦwww.saffronhousehotel.co.uk; ③), just a few minutes from the beach and with its own heated outdoor pool. If you want a **snack** – baguettes, home-baked bread and cakes, or cold meats – to eat in or take away, or a cream tea, drop in to the *Harbour Deli* on Borough Road (closed Sun). The *Foc's'le Inn*, overlooking the beach off Cross Street, is top choice for a **drink** and also does snacks, which you can enjoy from its outdoor benches.

Inland Exmoor

Watered by 325 miles of river, the upland plateau of inland Exmoor reveals rich swathes of colour and an amazing diversity of wildlife. The cheapest and best way to appreciate the grandeur of the moor is on foot, and endless permutations of **walking routes** are possible along a network of some 600 miles of public footpaths and bridleways. **Pony trekking** is another option for getting the most out of Exmoor's desolate beauty, and stables are dotted throughout the area. **Kayaking** and **mountain biking** are also increasingly popular pursuits. Whichever of these you are pursuing, bear in mind that over seventy percent of the National Park is privately owned and that access is theoretically restricted to public rights of way; special permission should certainly be sought before doing anything like camping or fishing.

There are four obvious bases for excursions: **Dulverton**, in the southeast and connected by bus #25B to Taunton and by #398 to Tiverton and Minehead, makes a good starting point for visiting the seventeen-span medieval bridge at Tarr Steps, about five miles to the northwest; you could also reach the spot from **Winsford** via a circular walk which takes in the prehistoric Wambarrows on the summit of Winsford Hill, and the ancient Caratacus Stone; on the B3224, **Exford** makes a useful base for the heart of the moor; and further west, **Simonsbath** is an excellent starting point for hikes, despite holding only a couple of hotels – Dulverton and Exford have most of inland Exmoor's accommodation.

Organized activities on Exmoor

One of the best ways to enjoy the full range of outdoor activities on Exmoor is as part of an organized group. Park visitor centres can supply a full list, but the most appealing options include the partly off-road **Land Rover tours** to view Exmoor ponies, red deer and other wildlife. The main operators are: Barle Valley Safaris (Ⓣ01643/851386, Ⓦwww.exmoor-barlevalley-safaris.co.uk), which leave from Dulverton, Dunster and Minehead; Exmoor Safari (Ⓣ01643/831229), which start their tours at the *White Horse Inn* in Exford, where you can also book; and Discovery Safaris based in Porlock (Ⓣ01643/863444, Ⓦwww.discoverysafaris.com), leaving from outside Porlock's tourist office (or any other prearranged spot). Excursions generally last 2–3 hours and cost £20–25 per person.

The National Park Authority and other local organizations have also put together a programme of **guided walks**, graded according to distance, speed and duration and costing £3–5 per person depending on the length of the walk. For more details, and for specific schedules, contact any of the park visitor centres or phone the National Park base at Dulverton (Ⓣ01398/323665).

Dulverton

On the banks of River Barle on Exmoor's southern edge, **DULVERTON** is one of the main gateways to the moor, and, as home to the National Park Authority's headquarters, makes a useful port of call before venturing onto the moor. The town is grouped around Fore Street and the High Street, which run parallel from the river towards the hilltop parish church. Fore Street has most of the shops and pubs, plus the post office, a bank with a cash machine and the **Exmoor Visitor Centre** (daily: April–Oct 10am–1.15pm & 1.45–5pm; Nov–March 10.30am–3pm; Ⓣ01398/323841, Ⓦwww.exmoor-nationalpark.gov.uk), which shares premises with the public library at no. 7. The centre has information on the whole moor and, at the back, a small exhibition on life on Exmoor with a film showing aspects of moor-management. Behind the visitor centre, and accessible from it, the **Guildhall Heritage Centre** (Easter–Oct daily 10am–4.30pm; free) has an absorbing museum of the village, including an art gallery, a reconstructed Victorian kitchen and bedroom, and an archive room holding an extensive photographic collection, tapes of oral history and films. The centre also holds regular exhibitions.

With the moor beckoning, you're unlikely to want to linger long in the town itself, but Dulverton does hold a wide spread of **accommodation**, convenient if you plan on doing some walking. Top choices are *Town Mills* (Ⓣ01398/323124, Ⓦwww.townmillsdulverton.co.uk; no under-12s; ⑤), a Georgian millhouse at the bottom of the High Street with good-size, pine-furnished bedrooms, including a family room, and the *Tongdam Thai Restaurant*, 26 High St (Ⓣ01398/323397, Ⓦwww.tongdam.com; ④), which has some small, modern and elegantly furnished rooms upstairs, the best of which has a separate sitting room and a balcony. If you hanker for beams and four-posters, try the *Lion Hotel* in Bank Square (Ⓣ01398/323444, Ⓦwww.lionhoteldulverton.com; ⑤), where rooms 9 and the slightly larger 11 have a nice prospect over the street. A couple of miles north of Dulverton, past the *Rock House Inn*, there are two **camping barns** at Northcombe Farm, with cooking facilities and hot showers but no linen (bed-mats can be rented), charging £8.50 per person per night (Ⓣ01398/323602).

For **food**, it's a choice between the bar menu at the *Lion Hotel*, or the more adventurous fare at *Tongdam Thai Restaurant*, 26 High St (Ⓣ01398/323397), where such dishes as marinated duck and prawn curry cost around £10, and *Woods*, a gastropub at 4 Bank Square (☎01398/324007) serving light lunches and fuller evening meals of organic chicken, lamb and seafood at £12–13 as well as excellent ales. *Lewis's Tea Rooms* on Fore Street serves hot and cold snacks and a range of **cream teas**, best of them the Dulverton (£9.50), including freshly made sandwiches and cake.

Moorland **horseriding** is offered at West Anstey Farm (☎01398/341354), a couple of miles west of Dulverton; there's also a camping barn here. Land Rover safaris leave from Dulverton; see box opposite for details.

Tarr Steps and around

Nestling in the deeply wooded Barle valley five miles northwest of Dulverton, the **Tarr Steps** clapper bridge is one of Exmoor's most tranquil spots. Many prefer to walk here (from Dulverton Bridge, simply follow the riverside track upstream); by road it's a left turn from Dulverton's Fore Street, and another left five miles along the B3223. If you're driving, leave your vehicle in the car park and walk the final 500m downhill, or else you can follow a tributary of the Barle to the bridge signposted from the car park.

Positioned next to a ford, the ancient **bridge** is said to be the finest of its type in Britain, constructed of huge gritstone slabs that are fixed onto piers by their own weight – which can be as much as two tonnes. Over 55m long with seventeen spans, it's normally about a metre above water level – much lower than when originally built due to the river silting up. Floodwaters now frequently cover the bridge, often causing damage – all but one of the slabs were washed away on the night of the 1952 Lynmouth deluge (see p.184). When this happens, however, the stones seldom travel far, and they are now numbered for easy repair; they're also protected by upstream cables that help to arrest flood debris charging down.

The bridge's age has been much disputed, with some claiming prehistoric origins, apparently backed up by the Bronze Age tracks found converging on the crossing, and its name, derived from the Celtic *tochar* meaning causeway. But

▲ Tarr Steps

A walk from Tarr Steps

Tarr Steps makes a great destination on foot from Dulverton or Winsford (a route is detailed opposite), and you can extend the walk by combining it with this exhilarating five-mile circular walk, which takes in Winsford Hill, near Winsford. It's not excessively challenging, and you should be able to complete the circuit in around four hours.

Follow the riverside path upstream from Tarr Steps, turning right about half a mile along Watery Lane, a rocky track that deteriorates into a muddy lane near Knaplock Farm. Stay on the track for three-quarters of a mile until you reach a cattle-grid, on open moorland. Turn left here, cross a small stream and climb up **Winsford Hill** for the 360-degree moorland views and the group of Bronze Age burial mounds (see opposite). If you want a refreshment stop, descend the hill on the other side to the village of Winsford (see below).

A quarter of a mile due east of the Barrows, via any of the broad grassy tracks, the ground drops sharply by over 60m to the **Punchbowl**, a bracken-grown depression resembling an amphitheatre. Keep on the east side of the B3223 which runs up Winsford Hill, following it south for a mile to the Spire Cross junction, where you should look out for the nearby **Caratacus Stone** (see opposite), partly hidden among the gorse. Continue south on the east side of the road, cross it after about a mile, and pass over the cattle-grid on the Tarr Steps road, from where a footpath takes you west another one- and- a- half miles back to the river crossing.

there's no proof of a previous construction to this one, the earliest record of which is from Tudor times. Most now agree that, like the clapper bridges on Dartmoor, it is likely to be medieval. According to legend, however, the bridge was made by the devil as a place to sunbathe. The Prince of Darkness vowed to destroy any creature attempting to cross, and when a parson was sent to confront him he was met by a stream of profanities. When the abuse was returned in good measure, the devil was so impressed he allowed free use of the bridge.

The ancient **woodland** around Tarr Steps largely consists of sessile oak – formerly coppiced for tan bark and charcoal production – and a sprinkling of beech, but you'll also see a mix of downy birch, ash, hazel, wych-elm and field maple, often with a thick covering of lichen. The hazel coppice forms an important habitat for dormice, and you may spot red deer on the riverbanks. Birds breeding hereabouts include redstart, wood-warbler and pied fly-catcher, and you'll probably catch sight of dippers, grey wagtails and kingfishers. There's a choice of **walks** to embark upon, either onto Winsford Hill (see box above); upstream of the river as far as Withypool (4 miles); or downstream to Dulverton. The visitor centre at Dulverton can equip you with itineraries for waymarked circular walks taking in Tarr Steps.

Above the Steps, *Tarr Farm*, a sixteenth-century riverside inn, restaurant and tearoom provides an excellent spot to contemplate the river, and also serves somewhat pricey evening meals, for which you should book (Ⓣ01643/851507, Ⓦwww.tarrfarm.co.uk). Upmarket **accommodation** in modern, fully equipped rooms is available here too (❽; no under-10s).

Winsford

Five miles north of Dulverton, and signposted a mile west of the A396, **WINSFORD** lays good claim to being the moor's prettiest village. A scattering of thatched cottages ranged around a sleepy green, Winsford is watered by a confluence of streams and rivers – one of them the Exe – giving it no fewer than seven bridges. Dominated, as it has been for centuries, by the rambling, thatched *Royal Oak Inn*, the village was the childhood home of the great trade union leader and Labour politician Ernest Bevin (1881–1951) – his birthplace, bearing a plaque, is across from the post office and stores.

Once you've admired the village's obvious charms, the best plan is to abandon them in favour of the surrounding countryside. The obvious walking excursion from the village is the climb up **Winsford Hill**, a heather moor cut through by the B3223 that's reached on foot by taking the Tarr Steps road past the *Royal Oak*; turn off onto the moorland where it turns sharp left after about three-quarters of a mile. About the same distance further west, the hill's round 1400-foot summit is invisible until you are almost there, but once you're at the top, your efforts are repaid by views as far as Dartmoor, and you can clamber around three Bronze Age burial mounds known as the **Wambarrows**. A mile southeast of the summit, near the turning for Tarr Steps, the B3223 runs close to the **Caratacus Stone**, an inscribed monolith thought to date from between 450 and 650 and referred to in medieval documents as the Longstone. It is not immediately easy to spot among the vegetation, though you'll probably pick out the roof of the comic "bus shelter" canopy built over it in 1906. The damaged inscription on the greyish-green monolith, four feet high, reads "Carataci Nepos" – that is, "kinsman of Caratacus", the last great Celtic chieftain who was defeated by the Romans in 46 AD. It's an easy walk from here to Tarr Steps, described in the box opposite.

The *Royal Oak Inn* (ⓣ01643/851455, ⓦwww.royaloak-somerset.co.uk; ❼–❽) is the obvious place for drinks, snacks and full restaurant meals, though the **accommodation** in spacious rooms with four-posters is expensive; the four less appealing rooms in a modern annexe are cheaper (❻). A hundred yards beyond the pub on Halse Lane, *Karslake House* (ⓣ01643/851242, ⓦwww.karslakehouse.co.uk; no under-12s; closed Feb & March; ❺), is a more affordable B&B with quality rooms – all en suite or with private bathrooms – and a relaxed **restaurant** that serves acclaimed three-course dinners (£27 for residents, £29.50 for others); it's open to residents Tuesday–Saturday but to nonresidents on Friday and Saturday

Exmoor wildlife

The establishment of the National Park has done much to protect Exmoor's diverse **wildlife**, from dormice and fritillaries to ravens and buzzards. The management of the coastal heath that makes up most of the terrain has allowed certain species of birds to thrive, while the gorse covering large parts of it has especially favoured the diminutive blue Dartford warbler and the orange-breasted stonechat. Most celebrated of the moor's mammals, though, are **Exmoor ponies**, a unique species closely related to prehistoric horses. Most commonly found in the treeless heartland of the moor around Exmoor Forest, Winsford Hill or Withypool Common, these short and stocky animals are not difficult to spot, though fewer than twelve hundred are registered, and of these only about two hundred are free-living on the moor. You probably won't get close to them, but if you do, don't try to feed them, and bear in mind that their teeth are sharp enough to tear up the tough moorland plants. Much more elusive are the **red deer**, England's largest native wild animal, of which Exmoor supports the country's only wild population. Over the centuries, hunting has accounted for a drastic depletion in numbers, but red deer have a strong recovery rate – about 2500 are thought to inhabit the moor today, and their annual culling by stalking as well as hunting is a regular point of issue among conservationists and nature-lovers. Porlock Visitor Centre (see p.180) organizes "Rutting Weekends" in autumn, a good opportunity to view the deer – advance booking essential.

evenings only. A mile southwest of the village, reached from Halse Lane, *Halse Farm* **campsite** (ⓣ01643/851259, ⓦwww.halsefarm.co.uk; closed Nov to late March) is not very well sheltered but has good facilities and, located on the edge of the moor, is convenient for walkers.

Exford

At an ancient crossing point on the River Exe, **EXFORD**, four miles northwest of Winsford, preserves an insular air, its sedate cottages and post office ranged around a tidy village green. A part of the Royal Forest of Exmoor from Saxon times until the early thirteenth century, Exford prospered as a junction for packhorse trains carrying wool and cloth. During the nineteenth century, it grew as a **sporting centre** and today, as the base of the Devon and Somerset Staghounds, local life is intimately involved with the **hunt**, particularly during the long season, which lasts from early August to late April. The village is also popular with walkers for the hike to **Dunkery Beacon**, Exmoor's highest point at 1704ft/518m (map ref SS891415); a four-mile hike to the northeast, the route is clearly marked along a track that starts from Combe Lane, just past the post office (turn right at the end of the playing fields). The bridleway here eventually becomes a rough track, which winds slowly round to the summit of the hill – a steady uphill trudge. A substantial cairn sits at the top, from where a majestic vista unfolds, with lonely moorland all about and South Wales often visible; there's also easy access by car, with a road passing close to the summit.

Hunting on Exmoor

For many, outdoor sports on Exmoor means hunting and shooting, practices which have been at the heart of local communities for centuries. Shooting mainly takes place between September and January, but **hunting** can go on all year – though mostly in winter – and plays a large part in the lives of many of Exmoor's inhabitants. Socially, too, the institution is central, since most hunts have full calendars of events. The voice of local hunt supporters is loud and clear: the **Countryside Alliance** (ⓦwww.countryside-alliance.org) pro-hunting lobby has strong support and "Fight Prejudice" stickers are evident everywhere,

In contrast, the true number of local **opponents** to the hunt will never be known – few want to risk taking a stand in Exmoor's close-knit communities. Alongside the cruelty argument, the two reasons most often cited for opposing hunting are the damage caused to farmland and gardens by dogs and horses, and the chaos created by the hunt followers – many of them city-folk – whose cross-country manoeuvrings can block up roads and show scant regard for either countryside or property. The National Trust's ban on stag-hunting on its land has added more fuel to the debate, since it has virtually ended the practice in many places.

What cannot be denied is the heavy dependence of Exmoor's economy – more than most other hunting areas in Britain – on the sport, not least in such villages as Exford, home to the kennels and stables of the Devon and Somerset Staghounds. If you're looking for a quiet time in these parts, you're best off keeping your views on the matter to yourself, since feelings run high.

You can find out about meets of the Devon and Somerset Staghounds in the local press where they are advertised (as are the hunt's puppy and horse shows, point to point races and other summer events). For the case against hunting, see the **League Against Cruel Sports**' website ⓦwww.league.org.uk.

It's common for the various hunters, walkers, shooters and fishers who frequent these parts to fill all of Exford's relatively wide range of **accommodation**. Sporty types are most evident in the two large inns that dominate the village: the impressively timbered and ivied *White Horse Inn*, by the bridge (ⓣ01643/831229, ⓦwww.exmoor-whitehorse.co.uk; ❼), and the more exclusive but equally old-fashioned *Crown Hotel* (ⓣ01643/831554, ⓦwww.crownhotelexmoor.co.uk; ❼), where rooms have dark furnishings and large bathrooms. Backing onto the village green on Chapel Street, the friendly *Exmoor Lodge* (ⓣ01643/831694, ⓦwww.exmoor-lodge.co.uk; no credit cards; ❷) is a considerably cheaper alternative, a B&B with small, plain, mostly en-suite rooms, and lots of local information on hand. Exford holds the moor's main **youth hostel**, a large, gabled Victorian house near the river (ⓣ0845/371 9634, ⓔexford@yha.org.uk). Most rooms have four to six beds (from £10), and family rooms and camping pitches are also available. Two and a half miles northwest of the village, beyond Edgcott, *Westermill Farm* (ⓣ01643/831238, ⓦwww.exmoorcamping.co.uk) provides a tranquil **campsite** in grass paddocks on the banks of the Exe. There are free hot showers and waymarked walks over the five-hundred-acre farm, plus a small, seasonal shop selling local meat. Apart from tent pitches, self-catering cottages are available.

Exford's two inns provide the village's main **restaurants**: the *Crown* has a bar menu as well as classy and quite expensive dishes such as roast loin of venison, while the *White Horse* has basic bar meals popular with walkers, hunters and hostellers, alongside a pricier restaurant menu. Both inns also serve afternoon teas.

Exmoor Forest and Simonsbath

At the centre of the National Park, **Exmoor Forest** is the barest part of the moor, scarcely populated except by roaming sheep and a few red deer – the word "forest" denotes simply that it was formerly a hunting reserve. It's also one of the moor's wettest and boggiest zones – walkers should carry waterproofs whatever the weather, and take note of local weather reports. In the middle of the area, and just over five miles west of Exford on the B3223, the village of **SIMONSBATH** (pronounced "Simmonsbath") consists of little more than a couple of hotels, a pottery and a sawmill at a crossroads between Lynton, Barnstaple and Minehead on the River Barle. The village was home to Midlands ironmaster John Knight, who purchased the forest in 1819 and, by introducing tenant farmers, building roads and importing sheep, brought systematic agriculture to an area that had never before produced any income. The Knight family also built a wall round their land – parts of which can still be seen – as well as the intriguing dam at Pinkworthy (pronounced "Pinkery") Pond, part of a scheme to harness the headwaters of the River Barle, though its exact function has never been explained.

Paths radiate from Simonsbath across epic moorland, for which park visitor centres can supply walking itineraries. One easy waymarked route starts from opposite the *Exmoor Forest Hotel* and leads through Birchcleave Wood, running more or less parallel to the Barle for a couple of miles to **Cow Castle**, site of an old hillfort, and four miles further to Withypool. In the opposite direction, you can follow the River Barle upstream from Simonsbath for about four miles to the dark, still waters of **Pinkworthy Pond** – keep a lookout for red deer drinking here in summer. If you don't want to walk all the way, the B3358 passes within a couple of miles of the lake.

There are a couple of good **accommodation** options here: *Simonsbath House Hotel* (Ⓣ01643/831259, Ⓦwww.simonsbathhouse.co.uk; no under-12s; ❻), former home of the Knight family and now a cosy bolt hole offering plush guest rooms with glorious moorland views, as well as self-catering cottages in a converted 350-year-old barn, and the *Exmoor Forest Inn* (Ⓣ01643/831341, Ⓦwww.exmoorforestinn.co.uk; closed Mon & Tues Jan to mid-Feb; ❺), with plain but adequate en-suite rooms and space for free **camping**. The bar at the *Inn* is good for quaffing local ales and serves meals for around £10 (closed Mon, also Sun eve Nov–March). Alternatively, treat yourself to a quality repast at the formal **restaurant** at *Simonsbath House Hotel*, where three-course dinners that might include guinea fowl and venison cost £35. In a converted barn next door, *Boevey's* (closed eves and all Dec–Jan) provides coffees, crusty rolls, pastas and other snack lunches (around £8), as well as **internet** access.

You'll find a pair of classic country **pubs** with real ales and excellent food further afield; one, the *Poltimore Arms* – renowned for its fish pie – lies a couple of miles southwest of Simonsbath at Yarde Down, on the Brayford road, while the award-winning *Black Venus* is at Challacombe, five miles west on the edge of Exmoor.

Travel details

Trains

Minehead to: Bishops Lydeard (4–8 daily; 1hr 15min); Dunster (4–8 daily; 6min). Service runs late March to early Nov.

Buses

Combe Martin to: Barnstaple (Mon–Sat 5 daily; 1hr–1hr 15min); Ilfracombe (Mon–Sat 1–2 hourly, Sun 3 daily; 20min); Lynmouth (late May to late Sept 3 daily, late Sept to late May Sat & Sun 2 daily; 1hr); Lynton (late May to late Sept 3 daily, late Sept to late May Sat & Sun 2 daily; 40min).

Dulverton to: Exford (Mon–Sat 2 daily; 40min); Minehead (Mon–Sat 6 daily; 1hr–1hr 20min); Winsford (Mon–Sat 2 daily; 25min).

Dunster to: Dulverton (Mon–Sat 6 daily; 50min–1hr 15min); Minehead (3–4 hourly; 10min); Winsford (Mon–Sat 2 daily; 50min).

Exford to: Dulverton (Mon–Sat 2 daily; 40min); Minehead (Mon–Sat 2–4 daily, also late May to late Sept Sun 2 daily; 45min–1hr); Porlock (late May to Sept Sat & Sun 2 daily, also late July to late Aug Tues & Thurs 2 daily; 35min); Winsford (Mon–Sat 2 daily; 15min).

Lynmouth to: Barnstaple (Mon–Sat 3 daily; 1hr 10min); Combe Martin (late May to late Sept 3 daily, late Sept to late May Sat & Sun 2 daily; 1hr); Ilfracombe (late May to late Sept 3 daily, late Sept to late May Sat & Sun 2 daily; 1hr 20min); Lynton (Mon–Sat 1–2 hourly, Sun 2–3 daily; 15min); Minehead (3–4 daily; 55min); Porlock (3–4 daily; 35min).

Lynton to: Barnstaple (Mon–Sat 10–11 daily; 55min); Combe Martin (late May to late Sept 3 daily; 40min); Ilfracombe (late May to late Sept 3 daily, late Sept to late May Sat & Sun 2 daily; 1hr); Lynmouth (Mon–Sat 1–2 hourly, Sun 2–3 daily; 15min).

Minehead to: Dulverton (Mon–Sat 6 daily; 55min–1hr 25min); Dunster (3–4 hourly; 10min); Exford (Mon–Sat 2–4 daily, also late May to late Sept Sun 2 daily; 45min–1hr); Lynmouth (3–4 daily; 55min); Porlock (Mon–Sat 2 hourly, Sun 3 daily; 15–20min); Porlock Weir (Mon–Sat every 2hr; 25min); Taunton (1–2 hourly; 1hr 10min); Winsford (Mon–Sat 2 daily; 55min).

Porlock to: Exford (late May to Sept Sat & Sun 1 daily, also late July to late Aug Tues & Thurs 1 daily; 1hr 35min); Lynmouth (3–4 daily; 35min); Minehead (Mon–Sat 1–2 hourly, Sun 3 daily; 15–20min); Porlock Weir (Mon–Sat every 2hr; 7min).

Winsford to: Dulverton (Mon–Sat 2 daily; 25min); Dunster (Mon–Sat 1–2 daily; 45min); Exford (Mon–Sat 1–2 daily; 15min); Minehead (Mon–Sat 1–2 daily; 55min).

7

North Devon and Lundy

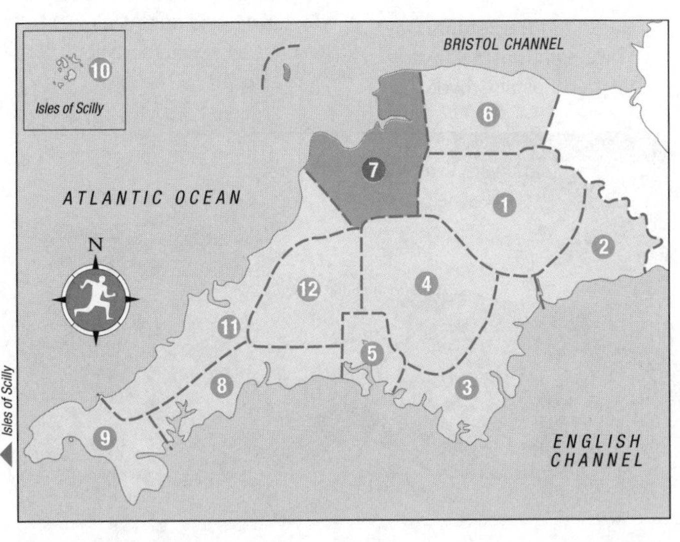

CHAPTER 7

Highlights

* **Barnstaple Pannier Market** The biggest of Devon's ancient covered markets offers a few bargains alongside the local craftwork and produce. See p.200
* **The Tarka Trail** This long walking and cycling route provides the ideal way to explore North Devon's coast and interior. See p.200
* **Surfing in Barnstaple Bay** Wave enthusiasts flock to the beaches at Croyde, Woolacombe and Saunton for Devon's best surf. See pp.202–203
* **A stroll through Appledore** The narrow lanes of this old port have an almost Mediterranean flavour, terrific estuary views and a brace of worthy sights. See p.209
* **Lundy Island** The ultimate escape, this flat splinter of land is broadside on to the Atlantic and dotted with unusual accommodation. See p.217

▲ Riding the Tarka Trail

7

North Devon and Lundy

Extending east from Exmoor to the Cornish border, the North Devon region encompasses a motley range of landscapes from banal beach resorts and picture-postcard villages to savage, wind-lashed rockscapes. Apart from a few pockets of more intense activity, it's a tranquil, unhurried region, less touristy than Devon's southern coast. The chief town, **Barnstaple**, at the end of a branch line from Exeter, is a good place to get started, with extensive transport connections and good accommodation and eating options. From here it's an easy run to some of Devon's best beaches, at **Croyde**, **Woolacombe** and **Saunton Sands**, all hugely popular with surfers. **Ilfracombe**, on the other hand, is a traditional tourist resort with strong Victorian trappings; to the east, the hilly seaboard stretching as far as the Exmoor coast (see Chapter 6) provides a strenuous but stimulating hiking route.

Enjoying a fine site on the Torridge River, the robust working town of **Bideford** is mainly a transit centre, with some decent accommodation and bus connections to all the towns on Bideford Bay. Easiest to reach is **Appledore**, sheltered in the mouth of the Torridge estuary. Inland, **Great Torrington** makes a good stop for walkers or bikers following the **Tarka Trail** (see box, p.200), which passes through some of the region's loveliest countryside. West of Appledore, **Westward Ho!** has a magnificent swathe of sand to compensate for the ugly holiday developments. The coast along the furthest reaches of Bideford Bay is dominated by cliffs, where the quiet hamlet of **Buck's Mills** and the tourist honeypot of **Clovelly** cling to the steep slopes amid thick woods. If you're put off by the crowds and artifice of the latter, follow the bay round to stormy **Hartland Point** at Devon's north-western corner, an intensely rural area well off the beaten track, and offering bracing cliff walks southwards as well as the more temperate appeal of Hartland Abbey. For remoteness, though, you can't do better than **Lundy Island**, a tract of wilderness in the middle of the Bristol Channel that makes a great bolt hole for a night or two, and affords tremendous views of England, Wales and, westwards, the Atlantic Ocean.

You'll find a wealth of **information** on North Devon at Ⓦwww.northdevon.com. The region has a good network of **public transport**; as well as the Tarka Line rail connection between Exeter and Barnstaple, bus routes cover most places – the most useful services are detailed in this chapter, and you can get

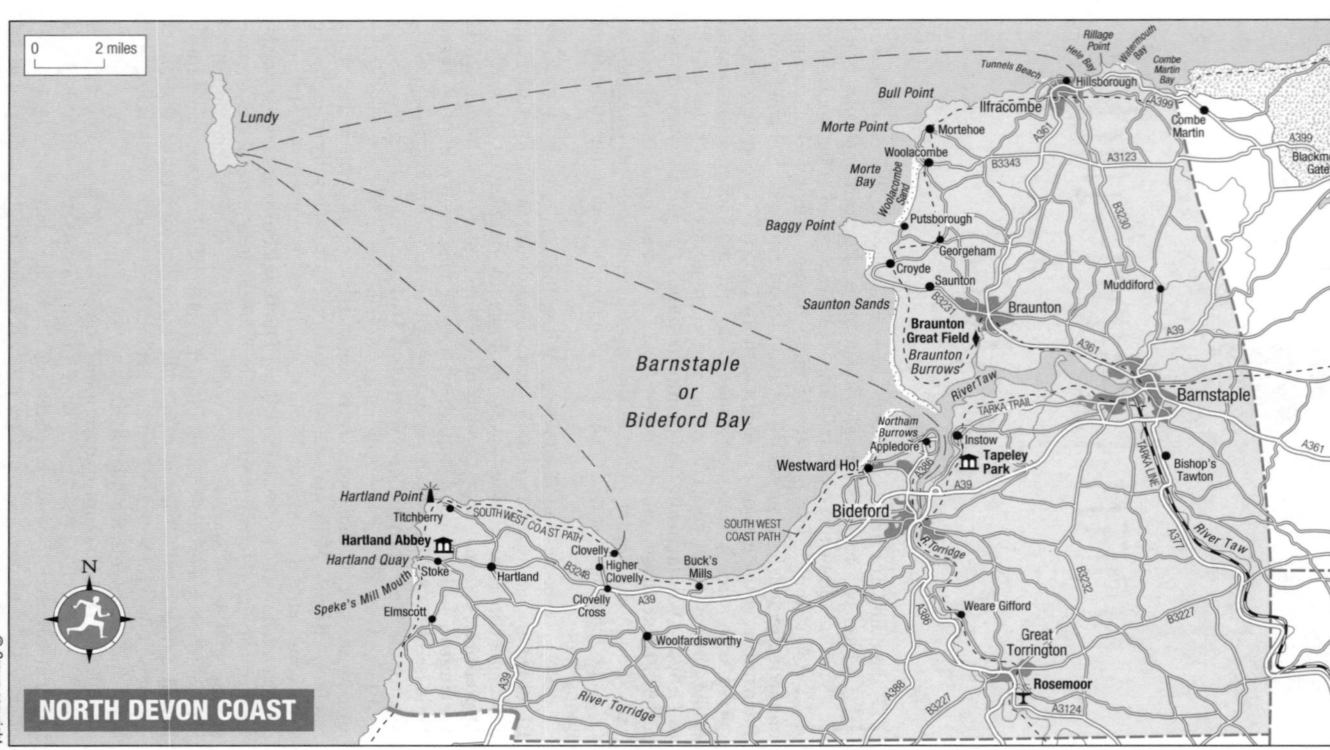
NORTH DEVON COAST
0 2 miles
N
Lundy
Barnstaple
or
Bideford Bay
Tunnels Beach
Hele Bay
Rillage Point
Watermouth Bay
Combe Martin Bay
Hillsborough
Ilfracombe
Bull Point
Combe Martin
Blackmoor Gate
A399
A3123
A361
B3343
B3230
Morte Point
Mortehoe
Woolacombe
Morte Bay
Woolacombe Sand
Putsborough
Baggy Point
Georgeham
Croyde
Saunton
Saunton Sands
B3231
Muddiford
Braunton
Braunton Great Field
Braunton Burrows
A39
River Taw
TARKA TRAIL
Barnstaple
Northam Burrows
Appledore
Instow
Tapeley Park
Westward Ho!
A386
Bishop's Tawton
TARKA LINE
A377
River Taw
Bideford
R. Torridge
SOUTH WEST COAST PATH
Hartland Point
Titchberry
Hartland Abbey
Hartland Quay
Stoke
Speke's Mill Mouth
Hartland
Elmscott
B3248
Clovelly
Higher Clovelly
Buck's Mills
Clovelly Cross
Woolfardisworthy
B3232
Weare Gifford
B3227
Great Torrington
Rosemoor
A3124
A388
River Torridge

more information from Traveline at ⓣ0871/200 2233, ⓦwww.traveline.org.uk. **Surfers** can check conditions at all the local beaches at ⓦwww.eyeball-surfcheck.co.uk.

Barnstaple

At the head of the Taw estuary, **BARNSTAPLE** has been North Devon's principal town since at least Norman times. Its significance as one of the rare ports on this coast was largely lost in the nineteenth century, however, when the river silted up, preventing large ships from docking, though smaller vessels still come to load up with sand (used for ballast). The local Taw and Torridge river-mouths have also provided large quantities of the red clay used in the famous **pottery** that has been produced in the Bideford and Barnstaple area since the thirteenth century, and was exported to Wales, Ireland, Northern Europe and the New World by the early seventeenth century. The local **Barum ware** enjoyed a further boost when it received Queen Victoria's patronage in 1885 – fine examples can be seen in the **Museum of North Devon**. Pottery-making has nothing like the same role nowadays, though the town retains its status as the region's chief administrative and commercial centre.

Arrival and information

Barnstaple's **train station** is on the south side of the Taw, a five-minute walk from the centre, where the **bus station** sits between Silver Street and Belle Meadow Road. There's a small but well-informed **tourist office** in the Museum of North Devon (Mon–Sat 9.30am–5pm; ⓣ01271/375000, ⓦwww.staynorthdevon.co.uk), covering the whole North Devon area including the Devon side of Exmoor; there's also a free **left-luggage** facility there (no bags can be left overnight). You can **rent bikes** from Tarka Trail Cycle Hire at the train station (April–Oct daily; ⓣ01271/324202, ⓦwww.tarkatrail.co.uk). Access the **internet** at the library on Tuly Street, where the first thirty minutes are free (then £1.50 for 30min), though you may have to wait for a terminal. The library is open from 9 or 9.30am until 7pm Monday, Tuesday and Friday, until 1pm Wednesday, until 5pm Thursday and until 4pm Saturday.

Accommodation

There's not a great choice of **accommodation** in town, but advance booking should secure a room in one of the best places.

Broomhill Art Hotel Muddiford ⓣ01271/850262, ⓦwww.broomhillart.co.uk. Set in lush countryside two miles north of Barnstaple and signposted off the A39, this place is a striking combination of gallery, restaurant and hotel, where the en-suite rooms overlook an impressive sculpture garden. A two-night minimum stay with half-board is required Fri & Sat. The frequent #30 and #301 Barnstaple–Ilfracombe buses (not Sun) stop outside. No credit cards. ❺

Mount Sandford Landkey Rd ⓣ01271/342354. A couple of miles southeast of the centre, this Georgian guesthouse is packed with flowers both inside and in the lovely garden, which all of the spacious en-suite rooms overlook. From the museum, follow Taw Vale, New Rd and Newport Rd, which leads to Landkey Rd. No credit cards. ❸

The Old Post Office 22 Pilton St ⓣ01271/859439, ⓦwww.theoldpostoffice-pilton.co.uk. Half a mile north of the centre, this elegant Georgian B&B has two rooms: one en-suite double, which overlooks the garden, and one at the front with private bathroom. Breakfasts are mainly free range and organic. No credit cards. ❺

The Old Vicarage Barbican Terrace, ⓣ01271/328504. Central but quiet B&B with period features and a great garden about half a mile southeast of Long Bridge, on the corner of Eastern Ave (the main A361 Tiverton road). The spacious rooms have fridges and broadband access, but may suffer from traffic noise. ❸

Royal and Fortescue Hotel Boutport St ⓣ01271/342289, ⓦwww.royalfortescue.co.uk. This plush Victorian hotel is one of Barnstaple's most central choices, right by the museum, and has surprisingly cheap room-only rates. It bustles with activity on the ground floor – where there's a bar, café and restaurant – but is quieter upstairs. ❹

Yeo Dale Hotel Pilton Bridge ⓣ01271/342954, ⓦwww.yeodalehotel.co.uk. Prominently sited near the River Yeo, on the main A39 Ilfracombe road, this place has smart and clean rooms – variously sized and reasonably priced – with or without bathrooms. ❺

The Town

Remote from the region's other main centres, Barnstaple has developed a very separate identity from Devon's south-coast towns, though reveals surprisingly little of great age or interest. Its centuries-old role as a marketplace for local foodstuffs, however, is perpetuated in the daily bustle around the huge timber-framed **Pannier Market**, off the pedestrianized High Street – the model for similar structures throughout North Devon. The market offers antiques (Wed), arts and crafts (Thurs April–Dec) and general goods and fresh local produce (Mon April–Dec, also Tues, Fri & Sat) – Friday is the liveliest day, attracting people from throughout the region. Alongside the market runs **Butchers Row**, a few of its 33 archways still holding butcher's shops.

Between the High Street and Boutport Street, which curves round to meet the High Street at its southern end, a grassy area holds Barnstaple's **parish church**, with its curiously twisted "broach" spire – octagonal, rising from a square tower. Close by lies the fourteenth-century **St Anne's Chapel**, an oddly shaped, part-battlemented building converted into a grammar school in 1549 and later numbering John Gay (1685–1732), author of *The Beggar's Opera*,

The Tarka Line and the Tarka Trail

Rated by some as one of the finest pieces of nature writing in the English language, Henry Williamson's *Tarka the Otter* (1927) has been enthusiastically adopted as a promotional device by North Devon's tourist industry. Partly set in the Taw valley, the book has lent its name to the **Tarka Line** – the scenic Exeter–Barnstaple rail route that follows the Taw for half its length – which itself forms part of the **Tarka Trail**, a 180-mile route that tracks the otter's wanderings in a giant figure-of-eight centring on the town of Barnstaple. For walkers and cyclists, the trail, marked by an otter's-paw symbol, makes an excellent way to get around as well as obtain a close-up look at the wildlife of the Taw estuary. To the north, the Tarka Trail penetrates Exmoor, then follows the coast back along the cuttings and embankments of the old Barnstaple–Ilfracombe rail line, passing through Williamson's home village of **Georgeham** on its return to Barnstaple. South, the path takes in Instow and Bideford, following the disused rail line to Meeth and continuing as far as Okehampton before swooping up to Eggesford, from where the Tarka Line covers the route back to Barnstaple. Tourist offices issue a free leaflet with a route map covering the whole trail.

The 21 miles of the Tarka Trail that follow former rail lines are ideally suited to **bicycles**, and there are rental shops at Barnstaple (see p.199), Bideford (see p.208), Braunton (see p.202) and Great Torrington (see p.211). Space for 2–6 bikes is available on Tarka Line trains, for which advance booking is recommended: call First Great Western (ⓣ08457/000125) at least two hours before departure.

among its pupils; it's now closed to the public unless on a guided tour (for which, apply to **Barnstaple Heritage Centre**, see below, or the council office at Barum House, The Square, opposite the tourist office).

On the riverbank at the end of Boutport Street, the lively miscellany of militaria, nature and pottery at the **Museum of North Devon** (Mon–Sat 9.30am–5pm; free) is well worth taking in. The ground floor illustrates local wildlife, focusing on the ecosystems of North Devon's estuaries and coastline, but there's more gripping material upstairs, where a room is devoted to **Barum ware**, the colourful work created by C.H. Brannam's studio, featuring lurid lizard and fish designs in greens and ochre-reds. You can also see examples of sgraffito, a traditional North Devon technique achieved by scratching through the slip to show the red clay underneath. Other first-floor rooms display war memorabilia – uniforms, flags, guns – connected to the Devonshire regiment and the Royal Devon Yeomanry, formed two centuries ago to protect the coast from Napoleon.

From the museum, you can pass under Long Bridge – the main crossing over the Taw – to reach, a couple of hundred yards west along the riverside, Queen Anne's Walk, a florid and colonnaded building built in the eighteenth century as a merchants' exchange and now housing the **Barnstaple Heritage Centre** (April–Oct Mon–Sat 10am–5pm; Nov–March Mon–Fri 10am–4.30pm, Sat 10am–3.30pm; £3.50), a survey of the town's history from Saxon times. Costumed mannequins, reconstructions of a medieval market and a ship's hold, and displays relating to the town during the Tudor, Stuart and Civil War eras entertainingly tell the story, and there are sections on John Gay and the Huguenot refugees who settled in Barnstaple during the seventeenth century (one of whose number married Samuel Pepys). Both the museum and Heritage Centre are on the **Tarka Trail**, allowing for a pleasant riverside stroll or cycle further afield.

Eating and drinking

With a couple of exceptions, Barnstaple's **restaurants** are nothing to write home about, but the following places have a good atmosphere and serve inexpensive or moderately priced food. You can also pick up simple snacks in and around the Pannier Market.

Kafé Karumba 10 Holland Walk, off High St. You'll find a cosy, contemporary ambience here, where you can order panini, pastries, a range of coffees and good smoothies. Closed eves & Sun.

Old Custom House The Strand ⓣ01271/370123. Intimate bistro with Modern-British dishes such as duck, pork and ragout of shellfish (£14–18). Good-value lunchtime snacks cost £4 each. Closed Mon lunch & Sun.

Old School Coffee House Church Lane. In a building dating from 1659 and located near St Anne's Chapel, this tearoom has oodles of traditional atmosphere and serves morning coffees, teas and inexpensive light lunches including pies and toasted sandwiches for £4–5. Closed eves & Sun.

Owl Vegan Café 1 Maiden St. Simple veggie and vegan café offering such predictables as nut roast, lentil bake and bean casserole, all for under £6. Special diets catered for, and wi-fi and board games available. Closed eves & all Sun.

Riverfront Café The Strand. By day, sandwiches, pizzas, pastas and cream teas are served in this bright modern building next to the Heritage Centre; in the evening, come here for drinks. There's outdoor seating in summer to enjoy the view over the river. Closed eves Sun–Wed.

Terra Madre Muddiford ⓣ01271/850262. North of town, and part of the *Broomhill Art Hotel* (see p.199), this relaxed place specializing in Mediterranean-style cuisine lays on bar snacks as well as delicious set-price three-course lunches (£14) and evening meals (£19). Live jazz evenings with tapas usually take place the first Wed of the month (book ahead). Closed Mon, Tues & Sat all day, open eves Fri & Sat. No credit cards.

Croyde and around

Eight miles west of Barnstaple, village gentility collides with youth culture at **CROYDE**, a cosy huddle of cottages alongside a leat, or channelled stream, that empties into the sea half a mile away at **Croyde Bay**.

Arrival and information

Bus #308 (not Sun in winter) travels from Barnstaple via Braunton and Saunton to Croyde. The **tourist office** in Braunton, on Caen Street (Easter–Nov Mon–Fri 10am–4pm, Sat 10am–2pm, also Sun 10am–2pm late July to early Sept; Dec–Easter Mon–Fri 10am–3pm; ⓣ01271/816400, ⓦwww.brauntontic.co.uk), covers the whole area. Braunton is also the place to **rent bikes**, from Otter Cycle Hire on Station Road (March–Nov; ⓣ01271/813339).

Accommodation

Booking ahead is essential for all of the **accommodation** in the Croyde Bay area. Croyde has the area's biggest selection, though **Georgeham**, up the road makes a pleasant alternative. Most of the **campsites** in the area are seasonal, and fill up quickly.

B&Bs

Breakers Rock Hill, Georgeham ⓣ01271/891169, ⓦwww.breakersgeorgeham.com. Excellent surfers' B&B close to the *Rock Inn*, with a nice garden for barbecues, and boards and wet suits to rent. No credit cards. ④

Bridge Farm Jones's Hill ⓣ01271/890422. Right at the centre of the village, and close to the beach, this thatched farmhouse with three large rooms is often booked up. The same people run *The Orchard* campsite. No credit cards. ④

Home House St Mary's Rd ⓣ01271/891259, ⓦwww.homehousecroyde.co.uk. Surfer- and family-friendly thatched, B&B with a contemporary makeover, ten minutes from the beach. ⑤

Kittiwell House St Mary's Rd ⓣ01271/890247, ⓦwww.relaxincroyde.co.uk. At the top end of the road, this thatched, sixteenth-century inn has sleigh beds and sunken baths, and has self-catering units. No under-10s. ⑥

Parminter St Mary's Rd ⓣ01271/890030, ⓦwww.parminter.co.uk. Beside the stream, this friendly place has three large rooms (one can be a family room) in two tastefully converted barns. No credit cards. ⑤

Campsites & hostel

Baggy's Surf Lodge Moor Lane ⓣ01271/890078, ⓦwww.baggys.co.uk. Clean and friendly hostel right above the beach, with four bunkrooms (£25 per person) and four doubles (⑤), mostly with great views; prices include breakfast. There's a café, free wi-fi and surfboard and wet-suit hire.

Bay View Farm ⓣ01271/890501, ⓦwww.bayviewfarm.co.uk. Five minutes from the centre of Croyde at the southern end of the village, this grassy, family-friendly campsite has good facilities, but it's expensive, and requires minimum-length stays at peak periods. Booking is only possible for weekends (and then at least a month ahead). No groups or credit cards. Closed mid-Oct to Easter.

The Orchard St Mary's Rd ⓣ01271/890422. Facilities are pretty rough-and-ready in this small,

Surfing in Croyde

You can **rent surf equipment** from stalls on Croyde's beach in summer, otherwise try Le Sport on Hobbs Hill, Croyde, open all year (but weekends only Oct–Easter); board and wet suit cost £12 for half a day, £18 for the whole day. **Tuition** is provided between April and October by Surf South West, in the Burrows Beach car park on the right-hand (northern) side of the bay (ⓣ01271/890400, ⓦwww.surfsouthwest.co.uk). For the latest on **local surf conditions**, check out the **surf reports** at ⓦwww.A1surf.com. A useful website for accommodation and other facilities in Croyde, including sea conditions, is ⓦwww.croyde-bay.com.

GoldCoast Oceanfest

The annual **GoldCoast Oceanfest** takes place around the third weekend of June in Croyde Bay, featuring a range of water- and beach-sports competitions; surfing looms large, but there's also volleyball and mountain biking as well as live music and workshops. See ⓦwww.goldcoastoceanfest.co.uk for info and tickets (around £35 for the weekend; book early).

sloping field, but it's cheaper than most sites hereabouts. You'll find it behind the post office in the centre of Croyde. No groups, telephone bookings or credit cards. Usually open all year.

Surfer's Paradise Sandy Lane ⓣ01271/890671, ⓦwww.surfparadise.co.uk. Superbly placed campsite next to the beach, but expensive, and with very basic facilities. Can be raucous. No electric hook-ups or telephone bookings. Closed Sept to mid-July.

The village

Backed by grassy dunes, the firm, sandy beach here has retained its secluded, undeveloped appeal, enhancing its role as a favourite **surfing** spot (it's lifeguarded May–Sept 10am–6pm). Drivers can park to the north of the sands at the bottom of Moor Lane, an equally good spot from which to explore the **Baggy Point** headland at the top of Croyde Bay. Here, the vertical cliffs are inhabited by nesting birds and, from September to November in particular, a swirl of gannets, shags, cormorants and shearwaters. In clear weather, you can see round Bideford Bay to Hartland Point, while out to sea lies the flat silhouette of Lundy Island.

South of Croyde, surfing is much in evidence at **Saunton Sands**, a very long strand magnificently exposed to long ranks of breakers. Extending behind the beach are the substantial sand dunes and mud flats of **Braunton Burrows**, the core of a UNESCO-designated Biosphere Reserve where the flora and aquatic birdlife are managed according to a sustainable programme of conservation, research and education. Constituting the largest sand dune system in England, the bleak area is interwoven with walking trails; the coastal path cuts right across, and you can also get here along quiet signposted lanes from the Tarka Trail, which passes through **BRAUNTON**, three miles inland. This small town is notable mostly for **Braunton Great Field**, a 340-acre area to the west of the Velator level-crossing that's one of the few remaining open-field systems surviving in the country. It's still strip-farmed according to medieval methods, the strips divided by grass balks, or ridges. You can view the field – and Braunton Burrows – from Braunton Beacon, at the top of West Hill.

A mile inland of Croyde, the pretty hamlet of **GEORGEHAM**, a scattering of thatched and beflowered cottages around a typical Devon church, holds Skirr Cottage, where **Henry Williamson** wrote *Tarka the Otter*. He's buried in the churchyard of St George's.

Eating and drinking

Food choices are fairly unexciting hereabouts. Bar snacks and full meals are served at Croyde's **pubs**, though these get fairly busy in summer and at weekends all year – Georgeham's inn has more character.

The Blue Groove 2 Hobbs Hill, Croyde ⓣ01271/890111. There's a young, funky ambience here in low season and at night, but it gets pretty overwhelmed at peak times. The menu ranges from salads, burgers and smoothies to Mexican pancakes and Massala mussels (£10–14); alternatively, just drop by for a beer in the evening. Closed mid-Oct to Easter.

The Manor St Mary's Rd, Croyde. Mainstream pub and restaurant at the top of the road, with a games room and outdoor seating. You can munch on baguettes or hot bar meals costing around £10.
The Rock Rock Hill, Georgeham ⓣ01271/890322. Traditional and highly popular local, with real ales, excellent bar meals and a conservatory. Booking recommended for evening meals.
Sands Café-Bar Saunton ⓣ01271/891288. Part of the *Saunton Sands Hotel*, this makes a great stop for freshly cooked food all day, with superb views, and mains at around £13. There's also a terrace bar, and the hotel's main, formal restaurant (ⓣ01271/890212) is a good venue for Sunday lunch. Closed Dec–Feb, limited opening in winter.
The Thatch 14 Hobbs Hill, Croyde. This pub is a buzzing surfers' hangout, with live music at weekends.

Woolacombe and around

North of Baggy Point, the pick of the beaches in **Morte Bay** is **Putsborough**. It's quieter and less crowded than **Woolacombe Sand**, the broad expanse stretching northward from here, which is very popular with surfers and families alike at its far end. Though splendidly positioned at the bottom of a valley, **WOOLACOMBE** lacks charisma, and amounts to little more than a collection of hotels, villas and retirement homes; things get animated in summer, but there's a rather drab feel at other times. The Blue Flag-awarded beach, of course, is the main attraction, and the surrounding coastline holds equal appeal. At its northern end, Morte Bay is bracketed by **Morte Point**, an area of grass and gorse that's good for walking, below which stretches a rocky shore whose menacing sunken reef inspired the Normans to give it the name Morte Stone. A break in the rocks makes space for pocket-sized **Barricane Beach** (signposted), famous for the tiny tropical shells washed up here from the Caribbean by Atlantic currents, and a favourite swimming spot. Walkers can take in the splendid rock contortions hereabouts by continuing a mile or so beyond Morte Point to **Bull Point**, where a lighthouse warns ships off the fractured reefs tapering away out to sea.

Practicalities

Buses pull in right by Woolacombe's seafront. On the Esplanade, the **tourist office** (Easter–Oct Mon–Sat 10am–5pm, Sun 10am–3pm; Nov–Easter Mon–Sat 10am–1pm; ⓣ01271/870553, ⓦwww.woolacombetourism.co.uk) has information on the coast from Saunton Sands to Ilfracombe, and offers **internet access** at £1 per 15 minutes. You can log on in more comfort at the *Eyeball* café on Barton Road. Several shops near the beach rent and sell **surf gear**.

Running downhill to the sand, Beach Road holds most of the **accommodation**, including *The Rocks Hotel* (ⓣ01271/870361, ⓦwww.therockshotel.co.uk; ➎), a surfer-friendly four-storey place close to the beach, with high-spec bedrooms and bathrooms and a breakfast room in the style of an American diner, complete with jukebox. Higher up the road, there's *Sandunes* (ⓣ01271/870661, ⓦwww.sandunesbedandbreakfast.co.uk; no credit cards; ➎), where the en-suite rooms are bright and modern, two of them with a large balcony. About a mile north of Woolacombe at Mortehoe, seek out *Victoria House*, an upmarket B&B overlooking Grunta Beach on Chapel Hill, (ⓣ01271/871302, ⓦwww.victoriahousebandb.co.uk; no credit cards; ➐); the rooms all have terrific sea views – one, the Beach House, has its own terrace – and healthy breakfasts include freshly baked bread.

The nearest **campsite**, *Woolacombe Sands Holiday Park* (ⓣ01271/870569, ⓦwww.woolacombe-sands.co.uk; closed Nov–Easter), lies a two-field uphill walk from the beach and has sea views and a two- or three-night minimum stay at weekends. However, with all the razzmatazz of heated indoor and outdoor pools, nightly entertainments in season and other organized amusements, you might prefer the relative peace of *North Morte Farm* (ⓣ01271/870381, ⓦwww.northmortefarm.co.uk; closed Oct–Easter), a five-minute walk from the pubs of Mortehoe village and 500m from the coast path and the rock-and-sand beach of Rockham Bay; it has an unsheltered camping area with electric hook-ups, a good shower block and panoramic views, and static caravans are available for weekly rent. About a mile inland, on the Georgeham road, *Little Roadway Farm* (ⓣ01271/870313; closed Dec–Easter) is a simple and cheap site, one of the few hereabouts that accepts groups (though groups, families and couples are all separated).

Just up from the beach, surf dudes and others congregate at the *Red Barn*, a **bar** and **restaurant** with a rank of surfboards in the roof, offering good beers, snacks and grills (£7–14). Next to the tourist office on the Esplanade, *The Boardwalk* (ⓣ01271/871115; reduced hours in winter and closed Dec to mid-Feb) is a quieter spot for teas, coffees, panini and pizzas, with fresh seafood dishes in the evening on set-price menus (£18–21). Off South Street, *The Courtyard* (ⓣ01271/871187; closed Nov–Easter, also Mon & Tues Easter–June & Oct) has a more refined feel, serving a small but toothsome selection of local meat and seafood; there are good lunchtime and early-evening deals (£13.50–16.50), otherwise mains cost around £13. Behind the *Red Barn* on Beach Road, the stylish *Bar Electric* has snacks, comfy chairs and beach views from its terrace, a mellow spot for summer evenings (closed Mon & Tues for food).

Ilfracombe and around

Squeezed between hills and sea five miles east of Morte Point, **ILFRACOMBE** is North Devon's most popular resort. With large-scale development restricted by the surrounding cliffs and outcrops, the town is essentially little changed since its evolution into a tourist destination in the nineteenth century, since when it has established itself as a full-on family resort. More recently, while continuing to draw elderly groups and the bucket-and-spade brigade, Ilfracombe has started to attract the surfer crowd and a hipper image, symbolized by the modernistic twin white chimneys of the **Landmark Theatre** on Wildersmouth Beach. The resort goes into overdrive in summer, when the relentless pressure to have fun and the ubiquitous smell of chips can become oppressive – though, as the chief attractions lie in the surrounding area, this shouldn't impinge too much.

Arrival and information

Buses #3 and #301 (not Sun) from Barnstaple, #31 (#302 on Sun) from Woolacombe, #30, #301 (neither on Sun) and #300 (weekends only in winter) from Combe Martin, and #300 (weekends only in winter) from Lynton all stop near Ilfracombe's harbour on Broad Street, at the bottom of the High Street and its continuation Fore Street. If you're planning to return by bus from a coastal hike, note that services can finish early and that few run on Sunday. By the Landmark Theatre on the seafront, the **tourist office** (Easter–Oct daily 10am–5pm; Nov–Easter Mon–Fri 10am–5pm, Sat 10am–4pm; ⓣ01271/863001, ⓦwww.visitilfracombe.co.uk) can provide bus timetables as well as selling tickets for coaches, trains and the boat for Lundy. You can log on to the **internet** at the library at the Candar, off Sommers Crescent, below Fore Street (Mon–Sat 9.30am–1pm, also Mon & Fri 2–5pm, Tues & Thurs 2–6.30pm); the first thirty minutes are free, then £1.50 per thirty minutes.

Accommodation

Ilfracombe has a good choice of **accommodation**, though space can be scarce in summer. There's a great **campsite** on cliffs outside town listed below; alternatively, try the sites around Morte Point (see p.204).

Inglewood Guest House Highfield Rd ⓣ01271/867098, ⓦwww.inglewoodhouse.co.uk. Above the High St, this Victorian B&B boasts panoramic sea views from most rooms – all are en suite. Home-cooked evening meals by arrangement. No credit cards. ❸

Little Meadow Lydford Farm ⓣ01271/862222, ⓦwww.littlemeadow.co.uk. Friendly, low-key campsite 3 miles east of Ilfracombe off the A399, and connected by footpath to Watermouth Castle and the beach. There are exhilarating sea views and a pub within walking distance. Book well ahead in summer. No credit cards. Closed Oct–Easter.

Ocean Backpackers 29 St James Place ⓣ01271/867835, ⓦwww.oceanbackpackers.co.uk. Excellent independent hostel centrally positioned near the bus station and harbour. A favourite with surf enthusiasts, it has a drying-room for wet suits, surf DVDs to watch and a decent kitchen. Dorm beds are £12.50–14, double rooms £35.

Sherborne Lodge Hotel Torrs Park ⓣ01271/862297, ⓦwww.sherborne-lodge.co.uk. Roomy Victorian villa close to Tunnels Beach on the western side of town, with a bar and dining room. ❹

Tracy House Belmont Rd ⓣ01271/863933. Also on the western side of town, a few minutes from the High St, this characterful old building stands within an acre of walled garden and has five en-suite rooms. Closed late Sept to Jan. ❸

The Town

Best appreciated outside the peak season, Ilfracombe's genuine appeal focuses on its compact **harbour**, protected by the grassy mound of Lantern Hill. Surmounting this headland, the fourteenth-century **St Nicholas Chapel** once offered refuge to pilgrims en route to Hartland Abbey (see p.216) and was later used as a lighthouse. There's usually some low-key fishing activity on the quayside, where crab and lobster are hauled up, and in summer it's the departure point for cruises to Lundy (see p.217), coastal tours and fishing trips, all bookable here. A former lifeboat house on the harbourside now holds **Ilfracombe Aquarium** (daily: mid-Feb to Easter 10am–3.30pm; Easter–June 10am–4.30pm; July & Aug 10am–5.30pm; Sept & Oct 10am–4pm; call ⓣ01271/864533 for winter opening; £3.50; ⓦwww.ilfracombeaquarium.co.uk), displaying a variety of denizens of rivers and seas in recreated watery habitats, from stream to rock pool and ocean.

Away from the harbour, next to the Landmark on Wilder Road, make time to visit the superlative **Ilfracombe Museum** (April–Oct daily 10am–5pm; Nov–March Tues–Fri 10am–1pm; £2.50), once a hotel laundry room, now crammed with photos and Victoriana relating to the area, alongside plenty of material about the local wildlife; there are giant stuffed gulls, thousands of butterflies, moths and beetles in cases and a small section devoted to Lundy Island. Many of the items were originally collected by the museum's founder, Mervyn G. Palmer, who had worked in London's British Museum and travelled extensively in Central and South America before settling in Ilfracombe in 1930.

West of the centre, past Wildersmouth Bay, rocky **Tunnels Beach** takes its name from the two tunnels bored through the cliffs by Welsh miners in the nineteenth century – still the main means of access. Privately owned (roughly open 9.30/10am–6/7pm; £1.95 for all-day entry; ⓦwww.tunnelsbeaches.co.uk), the Blue Flag beach has a protected rock bathing pool at low tide. Surfers will be more interested in the long, west-facing strands at Woolacombe (see p.204).

Above the seafront, the High Street and its continuation Fore Street hold most of the shops, as well as one curiosity at 6 High St, **Walker's Chocolate Emporium** (Mon–Sat 9am–5pm; free; ⓦwww.chocolate-emporium.co.uk), a shop specializing in quality confectionery handmade on the premises; upstairs there's a chocolate museum and a café selling a range of hot chocolates and luscious sweet snacks. Sugar-, gluten- and dairy-free products are also sold.

The town's best collection of antiques and paintings lies a mile east of the centre, off the A399 Combe Martin road, where you can join an hour-long guided tour of **Chambercombe Manor** (Easter–Oct Mon–Fri 10.30am–5.30pm, Sun noon–5.30pm, also Sat in July & Aug noon–5.30pm; £7; ⓦwww.chambercombemanor.org.uk). Although parts of this whitewashed huddle of buildings around a cobbled courtyard originate from the eleventh century, the furnishings are mostly Elizabethan and Jacobean. Highlights of the tour are the bedroom supposedly occupied for one night by Lady Jane Grey, and a next-door hidden chamber where a dummy recalls the skeleton of a young woman discovered here in 1865 – her dead body had apparently been secretly sealed in the room two hundred years earlier by a "wrecker" who, having stripped the valuables from a victim of a shipwreck that he had brought about, discovered that the corpse was that of his own daughter. The four acres of lovely gardens and woods are an added incentive to visit.

Outside town, one of Devon's loveliest coastal walks extends east towards Combe Martin (see p.186); it involves a stiff ascent up to the grassy heights of **Hillsborough**, about a mile from the centre, which offers a perfect prospect over Ilfracombe. Beyond, **Hele Bay**, its deep waters almost encircled by cliff, is the first of a sequence of undeveloped coves and inlets surrounded by jagged, slanting rocks and heather-covered hills. **Rillage Point** offers the occasional seal sighting, while the first-class sand beach at **Watermouth Bay**, three miles east of Ilfracombe (reachable on buses #30, #33, #300 and #301), is protected by yet more dramatic cliffs and rocky outcrops. Above the bay, the imposing, castellated **Watermouth Castle** (Mon–Fri & Sun: Easter to late July & Sept 10.30am–5.30pm, last admission at 3pm; late July & Aug 10am–6.30pm, last admission at 3.30pm; £12; ⓦwww.watermouthcastle.com), dating from the nineteenth century, is best admired from the outside – unless you have kids, who will appreciate the gnomes, dungeons and water rides.

Eating and drinking

Aside from Ilfracombe's most famous **restaurant**, *The Quay*, you'll find a succession of enticing eateries on Fore Street, a couple of minutes' walk from the harbour. For a quiet drink or bar meal, head for *The George and Dragon* near the bottom of the street, the oldest **pub** in town.

La Gendarmerie 63 Fore St ⓣ01271/865984. Ex-Victorian police station converted into a smart brasserie, with a select menu of Modern-European dishes (£14–17) and a relaxed ambience. Closed Mon and lunchtimes except Sun lunch in winter, also closed Tues in winter.

The Genie High St. Located in The Lantern community centre, this congenial café serves inexpensive salads, rolls and other snacks, and has internet access. Closed eves & all Sun.

Maddy's 26 St James Place. Award-winning fish and chips just steps away from the harbour.

The Quay 11 The Quay ⓣ01271/868090, ⓦwww.11thequay.co.uk. For its harbourside location as much as for its food, a meal here is the highlight of a visit to Ilfracombe. Co-owned by artist Damien Hirst (some of whose works are on display), the restaurant has mainly Mediterranean dishes using local ingredients (£16–20), for example roasted black bream and Devon beef fillet; a six-course summer tasting menu costs around £50 without drinks, while a Sunday roast comes to under £10. You can also order drinks and snacks in the more relaxed ground-floor area; the more formal rooms upstairs overlook beach and harbour to either side. Closed Sun eve, Mon & Tues.

Bideford

Serenely spread out along the west bank of the River Torridge, the estuary town of **BIDEFORD** formed an important link in the North Devon trade network. The long, tree-lined quayside retains its role as the town's focal point today, while the most conspicuous reminder of its former mercantile importance, **Long Bridge**, still straddles the broad expanse of the Torridge. First built around 1280, the bridge was reconstructed in stone in the following century and subsequently reinforced and widened – hence the irregularity of its 24 arches, no two of which have the same span.

From the Norman era until the eighteenth century, the port was the property of the Grenville family, whose most celebrated scion was **Sir Richard Grenville**, commander of the ships that carried the first settlers to Virginia, and later a major player in the defeat of the Spanish Armada. Grenville also featured in *Westward Ho!*, the historical romance by Charles Kingsley who wrote part of the book in Bideford and is thus commemorated by a statue at the quay's northern end. Behind it, extending up the riverbank, **Victoria Park** contains guns captured from the Spanish in 1588. Backing onto the park on Kingsley Road, the **Burton Art Gallery and Museum** (Mon–Sat 10am–4pm, Sun 11am–4pm, closes 5pm Mon–Fri July–Sept; free; Ⓦwww.burtonartgallery.co.uk) exhibits paintings from the eighteenth century to modern times and has regular exhibitions. Craftwork is also represented, including examples of the local slipware – once prized even more highly than that of Barnstaple. The museum section focuses on local personalities including Richard Grenville, and on such trades as lime-burning, saddlery, and glove- and collar-making; items on display include the original town charter sealed by Elizabeth I in 1583, and a scale model of Long Bridge at every stage from its beginnings to the present day. The gallery's *Café du Parc*, with outdoor tables in summer, makes a good refreshment stop.

At the other end of town, in Market Place, Bideford's **Pannier Market** is a diminutive version of the one in Barnstaple, open for crafts and produce on Tuesdays and Saturdays until 2 or 3pm. On the far side of Long Bridge, **East-the-Water** holds Bideford's disused station, where a converted carriage serves as an information point for the **Tarka Trail**, which runs alongside the river on this side.

Practicalities

All **buses** stop on Bideford Quay, at the north end of which the **tourist office** is located within the **Burton Art Gallery and Museum** and has the same hours (see above; Ⓣ01237/477676; Ⓦwww.torridge.gov.uk). You can buy day-return boat tickets to Lundy Island (see p.217) here – also available from the main ticket office on the quayside. You can **rent bikes** from Bideford Bicycle Hire, Torrington Street, 150m south of the bridge (open daily; Ⓣ01237/424123, Ⓦwww.bidefordbicyclehire.co.uk).

Bideford's best **accommodation** choices include the friendly *Cornerhouse*, 14 The Strand (Ⓣ01237/473722, Ⓦwww.cornerhouseguesthouse.co.uk; no credit cards; ④), two minutes from Victoria Park, which offers four rooms with shared bathrooms, and, further out on Northdown Road but linked to the centre by a footpath, the Georgian *Mount* (Ⓣ01237/473748, Ⓦwww.themountbideford.co.uk; ⑤), set in its own walled gardens, with elegant rooms, a separate lounge for guests and free wi-fi. You'll also find good options in nearby Appledore and Instow (see opposite).

For **food and drink**, check out the *Energy Bar*, 45a Mill St (closed eves & Sun), for nutritious snacks and smoothies; *Cafecino Plus*, 26 Mill St

(Ⓣ01237/473007; closed Mon eve & all Sun), a lively café/bistro with courtyard seating offering snacks as well as more elaborate dishes such as Moroccan lamb and roast duck (£10–13), or the much fancier *Lathwells*, 4 Cooper St (Ⓣ01237/476447; closed lunchtime & all Sun–Tues), just up from the Quay, a relaxed **restaurant** serving local meat and seafood, including excellent grilled lamb skewers (£13–19).

Appledore

The area's maritime heritage is more evident a couple of miles downstream at **APPLEDORE**, near the confluence of the Taw and Torridge rivers (bus #2 or #16 from Bideford's Quay, #2 from Barnstaple). This quaint old port is home to England's last purely commercial shipbuilder, providing one of the few North Devon industries entirely independent of tourism, though its future is uncertain, with liquidation looming, threatening mass redundancies locally. With most of the yards out of sight, however, the pastel-coloured Georgian cottages and placid quayside combine to lend the town a harmonious air, which extends to the tiny back lanes climbing above the quay. A few minutes' walk up Meeting Street or Bude Street, the **North Devon Maritime Museum**, housed in a typically elegant villa on Odun Road (Easter–April & Oct daily 2–5pm; May–Sept Mon–Fri 11am–1pm & 2–5pm, Sat & Sun 2–5pm; £1.50), gives an absorbing insight into the town's seafaring past and into maritime matters generally. The ship's figurehead, cannon and anchors arrayed outside give a good idea of the contents within: mainly roomfuls of salvaged equipment, along with photos and models, and an assortment of oddities from shipwrights' tools to mud shoes.

From Appledore's quayside, you can join **fishing trips** and estuary and river **cruises** between May and September (around £12 for two hours, £15 for three); look into Liz's Shop or The Quay Gift Shop on the Quay, or call Ⓣ01237/471033 for information and tickets.

Practicalities

Appledore has a very comfortable **B&B**, just off the seafront at 9 Myrtle St: *Raleigh House* (Ⓣ01237/459202, Ⓦwww.appledorebandb.co.uk; no credit cards; ❺), which has just one double bedroom available, with an en-suite bathroom and a private sitting room. Alternatively, you can enjoy magnificent views from the front rooms of the plain *Seagate Hotel*, The Quay (Ⓣ01237/472589, Ⓦwww.seagatehotel.co.uk; ❺), though back-facing rooms are slightly cheaper.

Moderately priced **meals** are available at the *Seagate*, but you'll find a far pleasanter ambience at either of the two traditional **pubs** on Irsha Street, at the northern tip of Appledore, where the *Royal George* and *Beaver Inn* share tranquil panoramic views across the estuary and serve good fish dishes – and the *Beaver* has live music every Saturday. *Schooners*, a **deli** at 25 Market St offers soups, pasties and other inexpensive items to eat in or take away.

Instow and around

On the eastern side of the Torridge estuary, **INSTOW** has an even calmer feel than Appledore. Stretching into the distance, and broadening to a muddy flat at low tide, the sandy beach – chosen by the US army for D-day rehearsals during World War II – is backed by a long quay dating from the seventeenth century.

There are a couple of good pubs and restaurants here, but Instow's main appeal is its understated charm.

A mile south of Instow and three miles north of Bideford, on the east bank of the Torridge, the ten acres of gardens at **Tapeley Park** (Easter–Oct Mon–Fri & Sun 10am–5pm; £4; Ⓦwww.tapeley-park.co.uk) were created in the nineteenth century by Sir John Belcher. The Italianate lawns overlooked by palm trees and topiary descend in ornamental terraces to a lake surrounded by huge Thuja-Plicata trees, the oldest of their kind in the country. There's an ilex tunnel; a brick, igloo-shaped Ice House; a Shell House plastered with broken shells and conches; and a walled kitchen garden. The red-brick, much-altered Queen Anne house (open only to groups) has been the home for three centuries of the Christie family – John Christie was the moving spirit in setting up Glyndebourne Opera, in Sussex in 1934. The present owner has given the place a New Age direction, with an ongoing project to make the estate entirely self-sufficient. Events and exhibitions take place throughout the summer, for which consult the website.

Practicalities

If you want to **stay** in Instow, try *Lovistone Cottage*, a charmingly furnished B&B on Antsey Way, at the southern end of the village and very close to the Tarka Trail (Ⓣ01271/860676, Ⓦwww.lovistone.co.uk; no credit cards; ❹), or the *Wayfarer Inn*, Lane End Road, off Marine Parade (Ⓣ01271/860342 Ⓦwww.thewayfarerinstow.co.uk; ❺), a popular pub with light and modern rooms upstairs, some with great views. You can also get quality bar meals here (around £9), or go round the corner where two adjacent **restaurants** on Marine Parade enjoy estuary views: *The Decks* (Ⓣ01271/860671; closed Sun & Mon, also lunchtime in winter), a chic and sleek affair with dishes at £15–20, and *The Boathouse* (Ⓣ01271/861292), a more down-to-earth pub and attached dining area, where evening mains cost £10–15.

Great Torrington and around

Five miles up the River Torridge from Bideford, connected by the Tarka Trail and the A386, **GREAT TORRINGTON** is a sleepy market town surrounded by woods and hills carpeted in gorse and bracken. It's a small and nondescript place, though the central **Square** makes a handsome ensemble, with the pink Georgian facade of the long Pannier Market and a porticoed town hall.

Torrington changed hands several times during the **Civil War**, and was the scene of the last great battle in 1646, at the end of which the New Model Army under Thomas Fairfax and Oliver Cromwell occupied the town. After the battle, two hundred Royalist soldiers were imprisoned in St Michael's church, just north of the Square where, unknown to their captors, eighty barrels of gunpowder had also been stored; somehow (for reasons never discovered) it was ignited, the ensuing explosion killing them all. In the churchyard of the rebuilt St Michael's, a large cobbled mound near the main entrance is reputed to be the burial place of the victims. The events are brought to life in **Torrington 1646** (April–Sept Mon–Fri 10am–5pm, also Sat in July & Aug 10am–3pm; last tour 2hr before closing; £7.95; Ⓦwww.torrington-1646.co.uk), a permanent exhibition at Castle Hill car park, a few steps along South Street from the Square; guides in seventeenth-century costume narrate the night of the battle and explosion and show you around the physic garden. In the Royalist encampment, you can play some of the games of the era and try on armour.

The village of **Weare Giffard**, a couple of miles northwest of town, makes a picturesque diversion: the houses run alongside the river for a mile or more, in a setting that inspired Henry Williamson when he wrote *Tarka the Otter* and was used in the 1979 film – the Tarka Trail runs through here.

On the A3142 Exeter road a mile south of Torrington, **Rosemoor** (daily: April–Sept 10am–6pm; Oct–March 10am–5pm; last entry 1hr before closing; £6.50; ⓦwww.rhs.org.uk) encompasses a huge range of plants but is most famed as a centre of rose cultivation, notably in summer when 2000 roses in 200 varieties are on display. However, the garden – one of four managed by the Royal Horticultural Society – makes a good outing at any time for its woodland walks, Winter Garden, Model Gardens, numerous tropical species and the exuberant herbaceous borders.

Practicalities

Bus #315 runs between Barnstaple, Bideford, Torrington and Exeter. The town's **tourist office** is next to the Torrington 1646 exhibition at Castle Hill car park (Easter–Sept Mon–Fri 10am–4.30pm, Sat 10am–1pm; Oct–Easter Mon, Tues, Thurs & Fri 10am–4pm, Wed & Sat 10am–1pm; ⓣ01805/626140, ⓦwww.great-torrington.com). The library, in the same building, offers **internet access**. You can **rent bikes** from Torrington Cycle Hire at the old station, a mile or so north, off the Bideford road (mid-Feb to late Oct daily; ⓣ01805/622633). If you want to **stay** centrally, try *Windsor House*, a B&B on New Road, at the edge of the town centre (ⓣ01805/623529, ⓦwww.windsorhousebandb.co.uk; ❸). It's a rather grand ex-farmhouse whose rooms have private bathrooms and which also offers snooker, darts, table football, a lock-up for bikes and evening meals on request.

There isn't much in the way of **restaurants** in town. However, you could do a lot worse than the *Plough Arts Centre* on Fore Street near the Square (ⓣ01805/624624, ⓦwww.plough-arts.org), which has a pleasant café (closed Sun & Mon) serving snacks and full meals as well as a gallery with arts and craftwork exhibitions, and a lively programme of films and events. Among the local **pubs** opt for the *Black Horse* on the Square, one of the oldest buildings in town (probably sixteenth-century) that briefly served as the headquarters of General Fairfax. You can pick up delectable picnic items from *Browns*, a deli at 37 South St (closed Sun & Mon), also serving coffees, teas and light snacks. Tarka trailers will appreciate the *Puffing Billy*, the old station just north of the village and on the trail, now converted into an informal daytime café serving panini and jacket potatoes (Easter–Sept only). In **Weare Giffard**, the *Cyder Press* pub makes a great refreshment stop.

Westward Ho!

Three miles northwest of Bideford and less than two miles southwest of Appledore, **WESTWARD HO!** is the only English town to be named after a book. **Charles Kingsley**'s bestselling historical romance, which he wrote while staying at Bideford, was set in the surrounding country, and it wasn't long after its publication in 1855 that speculators recognized the tourist potential of what was then an empty expanse of sand and mud pounded by Atlantic rollers. The town's first villa was built within a decade, but even its early development failed to inspire much enthusiasm. **Rudyard Kipling**, who spent four years of his youth here (as recounted in his novel *Stalky and Co.*), described the place as "twelve bleak houses by the shore". His presence is recalled in Kipling Terrace – the site of his school – and **Kipling Tors**, the heights at the west end of the three-mile sand-and-pebble beach.

Kingsley didn't think much of the new resort when he paid a visit, and he probably wouldn't care for it now, with its unsightly muddle of holiday chalets, Victorian villas, modern blocks and the Royal North Devon Golf Club – the country's oldest course, dating from 1864. Once you get past these, however, the broad sandy seafront has an undeniable grandeur. Popular with kite-flyers and kitesurfers, the **beach** offers fabulous swimming and surfing, as well as great views across Bideford Bay. Behind the sands, and protected from the sea by the long rocky foreshore and a high ridge of large pebbles, **Northam Burrows** is a flat, marshy expanse of dunes and meadows rich in flora and fauna, attracting plenty of migratory birds.

Practicalities

Buses #16 and #16A follow a circular route between Bideford Quay, Appledore and Westward Ho! (not Sun), and #1 connects Westward Ho! with Bideford and Barnstaple daily. You'll find **surfing** gear to buy or rent (£10 a day for wet suits or boards) at Surfers on Golf Links Road, and there are stalls on the beach in summer. The North Devon Surf School (Ⓣ01237/474663, Ⓦwww.northdevonsurfschool.co.uk), located at the Northam Burrows end of the beach, provides tuition.

Golf Links Road, the main route to the beach, holds most of the town's facilities. Its western end has a selection of fast-food shops and **restaurants**, including *Country Cousins* at 3 Westbourne Terrace (Ⓣ01237/476989), a large, traditional place offering everything from crab salads to mixed fish grill (£16), and *Potwallopers* (Ⓣ01237/474494; closed Sun eve and all Mon & Tues, reduced hours in winter), a more sophisticated Mediterranean bistro on Golf Links Road, where main courses cost £10–17. The *Waterfront Inn* at the western end of Golf Links Road provides bar food and beers as well as en-suite **accommodation** (Ⓣ01237/474737, Ⓦwww.waterfrontinn.co.uk; ❹), though it can get quite noisy here. Far better is to look further up from the beach, at *Culloden House*, which occupies a commanding position on the wooded Fosketh Hill (Ⓣ01237/479421, Ⓦwww.culloden-house.co.uk; ❹). One of the earliest houses to be built in the resort, it preserves its Victorian character and offers five spacious rooms, all en suite and with first-class views; two rooms face the sea and can accommodate families. Next-door on Kingsley Road, *Manorville* (Ⓣ01237/479766, Ⓦwww.manorvillehostel.com; limited opening Nov–Easter; ❹) is an excellent independent (but YHA-affiliated) **hostel** with modern dorms sleeping 2–7 (from £13.50 per person; £40 for an en-suite double), a well-equipped kitchen and a panoramic conservatory. The only **campsite** in Westward Ho! is *Braddicks* on Merley Road at the western end of town (Ⓣ01237/473263, Ⓦwww.braddicksholidaycentre.co.uk; closed Nov to mid-May), part of a gigantic, soulless accommodation complex where caravans are also available to rent.

Buck's Mills

West round Bideford Bay, the A39 steers inland of the coast, above an almost unbroken line of thickly wooded cliffs. The first village of any kind, tucked into a niche in the cliff wall, is **BUCK'S MILLS**, seven miles west of Bideford, at the bottom of a steep lane that weaves through woods tended by the Woodland

Trust and crossed by waymarked paths (bus #319 stops on the main road, a mile or so up). Though mills have long existed here, powered by the fast-flowing stream gushing through the valley, fishing was the mainstay of the small community until local stocks declined and villagers risked sailing to Lundy each day to work as quarrymen. In 1598, Richard Cole of Woolfardisworthy – said to be Old King Cole of the nursery rhyme – sought to provide better shelter for cargo vessels by building a quayside, of which only scanty remnants are now visible at low tide.

The sloping street ends where the stream thunders down to a stony beach overlooked by the ivy-covered, castle-like ruins of a lime-kiln, thought to date from 1760. Limestone and coal were brought here by boat from south Wales and burned in the local kilns to produce slaked or quick-lime, used in limewash, lime-water and as fertilizer for the local acidic soil. From the beach, you may be able to pick out the Gore, a submerged pebble bank that stretches out to sea for a quarter of a mile. This may have been man-made, though local lore attributes it to the devil who started building it as a causeway to Lundy, 18 miles distant, but gave up when the handle of his Devon shovel broke.

Clovelly

The impossibly picturesque village of **CLOVELLY** must have featured on more calendars, biscuit boxes and tourist posters than anywhere else in the West Country. It was put on the map in the second half of the nineteenth century by two books: Charles Dickens's *A Message From the Sea* and, inevitably, *Westward Ho!* – Charles Kingsley's father was rector here for six years. To an extent, the archaic tone of the village has been preserved by restricting hotel accommodation and banning holiday homes, but in the tourist season, when it's an obligatory stop for

▲ Clovelly

a regular stream of visitors, it's impossible to see past the artifice. Come out of season or after hours, however, and you'll find genuine charm – be prepared, though, for the hefty uphill slog over tricky cobbles on the way out.

Arrival and information

Unless you're coast-pathing, you have to pass through the oversized **visitor centre** to enter the village (daily: April–Oct 9am–6pm; Nov–March 10am–4pm; closing hours may vary), where you're charged £5.75 for access to shops, snack bars, an audiovisual show and use of the car park. You can reach Clovelly's visitor centre on bus #319, which traces a route from Barnstaple and Bideford to Hartland (not Sun in winter). Limited **information** is available at the ticket office (for times see above; ⓣ01237/431781, ⓦwww.clovelly.co.uk), which can supply a list of local **accommodation**.

Accommodation

With limited accommodation options in Clovelly itself, you'd be wise to book ahead even in winter if you wish to stay here. There's better value for money and greater availability in Higher Clovelly, a twenty-minute walk up from the visitor centre. The nearest **campsite** is at the very top of the road, on the corner with the A39: the very basic *Dyke Green Farm* (ⓣ01237/431279; no credit cards; closed Nov–Easter).

Donkey Shoe Cottage High St ⓣ01237/431601, ⓦwww.donkeyshoecottage.co.uk. Friendly and comfortable B&B whose three plainly furnished rooms are bigger than you might expect from the outside, and share a bathroom. No credit cards. ❸

East Dyke Farmhouse ⓣ01237/431216, ⓦwww.bedbreakfastclovelly.co.uk. Two-hundred-year-old building with a beamed and flagstoned dining room and quiet, spacious guest rooms with fridges and private bathrooms. It's right at the top of the village, near the A39 junction. No credit cards. ❸

Fuchsia Cottage Burscott Lane, Higher Clovelly ⓣ01237/431398, ⓦwww.clovelly-holidays.co.uk. This modern B&B feels right off the beaten track, but it's right in front of a path leading through fields to the bottom of the village in about ten minutes. One of the two en-suite doubles has sea views, and there's also a single. Packed lunches and luggage transfers can be arranged for walkers. No credit cards. ❸

New Inn High St ⓣ01237/431303, ⓔnewinn@clovelly.co.uk. Small, swish hotel with a luxurious feel and decor inspired by William Morris. Ask here about the much more stripped-down B&B rooms in an annexe across the road (❸), most with shared bathrooms. ❼

Red Lion The Quay ⓣ01237/431237, ⓔredlion@clovelly.co.uk. Enjoying the best position in the village, this hotel has a traditional atmosphere but bright, modern bedrooms, all with great views. ❼

The village

The cobbled, traffic-free High Street, known locally as Up-along or Down-along (according to which way you are going) plunges down past neat, flower-smothered cottages where battered sledges are tethered for transporting goods – the only way to carry supplies since the use of donkeys ceased. A couple of buildings here hold an exhibition devoted to Charles Kingsley and a restored nineteenth-century fisherman's home.

At the bottom of the village, Clovelly's stony beach and tiny **harbour** lie snuggled in a cleft in the cliffs; the jetty was built in the fourteenth century to shelter the only safe port on this coast between Appledore and Boscastle in Cornwall. A lifeboat now operates from here, but a handful of fishing boats and piles of lobster baskets are the only remnants of a fleet that provided the village's main business before the herring and mackerel stocks dried up in the first half of the twentieth century. In summer, kiosks at the harbourside advertise **boat trips**, providing a good way to see the bay and coastline, as well as cruises to Lundy (see p.217): sailing time is an hour each way, and you get at least six hours on shore (Ⓣ01237/431405 or 0777/419 0359, Ⓦwww.clovelly-charters.ukf.net; £35, plus £5 landing fee, waived for NT cardholders). The same operators can also arrange supervised swimming with the seals off the island's coast, as well as fishing and diving trips.

If you can't face the uphill climb back to the top of the village, take the Land Rover which leaves every fifteen minutes or so from behind the *Red Lion* pub to the visitor centre at the top (Easter–October; £2). Immediately below the visitor centre, **Hobby Drive** is a three-mile walk along the cliffs through woods of sycamore, oak, beech, rowan and the occasional holly, with grand views over the village (the coast path follows this route). From the visitor centre, pick up a free pamphlet of coast walks in the vicinity, noting the flora, fauna and points of historical and geographical interest to look out for.

Eating and drinking

As for **food and drink**, the *New Inn* on the High Street has bar **meals**, teas and set-price meals (£20–25) in its formal restaurant, while the *Red Lion* offers snacks in its Harbour Bar, with locals congregating to drink in the Snug Bar at the back; upstairs, the restaurant provides a three-course dinner for £30.

Hartland and around

Four miles west of Clovelly and about three from the coast, **HARTLAND** has a quiet, insulated air, remote from the main routes of the West Country. The village has three pubs and a couple of stores to supply nourishment, but it's the coast to the north and west that provides the main incentive for being here, reached – unless you're on the coastal path – along narrow, high-hedged lanes between cultivated fields. Three miles northwest, the Atlantic meets Bideford Bay at **Hartland Point**, one of Devon's most dramatic sights. A solitary lighthouse, 350 feet high, overlooks jagged black rocks battered by the sea, and when conditions are clear, the bare horizon is interrupted only by the long, low profile of Lundy (see p.217). Seals can sometimes be seen here or a mile east of the point at **Shipload Bay**, the only sandy beach between Westward Ho! and Cornwall. Walkers can reach it along the coastal path. By road, follow signs for Hartland lighthouse, park at East Titchberry Farm (500m before West Titchberry Farm), from where a signposted path leads 300m to the beach. Erosion and subsidence here have made access difficult in recent years and the last section of steps down to the beach is missing, but it's well worth the effort of negotiating the rather tricky clamber down.

South of the headland, **Hartland Quay** is a scatter of houses around the remains of a once-busy port, financed in part by the mariners Raleigh, Drake and Hawkins, but mostly destroyed by storms in the nineteenth century. The slate in the cliffs to either side reveals cross sections of spectacularly contorted rock strata, though its instability makes it inadvisable to approach the edge, climb or sit under the cliffs. Near the hotel here (see below), two upper rooms of the Quay Buildings, which once accommodated coastguards, labourers and traders, now house the **Hartland Museum** (Easter–Oct daily 11am–4.30pm; £1), displaying maps, models, photos and prints, as well as various salvaged items from the dozens of ships that have foundered around this stretch of coast over the centuries. Many more must have been prevented, though, by the tower of fourteenth-century **St Nectan's** – a mile inland in the village of **Stoke** – which acted as a landmark to sailors before the construction of the Hartland lighthouse at Hartland Point; at 128ft, it's the tallest church tower in North Devon. Inside, the church boasts a finely carved rood screen and a Norman font, all covered by a repainted wagon-type roof.

Half a mile east of Stoke and about a mile west of Hartland, gardens and lush woodland surround **Hartland Abbey** (house April to late May Wed, Thurs & Sun 2–5pm; late May to early Oct Mon–Thurs & Sun 2–5pm; gardens April to early Oct daily except Sat noon–5pm; £9, grounds only £5; Ⓦwww.hartlandabbey.com), an eighteenth-century country house incorporating the ruins of an abbey dissolved in 1539. It's an endearing old place, displaying fine furniture, old photographs and recently uncovered Victorian murals on Arthurian themes, copied from the House of Lords. The Regency library has portraits by Gainsborough and Reynolds, and George Gilbert Scott designed the vaulted Alhambra Corridor and outer hall. From the house, a path leads a mile through woodland strewn in spring with bluebells and primroses to cliffs and a small bay that's sandy at low tide.

Southwards down the coast, saw-toothed rocks and near-vertical escarpments defiantly confront the waves, with spectacular waterfalls tumbling over the cliffs. A mile or so south of Hartland Quay, **Speke's Mill Mouth** is a select surfers' beach – though the rocks and even fragments of wrecks lying just below the surface of the water make surfing ill-advised for anyone unfamiliar with the area. A mainly rocky cove, it's reached by steep steps from the coast path. There's no road access, and no facilities of any kind.

Practicalities

Hartland is served by bus #319 which, starting from Barnstaple, takes in Bideford and Clovelly on its route west. You'll find general **information** on the area at Ⓦwww.hartlandpeninsula.co.uk. Although the village's inns provide B&B **accommodation**, the best choice here is on North Street (off Fore Street) at *Two Harton Manor*, The Square (Ⓣ01237/441670, Ⓦwww.twohartonmanor.co.uk; no credit cards; ③), where there are two congenial rooms above an artist's studio – one en suite with a four-poster. Organic, locally sourced and Aga-cooked breakfasts are eaten in the flagstoned kitchen; woodcut printmaking courses are also offered here. Otherwise, the most appealing places are outside the village. Near Hartland Point, *West Titchberry Farm* (Ⓣ01237/441287; no credit cards; ③) offers simple rooms – one of them en suite, accommodating up to four – a warm guests' lounge and, with notice, evening meals (£14–16); a self-catering cottage is also available. To get to the farm, follow the frequent signs for Hartland lighthouse. For proximity to the sea, you can't do better than the *Hartland Quay Hotel* (Ⓣ01237/441218, Ⓦwww.hartlandquayhotel.com; ⑤), with spray flecking the windows on rough days – though the rooms are fairly ordinary, and the whole place has rather a musty air.

Inland at Stoke, *Stoke Barton Farm*, just opposite St Nectan's Church, provides basic **camping** facilities in a large, exposed field (Ⓣ01237/441238, Ⓦwww.westcountry-camping.co.uk; closed Nov–Easter). Five minutes' walk outside Hartland on South Lane, you can camp year-round at *Hartland Caravan and Camping Park* (Ⓣ01237/441242 or 441876). Two miles south of Stoke and about half a mile inland, Elmscott **youth hostel** occupies a converted Victorian schoolhouse (Ⓣ0845/371 9736, Ⓔjohn.goa@virgin.net; from £15). It's a remote spot, difficult to reach by public transport: take bus #319 to Hartland, from where it's a three-and-a-half-mile walk to Elmscott along the footpath from the west end of Fore Street. Food is not provided, but there's a self-catering kitchen.

Places to **eat and drink** include the *Anchor Inn*, at the western end of Hartland, which gets crowded in the evenings and has real ales, darts and a separate dining room, and the *Hartland Quay Hotel*, which has bar meals and Wreckers' Ale on tap. At Stoke, *Stoke Barton Farm* (see opposite) provides breakfasts, teas and home-made scones (Easter–Sept Sat & Sun).

Lundy Island

Disembarking on the windswept island of **LUNDY**, twelve miles northwest of Hartland Point, feels like arriving at the last outpost. A granite sliver three miles long and roughly half a mile wide, the island was home to an early Christian community in the fifth and sixth centuries, and today its twenty-odd full-time residents share it with the thousands of marine birds for which Lundy is a refuge. With no roads, one pub and one shop, little has changed since the **Marisco** family established itself here in the twelfth century, making use of the coves and shingle beaches to terrorize shipping up and down the Bristol Channel. The family's reign ended in 1242 when one of their number, William de Marisco, was found to be plotting against the king, whereupon he was hanged, drawn and quartered at Tower Hill in London.

After the Mariscos, Lundy's most famous inhabitants were **Thomas Benson**, MP for Barnstaple in the eighteenth century – mainly remembered for using slave labour to work the island's granite quarries and for his part in a massive insurance fraud – and **William Hudson Heaven**, a clergyman from Bristol who bought the island in 1834 and established what became known as the "Kingdom of Heaven". He reopened the quarries, which are said to have provided the tough granite for the Thames Embankment in London, though they closed soon afterwards. The National Trust acquired Lundy in 1969, and it's now managed by the Landmark Trust with the aim of restoring the many relics of former habitation that are scattered around – several of them converted into holiday accommodation – and preserving the primitive character of the place. Accordingly, you won't find any newfangled amusements to impinge on Lundy's pristine, low-tech ambience – all electricity is cut off at midnight each night – and returning to the mainland after a few hours here induces something close to culture shock.

Walking is really the only thing to do here, and tracks and footpaths interweave all over the island. Inland, the grass, heather and bog is crossed by dry stone walls and grazed by ponies, goats, deer and the rare Soay sheep. The shores – mainly cliffy on the south and west, softer and undulating on the east – shelter a rich variety of **birdlife**, including kittiwakes, fulmars, shags and Manx shearwaters, which often nest in rabbit burrows. The most famous birds, though, are the **puffins** from which Lundy is named – from the Norse *Lunde* (puffin) and *ey* (island). They can only be sighted in April and May, when they come ashore to mate. Offshore, **basking sharks**, which can grow to 25ft, can be seen from early July to mid-August, and grey seals can be observed all the year round. You'll find a few pockets of beach to swim off, but the cold waters are not exactly inviting, and swift currents are a risk, particularly at the northern end of the island.

Around the island

In spite of the lack of artificial entertainments, Lundy provides plenty of diversion, and an overnight sojourn allows you to experience the very different flavour after the day-trippers have departed. The few specific sights provide destinations for walks, but really the best advice is to wander at will. The island is divided into holdings by walls cutting across its width; a fast walk from wall to wall takes about twenty minutes, and you can calculate five or ten minutes to traverse from the cliffier western shore to the more protected east, along paths branching off to left and right of the central plateau.

Just up from the harbour, on the southeastern corner of the island, **Marisco Castle** was erected by Henry III in 1244, following the downfall of the Mariscos, and was paid for from the sale of rabbits – Lundy was a Royal Warren. The small keep has walls three feet thick, constructed of local granite and all inclining inwards, and was probably the main building on the island until the late eighteenth century. Rebuilt in the Civil War, it's now restored as holiday accommodation. From here, it's a few minutes on foot to the "**village**", a uniform cluster of buildings including the pub and shop. Just east of the pub stands **Millcombe House**, an incongruous piece of Georgian architecture in these bleak surroundings that was the home of William Hudson Heaven. South of the pub, the square-towered church of **St Helena** was built in 1896 by his son, Hudson Grosett Heaven, to the design of the eminent Victorian architect John Norton. Some of the loneliest parts and most dramatic landscapes of Lundy lie west of here, around the island's southern tip. Here, the **Devil's Limekiln** should be approached with care: it's a pit more than a hundred yards deep, into which the sea enters from the bottom.

North of the village, Lundy's main track heads along the north–south axis of the island, across the springy turf and heather of **Ackland's Moor** to the first of the island's three dividing walls. After the first or "quarter wall", climb down a steep path to the right to see the **Quarries** – last used in 1911 – and adjacent beach. At the western end of the wall, granite steps lead down to the remains of the cottages, magazine and gun-station which make up the **Battery**, dating from 1863, from which a cannon was fired every ten minutes in foggy conditions. The cannons are still there. Half a mile north of here, **Jenny's Cove** is named after a vessel reputed to be carrying ivory and gold that was wrecked here in the seventeenth century, and is the haunt of razorbills, guillemots and puffins.

Practicalities

The MS *Oldenburg* crosses to Lundy up to four times weekly from Bideford or Ilfracombe between April and October. In each case, day-return tickets cost £32.50, open returns £56 and journey-time is around two hours. Discounts on the ferry fare are available to National Trust members, seniors, students and families. Between November and March, a helicopter service from Hartland Point (see p.215) takes over, taking just seven minutes (currently Mon & Fri at 11am, £92 return); day returns are not available for helicopter flights. For sailing and flight reservations, and to check departures (sailings are dependent on the state of the seas, though cancellations are rare) call ☎01271/863636; day returns can also be booked from local tourist offices.

The *Marisco Tavern*, a cheerful hall with a balcony, whose only chilling note is supplied by the display of life-preservers from some of the ships foundered off the island's coasts, is very much Lundy's focal point. The buffet lunch and local ale are good enough to discourage some trippers off the ferry from venturing any further on the island. The village **shop** has a good range of provisions and, if you're staying on the island, you can arrange to have groceries delivered.

Accommodation on Lundy can be booked up months in advance, but it's worth enquiring about last-minute vacancies. Prices in midsummer are around £550–800 per week for accommodation for two. **B&B** – with breakfast in the *Marisco* – is available only in the rare gaps between rentals, and can only be booked within two weeks of the proposed visit; expect to pay £72 per night for a double room in peak season. All **bookings** done within a fortnight of the intended stay can be made at the Landmark Trust's shore offices on Bideford's Quay or, between March and October, Ilfracombe Harbour (Ⓣ01271/863636 for both); otherwise, contact the Trust's office in Maidenhead (Ⓣ01628/825925, Ⓦwww.landmarktrust.org.uk). Choices include the two-storey granite *Barn*, a hostel sleeping fourteen; the *Old House*, where Charles Kingsley stayed in 1849, and the *Old Light*, a lighthouse built in 1820 by the architect of Dartmoor Prison, one of the three lighthouses on the island (the other two are in use). The remotest place is the *Tibbetts*, about one and three-quarter miles from the village along the main track to the north, and lit by calor gas rather than electricity; it sleeps four in bunks. A single person might find the *Radio Room* cosy; it once housed the transmitter that was the island's only link with the outside world. In all cases, furnishings are chosen to suit the individual property. There's also a **campsite** near the *Tavern* in the village (open Easter–Oct); it's surrounded by a protective wall but can still get pretty wet and windswept in stormy weather. **Information** on transport and accommodation can be found on the island's website Ⓦwww.lundyisland.co.uk.

Travel details

Trains

Barnstaple to: Exeter (Mon–Sat hourly, Sun 6 daily; 1hr 15min).

Buses

Appledore to: Barnstaple (Mon–Sat 2 hourly, Sun hourly; 50min); Bideford (Mon–Sat 2–3 hourly, Sun hourly; 20–25min); Westward Ho! (Mon–Sat 3–4 daily; 12min).
Barnstaple to: Appledore (Mon–Sat 2 hourly, Sun hourly; 40–50min); Bideford (Mon–Sat every 5min, Sun 2–3 hourly; 25–30min); Braunton (Mon–Sat 4–5 hourly, Sun 1–2 hourly; 15–20min); Clovelly (Mon–Sat 6 daily, Sun in summer 2 daily; 1hr); Croyde (Mon–Sat every 30min, Sun in summer 5 daily; 40min); Exeter (Mon–Sat 15 daily, Sun 2 daily; 1hr 50min–2hr 35min); Great Torrington (Mon–Sat 1–3 hourly, Sun 4 daily; 40–50min); Hartland (Mon–Sat 6 daily, Sun in summer 2 daily; 1hr 25min); Ilfracombe (Mon–Sat 3 hourly, Sun hourly; 35–45min); Instow (Mon–Sat every 5–10min, Sun 2–3 hourly; 20min); Lynton (Mon–Sat hourly; 55min); Saunton (Mon–Sat every 30min, Sun in summer every 2hr; 30min); Tiverton (Mon–Sat 15 daily, Sun 4–5 daily; 50min–1hr 10min); Westward Ho! (Mon–Sat 2 hourly, Sun hourly; 40–50min); Woolacombe (Mon–Sat 5–6 daily, Sun in summer 3 daily; 45min).
Bideford to: Appledore (Mon–Sat 1–2 hourly, Sun hourly; 15–25min); Barnstaple (Mon–Sat every 5min, Sun 2–3 hourly; 25–30min); Clovelly (Mon–Sat 6 daily, Sun in summer 2 daily; 40min); Exeter (Mon–Sat 7–8 daily, Sun 2 daily; 2hr); Great Torrington (Mon–Sat 1–2 hourly, Sun 4 daily; 15–20min); Hartland (Mon–Sat 6 daily, Sun in summer 2 daily; 1hr); Westward Ho! (Mon–Sat 3 hourly, Sun hourly; 15–35min).
Braunton to: Barnstaple (Mon–Sat 4–5 hourly, Sun 1–2 hourly; 15–20min); Croyde (Mon–Sat every 30min, Sun in summer 5 daily; 20–25min); Ilfracombe (Mon–Sat 2 hourly, Sun hourly; 25min); Saunton (Mon–Sat every 30min, Sun in summer 5 daily; 12min); Woolacombe (Mon–Sat 5–6 daily, Sun in summer 3 daily; 20–30min).
Clovelly to: Barnstaple (Mon–Sat 6 daily, Sun in summer 2 daily; 50min–1hr 10min); Bideford (Mon–Sat 6 daily, Sun in summer 2 daily; 40min); Bude (Sun in summer 2 daily; 50min); Hartland (Mon–Sat 6 daily, Sun in summer 2 daily; 15min).
Croyde to: Barnstaple (Mon–Sat every 30min; 40–50min); Braunton (Mon–Sat every 30min; 20–25min); Saunton (Mon–Sat every 30min, Sun in summer 5 daily; 5–10min).
Great Torrington to: Barnstaple (Mon–Sat 1–3 hourly, Sun 4 daily; 40–50min); Bideford (Mon–Sat 1–2 hourly, Sun 4 daily; 15–20min).
Hartland to: Barnstaple (Mon–Sat 6 daily, Sun in summer 2 daily; 1hr 20min); Bideford (Mon–Sat 6 daily, Sun in summer 2 daily; 1hr); Bude (Mon–Sat 2–3 daily; Sun in summer 2 daily; 30min–1hr); Clovelly (Mon–Sat 6 daily, Sun in summer 2 daily; 15min).

Ilfracombe to: Barnstaple (Mon–Sat 3 hourly, Sun hourly; 35–45min); Braunton (Mon–Sat 2 hourly, Sun hourly; 25min); Lynton (late May to late Sept 3 daily; late Sept to late May Sat & Sun 2 daily; 1hr); Woolacombe (hourly; 25–30min).
Saunton to: Barnstaple (Mon–Sat every 30min, Sun in summer 5 daily; 20–30min); Braunton (Mon–Sat every 30min, Sun in summer 5 daily; 12min); Croyde (Mon–Sat every 30min, Sun in summer 5 daily; 5min).

Westward Ho! to: Appledore (Mon–Sat 5 daily; 12min); Barnstaple (Mon–Sat 2 hourly, Sun hourly; 40–50min); Bideford (Mon–Sat 3 hourly, Sun hourly; 25–30min).
Woolacombe to: Barnstaple (Mon–Sat 6 daily, Sun in summer 3 daily; 40min); Braunton (Mon–Sat 6 daily, Sun in summer 3 daily; 20min); Ilfracombe (hourly; 25–30min).

8

South Cornwall coast

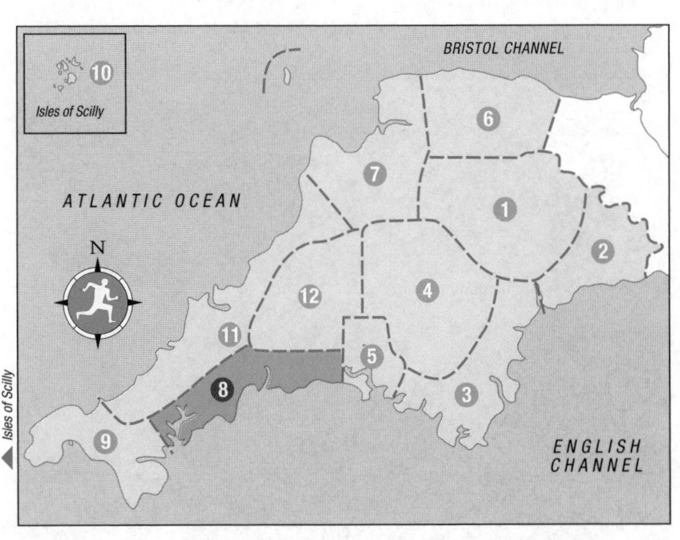

CHAPTER 8

Highlights

* **Fowey** With its beautiful location, this classic riverside town and its environs invite an extended exploration. See p.229

* **The Eden Project** Disused clay pit now home to exotic plants and crops, many reared in vast domes, and offering an extraordinary display of biodiversity. See p.233

* **Lost Gardens of Heligan** Exuberant and intriguing, this historic garden ranks among the country's finest. See p.238

* **The Roseland Peninsula** Seclusion and serenity reign in this remote haven, which also offers fabulous coastal walking. See p.245

* **Oyster Festival, Falmouth** Celebration of local seafood and a showcase of gastronomy in October, a must for foodies. See p.251

▲ The Eden Project

8

South Cornwall coast

Nearly all of Cornwall's rivers empty into the sea along the county's southern coast, providing a succession of estuaries which shelter the numerous small fishing ports strung along the seaboard. This combination of natural beauty and quaint old villages has ensured that the area is heavily visited, and most places are touched by varying degrees of commercialization, but the thrilling cliff-hung coastline – the best sections of which are accessible only on the South West Coast Path – always provides a convenient escape.

Tourism has certainly stamped its imprint on medieval ports such as **Looe** and **Polperro**, but their charm is well-nigh irresistible in low season, when they revert to the sleepy state that suits them best. The estuary town of **Fowey**, however, is big enough to transcend the summer influx, and as a working port has an agreeably self-sufficient air. West of here, **St Austell**, the capital of Cornwall's china-clay industry, lacks much intrinsic interest, but it's just a stone's throw from the unspoiled Georgian harbour village of **Charlestown**, the most appealing of the resorts on **St Austell Bay**, and is also the nearest stop to the extraordinary **Eden Project**, the region's most talked-about attraction. On a smaller scale, the **Lost Gardens of Heligan**, further west, are also spectacular, a salvaged Victorian garden that contains immaculate shrubs alongside swampy, jungle-like tracts. Close by, first impressions suggest that **Mevagissey** is just another over-exploited fishing village, but, again, it preserves a genuine allure with the added bonus of some fine restaurants. To the south, **Veryan Bay** is a sequestered nook mostly off the tourist track, though its gorgeous beaches are popular in summer.

Continuing west along the coast, **Carrick Roads**, the complex estuary basin which forms one of the finest deep-water anchorages in Britain, has pockets of frantic tourist activity counterbalanced by the rural calm of its creeks and muddy inlets. At its top, the county capital of **Truro** has Cornwall's best museum and one of Britain's most striking – and newest – neo-Gothic cathedrals, but the major resort in these parts is **Falmouth**, at the bottom of the estuary, where the mighty Pendennis Castle occupies a commanding site at the end of the promontory. Its sister-fort lies across the estuary mouth at **St Mawes**, the biggest village on the mercifully undeveloped **Roseland Peninsula**, where waterside churches are steeped in a timeless calm.

The main **train** line to Penzance runs through Lostwithiel, St Austell and Truro, but apart from these towns, and Falmouth and Looe, which lie at the end of picturesque branch lines, most of the places in this chapter are served by buses only. On the whole you'll find a good distribution of **accommodation** throughout the region, though many places close in winter. For full details, as well as attractions, activities and events, see Ⓦwww.visit-southeastcornwall.co.uk and www.visitthecornishriviera.co.uk.

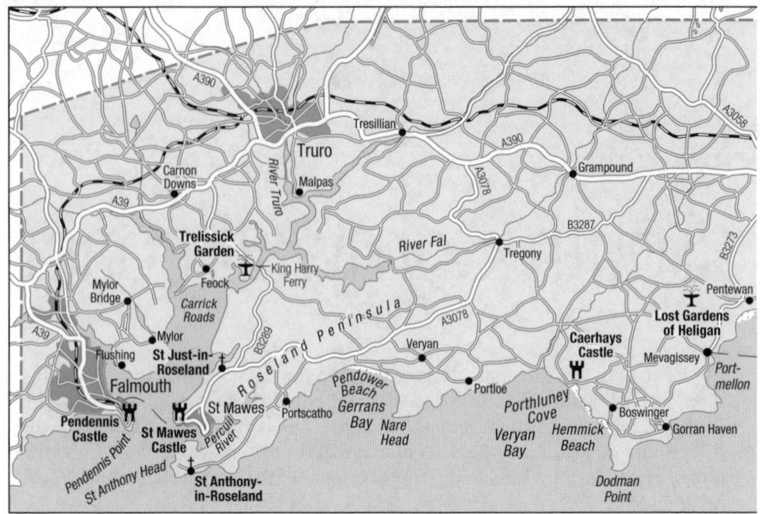

Looe

LOOE was drawing crowds as early as 1800 when the first bathing-machines were wheeled out, but the arrival of the railway in 1879 was what really packed its beaches. The town stands at the mouth of the East and West Looe rivers which meet here, the combined stream dividing East Looe, where most of the action is, from quieter West Looe, and crossed by a seven-arched bridge near the main car park. On the East Looe side, the main Fore Street runs south from the bridge, a long gaudy parade of shops and cafés that ends at the web of narrow lanes around Buller Quay and the harbour. If the tide's right, crossing by ferry from Buller Quay (40p) saves you the trek round by bridge to West Looe.

Arrival and information

The best way to approach Looe is on the **Looe Valley Line**, a branch line off the main rail line from Plymouth, which makes a scenic run along the course of the East Looe River from Liskeard. There are also regular **buses** from Liskeard (#573) and Plymouth (#572, not Sun), both of which go on to Polperro. If you **drive** into Looe, you're best off heading for the Millpool car park at the approach to the town, as the car park near the bridge fills up quickly; alternatively, there's free parking along Marine Drive in West Looe.

The **tourist office** is at the New Guildhall, halfway down Fore Street in East Looe (Daily: Easter and May to mid-Sept 10am–5pm; April & mid-Sept to Oct 10am–2pm; ⓣ01503/262072, ⓦwww.visit-southeastcornwall.co.uk). The office is also open on winter weekdays 10am–1pm, but unstaffed. You can log on to the **internet** here or at Looe Enterprise Centre (Mon–Fri 9.30am–4.30pm), in the arcade off Higher Market Street; both places charge £1.50 for thirty minutes. On Marine Drive, West Looe, Looe Divers (ⓣ01503/262727, ⓦwww.looedivers.com) provides equipment, **diving** instruction and excursions in an area exceptionally rich in sites.

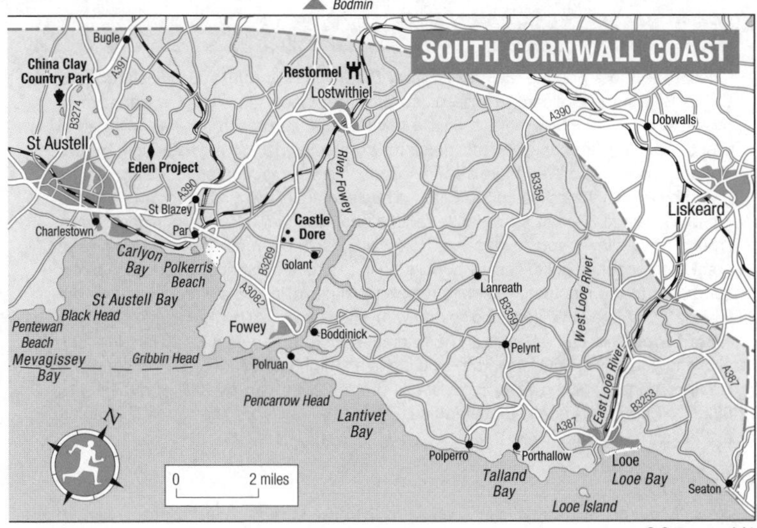

Accommodation

The plethora of **accommodation** in town helps to keep prices down. Among the local **campsites**, opt for *Tregoad Farm* (ⓣ01503/262718, ⓦwww.tregoadpark.co.uk), one and a half miles west of Looe via the B3253 Polperro road; it's quieter than most, with a shop, bar/bistro, pine-furnished washing facilities and a heated outdoor pool. It also has camping barns and camping pods – insulated "wooden tents" with or without electricity.

Ambleside Shutta Rd, East Looe ⓣ01503/263368, ⓦwww.looeamblesidebandb.co.uk. At the top of a steep climb – the narrow lane is not suitable for cars – from where you can soak up splendid river views from the two spotless rooms (one supplied with a telescope). You can also enjoy the panorama over the excellent breakfasts, which include good veggie and vegan options. Crabbing equipment available. No credit cards. ④

Marwinthy East Cliff, East Looe ⓣ01503/264382, ⓦwww.marwinthy.co.uk. In a peaceful, elevated position with lofty views, this friendly guesthouse has four unfussy rooms, some en suite. There's a panoramic veranda, and a choice of breakfasts. It's adjacent to the coast path. No credit cards. ②

Schooner Point 1 Trelawney Terrace, West Looe ⓣ01503/262670, ⓦwww.schoonerpoint.co.uk. Just 100m from Looe Bridge, this family-run guesthouse has great river views from most of its good-value rooms, which include a single. No credit cards. ③

Sea Breeze Lower Chapel St, East Looe ⓣ01503/263131, ⓦwww.seabreezelooe.com. Very close to the beach and harbour, this B&B has smallish rooms with shared or en-suite bathrooms, Egyptian cotton bedding, fluffy towels and free parking. No under-6s. ③

The Town

At the end of Fore Street in East Looe, the **Old Guildhall Museum** on Higher Market Street (Easter & late May to Sept Mon–Fri & Sun 11am–4pm; £1.80) is worth a visit, holding a diverse collection of maritime models and exhibits, household items and a collection of puppets. It's the building itself that most impresses, however; a beamed, fifteenth-century construction that once housed a magistrates' court and jail cells. Aside from the museum, it's East Looe's long **harbour** that holds all the interest. When not beset by milling crowds, it's an absorbing place to while away some time, its quays stacked with crates and lobster

Looe Island

One of the most popular excursions from Buller Quay is out to **Looe Island** (also called St George's Island), a mile or so offshore. Once the site of a Benedictine monastery, the low, green hump, just a few hundred yards across, was bombed in World War II by Germans who mistook it for a warship. In 1965 it was bought by two doughty sisters who lived there for nearly forty years, as recounted in *We Bought an Island* by Evelyn Atkins (see p.387). Now a bird sanctuary owned by Cornwall Wildlife Trust, the island is great for a gentle ramble on a trail that takes in its highest point (150m), and allows you to observe Cornwall's second-largest breeding colony of great black-backed gulls. The rat population is a constant threat to the nesting birds; according to the nineteenth-century novelist Wilkie Collins, rats were caught on the island, "smothered in onion" and "eaten with vindictive relish by the people of Looe".

Boat trips take place Easter and September (£5 return, plus a £2.50 landing fee), allowing you a two-hour stay; the excursions are highly dependent on the tides and weather conditions, however, so always check departures by calling ⓣ0781/413 9223, or contact Looe's tourist office. Take food and drink as there's nothing available on the island.

baskets. Moored alongside the sixty-odd fishing vessels that continue to work from here is a small flotilla of other craft used for summer **boat trips**, for which you sign up at boards lined up on the quayside. These days, Looe is something of a shark-fishing centre (it's the headquarters of the Shark Angling Club of Great Britain), so it's not surprising that **shark-fishing expeditions** are offered (around £45 for a full day), for which you should contact the Shark Angling Club, based on Buller Quay (ⓣ01503/262642). A more modest two-hour mackerel quest (£10) is enough for most, allowing you to see something of the coast, and you can also soak up the scenery on board a **cruise to Polperro** (£10). **River and estuary trips** are also available from Buller Quay (around £5 per hour).

Projecting south from the harbour, Banjo Pier – named for its shape – separates the river mouth from **East Looe Beach,** the handiest stretch of sand but, as the most popular of the town's beaches, with a flurry of stalls and activities advertised, it gets pretty congested; you'll find a choice of calmer and more varied strands to east and west. At the far end of the town beach, try the quieter and rocky **Second** or **Sanders Beach**, reached through a break in the rocks known locally as the Khyber Pass. More secluded and sandier beaches are accessible from here at low tide and also from the coastal path from Looe or by road. One of the best is **Millendreath**, a crescent of sand and shingle less than a mile east of Looe, backed by concrete terraces and holiday chalets but still scenic, with scattered rocks and green hills on either side; the swimming is good, too. In West Looe, you can escape from the glut of holiday-makers on the long stretch of **Hannafore Beach** at the end of Marine Drive. Shingly at high tide, it reveals rock pools at other times, and has good views over to Looe Island.

Eating and drinking

The narrow streets between East Looe's quay and seafront hold a crop of **restaurants** that get very busy in summer. Plainer, inexpensive fare is served at any number of places along Fore Street. For pasties, head to The Pasty Shop on Buller Street (closed Sun), with flavours such as lamb, leek and mint, and Chinese chicken – you can watch them being made. For a dazzling range of **ice cream** in wafer or waffle cones, including lemon meringue and white chocolate flavours, visit Treleavens opposite the car park on Fore Street.

Mawgan's Lower Market St, East Looe ⓣ01503/265331. You'll find a calm, easy-going ambience and a range of tasty dishes at this upmarket choice, from pork and scallops to vegetable balti and Thai green curry (£13–18). Closed daytime and Dec–March.

Old Sail Loft The Quay, East Looe ⓣ01503/262131. This oak-beamed former warehouse offers a brasserie menu at lunchtime and early evening, with mains at around £11, or a pricier evening menu when you can sample a trio of local fish or game (£19) or a lobster thermidor (£30). Closed lunchtimes Tues & Sun, also Tues eve in winter.

Squid Ink Lower Market St, East Looe ⓣ01503/262674. Stylish and contemporary, this offers fresh fish and such dishes as "surf and turf", mixing meat and seafood, for example steak and scallops (£15–19), and there are set-price menus: £15 for two courses, £20 for three. Closed daytime & all Sun & Mon.

Tom Sawyer's Marine Drive, West Looe ⓣ01503/262782. This bustling, family-friendly place is strong on seafood and steaks (£10–15), but you can also grab a baguette and a pint here, and the tables outside offer serene sea views.

Trawlers The Quay, East Looe ⓣ01503/263593. Looe's best seafood restaurant is more formal than the neighbouring *Old Sail Loft*, and has a classier menu, including such dishes as seafood linguini and roasted monkfish wrapped in pancetta (£16–19). Meat and vegetarian options are also available, and there's some outdoor seating. Closed daytime and all Sun & Mon.

Pubs

Ye Olde Fishermans Arms Higher Market St. Supposedly the oldest pub in town, this relaxed local serves real ales, local ciders and puts on Irish and other acoustic music on Friday and Sunday nights.

Ye Olde Salutation Fore St. Sloping slate floors, a gallery of shark photos on the walls and good, cheap pub meals and snacks. Good Doom Bar bitter.

Polperro and around

Smaller, quainter and just as overrun by summer visitors, **POLPERRO** is linked with neighbouring Looe, four miles east, by hourly bus #573, the summer-only #281 (not Sat or Sun) and the Sunday-only #81B. From the bus stop and car park at the top of the village, milk floats disguised as trams (85p single) and horses and carts (£2 single) tout for those who cannot manage the ten-minute walk alongside the River Pol to the minuscule harbour. The tightly packed houses rising on each side of the stream are undeniably pretty, little changed since the village's heyday of smuggling and pilchard fishing, though its straggling main street, the Coombes, is now an almost unbroken row of gift shops and cafés. Come after the crowds have departed – in the evenings or at any time out of season – and you'll fall under the spell of this truly quaint spot.

You can get some good background on the village at the **Polperro Heritage Museum of Smuggling and Fishing** (Easter–Oct daily 10.30am–5.30pm; £1.75), housed in the old pilchard factory on the Warren, to the eastern side of the harbour. Focusing on the fishing and smuggling communities that once inhabited Polperro's packed cottages, it's a pretty low-key display, but you'll find some intriguing photos from the 1860s among other works by Victorian artists attracted to the area, including some showing the local fishermen wearing their traditional "knitfrocks" (knitted sweaters), examples of which are also on view here.

In summer, there are the usual choice of **boat trips** from the harbour, including those to Polruan, Fowey and Looe (£10–15 return). The coast-walking, needless to say, is outstanding. West of Polperro, the five miles to **Polruan**, on the Fowey estuary, are among the most scenic stretches of South Cornwall's coastal path, giving access to some beautiful secluded sand beaches. For more on the village and neighbourhood, visit the community **website** ⓦwww.polperro.org, or consult the knowledgeable and helpful staff at the post office on Fore Street.

Polperro's Fishermen's Choir

If you're in the area in summer, it's worth catching a **quayside concert** by the Polperro Fishermen's Choir, usually taking place during July and August in Polperro on Wednesdays at 8pm and at other local villages on different evenings. Look out for posters for details, or there may be a notice outside Polperro's chapel on Fore Street.

Accommodation

Although Polperro deserves no more than a swift visit during the busy summer months, it makes a peaceful **place to stay** for a night or two at any other time, and is a useful bolt hole for coast walkers. All prices are much reduced out of season.

The Cottles Longcoombe Lane ⓣ01503/272578, ⓦwww.cottles-polperro.co.uk. At the top of the village (above the car park) is a good choice, with a conservatory and decking for relaxation, and with reflexology, reiki, aromatherapy and other treatments offered. Packed lunches for walkers available. ⑤

Old Mill House Mill Hill ⓣ01503/272362, ⓦwww.oldmillhouseinn.co.uk Close to the harbour but relatively secluded, this relaxed inn has seven cream-coloured rooms with antique furnishings. ④

Penryn House The Coombes ⓣ01503/272157, ⓦwww.penrynhouse.co.uk. One of Polperro's most congenial options, this has a country feel, cosy modern rooms – those at the back are quietest, but have no view – and friendly management. ⑤

Trenderway Farm Pelynt ⓣ01503/272214, ⓦwww.trenderwayfarmholidays.co.uk. For oodles of style and comfort, head a mile north of Polperro, where this sixteenth-century farmhouse offers superior rustic accommodation surrounded by 200 acres of working farmland. Local produce goes into the top-notch breakfasts, which can be taken in the conservatory or outdoors. Free wi-fi and a library are on hand, and self-catering cottages are also available. No children under 11. ⑥

Eating and drinking

Unsurprisingly, most of Polperro's numerous **restaurants** specialize in seafood, though you'll find a range of other dishes, including takeaway curries from *Somewhere*, a restaurant on Fore Street. For sit-down meals, it's best to reserve in summer and at weekends.

Blue Peter The Quay. Snug pub above the harbour where you can pick up a doorstep crab sandwich, among other snacks, or a full meal. The beers are excellent, and jazz or acoustic music is played live on Friday and Saturday nights and Sunday afternoons (less frequent In low season).

Couch's Great House Saxon Bridge ⓣ01503/272554. The best feed in town, this place insists on locally sourced ingredients for its contemporary dishes, like rump of lamb, wild sea bass and Cornish Brie and truffle. You'll pay £25 for three courses; £38 for a seven-course tasting menu. Closed daytime except Sun lunch, also Oct–April Tues except during school hols.

The House on Props Talland St ⓣ01503/272310. Supported by ancient struts over the Pol, this cosy spot has superb fish and meat dishes, for example trio of fish, steaks and mussel chowder (£10–15), not to mention scrumptious home-made cakes to accompany an afternoon tea or takeaway. Closed Sun eve & Nov–Jan.

Neville's Little Green, off Fore St. ⓣ01503/272459. Bow-fronted and beamed restaurant where the menu includes such items as Fisherman's Lunch, either crab or mackerel with salad (£7.25), a mild prawn curry (£9) and Crabber's Feast (£16.75). It's also famous for superlative steak and chips (a fillet steak is around £17) and gargantuan portions. Closed mid-Jan to Feb, also Sat lunch & all Sun.

Old Mill House Mill Hill ⓣ01503/272362. This easy-going pub has a separate, family-friendly restaurant where mains cost under £10, for example lasagne, chicken and the catch of the day.

Fowey and around

The frequent ferries that cross the River Fowey from Polruan afford a fine first view of the quintessential Cornish river port of **FOWEY** (pronounced "Foy"), a cascade of neat, pale terraces at the mouth of one of the peninsula's grandest riverscapes. Having become Cornwall's major south-coast port in the fourteenth century, Fowey became ambitious enough for Edward IV to strip the town of its military capability, but it continued to thrive commercially, coming into its own as the leading port for china-clay exports in the nineteenth century. Fowey retains its strong maritime flavour today: in addition to the bulky freighters docking at the wharves north of town, the harbour is crowded with trawlers and yachts, giving the town a brisk, purposeful character lacking in many of Cornwall's south-coast ports. The town's prosperous air is reflected in its premier annual event, **Regatta Week** in mid-August.

Arrival and information

Fowey is most easily accessible by ferry from Polruan or Bodinnick (see box, below) or hourly #25 **buses** from St Austell and Par train stations. **Drivers** will find that the Caffa Mill car park by the Bodinnick ferry crossing fills up quickly (though there's an overflow car park nearby); there's more space at the central car park off Hanson Drive and at the third more distant one above Readymoney Cove, both well signposted. A minibus (May–Sept daily continuously; Oct–April Mon, Wed, Fri & Sat every 15min; £1) shuttles between the main car parks and St Fimbarrus from 10am until about 6pm (in winter 11am–4pm), with an hourly connection to Par. Travellers to or from the west might make use of the **ferry** linking Fowey with Mevagissey (see p.237), which operates three to six times daily between late April and September (35min; £6, or £10 return). As well as being an excellent way to travel between the villages, it's a great excursion to view St Austell Bay, with the possibility of spotting the odd basking shark; check for sailings at ⓣ0797/720 3394, ⓦwww.mevagissey-ferries.co.uk.

Below St Fimbarrus on South Street, the **tourist office** (Mon–Sat 9.30am–5pm, Sun 10am–5pm; ⓣ01726/833616, ⓦwww.fowey.co.uk) can supply information on the area, a well as good local walking itineraries. You can access the **internet** at Fowey's library, on Passage Lane near the Caffa Mill car park (Mon & Wed 10am–5pm, Tues, Thurs & Fri 10am–5.30pm, Sat 10am–12.30pm; £1 per 30min).

Accommodation

Accommodation in Fowey is abundant, varied and of good quality, though can be expensive in high season, especially during Regatta Week in mid-August,

Crossing the Fowey

A car and passenger ferry runs between **Bodinnick** and **Caffa Mill**, at the north end of Fowey (April–Oct Mon–Sat 7am–8.45pm or dusk, Sun 8am–8.45pm or dusk; Nov–March Mon–Fri 7am–7pm, Sat 8am–7pm, Sun 9am–7pm; £2.70 per car, £1.20 per foot passenger). There's a large car park at Caffa Mill, which is connected by a separate ferry to Fowey's more central quays (May–Sept 10am–5pm; £1).

The **Polruan** passenger ferry (May–Sept Mon–Sat 7.15am–11pm, Sun 9am–11pm; Oct–April Mon–Fri 7.15am–7pm, Sat 7.30am–7pm, Sun 10am–5pm; £1.20, bikes 90p) connects with Fowey's more central quays.

when you should book well ahead. The area around town also throws up some excellent choices – we've recommended a couple below.

Hotels and B&Bs

Coombe Farm ⓣ01726/833123, ⓦwww.coombefarmbb.co.uk. Perfect rural isolation is available here, just twenty minutes' walk west of town, at the end of a lane off the B3269. The two en-suite rooms have sea views, and there's a bathing area at Coombe Haven 300m away. Cream teas are available in the walled garden in summer. No under-12s. No credit cards. ④

Marina Villa Hotel The Esplanade ⓣ01726/833315, ⓦwww.themarinahotel.co.uk. Dating from 1815, this waterside retreat has all the requisites for extreme pampering, and boasts a renowned restaurant (see opposite). The decor is gorgeous and there are wonderful views. ⑧

Old Ferry Inn Bodinnick ⓣ01726/870237, ⓦwww.oldferryinn.co.uk. Most of the rooms here have great views across the river to Fowey and are en suite (one has a four-poster). There are bars and a restaurant on the premises. ⑤

Old Quay House Hotel 28 Fore St ⓣ01726/833302, ⓦwww.theoldquayhouse.com. At the top end of the scale, this boutique hotel in a traditional setting offers abundant style, with eight of its twelve creamily opulent rooms enjoying estuary views and patios. ⑧

Safe Harbour 58 Lostwithiel St ⓣ01726/833379, ⓦwww.cornwall-safeharbour.co.uk. A brisk walk up from Fore St, but right in front of the bus stop, this pub has decent-sized rooms – all en suite except for two singles – and there's parking. ⑤

Ship Inn Trafalgar Square ⓣ01726/832230. Very central sixteenth-century pub offering B&B, 200m from the quay. Rooms have shared bathrooms and there's no breakfast, hence the very reasonable rates. Ask for the Oak Room, with original oak panelling. ③

Campsites and hostel

Golant Youth Hostel ⓣ0845/371 9019, ⓔgolant@yha.org.uk. Three miles north of town, overlooking the river outside the village of Golant, *Penquite House* is a Georgian mansion set in gardens and fourteen acres of woodland, and offers dorms and family rooms, with beds from £16. The #25 bus passes the end of the drive at Castle Dore crossroads, from where it's a one-and-a-half-mile walk.

Penhale ⓣ01726/833425, ⓦwww.penhale-fowey.co.uk. The nearest campsite to Fowey is a mile and a half west of town (also within walking distance of Polkerris beach, and 3.5 miles from the Eden Project). Facilities Include a games room and shop, and there are level pitches and great estuary views. Closed early Oct to mid-March.

Penmarlam ⓣ01726/870088, ⓦwww.penmarlampark.co.uk. Three-quarters of a mile up from the Bodinnick ferry crossing on the east bank of the river, a peaceful spot with a shop, well-maintained facilities and internet access. Closed Nov–March.

The town and around

Fowey's steep centre is dominated by the fifteenth-century church of **St Fimbarrus**, at the junction of the two main streets running parallel to the river – Fore Street upriver and the Esplanade towards the sea. The church marks the traditional end of the ancient **Saints' Way** from Padstow (see p.333), linking the north and south Cornish coasts. Below St Fimbarrus, the small **Literary Centre** at the back of the tourist office on South Street (and sharing the same times; free) is worth a glance; the exhibition is mainly devoted to the life and work of **Daphne du Maurier**, who spent her most creative years in and around Fowey, and includes a twelve-minute DVD about the author. There's also material on other writers with local connections: children's writer Kenneth Grahame and Sir Arthur Quiller-Couch, alias "Q", who lived on Fowey's Esplanade between 1892 and 1944, and whose writings helped popularize the place he called "Troy Town".

Behind St Fimbarrus stands **Place House**, an extravagance belonging to the local Treffry family, with a Victorian Gothic tower grafted onto the fifteenth- and sixteenth-century fortified building. Below the church, the *Ship Inn*, sporting some fine Elizabethan panelling and plaster ceilings, was originally home to the Rashleighs – a recurring name in the local annals – and held the local Roundhead HQ during the Civil War.

At its southern end, the Esplanade shrinks to a footpath that gives access to some exhilarating **coastal walks**. On the right, look out for the remains of a blockhouse that once supported a defensive chain hung across the river's mouth; a few minutes' walk past this will bring you to the small beach of **Readymoney Cove**. As the only town beach, it doesn't take long to get jam-packed, but you can escape along the wooded path which climbs steeply above the southern end of the cove to enjoy fine estuary views from the scant ruins of **St Catherine's Castle**, built by Thomas Treffry on the orders of Henry VIII – little more than a wall or two remain today. Across the river, **Polruan** itself is worth a visit for the magnificent views across Fowey harbour stretching south to the Lizard peninsula. From the small port, a two-mile signposted coastal walk curls round to **Lantic Bay**, sheltering a beautiful and relatively quiet beach; beware that currents can be very strong here.

There are also alluring **hikes** to be made **inland from Fowey**. You don't have to take on the entire thirty miles of the Saints' Way to get the flavour of this trail, but if you prefer a circular route you can try the **Hall Walk**, a scenic four-mile hike north of the village. More details are available from the tourist office, though it's simple enough: cross the river on the car ferry (at the car park north of town) to **Bodinnick**, walk downstream on the other side, crossing the footbridge over the narrow creek of Pont Pill, then take the passenger ferry back from Polruan. At Penleath Point, where the path turns from south to east into Pont Pill, there's a white memorial to Arthur Quiller-Couch. Continuing north beyond the west bank ferry stage, on the other hand, will bring you to **Golant**, a riverside hamlet three miles north of Fowey, from which a road leads just over a mile west to the Iron Age fort of **Castle Dore**, which features in Arthurian romance as the residence of King Mark of Cornwall, husband of Iseult. From Fowey, bus #25 passes close to the earthwork, with a five- or ten-minute walk from the stop on the crossroads. There's not a great deal to see, though you could combine an excursion here with a visit to the **Tristan Stone**, a tall monolith about a mile northwest of Fowey off the A3082, supposed to be the tombstone of Tristan, known in legend as Mark's nephew and rival in love. Its Latin inscription bears an alleged reference to Drustanus, a version of the name Tristan.

Back in town, things liven up considerably during the annual **Royal Regatta and Carnival**, a sailing extravaganza with evening entertainment, combined with what is rated as one of Cornwall's best carnivals, taking place over a week in mid-August. River races and aerial displays by day and fireworks by night pull in the crowds; see Ⓦwww.foweyroyalregatta.co.uk for details.

Eating and drinking

Fowey's **restaurants** have an excellent reputation. The area is also well provided with **pubs**, all of which offer meals, notably Golant's *Fisherman's Arms*, Bodinnick's *Old Ferry Inn* – whose back room is hewn out of the rock – and Polruan's excellent *Lugger Inn*, with high-backed settles.

The Other Place 41 Fore St Ⓣ01726/833636. There are muted colours and an airy, modern vibe at this upstairs restaurant where everything from lobster to fish and chips is offered (most main courses cost around £16), while you can buy takeaway snacks including some fifteen flavours of ice cream at its street-level outlet. Restaurant closed daytime and weekdays in winter.

Restaurant Nathan Outlaw 20 Fore St Ⓣ01726/833315. At the *Marina Villa Hotel* (see opposite), run by a Michelin-starred chef, this stylish eatery offers such classy concoctions as lobster risotto and duck with pistachios and cherries. Mains cost around £27, and a seven-course tasting menu is £70. It's all fairly swish, and there's a riverside terrace.

Activities around Fowey

Below Fore Street, the Town Quay is the departure point for **river cruises** which, between Easter and October, provide a great way to explore the harbour and waterways hereabouts (tickets £6–10). The Quay is also the embarkation point for Fowey Marine Adventures, 35 Fore St (Ⓣ01726/832300, Ⓦwww.fowey-marine-adventures.co.uk), which operates a range of **sea cruises** in a RIB, with an accent on wildlife-watching – basking sharks can often be seen (£16–35 for 40min–3hr) – and for **self-drive motorboat rental** from Town Quay Boat Hire (Ⓣ0798/999 1115; £15 for 30min, or £65 for 4hr, including petrol, for up to 5 people). For the trip across St Austell Bay to Mevagissey, see "Arrival and information" p.229. For accompanied **canoe trips** (£20–40), contact Fowey River Expeditions, 17 Passage St (Ⓣ01726/833627, Ⓦwww.foweyriverexpeditions.co.uk), or Encounter Cornwall (Ⓣ01208/871066, Ⓦwww.encountercornwall.com), based in the village of Lerryn, in a tranquil creek three miles north of Bodinnick. Encounter Cornwall also offers **kayak hire and tuition**, and can also arrange cycle rides, self-guided walks and accommodation, as well as **bike rental** with a delivery and collection service.

Closed lunchtime Sun–Thurs, also eves Sun & Mon in winter.

Sam's 20 Fore St. Popular café and bistro adorned with posters and pop memorabilia, serving good-quality burgers (£7.50–9) and bouillabaisse (£27 for two). It doesn't take bookings, so arrive early if you don't want to queue.

Q 28 Fore St Ⓣ01726/833302. By the waterside at the elite *Old Quay House* hotel (see p.230), this elegant but relaxed restaurant ranks among the top-quality places in town, specializing in Mediterranean takes on meat and seafood dishes for £11–17. Leave room for dessert. Closed lunchtimes Oct–May.

Tiffins 24 Fore St Ⓣ01726/832322. Brisk but pleasant family-friendly place for baguettes or a plate of mussels (around £9), and pricier evening meals (mains around £15). There's a quieter space upstairs where you can also repair for a cocktail.

Inland to Lostwithiel

Five miles north of Fowey, reachable by train from Par and St Austell or weekday bus #24 or the more frequent National Express coach from St Austell, **LOSTWITHIEL** is an old market town and tin-exporting port on the lowest bridging point of the River Fowey, with an appealing mix of comely Georgian houses and dark cobbled passageways. The main A390 passes through the centre of town along Queen Street, east of which lie Fore Street and the parallel North Street – the latter leading to the fifteenth-century granite bridge over the river, and the train station.

Tanning was a major industry in Lostwithiel until the late 1800s, so it's apt that **St Bartholomew's Church** (Easter to late Sept Tues, Thurs & Fri 11am–3pm) on Church Lane (off Fore St), with its thirteenth-century Breton-inspired octagonal spire, should be dedicated to the patron saint of tanners. Inside, the finely carved octagonal font is worth taking a look at, as is the **Lostwithiel Museum** at 16 Fore St (Easter–Sept Mon–Sat 10.30am–12.30pm & 2.30–4.30pm; free), which charts eight centuries of local history from the time the town claimed to be Cornwall's capital. The area's military heritage is most vividly captured in the imposing ruins of **Restormel Castle**, crowning a hill a mile or so north of Lostwithiel (April–June & Sept daily 10am–5pm; July & Aug daily 10am–6pm; Oct daily 10am–4pm; £3; EH). Thought to have been built by a Norman baron around 1100 to protect the port, and enlarged at the end of the thirteenth century, Restormel preserves the shale-built shell of its huge circular keep, surrounded by a deep moat. By the time of the Civil War, the castle was already in a sorry state, and Royalist forces under Sir Richard Grenville found it easy to prise it out of the hands of the Earl of Essex's Parliamentarian army in 1644, the last time Restormel saw any service – and the last time that it was inhabited, since the Royalists abandoned it almost immediately. It's a peaceful, panoramic spot, an easy walk from Lostwithiel and good for a picnic.

Practicalities

Signposted at the northern end of town from the A390, Lostwithiel's **tourist office** (Mon–Fri 10am–5pm, Sat 10am–1pm; ⓣ01208/872207, ⓦwww.lostwithieltic.org.uk) is located in the Community Centre on Liddicoat Road; there's a free car park nearby.

There are a couple of good local **accommodation** options hereabouts. Next to each other off the A390 southwest of town, less than five minutes' uphill walk from the centre, try either of the two well-preserved Victorian lodgings on the Terrace: *Penrose* (ⓣ01208/871417, ⓦwww.penrosebb.co.uk; ③) or *Tremont House* (ⓣ01208/873055, ⓦwww.tremonthouse.co.uk; ④); both have internet access and great views from the good-size rooms. *Restormel Farm*, close to Restormel Castle's entrance gate (ⓣ01208/872484; closed Nov–Feb no credit cards; ④), is an old-fashioned farmhouse with two large rooms with a shared bathroom and a separate lounge and dining room displaying a few finds from the fields. The grounds of Lanhydrock (see p.357) are a fifteen-minute walk away.

Lostwithiel also has a great **restaurant**, the intimate, elegant *Trewithen*, 3 Fore St (closed Sun & Mon; ⓣ01208/872373), where dishes are globally inspired and locally sourced, for example Cornish antipasti (£14) and salmon and halibut Thai curry (£17); there's a courtyard garden for lunches, when a two-course menu is served for £11. There are a couple of more modern options also worth investigating: the *Terra Nova*, a café-bistro further down Fore Street where lunch dishes are £5–7.50 and evening mains under £10 (including delicious vegetarian dishes), and *River Brasserie* close by on Parade Square (closed daytime Sun & Mon; ⓣ01208/872774), where meat and seafood dishes are £13–17. The equally contemporary *Royal Talbot* **pub** on Duke Street is good for salads and has comfy sofas.

The Eden Project

Some ten years after it opened, the **Eden Project**, four miles northeast of St Austell (April–Sept daily 9.15am–6pm, last entry 4.30pm, may close later during school hols; Oct–March Mon–Fri 10am–4pm, Sat & Sun 10am–6pm, last entry 3pm; £16; ⓦwww.edenproject.com), remains the most feted of South Cornwall's attractions. Designed to showcase the diversity of the planet's plant life in an innovative, sometimes wacky, but refreshingly ungimmicky style, Eden was the brainchild of Tim Smit, the leading light in the rescue of the Lost Gardens of Heligan (see p.238), who first envisaged the potential of this disused clay pit, 160ft deep and covering 34 acres. There's plenty to see and do here, worth setting aside a full day for a thorough exploration, ideally with frequent breaks as the whole experience can prove quite exhausting.

The awesome scale of the project becomes apparent only once you have passed the entrance at its lip, from which the whole site is revealed, stunningly landscaped with an array of various crops and flower beds on scimitar-shaped terraces. Taking centre stage are the vast geodesic "biomes", or conservatories, made up of eco-friendly, Teflon-coated, hexagonal panels. One cluster, the **Mediterranean Biome**, holds groves of olive and citrus trees, cacti and other plants more usually found in the Mediterranean, southern Africa and southwestern USA. Connected to it by a common entrance, the larger **Rainforest Biome** – claimed to be the biggest greenhouse in the world – contains plants from the tropics, including teak and mahogany trees, and there's even a waterfall and river gushing through. Things can get pretty steamy here, but you can take cool refuge in an air-conditioned bunker halfway along the course.

Equally impressive are the **external grounds** (described by Smit as "Picasso meets the Aztecs"), where plantations of bamboo, tea, hops, hemp and tobacco are interspersed with brilliant swathes of flowers and eye-catching artworks that range from intricate wire animals to beautifully crafted cork and deadwood sculptures of woodland species. Along the pathways, informative panels outline some of the more pressing ecological issues around the world, and helpful guides are on hand to provide information. Timed **talks** and "story-telling" sessions are advertised on notice boards. In the midst of the complex, a lawned, open-air **arena** is the venue for free events by day and full-on concerts on summer evenings (see box, The Eden Sessions, below). In winter (Oct–Feb), this becomes a skating rink, with extended evening opening hours.

Eden's constantly evolving "living theatre" should ideally be visited in different seasons. Fresh sculptures and new hands-on activities are regularly added, many aimed at children, who will also appreciate the grand exhibition space and workshops (among other amenities) in The Core educational centre. Abundant good food is readily available, and there's a free Land Train shuttling between the entrance and the bottom of the pit in case your feet give up.

Weekends are always the most congested time to visit, especially during school holidays, while things are generally quietest either earlier or later in the day. Some **bus** travellers to Eden can save money and queuing time by buying a combined bus pass and admission ticket, the Eden Rider, valid for all First services in Cornwall (£17). From St Austell, you can take First #101 or Western Greyhound #527 (not Sun), while First #24 (not Sat or Sun) leaves you within about half a mile of the Visitor Centre; service #527 also links Eden with Newquay. **Bikers** and **hikers** can claim a £4 discount and skip the queues by going straight to the fast-track ticket window – the site is accessible on the Clay Trails cycleways (see opposite) and on a network of footpaths and road routes from St Austell and Par (local tourist offices can provide maps).

The Eden Sessions

The amphitheatre-shaped arena in the centre of the Eden Project has become one of Cornwall's premier concert venues, marketed as the **Eden Sessions**. Held every July, the events have attracted big-name artists (Kasabian and Paul Weller are among recent acts) which can book up months ahead. Consult the website for news of events, or call ⓣ01726/811972. Most ticket prices are £35–40, with priority given to "Inside Track" members (£10 or £15 annual subscription). Concerts start at 7pm or later; **buses** leaving at midnight are available to transport concert-goers back to St Austell, Bodmin, Penzance and other towns, for which advance booking is advised.

St Austell, Charlestown and around

Six miles west of Fowey and the nearest centre to the Eden Project, **ST AUSTELL** is an unprepossessing place that often gets gridlocked during the summer months. The town developed on the strength of the china-clay industry after deposits were found locally in the eighteenth century (see box, p.238), and the conical spoil heaps left by the mines are still the dominant feature of the local landscape, especially on Hensbarrow Downs to the north, where the great green-and-white mounds make an eerie sight. At the top of the town stands the **St Austell Brewery**, still owned by the same Hicks family who established the brewery in 1893. The visitor centre offers one-hour **guided tours** round the building (Mon–Fri 9am–5.30pm, Sat 10am–4pm, also Sun July–Sept 11am–3pm; last tours 90min before closing; no under-8s; £8; Ⓦ www.staustellbrewery.co.uk) – a good rainy day option. Numbers on each tour are limited, but you can book on Ⓣ 01726/66022.

The main reason to come to St Austell, however, is for the access it provides to choicer destinations nearby on the coast or inland. Two and a half miles north of town on the B3274 at Carthew, **China Clay Country Park** (Easter to late July, Sept & Oct daily 10am–5pm; late July to Sept daily 10am–6pm; Nov & Dec daily 10am–4pm; Jan–Easter Wed–Sun 10am–4pm; last entry 2hr before closing; £7.50; Ⓦ www.chinaclaycountry.co.uk) reveals everything you ever wanted to know about the china-clay industry. It's an extensive and absorbing exhibition, allowing a close-up view of how the pits were operated, with tours round the old clay workings, along with the original locomotives and wagons used in the pits. There's also a nature trail on site, so allow at least two hours to see everything. There's an excellent two-mile walk or bike ride you can make to get here from St Austell train station, the "Green Corridor", part of the **Clay Trails** (Ⓦ www.claytrails.co.uk), a network of mainly off-road bike routes that also link up with the Eden Project. Mostly gravel-surfaced, the trails are equally good for walkers and riders – contact St Austell's tourist office for more information.

St Austell's nearest link to the sea is at **CHARLESTOWN**, an unspoilt port that's an easy one-mile walk downhill from the centre. It's named after the entrepreneur Charles Rashleigh who in 1791 began work on the harbour of what was then a small fishing community, widening its streets to accommodate the china-clay wagons that passed through daily. Still used until the 1990s for shipping clay, the wharves appear oversized beside the tiny jetties, and are often dressed up by elaborate old-fashioned film sets – it's a favourite location for movie-makers. The dock is now owned by the Square Sail Shipyard, and you'll usually see one of the company's three old-fashioned square riggers *in situ* – they can usually be visited between Easter and October for a small admission charge. Housed in an old "dry" house for china clay behind the harbour, the **Shipwreck & Heritage Centre** (March–Oct daily 10am–5pm; £5.80; Ⓦ www.shipwreckcharlestown.com) is entered through tunnels once used to convey the clay to the docks, and shows a good collection of photos and relics as well as tableaux of historical scenes.

On each side of Charlestown's dock are coarse-sand and stone **beaches** sprinkled with small rock pools, above which cliff walks lead to the beaches around St Austell Bay. Eastwards, you soon arrive at overdeveloped **Carlyon Bay**, whose main resort is **Par**. It's a popular spot with caravanners and campers, but much of the bay is dominated by the china-clay works, the beaches here get clogged with clay, and the water is of dubious quality – the best swimming is to be found by pressing on to the sheltered crescent of **Polkerris**, flanked by rocks and green cliffs and protected by a curving breakwater. The easternmost limit of St Austell Bay is marked by **Gribbin Head**, near which stands Menabilly House, where **Daphne du Maurier** lived for 24 years. The model for "Manderley" in

▲ Charlestown

Rebecca, the house is not open to the public and not visible from the path, but you can see where Rebecca met her watery end at **Polridmouth Cove** and find out more at Fowey's Literary Centre (see p.230).

Practicalities

Trains on the main Penzance line stop at St Austell station on Station Approach, in the centre of town off High Cross Street. Most buses connecting St Austell with other towns stop here too, including #25, #26 and #26B for Fowey and Mevagissey, #525 (not Sun) for Charlestown and #526 also to Mevagissey. You can pick up full transport timetables as well as general information on the area from St Austell's **tourist office** (Easter–Sept daily 9am–6pm; Oct–Easter Mon–Sat 10am–5pm; Ⓣ01726/879500, Ⓦwww.visitthecornishriviera.co.uk or Ⓦwww.visitcornwalluk.co.uk), located half a mile southeast of the centre at the Jet garage on Southbourne Road (the A390). You can log on to the **internet** here (£1 for 30min).

Charlestown holds the most appealing **accommodation** options, the best of them being *Broad Meadow House*, behind the Shipwreck Centre on Quay Road (Ⓣ01726/76636, Ⓦwww.broadmeadowhouse.com; no credit cards), which between May and September offers "tent and breakfast" in pre-pitched "posh tents" in a meadow by the sea, to which breakfast is brought in the morning (£19–24 per person). It also has a few pitches available all year for regular campers – who can also order breakfast baskets (£6 per person). Other options include *T'Gallants*, 6 Charlestown Rd (Ⓣ01726/70203; ⑤), an elegantly furnished Georgian B&B at the back of the harbour with en-suite rooms and cream teas served in the garden, and, a few steps behind it, the *Rashleigh Arms* (Ⓣ01726/73635, Ⓔrashleigharms@staustellbrewery.co.uk; ⑤), with bright, mainly spacious en-suite rooms, two with sea views. The nearest **campsite** is just inland of St Austell Bay at Bethesda: *Carlyon Bay*, near the beach at Carlyon Bay and just a mile and a half from the Eden Project (Ⓣ01726/812735, Ⓦwww.carlyonbay.net; closed Nov–March), though there are pleasanter sites around Pentewan (see opposite).

Behind *T'Gallants*, try the *Rashleigh Arms* in Charlestown for a range of pub **food** including vegetarian options and a Sunday carvery, and, by the harbour, the *Harbourside Inn*, serving food all day and good coffees, and with live music on Saturday nights – in both you can eat for under £10 and drink real ales. Further afield, head for the *Rashleigh Inn*, a former coastguards' station right above the jetty at Polkerris (signposted from the A3082), a great venue for a crab and prawn sandwich (£6) or fish stew (£9).

Mevagissey and Heligan

Until the nineteenth century, **MEVAGISSEY**, five miles southwest of Charlestown, was famed for the fast ships constructed here and used for transporting contraband as well as pilchards. Today, the tiny port might display a few stacks of lobster pots, but the real business is tourism, with day-trippers converging on the harbour and overflowing into its surrounding labyrinth of alleys, a tight cluster of picturesquely flower-draped fishermen's cottages. Despite the crowds, the minute inner harbour – separated from the larger outer harbour by a pair of breakwaters – has an irresistible lure, with its clamour of swirling gulls amid the apparatus of the small fishing fleet. Between late April and September, a **ferry** operates several times daily between here and Fowey (see p.229).

Arrival and information

Buses #26, #26B and #526 from St Austell stop on Fore Street, the main road running behind the harbour. Mevagissey's helpful **tourist office** is in the *Country Kitchen* café on St George's Square (Mon–Fri 10am–5pm, also Sat & Sun 10am–5pm during summer school hols; ⓣ01726/844440, ⓦwww.mevagissey-cornwall.co.uk). You can log on to the **internet** here (£2 for 15min). If you want to get around **by bike**, head for Pentewan Valley Cycle Hire, Pentewan, one and a half miles north of Mevagissey (ⓣ01726/844242, ⓦwww.pentewanvalleycyclehire.co.uk).

Accommodation

Mevagissey's **accommodation** struggles to cope with the influx of summer visitors, though at any other time availability should be easy to come by. There's a cluster of pleasant **campsites** north of the village off Pentewan Road; most are family-friendly affairs with pools and play areas, for example *Sun Valley* (ⓣ01726/843266, ⓦwww.sunvalley-holidays.co.uk); the more peaceful *Meadows* is more basic and is edged by woodland (ⓣ01726/842547, ⓦwww.themeadowspentewanvalley.co.uk; closed Dec–March).

Corran Farm St Ewe ⓣ01726/842159, ⓦwww.corranfarm.co.uk. Handy for the Lost Gardens of Heligan (a signposted half-mile away), this spick-and-span, tile-hung farmhouse has three en-suite rooms and a wi-fi connection. Guests receive a complimentary cream tea, and the guest lounge has a log fire. No credit cards. ❸

Fountain Inn Cliff St, off East Quay ⓣ01726/842320. In the heart of Mevagissey, this flower-bedecked fifteenth-century inn has two stylish and airy en-suite rooms in the ❹ category, the cheaper double has separate facilities. ❷

Old Parsonage 58 Church St ⓣ01726/843709, ⓦwww.oldparsonage.net. Away from the harbour crowds, this wi-fi-enabled B&B has simply furnished single, double and twin rooms, on the small side, but all with en-suite or private bathrooms. Pick-ups from St Austell station and Newquay airport can be arranged. No single-night bookings at weekends in high season. ❹

Ship Inn Fore St ⓣ01726/843324, ⓦwww.staustellbrewery.co.uk. Colourful, modern bedrooms are available at this central spot, all en suite. No parking facilities. ❹

China clay

The extraction of **china clay**, or kaolin, is a Cornish success story. An essential ingredient in the production of porcelain, kaolin had, until the mid-eighteenth century, only been produced in northern China, where a high ridge, or *kao-lin*, was the sole known source of the raw material. In 1756, one **William Cookworthy** discovered deposits of kaolinite near Helston and subsequently in the hills west of St Austell, so kicking off the industry in Cornwall. The china clay was originally extracted to supply ceramics producers such as Wedgwood and Spode, but further uses were soon found. Among its many applications today, china clay improves the properties of paint and makes expensive prime-colouring pigments go further; it adds strength and resistance to rubber and plastics used for electrical insulation; and it's also used as an anti-caking agent in fertilizers, in insecticides, and as an ingredient in medicines – notably for quelling upset stomachs.Its most important use, though, is in **paper production**, and it remains the most widely used material after wood pulp. Still a vital part of Cornwall's economy, some 80 percent of the county's china clay is exported abroad through the ports of Fowey and Par to Western Europe (Scandinavia in particular).

The village and around

Other than its harbour, Mevagissey's main specific attraction is its **museum** at the end of East Quay, the road running alongside the harbour (Easter–June, Sept & Oct daily 11am–4pm; July & Aug daily 10am–5pm; free). The building has as much history as the exhibits inside: it was built in 1795 for the construction and repair of smugglers' boats, and most of its roof beams were recycled from the revenue-dodgers' old vessels. Alongside evocative photographs and other items illustrating the history of the region is a display devoted to Mr Pears, the local chemist who made his fortune from soap.

Many visitors to Mevagissey end up on the broad, sandy **Pentewan Beach**, a mile to the north, much of which is dominated by a caravan site, or at the awesome display of greenery at the **Lost Gardens of Heligan** (daily: April–Sept 10am–6pm; Oct–March 10am–5pm; last entry 90min before closing; £8.50; ⓦ www.heligan.com), two miles northwest of the village via the B3273. At their prime in the late 1800s, the gardens later fell into neglect and have only been rescued from their ten-foot covering of brambles in the last decade, largely under the instigation of Tim Smit, of Eden Project fame (see p.233). The marvellously abundant palm trees, giant Himalayan rhododendrons, immaculate vinery and glasshouses scattered about the garden all look as if they've been transplanted from warmer climes. Near the entrance, the northern gardens contain huge flower and vegetable plots, including pineapple pits dating from 1720, where the first pineapples in 150 years were coaxed into life a few years ago by the original manure heating system. A boardwalk takes you past interconnecting ponds, through a jungle and under a canopy of bamboo, ferns and palms down to the Lost Valley, where there are lakes, a wild-flower meadow and leafy oak, beech and chestnut rides. To get the most out of the gardens, it's worth joining one of the **guided tours** that take place daily in summer at 11.30am (£1.50). You can sample produce from the gardens at the *Steward's House* above the jungle area (closed in winter), or in the *Willows* restaurant near the entrance.

To reach Heligan, there's a virtually traffic-free trail from Mevagissey or St Austell for walkers and cyclists – ask local tourist offices there for full details – or take Western Greyhound bus #526 from either place.

Eating and drinking

It goes without saying that Mevagissey's **restaurants and pubs** specialize in fish, the menus changing according to the catch of the day.

Alvorada 17 Church St ⓣ01726/842055. You'll find a Portuguese slant to the tapas and main meals at this daintily decorated restaurant, where most main courses cost around £15. Specialities include *caldeirada*, or fisherman's casserole (£16). Closed lunchtime Mon & Sat, all Sun (but open Sun eve in Aug), also all Mon–Thurs & Fri lunch in winter.

Fountain Inn Cliff St. Economical lunches and evening meals are served in this fifteenth-century tavern, with all dishes at £6–15, and takeaway fish and chips also available. The beers are good and there's a piano for entertainment. No food Sun eve.

Roovray's 16 Fore St ⓣ01726/842672. Reserve a table here for a French take on dishes including fresh lobster and fruits de mer, though you may also find beef, duck, rabbit and Breton pancakes listed (£13–17); set-price two- and three-course early-evening menus (£14.50 and £18) help to keep the price down. Closed Tues & lunchtime Oct–Easter.

Ship Inn Fore St. Traditional pub with St Austell's ales and a range of bar meals plus fish specials, average price £8.50. There's regular live music at weekends.

Veryan Bay

Past the headland to the south of Mevagissey, the small sandy cove of **Portmellon** retains little of its boat-building activities but is reasonably free of tourists. Further still, **GORRAN HAVEN** was formerly a crab-fishing village but now looks merely suburban, though it has a neat rock-and-sand beach, and a footpath that winds round to the even more attractive **Vault Beach**, half a mile south. Curving west between Dodman Point and Nare Head, the five-mile parabola of **Veryan Bay** is barely touched by commercialism. Bounding the bay on the east, **Dodman Point** ranks as one of South Cornwall's most dramatic headlands, and has been the cause of many a wreck. From its gorse-covered heights, you can look down on a chaos of reefs and rocks, and splendid views extend westward across Veryan Bay. The promontory is topped by a stark granite cross built by a local parson as a seamark in 1896, and holds the substantial remains of an Iron Age fort, with a bulwark of earth cutting right across the point. Less than a mile west, sandy **Hemmick Beach** makes an excellent swimming spot, with rocky outcrops affording a measure of privacy. You'll find a little more commotion a mile or so west at **Porthluney Cove**, where the safe swimming tends to attract families. In a beautiful setting of wood, stream and pasture, the sandy beach is backed by the battlemented **Caerhays Castle** (house: mid-March to May tours at noon, 1.30pm & 3pm; gardens: mid-Feb to May daily 10am–5pm, last entry 4pm; house £5.50, gardens £5.50, combined ticket £9.50; ⓦwww.caerhays.co.uk), built in 1808 by John Nash. If you're here during the very limited opening period, you can join a thirty-minute tour of the house, mainly of interest to anyone who has seen Hitchcock's 1940 film of *Rebecca*, which was shot here. Call to reserve a place on ⓣ01872/501310. The beautiful wooded garden is more compelling, displaying world-famous collections of camellias, magnolias and rhododendrons.

Three miles further west, the minuscule and whitewashed village of **Portloe** is fronted by jagged black rocks that throw up fountains of seaspray, giving it a bracing, end-of-the-road kind of atmosphere. A mile or so inland of here, **VERYAN** itself has a pretty village green and pond, but is best known for its curious circular, white **houses** built some two hundred years ago by one Reverend Jeremiah Trist, apparently to guard the village from devils, which would be unable to hide in corners; for additional protection, the thatched roofs are topped by crucifixes.

A lane from Veryan leads a mile down to **Pendower Beach**, one of southern Cornwall's cleanest swimming spots. Two-thirds of a mile long and backed by dunes, Pendower joins with the neighbouring **Carne Beach** at low tide to create a long sand-and-shingle continuum.

Practicalities

If you want a drink or a bed in Veryan, head for the *New Inn* near the pond, a friendly pub with a quiet garden, where you can feast on wholesome meals such as duck with forest mushrooms (£10.50), and sleep in one of the spacious B&B rooms (ⓣ01872/501362, ⓦwww.newinnveryan.co.uk; ⑤). Otherwise try *Elerkey House* (ⓣ01872/501160, ⓦwww.elerkey.co.uk; ③), a large comfortable ex-farmhouse with three airy, en-suite rooms, a spacious garden and an adjoining art gallery; it's the first on the left after the church. If you prefer to wake up to the sea, however, stay in **Portmellon**, where the weathered old *Rising Sun Inn* (ⓣ01726/843235, ⓦwww.risingsunmevagissey.com; closed late Dec to Feb; ⑤) confronts the waves. If you're after something altogether classier, you can't do better than the *Lugger Inn* (ⓣ01726/501322, ⓦwww.luggerhotel.co.uk; ⑧) by the sea at **Portloe**; converted from a cluster of seventeenth-century cottages, this chic hideaway has modern furnishings, an excellent seafood restaurant and a terrace for drinks and sunbathing, with rugged coastline on either side.

At the other end of the scale, there's a great **youth hostel** (ⓣ0845/371 9107, ⓔboswinger@yha.org.uk; closed Nov–March; from £16) in a former farmhouse at **Boswinger**, a remote spot half a mile from Hemmick Beach; difficult to reach without your own transport, it's about a mile from the bus stop at Gorran Church Town, served infrequently by some #526 buses from St Austell and Mevagissey. Boswinger also has a **campsite**, *Sea View International* (ⓣ01726/843425, ⓦwww.seaviewinternational.com; closed Nov–March), with, as the name implies, a panoramic position overlooking Veryan Bay, on the road between Gorran Haven and Caerhays, near Hemmick Beach; with a heated outdoor pool, it's popular, so you'd be advised to book ahead in July and August.

Truro

Connected to the Carrick Roads estuary by the Truro River, the city of **TRURO** developed as a protected inland port, shipping tin to Europe and copper to Wales. One of Cornwall's original Stannary towns, it was a long-standing rival to Falmouth and although the silting of the river led to Truro's decline in the seventeenth century, prosperity returned with the tin-mining boom of the 1800s, as reflected in the solid Georgian houses. The arrival of the railway in 1859 and the granting of city status in 1877 ensured that Truro has remained Cornwall's commercial and administrative centre. However, it's more of a tourist crossroads than a holiday centre, lacking enough diversion to keep you away from the coast for long. In its favour, the accommodation here is generally cheap, and there's a good range of pubs and restaurants.

Arrival and information

Buses – including services #88 from Falmouth and #89 and #90 from Newquay (not Sun) – stop at the Lemon Quay **bus station** in the city centre, or near the **train station** on Richmond Hill. Truro's **tourist office** lies on Boscawen Street (April–Oct Mon–Fri 9am–5.30pm, Sat 9am–5pm; Nov–March Mon–Fri 9am–5pm; ⓣ01872/274555, ⓦwww.truro.gov.uk).

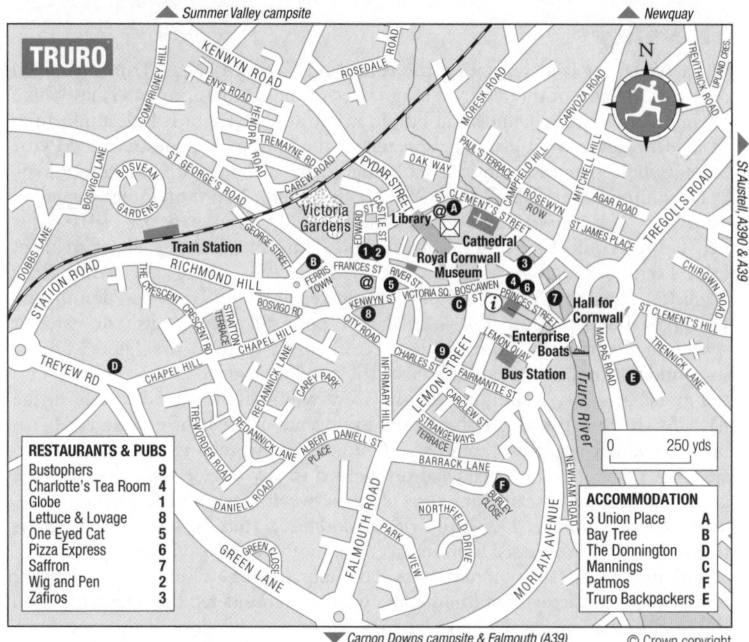

Accommodation

Accommodation in Truro is limited; it can get booked up in August but you shouldn't have much problem the rest of the year. The nearest **campsites** are the small *Summer Valley*, near Shortlanesend, two and a half miles northwest of town on the B3284 (ⓣ01872/277878, ⓦwww.summervalley.co.uk; closed Nov–March), and *Carnon Downs*, three miles southwest of Truro on the A39 Falmouth road (ⓣ01872/862283, ⓦwww.carnon-downs-caravanpark.co.uk), a large, flat and sheltered site with first-class washing facilities and steepish rates; it's one of the few campsites hereabouts that remain open all year.

3 Union Place ⓣ01872/263778. Convenient for the centre, in a Georgian terrace on a quiet cul-de-sac, this B&B has simple rooms with river or cathedral views. Bathrooms are shared, and there are flexible breakfast times and a discounted no-breakfast option if you prefer. No credit cards. ③

Bay Tree 28 Ferris Town ⓣ01872/240274, ⓦwww.baytree-guesthouse.co.uk. Smartly restored Georgian house in the centre with friendly management and shared bathrooms. Singles available. Advance booking recommended. No credit cards. ③

The Donnington 41–43 Treyew Rd ⓣ01872/222552, ⓦwww.donnington-guesthouse.co.uk. Smart and spacious Victorian B&B on the western side of town. Apart from two singles with private facilities, rooms are en suite, and there's a separate self-catering coach house at the back that would be handy for families. ④

Mannings Lemon St ⓣ01872/270345, ⓦwww.manningshotels.co.uk. Central and modern behind its Georgian facade, this casually smart, business-oriented place has eschewed traditional trappings in favour of a bright, contemporary feel, and has a good, informal brasserie. Wi-fi available. ⑥

Patmos 8 Burley Close, off Barrack Lane ⓣ01872/278018, ⓔb.ankers@tiscali.co.uk. Split-level modern house with friendly hosts; the larger en-suite room with views over the river (other room has private facilities). Breakfast includes options for special diets. It's a few minutes from the centre and station pick-ups can be arranged. No credit cards. ③

Truro Backpackers 10 The Parade ⓣ01872/260857 or 0781/375 5210, ⓦwww.trurobackpackers.co.uk. Relaxed hostel in a Georgian large terrace house close to the centre. There's a self-catering kitchen with an Aga stove, lounge and pleasant veranda. Dorm beds £18, single rooms £25 and doubles or twins £40.

The City

On a wedge of land separating the Allen and Kenwyn rivers, Truro's cobbled centre has plenty of interest, retaining traces of the medieval town's lanes where "kennels" or water channels still burble in the streets. There is little uniformity of style, however, most glaringly apparent at the bottom of pedestrianized Pydar Street, where the brisk modern shopping centre collides with the chronologically confused **Cathedral** (Mon–Sat 7.30am–6pm, Sun 7am–5pm; suggested donation £3; Ⓦwww.trurocathedral.org.uk). Completed in 1910, this neo-Gothic confection of local granite and Bath stone is the result of architect John Loughborough Pearson's controversial decision to revert to the Early English style, rather than something more in keeping with Truro's predominantly Georgian lines. Nonetheless, it makes a powerful impact, its tall exterior sprouting dramatically from the heart of the city, without the "close" usually surrounding English cathedrals. In fact, the building had to be shoe-horned into the available space, accounting for the skew-whiff alignment noticeable in the nave. Apart from this slight aberration, the overall effect is of orderly, clean-cut lines – a rather academic exercise in Gothic church-building which, a century later, has not noticeably mellowed or blended to any degree with the city. Free guided tours of the cathedral take place between April and October (Mon–Thurs & Sat 11am, Fri 11.30am), with an additional tour during school holidays (Mon–Fri 2pm). You need a permit to take photographs or videos (£1).

With its emphatically pointed arches and elaborate roof vaulting, the airy interior is notable for its Victorian **stained-glass** windows, considered the finest collection in the country. The most impressive include the rose window of the west front, depicting the Creation, and those in the north and south transepts. The south (right) aisle has a fine **baptistry**, with arcading and a font with pillars fashioned from Cornish serpentine. Further up on the same side, to the right of the choir, **St Mary's Aisle** is a relic of the Perpendicular church that formerly occupied the site, mostly demolished to make way for the new construction. You can see etchings of its original appearance at the back of the aisle, where there's also a copy of a letter of thanks from Charles I to the Cornish for their loyalty during the Civil War. The medieval-looking triptych behind the altar here is the work of Frank Pearson, the son of the cathedral's architect, who completed the project after his father's death. As well as the other fragments of the original church scattered about, there are some colourful Jacobean tombs worth viewing – and, in a different vein, look out for the matchstick model of the cathedral on the south aisle: it took 1600 hours and some 42,000 matches to assemble.

If you're spending any time in the county, a visit to the **Royal Cornwall Museum** (Mon–Sat 10am–4.45pm; free; Ⓦwww.royalcornwallmuseum.org.uk) on River Street provides some essential context to your travels. The **main gallery** on the ground floor illustrates diverse aspects of Cornwall's past, and includes, by the stairs, a Celtic inscription found at Tintagel (see p.341), and a portrait of Anthony Payne, "the Cornish giant" of Stratton (near Bude), in the uniform of a halberdier, thought to have been commissioned by Charles II. To either side, the **Nature Gallery** is dedicated to Cornwall's natural history, while the **Mineral Gallery** illuminates the county's geological make-up. Its collection of specimens is internationally important and includes examples of cassiterite (the only tin mineral of economic importance), mirror-surfaced iron pyrites and copper, asbestos and, in its various mottled forms, serpentine from the Lizard peninsula. You can also learn about Delabole slate and china clay via a diorama of a china-clay pit.

Upstairs, take a glance at the **Egyptian Gallery** showpieces – an unwrapped mummy and two detached feet from Roman-period mummies – on your way to the **Philbrick Gallery** of Cornish art, which features some outstanding paintings by the Newlyn School, including Harold Harvey's famous *St Just Tinminers*, a jaunty group of freshly turned out miners on their way down to the pits. There's also work by Stanhope Forbes and some sentimental but occasionally striking paintings by Henry Scott Tuke: maritime subjects, a small selection of his homoerotic nudes and a self-portrait. (For more on the arts in Cornwall, see Contexts, pp.383–386.)

The upstairs **balcony** shows decorative art, including Roman jewellery, Greek coins, fragments of Gothic churches and Renaissance items. Three further rooms show Old Master drawings and other items from the museum's art collection, textiles and costumes. If you want to delve deeper into Cornwall's past and present, the museum's Courtney Library is an invaluable archive of manuscripts, newspapers from 1798, reference works and art books; call ⓣ01872/272205 to arrange a visit.

Skirting the centre to the east, the Truro River appears rather dwarfed by the busy roads running alongside and over it. You can experience the best of it on a **river cruise** from the quayside: between May and September, Enterprise Boats operates a service downstream to Falmouth six times daily and to St Mawes twice daily (both £7.50 single, £12–15 return; ⓣ01326/374241, ⓦwww.enterprise-boats.co.uk), or you can just go as far as Trelissick Garden (see p.246; £4.50) – call for winter services. The highly scenic full trip takes about an hour as far as Falmouth or St Mawes. At low tide, departures are from **Malpas**, a village a couple of miles downstream, connected by a double-decker bus run by the boat company.

Eating and drinking

A good selection of Truro's **cafés and restaurants** lie on or around Kenwyn Street, west of the centre. There is a pair of decent **pubs** on the corner of Frances Street and Castle Street: the *Wig and Pen*, with real ale and patio seating, and the next-door *Globe*, which also serves a range of good food – there's a Sunday carvery (£11 including a beer); both places stage regular live music. On Boscawen Street, *Charlotte's Tea Room* above the *Pizza Express* (see below) is the best spot in town for **cream teas** in a Victorian setting (closed Sun).

Bustophers 62 Lemon St ⓣ01872/279029. Elegant wine bar and bistro where you sip a drink in the courtyard and sup on fresh local seafood or lamb. Most main dishes are around £12, and there's a set-price lunchtime and early-evening menu for £14. Closed Sun.

Lettuce & Lovage 15 Kenwyn St ⓣ01872/272546. Excellent wholefoods to eat in or take away, with a choice of Belgian beers. There are sandwiches (£3–4) and a dish of the day at lunchtime (£6.70), and main courses in the evening cost £9. There's an outdoor eating area. Closed eves Mon–Thurs & all Sun.

One Eyed Cat 116 Kenwyn St ⓣ01872/222122. Cool and contemporary restaurant and "drinkery" in a converted church, with tapas (£4–7) and mussels (£15) on the menu, as well as local steaks (£9–14). You can eat upstairs or on the ground floor, or just come for drinks. There are occasional DJs and live acoustic music. Closed Sun eve.

Pizza Express Boscawen St ⓣ01872/263617. Near the tourist office, this outlet for good, reliable pizzas is housed in the imposing old Coinage Hall, which sports carpets on the walls alongside portraits of George II and other notables. Pastas, pizza and salads cost £6–10.

Saffron 5 Quay St ⓣ01872/263771. Originally prepared fish and meat dishes are offered here in congenial surroundings, for example grilled red gurnard and chicken and lobster fricassee (£10–16). There's an especially good-value early-evening menu (£10 or £13 for two or three courses) as well as brunches on Sat. Closed Sun, also Mon eve Jan–May.

Zafiros 3 New Bridge St. Modern coffee and drinks lounge, with blue and red lighting, screens everywhere, free wi-fi and food – burgers, salads and the like (£6–8) – served until 7pm. There's regular live music and *The Office* nightclub stays open most nights until 2 or 3am. Gets especially busy at weekends. Closed Sun.

Listings

Banks Branches of all the main banks are scattered around Boscawen St and St Nicholas St.

Bike rental Bike Chain on the Mineral Tramway Cycle Trail at Bissoe, five miles southwest of Truro and signposted off the A39 at Devoran (☎01872/870341, ⓦwww.cornwallcyclehire.com; open daily until 6pm, or 5pm in winter), rents out bikes for exploring the old tramway system (see p.321) at £10–15 per day. Delivery and collection service available. Truro's tourist office can supply a free booklet outlining mountain bike routes.

Car hire Avis, Tregolls Rd ☎01872/262226, ⓦwww.avis.co.uk; Hertz, train station ☎01872/270238, ⓦwww.hertz.co.uk; Vospers, Newham Industrial Estate ☎01872/264664.

Hospital There's a 24hr accident and emergency department at the Royal Cornwall Hospital (Treliske), Higher Town (☎01872/250000), about a mile west of the centre on the A390 Redruth road.

Internet access Log on at Truro's library on Union Place and Pydar St (Mon, Tues, Thurs & Fri 8.30am–6pm, Wed Sat 9am–4pm; £1.80 for 30min), where booking at ☎01872/272702 is advisable, or Truro Computer Services, Frances St (Mon–Sat 9am–5pm; 50p for 10min).

Markets A flea market takes place three or four days weekly in the Hall for Cornwall, with entrances on Boscawen St and Back Quay (days vary: see inside Hall for details). Nearby Lemon Quay is the venue for a farmers' market on Wed & Sat.

Post office Opposite the cathedral, open Mon & Wed–Sat 9am–5.30pm, Tues 9.30am–5.30pm; has *bureau de change*.

Taxis A1 Taxis ☎01872/275981; Avacab Taxis ☎01872/241214.

Theatre The main regional venue is Hall for Cornwall, with entrances on Boscawen St and Quay St (☎01872/262466, ⓦwww.hallforcornwall.co.uk), which stages a programme of concerts and plays throughout the year.

St Mawes and the Roseland Peninsula

In a secluded spot at the mouth of the Percuil estuary and across the neck of the Carrick Roads from Falmouth, **ST MAWES** is an elite enclave of cottages, villas and abundant gardens, sloping above a simple harbour. A stroll around the village could take in St Mawes Castle, a good spot to soak up the stirring estuary views. Above all, make time for an exploration of the secretive lanes and rocky coast of the **Roseland Peninsula**, one of Cornwall's most ravishing corners.

Arrival and information

Bus #50 links St Mawes with Truro every two hours (three times daily on Sun), though it's more romantic to get here by boat, either by ferry from Falmouth (twice hourly in summer, less frequently in winter; ☎01872/861910, ⓦwww.kingharryscornwall.co.uk; £4.50 or £7 return; 20min) or from Truro (see p.243). The village has no tourist office but the **websites** ⓦwww.stmawesandtheroseland.co.uk and www.stmawes.info are useful for places to stay and eat and for general information.

Accommodation

St Mawes has far fewer **accommodation** options than Falmouth, but, if you're flush, this is the place for atmosphere and some seriously ritzy retreats. For those on a more modest budget, there are a handful of cheaper **B&Bs**, and there's a **campsite** with clean, modern facilities three miles north of St Mawes outside St-Just-in-Roseland, signposted off the A3078 and B3289: *Trethem Mill* (☎01872/580504, ⓦwww.trethem.com; closed early Oct to March).

Hotel Tresanton Lower Castle Rd ⓣ01326/270055, ⓦwww.tresanton.com. Cornwall doesn't get much more jet-setting than this, a Mediterranean-style oasis of luxury with bright, sunny colours and a yacht and speedboat available in summer to guests. 9

Little Newton Newton Rd ⓣ01326/270664. Two small but smart and modern en-suite rooms are available here, a steep ten-minute walk up from the seafront from behind the *Victory Inn*. No credit cards. Closed Nov–Feb. 3

Lowen Meadows Newton Rd ⓣ01326/270036. A little further up from *Little Meadows*, just off Castle Rd (easily accessed by drivers without having to enter the village), this modern B&B offers one large en-suite room with a wonderful river view. Closed Oct–March. No credit cards. 5

St Mawes Hotel Marine Parade ⓣ01326/270266, ⓦwww.stmaweshotel.co.uk. It doesn't have the panache of the *Tresanton*, but this slightly more affordable seafront place can also boast an exclusive air, with crisply contemporary rooms (those with estuary views cost more). 7

The village and around

At the village's western end, the small and pristine **St Mawes Castle** (April–June & Sept Mon–Fri & Sun 10am–5pm; July & Aug Mon–Fri & Sun 10am–6pm; Oct Mon–Fri & Sun 10am–4pm; Nov–March Fri–Mon 10am–4pm; may close 4pm on Sun & Fri in summer; £4; EH) was, like Pendennis across the water in Falmouth (see p.250), built during Henry VIII's reign between 1539 and 1543, based on designs by the king's German military architect Stefan von Haschenberg. Both castles adhere to the same clover-leaf design, with a central round keep surrounded by robust gun emplacements, but this is the more architecturally interesting of the pair, with three semicircular bastions surrounding the four-storey central tower, and some of the best examples of decorative stonework of all Henry's fortified works. The castle lacks much drama, however, partly on account of its immaculate condition, which it owes to its early surrender when placed under siege by General Fairfax's Parliamentary forces in 1646. The bloodless takeover eased the way for Fairfax's harder-fought acquisition of Pendennis Castle a few weeks later.

Among the examples of Tudor stone-carving and stone-dressing, look out for a Latin inscription to Henry (with a back-to-front "S") at the entrance. There are few other signs of finesse here, however, the strictly utilitarian design offering little scope for comfort or privacy for the lonely garrison, with scarcely a passage or stairway not overlooked by slits and spyholes. Although its design was considered revolutionary at the time, it retained such medieval features as the terrifying *oubliette*, a deep, square shaft just inside the entrance on the right where prisoners were detained, now covered by a glass roof. The cellar kitchen and the gun installations constitute the main points of interest, though you'll learn plenty about the castle's background as well as local history with the free audioguide. The guidebook (£3.99) represents good value if you're planning to visit Pendennis Castle too (see p.250), which it also describes.

Within easy distance of St Mawes, the backwaters of the **Roseland peninsula**, a deeply serene area of narrow lanes and idyllic waterside retreats, make an irresistible excursion. You can get a taste of it on a trip to one of Cornwall's most picturesque churches, **St Anthony-in-Roseland**, a twelfth- to thirteenth-century building reachable in fifteen minutes from St Mawes harbour by the seasonal **ferry** across the Percuil River (Easter–Oct daily around every 30min 9.30am–5.15pm; £3.50, or £5.50 return, £3.50 one way for bikes). The peninsula's rocky southern coast, where a lighthouse at **St Anthony's Head** marks the entry into Carrick Roads, is well worth exploring, especially for the throngs of sea birds that nest hereabouts.

St Anthony-in-Roseland's charm is if anything eclipsed by that of a second church lying three miles north of St Mawes, **St Just-in-Roseland**, reachable by road or on signed paths. On the shore of a creek surrounded by palms and subtropical shrubbery, with granite gravestones tumbling right down to the water's edge, the small grey church dates from 1261 but has a fifteenth-century tower.

A couple of miles further north of St Just, the chain-driven **King Harry ferry** crosses the River Fal about every twenty minutes (April–Sept Mon–Sat 7.30am–9.30pm, Sun 9.10am–9.30pm; Oct–March Mon–Sat 7.30am–7.30pm, Sun 9.50am–6.30pm; cars £4.50, or £7.50 day return, bikes 50p, foot-passengers 20p; ⓣ01872/862312, ⓦwww.kingharryscornwall.co.uk), significantly shortening the route to Truro or Falmouth. The ferry docks close to **Trelissick Garden** (daily: mid-Feb to Oct 10.30am–5.30pm or dusk; Nov to mid-Feb 11am–4pm or dusk; £7; NT), celebrated for its hydrangeas and other Mediterranean species, rhododendrons and camellias, and there's a splendid woodland walk along the Fal (free access all year). Take bus #93 (not Sun) from Truro to get here, or, in summer, join a river trip from Truro, (see p.243) Falmouth (see p.249) or St Mawes (see p.244).

Eating and drinking

There isn't a great deal of choice when it comes to **food** and **drink** in St Mawes, though prices are reasonable and the quality is generally high. A supermarket near the harbour can supply picnic needs.

Café Chandlers Harbourside. Simple and cheap fare is offered here, from sandwiches to salads and hot snacks, plus good coffees and fresh fruit juices. Locally sourced deli items also available. Closed eves.

St Mawes Hotel Marine Parade ⓣ01326/270266. A relaxed spot for a drink or a meal in the ground-floor café-bar, and you can enjoy panoramic views from the upstairs restaurant, where roast mackerel with coconut, lime and chilli (£8.50) and rump steak (£12) are on the menu.

Tresanton Lower Castle Rd ⓣ01326/270055. Chic cuisine with a Mediterranean flavour, strong on seafood and local meat. The set-price dinner weighs in at £42 for three courses, and there are terraces for dining alfresco.

Victory Inn Victory Steps. Atmospheric, oak-beamed pub opposite the harbour, serving local ales and fine seafood meals at the bar or in the more up-to-date restaurant upstairs, where mains are around £11. The crab risotto is especially good. A couple of elegant rooms are also available here (ⓣ01326/270324, ⓦwww.victory-inn.co.uk; ❼).

Falmouth and around

The construction of Pendennis Castle on the western side of the Carrick Roads estuary mouth in the sixteenth century prepared the ground for the growth of **FALMOUTH**, then no more than a fishing village. The building of its deep-water harbour was proposed a century later by Sir John Killigrew, one of a mercantile dynasty that long dominated local life, and Falmouth's prosperity was assured when it became chief base of the fast Falmouth Packets in 1689, which sped mail and bullion to the Mediterranean and the Americas. In the twentieth century, however, Falmouth lost most of its Cornish character in the process of becoming a full-time tourist resort, but has latterly assumed another identity as a centre of the local **arts scene**, providing a vital antidote to the predominant eating-and-shopping tone of its main street. The castle, of course, is the chief attraction, and some good beaches and eating and sleeping choices add to the town's allure. There are also some excellent river cruises for exploring the ins and outs of the Carrick Roads, and even the twenty-minute crossing to St Mawes (see p.244) makes a great way to view Pendennis as well as St Mawes Castle and St Anthony's Head.

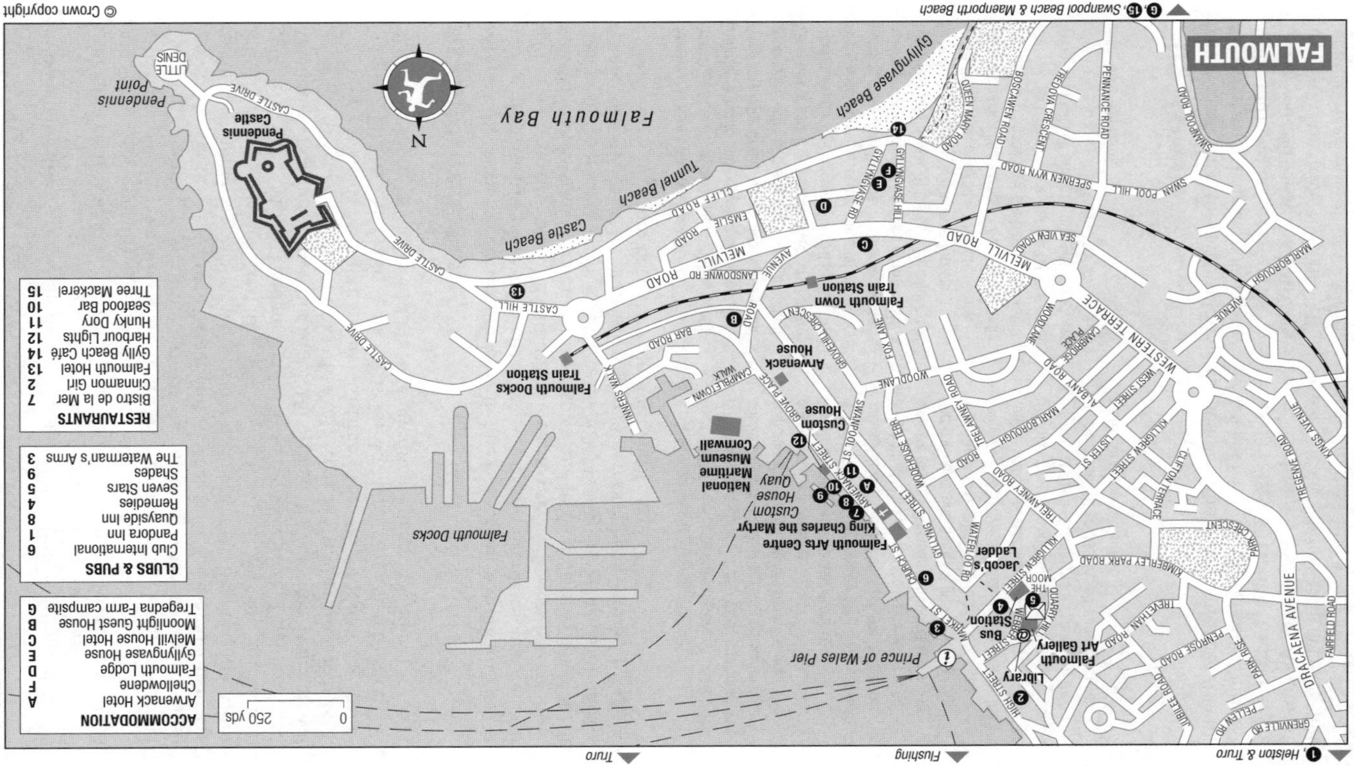

FALMOUTH
ACCOMMODATION
Arwenack Hotel A
Chellowdene F
Falmouth Lodge D
Gyllyngvase House E
Melvill House Hotel C
Moonlight Guest House B
Tregedna Farm campsite G
CLUBS & PUBS
Club International 6
Pandora Inn 1
Quayside Inn 8
Remedies 4
Seven Stars 5
Shades 9
The Waterman's Arms 3
RESTAURANTS
Bistro de la Mer 7
Cinnamon Girl 2
Falmouth Hotel 13
Gylly Beach Café 14
Harbour Lights 12
Hunky Dory 11
Seafood Bar 10
Three Mackerel 15
0 250 yds
St Mawes
Helford River
Truro
Flushing
1, Helston & Truro
G, 15, Swanpool Beach & Maenporth Beach
© Crown copyright
Falmouth Docks
Falmouth Bay
Pendennis Castle
Pendennis Point
Little Denis
Castle Beach
Tunnel Beach
Gyllyngvase Beach
Prince of Wales Pier
Falmouth Docks Train Station
Falmouth Town Train Station
National Maritime Museum Cornwall
Custom House Quay
Custom House
Arwenack House
Falmouth Arts Centre
King Charles the Martyr
Jacob's Ladder
Bus Station
Library
Falmouth Art Gallery
N
CASTLE DRIVE
CASTLE HILL
TINNERS WALK
BAR ROAD
CAMPBELTOWN WALK
GROVE PLACE
AVENUE ROAD
LANSDOWNE RD
MELVILL ROAD
EMSLIE ROAD
CLIFF ROAD
GYLLYNGVASE RD
GYLLYNGVASE HILL
QUEEN MARY ROAD
BOSCAWEN ROAD
TREDOVA CRESCENT
PENNANCE ROAD
SWANPOOL ROAD
SWAN POOL HILL
SPERNEN WYN ROAD
SEA VIEW ROAD
MARLBOROUGH AVENUE
WOODLANE
WESTERN TERRACE
CAMBRIDGE PLACE
ALBANY ROAD
WEST STREET
KILLIGREW STREET
LISTER ST
MARLBOROUGH ROAD
TRELAWNEY ROAD
FOX LANE
GROVEHILL CRESCENT
SWANPOOL ST
ARWENACK STREET
CHURCH ST
MARKET ST
GYLLYNG STREET
WODEHOUSE TERR.
WATERLOO RD
KILLIGREW STREET
THE MOOR
QUARRY HILL
WEBBER STREET
HIGH STREET
TREVETHAN ROAD
KIMBERLEY PARK ROAD
PARK CRESCENT
CLIFTON TERRACE
TREGENVE ROAD
KINGS AVENUE
DRACAENA AVENUE
FAIRFIELD ROAD
PARK RISE
PENROSE ROAD
JUBILEE ROAD
PELLEW RD
GRENVILLE RD

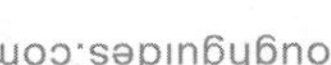

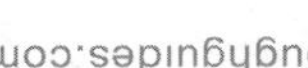

Arrival, getting around and information

A branch line from Truro runs daily to Falmouth, stopping at Falmouth Town and Falmouth Docks **train stations**, nearest the beaches and castle respectively, and each around ten minutes' walk from the centre. **Buses** #88, #88B and #400 (not Sun) from Truro and National Express coaches stop on the Moor, the old town's main square at the western end of the long main street that runs almost the whole length of the harbour, variously called High Street, Market Street, Church Street and Arwenack Street. **Local buses** are useful for linking the various parts of town, chiefly #41, between the Moor and Gyllyngvase Beach, and the #400 (neither runs on Sun in winter), connecting the Moor, Pendennis Castle and Gyllyngvase, Swanpool and Maenporth beaches. Below the Moor, the Prince of Wales Pier is the arrival point for passenger **ferries** from St Mawes (see p.244) and Truro (see p.240). The pier also holds Falmouth's **tourist office** (April–Oct Mon–Sat 9.30am–5.15pm, July & Aug also Sun 10.15am–1.45pm; Nov–March Mon–Fri 9.30am–5.15pm; ⓣ01326/312300, ⓦwww.discoverfalmouth.co.uk).

Accommodation

Most of the town's **accommodation** lies near the train stations and beach area; expect to pay more for the latter. Among the overdeveloped caravan parks on the coast south of Falmouth, the **campsite** at *Tregedna Farm* is more tent-friendly, two and a half miles from town and half a mile from Maenporth Beach and the coast path (ⓣ01326/250529, ⓦwww.tregednafarmholidays.co.uk; closed Oct–March); there are also bunkrooms here. See also p.241 for a good year-round site between Falmouth and Truro.

Arwenack Hotel 27 Arwenack St ⓣ01326/311185, ⓔarwenack@hotmail.com. Centrally located on the busy main street, this workaday hotel in a 250-year-old building offers good value without many trimmings, though the top room boasts a superb view. No credit cards. ❸

Chellowdene Gyllyngvase Hill ⓣ01326/314950, ⓦwww.chellowdene.co.uk. Unusual deep-roofed building 50m from the beach, with all rooms having private facilities, and two of the rooms with balconies with a view of the sea. No under-10s. ❺

Falmouth Lodge 9 Gyllyngvase Terrace ⓣ01326/319996 or 0752/572 2808, ⓦwww.falmouthbackpackers.co.uk. Clean and friendly backpackers' hostel near the beach, decorated with mementoes of Africa and the Caribbean, and with use of kitchen and free internet. Bunks cost from £19, and there are doubles for £42 or £50 en suite. No credit cards.

Gyllyngvase House Gyllyngvase Rd ⓣ01326/312956, ⓦwww.gyllyngvase.co.uk. Staid but comfortable choice within its own grounds two minutes from the sea. There's a nice lounge bar with sea views and a couple of rooms also have bay views. Free wi-fi. ❺

Melvill House Hotel 52 Melvill Rd ⓣ01326/316645, ⓦwww.melvill-house-falmouth.co.uk. A few minutes' walk from the beach, this pink-fronted Victorian terrace house offers functional, en-suite rooms with small bathrooms and sea or harbour views, and there's a guests' lounge. ❸

Moonlight Guest House 6 Anwyn Cottages, Avenue Rd ⓣ01326/315262. Convenient for the centre, station, beaches and castle, this good-value B&B has three en-suite rooms with woody decor, the best of them (slightly more expensive) the spacious attic. Breakfast is self-catering in your room. No credit cards. ❶

The Town

The logical place to start exploring Falmouth is **the Moor**, the Old Town's elongated central square, now mainly used as a bus terminus and car park. One side of the square offers access to the precipitous 111 steps of **Jacob's Ladder**, from where you can enjoy the bird's-eye view of the harbour and estuary. At ground level, you can trace the busy **High Street** and its continuations Market and Church streets from the Moor, running parallel to the harbour.

A landmark halfway along is Falmouth's parish church of **King Charles the Martyr**, consecrated in 1662 when the town was once again able to assert its royalist allegiances. It's unusual for its round arches and huge granite Tuscan columns within, and has some good Victorian stained and enamelled glass in the north aisle, though successive alterations have stripped it of much of its character. Further along Arwenack Street, the white-columned facade of the **Custom House** (1820) stands in front of the lively **Custom House Quay**, the spur of Falmouth's development as a port after it was built in 1670 by the Killigrews. Note the King's Pipe on the Quay, a brick chimney used to incinerate seized contraband tobacco.

The Killigrews' home, the Tudor **Arwenack House** (not open to the public), still stands at the southern end of Arwenack Street, and is Falmouth's oldest example of domestic architecture, though only fragments of the fourteenth-century house remain following remodelling in the sixteenth and eighteenth centuries. The odd granite pyramid standing opposite the house, built in 1737, is probably intended to commemorate the local family, though its exact significance has never been clear. The dynasty's most eminent member was Thomas Killigrew, a former companion-in-exile to Charles II and an indifferent Restoration dramatist who was also manager of the king's company of actors. As the founder of London's Theatre Royal in Drury Lane, he obtained permission to use female actors for the first time on stage – thereby introducing Nell Gwynne to the king's notice.

Falmouth's **National Maritime Museum Cornwall** stands on the seafront opposite Arwenack House (daily 10am–5pm; £8.75; Ⓦwww.nmmc.co.uk). The large, purpose-built exhibition centre offers a fascinating exploration of water-borne craft, with diverse examples from all over the world. Many of these are spectacularly suspended in mid-air in the **Flotilla Gallery**, the cavernous centrepiece of the museum, where the vessels can be viewed from three different levels. The exhibits are re-hung annually to illustrate different maritime themes. In addition, there are numerous smaller galleries that focus on boat-building and repairing skills, seafaring history, Falmouth's packet ships and Cornwall's various other links with the sea, including fishing. There's plenty of interactive gadgetry, and at one end of the museum, a lighthouse-like lookout tower offers lofty views over the harbour and estuary.

Falmouth's arts scene presents a very different side to the town, which you can investigate at Church Street's **Poly**, a general arts centre (daily 10am–5pm; free),

Ferries and cruises from Falmouth

From the Prince of Wales Pier, below the Moor, or (less frequently) from Custom House Quay, ferries leave for **St Mawes** once or twice an hour all year (£4.50, or £7.50 return, bikes £3.50), a twenty-minute crossing between about 8.30am (9.30am on Sun) and 9pm in summer (check winter times). Ferries from Prince of Wales Pier also connect up with **Truro** up to five times daily (see p.243), taking around an hour each way and costing £12 return, and with **Trelissick Garden** (£4.50 one way). In addition, there are once- or twice-hourly crossings to the placid hamlet of **Flushing**, across the Penryn River (roughly 8.45am–5.15pm, with a lunch-break; adults & bikes £2, pay on board) and various river cruises (from £6), including to the **Helford River** (twice daily in summer; £12), bookable from kiosks on the pier. You can find out more about all boat trips by consulting Ⓦwww.falriverlinks.co.uk. **Self-drive cabin boats** carrying up to six people are available from Custom House Quay (around £20 per hour), for which no experience is necessary. You can arrange rental at the Quay or by calling one of the operators listed at the tourist office.

and **Falmouth Art Gallery** on the Moor (Mon–Sat 10am–5pm; free), both of which have small but eclectic collections of contemporary art, with regular exhibitions. There are plenty of private art galleries in town as well as open studio events, publicized on flyers, posters and at the tourist office, generally showing a more dynamic slant than much of the artwork on display at the region's other arts centre, St Ives. Round the corner from Falmouth Art Gallery, the northern end of the **High Street** continues the bohemian theme, with good restaurants and cafés around Old Brewery Yard.

Pendennis Castle and the beaches

Falmouth's most popular attraction, **Pendennis Castle** (daily: April–June & Sept 10am–5pm, closes 4pm on Sat; July & Aug 10am–6pm, closes 4pm on Sat; Oct–March 10am–4pm; £5.70; EH), occupies the tongue of land at the eastern end of town. Standing sentinel at the entrance to Carrick Roads, it's a less refined contemporary of the castle at St Mawes (see p.245), but the site on its own pointed peninsula wins hands down, the stout ramparts offering superb all-round views. Although now much larger and more imposing than St Mawes Castle, Pendennis was originally the same size, consisting of the circular keep and curtain wall erected by Henry VIII. Spurred to action by the Spanish Armada and the Spanish attack on Penzance in 1595, Elizabeth I added the bastioned outer defences which were to prove crucial during the Civil War a half-century later, when it endured a five-month siege by the Parliamentarians that ended only when nearly half its defenders had died and the rest had been starved into submission.

The central **Keep** now holds a collection of cannonry, and its gun deck is the scene of regular re-enactments of a battle. The structure formerly housed the garrison as well as the guns, and is joined to a domestic block that accommodated the governor, and also army officers during both world wars (accounting for the somewhat incongruous panelling in some of the rooms).

Near the keep, the fifteenth-century **Gunshed** has an exhibition where you can hone your Morse code and aiming abilities. In front, next to the One-Gun Battery, the Sally Port is the entrance to tunnels leading to the camouflaged **Half-Moon Battery**, first built in 1795 as a cannon platform, after which it remained the castle's most important gun emplacement for some 150 years. Together with the battery on St Anthony's Head on the opposite side of the estuary, Pendennis provided Falmouth's main defence during both world wars, though the guns visible now are 1946 models. There's a good view out to sea from the **Battery Observation Post**, where sightings were taken and relayed to the battery itself; it's now restored to how it might have looked during World War II, with instruments and charts, radio equipment and taped conversations adding to the ambience.

Out on the headland, beyond the walls, **Little Dennis** is the original blockhouse built by Henry VIII, reachable from the car park on Castle Drive from outside the castle. It's a breezily exposed point to visit at any time, with terrific views of Falmouth Bay and the estuary. Displays of jousting and open-air evening **concerts** and theatre productions are occasionally staged in Pendennis Castle grounds in summer, and there are ghost tours in winter; call ⓣ01326/316594 for dates and details.

West of Pendennis Point stretches a series of long sandy bays. The most popular of the **beaches** here is **Gyllyngvase Beach**, though neighbouring **Swanpool Beach** – accessible by cliff path from Gyllyngvase – is pleasanter, with an inland lake and a great café/restaurant (see opposite). Both beaches have good facilities and boats for hire. You'll find less paraphernalia a couple of miles further on at **Maenporth**, from where there are some fine cliff-top walks.

Eating

Pasties, pizzas and chips are available everywhere in Falmouth. You'll find good, freshly baked **pasties** from the Cornish Miner at Custom House Quay and from Morris at 60 Church St; both have vegetarian options. For self-caterers, there's a useful **wholefood shop**, The Natural Store, at 16 High St.

Bistro de la Mer 28 Arwenack St ⓣ01326/316509. Serious fish restaurant with large cellar-room, offering set lunches (£9.50–17.50); in the evenings, sample such dishes as Cornish fish soup (£18.50), tiger prawn kebab (£18.50) or duck (£15.50). Closed lunchtime Sun & Mon.

Cinnamon Girl Old Brewery Yard ⓣ01326/211457. Wholefood, vegetarian and vegan café that makes a pleasant place for a pause during the day for thoughtfully prepared snacks such as puy lentils and spicy goat's cheese on toast, and opens three nights a weeks for a selection of "evening bites" (£3 each or four for £10) and organic wines. Closed Sun & eves Sun–Wed.

Falmouth Hotel Castle Beach ⓣ0844/502 7587. This classic Victorian seaside palace overlooking lawns and beach offers a grandiose three-course dinner (£30) beneath overhanging chandeliers in its *Trelawney Restaurant*, for which booking is essential. Alternatively, you can sample the atmosphere while tucking into the more reasonably priced bar menu (lunch or dinner) or over an afternoon cream tea.

Gylly Beach Café Gyllyngvase Beach. Right on the beach with a decked area, this cool hangout serves everything from iced drinks to grills and pizzas, with lunch dishes at £6–9, evening mains £10–15. A good spot for breakfast or a summer barbecue (from 5pm), and there's live music on Sunday evenings. Closed Mon–Wed eves in winter.

Harbour Lights Arwenack St, near Custom House Quay. You can enjoy views over the harbour while enjoying award-winning fish and chips and other inexpensive snacks, or else sampling local mackerel or haddock (£7–10). Also good for takeaways.

Hunky Dory 46 Arwenack St ⓣ01326/212997. Smart, modern eatery for quality seafood, meat and vegetarian dishes (mostly £15–18). Leave space for some delectable desserts. Closed daytime.

Seafood Bar Lower Quay Hill (also known as Quay St) ⓣ01326/315129. Hidden below the *New Bamboo House* Chinese takeaway, this place offers a secluded ambience to sample excellent fish dishes (£12–18). Try the fish chowder or king prawns and scallops, or splash out on lobster. Closed daytime, also Oct–June all Sun & Mon.

Three Mackerel Swanpool Beach ⓣ01326/311886. Lovely spot overlooking the beach with a contemporary, easy-going atmosphere, offering such ambitious dishes as "Seafood Operetta" – red mullet, crevets, mussels, scallops and fennel – though delicious meat and vegetarian dishes are also on the menu. Mains in the evening cost £16–20, the simpler lunchtime fare £9–13. Book early for one of the tables by the window. Tapas are also served outside on the deck. Closed Sun eve Nov–Easter.

Drinking, nightlife and entertainment

Signifying the start of the oyster-dredging season, Falmouth's **Oyster Festival** (ⓦwww.falmouthoysterfestival.co.uk), stretching over four days in mid- or late October, features races in the harbour, celebrity chefs, twice-daily seafood-cooking shows and oysters on offer in the Oyster Bar, all to folk and jazz accompaniment. The main venue is Custom House Quay.

Falmouth is not especially renowned for its **clubbing** scene, but there are a couple of fair options: *Club International* in St George's Arcade (ⓣ01326/311284), *Shades* on Lower Quay Hill (ⓣ01326/311323) and *Remedies* on the Moor (ⓣ01326/414454), As well as its four exhibition galleries, **Falmouth Arts Centre** (ⓣ01326/212300, ⓦwww.thepoly.org) has a crowded schedule of film, drama, dance, talks, recitals and live-music events.

Pubs

Pandora Inn Restronguet, four miles north of Falmouth. Drivers, bikers or boaters might venture out to this riverside pub, where superior bar food is available at lunchtime and cream teas every summer afternoon. You can also wine and dine on fresh seafood in the upstairs restaurant (ⓣ01326/372678).

Quayside Inn 41 Arwenack St. The pick of the pubs, with local Sharp's and Skinner's ales, waterside tables and seafood on the bar menu, and occasional live music.
Seven Stars The Moor. For an old-fashioned tipple, this museum-like pub has a quiet atmosphere and a vicar-landlord whose family has operated the pub since 1873. Try the local Grandma's Weapon's Grade Ginger Beer.
The Waterman's Arms Off Market St. Popular with locals, with ample seating overlooking the harbour and free wi-fi.

Listings

Banks Barclays is on Killigrew St; HSBC and NatWest are on Market St; Lloyds TSB is on Killigrew St and Church St.
Bus information All routes and schedules at ⓣ0871/200 2233, ⓦwww.traveline.info, otherwise call First ⓣ0845/600 1420
Car rental Falmouth Garages, Church Rd, Penryn ⓣ01326/377246; Europcar, Yacht Marina, North Parade ⓣ0845/758 5375.
Internet Log on at the library on the Moor (Mon, Tues, Thurs & Fri 9.30am–6pm, Sat 9.30am–4pm; £1 for 30min). You can book a terminal by calling ⓣ0300/123 41115.
Police Dracaena Ave ⓣ0845/277 7444.
Post office The main office in The Poundshop on the Moor (Mon & Wed–Fri 8.30am–5.30pm, Tues 9am–5.30pm, Sat 9am–3pm, Sun 9am–12.30pm) has a *bureau de change*.

Travel details

Trains

Falmouth to: Truro (1–2 hourly; 25–30min).
Looe to: Liskeard (Mon–Sat hourly, Sun mid-June to mid-Sept 8 daily; 30min).
Par to: Newquay (Mon–Sat 5–7 daily, Sun mid-June to mid-Sept 5 daily; 50min–1hr 10min); Penzance (1–2 hourly; 1hr–1hr 15min); Plymouth (1–2 hourly; 45min–1hr).
Truro to: Bristol (3–5 daily; 3hr 20min–3hr 50min); Exeter (1–2 hourly; 2hr 20min); Falmouth (1–2 hourly; 25min); Liskeard (1–2 hourly; 45–50min); London (10 daily; 4hr 20min–5hr); Penzance (1–2 hourly; 50min); Plymouth (1–2 hourly; 1hr 10min–1hr 25min).

Buses

Charlestown to: St Austell (Mon–Sat hourly; 15min).
Falmouth to: Helston (Mon–Sat 15 daily, Sun 3 daily; 50min–1hr 5min); Penzance (Mon–Sat 8 daily; 1hr 40min); Plymouth (2 daily; 2hr 30min); St Austell (2 daily; 1hr 10min); Truro (Mon–Sat 4–5 hourly, Sun 1–2 hourly; 35–50min).
Fowey to: Mevagissey (Mon–Sat 4 daily, Sun hourly; 1hr); St Austell (1–2 hourly; 45min).
Gorran Haven to: Mevagissey (Mon–Sat 5 daily, Sun 2 daily; 20min).
Looe to: Liskeard (Mon–Sat hourly, Sun 5 daily; 25min); Plymouth (Mon–Sat 6–7 daily; 1hr 10min); Polperro (Mon–Sat 1–2 hourly, Sun 5–10 daily; 20min).
Lostwithiel to: St Austell (5–9 daily 25–50min).
Mevagissey to: Fowey (Mon–Sat 4 daily, Sun hourly; 1hr); Gorran Haven (Mon–Sat 4–5 daily, Sun 2 daily; 20min); St Austell (1–2 hourly; 20min).
Polperro to: Liskeard (Mon–Sat hourly, Sun 5 daily; 45–55min); Looe (Mon–Sat 1–2 hourly, Sun 5–10 daily; 20min).
St Austell to: Charlestown (Mon–Sat hourly; 15min); Eden Project (1–2 hourly; 20–25min); Falmouth (2 daily; 1hr); Fowey (hourly; 45min); Lostwithiel (Mon–Sat 6–11 daily, Sun 6 daily; 20–50min); Mevagissey (1–2 hourly; 20min); Newquay (Mon–Sat 2 hourly, Sun 6 daily; 1hr); Par (2 hourly; 30min); Truro (1–3 hourly; 30–45min).
Truro to: Falmouth (Mon–Sat 4–5 hourly, Sun 1–2 hourly; 30–50min); London (4 daily; 8hr); Newquay (Mon–Sat 7 hourly, Sun 2 hourly; 45min–1hr 25min); Penzance (Mon–Sat 1–2 hourly, Sun 4 daily; 1hr 10min–1hr 25min); Plymouth (6 daily; 2hr); St Austell (1–3 hourly; 25–40min); St Ives (Mon–Sat hourly, Sun 4 daily; 1hr 35min).

Ferries

Falmouth to: St Mawes (late May to Sept 2 hourly, Oct to late May 7–10 daily; 20min); Truro (May–Sept 5 daily; 1hr).
Fowey to: Mevagissey (late April to Sept 3–6 daily; 35min).
Mevagissey to: Fowey (late April to Sept 3–6 daily; 35min).
St Mawes to: Falmouth (late May to Sept 2 hourly, Oct to late May 6–10 daily; 20min); Truro (May–Sept 2 daily; 1hr).
Truro to: Falmouth (May–Sept Mon–Sat 6 daily; 1hr); St Mawes (May–Sept 2 daily; 1hr).

9

The Lizard and Penwith peninsulas

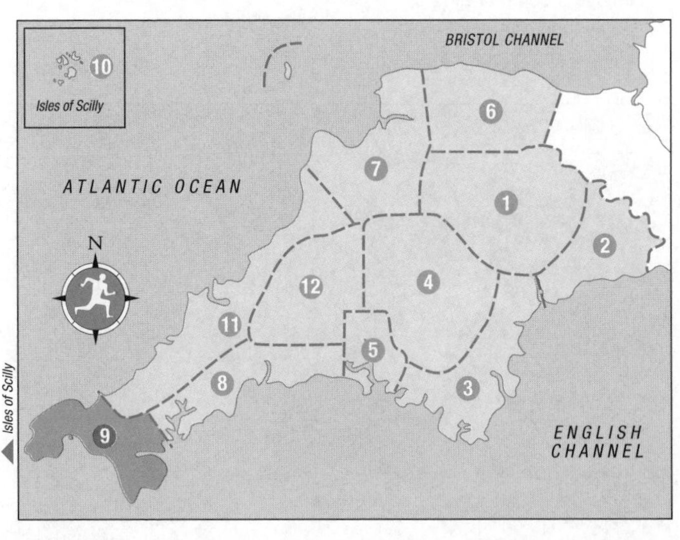

CHAPTER 9

Highlights

* **Lizard Point** England's southernmost cape preserves a bracing, windswept appeal, with exhilarating walks and a diverse range of flora. See p.262

* **Kynance Cove** One of Cornwall's grandest beaches, framed by dramatic cliffs and rocky isles. See p.262

* **St Michael's Mount** This partly fortified isle enjoys a commanding position in Mount's Bay, with rooms packed with interest and panoramic views. See p.272

* **An evening at the Minack Theatre** A unique open-air venue for drama and other performances, right on the cliff edge. See p.278

* **Barbara Hepworth Museum, St Ives** Absorbing gallery and subtropical garden packed with the sculptor's abstract works, inspired by the Penwith landscape. See p.291

▲ Lizard Point

9

The Lizard and Penwith peninsulas

Jutting like pincers into the Atlantic, the twin prongs of the Lizard and Penwith peninsulas, respectively the mainland's most southerly and westerly points, comprise one of the country's most scenically spectacular coastal areas, a succession of wave-pounded cliffs interspersed by a variety of exquisite beaches, and encompassing wide expanses of undeveloped moorland. Additionally, the mild climate favours a range of exotic vegetation, with fiery monbretia and rich, purple foxgloves crowding every roadside, while bright geraniums and lobelia spill from the grey granite that's the region's primary building material. Indeed granite is ubiquitous, evident everywhere from farmsteads to dry-stone walls, churches and castellated cliffs. Much of the Lizard is also made up of greenish-brown serpentine, a soft hydrated magnesium silicate that's sometimes mottled or spotted like a serpent's skin (hence the name) and is the staple material of craft shop trinkets.

The **Lizard peninsula** is the less developed of the two, its mostly flat and bare interior giving way to precipitous bluffs and cliff-girt coves where it meets the sea. Most of the holiday traffic is concentrated around these rugged bays with their superb beaches – places like **Kynance Cove**, theatrically framed by rocky pinnacles and serpentine cliff walls – though of course there's always a stream of pilgrims to **Lizard Point**, at the southern tip of the peninsula. Apart from the region's chief town of **Helston** and its nearby port of **Porthleven**, where a small fishing fleet lends a slightly brisker feel, most of the spartan villages hereabouts are tiny, unflustered havens buried away at the end of remote lanes, such as **Mullion Cove** and **Coverack**. You can reach the most appealing ones along the coastal path, which allows access to the awe-inspiring coastal scenery, though you might also consider exploring the peninsula **by bike** – a great way to get the best out of the network of narrow lanes connecting the villages and beaches.

The raw granite landscape predominates once more on the **Penwith peninsula**, where there are also some cracking sand beaches that attract throngs of tourists in summer. The principal town, **Penzance**, is big enough to preserve an independent identity, however, and has a first-rate museum giving a fascinating insight into the cultural life that existed here at the turn of the twentieth century. Many artists congregated in the neighbouring port of **Newlyn**, now the South West's biggest fishing centre, where there still exists a good collection of contemporary art, while later waves of artists were attracted across the neck of the

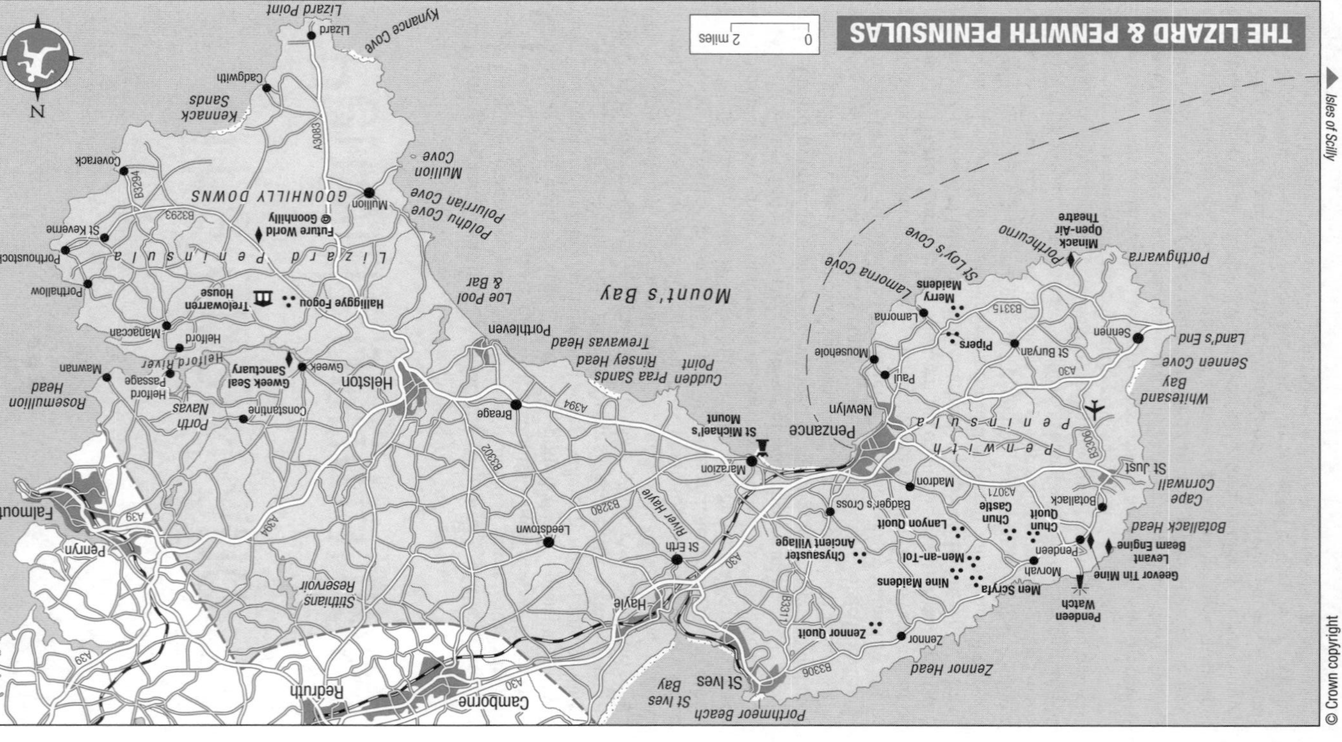
THE LIZARD & PENWITH PENINSULAS
0 2 miles
N
Falmouth
Penryn
Redruth
Camborne
Rosemullion Head
Mawnan
Helford Passage
Helford River
Porth Navas
Constantine
Manaccan
Helford
Porthallow
Porthoustock
St Keverne
Coverack
Trelowarren House
Gweek Seal Sanctuary
Gweek
Halliggye Fogou
Future World @ Goonhilly
GOONHILLY DOWNS
Lizard Peninsula
Kennack Sands
Cadgwith
Lizard
Lizard Point
Kynance Cove
Mullion
Mullion Cove
Poldhu Cove
Polurrian Cove
Helston
Loe Pool & Bar
Porthleven
Trewavas Head
Rinsey Head
Praa Sands
Cudden Point
Breage
Leedstown
Stithians Reservoir
Mount's Bay
St Michael's Mount
Marazion
River Hayle
St Erth
Hayle
St Ives Bay
St Ives
Porthmeor Beach
Zennor Quoit
Zennor
Zennor Head
Chysauster Ancient Village
Badger's Cross
Penzance
Newlyn
Mousehole
Paul
Lamorna
Lamorna Cove
Merry Maidens
St Loy's Cove
Pipers
St Buryan
Porthcurno
Minack Open-Air Theatre
Porthgwarra
Land's End
Sennen
Sennen Cove
Whitesand Bay
Penwith Peninsula
Madron
Lanyon Quoit
Men-an-Tol
Nine Maidens
Men Scryfa
Chun Castle
Chun Quoit
Morvah
Pendeen
Pendeen Watch
Geevor Tin Mine
Levant Beam Engine
Botallack
Botallack Head
Cape Cornwall
St Just
Isles of Scilly
A30
A39
A394
A3083
A3071
B3293
B3294
B3302
B3280
B3311
B3306
B3315

peninsula to the busy holiday town of **St Ives**, where a branch of the Tate Gallery showcases their work within earshot of the sea. The peninsula's main draw, however, lies in its dramatic coastline – an inhospitable ring of cliffs, unbroken on the northern coast, but punctuated by some of Cornwall's best sandy beaches to the south, for instance at **Porthcurno**. Most visitors bypass the most interesting bits on their way to **Land's End**, whose position at Britain's westernmost point has endowed it with a mythic significance, and also with a brash entertainment complex. However, the jagged coast on either side has been spared, and offers some of the most rewarding coastal walking in the county. North of Land's End, **Cape Cornwall** retains its desolate air, the abandoned chimney stacks of Penwith's once-flourishing mining industry only adding to the majesty; you can soak up the flavour of the interior at villages such as **Zennor**, whose granite integrity attracted D.H. Lawrence during World War I, or by exploring the remnants of the peninsula's prehistoric societies amidst bleak, hilly moorland.

For practical and general information on the region, see the **website** Ⓦwww.visit-westcornwall.com, which lists accommodation, attractions and events, as well as including a beach guide, information on transport and numerous links.

The Lizard peninsula

The bare plateau of the **Lizard peninsula** – from the Celtic *lys ardh*, or "high point" – has plenty of primitive appeal, but you'll need to make a little effort to unearth some of the more out-of-the-way places. If the peninsula can be said to have a centre, it is **Helston**, known for its folk museum and the centuries-old tradition of the Furry (or Flora) Dance; it's a useful transport hub for buses. From here, it's a broad, treeless landscape as you follow the solitary A3083 to the southern headlands and the village known simply as **The Lizard**, at the peninsula's tip. On either side of the A3083, roads branch off westwards towards obvious attractions such as **Loe Pool**, Cornwall's largest natural lake and a haven for wildlife, or remote hamlets such as **Mullion Cove**, little more than a scattering of cottages set around a thick-walled harbour. Though the neighbouring beaches of **Polurrian** and **Poldhu** are more popular with surfers, **Kynance Cove**, west of Lizard village, is the peninsula's most appealing place to swim. The eastern coast is also sparsely settled, though such villages as **Coverack** attract a good deal of summer traffic for their lovely secluded settings. In contrast, the insular communities and secretive creeks of the **Helford River** have a very different tone, its muddy banks lapped by the occasional pleasure boat.

All **bus routes** to the Lizard peninsula pass through Helston, which is linked to Penzance by frequent First buses #2 (not Sun) and #2A, to Falmouth by #2 (not Sun) and #35, and to Truro by #82 (not Sun) and #82A. From Helston, #32 connects the east-coast villages of St Keverne and Coverack, and #33 runs to Mullion and The Lizard, while #35 takes in Gweek and Helford Passage en route to Falmouth. Porthleven, Rinsey and Praa Sands can be reached on buses #2 and #2A. For twice-daily weekday services connecting villages on the peninsula's east side, including Porthallow and Helford, contact East Lizard Dial-a-Ride at Ⓣ01736/757364. Some services are reduced in winter.

Helston's Furry Dance

Helston is most famous for its annual **Furry Dance** (also called Flora Dance), a complex ritual held on Flora Day, May 8 (unless this date falls on a Sunday or Monday, when the procession takes place on the previous Saturday). It's the high point on the town's calendar, for which preparations are made months in advance. It is said to commemorate an apparition by St Michael, the town's patron saint, but the revelry probably predates Christianity as a spring fertility ritual; it formerly involved a ceremony in the woods close to town followed by a dance back to the centre, now commemorated by the Hal-an-Tow ceremony, the second dance of the day. Of the five separate dances, the first begins at 7am, and is the least crowded; others take place at 8.30am, 9.30am, noon and 5pm. The midday dance is the most important: a stately procession of top-hatted men and summer-frocked women solemnly twirling through the town's streets, gardens and even houses, led by the Helston Brass Band. Give yourself plenty of time for this and the other dances, to guarantee a good viewing spot.

Bizarrely, there is at present no tourist office on the whole Lizard peninsula, though the office at Falmouth has some **information** (see p.248). You'll find brief descriptions of the main villages, local walks and accommodation options on the **website** of the Lizard Peninsula Tourism Association, Ⓦwww.lizard-peninsula.co.uk.

Helston

Three miles from the sea at the northern end of the Lizard peninsula, **HELSTON** is a sleepy, hilly place, very different nowadays from its former appearance when, as Hellaz, it was a busy port on the River Cober. This all changed around 1300, when its sea outlet became silted up by deposits from upstream tin-workings, which resulted in both the formation of Loe Pool (see p.260) and the frequent flooding which afflicted the town until the 1980s. These days the water level is controlled by a sluice and culvert at Loe Bar (see p.260) and by giant tanks in the town. Despite losing its role as a port, Helston remained an important centre as a Stannary town (where tin was brought to be assayed and taxed), as recalled in the name of its broad main thoroughfare, Coinagehall Street, which meets Helston's second axis, Meneage Street, at the Neoclassical **Guildhall**, itself the starting point for the town's celebrated **Furry** or **Flora Dance** (see above).

You can learn more about the Furry Dance and other aspects of the town's history at the eclectic **Helston Folk Museum** (Mon–Sat 10am–1pm, closes 4pm school hols; free), housed in former market buildings behind the Guildhall on Church Street. The long exhibition space, leading up through the old butter market to the fish and meat markets, is filled with a happy assortment of bric-a-brac relating to local trades, and includes sections on the telegraphy pioneer Marconi and on Helston's native son, **Bob Fitzsimmons** (1863–1917), the first boxer to be world middleweight, light heavyweight and heavyweight champion, and the only Briton to achieve this triple. The reconstructed Victorian classroom, with examples of canes and a leather tawse for beating children, and an upstairs section on mining and quarrying are also worth taking in.

Helston lay at the centre of one of Cornwall's most intensely mined regions, near to the biggest tin mine in the country, owned by the mighty Godolphin family, who had their town house in what is now the *Angel Hotel*, almost opposite the Guildhall on Coinagehall Street. At the bottom of this street, the arched and turreted **Grylls Monument** was erected in honour of a local banker and benefactor on the former site of Helston's castle, once guarding the Cober valley but already a ruin by 1478. After you've done a circuit of Helston's hilly backstreets, there's little else to detain you unless you're tempted by **Flambards Theme Park** (Easter to late July daily 10.30am–5pm; late July to early Sept daily 10.15am–5.45pm, closes 9.30pm for fireworks evenings on Wed in Aug; early Sept to late Oct daily 10.30am–4.30pm; Nov to late Dec & Feb–Easter Tues–Thurs, Sat & Sun 11am–4pm; last entry at 3.30pm Easter–Oct, 3pm Nov to late Dec & Feb–Easter; may also close Mon & Fri Easter to May & early Sept to late Oct, call to check £16.50 in summer, £7.95 after 2.15pm or 6pm on fireworks evenings, £5.95 in winter; ⓣ0845/601 8684; ⓦwww.flambards.co.uk), packed with various family amusements, such as a re-created Victorian village and a choice of white-knuckle rides. Fireworks evenings take place here on Wednesdays in August. Some rides and attractions are closed in winter. A marquee on the site, the **Kingsford Venue** (ⓣ01326/573404, ⓦwww.flambards.co.uk/flambardslive), stages concerts and other performances throughout the year. Flambards is well signposted from the A394 and A3083, on the eastern side of town.

Practicalities

Most **buses** stop on Coinagehall Street, including the frequent #2 and #2a from Falmouth and Penzance, and #82 and #82A from Truro. A couple of **accommodation** options are conveniently located nearby: *No. 52* at 52 Coinagehall St, a smart **B&B** with solid old furnishings in good-sized rooms to front and rear (ⓣ01326/569334 or 562821, ⓦwww.spingoales.com; ❸) – ask at the adjacent *Blue Anchor* if there's no reply – and, up the street at no. 16, the *Angel Hotel* (ⓣ01326/572701; ❸), slightly run-down, but with spacious bedrooms, and retaining some features from its five-hundred-year history, including a minstrels' gallery and a deep well in the bar.

For a drink or a **pub** snack, the *Blue Anchor* is an essential stop, a fifteenth-century monks' rest house with a series of snug flagstoned rooms, a skittle alley and a small garden; brewed on the premises, the excellent Spingo beer is available in three strengths (plus an extra-strength version at Christmas). There's live music here every weekend. Next door, *No. 52* has elegant green walls and offers seafood and chargrills for £12–16 (closed Sun). *Giuseppe's* at 4 Wendron St (closed Mon) has pastas and pizzas (£6–9) as well as meat and seafood dishes (around £11) in a simple, modern setting. If it's just a quick bite you're after, *Hutchinson's*, 95 Meneage St, serves award-winning fish and chips to eat in or take away (closed Sun except during peak summer period).

Porthleven and around

Three miles southwest of Helston on the B3304, **PORTHLEVEN** is a sizable port that once served to ship tin ore from the inland mines. Characterless houses now ring the top of village, but the harbour is of more interest, healthily packed with fishing boats and protected by two sets of stout walls. A brace of cannons sits on the outer walls, salvaged from the HMS *Anson*, a frigate wrecked on Loe Bar in 1807 with the loss of 120 sailors; the guns are said to have fired on Napoleon's navy at the Battle of Brest.

There are plenty of good **beaches** within easy reach of Porthleven: the best for swimming are around **Rinsey Head**, three miles northwest along the coast, including the sheltered Praa Sands. In the other direction, one and a quarter miles southwest, **Loe Bar** is a lovely bank of sand and shingle, accessible via the coast path from Porthleven's harbour – though swimming here is not recommended, due to the steeply shelving bottom and the strong currents. The Bar separates the sea from the freshwater **Loe Pool**, a lake stretching one and a quarter miles inland, and formerly extending much further up the valley of the River Cober towards Helston. Loe Pool is one of two places where it is claimed King Arthur's sword Excalibur was restored to its watery source (the other is on Bodmin Moor; see p.360); another local superstition warns that the pool claims a victim every seven years. A five-mile waymarked path round its perimeter allows you to explore the lovely creeks and woods surrounding it, accessible also from Helston (from the park on the Porthleven road).

In you fancy taking to sea for a while, you can arrange **fishing trips and coastal cruises** to see local caves and cliff faces at Porthleven Angling Centre on Porthleven harbour (Ⓣ01326/561885, Ⓦwww.porthlevenangling.co.uk), where prices range from £14 for two hours to £40 for eight hours at sea per person.

Practicalities

Buses #2 and #2a connect Porthleven with Helston and Penzance. The best **accommodation** choice here is *The Copper Kettle*, 33 Fore St (Ⓣ01326/565660, Ⓦwww.cornishcopperkettle.com; ④), offering spacious rooms with fridges, including a single and, on the ground floor, a whole suite including self-catering facilities; there's a patio, and five-course breakfasts. Alternatively, try the *An Mordros Hotel* on Peverell Terrace (Ⓣ01326/562236, Ⓦwww.anmordroshotel.com; ④), which offers rooms with views across the harbour and a luggage-transport service for walkers (£15), or the two smartly furnished rooms above *Kota* restaurant, at Harbour Head (Ⓣ01326/562407, Ⓦwww.kotarestaurant.co.uk; ⑤), the larger one benefiting from a glorious vista for which you pay £15 more.

The semi-formal *Kota* is Porthleven's top **restaurant**, where fishy mains cost £12–19 and there are two-course menus available between 5.30 and 7pm for £14 (Ⓣ01326/562407; closed lunchtime Sun–Thurs, all Sun & Mon in winter, and all Jan). On Fore Street, you can pick up excellent snack food, including pizzas made in a wood-fired oven, at the Corner Deli (closed Sun Oct–Easter), available until 9pm daily in summer and Wednesday–Saturday in winter. Meals are also served at two **pubs** enjoying great harbourside locations: the *Ship Inn*, on the north side of the harbour, and, on the south side, the *Harbour Inn*, with outside seating on the quayside, wood-panelled walls and live music on Saturdays (less frequent in winter).

Mullion and around

Three miles south of Helston, a right turn off the A3083 brings you to the inland village of **MULLION**. Here, a triangle of quiet roads encloses the fifteenth- to sixteenth-century church of **St Mellanus**, dedicated to the Breton St Mellane (or Malo). The short tower is partly constructed of serpentine, and the interior has some knobbly oak bench-ends showing a jester, a monk and cherubs with a chalice and barrel. Look out, too, for the dog-flap in the south door, originally for the ejection of unruly shepherds' dogs. Otherwise, the village is nothing special, but makes a useful base for the beaches and coves hereabouts.

Signposted a mile and a quarter southwest of the village, a scattering of picturesque cottages amid gorse- and bracken-smothered slopes look down on the gorgeous, enclosed little harbour of **Mullion Cove** – also known as Porthmellin – where a handful of fishing boats are sheltered behind thick brick jetties and rocky outcrops. Rocky strips of sand lie around the cove, but there's much better swimming at cliff-flanked **Polurrian**, a popular surfing beach less than a mile north along the coast path, while a further mile or so north, **Poldhu** is a generous expanse of sand wedged between acres of wild moorland; both beaches are accessible on the minor Mullion–Helston coast road (from Mullion, take The Commons, which turns into Poldhu Road).

If you're walking the coast path from Polurrian, you'll pass, on Poldhu's southern cliff edge, the **Marconi Monument**, a solitary obelisk erected in 1937 to mark the spot from which the first transatlantic radio transmission was made by Guglielmo Marconi in 1901. Poldhu continued as a commercial radio station until 1922, and during World War II was a vital link between Britain and the Atlantic convoys bringing men, munitions and food.

You can take **fishing trips and pleasure cruises** to local sea caves from Mullion Cove between Easter and October (ⓣ01326/240345 or 0797/480 3924; £12 per person for 1hr), and **riding** in the area is offered at Newton Farm on Polhorman Lane, a right turn off the Poldhu Road from Mullion (ⓣ01326/240388, ⓦwww.newton-equestrian.co.uk). Look out for peregrine falcons and choughs on your ramblings – the latter have recently begun to breed in the vicinity. Just south of the village on the A3083, the Lizard Cider Barn (Easter–Oct daily 10am–5pm, closes 6pm July–Sept) sells local ciders, wines, meads and liqueurs, and offers free tastings.

Practicalities

There are a few good **accommodation** options in **Mullion**, including *The Old Vicarage*, at the top of Nansmellyon Road (ⓣ01326/240898, ⓦwww.cornwall-online.co.uk; no credit cards; ❺); a large building fronted by a lawn and enclosed within a tall hedge garden, it offers four elegant and spacious rooms, either en suite or with private bathroom. Close by on Churchtown, *The Mount's Bay* is a stylish modern inn with comfortable accommodation and sea views from the rear rooms (ⓣ01326/241761, ⓦwww.mountsbayguesthouse.co.uk ❹). Five minutes' walk along The Commons (at the top of Churchtown heading west towards Poldhu) and around half a mile from the sea, *Campden House* (ⓣ01326/240365; no credit cards; ❸) is a friendly B&B with a fuschia-filled garden where cream teas are served; snacks and dinners are also available on request. In **Mullion Cove**, the Victorian *Mullion Cove Hotel* (ⓣ01326/240328, ⓦwww.mullion-cove.co.uk; ❽) is spectacularly situated high above the harbour, with its own diminutive outdoor pool. Sea-facing rooms cost more, and if you want to include a four-course evening meal, it's an extra £10 per person.

Most of the local **eating** options are in Mullion where, just down from the church on Nansmellyon Road, you'll find pastas (£7–9), two sizes of pizza (£6–9) and fish dishes at the Italian *Courtyard Restaurant* (ⓣ01326/241556). You can pick up home-baked pies and quiches at *Colroger Deli* on Lender Lane, which also has a few tables for coffees and snacks (closed Sun Sept–March). Pub food and real ales are served at the sixteenth-century *Old Inn*, which has ranks of tables outside, and at *Mount's Bay*, where there is a beer garden and regular evening entertainment. In Mullion Cove, nonresidents can stop at the *Mullion Cove Hotel* for teas, snacks in the bistro or set-price evening meals (£32), or you can sample delicious cakes, cream teas, crab sandwiches and pasties at the relaxed *Porthmellin Tea Rooms* right by the harbour (closed Nov–Easter).

The Lizard and around

Around four miles after the Mullion turn-off from the A3083, the non descript village of **THE LIZARD** is the main centre at the peninsula's southern end. Likened by John Betjeman to "an army housing scheme given over to visitors", it holds shops and a handful of places to sleep and eat, but unless you're looking for serpentine souvenirs or refreshment, it has a strictly functional appeal. A web of footpaths radiates out from the village towards the sea, the most popular being the mile-long track running parallel to the road leading to mainland Britain's southernmost tip, **Lizard Point**. Here, a couple of low-key cafés and gift shops look down on a ceaselessly churning sea and a tiny sheltered cove holding a disused lifeboat station. It's all quite unspoiled, a far cry from the paraphernalia surrounding Land's End (see p.279), and the coast on either side is no less impressive, a succession of rugged chasms and caves hollowed out by the sea from where you can occasionally spot grey seals, basking sharks and dolphins. You can tour the orderly, bright white **Lizard Lighthouse**, dating from 1752, and adjoining Heritage Centre, where you'll find a small display of equipment (open Easter–Dec from 11am or noon until 4–7pm according to month; usually closed Thurs & Fri, also Sat Oct–Dec, but open daily July & Aug; for specific times, call ⓣ01255/245011 or see ⓦwww.lizardlighthouse.co.uk; £5). The coast path leads east past the **Lion's Den**, a huge cavity in the cliffs caused by the collapse of a sea cave, to **Housel Cove**, where Marconi conducted his early radio experiments from a bungalow that's still visible above the small sandy beach (accessed via a steep cliff path). Beyond Marconi's bungalow, the prominent white, castellated building on **Bass Point** was constructed by Lloyd's insurers in 1872 to enable its company agents to semaphore passing ships and relay news of cargoes to merchants in London; it's now a private house. Half a mile further east and north of here, **Church Cove** is the site of the lifeboat station that replaced the one at Lizard Point. The cove lies at the end of a lane linking it with the hamlet of **LANDEWEDNACK**, whose fifteenth-century church is said to be the last place where a sermon was preached in the Cornish tongue, in 1674.

From here it's less than a mile by road back to The Lizard. Alternatively, from Church Cove continue northeast along the coast path for about a mile to **CADGWITH**, an idyllically snuggled fishing village of thatched roofs between headlands. Just before the village you can look down from the top of the cliff into the **Devil's Frying Pan**, where waves swirl around a collapsed sea cave.

A mile northwest of The Lizard, the peninsula's best-known beach, **Kynance Cove**, lies at the end of a toll-road (Easter–Oct £3.50; Nov–Easter free), signposted west off the A3083. In all, it's about a forty-minute walk from Lizard Point, including a final fifteen-minute clamber down steep steps to the shore. The white-sand beach is encircled by sheer 200-foot cliffs in which the olive-green serpentine is flushed with reds and purples, and faces the stacks and arches of offshore islets which are joined to shore at low tide. The biggest of these, **Asparagus Island**, takes its name from the wild asparagus that grows there. Masses of other wild flowers adorn the rocks on every side, giving the scene a wild grandeur. The water quality is excellent, too, though bathers should take care not to be stranded on the islands by the sea, which submerges the entire beach at high tide – fierce currents and creeping tides are a feature of all the beaches hereabouts. Kynance Cove has an excellent seasonal **café** and there are toilets.

The Lizard's coastal flowers

Much of the Lizard peninsula is designated a Site of Special Scientific Interest (SSSI) and is a protected nature reserve, with a total of eighteen nationally rare plant species growing locally, making this one of the top ten botanical sites in Britain. Ever since John Ray ("the father of British botany") discovered the fringed rupture-wort and the very rare wild asparagus at Lizard Point in 1667, visitors have flocked to the area in search of **cliff flowers**, many of them Mediterranean in origin. The hottentot fig, a showy South African succulent with pink and white flowers that was introduced in the nineteenth century, now dominates large areas of the cliffs despite efforts by the National Trust and Natural England to control its spread, while bluebells and thrift create extravagant swathes of colour in spring. Look out, too, for dropwort, harebells, bloody cranesbill and the rare and colourful Cornish heath that grows only on the magnesium-rich serpentine and gabbro rocks hereabouts.

Practicalities

Hourly #33 **buses** link The Lizard to Mullion and Helston. The village has a good choice of **accommodation**, including the *Caerthillian*, a pale blue Victorian B&B in the centre of the village (ⓣ01326/290019, ⓦwww.thecaerthillian.co.uk; no credit cards; ④), with all clean and bright rooms en suite or with private bathroom – room 3 has great views to Kynance Cove. There are a couple of excellent possibilities on Penmenner Road: *Parc Brawse House* (ⓣ01326/290466, ⓦwww.cornwall-online.co.uk; ④), a solid, brilliant-white building with large windows in its two rooms, and a self-catering cottage available, and *Penmenner House* (ⓣ01326/290370, ⓦwww.penmenner.co.uk; ⑤), where the poet Rupert Brooke once stayed, with richly coloured rooms, a guests' lounge and tasteful knick-knacks from around the world; neither place accepts credit cards. One of the region's best-situated **youth hostels** (ⓣ0845/371 9550, ⓔlizard@yha.org.uk; closed Nov–Easter; from £16) is housed in one of mainland Britain's most southerly buildings, a classic Victorian ex-hotel right on the coast, with smart facilities and majestic views – it's signposted from the village. The Lizard has little in the way of fine **restaurants**, though the old-fashioned *Witch Ball Restaurant* (ⓣ01326/290662; closed Sun eve) has grills (£11–16.50) and lobster (£26) alongside its soups and ciabattas. Across the road, the raftered *Coast Coffee Bar & Bistro* has baguettes, smoothies and outside seating (closed eves, also mid-Nov to Dec Mon & Sat and all Jan & Feb). The mainland's southernmost **pub**, the *Top House*, stands at the centre of the village, serves snack lunches and full meals (mains around £10) and has a few outside tables; folk performances take place on Mondays.

Goonhilly Downs and Coverack

West of the A3083 Helston–Lizard road, the lonely B3293 crosses the broad windswept plateau of **Goonhilly Downs**, where the futuristic saucers of an extensive satellite station and the nearby ranks of wind turbines make somewhat spooky intrusions. The tracking dishes appear deceptively small when seen from afar; close up they're enormous – the largest, "Merlin", is 32m in diameter. Claiming to be the world's largest satellite station, **Future World @ Goonhilly** (April to late June & early Sept to Oct daily 10am–5pm; late June to early Sept daily 10am–6pm; call ⓣ0800/679593 for winter times; £7.95; ⓦwww.goonhilly.bt.com) is capable of handling 600,000 phone, fax, video and data calls worldwide at any one time. You can find out more about its operations at the multimedia visitor centre, largely a customer-relations exercise on the part of British Telecom, but you'll take in some pretty spectacular views as well as all the statistical gush and technological wonders on the guided tours round the site; there are also interactive displays and a film showing how satellite technology developed from ideas by science fiction author Arthur C. Clarke.

Continuing east, the B3293 meets the coast at the fishing port of **COVERACK**, once a notorious centre of contraband. The sequestered village presents a placid picture, its thatched and lime-washed granite cottages overlooking a curve of beach that almost disappears to nothing at high tide; watch out for dolphins frolicking in the bay. At the southern end of the village, a tiny walled harbour is crammed with boats and there's a small selection of cafés and **restaurants**.

Practicalities

Coverack would make an ideal **place to stay** for rest and recuperation, though the few options are frequently fully booked. Try *Fernleigh*, on Chymbloth Way, a turn-off from Harbour Road (Ⓣ01326/280626, Ⓦwww.fernleighcoverack.co.uk; no credit cards; ❺), which has three spacious en-suite rooms, a small garden with bay views and amiable proprietors, who can provide a good three-course meal (£15) as well as packed lunches and luggage transfers, or, further up, five minutes from the beach, *Boak House* (Ⓣ01326/280608; closed Nov–Easter; no credit cards; ❸), offering good-value B&B with sea views and shared bathrooms. Alternatively, the *Paris Hotel*, right above the harbour (Ⓣ01326/280258, Ⓦwww.pariscoverack.com; ❺), also enjoys excellent views and has all rooms en suite. There's a **youth hostel** 200m west of here (up School Hill, signposted opposite the harbour), which has panoramic views, a pool table and good food (Ⓣ0845/371 9014, Ⓔcoverack@yha.org.uk; from £16). There are en-suite family rooms here as well as some camping pitches. *Little Trevothan,* just under a mile inland, is a quiet **campsite** with level pitches and caravans and a yurt for weekly rent (Ⓣ01326/280260, Ⓦwww.littletrevothan.com; closed Jan & Feb); it's signposted on the right of the B3293 as you approach Coverack, near the St Keverne fork.

Back in the village, you can **eat** well at the *Lifeboat House Seafood Restaurant* (Ⓣ01326/281212; closed Mon & Oct–May) – it's pricey and often fully booked, but the fresh seafood is superb with main dishes £10–15; you can also pick up first-class fish and chips from the attached takeaway (open daily all year). The nearby *Paris Hotel* has bar meals (mains around £10) and a garden.

Below the post office, the Coverack Windsurfing Centre, offers **windsurfing** courses and rents out surf-skis (April–Nov; Ⓣ01326/280939, Ⓦwww.coverack.org.uk). The community **website** Ⓦwww.coverack.org.uk is worth viewing for its useful visitor **information**.

St Keverne and around

Five miles north of Coverack via the B3293, connected by buses #T2 and #T3 (neither running Sun in winter), the inland village of **ST KEVERNE**, set around a pretty square, is the main centre for shops and facilities around these parts. Here, the ribbed, octagonal spire of **St Akeveranus** has served as a marker for sailors over the centuries; in the adjoining churchyard are the tombs of those claimed off this treacherous stretch of coast. The two pubs on the square, the *White Hart* (Ⓣ01326/280325; ❹), with three en-suite rooms, and the *Three Tuns* (Ⓣ01326/280949, Ⓦwww.three-tuns-pub.co.uk; ❸), with private or shared bathrooms, offer plain **accommodation**; both have gardens and moderately priced **restaurants**. *The Greenhouse*, just off the square on the High Street (Ⓣ01326/280800; closed Sun eve, all Mon and daytime Tues–Sat, all Tues in winter), serves organic, locally sourced and seasonal meals, for example slow-roasted pork belly (£13), baked megrim sole (£14) and a good range of vegetarian dishes (£9–10); in winter there are set menus for £15–20.

Less than a mile south of St Keverne (signposted off the Coverack road), **Roskilly's** (daily: summer 9am–9pm; winter 9am–5pm or 9am–3pm; Ⓦwww.roskillys.co.uk) produces some of Cornwall's best organic ice creams, available in fifty-odd flavours. You can purchase these, as well as yoghurt ices and other goodies, in the shop and restaurant, which stays open late for barbecues in summer, and you can also wander around the surrounding ponds, glades and wetlands, created to shelter wildlife.

Several mainly stony **beaches** lie within a short distance of the village and are perfect for a swim if you don't mind the rocks. The nearest of these is **Porthoustock**, a mile east of St Keverne, via the road to the right of the *White Hart* (turn off along the signposted lane to the right); its a stone-and-shingle strip flanked by quarry workings which faces the dreaded Manacles rocks three miles offshore – cause of numerous shipwrecks over the centuries. Alternatively, stay on the road from the *White Hart* for a couple of miles to reach **PORTHALLOW**, where there's a small grey-sand beach and a cluster of cottages around the harbour. Right on the shore here, the *Five Pilchards Inn* serves sizzling steaks and succulent, fresh-off-the-boat fish and lobster at £10–15 (no food Tues eve).

Along the Helford River

At the northeastern side of the Lizard peninsula, the **Helford River**, actually a ria or drowned river valley, reveals a range of different faces along its length, from sheltered muddy creeks upstream to its rocky, open mouth, all of which repay exploration on foot or by boat. On its south side, **Frenchman's Creek**, one of a splay of inlets running off the river, was the inspiration for Daphne du Maurier's novel of the same name, and her evocation of it still holds true: "still and soundless, surrounded by the trees, hidden from the eyes of men".

The creek is reachable on a footpath (signposted uphill in front of the *Shipwright's Arms* – see below) and road from **HELFORD**, less than a mile east. Surrounded by woods and lying at the bottom of a steep and narrow lane, this agreeable old smugglers' haunt has a neat, gentrified appearance nowadays, immersed in a comfortable lethargy. Overlooking the river, the *Shipwright's Arms* is a fine spot to soak up the atmosphere and eat **pub** lunches in the garden. You can cross to Helford River's north bank – and this is the route of the South West Coast Path – by the seasonal passenger ferry (April–June, Sept & Oct 9.30am–5.30pm; July & Aug 9.30am–9.30pm; £4) to the hamlet of **Helford Passage**. Both Helford and Helford Passage make good starting points for riverside walks, or you can **rent boats** (£50 for two hours) or kayaks (£10 per hour) from Helford River Boats, Helford Passage (Ⓣ01326/250770, Ⓦwww.helford-river-boats.co.uk), which operates a kiosk in season in front of the *Ferryboat Inn*.

In contrast to these inland locations, the village of **MAWNAN** stands close to the mouth of the Helford River, a couple of miles east of Helford Passage, its granite church of St Maunanus set apart from the village on a height. **Rosemullion Head** juts out into Falmouth Bay about a mile northeast of here, strewn with wild flowers in spring and summer and reachable on the coast path which winds round to Maenporth and beyond to Falmouth (see p.246).

Near the westernmost reaches of the river, outside the village of Mawgan (signposted from Garras), the old Cornish manor of **Trelowarren House (Ⓦwww.trelowarren.com)** has been in the hands of the local Vyvyan family, famous for their Royalist sympathies during the Civil War, since 1427. The mainly sixteenth-century house – described by Daphne du Maurier as "the last of England as I will ever know it" – boasts exquisite plasterwork and can be viewed on **guided visits** (call Ⓣ01326/221224 for details), enabling you to view the medieval stained glass of the Rococo Chapel. The extensive estate holds an "eco-community" of cottages available for self-catering, and between April and September you can explore waymarked **woodland walks** beyond the walled gardens and orchards at the centre of the estate, one of them leading to Tremayne Quay on the Helford River, nearly four miles away. The grounds also hold an intriguing late Iron Age construction, **Halliggye Fogou**, a stone-walled tunnel several metres long in an earthwork that once enclosed a settlement (free access during daylight hours April–Sept). A keyhole-shaped slit in the earth provides access to the chamber, which is high enough to stand in without stooping; you'll need a torch as it's very dark – though there's little to see.

For refreshments and gourmet dining, drop in on the *New Yard* (Ⓣ01326/221595; closed Sun eve, also Mon in winter), a classy **café/restaurant** in a converted coach house, where you can have snacks, full lunches (set-price menus are £16 or £19.50) or cream teas during the day, more sophisticated dishes costing £14–17 in the evenings (when there's a set-price menu for £23.50).

Nestled in a tranquil setting a mile or two north of Mawgan, outside the village of Gweek, the **National Seal Sanctuary** (daily: summer 10am–5pm, winter 10am–4pm; £13; Ⓦwww.sealsanctuary.co.uk) is a rehabilitation and release centre for the increasing number of injured seals being rescued from around Cornwall and beyond. Low-key and functional, it provides an informative insight into the lives of seals and the measures taken to care for them. There's plenty of entertainment in watching the seals at play, especially the pups, which can usually be seen between September and February. The ultimate aim is to get the seals back in the wild, but as this is sometimes impossible on account of their condition, the centre also offers a "retirement home". Other creatures, such as sea lions, otters, ponies and goats, are also cared for.

The Penwith peninsula

Though more densely populated than the Lizard, and absorbing a heavier tourist influx, the **Penwith peninsula** (also known as West Penwith, or the Land's End peninsula) retains the elements which have always marked it out – craggy, wave-pounded granite cliffs and a string of superlative sand beaches, encompassing wild, untrammelled moorland. The main town, **Penzance**, the terminus for trains from London and Birmingham and the embarkation point for the Isles of Scilly (see Chapter 10), is never overwhelmed by the weight of tourist traffic passing through and preserves a lively, unpretentious feel as well as some handsome Regency architecture. Its choice of accommodation, shops and restaurants and good transport links make it an obvious starting point for forays to nearby sights: the offshore bastion of **St Michael's Mount**, the well-preserved Iron Age village of **Chysauster**, the neighbouring fishing centre of **Newlyn**, or, just beyond, the bijou **Mousehole**. On the other hand, you shouldn't be deterred from pushing on further round the coast to be nearer beaches such as **Porthcurno**, site of one of the country's most famous performance venues, the cliff-hewn **Minack Theatre**. The raw appeal of Penwith's rugged landscape is still encapsulated by **Land's End**, though the headland's commercialization leads many to prefer the unadulterated beauty of **Cape Cornwall**, four miles north. A couple of miles inland from here, **St Just-in-Penwith** is the largest village on this extreme western seaboard, though it has little to detain you apart from its facilities and services. More compelling are the remnants of the mining industry around **Pendeen**, the remote prehistoric remains dotted inland of here, and the compact granite village of **Zennor**. Penwith's northern coast has few beaches to compare with its southern side, with the exception of the generous sands surrounding **St Ives**, whose tight knot of flower-filled lanes and Mediterranean ambience have long made it a magnet for artists and holiday visitors alike.

Penwith is more easily accessible than the Lizard, with a road circling its coastline and a good **bus** network from St Ives and Penzance, though transfers onto different routes can involve some lengthy waiting and services on Sundays and in winter are reduced or nonexistent. **Train** passengers to St Ives should change at St Erth, for the four-mile branch line that qualifies as one of Britain's most scenic railway tracts. Hikers have the option of walking the eight miles separating Penzance from St Ives along the old **St Michael's Way**, a waymarked pilgrims' route for which the tourist office in both these towns can provide a booklet including a route-map (£2). Bikers can ask at the tourist offices for the *Cycling in Penwith* pamphlet (50p), which details ten **cycling routes** around the peninsula of 14 to 28 miles.

Penzance

Occupying a sheltered position at the northwest corner of Mount's Bay, **PENZANCE** has combined a busy working atmosphere with the trappings of the holiday industry since the rail link to London was established in the 1860s. Most traces of the medieval town were obliterated at the end of the sixteenth century by a Spanish raiding party, and the predominant style now is Regency and Victorian, most conspicuously on the broad promenade west of the harbour and in the centre. The twin axes of Market Jew Street, climbing up from the train station, and the more attractive Chapel Street, swinging back downhill from its top, hold most of the shops, banks and other facilities, while the main residential area, and most of the accommodation, lie west of here.

Arrival and accommodation

Penzance's **train and bus stations** are next to each other by the seafront at the eastern end of town, also the location of the town's **tourist office** (Easter–Sept Mon–Fri 9am–5pm, Sat 10am–4pm, July & Aug also Sun 9am–1pm; Oct–Easter Mon–Fri 9am–5pm; ⓣ01736/362207, ⓦwww.visit-westcornwall.com), which can supply information on the whole Penwith peninsula. There are one or two **B&Bs** nearby at the bottom of Market Jew Street, but better choices lie either on Chapel Street, or west of the centre on Morrab and Alexandra roads.

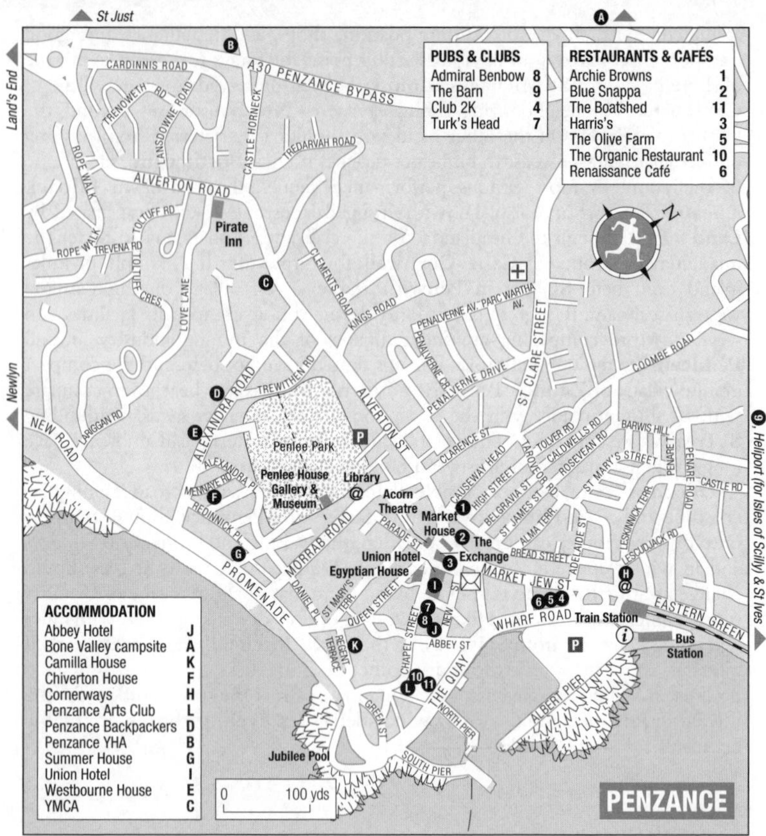

As well as the **campsite** listed opposite, there's a camping field much nearer the centre open in July and August only, well signposted in a field near the Tesco roundabout as you come into town off the A30; facilities are very basic, but rates are low and there are hot showers (Ⓣ01736/331974).

Hotels and B&Bs

Abbey Hotel Abbey St Ⓣ01736/366906, Ⓦwww.theabbeyonline.co.uk. This blue-painted seventeenth-century house – now owned by former model Jean Shrimpton and her husband – combines an eclectic mix of antiques and *objets d'art* with a homely, casually chic style, plus a well-stocked library, a quality restaurant and fantastic views over Mount's Bay. 8

Camilla House 12 Regent Terrace Ⓣ01736/363771, Ⓦwww.camillahouse.co.uk. Just off the seafront Promenade, this flower-decked Regency B&B is convenient for the harbour and has sea views from most rooms (the top rooms are cosiest). The owners also arrange cycle tours. Internet access throughout. 5

Chiverton House 9 Mennaye Rd Ⓣ01736/332733, Ⓦwww.chivertonhousebedandbreakfast.co.uk. Smart, granite Victorian guest-house steps from the seafront, where the clean, modern rooms have fresh decor and wi-fi access. Special diets catered for in the choice of breakfasts. No credit cards. 4

Cornerways 5 Leskinnick St Ⓣ01736/364645, Ⓦwww.penzance.co.uk/cornerways. Small, friendly B&B very close to the bus and train stations, with all four of the simply furnished rooms en suite. Evening meals are available (£16.50) as are packed lunches (£4.50). 4

Penzance Arts Club Chapel House, Chapel St ⓣ01736/363761, ⓦwww.penzanceartsclub.co.uk. You'll find a raffish whiff of bohemia in this flamboyant if slightly scruffy place, formerly the Portuguese embassy, dating from 1781. There are seven boldly painted rooms, regular talks and events and a good café/restaurant (see p.271). ⑥

Summer House Cornwall Terrace ⓣ01736/363744, ⓦwww.summerhouse-cornwall.com. This Regency-period restaurant-with-rooms run by an Anglo-Italian couple is well positioned for the promenade and centre, without suffering from excessive noise. The boutiquey rooms are smart and colourful and the restaurant is well worth trying. ⑥

Union Hotel Chapel St ⓣ01736/362319, ⓦwww.unionhotel.co.uk. This Georgian coaching inn is a fine place to soak up some local history, with breakfast served in the beautifully restored Assembly Room. It's a bit weathered, but good value. ④

Westbourne House Alexandra Rd ⓣ01736/350535, ⓦwww.westbourneguesthouse.co.uk. Fairly standard guesthouse that was once the home of Newlyn School artist Walter Langley. Rooms are large and clean and all en suite, and the landlord can provide tips on surfing, cycling and walking in Penwith. ④

Hostels and campsite

Bone Valley Heamoor ⓣ01736/360313. The nearest campsite to Penzance that's open all year round lies two miles north of town, reachable on buses #17, #17A and #17B. It's sheltered, clean and well equipped, but small, so call ahead at any time of year.

Penzance Backpackers Alexandra Rd ⓣ01736/363836, ⓦwww.pzbackpack.com. One of the region's tidiest and most welcoming hostels, with kitchen, lounge, laundry and wi-fi internet access. Dorm beds are £15 and there are also a few doubles (①).

Penzance Youth Hostel Castle Horneck, Alverton ⓣ0845/371 9653, ⓔpenzance@yha.org.uk. Less than two miles northwest of town, this Georgian mansion has storage lockers, a kitchen, internet access and no curfew, and serves tasty pizzas in the café. Dorm beds cost from £16, and there are also private rooms (①) and camping facilities. It's a 25-minute walk from the station up Market Jew St to Alverton Rd, then turn right at the *Pirate Inn*, or take bus #5 or #6 as far as the *Pirate Inn*. There are regular bus excursions to such places as the Minack Theatre in summer.

YMCA The Orchard, Alverton ⓣ01736/365016, ⓦwww.cornwall.ymca.org.uk. Just past Alexandra Rd, this hostel has an institutional feel, but is well equipped, with a kitchen, a large common room, internet access, and games and sports facilities. Dorm beds cost £17, and private singles and doubles are available (①).

The Town

At the top of Penzance's main traffic artery, **Market Jew Street** (from *Marghas Jew*, meaning "Thursday Market"), the pillared **Market House**, dating from 1836 and now a bank, marks the centre of town, its silver dome conspicuous from miles around. In front stands a statue of **Humphry Davy** (1778–1829), the local woodcarver's son who became one of the leading scientists of the nineteenth century. A pioneer in the field of electrochemistry, he identified six new elements including potassium and sodium, discovered the use of nitrous oxide ("laughing gas") for anaesthetic use in 1798, and invented the life-saving miners' safety-lamp, which bears his name and which his statue holds. A left turn immediately past it brings you to the top of the elegant **Chapel Street**, which has some of the town's finest buildings, including the flamboyant **Egyptian House**, built in the 1830s as a museum and geological repository but subsequently abandoned until its restoration thirty-odd years ago. Colourfully daubed with lotus-bud capitals – an "Egyptian" style harking back to the vogue spawned by Napoleon's campaign in Egypt in 1798 – the building currently holds holiday apartments. Across the street, the **Union Hotel**, dating from the seventeenth century, originally housed the town's assembly rooms; the news of Admiral Nelson's victory at Trafalgar and the death of Nelson himself were first announced from the minstrels' gallery here in 1805.

A turning at the top of Chapel and Market Jew streets brings you to **The Exchange**, a strikingly refurbished telephone exchange in Princes Street that now holds a modern art gallery (Easter–Oct Mon–Sat 10am–5pm; Nov–Easter Tues–Sat 10am–5pm; free). The white walls of the interior encompass Devon

▲ Jubilee Pool

and Cornwall's largest contemporary art space, with regular exhibitions of local, national and international artists.

Chapel Street dwindles to a narrow lane as it descends to the **harbour**, departure point for ferries to the Isles of Scilly (see p.297). South of the harbour, sited on a small promontory bulging out into Mount's Bay, the Art Deco **Jubilee Pool** (late May to mid-Sept daily 10.30am–6pm; £4) is a tidal, saltwater (though chlorinated) open-air swimming pool, built to mark the Silver Jubilee of George V in 1935. It's a classic example of the style, and non-swimmers can stroll around as a visitor (£1.30) to get a closer view of the pool and bay.

Penzance's long promenade extends west from here. A right turn brings you into Morrab Road, near the top of which lies **Penlee House Gallery and Museum** (Mon–Sat: Easter–Sept 10am–5pm; Oct–Easter 10.30am–4.30pm; £3, free on Sat; Ⓦwww.penleehouse.org.uk), a must for anyone interested in the art scene that flourished hereabouts at the end of the nineteenth century (you can also reach it from Alverton St, a continuation of Market Jew St). The gallery holds the country's largest collection of the works of the Newlyn School, though only a limited number of works are on display at any one time. Frequently sentimentalized but often bathed in an evocatively luminous light, impressionistic maritime scenes rub shoulders with portraits of Newlyn's fishing community by the likes of Stanhope Forbes and Norman Garstin – whose atmospheric masterpiece *The Rain It Raineth Every Day* is here – while temporary exhibitions highlight particular artists or themes (for more on Penwith's art schools, see Contexts, pp.383–386). The museum also has displays on local history. Penlee House itself is a creamy Italianate Victorian villa from 1865, which was inherited in 1918 by Alfred Branwell, a keen horticulturalist who introduced rare trees and shrubs from China, South America and Australia into its surrounding gardens, which make a fine spot for a picnic or a snooze.

Eating, drinking and nightlife

Penzance has few **restaurants** that rise above the average, though there are some reasonably priced eateries in the centre. If you're after an authentic **pasty**, head to

W.C. Rowe at 71 Causeway Head, while the Olive Farm, on Wharf Road below the Wharfside Centre, is the place for delicious ciabattas and other **takeaway** snacks, and you can pick up fresh fish from the Fish Boutique, a few doors along.

Restaurants and cafés

Archie Browns Bread St. Reasonably priced soups, salads, quiches and other vegan and veggie delights are available at this spacious and relaxed café/restaurant located above a health shop. It's normally open daytime only, but hosts occasional theme nights. Closed Sun.

Blue Snappa 35 Market Place ⓣ01736/363352. Congenial café-bar serving ciabattas, salads, tapas and evening meals. Stonebaked pizzas are £7, salmon steaks £9. Closed Sun eve, all Sun in winter.

The Boatshed Wharf Rd ⓣ01736/368845. A pleasant snack stop during the day, this café-bar with granite walls and ship's timbers offers tasty vegetarian dishes (around £8), meat and seafood (around £8–14) and pizzas (around £7.50) in the evening. Choose between the booth seating, window seats or tables outside.

Harris's 46 New St ⓣ01736/364408. Quality cuisine in formal surroundings. Seafood is the speciality, though such meat dishes as grilled breast of guinea fowl are also available. Main courses cost around £18–20. Closed Mon lunch & all Sun.

The Olive Farm Wharf Rd ⓣ01736/359009. Above a delicatessen specializing in olives, this long, narrow room with orange and lime shades and tables with seafront views offers a strongly Mediterranean menu, which includes such items as goat's cheese bruschetta (£6.50), mushroom stroganoff (£10.25) and seafood risotto (£14).

The Organic Restaurant 46 Chapel St ⓣ01736/874976. Below the Penzance Arts Club, this place uses the best local ingredients for such dishes as monkfish linguini, beefburgers, butternut squash and chickpea curry, and mushroom and tomato tagliatelle. Most main courses cost less than £10. Closed daytime & all Sun.

Renaissance Café Wharfside Centre, entered from Market Jew St or Wharf Rd. Popular and inexpensive café/restaurant with a small outdoor terrace that offers views over Mount's Bay, and there's wi-fi access.

Pubs

Admiral Benbow 46 Chapel St. Crammed with gaudy ships' figureheads and other nautical items, this historic pub has a restaurant made to resemble a ship's galley. Look out for the armed smuggler on the roof. The meals are family friendly but fairly mediocre – lunchtime dishes for around £8, Newlyn cod or steak and ale pie in the evening £10–15.

Turk's Head 49 Chapel St. The town's oldest inn, reputed to date back to the thirteenth century, and a great place for a drink or meal. The beer is good and menu items range from ciabattas to cod in saffron and beer batter, and *moules marinières* (£6 or £11). There's a maze of low-ceilinged rooms and a small walled garden.

Entertainment and nightlife

Over ten days in mid- to late June, the **Golowan Festival** (ⓣ01736/332211, ⓦwww.golowan.com) features fireworks, roots music and other entertainments, culminating in Mazey Day, with parades and a free programme of music and dance events at the festival marquee. One of the main venues is a converted chapel on Parade Street (west of Chapel St), the Acorn Theatre (ⓣ01736/365520, ⓦwww.acorn-theatre.co.uk), which at other times shows films and stages concerts and **theatre** and dance productions; the funky basement café also hosts live music and DJ nights. At the bottom of Chapel Street, *Penzance Arts Club* has a range of exhibitions and (often surreal) live performances, including poetry readings and small concerts (ⓣ01736/363761).

There are two permanent **dance** spots in town: the more central *Club 2K* (ⓣ01736/331211, ⓦwww.club2k.co.uk), opposite the tourist office, and, further out, *The Barn* (ⓣ01736/365754, ⓦwww.barnclub.com), near the Tesco roundabout off the A30, a mile east of the centre – both playing mainly house, hip-hop and chart music; *Club 2K* also has occasional live **concerts**.

Listings

Bike rental The Cycle Centre, 1 New St ☎01736/351671; £10 per day.
Boat trips Contact Mermaid Pleasure Trips ☎0790/173 1201, Ⓦwww.cornwallboattrips.co.uk or Marine Discovery ☎01736/874907 or 0774/927 7110, Ⓦwww.marinediscovery.co.uk for coastal cruises and wildlife-watching trips in search of seals, sea birds, dolphins, porpoises, sharks and more, from one hour (£10–18) to two and a half hours (£38), leaving daily in summer from the harbour.
Car hire Europcar, train station ☎01736/368816; Enterprise, The Forecourt, Long Rock ☎01736/332000.
Car parks There are car parks by the train and bus stations and tourist office, and a cheaper one off Alverton Rd (convenient for Penlee House). Travellers to the Isles of Scilly can deposit their vehicles at Avalon car park at South Place, near the harbour (☎01736/364622), for £5 per day.
Diving See St Ives Listings, p.294.
Hospital West Cornwall Hospital, St Clare St ☎01736/874000, 24hr accident and emergency department.
Internet access Library, 62 Morrab Rd ☎01736/363954 (Mon–Fri 9.30am–6pm, Sat 9.30am–4pm; 30min free, then £1 per 1hr). The Polyclean laundry (see below) also has a couple of terminals, as does the café inside the train station (Mon–Sat 7.30am–5pm), both 5p per min.
Laundry Polyclean, 4 East Terrace, opposite train station; open daily 9am–8pm.
Post office The main office is on Market Jew St (Mon–Fri 9am–5.30pm, Sat 9am–12.30pm).
Taxis Rank at train station, also Penzance Taxi Co ☎01736/366366.
Tours Harry Safari ☎0845/644 5940 can arrange tours of the prehistoric, Celtic and druidic sites of the peninsula lasting for half a day (£20 per person) or a full day (£30). You can also go on wacky one-hour evening "ghost tours" around Penzance (April–Sept Thurs, also Sun July & Aug; ☎01736/331206, Ⓦwww.ghosthunting.org.uk; £5): walks begin at 8.30pm from outside the tourist office. See also Ancient Stones of Kernow tours in St Ives (p.294).

Marazion and St Michael's Mount

Reached by frequent buses from Penzance, **MARAZION**, five miles east, is one of Cornwall's oldest chartered towns. Its biblical-sounding moniker is in fact a corruption of the names of local markets which were traditionally held here as early as 1070: Marghas Byghan ("Small Market") and Marghas Yow ("Thursday Market"). These days, the town attracts a regular stream of visitors, including many from Penzance who come here in summer for the wide, sand beaches, though most are here for the offshore isle of **St Michael's Mount**, whose chimneys and towers are an irresistible lure to anyone travelling along the long curve of Mount's Bay.

You're unlikely to want to linger in the busy main street of Marazion, spoiled by a steady procession of cars and coaches, unless you're tempted by the collection of photos and the reconstructed police cell in **Marazion Museum**, housed on the ground floor of the town hall on Market Place (Easter & late May to Oct Mon–Fri 10am–4pm; £1). You'll find more tranquillity at **Marazion Marsh**, an area of wetland behind the beach on the Penzance road, where there's an RSPB reserve (always open; free). The passage of trains on the main Penzance line seems to have little effect on the wildlife here: migratory birds and residents such as Cetti's warbler thrive, as do migrant dragonflies and butterflies.

St Michael's Mount

Just 400m from the mainland, the promontory holding **St Michael's Mount** can be approached on foot along a cobbled causeway at low tide; otherwise by frequent small ferries sailing from one of three different landings in Marazion, according to the state of the tide (£1.50 each way).

The Sea, The Sea...

Ever-present, ever-different, inescapable and irresistible, the sea is without doubt the principal single attraction of Devon and Cornwall. The Atlantic Ocean presses against the peninsula on all sides, wrapping it in a salty, wet embrace and imbuing it with its temperamental character. The cliffs, creeks, bays and beaches along the four hundred or so miles of coastline have long been a source of inspiration for generations of painters, poets, sailors and walkers.

Godrevy Beach, North Cornwall ▲

Beer Beach, East Devon ▼

Par Beach, St Martin's ▼

Beaches

Blessed by Britain's sunniest climate and enhanced by fine sands and a backdrop of cliffs, the **beaches** of the South West are hard to beat. Surfers, families and fashionable beach bums alike are drawn to the broad shores of cliffy North Devon, the shingly strands of East Devon, the intimate coves and creeks of South Cornwall or the huge, usually empty expanses of the Isles of Scilly. Extreme tidal shifts can transform a beach within the space of half an hour, inundating sandcastles and exposing rocks and rock pools that invite endless pottering. Although **pollution** continues to be a problem, in general West Country beaches are as clean as any in Europe. The best ones have been awarded the prestigious Blue Flag award (Ⓦwww.blueflag.org).

Best family beaches

▸▸ **Blackpool Sands**, South Devon. A crescent of coarse white sand sheltered by pines and with full facilities in season, this Blue Flag beach retains its appeal despite the crowds. See p.116.

▸▸ **Watergate Bay**, Newquay, North Cornwall. Newquay's most spectacular spot for sunning and swimming, overlooked by Jamie Oliver's *Fifteen* restaurant and with the Extreme Academy offering watersports. See p.330.

▸▸ **Kynance Cove**, Lizard Peninsula, West Cornwall. Dramatically framed by pinnacles of rock, with fine white sand and grassy areas. See p.262.

▸▸ **Porthcurno**, Penwith Peninsula, West Cornwall. This southeast-facing wedge of sand has a museum and open-air theatre nearby. See p.277.

▸▸ **Par Beach**, St Martin's, Isles of Scilly. Like most of the archipelago's beaches, this is immense, unspoiled, has perfect fine sand, and you'll usually have it all to yourself. See p.309.

Best surfing beaches

▸▸ **Woolacombe**, North Devon. Miles long, this long-established surfing beach has space for surf dudes and families alike. See p.204.

▸▸ **Croyde**, North Devon. One of Britain's best beach breaks, with sand dunes all around. Also very popular with swimmers and sunbathers. See p.203.

▸▸ **Polzeath**, North Cornwall. A famous surfing locale for all levels, though gets crowded in summer with families and fashionable young types. See p.338.

▸▸ **Fistral**, Newquay, North Cornwall. Surfers' paradise, getting plenty of swell and the best breaks of all Newquay's beaches. See p.330.

▸▸ **Sennen Cove**, Penwith Peninsula, West Cornwall. The mainland's most westerly beach picks up any surf that's going, also family-friendly. See p.280.

Seaside shenanigans

People are drawn to the coasts for a range of pursuits beyond simply swimming and sunbathing. For the most popular, **coast-walking**, nothing is required beyond a decent pair of shoes and a waterproof. Ringing the peninsula from Minehead in Somerset to Dorset, the magnificently scenic **South West Coast Path** is Britain's longest National Trail. For more challenging exertions, try **coasteering**, a high-energy cross between canyoning and cliff jumping.

Sailors will find a natural home in such resorts as Dartmouth, Salcombe and Falmouth, and every coastal town offers summertime **boat trips** in summer. If you want to get wet, have a go at **surfing** on the wave-battered north and west coasts, and **diving** is increasingly popular, particularly in West Cornwall and the Isles of Scilly.

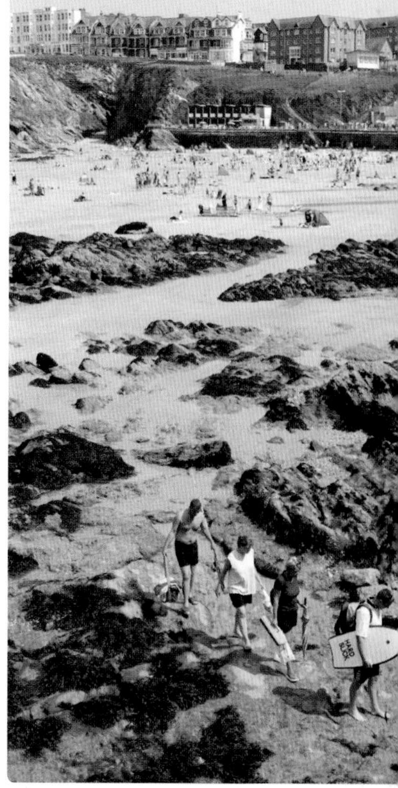

▲ Newquay Beach, North Cornwall

▼ Fistral Beach, Newquay

Sidmouth seafront, East Devon ▲

Newlyn lobsters ▼

Ports and resorts

Devon and Cornwall have their share of traditional and uniquely English **seaside resorts**. In season you'll find them animated by the screeching of seagulls, the hubbub of beaches and the whiff of takeaway fish'n'chips; in winter you can experience them in a more introspective mood. The brasher family resorts of Torquay, Falmouth and Newquay are full-on affairs where surfers and clubbers jostle along with young families; a more sedate air prevails in elegantly old-fashioned Sidmouth and Ilfracombe, while a thick helping of art gets mixed into the blend at St Ives.

Seemingly besieged by the sea, the region's often minuscule **fishing ports** are lower-key in style, but can still get lively in high summer. After the crowds have gone, such hideaways as Polperro, Mousehole and Port Isaac exude romance, worth savouring over a leisurely evening drink.

The sea at work

The sea continues to have a primary role in the West Country economy. Even with much-diminished fleets, Brixham in Devon and Newlyn in Cornwall are among the country's busiest **fishing** ports, with most of the catch transported across England to supply the nation's restaurants; fresh seafood is a staple on many West Country menus.

In the past, the sea has been linked to activities of a more nefarious nature, notably **smuggling** – almost every portside pub in Cornwall has a story to tell – and **wrecking**, involving the plundering of wrecked ships (sometimes deliberately wrecked by luring them onto the rocks with false lights). The former is the subject of pride and humorous yarns, the latter not so fondly remembered.

A vision of the archangel Michael to some local fishermen led to the construction of a church on this granite pile in the fifth century, and within three centuries a Celtic monastery had been founded here. The present building derives from a chapel raised in the eleventh century by Edward the Confessor, who handed over the abbey to the Benedictine monks of Brittany's Mont St Michel, another island-abbey inspired by a vision of Saint Michael, and the model for this one. The monastery complex was appropriated by Henry V during the Hundred Years' War, and it became a fortress following its dissolution a century later. After the Civil War, when it was used to store arms for the Royalist forces, it became the residence of the St Aubyn family, who still inhabit parts of the castle.

Although there's no arguing with its eye-catching site, the fortress-isle has a milder, more pedestrian feel than its prototype off the Breton coast. Above the island's harbour – historically used by the fishermen of Marazion, which never possessed its own – and past a restored **dairy** that formerly served a small herd of Jersey cows, it's a steep climb up the cobbled Pilgrims' Steps to the **castle** itself (April–June, Sept & Oct Mon–Fri & Sun 10.30am–5pm; July & Aug Mon–Fri & Sun 10.30am–5.30pm; Nov–March guided tours Tues & Fri at 11am & 2pm; call to check; £6.60; NT; Ⓣ01736/710507; Ⓦwww.stmichaelsmount.co.uk). The series of surprisingly small rooms within displays a wealth of weaponry and military trophies, period furniture and a feast of miniatures and larger paintings. The highlight of the tour is undoubtedly the **Chevy Chase Room**, the former monks' refectory given a seventeenth-century makeover. Sadly unconnected to the Hollywood actor, the name refers to a medieval hunting ballad ("Chevy" is either from the Cheviot Hills or the French *chevaux*, horses), which is illustrated by a simple plaster frieze on the walls. Apart from this, the room is dominated by the royal coat of arms given by Charles II in recognition of the St Aubyns' support during the Civil War.

The family is well represented in the portraits covering the walls in other parts of the castle, and in the inscriptions in the battlemented **chapel** that crowns the island's summit. The Georgian finery and "Gothick" style of the **Blue Drawing Room**, embellished with Rococo twirls and fancy plasterwork, makes a refreshing contrast to all the militaria, while the model of the house made of champagne corks in the **Map Room** also suggests less-than-martial pursuits. The castle's primary function, however, is remembered in the **Garrison Room**, where the Armada was first sighted on July 30, 1588; the beacon fire that was lit was the first to warn the nation that the Spanish invasion had come. The full story is recounted on a video screened down by the entrance, which is also where you can find **refreshment** at the *Sail Loft* café/restaurant, though the *Island Café* beyond the harbour is a pleasanter spot, with tables outside overlooking the sea. Both places are open April–October only. Local bands play beside the harbour on most Sundays in July and August.

Practicalities

In Marazion's centre, Philps Bakery, opposite the ferry embarkation point, is renowned for its **pasties**. If you want to sit down, the *Marazion Hotel* in the Square has a relaxed **restaurant**, and also serves teas, coffees and cakes. The hotel wouldn't make a bad choice to stay if you're seeking **accommodation** in the area: some rooms have stunning views – and cost extra – and all are clean, spacious and comfortable (Ⓣ01736/710334, Ⓦwww.marazionhotel.co.uk; ⑥). The best alternative is the *Blue Horizon*, at the eastern end of Fore Street (Ⓣ01736/711199, Ⓦwww.holidaybreaksmarazion.co.uk; ③), a Victorian

The Cornish pilchard industry

Actually a mature Breton sardine, the **pilchard**, or *sardina pilchardus*, has been caught, salted and pressed in Cornwall for over four hundred years. Migrating annually to breed in Cornish waters between August and December, the fish were traditionally caught in **seines**, encircling nets with floats at the top and weights at the bottom. Pilchards have always found a better market abroad than in England, and in the late seventeenth and early eighteenth centuries were even shipped to the West Indies to feed slaves working on sugar plantations, the cargoes frequently paid for in rum.

Around the middle of the nineteenth century, the pilchard fishery shifted its centre from the South Cornish coast to St Ives and the Mount's Bay ports, but by the 1870s over-fishing meant that the industry was already in decline. This, in turn, was largely due to the increasing use of **drift nets**, which effectively dispersed the shoals further out to sea, and to the change from sail- to steam-power and subsequently to the internal combustion engine adopted by the "drifter" boats just before World War I. By 1920 seine catches were rare, while drift-net fishing itself suffered a significant decline in the mid-1930s due to falling stocks. Nowadays, the pilchard catch is a tiny fraction of its former size, although, despite the limited demand for Cornish salted pilchards in Britain, a considerable **export** market survives in France, Spain and Italy. Italy was and remains the largest market, where *salacche inglesi* are traditionally eaten during Lent and form part of such pasta dishes as *spaghetti alla puttanesca* and *pasta con le sarde*. In Cornwall, you'll occasionally encounter pilchards on restaurant menus, and nowadays fresh "Cornish sardines" are cropping up too, but you're probably more likely to find them **tinned** in gift shops and speciality food stores.

B&B with, again, superb sea views from most rooms (costing more), wi-fi, a kitchenette and a patio overlooking Mount's Bay on which breakfast can be taken. A washing machine, a spa cabin and bike rental are also available.

Newlyn

Well protected behind two long piers immediately south of Penzance, **NEWLYN** is Cornwall's biggest fishing port and an important market and distribution point for the catches of smaller West Cornwall ports. **William Lovett** (1800–77), leader of the radical Chartist movement, was born in Church Lane, here, the son of a master-mariner. The town was also the focus of Cornwall's first "artists' colony", when a group of artists gathered here in the wake of the painter Stanhope Forbes in the late nineteenth century. Their work is displayed at Penlee House in Penzance (see p.270), but Newlyn's pioneering artistic spirit is perpetuated in **Newlyn Art Gallery**, occupying a detached Victorian building on the seafront at 24 New Rd (Easter–Oct Mon–Sat 10am–5pm; Nov–Easter Tues–Sat 10am–5pm; free). Elegantly modernized within, the newly extended gallery concentrates on contemporary works, but its regular exhibitions often focus on local artists, giving an insight into how the local tradition has evolved. For more on the arts scene in Newlyn, see Contexts, p.384.

You can get a feel of Newlyn's bohemian society at the start of the twentieth century by delving into some of the town's more picturesque corners away from the seafront. Off the Strand, which backs the harbour, **Orchard Place**, **Chapel Street** and **Fragdan Place** preserve a cobbled and unspoiled appearance, adorned with flowers and palms. Off Fore Street – a continuation of the Strand – climb **Trewarveneth Street** to another enclave in the higher town, where one of the alleys was lightheartedly named Rue des Beaux Arts by the Victorian painters who lived here (though, confusingly, this is not the lane to the left which currently bears that name). A smattering of present-day artists and craftspeople now inhabit the area.

Newlyn's artistic profile is dwarfed, however, by the **fishing** business, whose vitality – despite huge problems concerning falling stocks, quotas and foreign (particularly Spanish) competition – is a refreshing contrast to the dwindling activity evident in most of Cornwall's other ports.

Practicalities

The **Newlyn Fish Festival** takes over the town over the holiday weekend in late August, with samplings of local seafood as well as exhibitions of craftwork and Cornish entertainment (£4 entry; Ⓦwww.newlynfishfestival.org.uk). At other times, you can sample the local catch at the various shellfish and seafood outlets scattered around the harbour. For a well-prepared seafood **supper**, try *The Smugglers* (Ⓣ01736/331501; closed daytime & all Mon, also Tues–Thurs & Sun in winter), above the harbour on Fore Street, where you can enjoy, for instance, hake fillet on saffron risotto cake or sea-bass thermidor (main courses are around £16) while taking in the views over Mount's Bay. Just up from Newlyn Art Gallery on New Road, the stylish *Pizza Patio* (Ⓣ01736/363446; closed daytime) has delicious pizzas for £8–9 – also to take away – alongside a few salads and meat dishes. For a quick refueller by day, Aunty May's Pasty Company, at the bottom of the Coombe, has good **pasties** as well as quiches and baguettes (closed Sun). The cheapest place in town, however, is the canteen of the Royal National Mission to Deep Sea Fishermen, right by the harbour, where you can indulge in a no-nonsense fry-up for next to nothing (open weekdays 7am–2pm, Sat 8am–noon). If you're in Newlyn in the evening, you can sample some extra-strong Cornish mead wines and fruit wines at *The Meadery*, on the Coombe, along with chicken, scampi and chips (most dishes around £9), and there are a few tables outside.

As for **pubs**, the snugly beamed *Tolcarne Inn* has outdoor tables by the beach behind the art gallery, and serves inexpensive meals and real ales; jazz duos play live at Sunday lunchtimes. The local fishing folk tend to congregate in the two stripped-down bars of the *Swordfish Inn* – the "Shallow End" and the "Deep End" – on the harbourfront, or at the *Star Inn* two doors along, both of which can get quite boisterous after the boats have come in.

Penzance is a more agreeable **place to stay**, though Newlyn does have a few decent options, for example *Harbour View*, 22 Fore St, which has small, modern rooms with great views and a minimum two-night stay (Ⓣ01736/331315, Ⓦwww.harbourviewnewlyn.co.uk; ❸), and the *Swordfish Inn* (Ⓣ01736/362830, Ⓦwww.swordfishinn.co.uk; ❹), offering simple, soundproofed en-suite rooms; both have wi-fi internet.

Mousehole and Paul

Accounts vary as to the derivation of the name of **MOUSEHOLE** (pronounced "Mowzle"), three miles south of Penzance, to which it's linked by buses #6 and the infrequent #504. Originally the village was named Porth Enys ("port of the island"), a reference to St Clement's Isle, a low, bare reef that faces the village a few hundred yards offshore, while its present name may have been taken from a smugglers' cave just south of town. In any

Christmas at Mousehole

It's particularly worth stopping over in Mousehole during the Christmas and New Year period, when the **Christmas illuminations** are a regular crowd-puller. Reckoned to rival those of Manchester and Oxford Street, the lights are erected all over the village, including on the harbour walls and out to sea, and can be seen in all their glory every evening between the middle Saturday of December and the Friday at the end of the first week of January. The various dazzling displays range from spouting dolphins to dancing reindeer, a multicoloured serpent and a Christmas pudding. You can even take a helicopter flight from Penzance to view the illuminations from above – contact Penzance tourist office (see p.267) for details. The climax of the events is **Tom Bawcock's Eve** on December 23, to commemorate the stormy night long ago when a local fisherman – Tom Bawcock – managed to haul in enough fish to feed the hungry village. A local seafood dish known as Star Gazy (or Starry Gazy) Pie is prepared at the *Ship Inn* and brought out at midnight amid much carousing, and an image of the pie is always to be seen in lights. Nearby Newlyn (see p.274) has its own version of Christmas illuminations.

case, it perfectly encapsulates the village's minuscule round harbour cradled in the arms of a granite breakwater and encircled by a compact huddle of cottages. As the village attracts more visitors than it can handle, you'd do well to avoid the peak holiday periods when exploring its tight tangle of lanes, where many of the neat whitewashed or granite-grey cottages are draped with jasmine, fuschia and even cacti. Most are rented out as holiday homes in summer, giving the place a rather artificial air, though at least there is little modern development and no motor traffic.

If you're driving into Mousehole from the north, it's best **to park** on the roadside or in the car park before entering the village; steps here lead down to a concrete path by the water which takes you directly into the village. A stroll through the village will soon bring you to Keigwin Place, just up from the harbour, and site of Mousehole's oldest house, the porched **Keigwin House** (closed to visitors). Dating from the fourteenth century, it survived the famous raid on July 23, 1595, when four hundred Spanish arquebusiers and pikemen landed in the village and set upon the local inhabitants, slaying Squire Jenkyn Keigwin but sparing his house. The rest of the village and the church in nearby Paul were torched. Outside the tight knot of cottages, further diversion can be had poking around the rocky foreshore north of the harbour, where there are good views across the bay to St Michael's Mount.

Half a mile inland, at the top of steep Mousehole Hill, the churchyard wall at **PAUL** holds a memorial to Dolly Pentreath, a Mousehole resident who died in 1777 – reputedly aged 102 – and is said to have been the last person to speak solely in Cornish. Whether this is true or not, the tablet has become a shrine to the death of the language, and the inscription includes a Cornish translation of a verse from the Bible.

Practicalities

Mousehole has several good **accommodation** possibilities, but they're not cheap. The best options are the swish *Old Coastguard Hotel* (Ⓣ01736/731222, Ⓦwww.oldcoastguardhotel.co.uk; ❼), just north of the centre on the Parade, where the wooden-floored brasserie, sloping garden and most of the rooms overlook the sea, and the three maple- and walnut-furnished rooms at the *Cornish Range*, an ex-pilchard factory turned "restaurant with rooms", at 6

Chapel St (Ⓣ01736/731488, Ⓦwww.cornishrange.co.uk; ❼). Right on the harbour, the *Ship Inn* also has some cramped rooms (Ⓣ01736/731234; ❺) – those with a view cost slightly more.

The village punches above its weight when it comes to dining, including two first-class **restaurants** worth booking ahead: *2 Fore St* (Ⓣ01736/731164; closed Jan), a fashionable, modern bistro just back from the harbour, where you can dine on fresh seafood (around £14.50 for mains) in the gravelly garden, and the more formal *Cornish Range*, with local art on the walls and a smart Mediterranean feel, offering local meat and fish dishes (mains cost around £18, and there's an early-evening two-course menu for £17.50). Alternatively, the *Ship Inn* provides good ales and bar meals for under £10, while *Pam's Pantry*, 3 Mill Lane, is the place for daytime crab sandwiches and yummy breakfasts, and *Janner's* on Commercial Road serves ample and tasty fish and chips. Apart from the *Ship*, all the above have reduced opening in winter.

Lamorna Cove and around

Four miles southwest of Mousehole, **Lamorna Cove** is squeezed between granite headlands, accessible along a deeply wooded lane from the comfortable old *Lamorna Wink* pub – as the sign shows, it was the wink that signified that contraband spirits were available. Placid and unspoiled, the cove has a small crescent of sand that's covered at high tide, and is sheltered by a sturdy pier and backed by a disused granite quarry gouged out of the rock. The spot makes a nice starting point for exploring the coast path: following it westwards takes you round Boscawen Point to **St Loy's Cove**, a couple of miles' hike, where *Cove Cottage* offers romantic **B&B** in one huge en-suite double room (Ⓣ01736/810010, Ⓦwww.cornwall-online.co.uk; closed Dec to mid-Feb; no credit cards; ❻), with a four-poster and a fabulous panorama. There are numerous **campsites** on the coastal B3315, which runs parallel to the path, all rather exposed; try *Treverven*, a couple of miles south of Lamorna Cove (Ⓣ01736/810200; closed Nov–Easter), with two long fields for pitches, a games area and distant sea views.

If you're following the B3315, it's easy to drop in on the signposted **Merry Maidens**, a ring of nineteen stones in an open field about a mile west of the road junction for Lamorna – there's a small lay-by for parking. The rough-hewn circle is said to be all that remains of a group of local women turned to stone as a punishment for dancing on Sunday. Half a mile to the north, in a field on the other side of the road, the **Pipers** are two tall upright stones supposedly representing the musicians petrified by the same spell. Other than the likelihood that the ring and uprights date from some time between 2400 and 800 BC, nothing is known about their origin or significance though they were probably the focus of some ceremonial function.

Porthcurno and around

On one of the peninsula's loveliest stretches of coast and five miles west of Lamorna, **PORTHCURNO** stands above a succession of picturesque coves and generous sand beaches set against a jagged granite backdrop. The scattered hamlet lies around – but mostly out of sight of – the most popular of the beaches, **Porthcurno Beach**, protected by high cliff walls and reachable along a path from the village car park. On the western side of the beach, just along from the date 1812 carved into the granite by an unknown hand, lies a beach-house built by local benefactress Rowena Cade for her nieces and nephews, artfully sandwiched within a fissure in the rock and now sadly cemented up. Cade was the founder of Porthcurno's famous **Minack Theatre**, situated at the top of the cliff 200ft above the sea, and reached by steep steps from the beach. Originating as a venue for amateur plays put on by Cade's friends and family, the theatre staged its first production (*The Tempest*) in 1932, and subsequently expanded as its fame spread – it now holds 750 seats, though the basic Greek-inspired design remains intact. The spectacular backdrop of Porthcurno Bay makes this one of the country's most inspiring theatres and productions are frequently sold out during the seventeen-week season, lasting from late May to late September, when an eclectic range of plays, opera and musicals are produced (see box opposite). The weather can be cold and blowy but cancellations are rare. If you can't make it to a performance, you can at least nose around the site and follow the story of the theatre's creation at the **Exhibition Centre** (daily: April to late Sept 9.30am–5.30pm, but 9.30am–noon when there are matinée performances, usually June–Sept Wed & Fri; late Sept to Oct 10am–5pm; Nov–March 10am–4pm; £3.50).

You can reach more fine beaches along the coast path from here, your steps accompanied to the west by the moaning of the whistling buoy at the Runnel Stone a mile offshore. The path runs westwards half a mile to **Porthchapel**, a wedge of smooth, clean sand, and beyond to a much narrower cleft in the cliffs at **Porthgwarra**, where a tunnel has been bored through a huge boulder to the rocky shore. Continuing west along the coast path from here brings you past **Nanjizal**, where there's access to a sandy beach, and eventually to Land's End – all in all, one of the best stretches of coastal walking anywhere.

Half a mile east of Porthcurno, the coast path skirts the beach of **Pednevounder**, a steep climb down and traditionally popular with naturists, but now equally frequented by the clothed. The Iron Age fort of **Treryn Dinas** once occupied the headland on the eastern prong of Porthcurno Bay, though nothing remains today beyond the earthworks comprising a ditch and bank. The most interesting feature here lies above it and a few steps back on top of a cluster of granite slabs: the rounded square of **Logan's Rock**, a seventy-tonne monster that for centuries rocked – reputedly at the merest touch – until it was knocked off its perch by a nephew of playwright Oliver Goldsmith and a gang of sailors in 1824. In the outcry that followed, they somehow replaced the boulder, but it rocked no more. Half a mile beyond Treryn Dinas, the coast path sweeps down to more sandy beaches near the cluster of cottages and a handful of fishing vessels at **Penberth Cove**, where the National Trust has restored the heavy wooden capstan that once used to haul boats up the slipway.

Halfway between Porthcurno and Logan's Rock, a white pyramid adjacent to the coast path marks the spot where an undersea telegraph cable was landed in 1870, recalling Porthcurno's important role as a terminus for a network of cables which reached across the world. The history of the telegraphy station, including the serious competition it faced from Marconi's innovations in "wireless" transmissions, is related in the **Porthcurno Telegraph Museum** (Easter–Oct daily 10am–5pm, closes 7.30pm Wed late May to mid-Sept; Nov–Easter Sun & Mon 10am–5pm, daily during school hols; last admission 4pm; £5), housed in a bomb-proof, gas-proof, underground communications bunker from World War II, just up from Porthcurno Beach, behind the car park. Brass and mahogany instruments and etchings give a vivid sense of the pioneering work undertaken by the marine engineers

Performances at the Minack

Tickets for shows at the Minack Theatre for afternoon (1.30 or 2pm) or evening (8pm) performances cost £8.50 for the main auditorium or £7 for upper-terrace seating. You can book in person at the box office (Mon–Fri 10am–5.30pm, also Sun in summer; closes 8pm on performance evenings), by phone (same hours; ⓣ01736/810181) or on the website (ⓦwww.minack.com). Bring a cushion and a rug. Programmes are available in local tourist offices or on the website.

and the problems they faced with cables getting broken or snagged – one photo from 1947 shows a fisherman staring in dismay at a tangle of trawl gear entwined with cable. Most cables today are buried under the seabed; a model of one of the submersible vehicles used for putting them in place is also on show. Apart from this, there's material on the Victorian version of the internet and the secret communications systems of World War II.

Practicalities

Buses #1, #1A, #300 (summer only) and #504 (not Sun) stop at Porthcurno on their run between Penzance and Land's End. The museum's **website**, ⓦwww.porthcurno.org.uk, provides general information about Porthcurno and the vicinity, with rough maps and directions for a local walk. **Refreshments** can be found nearby on the road climbing above the beach to the car park, where the *Porthcurno Beach Café* (closed weekdays Oct and all Nov–Easter) provides baguettes, cakes and coffees, and the *Cable Station Inn* (closed Oct–Feb) serves standard pub grub, most hot dishes costing around £8.50, and has a veranda, pool table, table tennis and darts (you can also apply here to use the nearby tennis courts).

A couple of local B&Bs offer alluring **accommodation**: the detached, self-contained *Driftwood Studio* (ⓣ01736/810796, ⓦwww.cornwall-online.co.uk; ❺), just 500m from the Minack, with a lounge, sea views and a three-night minimum stay in summer, and *Sea View House* (ⓣ01736/810638, ⓦwww.seaviewhouseporthcurno.com; ❺), which also has views and provides picnics and evening meals for £15 or £20. Neither place accepts credit cards.

Land's End

Four miles west of Porthcurno, **Land's End** can be reached via buses #1, #1A and #504 (not Sun) from Penzance, or the summer-only open-top #300, which follows a circular route taking in Penzance, Marazion, St Ives, Zennor, St Just and Sennen Cove. Unarguably, however, the best way to approach England's extreme western tip is on foot via the coastal path. Although it would be hard to efface the potency of this majestic headland, the amusements complex that dominates the land approach comes close to irreparably violating the spirit of the place. Once past it, however, you can relax: turf-covered cliffs sixty feet high provide a platform to view the Irish Lady, the Armed Knight, Dr Syntax Head and the other wind-eroded outcrops dotted around, beyond which you can spot the Longships lighthouse, a mile and a half out to sea, and sometimes the Wolf Rock lighthouse, nine miles southwest (flashing every fifteen seconds), or even the dim outline of the Isles of Scilly, 28 miles away. From the point or the coast path on either side, look out too for the area's richly diverse **wildlife**, from busy fulmars and herring gulls, to Atlantic grey seals "cottling" out to sea (drifting, as though asleep, with just their heads above the water). In early September, colonies of seals haul themselves out of the water to breed on the rocks below Longships lighthouse. Other regular passengers on the fast currents include dolphins, porpoises and basking sharks, for which a pair of binoculars would be useful.

You'll almost always have to share the point with crowds of other visitors, often queuing for the traditional Land's End souvenir: a photo taken next to a signpost showing distances to New York (3147 miles), John O'Groats (874 miles) and the hometown of their choice. It's harmless, unobtrusive fun, unlike the trivializing **Land's End Experience** (daily from 10am, or 10.30am in winter, closing times vary – call ⓣ0871/720 0044; free entry but all-day parking costs £2–4; ⓦwww.landsend-landmark.co.uk), which substitutes a panoply of lasers and unconvincing sound effects for the real open-air experience. If you have kids in tow, you might be swayed to sample the exhibitions and amusements, most of which cost £3–4; you can also buy an all-inclusive ticket for £10.95, or £8.95 in winter. One exhibition is dedicated to the "**end-to-enders**" – those who have walked, ridden or driven from Land's End to John O'Groats (or vice versa) – showing some of the various means of transport used, for example a motorized bar stool and a powered supermarket trolley. If you opt for one of the sound-and-light shows, the best is probably the Return to the Last Labyrinth, "an exciting multi-sensory experience" which somehow blends the stories of smugglers, wreckers and King Arthur. In August, many come here for the **fireworks displays** that take place on Tuesdays and Thursdays at around 9.30pm.

Practicalities

Just behind the point, the *First and Last House* has unremarkable light **refreshments**, but if you want a full meal, the only option is *Longships Restaurant*, part of the *Land's End Hotel*, which has tables outside overlooking the sea and in a conservatory. You might even be tempted to stay in the fancily furnished rooms at the **hotel** itself (ⓣ01736/871844, ⓦwww.landsendhotel.co.uk; ❼; may close Sun–Tues in winter); though not all have sea views. The nearest **campsite**, *Seaview* (ⓣ01736/871266, ⓦwww.seaview.org.uk), is just a ten-minute walk away on the B3315; there's a heated outdoor pool, and Whitesand Bay is close by, though the site is poorly maintained.

If you don't want to depend on your feet for exploring the coast around Land's End and Sennen, you might consider excursions on **horseback**, offered by Land's End Riding Centre at Trevescan Farm, 200m from the Land's End–Porthcurno junction on the B3315 (ⓣ01736/871989), or on a **scenic flight**, available from Land's End Airport, midway between Land's End and St Just on the B3306; a ten-minute flight costs £35 per adult (£45 for single occupancy). Call ⓣ01736/788771 to book.

Whitesand Bay

The rounded granite cliffs fall away a mile and a quarter northeast of Land's End at **Whitesand Bay** to reveal a glistening mile-long shelf of sand, the only substantial beach at this end of the peninsula, and one of the largest in West Cornwall. The rollers here make for good surfing, and boards can be rented and lessons arranged at the more popular southern end of the beach, **Sennen Cove**, where Sennen Surfing Centre, occupying a kiosk in summer, can arrange two- to three-hour lessons or longer **surfing** courses, with all equipment provided (ⓣ01736/871227 or 871561, Ⓦwww.sennensurfingcentre.com). Alternatively, just hire a wet suit and board from the hire shop below *The Beach* (see below; each costs around £10 per day, plus a £10 deposit).

For snacks and full **meals**, there's *The Beach* (Ⓣ01736/871191; closed Jan, and may close daytime & Sun–Thurs in winter), a café/restaurant where breakfasts, snack lunches, such as pizzas, crab soup and falafel (all around £8), and steaks and seafood in the evening (£17–20) are all on offer. The adjacent esplanade holds more snack bars and a popular **pub**, the *Old Success Inn*, where you can munch bar food or dine on fish, meat and veggie dishes in the moderately priced restaurant. If you want to stay in Sennen Cove, there is a pair of cosy **B&Bs** tucked away on Old Coastguard Row at the southern end of the Strand and right on the coast path: *Myrtle Cottage* (Ⓣ01736/871698, Ⓦwww.cornwallfarwest.co.uk/cfwmyrtle; no credit cards; ❸), with three rooms – one en suite – as well as a fine café with a patio overlooking the sea (open to nonresidents), and *Pengelly House* (Ⓣ01736/871866, Ⓦwww.pengellyhouse.com; no credit cards; ❹), offering three rooms but no breakfast. If you don't mind being a twenty-minute walk inland (and uphill), try the *Whitesands Hotel* (Ⓣ01736/871776, Ⓦwww.whitesandshotel.co.uk), located on the A30 above the cove, with six themed rooms for B&B (❹), a separate upmarket **surf lodge** in four bunkrooms with self-catering facilities (Ⓦwww.whitesandslodge.co.uk; £21), and two heated and decked **tipis**, each sleeping up to four (from £16 per person), available between April and September. Hotel and lodge have a two-night minimum stay, and reduced opening in winter. Also on the premises are a **restaurant** and café with barbecues in summer, open to all for light snacks (£5–8), and grills and seafood dishes (£9–17); again, it may be closed in winter.

St Just-in-Penwith and Cape Cornwall

Three miles north of Whitesand Bay and half a mile inland from the sea, **ST JUST-IN-PENWITH** is the main centre at the peninsula's western end – not to be confused with St Just-in-Roseland (see p.246). Quiet most of the time, it gets quite lively in summer with visitors drawn to its limited range of shops, pubs, restaurants and B&Bs. It's the coast that is the main attraction, not least the rocky headland of **Cape Cornwall**, a rather desolate spot, thankfully undeveloped. See the website Ⓦwww.landsendarea.co.uk for downloadable **self-guided walks** and general information.

Arrival and information

St Just is reachable from most places in Penwith on **buses** #17, #17A, #17B, #300 (summer only) and #504 (not Sun). There's a **tourist office** in the library on Market Street (Mon–Fri 10am–1pm & 2–5pm, Sat 10am–1pm, closed Thurs Oct–March; Ⓣ01736/788165, Ⓦwww.visit-westcornwall.com), where you'll also find year-round **internet** access (90p for 15min), a little further up from the area's main **post office**.

Accommodation

St Just has a concentration of **accommodation**, though even here choice can be limited, and you'll need to book early in high season. Note that the *Kelynack* campsite (see below) also offers B&B and bunkhouses.

Hotels and B&Bs

Boscean Country House Boswedden Rd ⓣ01736/788748, ⓦwww.bosceancountryhotel.co.uk. A mile or so northwest of the village, you'll find luxurious touches here, with a generous walled garden, oak-panelled public rooms and log fires. Clean, bright rooms and free internet. Closed Nov–March. ⑤

Commercial Hotel Market Square ⓣ01736/788455, ⓦwww.commercial-hotel.co.uk. The best of the two inns on the central square has plain but modern en-suite rooms, with friendly staff and a complimentary bottle of wine for guests. The top room is accessed via steep stairs. ⑤

No 11 11 Fore St ⓣ01736/786767, ⓦwww.11forestreet.co.uk. Traditional but sympathetically modernized granite cottage offering B&B in two rooms – one en suite – with oak beds, organic toiletries, plasma TVs and wi-fi. There's a lovely garden at the back, and the helpful hosts can arrange baggage-forwarding and packed lunches. No under-10s. ④

Old Fire Station 2 Nancherrow Terrace ⓣ01736/786463, ⓦwww.oldfirestationstjust.co.uk. Central, modern B&B with an open-plan lounge and breakfast room and three smallish, white-painted en-suite bedrooms, one on the ground floor, the top two with distant sea views. ④

Campsite and hostel

Kelynack Caravan and Camping Park Kelynack ⓣ01736/787633, ⓦwww.kelynackcaravans.co.uk. Secluded site just outside the hamlet of Kelynack, a couple of miles south of St Just, offering sheltered pitches – a rarity on Penwith. There's also accommodation available in a couple of small and clean bunkhouses (£12), available all year, and in two simple rooms for B&B (book ahead; ④). Closed Nov–Easter.

Land's End Youth Hostel ⓣ0845/371 9643, ⓔlandsend@yha.org.uk. Less than a mile south of St Just and a convenient half-mile from the coast path, this hostel has beds from £10 and camping facilities, and a kitchen and cooked meals are available. To get here on foot, take the left fork past the post office in St Just and follow the track at the bottom of the road; by car, take the B3306 Land's End road, turning right at the hamlet of Kelynack. Call ahead at all times.

The village and around

Once a close-knit mining community serving the local tin and copper industry, St Just retains its rows of trim grey cottages, radiating out from the central Market and Bank squares. Just off the squares, behind the clocktower, **Plen-an-Gwary**, or "play place", is a grassy open-air theatre that was once a venue for old Cornish miracle plays and was later used by Methodist preachers as well as local wrestlers. These days, the occasional concert or play is staged here.

There could be no greater contrast to the prosaic tenor of St Just than the dramatic coastline two miles west at **Cape Cornwall**, for which the village is the main access point (from Cape Cornwall Road, off Bank Square). For years this headland – topped by the stack of the Cape Cornwall Mine (closed in 1870) – was thought to be England's westernmost point, until more accurate means of measurement decided the contest in favour of Land's End. In many ways, though, Cape Cornwall is the more stirring of the two promontories: there are no towering outcrops or lighthouses to look out onto, but neither are there cafés, entertainments or car parks to distract from the vista. Sheltered by the cape, the cove has a few boats hauled up and a foreshore with plenty of rock pools to explore, though there's no beach to speak of. Southward, the coast path takes in some spectacular cliff scenery on its route to Land's End, while northward towards Pendeen, away from the crowds, it passes close to one of Cornwall's most dramatic engine houses at **Botallack** (see opposite).

Eating and drinking

You don't need to travel out of St Just for a bite to **eat or a pint of ale**. However, a short excursion will bring you to other good alternatives, such as the *Queen's Arms* a mile up the road in Botallack, which lays on decent bar food, or the excellent *Gurnard's Head* gastropub (see p.287).

Commercial Hotel Market Square. With two bars, a beer garden and a pool table, this pub also has a conservatory restaurant where you can order local sardines (£9), among other dishes.
The Cook Book 4 Cape Cornwall Rd ⓣ01736/787266. For coffees, teas and lunches, this easy-going place should satisfy, with soups and home-made cakes, tables outside and second-hand books for sale.
Kegen Teg 12 Market Square ⓣ01736/788562. Organic, local and mainly vegetarian food is offered here, for example falafel (£9.60) and Welsh rarebit (£6.40). Tasty breakfasts, cakes, smoothies and organic ice cream are also available. Closed eves, also weekends in winter, and all Jan & Feb.
Star Inn 1 Fore St. Old-fashioned gem of a pub, full of traditional character, where you can sample Tinners and other local ales, and there's a rear yard. No food is served, but you can bring in a pasty or other non-odorous snack. Live music Mon, Thurs and some Sat.
Wellington Hotel Market Square. The pub here has real ales and a beer garden, and there's a separate upstairs restaurant serving, for example, crab salad and smoked fish platter (£7.50–11).

Penwith's mining heritage

Two miles north of St Just on the B3306, **Geevor Tin Mine** (Easter–Oct Mon–Fri & Sun 9am–5pm, also Sat in July & Aug; Nov–Easter Mon–Fri 10am–4pm; last entry 1hr before closing; £8.50; ⓦwww.geevor.com) was the area's last working mine, ceasing operations in 1990. Since then, the building has been restored and opened up to visitors to allow a fascinating close-up view of the Cornish mining industry. You can wander at will among the surface machinery and through the vast mill where 98 percent of the valueless rock was separated from the tin ore, but the most thrilling part is the guided tour of an adit, or horizontal passage running into the rock (the main underground area is now flooded to sea level). Here, the hellish working conditions of a tin miner are graphically described by the knowledgeable guides, and you can peer down into the murky depths of vertical shafts, or up them to the sky. A small **museum** shows a model of the mine and explains the complex process of tin production. You might finish up in the on-site **café**, which affords distant views west to the coast, as far as the engine house of the Levant Mine, closed since 1930 when its workings were absorbed within the Geevor mine.

Perched on the cliff edge outside **Trewellard**, the brick buildings of the former mine now hold the **Levant Beam Engine** (early to late March Fri 11am–5pm; April, May & Oct Wed & Fri 11am–5pm; June Wed–Fri & Sun 11am–5pm; July–Sept Tues–Fri & Sun 11am–5pm; early Nov to Feb Fri 11am–4pm; £5.80; NT), Cornwall's oldest beam engine now restored and functioning, as well as a small exhibition. Already locally famous for the number of its "cappens" (captains, or foremen) and for its use of pit ponies – rare in Cornwall – Levant was the scene of a major disaster in 1919, when the beam holding the "man-engine", or mechanical lift, broke away from its upper coupling, resulting in the deaths of 31 men and serious injuries to many others. There's a short underground tour and an explanatory film (but note that the engine is not in operation, or "steaming", between Nov and Feb). If you don't want to hike it from Geevor to Levant, the site can be reached on Levant Road, which branches off the St Just road at the *Trewellard Arms Hotel*.

From Levant, a three-quarter-mile walk south along the coast path brings you to the evocative, cliff-clinging remains of **Botallack Mine**, whose workings once extended under the sea. The Count House here (the old accounting office), restored by the National Trust, contains displays on the area's mining history, geology and wildlife (daily 10am–4pm; free), and you can enter the "labyrinth chambers" – the decontaminated arsenic works.

Pendeen and around

Immediately east of Geevor, two ruined engine houses guard the approach to **PENDEEN**, an unexceptional ex-mining village which has some appealing excursions within an easy radius. The nearest is to see an example of a **fogou**, or prehistoric underground chamber, in nearby farmland; to get there, take the narrow lane to the right of Boscaswell Stores, signposted for the lighthouse, and then take the signposted right turn for *Pendeen Manor Farm*, where you can ask to view the chamber which is reached across a muddy farmyard. A torch is essential: the steep entrance leads down to a stone tunnel which bends sharply left after a few yards, and there is a further stretch accessible only on hands and knees. Though the fogou's function is unknown, it suggests the presence of an Iron Age village, possibly on the site of the farm. One of Cornwall's greatest scholars, the antiquary and naturalist William Borlase (1696–1772), was born in *Manor Farm*, which also provides snacks and **cream teas**.

Past the turn-off for *Manor Farm*, the lighthouse road meets the sea at the slate promontory of **Pendeen Watch**. Poised on the edge of this grassy knoll, **Pendeen Lighthouse** affords superb views over the craggy coast and towards the derelict engine houses dotted around the surrounding hills. The squat, white tower – in service since 1900 – has the last working twelve-inch fog siren in the country – be warned that this can sound without warning, a potentially traumatic experience. The headland also gives access to the lovely rocky **Portheras Cove**, a ten-minute walk east, where you'll find an excellent sandy beach, though there are signs warning of metal fragments from a dynamited shipwreck.

Inland: prehistoric remains

East of Pendeen and inland, the granite and hilly moorland is an apt setting for the cluster of enigmatic relics of Cornwall's prehistory scattered about here. They're worth winkling out if only for their lonely setting, but are mostly fairly remote and difficult to track down; information and detailed maps are available at local tourist offices. With a compass to hand, the sites could equally be visited from Zennor or from one of the roads linking the B3306 with Penzance.

Chun Quoit and Chun Castle

Less than a mile southeast of Pendeen, off the B3318 Penzance road, a lay-by on the left marks the start of a track that winds onto the moor and to **Chun Quoit** (map ref SW402339), one of the most dramatic of Penwith's quoits – dolmens, or granite rocks arranged into what may have been burial chambers, whose outer covering of earth has washed away over the centuries. Chun resembles a giant mushroom from afar, the "capstone" poised precariously on four upright slabs, together enclosing a chamber within which bones of ancestors may have been laid.

Visually less arresting remains of Penwith's past inhabitants can be reached along a path that threads about a quarter of a mile eastwards from Chun Quoit to the top of a hill, where a rubble of rocks and two upright stones marking a gateway are all that's left of the Iron Age **Chun Castle** (map ref SW405339). At this ancient hillfort, archeologists have found traces of slag in smelting pits, suggesting that tin mining existed here at least two thousand years ago. From

Chun Castle, a track leads southeast and downhill to a farm, from where a lane leads northeast for less than a mile to meet the minor Morvah–Madron road (which drivers can access from the coastal B3306, taking a right turn for Madron and Penzance just past the village of Morvah).

Men-an-Tol and Men Scryfa

Almost opposite the lane from Chun Castle, and a mile from Morvah, a signposted track wanders northeast for just under a mile to where a marked path to the right goes through fields to **Men-an-Tol** (map ref SW426349), or "stone of the hole". Also called the "Devil's Eye", this rock hoop in open moorland – probably the remains of a neolithic tomb – suggests nothing so much as a giant doughnut. Similar "hole stones" have been found elsewhere as entrances to burial chambers, and in the Middle Ages this one was thought to have great healing powers: people crawled through the hole to rid themselves of rheumatism, spine troubles or ague, while children with scrofula or rickets were passed three times through it before being dragged round it through the grass.

Further up the track from the Morvah–Madron road, another five minutes' walk brings you to **Men Scryfa** (map ref SW427353), a standing stone with a Latin inscription commemorating "Rialobran, the son of Cunoval" – probably a reference to a sixth-century Celtic chieftain.

Lanyon Quoit

Another mile or so down the Morvah–Madron road, and less than two miles northwest of Madron, **Lanyon Quoit** (map ref SW430337) is more easily visited, its roadside location partly accounting for its status as best known of Cornwall's quoits. Its local name, "Giant's Table", is a plain reference to its form – a broad top slab balanced on three upright stones. The quoit has not survived intact over time however: in 1815 a storm caused the structure to collapse, and it was re-erected nine years later with only three of the four original supports. Consequently it is not so high as it once was, though it still makes an arresting sight in the midst of the moor.

Chysauster

One and three-quarter miles from the turn-off on the B3311 Penzance–St Ives road (the route of the #516 bus) at Badger's Cross, the Iron Age village of **Chysauster** (map ref SW472350) occupies a windy hillside with views over Penzance (daily: April–June & Sept 10am–5pm; July & Aug 10am–6pm; Oct 10am–4pm; £3; EH). The best-preserved ancient settlement in the South West, it dates from about the first century BC and consists of the shells of eight stone buildings, each holding an open courtyard from which small chambers lead off. The largest structures are likely to have been farm dwellings, probably thatch-roofed with walls coated with wattle and daub, while other rooms were probably barns, stalls or stables, or even protected vegetable gardens. Huts three, four and six are the best preserved and give the most vivid impression of the grandeur of the dwellings, where open hearths, stone basins for grinding corn and covered drains have been identified.

The site was used as an open-air pulpit by Methodist preachers at the beginning of the nineteenth century and was first excavated in the 1860s. The surrounding heather and gorse give the place a bracing, wild feel, though it's a mystery why the original inhabitants would have chosen such a high exposed position for their village.

Zennor and around

Back on the coastal B3306, the road snakes eastward from Morvah, bringing you after five or so miles to **ZENNOR**, an ancient village known by literati for its associations with **D.H. Lawrence** (see box, below). The village retains no trace of Lawrence's presence today, though you might invoke his memory in the *Tinners Arms* – the pub that lent him the title of a short story which A.L. Rowse grudgingly conceded to be "more true to Cornish life than most other things written about us by foreigners".

At the bottom of the village, next to the old Methodist chapel, the **Wayside Museum** (daily: Easter–May & Oct 11am–5pm; May–Sept 10.30am–5.30pm; £3.75) is dedicated to Cornish life from prehistoric times. It's a densely packed and eclectic compendium of over five thousand items crammed into fifteen rooms, where you can rummage to your heart's content among the painstakingly labelled exhibits, many of which were found under hedges and in fields. Ancient tools used by carpenters, wheelwrights, plumbers and cobblers are displayed alongside primitive agricultural threshing machinery, ploughs and sheep-shearers, and there are granite pounders and mortars for crushing seed and corn which date from around 3000 BC. You'll also see a reconstruction of a traditional parlour and kitchen, with thick stone walls and a very low doorway to keep out the wind, while, on a very different note, cuttings and photos give the background to Zennor's various literary connections. On your way out, look for the "plague stone" just outside the building – its bowl was filled with vinegar for disinfecting visiting merchants' money during cholera outbreaks in the nineteenth century.

Above the museum, the simple granite church of **St Senara** has a barrel-vaulted roof typical of many of Penwith's churches, but its most famous feature is the **Mermaid Chair**, made from two sixteenth-century bench-ends carved with an image of a mermaid holding a mirror and a comb. The carving relates to a local

D.H. Lawrence in Zennor

Seeking escape from the London literary scene as well as inspiration from the "fine thin air which nobody and nothing pollutes", D.H. Lawrence came to live in Cornwall in December 1915, and moved to Zennor the following March. Installed with his wife **Frieda** at Higher Tregerthen, one of a group of cottages about a mile east of the village, he was evidently smitten by the place, describing it in a letter to **John Middleton Murry** and **Katherine Mansfield** in March 1916 as "a tiny granite village nestling under high shaggy moor hills, and a big sweep of lovely sea, lovelier even than the Mediterranean ...It is all gorse now, flickering with flowers, and then it will be the heather; and then, hundreds of foxgloves. It is the best place I have been in, I think." The following month Murry and Mansfield came to join the Lawrences in what Lawrence envisaged as a writers' community to be called **Rananim**. The experiment was unsuccessful, however; alienated by Lawrence and Frieda's violent quarrels and by Lawrence's evident disapproval of the newcomers' own relationship, Murry and Mansfield left after two months for a more sheltered spot near Falmouth. Lawrence stayed on to write **Women in Love**, spending a year and a half in Zennor in all, though his enthusiasm for the place was gradually eroded by the hostility of the local constabulary and the residents, who took a dim view of the couple's unorthodox lifestyle, not to mention Frieda's German associations (her cousin was air ace Baron von Richtofen, the "Red Baron"). In October 1917, after police had ransacked their cottage, the Lawrences were brusquely given notice to quit. His Cornish experiences were later described in **Kangaroo**, while Mansfield and Murry were peeved to find themselves characterized as Gudrun and Gerald in **Women in Love**, with the Lawrences themselves re-created as Birkin and Ursula.

legend according to which a mermaid was so entranced by the singing of a chorister in the church choir that she lured him down to the sea, from which he never returned – though his singing can still occasionally be heard. On the left of the church doorway, a plaque commemorates the memory of John Davey of Boswednack, supposed to be the last person to possess a working knowledge of the Cornish language when he died in 1891 – one of several claiming this honour.

Behind the *Tinners Arms*, next to the church, a fairly level path leads less than a mile northwest to the sea at **Zennor Head**, where there is some awe-inspiring cliff scenery above the sandy **Pendour Cove** (the fabled home of Zennor's mermaid). The six-and-a-half-mile hike to St Ives from here is testing but highly rewarding, taking three or four hours. If you're doing a round trip, you might consider the inland route on one leg, taking the path between Zennor's churchyard and the village hall across fields and through a sequence of tiny hamlets. The path passes close to **Higher Tregerthen**, where D.H. Lawrence lived after his stay at the *Tinners Arms*, reachable in about fifteen minutes from Zennor. Above the house, another path leads south off the St Ives road behind the Eagle's Nest – for many years the home of St Ives painter Patrick Heron – for around a mile to **Zennor Quoit** (map ref SW469380). This chambered tomb, which has one of the widest roof slabs of all Cornwall's quoits – at an angle, as it has slipped over time – is a rare example of a quoit with two central chambers, thought to be some 4500 years old.

Practicalities

From Penzance and St Ives, buses #508 (not Sun) and the summer-only #300 run to Zennor. The *Tinners Arms* provides a homely spot for a **drink** or pub snack or full meal and outdoor tables. Alternatively, baguettes and scrumptious cakes are available from the ground-floor **café** at the *Old Chapel*, a hostel in the former Wesleyan chapel next to the Wayside Museum. If you don't mind sleeping up to six to a room, the hostel makes a fun place to **stay** (Ⓣ01736/798307, Ⓦwww.zennorbackpackers.co.uk/; £15); a room sleeping four costs £50, and camping pitches are available. Otherwise, you'll find more comfort at the *Tinners Arms* (Ⓣ01736/796927, Ⓦwww.tinnersarms.com; ⑤), which, in an adjacent building, offers two bright en-suite doubles and two singles with a shared bathroom. West of the village, right by the turn-off to Zennor on the St Just–St Ives road, the remote *Tregeraint House* (Ⓣ01736/797061, Ⓦwww.cornwall-online.co.uk/tregeraint-house; no credit cards; ⑤) is run by a potter and boasts cliff-top views from two of its three rooms, all of which have washbasins and share a bathroom; the owner can provide transport for pick-ups. A couple of superb choices lie about a mile further, near Gurnard's Head: *Cove Cottage* (Ⓣ01736/798317, Ⓦwww.cornwall-online.co.uk/cove-cottage; ⑥), whose elegant rooms are set above an isolated cove where you can enjoy peaceful swimming and sunbathing, and breakfast can be taken on the terrace, and the *Gurnard's Head* (Ⓣ01736/796928, Ⓦwww.gurnardshead.co.uk; ⑥), a highly rated but laid-back gastropub with smallish rooms and simple but expertly prepared food, for which booking is recommended; mains cost £12–16.

St Ives

East of Zennor, the road runs four hilly miles to the steeply built town of **ST IVES**, which has smoothly undergone the transition to holiday haunt from its previous role as a centre of the fishing industry. So productive were the offshore waters that a record sixteen and a half million fish were caught in one

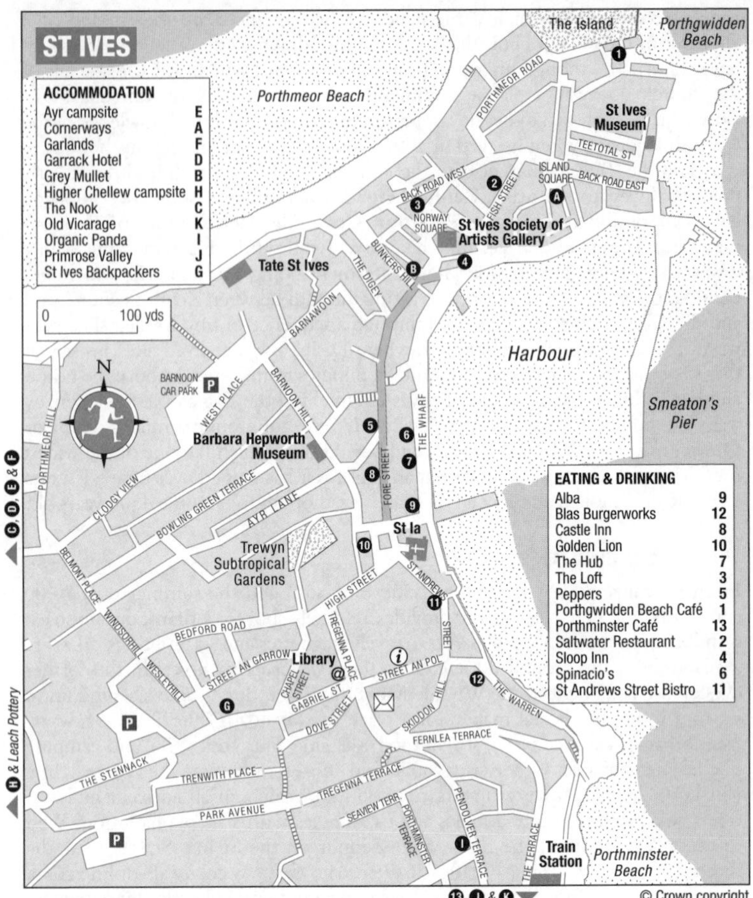

net on a single day in 1868, and the diarist Francis Kilvert was told by the local vicar that the smell was sometimes so great as to stop the church clock. Virginia Woolf, who spent every summer here to the age of twelve, described St Ives as "a windy, noisy, fishy, vociferous, narrow-streeted town; the colour of a mussel or a limpet; like a bunch of rough shell fish clustered on a grey wall together". By the time the pilchard reserves dried up in the early 1900s, St Ives was beginning to attract a vibrant **artists' colony**, precursors of the wave later headed by Ben Nicholson, Barbara Hepworth, Naum Gabo and the potter Bernard Leach, who in the 1960s were followed by a third wave including Terry Frost, Peter Lanyon and Patrick Heron.

St Ives' dual artistic and fishing legacies are continued today in the numerous **galleries** jammed into its narrow alleys, and in the daily landing of **fishing** catches on Smeaton's Pier. The town has little in common with the rest of the Penwith peninsula, its broad sand beaches, higgledy-piggledy flower-decked lanes (bearing such melodious names as Teetotal St and Salubrious Place), and the modern architecture of the Tate putting it into an altogether different category from the austere granite villages and jagged cliffs that characterize most of West Cornwall. It also receives most of the tourism but, however inundated it gets, St Ives always repays a visit, and its range of accommodation makes it a great base for excursions to the rest of the peninsula.

Arrival and information

To reach St Ives by **train**, change at St Erth on the main London–Penzance line, or take a direct service from Penzance. St Ives' train station lies at the eastern end of town, behind Porthminster Beach, and below Station Hill, where **buses** #17, #17A #17B, #300 (summer-only), #508 and #516 from Penzance, #14 from Truro and National Express services all stop. A few minutes' walk away on the narrow Street an Pol, the **tourist office** (April, May & Oct Mon–Fri 9am–5pm, Sat 10am–4pm; June–Sept Mon–Fri 9am–5pm, Sat 10am–4pm, Sun 10am–2pm; Nov–March Mon–Fri 9am–5pm, Sat 10am–1pm; ⓣ01736/796297, ⓦwww.visit-westcornwall.com) can book **accommodation** for £3. Drivers should park as soon as possible or, better still, use the car park at Lelant Saltings (or one of the other stations on the branch line from St Erth) and take the train in. Alternativley, park at Carbis Bay and walk a mile along the coast from there, an easy and pleasant stroll. Taxis in St Ives are generally cheap.

Accommodation

Even with West Cornwall's greatest concentration of hotels and guesthouses, St Ives can still run short of rooms in midsummer, and advance booking is essential. Some places ask for a week's minimum stay in peak season; out of season, rates drop significantly. Most of the following choices are fairly central, and most offer one or two parking spaces.

Hotels and B&Bs

Cornerways 1 Bethesda Place ⓣ01736/796706, ⓦwww.cornerwaysstives.com. Daphne du Maurier once stayed in this tasteful modern cottage conversion, which has friendly management and contemporary en-suite rooms named after Daphne du Maurier characters – ask for the top room. No credit cards. ⑤

Garlands 1 Belmont Terrace ⓣ01736/798999, ⓦwww.cornwall-online.co.uk/garlands. Stripped floors enlivened by upbeat, colourful touches make this family-run B&B in the higher part of town a great choice. Two rooms share a bathroom. Three-night minimum stay in July & Aug. No credit cards. ④

Garrack Hotel Burthallan Lane ⓣ01736/796199, ⓦwww.garrack.com. Suitably secluded for a pampered stay, but within walking distance of Porthmeor Beach, this sedate, family-run hotel has a variety of rooms (mostly ⑧) plus an indoor pool, a sauna and an excellent restaurant. ⑦

Grey Mullet 2 Bunkers Hill ⓣ01736/796635, ⓦwww.touristnetuk.com/sw/greymullet. Oak-beamed and drowned in flowers and pictures, this eighteenth-century house – claimed to be the oldest in town – is 20m from the harbour on a cobbled lane. Rooms are en suite but some are cramped. No under-15s. ④

The Nook Ayr, off Ayr Terrace ⓣ01736/795913, ⓦwww.nookstives.co.uk. In a quiet lane at the top of a steep hill, this modern, tastefully decorated B&B has spotless, well-equipped rooms – some small – and free wi-fi, a decked patio and parking spaces. It's a ten-minute walk down to the centre, longer on the ascent. No credit cards. ⑤

Old Vicarage Brush End, Lelant ⓣ01736/753324, ⓦwww.oldvicaragelelant.co.uk. Away from the bustle in its own abundant garden, this nineteenth-century house is close to Lelant Salting train station for quick access to St Ives, and mixes period furnishings with modern art. No young children. No credit cards. Closed Nov to mid-March. ⑤

Organic Panda 1 Pendolver Terrace ⓣ01736/793890, ⓦwww.organicpanda.co.uk. As the name suggests, everything is organic and sustainable in this stylish B&B close to the stations, including the plush cotton bedding and bamboo towels. Two of the bright, white rooms have inspiring views, and there's free wi-fi and delicious, healthy breakfasts at the communal table. No under-3s. ⑥

Primrose Valley Porthminster Beach ⓣ01736/794939, ⓦwww.primroseonline.co.uk. Relaxed, eco-friendly hotel separated from Porthminster Beach by the railway. Contemporary-style rooms, some with balconies, are spacious, fresh and light, and four have (sideways) sea views. Wi-fi enabled. There are three- or four-day minimum stays in July and Aug. No under-8s. Closed most of Jan. 7–8

Campsites and hostel

Ayr Higher Ayr ⓣ01736/795855, ⓦwww.ayrholidaypark.co.uk. St Ives has no campsites right on the seafront but this large complex with caravans and holiday homes, half a mile west of the centre above Porthmeor Beach, has a good sea prospect and first-class facilities – making this an expensive site – though it doesn't have much in the way of shelter. It's near to the coast path, and buses #339 and #516 pass close by.

Higher Chellew Nancledra ⓣ01736/364532, ⓦwww.higherchellewcamping.co.uk. Good out-of-town alternative to *Ayr*, and much cheaper. It's small, tidy and friendly, with basic but clean facilities, including a washing machine, however there are no shops nearby. On the B3311, equidistant between St Ives and Penzance (on the #344 bus route), it's a good base for exploring the whole peninsula. No credit cards. Closed Nov–Easter.

St Ives Backpackers The Stennack ⓣ01736/799444, ⓦwww.backpackers.co.uk/st-ives. Restored Wesleyan chapel school from 1845, usefully located in the centre of St Ives, with table tennis and pool, and barbecues in summer. Dorms have four, six or eight beds for up to £18 per night, and there are double and twin rooms (1). Rates drop in winter. There's a kitchen and internet access.

The Town

Squeezed between no fewer than four beaches – if you count the sands of the harbour – and steep slopes and headlands, St Ives is a town of picturesque nooks and eye-catching vistas. The pedestrianized **Fore Street** threading through its centre is usually a mass of shuffling tourists who spill out onto the wide harbour, where the piercing shrieks of gulls add to the hubbub. Above and at either end of the main drag is a disorienting maze of lanes packed with restaurants, bars and galleries.

The galleries

On the north side of town, reached from Back Road West or over Barnoon Hill, Porthmeor Beach is overlooked by the town's greatest cultural asset, **Tate St Ives** (March–Oct daily 10am–5.20pm; Nov–Feb Tues–Sun 10am–4.20pm, closes 1 week three times a year, call to check ⓣ01736/796226, ⓦwww.tate.org.uk/stives; £5.75; combined ticket with Barbara Hepworth Museum £8.75). Free half-hour **tours** of the gallery usually kick off from Patrick Heron's stained-glass window at 11.30am (not Sun).

Anyone expecting something on the same scale as Britain's other Tate galleries may be disappointed by the St Ives collection, which has a much smaller and more local feel, though few would deny the splendour of its beachfront location. The seaside sounds are a constant presence inside the airy white building, creating a lively soundtrack to the paintings, sculptures and ceramics, most of which date from the period 1925 to 1975, and many inspired by St Ives itself. Near the entrance, the tone is set by a massive stained-glass window by **Patrick Heron**, said to be the largest unleaded stained glass in the world, whose great slabs of colour recall the brilliance of the sun, sand and sea outside. Contrastingly, the work of the local naive painter **Alfred Wallis** shows more muted tones, as in his *Houses at St Ives, Cornwall* and *Newlyn Harbour*. Depicting cottages in front of The Island, with the harbour and a glimpse of the open sea with the local fishing fleet, Wallis's *St Ives* was one of the first paintings he sold, bought by Ben Nicholson on his visit to the town in August 1928. The influence of Wallis's diagrammatic designs is apparent in some other work here, for example *Island Sheds* by **Wilhelmina Barns-Graham** and *St Ives from the Cemetery* by **Bryan Pearce**. The interplay between the different generations of artists can also be seen in the painted aluminium and wood *Construction* by **Peter Lanyon**, which shows a debt to the constructivist **Naum Gabo**, who lived in St Ives during World War II and is also represented here. Check out, too, Lanyon's tall, chaotic, partly abstract harbour view, *Porthleven*, in the Lower Gallery, and **John Wells'** *Seabird Forms*, which strikingly depicts the movement and flight patterns of sea birds, in a similar blend of figurative and abstract ideas.

The crescent-shaped **Gallery 2**, which overlooks the beach, has displays of pottery and stoneware by **Bernard Leach** and his school, including **Michael Cardew** and **Shoji Hamada**, mostly very simple designs of jugs, cups, plates and bowls. **Barbara Hepworth**'s sculpture *Sea Form (Porthmeor)* is her response to the beach, while her *Menhirs*, carved from a single piece of slate, and *Landscape Sculpture*, a bronze from the late 1950s, take their inspiration from what she called "the pagan landscape" of the Penwith peninsula. As well as this permanent collection, there are constant exhibitions focusing on the St Ives artists and others, usually with a local connection. Finish up your visit at the museum's rooftop **café**, one of the best places in town for tea and cake, with a stupendous panorama (you don't need a gallery ticket to visit the café).

If your appetite has been whetted by Hepworth's elemental sculpture, the **Barbara Hepworth Museum** (same times as Tate St Ives, but closes at dusk if earlier; £4.75; combined ticket with the Tate £8.75) is an essential stop, a short distance away on Barnoon Hill. One of the foremost nonfigurative sculptors of her time, Hepworth lived in the building from 1949 until her death in a fire here in 1975. Apart from the sculptures, the museum has masses of background on her art, from letters to catalogues and reviews; her photos of Cornish quoits and landscapes provide clues to the inspiration behind her sleek monoliths. The clean all-white space is a superb setting for such works as *Infant*, a shiny, alien-looking child carved from Burmese wood. In the adjoining garden, a lush area planted with subtropical trees and shrubs, Hepworth herself arranged her stylistically diverse works in striking settings: in one grassy corner, *Conversation with Magic Stones* consists of six irregularly shaped pieces in an intimate huddle, opposite the wildly different *Apollo*, a steel rod fashioned into a geometric shape. At the centre of the garden, the mammoth *Four Square (Walkthrough)* is the most massive work, while *Meridian* is perfectly placed under a tree surrounded by a bush and bracken. Hepworth's famous "wired" pieces, in which the different planes are linked by the threaded string, are also well represented, for example *Spring 1966*. Though the garden attracts plenty of visitors, it remains a tranquil escape from the town's bustling activity. There are a few other Hepworth works dotted around St Ives, including the rather uncharacteristic *Madonna and Child*, a tender work in memory of her son killed during RAF service in 1953, donated to the harbour-side church of **St Ia** (irregular opening), where the High Street meets Fore Street. The steel candlesticks that stand in front of the work are also by the sculptress. The church itself is a fifteenth-century building dedicated to a female missionary said to have floated over from Ireland on an ivy leaf.

Many of St Ives' private galleries are small, and their contents can usually be glimpsed from outside, but most welcome visitors. The **St Ives Society of Artists Gallery** (Mon–Sat 10.30am–5.30pm, also Sun 2.30–5.30pm Easter to mid-Oct; free; ⓦwww.stisa.co.uk) is a much bigger affair, occupying the old Mariners' Church on Norway Square – as it has done since 1945 when its members included Lamorna Birch, Barbara Hepworth and Ben Nicholson. Following the split with the abstract group in 1947, the gallery has shown chiefly figurative work, much of it of a high quality. In the main gallery upstairs, the members' paintings and sculptures – virtually all on local themes – are constantly replaced by new works, giving a good overview of the group's varying styles, while the Crypt Gallery below is used for private exhibitions (free).

Devotees of Bernard Leach's Japanese-inspired ceramics can visit his studio, the **Leach Pottery** (March–Oct Mon–Sat 10am–5pm, Sun 11am–4pm; Nov to early Jan Tues–Sat 10am–4pm; £4.50; Ⓦwww.leachpottery.com), in the Higher Stennack neighbourhood, three-quarters of a mile outside St Ives' centre on the Zennor road. You can see the original workshops used by Leach and Shoji Hamada in 1920, and later by Michael Cardew, Janet Leach and others, as well as an exhibition room, shop and contemporary gallery.

For more on the arts in St Ives, see Contexts p.385.

The rest of town and the beaches

Housed in an old Sailors' Mission at Wheal Dream, between the harbour and Porthgwidden Beach, **St Ives Museum** (Easter–Nov Mon–Fri 10am–5pm, Sat 10am–4pm; £1.50) will appeal to anyone with a magpie curiosity and lots of energy. A wide-ranging trawl through Cornish history, and more particularly that of Penwith and St Ives, the densely crowded rooms on two floors throw up such nonessential bric-a-brac as a collection of kettles, a bardic robe, a stuffed turtle that had wandered over to Cornwall from Mexico and a collection of photos including some of the St Ives artists. The sections devoted to the railway in Cornwall, the pilchard industry and of course mining, with a model of the Levant mine "man-engine" which crashed in 1919 (see p.283), entertainingly fill out the picture. Below the museum, there are views across the bay to Hayle Sands and, directly below, over tiny **Porthgwidden Beach**, a sheltered spot for a quiet paddle on a hot day.

If you need relief from the claustrophobic lanes of St Ives, take a picnic or just a breather in **Trewyn Subtropical Gardens** (8am – sunset), a miniature haven furnished with benches, banana trees and wooden sculptures of musicians round the lawns; it's tucked away off Bedford Road, above the High Street. For a bit more space, however, you can't do better than a bracing climb up to **The Island**, the undeveloped headland (also known as St Ives Head) that separates the harbour and Porthgwidden Beach from Porthmeor Beach. **St Nicholas Chapel** sits in isolation on this heathy promontory, and there are inspiring views across St Ives Bay.

At some point, you'll fetch up on the wide expanse of **Porthmeor Beach**, dominating the northern side of St Ives. Unusually for a town beach, the water quality is excellent, meriting a Blue Flag award in 2009, and the rollers make it popular with surfers (boards are available for rent below the Tate); there's also a good open-air café here. South of the train station, **Porthminster Beach**, another favourite spot for sunbathing and swimming, is an even longer stretch of smooth yellow sand, but more sheltered. Further east, some of the region's best beaches lies on either side of the Hayle estuary, usually less crowded than the town beaches. Reached from Hayle, three miles of pearly sands stretch from the estuary to Godrevy Point.

Eating and drinking

The huge range of **restaurants** in St Ives stretches from Penwith's most sophisticated eateries to pizzerias and places serving simple fish and chips and other seaside snacks. Self-caterers and picnickers will find plenty of choice among the town's shops and supermarkets. Dozens of flavours of **ice cream** (including orange mascarpone and pistachio) as well as frozen yoghurts, milk shakes and slush puppies can be had at Willy Wallers, adjacent to the *Sloop* on the Wharf.

Alba The Wharf ⓣ01736/797222. This sleek harbourside restaurant on two floors of a converted lifeboat house cooks up some of the best food in town. Starters include Provençael fish soup and among the mains (all £12–17) are cassoulet of monkfish, black bream with feta and olive mash, and confit of duck leg. There are two- and three-course set menus (£13.50 and £16.50) for lunch and early evening.

Blas Burgerworks The Warren. This "alternative burger bar" doles out what are probably the best burgers you'll ever have, served in a variety of ways using the best local ingredients (£7.50–10). There's just one small room with four communal tables made from found or reclaimed wood. No reservations. Closed Sun & Mon in winter.

The Hub 4 The Wharf. Grilled breakfasts in the morning, sandwiches, burgers and crab linguine (£5–12) at lunchtime, and drinks in the evening make this café-bar a lively stop, open until late. There's a small terrace at street level, and a balcony upstairs overlooking the harbour.

The Loft Norway Lane ⓣ01736/794204. Bright and stylish, this is set in a long, conservatory-like space with an outdoor terrace for views over the town. Mains cost around £16, The Seafood Marinière is one of the most popular dishes; non-seafood items include duck and steak. Closed Oct–Easter Sun & Mon.

Peppers 22 Fore St ⓣ01736/794014. Mellow and friendly pizza parlour, also serving pasta (£6–8) and steaks (£11–15). Pizzas cost £6–11 according to size, and you can create your own. Closed daytime.

Porthgwidden Beach Café Porthgwidden Beach ⓣ01736/796791. A bustling offshoot of the *Porthminster Café* in the Downalong area of town, this summery place with a stone terrace offers simple fare such as burgers, fish and chips, pastas and steaks as well as more ambitious dishes, for example baked mackerel with spinach and seafood pancakes with mussels, all around £10. Breakfasts include scrambled egg and smoked salmon (£5); or just order a a coffee or tea. Oct–Easter closed Mon, also eves Sun, Tues & Wed.

Porthminster Café Porthminster Beach ⓣ01736/795352. With its fantastic beach location, this makes a superb spot for coffees, lunches, cream teas and full evening meals. Lunchtime meals (£8.50–13.50) include crab cakes, mackerel and grilled sea bream, while innovative dishes such as monkfish curry and baked cod with spicy tiger prawns and chorizo (£18–19) are served at dinner. Nov–March closed Mon and eves Sun & Tues–Thurs.

Saltwater Restaurant 14 Fish St ⓣ01736/794928. Bright, beachy, fishy paintings on the walls and a good choice of seafood, from swordfish to grilled scallops, priced at £12–15. The leek and chestnut mushroom risotto is also good (£11.50). Closed daytimes, all Sun & Mon and mid-Nov to mid-Feb.

Spinacio's The Wharf ⓣ01736/798818. In this L-shaped room with wooden floors and posters on white walls, you can enjoy views over the harbour as you tuck in to such vegetarian delights as mushroom and bean burger or roast vegetable and cheese tart for around £11. Friendly and relaxed. Closed daytime and Nov–Easter.

St Andrews Street Bistro 16 St Andrews St ⓣ01736/797074. Rugs on the wooden floor and tall white walls filled with *objets d'art* help to create a great low-lit, boho ambience. The food is good, too: Modern-British with exotic elements, for example ostrich fillet and Jamaican goat curry (mains are £12–17). Occasional live music. Closed daytime; call for winter opening.

Nightlife and entertainment

Nightlife in St Ives is limited, and decent **pubs** are few and far between – and often packed: the *Castle Inn* on Fore Street and the *Golden Lion* on Market Place are the best places for real ales (the *Golden Lion* also has a beer garden and live music in the back bar on Fridays and Sundays), while the *Sloop Inn* on the Wharf has slate floors, beams and work by local artists on display, but gets very touristy.

Over a fortnight in September, the **St Ives Festival** features jazz, blues, classical and roots music, as well as poetry, plays and exhibitions; for more information, call ⓣ01736/366077 or see ⓦwww.stivesseptemberfestival.co.uk.

Listings

Banks HSBC, Barclays and Lloyds TSB on the High St; NatWest on nearby Tregenna Hill; all have ATMs.

Boat trips A range of excursions are touted at the harbour in summer; a 40minute coastal cruise costs around £7, a two-hour fishing trip £15.

Bus information First ⓣ0845 600 1420; Western Greyhound ⓣ01637/871871; otherwise, for all timetable and route enquiries call ⓣ0871/200 2233.
Car hire St Ives Car Hire ⓣ0845/057 9373, ⓦwww.stivescarhire.co.uk; St Ives Motor Company ⓣ01736/796695, ⓦwww.stivesmotor.co.uk.
Diving Undersea Adventures, 7 Hayle Industrial Park, Hayle (ⓣ01736/751066, ⓦwww.undersea.co.uk), has courses and guided dives around Penwith for all abilities.
Hospital The Minor Injury Unit at Stennack Surgery, at the bottom of Bullans Lane on the Stennack (ⓣ01736/793333), can deal with most casualties, otherwise head for Penzance (see p.272).
Internet Log on at the library, Gabriel St, open Tues 9.30am–9.30pm, Wed–Fri 9.30am–6pm or 9.30am–8pm in summer, Sat 9.30am–12.30pm; £1.80 per half-hour. The *Sloop* pub is *a* wi-fi hotspot.
Post office Main office on Tregenna Hill, where there's a *bureau de change*; there's a smaller branch at the bottom of Fore St, off the Wharf. Both are open Mon–Fri 9am–5.30pm Sat 9am–12.30pm.
Riding Penhalwyn Trekking Centre, Halsetown ⓣ01736/796461 offers hourly, half-day and day treks over Penwith's moors.
Supermarket The Cooperative on Lower Stennack stays open until 11pm in summer.
Surfing Shore Surf, 46 Mount Pleasant, Hayle (ⓣ01736/755556 or 0785/575 5556, ⓦwww.shoresurf.com), offers half-day (£25) or full-day courses (£40). St Ives Surf School (ⓣ0779/226 1278, ⓦwww.thesurfschooluk.com) which operates from St Ives Bay has a kiosk on Porthmeor Beach in summer, offering lessons from £25. All equipment included for both.
Taxis Ranks at the bus and train stations. Ace Cars ⓣ01736/797799; St Ives Cars ⓣ01736/799200; St Ives Taxis ⓣ01736/793000.
Tours Ancient Stones of Kernow focuses on the prehistoric monuments of the Penwith peninsula; full-day tours, usually on Thurs & Fri, cost £30 per person (ⓣ01736/797312, ⓦwww.ancientstonesofkernow.co.uk). Evening "ghost tours" of St Ives, starting from the tourist office, begin at 8.30pm, also Wed at 10.15pm in Aug (April–Oct Tues, also Wed June–Sept; ⓣ01736/331206, ⓦwww.ghosthunting.org.uk; £5). For other tours around Penwith, see Harry Safari (p.272).

Travel details

Trains

Penzance to: Bodmin (1–2 hourly; 1hr 15min); Exeter (13 daily; 3hr); London (10 daily; 5–6hr); Plymouth (1–2 hourly; 2hr); St Erth (1–2 hourly; 10min); St Ives (2–5 daily; 30min); Truro (1–2 hourly; 40min).
St Erth to: Penzance (1–2 hourly; 15min); St Ives (1–2 hourly; 15min).
St Ives to: Penzance (2–5 daily; 25min); St Erth (1–2 hourly; 15min).

Buses

Helston to: Coverack (Mon–Sat 8 daily, Sun 2 daily; 30–40min); Falmouth (Mon–Sat 13 daily, Sun 2 daily; 40min–1hr 10min); The Lizard (Mon–Sat hourly, Sun 5 daily; 40–50min); Mullion (Mon–Sat hourly, Sun 5 daily; 25min); Penzance (Mon–Sat hourly, Sun 6 daily; 55min); Truro (Mon–Sat hourly, Sun 5 daily; 50min–1hr).
Penzance to: Helston (Mon–Sat hourly, Sun 6 daily; 50min); Land's End (June–Sept Mon–Sat hourly, Sun 5–8 daily; Oct–May 5–10 daily; 55min); Mousehole (Mon–Sat 2–3 hourly, Sun hourly; 15–20min); Newquay (2 daily; 1hr 30min–2hr); Plymouth (6 daily; 3hr–3hr 40min); St Austell (2 daily; 1hr 30min–2hr 15min); St Ives (Mon–Sat 2–3 hourly, Sun 1–2 hourly; 35–45min); St Just (Mon–Sat 2–3 hourly, Sun 9–11 daily; 35min–1hr 30min); Truro (Mon–Sat 1–2 hourly, Sun 5 daily; 1hr 40min).
St Ives to: Land's End (June–Sept 3–5 daily; 1hr 40min); Newquay (5 daily; 1hr 30min); Pendeen (June–Sept 3–5 daily; 45min); Penzance (Mon–Sat 2–3 hourly, Sun 1–2 hourly; 30–45min); Plymouth (4 daily; 3hr–3hr 20min); St Austell (2 daily; 1hr 45min); St Just (Mon–Sat 2–3 hourly, Sun 8–10 daily; 1hr–1hr 20min); Truro (Mon–Sat hourly, Sun 6 daily; 1hr 10min–1hr 40min); Zennor (Mon–Sat 4–9 daily, Sun in summer 3–5 daily; 15–25min).

Flights (all Mon–Sat)

Land's End to: St Mary's, Isles of Scilly (mid-March to Oct frequent flights; Nov to mid-March 1–4 daily; 20min).
Penzance to: St Mary's, Isles of Scilly, by helicopter (late March to Oct 7–17 daily; Nov to late March 3 daily; 20min); Tresco, Isles of Scilly, by helicopter (late March to Oct 4–6 daily; Nov to late March 2 daily; 20min).

10

The Isles of Scilly

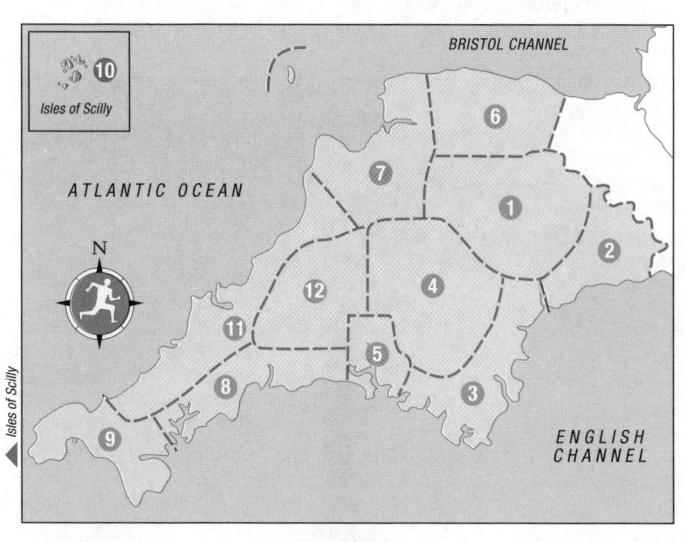

CHAPTER 10 Highlights

* **Gig racing** All the islands participate in this exciting boat race, Scilly's primary sport, best viewed from accompanying boats out at sea. See p.302
* **Tresco Abbey Gardens** An oasis of exotic greenery built around the ruins of the old priory. See p.306
* **Great Bay, St Martin's** Among the dozens of stunning beaches in the Scillies, this crescent of creamy white sand takes some beating. See p.310
* **Diving** The clarity of the waters and the numerous wrecks make the archipelago one of Britain's best dive sites. See p.304 & p.310
* **Boat excursions to the Western Rocks** This remote and scattered rockscape has been the scene of countless shipwrecks and today is a teeming sanctuary for birds and seals. See p.313

▲ Bishop Rock Lighthouse, Western Rocks

10

The Isles of Scilly

Lying 28 miles southwest of Land's End, the Isles of Scilly (the name "Scilly Isles" is strongly disapproved of) are a compact archipelago of 100–150 islands – counts vary according to the definition of an island and the height of the tide. None is bigger than three miles across, and only five of them are inhabited. Though they share a largely treeless and low-lying appearance – rarely rising above 30m – each island nonetheless has a distinctive character, revealing new perspectives over the extraordinary rocky seascape at every turn.

Free of traffic, theme parks and amusement arcades, the Scillies provide a welcome respite from the mainland tourist trail. The energizing briny air is constantly filled with the cries of sea birds, while the **beaches** are well-nigh irresistible, ranging from minute coves to vast untrammelled strands – though swimmers must steel themselves for the chilly water. Other attractions include Cornwall's greatest concentration of **prehistoric remains**, some fabulous **rock formations**, and masses of **flowers**, nurtured by the equable climate and long hours of sunshine (the archipelago's name means "Sun Isles"). Along with tourism, the main source of income here is flower-growing, and the heaths and pathways of the islands are also dense with a profusion of wild flowers, from marigolds and gorse to sea thrift, trefoil and poppies, not to mention a host of more exotic species introduced by visiting foreign vessels.

The majority of the resident population of just over two thousand is concentrated on the biggest island, **St Mary's**, which has the lion's share of facilities in its capital, **Hugh Town**. Among the "off islands", as the other inhabited members of the group are known, **Tresco** is the largest, and presents an appealing contrast between the orderly landscape around its abbey – whose subtropical **gardens** are the archipelago's most popular visitor attraction – and the bleak, untended northern half. West of Tresco, **Bryher** has the smallest population, the slow routines of island life quickening only in the tourist season. The bracing, back-to-nature feel here is nowhere more evident than on the exposed western shore, where **Hell Bay** sees some formidable Atlantic storms. East of Tresco, **St Martin's** has a reputation as the least striking of the Scillies with the most introverted population, but its beaches are impressively wild and it boasts stunning views from its cliffy northeastern end. On the southwest rim of the main group, the tidy lanes and picturesque cottages of **St Agnes** are nicely complemented by the weathered boulders and craggy headlands of its indented shoreline.

A visit to the isles would be incomplete without a sortie to the **uninhabited islands**, sanctuaries for seals, puffins and a host of other marine birdlife. On the largest of them, **Samson**, you can poke around prehistoric and more recent remains that testify to former settlement. Some of the smaller islets also repay a visit for their delightfully deserted beaches, though the majority amount to no more than bare rocks. This chaotic profusion of rocks of all shapes and sizes, each bearing a name, is densest at the archipelago's extremities – the **Western Rocks**, lashed by ferocious seas and the cause of innumerable wrecks over the years, and the milder **Eastern Isles**.

Although you can get a taste of the islands' highlights on a day-trip from Penzance, the Scillies deserve a much longer visit. The chief drawbacks are the high cost of reaching them and the shortage of **accommodation** (advance booking is essential throughout the year). Note that many B&Bs on the off islands offer – and often insist on – a dinner, bed and breakfast package, and this is anyway usually the most convenient option, considering the tiny choice of places to eat. Many hotels and B&Bs closed in winter, but there are usually enough to cater for the trickle of visitors who come in these months. The alternative is a **self-catering** deal, almost always available by the week, and you'll need to book some time in advance. Apart from Tresco, each island also has one **campsite**, mostly unsheltered with basic facilities; all closed during winter, when it would be impractical to pitch a tent in any case – camping elsewhere is not allowed.

Food is available in pubs, cafés and restaurants on all five inhabited islands, and you can find basic groceries on each (though at higher prices than on the mainland). Again, choice is very limited in winter, when pubs on the off islands have reduced opening.

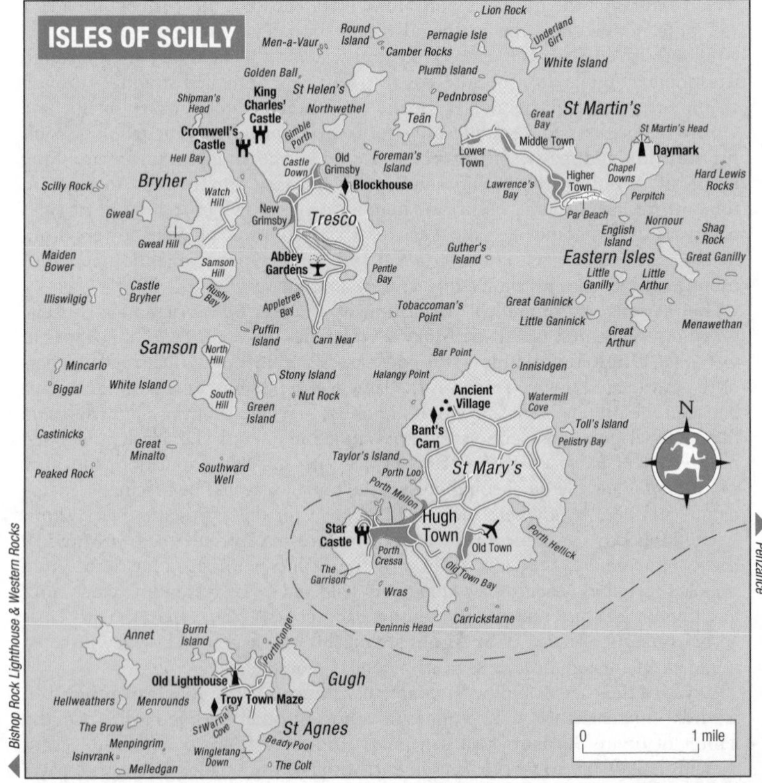

Getting to the islands

Whether you choose to arrive on the islands by sea or air, it's advisable to book in advance – several days ahead if it's high season. Travelling by sea is cheapest, and allows you to view the magnificent Penwith coastline (though seas can be nauseatingly rough). **Ferries** to St Mary's are operated by Isles of Scilly Travel (Ⓣ0845/710 5555, Ⓦwww.ios-travel.co.uk) from Penzance's Lighthouse Pier, where there's a ticket office. Sailings take place on Monday, Wednesday, Friday and Saturday in early April and all October, Monday–Saturday between early April and September. There is no service between November and early April. Departures are mainly at 9.15am, with most returns from St Mary's at 4.30pm; journey time is about two and three-quarter hours. One way tickets cost £47.50, returns £95, "Saver Returns" (travelling both ways on any Tues, Wed or Thurs) £80, with discounts for families on day returns and for under-16s on all fares. **Day returns** are especially good value at £35 (you can't use these as one way tickets, as names are checked and only hand luggage is allowed). It's worth asking the ticket office about special offers for discounted ferry tickets, sometimes available with vouchers from local newspapers in Cornwall.

Arriving by **air** is much more expensive, but quick and memorable, affording a terrific overview of the archipelago and its surrounding litter of rocks (and incidentally revealing how shallow the waters are around here). Fares vary according to whether you opt for a "Saver" or an open return. A Saver is valid for off-peak flights and none on Saturday (or Mon & Fri from Exeter, Bristol or Southampton). The departure points for Skybus aeroplane flights (also operated by Isles of Scilly Travel, see above) are Land's End Airport, near St Just (Mon–Sat frequent flights; 20min; £109–129 return), Newquay (Mon–Sat 2–4 daily; 30min; £125–149 return), Exeter (Mon–Sat 1–2 daily; 1hr; £199–239 return), Bristol (Mon–Sat 1–2 daily; 1hr 15min; £242–289 return) and Southampton (Mon–Sat 1 daily; 1hr 30min; £256–309 return). Day-return tickets are also available from Land's End (£86) and Newquay (£96) airports. In winter (usually Oct–March or Easter), there is a significantly reduced service from Land's End, Newquay and Exeter only. A subsidized transfer service is available from Penzance train station to Land's End Airport (£4), which should be arranged when you book your flight. Passengers arriving at St Mary's can make use of a transport service to any destination on St Mary's (£3.50).

Isles of Scilly Travel also offers a **combination day return**, allowing you to depart from Penzance by air and return by sea, or vice versa (£70).

British International (Ⓣ01736/363871, Ⓦwww.islesofscillyhelicopter.com) runs **helicopter flights** throughout the year from the heliport a mile east of Penzance to St Mary's (late March to Oct Mon–Sat 7–17 daily; Nov to late March Mon–Sat 3 daily) and Tresco (late March to Oct Mon–Sat 4–6 daily; Nov to late March Mon–Sat 2 daily). Journey time is about twenty minutes, though note that helicopters are more subject to delays due to mechanical failure than other transport options. Fares are £96 for a day return, £170 for an open return; a Standby Day Return, only bookable up to 24 hours in advance, costs £75 and an Excursion Fare for weekday travel outside peak times is £140. Fares for under-16s and infants are further discounted. A shuttle **bus service** connects Penzance train station with the heliport, leaving 45 minutes before each scheduled departure (£2).

Once on the islands, you'll have no difficulty travelling between them, with **inter-island launches** (£4) operated by St Mary's Boatmen's Association (Ⓣ01720/423999, Ⓦwww.scillyboating.co.uk), leaving from the quayside for the other islands (the "off islands") soon after the ferry arrives in St Mary's; luggage destined for the off islands should be clearly marked with the name of the island, so that bags can be deposited in the right pile on the dock. Note, however, that there is a much-reduced service in winter and none at all in bad weather – even in summer, the waves can be frighteningly high.

The only **tourist information** office is on St Mary's (see opposite), covering the whole archipelago. However, it's worth looking at the **websites** Ⓦwww.simplyscilly.co.uk and Ⓦwww.scillyonline.co.uk, which have a wealth of information on all aspects of the islands including advice for visitors.

A history of the islands

In the annals of folklore, the Scillies are the peaks of the submerged land of **Lyonnesse**, a fertile plain that extended west from Penwith before the ocean broke in, drowning the land and leaving only one survivor to tell the tale. The story may not be complete fantasy, in so far as the isles form part of the same granite mass as Land's End, Bodmin Moor and Dartmoor, and may well have been joined to the mainland in the distant past.

The early human history of the Isles of Scilly is equally obscure. Many have tried to prove that the archipelago was the group of islands referred to in classical sources as the Cassiterides, or "Isles of Tin", where the Phoenicians and Romans obtained their supply of the precious metal – though no trace of tin mining remains today – while some have also identified the Scillies as the legendary "Isles of the Blest" to which the dead heroes and chieftains of the mainland were conveyed in order to find peace and immortality. This theory is apparently supported by the unusual quantity of **Bronze Age** burial chambers found here, though it is more likely that these were rather the tombs of the first Scillonians, dating from some time between 1900 and 800 BC.

There is evidence of **Roman occupation** from the third and fourth centuries AD, when the isles are thought to have been used as a place of exile for undesirables. Recorded history, however, begins in the twelfth century, when Henry I granted the Scillies to the Benedictine abbey of Tavistock, in Devon, whose monks established a priory on Tresco. Although the **Benedictines** had nominal control for the next four hundred years, their rule was always limited by the activities of pirates, and as conditions were extremely tough anyway, the resident monks probably welcomed the opportunity to return to the mainland following the Dissolution in 1539. In 1571, the isles were leased to the **Godolphin family**, a Cornish dynasty which held the archipelago for the crown until 1831, introducing a degree of order and generally improving the lot of the islanders by such measures as dividing the land into manageable plots. They also provided a much-needed protective garrison, though the construction of Star Castle on St Mary's in 1593 was at the behest of Elizabeth I, motivated by the fear of Spanish invasion. The presence of the fort ensured that Hugh Town, rather than Tresco, site of the abbey, should be the islands' capital. It also meant that the islanders were left alone by the pirates, and stability reigned until the eruption of the **Civil War**, when the Scillies upheld the Royalist cause long after the mainland had capitulated to the Parliamentarians. After a brief sojourn by the Prince of Wales (later Charles II) in 1646, the archipelago was occupied by a Roundhead army, whose legacy was Cromwell's Castle in Tresco.

As soon as the Roundheads had departed, the Godolphins resumed their tenure, though their new official responsibilities after the Restoration – a reward for their loyalty to the crown – meant that they were rarely present on the islands. The maladministration and corruption of their local stewards, who demanded high rents while neglecting the plight of the Scillonians, combined with regular crop failure, reduced the local population to a fruitless struggle for subsistence over the next 150 years. Although fishing and piloting continued to be the economic mainstays, the development of agriculture was impeded by the short leases granted to the tenant farmers, which discouraged any long-term planning. Conditions improved only with the arrival in 1834 of a new proprietor,

Flower-farming in the Scillies

After tourism, **flower-farming** is the most important commercial activity on the isles. The flower farms shape much of the landscape with their narrow fields, or "pieces", intricately divided by tall windbreaks of hardy veronica, pittosporum, euonymus and escallonia, lending a maze-like appearance to some of the inland tracts. Most of the crop consists of various species of narcissi, first appearing well before Christmas and creating a spectacular effect in March and April when they are in full flower. Harvesting takes place throughout the winter, just before they flower, when the crop is flown or shipped directly to markets in London and other mainland centres in Britain and abroad.

Augustus Smith, a landowner from Hertfordshire who, despite his despotic methods, implemented far-reaching reforms that included the construction of roads, the overhaul of the land-tenure system and the introduction of compulsory education thirty years before it became law on the mainland. Smith's work was continued after his death in 1872 by his nephew Lieutenant Dorrien-Smith, who was mainly responsible for introducing **flower-farming** to the archipelago (his descendant, Robert Dorrien-Smith, is the current leaseholder of Tresco and owner of Bryher's *Hell Bay Hotel*). This quickly became the economic lifeblood of the community and continues to be of prime importance today, though the advent of **tourism** over the last forty years has overtaken it in terms of revenue. The growth of the holiday industry dates chiefly from the 1960s, when the islands were the favourite resort of the then prime minister Harold Wilson. The subsequent demand for second homes and retirement bungalows has transformed the local landscape, most prominently on St Mary's, though development of the off islands has been much less conspicuous.

St Mary's

An indented oval with a pair of pincer-like projections from its southwestern edge, **ST MARY'S** is the largest of the Isles of Scilly, measuring about three miles across at its widest point. Despite holding the archipelago's highest point, Telegraph Hill, St Mary's is in places as low-lying as its neighbours, with constant fears of flooding in the capital, **Hugh Town**, which straddles the isthmus connecting the island's western limb.

Though pleasant enough, and holding the bulk of the Scillies' accommodation and services, Hugh Town has little to occupy your time once you've exhausted the harbour and museum. The best attractions, which consist of a handful of prehistoric remains and some tempting beaches, are dispersed around the island; all can be reached by easy hikes, and some are accessible by bus or bike.

Arrival, information and getting around

Ferry passengers disembark at the harbour on Hugh Town's sheltered north side, also the departure point for launches to the other islands, while the **airport** lies a mile east of town, connected by regular buses to the centre, whose departures are timed to coincide with flight arrivals. The main drag, Hugh Street, runs between the bus stand at the Parade, at its eastern end, and the harbour, and holds the archipelago's only two banks and the **tourist office** (Easter–Oct Mon–Fri 8.30am–6pm, Sat 8.30am–5pm, Sun 9am–2pm; Nov–Easter Mon–Fri 9am–5pm;

Gig racing in the Scillies

If you're coming to the Isles of Scilly between May and September, try to time your visit to be here on a Wednesday or Friday evening to witness the **gig races**, the most popular sport on the Scillies. Some of the gigs – six-oared vessels some 30ft in length – are over a hundred years old, built originally to carry pilots to passing ships. The races are usually performed by women on Wednesdays, men on Fridays; they usually start off from Nut Rock, to the east of Samson, finishing at St Mary's Quay, and can be followed on launches that leave about twenty minutes before the start of each race (£4, pay on board).

ⓣ01720/424031, ⓦwww.simplyscilly.co.uk). The staff has information on all the islands, and can advise on accommodation, walks, diving and other activities. You can log on to the **internet** here (£1/15min) or at the library in Buzza Street, behind Porthcressa beach (Mon–Fri 9.30am–noon & 3.30–6pm, Sat 9.30am–noon; £1.45 for 15min), while the whole harbour area is a wi-fi hotspot. Further news and information can be found by tuning in to the excellent Radio Scilly (107.9 FM), including boat times.

The town can easily be negotiated on foot, and you don't really need any transport to explore the rest of St Mary's. However, you can get around the island fast by means of the circular **bus** service leaving from outside the town hall on the Parade (Easter to mid-Oct 6–7 daily; £1.50). **Taxi** companies include Scilly Cabs ⓣ01720/422901, Q Cabs ⓣ01720/422260 and Island Taxis ⓣ01720/422126. You can **rent bikes** from St Mary's Bike Hire (ⓣ0779/663 8506), with an outlet on the Strand open between Easter and October; it's £7 9am–5pm, £9 for 24 hours. However, roads do not give access to the island's remoter coastal sections, which are reachable only on foot (off-road biking is not viable).

If you want to experience the island on a **bus tour** with commentary, contact Island Rover (ⓣ01720/422131; 1hr 10min; £7) or Classic Tours (ⓣ01720/422479; 1hr 30min–2hr; £30 for two people, £40 for three), which uses a vintage open-top Riley from 1929. Nature specialist Will Wagstaff (ⓣ01720/422212, ⓦwww.islandwildlifetours.co.uk) offers **wildlife tours** around St Mary's and other islands, highlighting the local flora and fauna, particularly birdlife, with aspects of local history thrown in. Dates and times are advertised at the tourist office and St Mary's Quay; tours of St Mary's normally meet behind the town hall above Porthcressa Beach at around 10am, those for the other islands at the Quay (£10 per person for a full day, plus ferry fares to the other islands). All tours run roughly from Easter to mid-October,

Accommodation

Hugh Town is relatively well supplied with **hotels and B&Bs**, all within easy walking distance of the harbour. There is much to be said for staying outside Hugh Town, where you can be assured of peace and quiet – one option is listed below. The island's only **campsite** is *Garrison Campsite* near the playing field at the top of the Garrison in Hugh Town (ⓣ01720/422670, ⓦwww.garrisonholidays.com; closed Nov–Easter). Camping elsewhere on St Mary's is not allowed.

Beachfield House Porthloo ⓣ01720/422463, ⓔwhomersley@supanet.com. Less than a mile north of town and just steps from the beach, this B&B offers peaceful accommodation even in high summer. The six en-suite rooms – four with sea views – are available all year. No credit cards. ❺

Lyonnesse Guest House The Strand ⓣ01720/422458. Right on the harbourfront, this friendly B&B has good views and offers evening meals. No under-5s. No credit cards. Closed Nov–March. ❺

Mincarlo Carn Thomas ☎01720/422513, Ⓦwww.mincarlo.force9.co.uk. Bright, airy and modern B&B at the eastern end of Town Beach, with white walls, grand views and free wi-fi access. All rooms are en suite and most have big windows, though the cheapest, on the ground floor, don't enjoy the sea vista. ❺

Schiller Pilot's Retreat, Church Rd ☎01720/423162, Ⓦwww.schiller-scilly.co.uk. Away from the port (a ten-minute walk) and well placed for Old Town Bay and Peninnis, this place has modern, en-suite, pine-furnished rooms with their own dining areas, where breakfast is self-served (hot croissants or raisin buns are delivered to your door). ❹

Star Castle Hotel The Garrison ☎01720/422317, Ⓦwww.star-castle.co.uk. The island's most atmospheric hotel, where the steep rates get you richly furnished, irregularly shaped rooms and access to an indoor pool and tennis court. Double B&B here starts at £235, though you may find last-minute discounts. Closed Dec to mid-Feb. ❾

Veronica Lodge The Garrison ☎01720/422585, Ⓦwww.veronicalodge.4t.com. Large, solid house with a sheltered, spacious garden and great sea vistas from its comfortable bedrooms. No under-14s. No credit cards. Closed Dec–Feb. ❺

Hugh Town

Although it can get inundated by ambling tourists in summer, **HUGH TOWN** never feels overwhelmed in the way that many mainland towns do, partly on account of the absence of much motor traffic. The twin centres of activity are Hugh Street, lined with shops and pubs, and the **harbour**, protected by a long pier, where the coming and going of ferries, launches and yachts creates a mood of quiet industry. As well as the inter-island launches departing from here (see box, p.299), there are daily **boat trips** to view seals and sea birds (excursions to see the puffins run between April and mid-July only): schedules and prices are posted on boards on the quayside and outside the Isles of Scilly Travel office, behind the tourist office on Hugh Street.

From the Bank at the western end of Hugh Street, Garrison Hill climbs up to the high ground west of Hugh Town known as the **Garrison**, after the ring of fortifications erected around this headland in the eighteenth century. The promontory was already the site of the archipelago's major defensive structure, **Star Castle**, which still dominates the height today just up from Garrison Hill. Built in the shape of an eight-pointed star in 1593 after the scare of the Spanish Armada, it sheltered the future Charles II in 1646 when he was on the run from Parliamentary forces, and later became the headquarters of the famous Royalist privateer, Sir John Grenville, under whom it was the last Cavalier stronghold until stormed by Admiral Blake in 1651. Now converted into a hotel (see above), the castle is not visitable today unless you're a guest or are eating or drinking at the restaurant or bar (see p.306); the interior holds little of the original structure in any case. However, there is plenty of amusement to be had on the circular **rampart walk** around the headland, which you can complete in less than an hour and which affords spectacular views over all the islands and the myriad rocky fragments around them.

The only other essential stop in town is the engaging **Isles of Scilly Museum** on Church Street, which begins at the Parade (Easter–Sept Mon–Fri 10am–4pm, Sat 10am–noon; Oct–Easter Mon–Sat 10am–noon; £3.50), well worth an hour or two's wander for background on the archipelago. Most of the exhibits are items that have washed up on the islands' shores, for example the two cases of clay pipes, and relics salvaged from the many ships that have foundered on or around the islands. Among the latter, there's an entertaining ragbag of finds recovered from the *Cita*, which sank off St Mary's Porth Hellick in March 1997; much of its cargo, ranging from tobacco to trainers, found its way into the islanders' homes.

Adjacent to the harbour on the north side of Hugh Town, the murky waters of the **town beach** do not invite any more than a paddle, and the neighbouring

Porthmellon Beach, looking out onto a mass of small boats, is not much better, though space can be found for **windsurfing**, with hire and instruction facilities on hand; sailing dinghies, snorkelling gear and wet suits are all also available from the Sailing Centre here (Ⓣ01720/422060, Ⓦwww.sailingscilly.com). Both beaches pale in comparison to **Porthcressa Beach**, a lovely sandy hollow in the sheltered bay on the south of the isthmus.

Around the island

East of Hugh Town, St Mary's is a chequerboard of meadows and box-like flower patches, though the most attractive parts are all on the coast, which is best explored on foot. From Hugh Town's Porthcressa Beach, a path wanders south, skirting the jagged teeth of **Peninnis Head**, and passing some impressive sea-sculpted granite rocks on the way, including the formation known as the **Kettle and Pans**, 100m north of Peninnis lighthouse, where immense basins have been hollowed out by the elements. Past here, the path follows the coast to placid **Old Town Bay**, where the scattered modern houses of **Old Town** give little hint that this was the island's chief port before Hugh Town took over that role in the seventeenth century. These days, Old Town boasts a few decent cafés and a sheltered south-facing **beach**, where Island Sea Safaris offers one- or two-hour **sea trips** around the uninhabited islands, and also has **diving** and snorkelling equipment for hire, with excursions to

Sir Cloudesley Shovell

Of all the wrecks that litter the seabed around the Isles of Scilly, the most famous are those belonging to the fleet led by Rear-Admiral **Sir Cloudesley Shovell** (1650–1707), a hero of many naval battles including an attack on Tripoli and the capture of Gibraltar and Barcelona. On September 19, 1707, a month after sailing for England from Gibraltar, 21 ships of the Mediterranean squadron under Shovell's command were beset by gales and fog, which made accurate navigation impossible. The concerned commander convoked a meeting on board his flagship, the HMS *Association*, to establish their position, at which the consensus was that they were off the island of Ushant, 26 miles northwest of Brittany, with the English Channel open and clear before them. Strangely for such experienced mariners, they were completely wrong: in fact they lay some hundred miles north of that position, so when Shovell issued the command to steer in a northeasterly direction, the fleet converged directly onto the Isles of Scilly. In all, **five ships** and nearly **2000 men** were lost; four ships foundered on the Western Rocks, two – including the *Association* – with all hands lost. One vessel, the *Phoenix*, unintentionally and quite miraculously sailed through Broad Sound, but hit rocks and was beached near New Grimsby on St Agnes, where it was quickly reduced to a total wreck. According to one ghoulish story, Shovell himself escaped the wreckage at first, putting to sea in a small boat accompanied by his treasure chest and pet greyhound, but was wrecked a second time – years later, a St Mary's woman confessed on her deathbed to finding the admiral lying exhausted on the beach and finishing him off for the sake of his gold rings. Other reports, however, claim that his body was found at sea. He was buried on the sands at Porth Hellick where a memorial stone still stands.

Despite his evident responsibility for the tragedy, Shovell's reputation became, if anything, enhanced by it, and he was glorified as a much-decorated war hero who went down with his ship: Queen Anne ordered that his body be exhumed and conveyed to London for an elaborate funeral in Westminster Abbey, where his tomb lies to this day. In 1967, local divers recovered many of the **treasures** carried in his fleet, which included a hoard of Spanish "**pieces of eight**" – one of the greatest troves ever found around the British Isles.

reefs and wrecks (Ⓣ01720/422732 or 0774/761 5732, Ⓦwww.islandseasafaris.co.uk). Back from here, the church cemetery holds the grave of Harold Wilson, Labour Prime Minister 1964–70 and 1974–76.

Three-quarters of a mile east of Old Town, past the airport's perimeter, **Porth Hellick** is the next major inlet on St Mary's southern coast, marked by a rugged quartz monument to the fantastically named admiral Sir Cloudesley Shovell (see box opposite), sited at the bottom of the bay just back from the beach. On the seaward side of the monument is another rock shape, the aptly named **Loaded Camel**. At the eastern end of the bay, a gate leads to a path over the hill, from which a signpost points right to a 4000-year-old **barrow**, or passage grave, probably used by the Scillies' first colonists. The grave is covered by a circular mound, some 40ft in diameter, with a curving passage leading to the central chamber, composed of large upright stones and four large slabs for a roof.

On the **eastern side** of St Mary's, less than two miles from Hugh Town and a mile north along the coast from Porth Hellick, **Pelistry Bay** is one of the most secluded spots on the island, its sandy beach and crystal-clear waters sheltered by the outlying **Toll's Island**. The latter, joined to St Mary's at low tide by a slender sand bar, holds the remains of an old battery known as Pellow's Redoubt as well as several pits in which kelp was burned to produce a substance used for the manufacture of soap and glass. Grey seals are also a common sight here. The *Carn Vean* **café** nearby offers sandwiches, snack lunches and tea and cakes, with tables outside (closed eves & Nov–Feb). Inland of here, next to the main road between Pelistry and Maypole, St Mary's Riding Centre (Ⓣ01720/423855) offers **riding** excursions (£25 for an hour's hack, £45 for 2hr); tuition is also available (£25–50 per hour).

The best remnants of early human settlement on the Scillies are in the north of the island, reached by path and – part of the way – by road. A mile or so north of Hugh Town, overlooking the sea near the island's cluster of tall TV masts, **Halangy Down**, dating from around 2000 BC, consists of an extensive complex of stone huts, the largest of which gives onto a courtyard with interconnecting buildings. Though evocative enough, the site is not as complete as **Bant's Carn**, above the village at the top of the slope, a long rectangular chamber topped by four large capstones used for cremations. Part of a much earlier site, the Carn is probably contemporaneous with the barrow at Porth Hellick.

Eating and drinking

Hugh Town has the vast majority of **places to eat** on St Mary's, though there's one good exception a short walk out of town, listed below. During high season, it's usually necessary to book evening meals in advance.

The Boat Shed Porthmellon Ⓣ01720/423881. With a prime location overlooking the harbour and beach, this child-friendly café-bistro has local crab and tapas among other snacks on offer during the day, and a more expensive evening menu specializing in seafood (booking advised). Glass doors give onto a decked area on the beach. Closed Sat, daytime Sun, and all Oct–March.

The Deli Hugh St. Right opposite the tourist office, this is a great stop for smoothies and juices, as well as a range of wholesome daytime snacks and takeaway items, Including freshly baked pizzas. Open some evenings in summer. Closed Sun.

Dibble and Grub Porthcressa Beach Ⓣ01720/423719. This place has a vibrant Mediterranean feel, good music and superb views, with tables outside; it's open during the day for fresh fruit juices, snacks and coffees, in the evening for tapas, succulent steaks, seafood and vegetarian dishes (mostly £12–17). Closed Sun, also some eves in summer, and daytime & most eves Nov–March.

Juliet's Garden Restaurant Ⓣ01720/422228. Out of town, above the seashore between Porthmellon and Porthloo beaches and below the golf course, this is one of the island's most congenial places to eat, serving scrumptious cakes, teas, cold meats and home-made pâtés and pickles by day, pastas and more elaborate seafood and meat dishes (£11–16) in the evenings, both indoors and in its panoramic garden. Evening opening varies according to season and demand, but usually closed Tues eve June to mid-Sept & all Nov to mid-March.

Star Castle Hotel The Garrison ⓣ01720/422317. Of the three eateries here, the atmospheric *Castle Restaurant*, with a magnificent granite fireplace, is good for high-quality meat and vegetarian dishes; the larger and less formal *Conservatory* (open mid-March to mid-Oct only), gives onto the garden and concentrates on seafood, while the *Dungeon Bar* (lunch only) offers snacks and full meals – salads, jacket potatoes and steaks – and has tables on the ramparts. Booking is essential for the *Castle* and *Conservatory*; a four-course meal in either costs £34.50.

Tresco

Measuring two miles by one mile, **TRESCO** is the second largest of the islands, and also the most visited of the "off islands". Despite its regular boatloads of day-trippers, however, it never feels crowded, and there are ample opportunities to find a solitary beach. There are also more trees and vegetation than on the other Scillies, and the island is less windy than the rest of the group. Once the private estate of Devon's Tavistock Abbey, and later the home of the "benevolent despot" Augustus Smith and his family, Tresco retains a privileged air, with short-term accommodation confined to a couple of exclusive lodgings.

According to the tide, **boats** pull in at either New Grimsby, midway along the west coast, the smaller quay at Old Grimsby, on the east coast, or Tresco's southernmost point, Carn Near. Wherever you land, it's only a few minutes' walk along signposted paths to the entrance of **Abbey Gardens** (daily 9.30am–4pm; £10), where the sparse ruins from the Benedictine priory of St Nicholas lie amid extensive subtropical gardens first laid out by Augustus Smith in 1834. Immediately on taking up office as Lord Proprietor of the islands, Smith established his residence in the present abbey, a tall Victorian mansion to the west of the gardens, and set about clearing the wilderness of undergrowth which then

▲ Grey seals

covered most of the island's southern half. Planting belts of cypress and Monterey pines from California as windbreaks, and erecting a tall wall, he introduced plants and seeds from London's Kew Gardens which formed the core of the botanical garden. His work was continued by his successors – including the present Dorrien-Smith – and was augmented by seedlings brought from Africa, South America and the Antipodes, often by local mariners. Today's dense abundance of palms, aloes, cacti and other tropical shrubs lends an almost jungle-like air, with some strategically sited statuary adding to the exotic ambience. The entry ticket also admits you to **Valhalla**, housed in a building near the entrance, a colourful collection of figureheads and name plates taken from the numerous vessels that have come to grief around here.

Tresco's alluring sandy **beaches** are equally easy to reach: one of the best – **Appletree Bay**, a dazzling strand of white sand and shells – is only a few steps from the ferry landing at Carn Near. Further up the island's western shore, there's another gorgeous sandy bay around the cluster of cottages that make up **New Grimsby**, where there's a store, gallery and the island's sole pub, the *New Inn*. From the pub, a lane heads across the narrow waist of the island to the village of **Dolphin Town** – named after an early Lord Proprietor of Scilly, Sir Francis Godolphin – where the stout grey church of **St Nicholas** is ringed by fields and trees. The lane then continues across to Tresco's eastern side, where **Old Grimsby** has a pier and another couple of sandy beaches. Based on the beach here close to the *Island Hotel* in July and August, the Isles of Scilly Sailing Centre offers **kayaks**, **sailing dinghies** and **wet suits** for rent, as well as **sailing lessons** (Ⓣ01720/422060, Ⓦwww.sailingscilly.com). The granite shell on the high ground at the southern end of Old Grimsby's harbour is the **Blockhouse**, a gun platform built to protect the harbour in the sixteenth century. South of Old Grimsby stretch a succession of wide strands, ending at the glorious curve of **Pentle Bay**, which are probably the island's finest.

North of the road between the two Grimsbys, tidy fields give way to the heathland of **Castle Down**, an elemental expanse of granite, gorse and heather crossed by narrow paths. Skirting Castle Down from New Grimsby, a path traces the coast to the scanty ruins of **King Charles' Castle**, built in the 1550s. Strategically positioned on high ground to cover the lagoon-like channel separating Tresco and Bryher, this artillery fort was in fact badly designed, its guns unable to depress far enough to be effective. It was superseded in 1651 by the much better-preserved **Cromwell's Castle** nearby, a round granite gun-tower built at sea level next to the pretty sandy cove of **Castle Porth**.

The shore path continues from Castle Porth round the serrated northern edge of Tresco to **Piper's Hole**, a long underground cave accessible from the cliff edge, which is the source of several legends that variously identify it as the abode of mermaids, ghosts or smugglers. The entrance can be a little difficult to negotiate but it's worth pressing ahead to the freshwater pool some 60ft within, for which a torch is essential. South of here, the deep indentation of **Gimble Porth** is one of the few sheltered inlets of this northern promontory, its shores crowded by dense ranks of rhododendrons, beyond which extend the orderly fields and flower plantations of Tresco's southern half.

Practicalities

If you're in the money, you can join the elite at the *Island Hotel* at Old Grimsby (Ⓣ01720/422883; closed Nov–Feb; ⑨), a sumptuous modern retreat with panoramic views and numerous facilities including a pool and tennis – short breaks in low season are best value – or head for the less grand *New Inn* at New Grimsby (Ⓣ01720/422844; ⑧), where rooms are spacious and airy, those with sea views slightly more expensive (there's an outdoor pool here too). Otherwise the only **accommodation** on the island comprises self-catering homes, usually available by the week only, though it's worth asking if you want a shorter period (there's rarely any availability at all in July and Aug). Prices run from £400 to £5000 per week, according to season and size: contact *Borough Farm* (Ⓣ01720/422843, Ⓔbruce.christopher@unicombox.co.uk) or Tresco Estate Office (Ⓣ01720/422849) for bookings and further details.

Fresh fish and local beef take pride of place at the *New Inn*'s **restaurant** where you can eat in the bar or garden (mains are mostly £10–17). For gourmet cuisine, head for the restaurant at the *Island Hotel*, where seafood is also the speciality and a three-course evening menu costs £39 (booking essential); there's a cheaper lunchtime menu in the Terrace Bar here. **Information** on Tresco, including anything to do with accommodation, is available on the island's website Ⓦwww.tresco.co.uk.You can **rent bikes** for £10 a day from the estate office at New Grimsby (Ⓣ01720/422849).

Bryher

Covered with a thick carpet of bracken, heather and bramble, **BRYHER** is the smallest of the populated islands, and also the wildest. The prevailing feeling here is of a struggle between man and the environment, with the cultivable parts of the island regularly threatened by the encroaching sea. The eighty-odd inhabitants have introduced some pockets of order in the form of flower plantations, mostly confined to the scattering of houses just up from the main quay that makes up the grandly named **Bryher Town**, facing Tresco on Bryher's eastern side. Just 50m from the granite jetty, the church of **All Saints**, dating from 1742, is the archipelago's oldest, its churchyard chock-full of gravestones marked Jenkins, showing the extent to which this Welsh family, that settled here over three hundred years ago, once dominated island life.

To the north of Bryher Town, more flower patches creep up **Watch Hill**, one of the island's five Scillonian-scale "hills", whose comparatively steep slopes makes it seem taller than its 42m/138ft. A brief ascent allows you to take in a grand panorama of the whole group of islands. Nearer to hand, the calm corridor of water between Bryher and Tresco, **New Grimsby Channel**, is one of the archipelago's best anchorages, and consequently often crowded with a small flotilla of moored boats. Thrusting out of the water in mid-channel, you'll see the jagged rock pile of **Hangman Island**, which takes its name either from the execution of pirates or of the Cavaliers who were dispatched here during the Civil War.

Barren heathland soon asserts itself to the north, extending as far as the impressive granite promontory of **Shipman Head**, another terrific vantage point offering dizzying views over the foaming Atlantic. Bryher's exposed western seaboard takes the full brunt of the ocean, and nowhere more spectacularly than at the aptly named **Hell Bay**, cupped by a limb of land below Shipman Head, and frequently blasted by ferocious winds and savage waves. It's worth following the island's serrated western coast down its full length to get the full value of the sound and fury, which is the rule even in relatively calm weather. By contrast, peace usually reigns in the south-facing **Rushy Bay**, a small, sheltered and sandy crescent, surrounded by a mass of flowers, that counts among the island's best **beaches**. Its name is derived from the rushes, marram grass and other plants grown here by Augustus Smith in the 1830s in order to stabilize the shore from erosion. Above the bay, **Samson Hill** has a few megalithic barrows submerged beneath a coating of gorse, foxgloves, campion and other wild flowers, and boasts views as good as those from Watch Hill.

From Bryher's quay, Bryher Boat Services (ⓣ01720/422886, ⓦwww.bryherboats.co.uk) operate a regular year-round ferry service to the other islands (£7.60 return) and offer **tours** to seal and bird colonies on the outlying rocks as well as fishing expeditions (£14). You can **rent boats** – mainly kayaks (£10–15 per hour) and sailing dinghies (£20 per hour) – from Bennett Boatyard at Green Bay (ⓣ0797/939 3206, ⓦwww.bennettboatyard.com), south of the main quay on the eastern side.

Practicalities

Bryher has a tiny range of **accommodation** which, apart from the one hotel, is usually fully booked in August. The cheapest choices are the B&Bs *Soleil D'Or* (ⓣ01720/422003, ⓦwww.bryher-ios.co.uk/sd; closed Nov–Feb; no credit cards; ❺), north of the main quay and with views over to Tresco, and *Bank Cottage*, on the western side near Gweal Pool (ⓣ01720/422612, ⓦwww.bank-cottage.com; no under-10s; closed Nov–March; no credit cards; ❻), where all rooms are en suite or with private facilities, and all enjoy sea views. Guests in *Bank Cottage* can use a kitchen to prepare light meals, or the barbecue in the luxuriant garden, and have use of a rowing boat; there's a week minimum stay May–Aug. Halfway down the other side of the island, the extremely swish *Hell Bay Hotel* (ⓣ01720/422947, ⓦwww.hellbay.co.uk; closed Nov–Feb; ❾) is beautifully situated next to the placid and brackish Bryher Pool, below the Gweal Hill promontory. Decorated in a style that combines Caribbean, New England and Cornish elements, each room has its own sitting room, and public rooms are filled with art by the likes of Barbara Hepworth. Half- or full-board is obligatory, but discounts are available for short breaks in spring and autumn. *Jenford Farm* offers basic **camping** facilities in a relatively sheltered site on Watch Hill (ⓣ01720/422886, ⓦwww.ryher-ios.co.uk/cs; closed Nov–March).

For refreshment, the *Hell Bay Hotel* has a bar and a good **restaurant** open to nonresidents; early booking is essential for evening meals, when set-price menus cost £35. The friendly *Vine Café*, below Watch Hill (ⓣ01720/423168; no credit cards; closed Sat, also eves Tues, Thurs & Fri in winter, Fri in summer, and all Nov–Feb) sells hot snacks, sandwiches and cakes during the day, and has set evening meals (£16.50) for which booking is essential – bring your own beer or wine. You can also eat inexpensively at the *Fraggle Rock Café* near the post office north of the main quay (ⓣ01720/422222; closed weekdays Nov–March), famous for its crab double-decker sandwiches; there's an upstairs restaurant for which booking is advised (Friday is fish-and-chips night) and there's wi-fi and terminals for **internet access**. The island's post office doubles as a general store, selling a limited range of food and good fresh bread; you can also buy fresh veg (and, in season, strawberries) from Hillside Farm, just south of the church, or from the nearby stall it supplies between late May and September.

St Martin's

The third largest of the Isles of Scilly and a mile east of Tresco, **ST MARTIN'S** is a narrow ridge some two miles in length, its northern side wild and rugged, the southern side sloping gently to the sea and chiefly given over to flower-growing. The main landing stage is on the promontory jutting out from this more sheltered side, at the head of the majestic sweep of **Par Beach**, a bare wedge of pure-white sand. From the quay, a road leads uphill past a public tennis court to **Higher Town**, the island's main concentration of houses and the location of the only shop as well as St Martin's Diving Centre (Ⓣ01720/422848, Ⓦwww.scillydiving.com), which offers **scuba and snorkelling** excursions with equipment for rent as well as tuition at all levels. Free of plankton or silt, the waters around St Martin's are said to be among the clearest in Britain, and are much favoured by scuba enthusiasts. Non-divers can go snorkelling among the seals around the nearby Eastern Isles (see p.313).

Beyond Higher Town's church, a road runs westwards along the island's long spine to **Middle Town** – actually little more than a cluster of cottages and a few flower-packing sheds – and from there to the western extremity of the isle. Here, **Lower Town** has a slightly larger collection of houses nestled under Tinkler's Hill, as well as a pub and a second quay, all overlooking the uninhabited isles of Teän and St Helen's (see p.313).

From Lower Town, there's easy access to the long, sandy continuum of **Lawrence's Bay** on St Martin's southern coast, backed by large areas of flowerbeds. However, the best beaches – among the grandest ones in the Scillies – lie on the desolate northern side: the beautiful half-mile recess of sand at **Great Bay** and the adjacent **Little Bay** reachable from paths branching north off the main east–west track. Utterly secluded and backed by grassy dunes, this stretch is ideal for swimming and is also a nice place to do some exploring. From Little Bay, you can climb across boulders at low tide to the hilly and wild **White Island** (pronounced "Wit Island"), on the northeastern side of which you'll find a vast cave, **Underland Girt**; it's accessible at low tide only, so take care not to be stranded by the returning high waters.

East of Great Bay, paths weave round the rocky coves to the island's northeastern tip, where the heathland of **Chapel Downs** is dominated by a conspicuous red-and-white Daymark, erected in 1683 (not 1637 as inscribed) as a warning to shipping during the day. On the edge of the heathland, the sheer cliffs of **St Martin's Head** confront crashing seas; on a clear day you can make out the foam breaking against the Seven Stones Reef seven miles distant, where the tanker *Torrey Canyon* was wrecked in 1967, causing one of the world's worst oil spills. Working your way round the perimeter of Chapel Downs you can reach another fine beach, **Perpitch**, on the southeastern shore facing the scattered Eastern Isles (see p.313).

In summer, there's **boat rental** from the beach at **Lawrence's Bay** near Higher Town, operated by Bennett Boatyard (Ⓣ0788/180 2964; see p.309 for prices).

Practicalities

Visit the website Ⓦwww.st-martins-scilly.co.uk for general **information** on the island, including a good map and **accommodation** details. St Martin's has a better choice of **B&Bs** than most. *Polreath*, in Higher Town (Ⓣ01720/422046, Ⓦwww.polreath.com; closed Nov–March; ❼), with a restaurant, conservatory and extensive garden, has two en-suite rooms with all-round views and requires a week's minimum stay May–September, three nights at other times. *Ashvale House*, near the pub in Lower Town (Ⓣ01720/422544, Ⓔashvalehouse@btinternet.com; no credit cards; closed Oct–Easter; ❺), offers two en-suite rooms with sea views, a lounge and a garden. *Fuchsia Cottage*, in Middle Town (Ⓣ01720/422023, Ⓦwww.scillyman.co.uk; closed Nov–Feb; ❺), with home-made bread and jam for breakfast and free wi-fi, has two rooms with en-suite or shared facilities. The island's sole **hotel** lies just around the corner from here, the posh *St Martin's on the Isle* (Ⓣ01720/422090, Ⓦwww.stmartinshotel.co.uk; closed Nov–Feb; ❾), a cluster of cottages with modern rooms looking onto a sandy beach. Amenities include a snooker room and a heated indoor pool with a sun patio. The **campsite** in Middle Town (Ⓣ01720/422888, Ⓦwww.stmartinscampsite.co.uk; closed mid-Oct to mid-March), just off the road near Lawrence's Bay, enjoys a degree of shelter behind its tall hedges, and is the best equipped of the Scillies sites, with clothes-washing, drying and ironing facilities. Stays during the summer holiday season are usually booked months in advance.

If you're looking for **snack** food, you can't do better than the acclaimed pasties, pizzas, pastries and other mainly organic goodies sold at the bakery/deli on Moo Green, Higher Town. For **meals**, *Polreath* has an excellent tea garden serving baguettes and such specialities as smoked mackerel salad at lunchtime, and a range of home-baked cakes and pastries for tea (closed Sat). Its airy conservatory restaurant is open for evening meals on Monday (curry night) and Wednesday ("family favourites") – residents can also dine on Thursday and Friday evenings. Down the valley south of Higher Town, the wholefood café at *Little Arthur Farm* offers a range of delicious cakes and organic, farm-grown snacks by day, and opens in the evening for bistro food on Mondays and Fridays, when mains are £8.50–12.50, and for fish and chips on Tuesdays and Thursdays (Ⓣ01720/422457; closed Oct–March no credit cards;). For a filling lunch or supper, the popular *Round Island Bar and Bistro* at the *St Martin's on the Isle* hotel offers such dishes as stir-fried squid and vegetarian risotto for around £8 for starters, £15 for main courses (closed Mon eve). The hotel's *Teän Restaurant* provides a more formal ambience and wonderful panoramic views to accompany its gourmet meat, fish and vegetarian dishes (£47.50 for three courses). The only **pub** on the island is the *Seven Stones* in Lower Town, where snacks and meals are available for £8–12.

St Agnes

The southern- and westernmost of the inhabited isles, **ST AGNES** – known simply as "Agnes" locally – is also the craggiest, its rocks weathered to fantastic shapes. Visitors disembark at **Porth Conger** in the north of the island, from where a road leads inland past the most significant landmark on St Agnes, the disused **Old Lighthouse** – dating from 1680, it's one of the oldest in England. From the lighthouse the right-hand fork in the road leads to the western side of the island and **Periglis Cove**, a picturesque spot and a popular mooring for boats, while the left-hand fork heads south to **St Warna's Cove**, where the patron saint of shipwrecks is reputed to have landed from Ireland; the exact spot is marked by a holy well. It's said that in the old days, locals would cast coins into it to persuade the saint to send them a wreck. Between the two coves is a fine coastal path which passes the **Troy Town Maze**, a miniature maze of stones thought to have been created a couple of centuries ago, but possibly much older. Kept in good order over the years, the circular formation appears rather paltry next to the mighty granite boulders close by.

South beyond St Warna's Cove, the path continues past some of the island's most spectacular sections of shoreline, with views over to the Western Rocks (see p.313). St Agnes's southern segment is mostly taken up by the wild heathland of **Wingletang Down**. At its tip, the headland of **Horse Point** has more tortuously wind-eroded rocks. On the eastern side of Wingletang Down the inlet of **Beady Pool** gained its name from the trove of beads washed ashore from the wreck of a seventeenth-century Dutch trader; some of the reddish-brown beads still occasionally turn up. Above the cove, the **Giant's Punchbowl** is one of the island's most remarkable rock sculptures: two immense boulders, one poised above the other, with a wide basin 3ft deep in its top.

The eastern side of St Agnes harbours one of the island's best beaches, the small, sheltered **Covean** (accessible from the path opposite *Covean Cottage*, above Porth Conger). Between the cove and Porth Conger, a broad sand bar appears at low tide to connect the smaller isle of **Gugh** (pronounced to rhyme with Hugh), creating another lovely sheltered beach. You can cross the bar to Gugh to wander around a scattering of untended Bronze Age remains – including the **Old Man of Gugh**, a tilting standing stone on the eastern side of the island – and to admire the wonderful panorama from the hill at Gugh's northern end. Take care not to be marooned on the isle by the incoming tide, which creates an extremely fierce current over the bar. Swimming is not advised at high tide here.

From Porth Conger, there are **boat trips** to all the islands, and also, tides and weather permitting, **catamaran trips** on the *Spirit of St Agnes* to St Mary's (April–Oct 2 daily at 10.15am and 3.15pm, returning at 12.30pm and 4.30pm; Nov–March 3 weekly; £7.40 return), to the off islands (Mon–Fri; £7.60) and to the Bishop Rock lighthouse (once or twice weekly in summer; £15 for two hours). Schedules are posted at all St Agnes accommodation and at the *Turk's Head* pub; alternatively see Ⓦwww.st-agnes-boating.co.uk, or call Ⓣ01720/422704. Contact the same number for a **sea taxi** service available all year, costing £27 per trip to go anywhere in the archipelago.

Practicalities

The community website Ⓦst-agnes-scilly.org has **information** on all accommodation on St Agnes, including a page showing self-catering availability. There's a slim choice of **B&Bs**: the friendly *Covean Cottage* above Porth Conger (Ⓣ01720/422620; closed Nov–March; ❺) has comfortable rooms – en suite or with shared bathrooms – and three-course evening **meals** (£17.50; not available Tues, Fri & Sat), while *Hellweathers*, abutting the sea between the church and Periglis Cove (Ⓣ01720/422430, Ⓔmichael.crompton@virgin.net; closed Nov–Easter; no credit cards; ❺), has two rooms enjoying views towards the isle of Annet and Bishop Rock lighthouse, and evening meals on request. There's a **campsite** at at Periglis Cove, *Troytown Farm* (Ⓣ01720/422360, Ⓦwww.troytownscilly.co.uk; closed Nov–March), fairly exposed but right at the water's edge, and also enjoying first-rate views over to the Western Rocks. Home-produced beef, pork, vegetables and milk – which goes into lip-smacking ice cream – are sold at the farm shop.

Covean Cottage has a tea garden for **snacks** during the day (closed Sat). *Coastguards Café*, one of a row of cottages past the Old Lighthouse and post office on the island's western side, serves soups, salads, toasties, crab rolls and seafood platters by day, with tables inside and out, and great views towards the Western Rocks (closed Sun & Nov–March). In the evening this becomes *High Tide* (Ⓣ01720/423869), a licensed restaurant where local seafood dishes with Pacific Rim elements are served for £12–15 (closed Sun & winter). Just above the jetty at Porth Conger, the perfectly sited *Turk's Head* **pub** serves superb St Agnes pasties and full meals to accompany its local beers.

The uninhabited isles

Many of Scilly's **uninhabited islands** were previously settled and reveal fascinating traces of the former habitations and commercial activities. The prevailing impression, though, is of nature holding sway, from the teeming birdlife perched on every ledge to the ocean in full spate beating against their exposed shores.

Weather permitting, there are regular boat excursions from Hugh Town's harbour, run by the St Mary's Boatmen's Association (☎01720/423999), and also frequent services from the nearest inhabited islands.

From Bryher's quay, it's just a quick hop to **Samson**, the largest of the uninhabited isles and marked out by its mammary-like twin hills. The island has been abandoned since 1855 when the last impoverished inhabitants were ordered off by Augustus Smith, then the proprietor of all the islands, who decided that their continued existence there was unsustainable. Wildlife reigns supreme, the slopes thickly grown with gorse and sea holly and populated chiefly by divebombing gulls and colonies of black rabbits. Boats usually pull up on a beach on the island's eastern side, from which a path leads up over **North Hill**, the site of several primitive burial chambers dating from the second millennium BC. One of these – without its cover and exposed to the elements on the summit – is thought to be the sepulchre of a tribal chief. Most of the abandoned cottages of the nineteenth-century inhabitants are on **South Hill**, many still with limpet shells piled outside their doors, left over from when these were collected and traded.

There are also regular excursions from Lower Town in St Martin's to the uninhabited isles of Teän and St Helen's, just a quarter of a mile away. **Teän**, a flattish, meandering island with several crescents of sandy beach, was formerly used by families from St Martin's for burning kelp and to graze their cattle; their ruined cottages can still be seen. Behind Teän, **St Helen's** holds the remains of the oldest church on the archipelago, a tenth-century oratory, together with monks' dwellings and a chapel. At the base of the island's hill, which reaches almost 45m, you can see the melancholy ruins of a "pest house" erected in 1756 to house plague-carriers entering British waters.

Out beyond St Agnes, the **Western Rocks** are a horseshoe of islets and jagged rocks which have been the cause of innumerable wrecks, from Cloudesley Shovell's *Association* (see box, p.304) to the American schooner *Thomas W. Lawson*, the largest pure sailing vessel ever built and the only one with seven masts. It came to grief here in 1907, creating what may have been the world's first spillage disaster when its cargo of crude oil washed up on St Agnes. The biggest of these outcrops is **Annet**, probably never inhabited and notable as a nesting-place for a rich variety of **birds**, such as the stormy petrel and Manx shearwater as well as colonies of puffins and shags; however, many species have been chased out or slaughtered in recent years by the predatory great black-beaked gull, largest of the gull family. The island cannot be visited during the nesting season, which is probably just as well, as the screeching clamour and the stench of the birds' effluvia are said to be unbearable.

The islands forming the western arm of the group are the best place to see **grey seals**, who prefer these remote outposts for breeding. Many visitors come to this farthest edge of Scilly just to view the **Bishop Rock Lighthouse**, however, a lonely column five miles out – at 175ft, it's the tallest in the British Isles and the westernmost one on this side of the Atlantic. The men who built it between 1847 and 1850 lived on the nearby rocky islet of **Rosevear** – hard to believe, given the extremely harsh conditions, especially in light of the fact that they grew their own vegetables here, established a blacksmith's shop and even organized a ball to which guests from St Mary's and other islands were invited. Remains of their constructions can still be seen.

On the other side of the group, scattered between St Martin's and St Mary's, the **Eastern Isles** are mere slivers of rock to which boat-trippers make forays to view puffins and grey seals. Protected from the Atlantic currents by the other islands, these outcrops generally have more soil than the Western Rocks, and several have excellent beaches – notably **Great Arthur** and **Great Ganilly**. Both of these also have prehistoric remains; on **Nornour**, reached at low tide along a rocky bar from Great Ganilly, dwellings have been unearthed which date back to the first century AD – the finds are now on show in the museum on St Mary's (see p.303).

Travel details

Ferries

St Mary's to: Penzance (April–Nov 4–6 weekly; 2hr 45min).

Flights (all Mon–Sat)

St Mary's to: Bristol (late March & Oct 3 weekly; April–Sept 1–2 daily; 1hr 15min); Exeter (late March & Oct 3 weekly; April–Sept 1–2 daily; Nov to mid-March, via Newquay, 2 weekly; 1hr–1hr 30min); Land's End (mid-March to Oct frequent flights; Nov to mid-March 1–4 daily; 20min); Newquay (mid-March to Oct 2–5 daily; Nov to mid-March 1–2 daily; 30min); Penzance by helicopter (late March to Oct 7–17 daily; Nov to late March 3 daily; 20min); Southampton (late March & Oct 3 weekly; April–Sept 1 daily; 1hr 30min).

Tresco to: Penzance by helicopter (late March to Oct 4–6 daily; Nov to late March 2 daily; 20min).

11

Cornwall's Atlantic coast

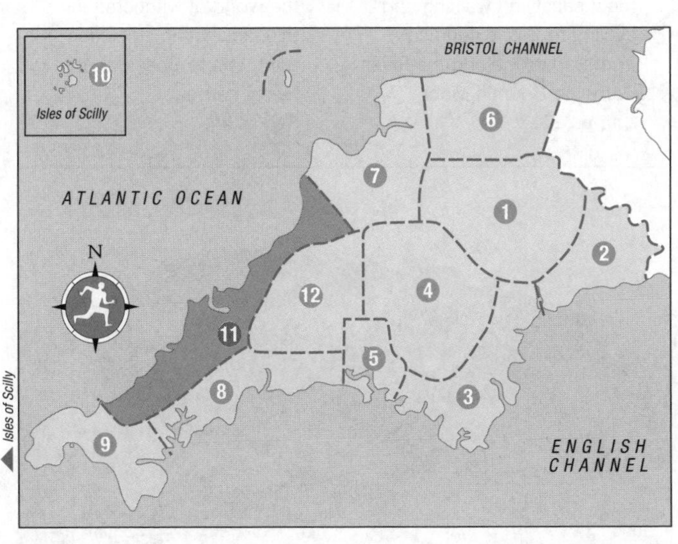

CHAPTER 11

Highlights

* **The beaches** The cliffy, west-facing beaches lining the Atlantic coast are not only spectacular but ideal for swimming and surfing.
* **Seafood in Padstow** The bijou harbour town can boast an extraordinary concentration of gastronomic excellence, well worth a splurge. See p.336
* **Camel Trail** One of Cornwall's most satisfying walking and cycling routes, extending from Padstow along the River Camel to Bodmin Moor. See p.337
* **St Enodoc** Burial place of John Betjeman, this ancient church nestles in a peaceful spot within sight of the sea. See p.338
* **Tintagel Castle** A ruined, fairy-tale fortress on the cliff edge, rich with Arthurian associations. See p.342
* **Museum of Witchcraft, Boscastle** Delve into the world of witchcraft in this fascinating collection right next to Boscastle's twisty harbour. See p.344

▲ Tintagel

11

Cornwall's Atlantic coast

Cliffier and more ragged than the county's southern seaboard, North Cornwall's Atlantic coast from St Ives Bay to the Devon border is punctuated by a sequence of small resorts which have sprung up around some of the finest beaches in England. Standing aloof from the holiday traffic and caravan parks that these have generated are the derelict stacks and castle-like ruins of the engine houses that once powered the region's mining industry, complemented by the grey Methodist chapels that testify to the impact of the great evangelist **John Wesley** on the local communities. His open-air meetings attracted thousands of listeners in such places as Gwennap Pit outside **Redruth** and **Camborne**, the twin centres of copper and tin production. Relics of both mining and Methodism are also evident in the area around **St Agnes**, a steep and dispersed village to the north that preserves its old miners' dwellings. On the nearby coast, however, the accent is on recreation, especially **surfing**. Surrounded by splendid beaches, **Newquay** is acknowledged as the country's surfing capital, and has become the centre of Cornwall's party culture. The surf scene extends north to the beaches around the fishing port of **Padstow**, on the Camel estuary, though the town itself has forged a separate identity as a gastronomic hotspot, thanks largely to the efforts of master-chef **Rick Stein**, who has carved out a veritable empire here with the emphasis firmly on fresh seafood. Another reason to come to Padstow is for the **Camel Trail**, a cycle and walking route which weaves inland along the Camel River to the rather nondescript town of **Wadebridge**, and beyond to Bodmin Moor.

North of the Camel, the coast is an almost unbroken line of cliffs as far as the Devon border; the gaunt, exposed terrain shelters such peaceful nooks as **Port Isaac**, and makes a theatrical setting for **Tintagel**, whose atmospheric ruined castle and mythical links with King Arthur have made it the most popular sightseeing destination on this coast. A few miles further on, the craggy village of **Boscastle** has strong associations with Thomas Hardy that can be traced on an inland riverside walk. Sand and surf re-establish themselves at **Bude**, where the wide strand and choice of beaches draw legions of surfers in season. **Walkers**, too, will enjoy the memorable cliff paths around here, particularly those running due north to the Devon border, seven miles away.

North Cornwall's network of **public transport** covers all the places described in this chapter. **Newquay** is the terminus for the cross-peninsula **train route** from

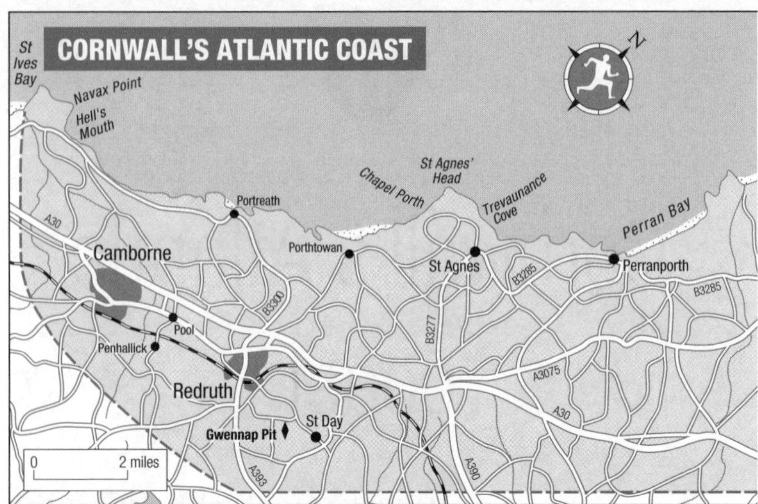

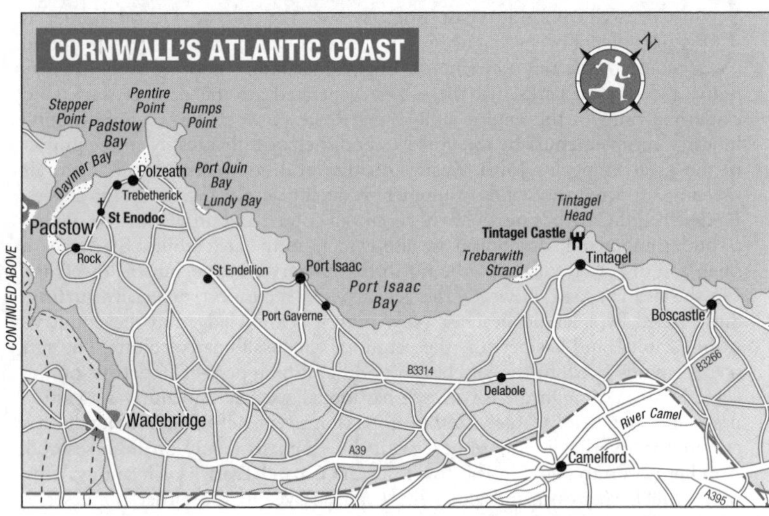

CONTINUED ABOVE

Par, a stop on the main line to Penzance; other stops include Camborne and Redruth. The latter is connected to St Agnes on the #315 bus route (not Sun). The weekday #403 takes in Newquay, Perranporth, St Agnes and Truro, and Western Greyhound's #585, #586 and #587 connect Newquay and Truro. Newquay and Padstow are connected along the coast by Western Greyhound #556, and Padstow is also served by the frequent #555 from Bodmin. Service #584 connects Wadebridge with Polzeath, Port Isaac and Camelford, #594 links Camelford with Tintagel and Boscastle, and #595 runs from Boscastle to Bude (none of these routes is served Sun November–March). Bude is linked to Okehampton and Exeter by #X9 and #X90 (not Sun). Two or three National Express coaches daily link Penzance, St Ives, Camborne, Redruth, Newquay, Bodmin and Plymouth.

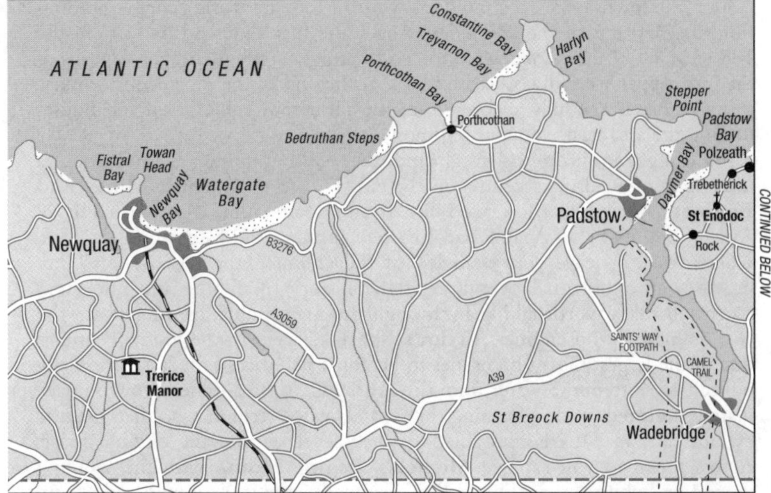

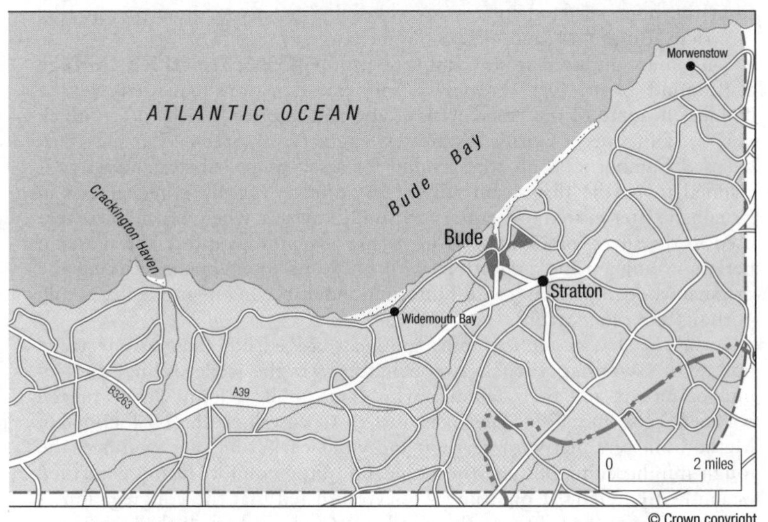

A useful **website** for the area is Ⓦwww.atlantic-heritage-coast.co.uk, which has info on the coast from Newquay to Bideford Bay, including accommodation, activities, attractions, a beach guide, with maps.

Camborne, Redruth and around

Ten miles west of Truro, the unprepossessing towns of **REDRUTH** and neighbouring **CAMBORNE** are largely bypassed by tourists speeding down the A30, but merit a stop for anyone interested in Cornwall's industrial history. Nowadays an amalgamated conurbation spreading for six miles along the

A3047, the towns once accounted for two-thirds of the world's copper production, the 350 pits in the area employing some fifty thousand workers in the 1850s. Many of the miners were forced to emigrate when cheaper deposits of tin and copper were discovered overseas at the end of the nineteenth century; the area has never fully recovered, as the numerous ruins of engine houses dotting the area bear eloquent testimony.

You can get an intriguing insight into the world of mining at **Pool**, about a mile west of Redruth's centre on the A3047, site of **Cornish Mines and Engines** (April–Oct Mon, Wed–Fri & Sun 11am–5pm, also Sat in July & Aug; £5.80; NT) on Agar Road (reached through the Morrisons' car park, where you can leave your vehicle). At the entrance, the Discovery Centre provides an audiovisual overview of the history of mining and miners in Cornwall that's worth taking in, though the main points of interest are the two dramatic beam engines. **Taylor's Shaft**, adjacent to the visitor centre, is one of the largest Cornish engines to be constructed (and the last), originally built in 1892 to pump water from the nearby Carn Brea mines. Now immaculately restored with gleaming brass and wood trimmings, the gigantic cylindrical apparatus is viewable on three levels within the engine house. Across the road you can see **Michell's Engine House** with the winding engine or "whim" in clanking action, originally used to haul men and ore up from the mine shaft when it was worked by steam, and now powered by electricity. Buses #14 and #18 pass by here.

Half a mile southwest from Camborne off the B3303, **Trevithick Cottage** at Penponds (April–Oct Wed only 2–5pm; free, donations requested) was the childhood home of the "mercurial, erratic and inspired" Richard Trevithick (1771–1833), one of Cornwall's greatest engineers. Between 1796 and 1801, he used Camborne as his trial ground for a self-propelled steam carriage – claimed to be the first steam railway locomotive. Largely unrecognized in Britain, he later moved to Central and South America, where his engines were used in the silver mines. Despite his richly adventurous career, the museum here is a rather paltry collection, with only one room open, retaining the original wooden panelling and shuttering, and displaying memorabilia, family portraits and photographs.

Outside St Day, a couple of miles southeast of Redruth, the grassy, terraced hollow of **Gwennap Pit** (always open; free) was the scene of huge gatherings of miners and their families who came to hear John Wesley preach between 1762 and 1786. The first visits to Cornwall by the co-founder of Methodism were met with derision and violence, but he later won over the tough mining communities who could find little comfort in the gentrified established Church. At one time Wesley estimated that the congregation at Gwennap Pit exceeded thirty thousand, noting in his diary, "I shall scarce see a larger congregation till we meet in the air." The present tiered amphitheatre was created in 1805, with seating for twenty thousand, and is today the venue of Methodist meetings for the annual Whit Monday service, drawing adherents from all over Cornwall.

Four miles southwest of Gwennap Pit outside Troon, **King Edward Mine** is Cornwall's oldest complete mine site, now a museum where you can view the machinery and devices used to break down and sort the tin ore and tour the various parts of the site (May & June Wed, Thurs, Sat & Sun 10am–5pm; July & Sept Mon & Wed–Sun 10am–5pm; Aug daily 10am–5pm; Oct–April Sun 9am–noon; last admission 1hr before closing; £4.50). You can also learn about the network of **mineral tramways** that provide a useful way of accessing King Edward Mine and for touring the area (see box).

Cornwall's Mineral Tramways

Built in the heyday of the mining era between 1750 and 1860 for the transportation of tin and copper ore, Cornwall's **Mineral Tramways** have been restored as mainly off-road **walking**, **cycling** and **horseriding routes**. Some of the tracks follow the route of the Redruth and Chacewater Railway – built to carry ore from the mine at Gwennap to the coast (and becoming Cornwall's first proper railway when it converted to steam in 1853) – and the rival Portreath Tramroad, which traverses fairly flat terrain to Portreath harbour on the northern coast. Of the network of eight routes planned, only three are up and running: the **Coast-to-Coast** trail, linking Portreath with Devoran at the top of the Carrick Roads estuary on the south coast (eleven and a half miles); the **Great Flat Lode Trail**, a circular seven-and-a-half-mile trail around the Carn Brea hill that can be accessed from King Edward Mine (see opposite), and the **Tresavean Trail**, which follows an old branch line of the Hayle railway for just over a mile.

Books and route maps can be bought at local tourist offices or from local **bike rental** shops: Bike Chain at Bissoe, signposted off the A393 near Gwennap (Ⓣ01872/870341, Ⓦwww.cornwallcyclehire.com; open daily), and Bike Barn, Portreath (see p.322), both offering **bikes** for £12–15 per day.

Practicalities

Camborne and Redruth are both **train stops** on the Plymouth–Penzance main line. Camborne's station is south of the centre on South Terrace Road, while Redruth's is just south of the main thoroughfare, Fore Street, on Station Road – frequent **buses** run between the two centres. Buses #14, #18, #40, #41 and #47 connect the towns with Truro, Falmouth, Penzance and St Ives. If you need **accommodation**, try Redruth's turreted Edwardian *Lansdowne House*, five minutes from the bus and train stations at 42 Clinton Rd (Ⓣ01209/216002, Ⓦwww.lansdowne-guesthouse.co.uk; ❹), with amiable management and rooms with or without en-suite bathrooms. Best of the bunch in Camborne is the eighteenth-century coaching inn, *Tyacks Hotel*, prominently sited on Commercial Street, just north of the station (Ⓣ01209/612424; ❺). Granite-built and faced with stone from local mines, it has pine-furnished rooms and a wi-fi facility. Guests and nonresidents can dine on a moderately priced international menu in its *Trevithick Restaurant*; bar food is available at lunchtime.

Portreath and around

Redruth's former harbour – once serving the local mining industry and a working harbour until the 1960s – lies two and a half miles northwest at **PORTREATH**. These days the village is better known as a holiday resort, a collection of modern houses surrounding a sea wall which backs onto a sand-and-shingle beach, which is a draw for surfers from far and wide, despite the local sewage outlets. On the east side of the beach, a sea-water pool has been formed by adding a retaining wall to a natural rock pool; on the west side, **Lady Basset's Baths** consist of six bath-shaped pools, hewn from the rock at different levels to catch the tide, created around 1800 for Lady Frances Basset, whose father believed in the healing powers of cold sea water (just over a mile down the coast at Basset Cove, the Basset family had a winch installed to take them down the 250-foot cliff in a cage). One bath is inside a cave and was reached by a metal ladder.

Though you might be content with the beach in town, Portreath is within walking distance of other coastal attractions, notably the awe-inspiring **Hell's Mouth**, a cauldron of waves and black rocks at the base of two-hundred-foot cliffs, five miles south along the coast. Three miles north of the village, **Porthtowan** is another popular surfing beach which, unlike many of the cliff-bordered beaches around here, still catches the sun from late afternoon on. The good water quality here merited a Blue Flag award in 2009.

Portreath is connected with Camborne bus station and Redruth train station by **buses** #43 and #44 (not Sun), and with St Ives and Newquay by the summer-only #501 (not Sat). **Accommodation** is fairly limited, with the best choices being the light and airy *Cliff House*, a two-hundred-year-old cottage just off the harbourside on the Square (Ⓣ01209/843847, Ⓦwww.cliffhouseportreath.com; ❹), where the plain, smallish rooms have en-suite or private bathrooms and free wi-fi. Alternatively, venture a little further out to the charmingly old-fashioned restored Georgian mansion *Glenfeadon House*, Glenfeadon Terrace (Ⓣ01209/842650, Ⓦwww.glenfeadonhouse.co.uk; ❺), about a quarter-mile from the sea – take the second left turning after the school on the B3300; all rooms are en suite, there's a large wooded garden and luggage transfer can be arranged for walkers. **Campers** will find a well-sheltered site at Cambrose, between Portreath and Porthtowan: *Cambrose Touring Park* (Ⓣ01209/890747, Ⓦwww.cambrosetouringpark.co.uk; closed Nov–Easter), with free hot showers, a heated pool and a small store.

For **meals**, choose between Portreath's two **pubs**: the traditional *Portreath Arms*, right next to *Cliff House*, and the more modern and quieter *Basset Arms*, off Beach Road and with outdoor seating, both serving simple dishes for around £10. You'll eat far better, though, at *The Blue Bar*, right above the beach at Porthtowan, one of the area's most congenial **eateries**, much favoured by the surf crowd, offering baps and pitta bread at lunch time, pizzas, and all-day breakfasts at weekends and more formal evening meals; live bands play on most Saturday evenings (also Fri in summer). **Surfing gear** in Portreath can be rented from Savage Surf on Beach Road (£4.50 per hour for board and wet suit). At Cambrose, you can **rent bikes** from the Bike Barn, Elm Farm (Ⓣ01209/891498, Ⓦcornwallcycletrails.com; £12 per day), right on the Coast-to-Coast trail. Bike courses and B&B (❸), self-catering and camping accommodation are also offered here.

St Agnes and around

Five miles north of Redruth and a mile from the coast, and surrounded by ghostly engine houses, the old mining town of **ST AGNES** gives little hint today of the conditions in which its population once lived. Immaculate flower-filled gardens front the straggling streets of grey-slate and granite cottages in **Peterville**, the lower part of the village, and **Churchtown**, the upper, more central part. The two ends are connected by the steep Town Hill, with its picturesque terrace of cottages known as "Stippy-Stappy", a Cornish colloquialism for going uphill.

Before heading for the beaches, there are a couple of sights in and around town that are worth exploring, starting with the unprepossessing **St Agnes Church** in Churchtown, dedicated to a 13-year-old Roman girl martyred in 304. Though dating from 1849 in its present incarnation, the church merits a glance for its much older relics, including a quirky Elizabethan alms box supported by the figure of a hungry man, his hands pressed against his empty stomach. The stones for the altar were taken from the harbour's ruined jetty. On the outskirts of the village south of Churchtown, occupying a former chapel of rest, **St Agnes Museum** on Penwinnick Road (Easter–Oct daily 10.30am–5pm; free) holds a low-key collection of items related to the town's history and culture. Displays include a model of the harbour before its destruction by the sea in 1916, a self-portrait of John Opie, the first Cornish Royal Academician who was born in the vicinity (see Contexts, p.383), and exhibits relating to the local fishing industry, folklore and tin mining. A handsome leatherback turtle greets visitors by the door.

If you're intrigued by Cornwall's tinning industry, you can find out everything you need to know at **Blue Hills Tin Streams**, a wild spot at Trevellas Coombe, a mile or so northeast of St Agnes (Easter–Oct Mon–Sat 10am–4pm; £5.50; Ⓦwww.bluehillstin.com). A member of the resident family will guide you through the processes of vanning, panning and jigging – stages in the process of tin extraction – and point out examples of tin in its various smeltings in their workshop. There are products fashioned from the tin on sale in the shop. From St Agnes take the B3285 towards Perranporth, turning left for Wheal Kitty after 250m and right at the grass triangle (signposted).

The real pull around St Agnes, however, is the cliffy, sometimes sandy coast. The best place to take it all in – and one of Cornwall's most famous vantage points – is from **St Agnes Beacon**, 192m high, from where views extend inland to Bodmin Moor and even across the peninsula to St Michael's Mount. The easiest access is from the free car park on Beacon Drive, a mile west of the village, from where it's a ten-minute walk to the top (look out for the remains of Bronze Age barrows).

A mile or so northwest of the beacon, the knuckle of land that is **St Agnes Head** is edged by cliffs which support the area's largest colony of breeding kittiwakes, fulmars and guillemots, while grey seals are a common sight offshore. There are good beaches on either side: a couple of miles north, **Trevaunance Cove** has a fine sandy beach much favoured by surfers and boasts excellent water quality, while south of St Agnes Head and beneath the cliff-top relics of **Wheal Coates** tin mine, **Chapel Porth** is a wide expanse of white sand at low tide, rocky and stony at other times – swimmers and surfers should, however, be aware of the strong currents and undertows.

Practicalities

St Agnes is connected to Redruth train station by **bus** #315 (not Sun). The local **tourist office** is currently housed in the Churchtown Arts gift shop at 5 Churchtown (Mon–Sat 9.30am–5.30pm, Sun 10am–5pm; Ⓣ01872/554150, Ⓦwww.st-agnes.com), though is destined to move – ask around for the latest location. Surfboards and wet suits can be rented from Aggie Surf Shop at 4 Peterville Square, which can also arrange lessons.

There's a good choice of **accommodation** in and around the town, including Peterville's eighteenth-century *Malt House*, once the village brewing-house, which has a relaxed, bohemian atmosphere and offers four rooms with shared or en-suite bathrooms, six-course breakfasts and use of kitchen facilities (Ⓣ01872/553318, Ⓦwww.themalthousestagnes.co.uk; no credit cards; ❸). At the southern edge of the village, on Penwinnick Road (the B3277), the creeper-clad *Penkerris* (Ⓣ01872/552262, Ⓦwww.penkerris.co.uk; ❸) is a spacious and homely Edwardian B&B, with log fires in winter, a garden, and dinners available for £15.

If you want to be near the beach, head down to Trevaunance Cove, where the whitewashed *Driftwood Spars* (ⓣ01872/552428, ⓦwww.driftwoodspars.com; ⑤), originally a seventeenth-century tin miners' warehouse, offers maritime-themed rooms, some – costing more – facing the sea. There's a useful **campsite** a mile south of the centre of St Agnes on Penwinnick Road at *Presingoll Farm* (ⓣ01872/552333, ⓦwww.presingollfarm.co.uk; closed Nov–Easter), equipped with laundry facilities and free hot showers.

Right in the centre of town opposite the church, the large and lively **bar** at the *St Agnes Hotel* serves sandwiches, jacket potatoes and burgers for under £10, while the *Tap House* on Peterville Square attracts a young and lively crowd, thanks to its inexpensive Mexican and Indian food and **live bands**. By the sea, the *Driftwood Spars* is always busy, with hot and cold food at the three bars for under £10 as well as Cuckoo Ale, brewed on the premises, and live music at weekends; imaginatively prepared fish dishes are served in the upstairs restaurant (£15–20), where it's worth booking. The traditional-looking *Railway Inn* at 10 Vicarage Rd (a continuation of Churchtown) has a good selection of ales and meals and is a wi-fi hotspot (no food Sun eve).

Perranporth

Past the old World War II airfield three miles northeast of St Agnes, the resort of **PERRANPORTH** lies at the southern end of Perran Beach, a three-mile expanse of sand enhanced by caves and natural rock arches, and backed by turf-covered dunes. Once devoted to tin and copper mining, it's now a compact holiday resort that hasn't changed much since the 1930s, when John Betjeman poured scorn on its "bungalows, palm-shaded public conveniences and amenities, and shopping arcades in the cheapest style so that Newquay looks almost smart by comparison". However, the resort's aesthetics have little impact on the thousands of surfers who flock here year-round, drawn by the long ranks of rollers coming in straight off the Atlantic.

Perranporth is connected to St Agnes by **buses** #403 (not Sat or Sun), #501 (summer only; not Sat) and #583 (Sat only). From Newquay or Truro, take bus #403 or #587. Duchy Holidays, a letting agency at 8 Tywarnhayle Square, provides local **information** (Mon–Sat 9am–5pm in summer, 10am–4pm in winter; ⓣ01872/575254, ⓦwww.perranporthinfo.co.uk). **Surfing equipment** can be rented from Bathsheba Surf, nearby at 19 St Piran's Rd (ⓣ01872/573748); tuition can also be arranged here.

The **accommodation** provided in the *Seiners Arms*, right by the beach (ⓣ01872/573118, ⓦwww.seiners.co.uk; ⑤), is fairly basic and tired-looking, but there are magnificent views from its upstairs rooms. You'll find considerably more peace and luxury out of town at *Lambriggan Court*, Penhallow, a couple of miles south of Perranporth off the A3075 (ⓣ01872/571636, ⓦwww.lambriggancourt.com; ⑤); it has spacious rooms in a fresh, contemporary style, and extensive grounds with lakes and a menagerie of exotic animals.

The local **youth hostel** (ⓣ0845/371 9755, ⓔperranporth@yha.org.uk; closed Oct–Easter; from £16) is dramatically sited in a former cliff-top coast-guard station less than a mile west of Perranporth; call ahead to check opening. Reached from the coast path (signposted left off Tywarnhayle Road on the B3285 to St Agnes), it has four- and eight-bed rooms and a kitchen. The nearest **campsite**, *Perranporth Camping and Touring Park* (ⓣ01872/572174; closed Nov–Easter), lies half a mile northeast of the centre on Budnick Road, a five-minute walk across the dunes from the beach; it's equipped with a pool and a bar and

Lowender Peran

In mid to late October Perranporth hosts the **Lowender Peran festival**, a celebration of all things Cornish and Celtic, taking place over five days in the *Ponsmere Hotel*, Ponsmere Road, and featuring workshops, craft displays, ceilidhs and concerts. Day tickets cost around £5, evening events £10. For information, call ⓣ01872/553413 or see ⓦwww.lowenderperan.co.uk.

shop open in peak season. The quiet and clean *Tollgate Farm*, Budnick Hill, a mile east of town on the B2285 (ⓣ0845/166 2126, ⓦwww.tollgatefarm.co.uk; closed Oct–Easter), is more appealing, however, and very friendly.

Next to Duchy Holidays on Tywarnhayle Square, *The Cove* provides daytime **snacks** for under £5 and a friendly atmosphere, while bar food is served at the beamed, wood-panelled *Seiners Arms*, which has a sheltered terrace overlooking the beach, and more formal meals are available at the separate restaurant. Located right on the beach, the tropical-looking *Watering Hole* (ⓣ01872/572888, ⓦwww.the-wateringhole.co.uk; closed Oct–Easter Mon–Thurs) is a great place for breakfasts, burgers (£8) and steaks (£12–14), or just for a drink; it buzzes all year round and puts on live music – everything from folk to funk – on Saturdays (also Fri in summer) and barbecues in summer (Thurs & Sun).

Newquay and around

Straddling a series of rocky bluffs seven miles north of Perranporth, **NEWQUAY** has a defiantly youthful air, making it difficult to imagine the town enjoying any history extending more than a few years back. In fact the "new quay" was built as long ago as the fifteenth century in what was already a long-established fishing port, previously more colourfully known as Towan Blystra (Cornish for "boat cove in the sand hills"), concentrated in the sheltered west end of Newquay Bay. For many years the town thrived on the local pilchard industry which reached its peak in the late eighteenth century, when large quantities were exported to the Mediterranean (principally Italy). A century later the town's harbour was expanded for coal imports and a railway was constructed across the peninsula to carry shipments of china clay from the pits around St Austell to Newquay for export. With the trains came a swelling stream of seasonal visitors, drawn to the town's superb position and fine golden sands. These natural advantages, combined with the Atlantic rollers, continue to pull the crowds today, making Newquay North Cornwall's premier resort for **surfers**, while an infusion of smart **new bars** and restaurants have given the resort a cool, modern edge.

Arrival, information and accommodation

Newquay's **train station** is off Cliff Road, a couple of hundred yards from the **bus station** on East Street. All buses for the beaches stop on Cliff Road and its extension Narrowcliff, and at the bus station on Manor Road, five minutes from the town's **tourist office** on Marcus Hill (April–Sept Mon–Fri 9am–5.30pm, Sat & Sun 10am–4pm; Oct–March Mon–Fri 10am–4pm, Sat & Sun 10am–3pm; ⓣ01637/854020, ⓦwww.visitnewquay.org). The websites ⓦwww.newquay.co.uk, www.newquay.org.uk and www.surfnewquay.co.uk also have copious local info, and the latter has surfing news for the whole coast.

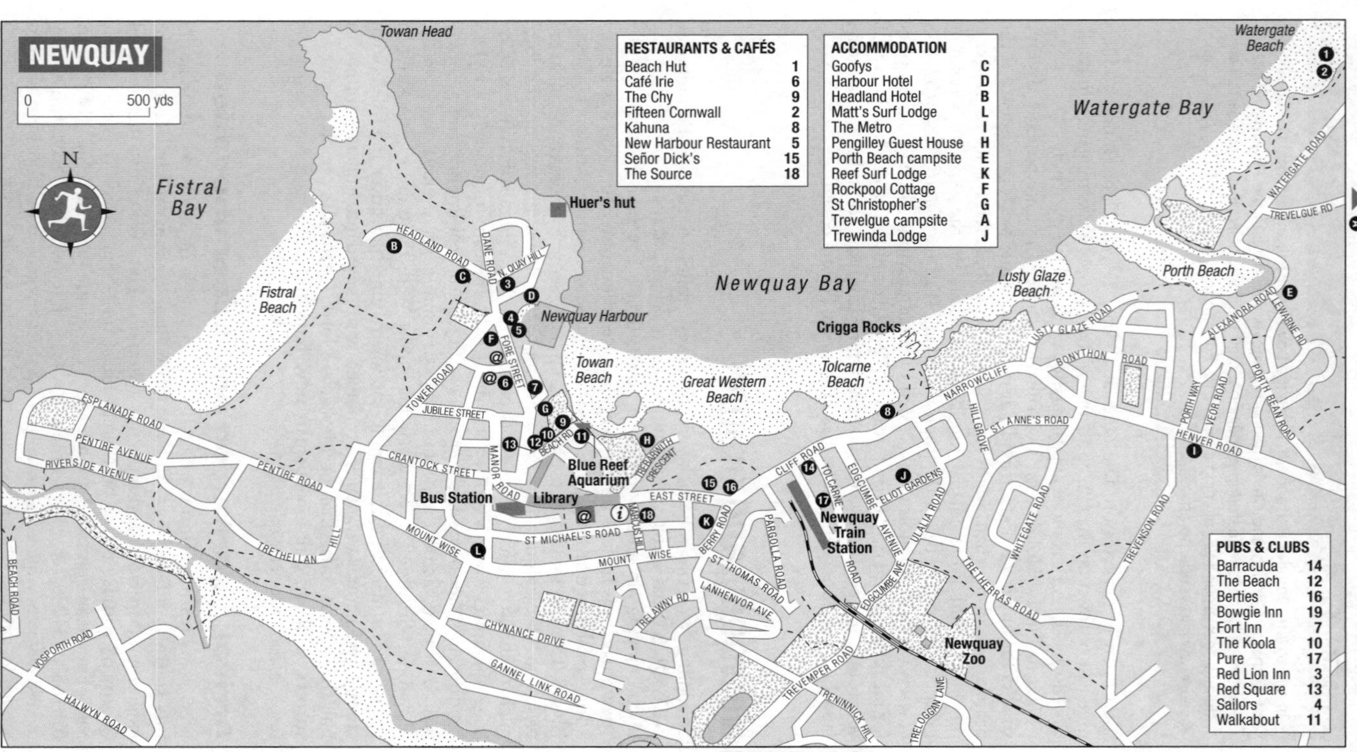
NEWQUAY
0 500 yds
N
RESTAURANTS & CAFÉS
Beach Hut 1
Café Irie 6
The Chy 9
Fifteen Cornwall 2
Kahuna 8
New Harbour Restaurant 5
Señor Dick's 15
The Source 18
ACCOMMODATION
Goofys C
Harbour Hotel D
Headland Hotel B
Matt's Surf Lodge L
The Metro I
Pengilley Guest House H
Porth Beach campsite E
Reef Surf Lodge K
Rockpool Cottage F
St Christopher's G
Trevelgue campsite A
Trewinda Lodge J
PUBS & CLUBS
Barracuda 14
The Beach 12
Berties 16
Bowgie Inn 19
Fort Inn 7
The Koola 10
Pure 17
Red Lion Inn 3
Red Square 13
Sailors 4
Walkabout 11
Towan Head
Watergate Beach
Watergate Bay
Fistral Bay
Fistral Beach
Huer's hut
Newquay Bay
Newquay Harbour
Towan Beach
Great Western Beach
Tolcarne Beach
Lusty Glaze Beach
Porth Beach
Crigga Rocks
Blue Reef Aquarium
Bus Station
Library
Newquay Train Station
Newquay Zoo
HEADLAND ROAD
DANE ROAD
N. QUAY HILL
FORE STREET
TOWER ROAD
JUBILEE STREET
BEACH RD
MANOR ROAD
CRANTOCK STREET
TREBARWITH CRESCENT
EAST STREET
MARCUS HILL
ST MICHAEL'S ROAD
MOUNT WISE
ESPLANADE ROAD
PENTIRE AVENUE
RIVERSIDE AVENUE
PENTIRE ROAD
TRETHELLAN HILL
BEACH ROAD
VOSPORTH ROAD
HALWYN ROAD
CHYNANCE DRIVE
GANNEL LINK ROAD
TRELAWNY RD
LANHENVOR AVE
ST THOMAS ROAD
BERRY ROAD
PARGOLLA ROAD
CLIFF ROAD
TOLCARNE ROAD
EDGCUMBE AVENUE
EDGCUMBE AVE
ELIOT GARDENS
ULALIA ROAD
TREVEMPER ROAD
TREINNICK HILL
TRELOGGAN LANE
TRETHERRAS ROAD
WHITEGATE ROAD
TREVENSON ROAD
HILLGROVE
ST. ANNE'S ROAD
NARROWCLIFF
BONYTHON ROAD
LUSTY GLAZE ROAD
PORTH WAY
VEOR ROAD
PORTH BEAN ROAD
HENVER ROAD
ALEXANDRA ROAD
LEWARNE RD
TREVELGUE RD
WATERGATE ROAD
Crantock Beach & 19
Trerice Manor (3 miles)
© Crown copyright

There are streetfuls of **accommodation** in all categories, though rooms are at a premium in July and August, when it's strongly advisable to book ahead. The town has the West Country's biggest selection of **independent hostels**, some fairly scruffy and jam-packed in peak season, but all with TVs, kitchens and places to store your surfboard. In some, regular stag and hen parties can make for disturbed nights, however, and most don't accept credit cards.

Campsites in the area are mainly mega-complexes, many of them geared to families and unwilling to take same-sex groups, or even couples, in order to minimize rowdy behaviour. The majority are located east of the centre, and are closed in winter.

Hotels and B&Bs

Harbour Hotel North Quay Hill ⓣ01637/873040, ⓦwww.harbourhotel.co.uk. Poised in a prime position overlooking the harbour, select lodgings with plush, balconied but smallish bedrooms facing seaward, and free wi-fi. There's a gourmet-quality restaurant. ❼

Headland Hotel Headland Rd ⓣ01637/872211, ⓦwww.headlandhotel.co.uk. Commanding unrivalled views over Fistral Beach, this Victorian pile has four-star facilities, including tennis courts and indoor and outdoor swimming pools. It's an extravagant but memorable treat. ❽

The Metro 142 Henver Rd ⓣ01637/871638, ⓦwww.metronewquay.co.uk. Clean, contemporary B&B out from the centre but just ten minutes' walk from Porth and Lusty Glaze beaches, with leather sofas, wide-screen TVs and internet access. Buffet-style Continental breakfasts are available until 11am, and you can use the breakfast room during the day. There's a busy road at the front, but back-facing rooms look onto fields. Closed Jan–Easter. ❺

Pengilley Guest House 12 Trebarwith Crescent ⓣ01637/872039, ⓦwww.pengilley-guesthouse.co.uk. Very close to the main town beach and with friendly management, this has tasteful, en-suite rooms – one has an antique brass bed and the top one has a small balcony – and a guests' lounge. No credit cards. ❸

Rockpool Cottage 92 Fore St ⓣ01637/870848, ⓦwww.rockpoolcottage.co.uk. Run by a former surfing champion, this B&B is beautifully furnished and convenient for the town centre and Fistral Beach. Breakfast is served in the rooms, each of which has a mini-fridge and en-suite bathroom. Closed Oct–Easter. ❹

Trewinda Lodge 17 Eliot Gardens ⓣ01637/877533, ⓦwww.trewindalodge.co.uk. Tasteful decor in the en-suite rooms of this friendly B&B, just a few minutes' walk from the train station and Tolcarne Beach, with access at all times. The owner, who runs a surf school, can give informed advice to surfers. ❸

Hostels

Goofys 5 Headland Rd ⓣ01637/872684, ⓦwww.goofys.co.uk. More minimalist and stylish hostel than most, more like a B&B and family-run, this has single, double and bunk beds in clean, en-suite rooms costing £32.50–40 per person in peak season. It's very close to Fistral Beach and the harbour, with sea views. Included in the price are help-yourself breakfasts, a modern kitchen and a child-friendly lounge.

Matt's Surf Lodge 110 Mount Wise Rd ⓣ01637/874651, ⓦwww.matts-surf-lodge.co.uk. Set slightly further out than the other hostels, but with friendly staff and a licensed bar (and free tea and coffee are available all day). In summer, dorm beds are £15–20, and en-suite double rooms ❸, but winter prices are much lower, and there's a special rate of £45 per week from Sept–May (prices include breakfast). Ask about three-day surf packages in low season.

Reef Surf Lodge 10–12 Berry Rd ⓣ01637/879058, ⓦwww.reefsurflodge.info. Central, upmarket hostel, with a sleek, contemporary feel – stainless steel everywhere, surf videos on plasma screens, and CD players and wide-screen TVs in the en-suite bunkrooms. Prices in summer are high (£40–45) but drop considerably in low season and there are good discounts for longer stays. There's bar food, live entertainment, beach parties and a surf centre.

St Christopher's 35 Fore St ⓣ01637/859111, ⓦwww.st-christophers.co.uk. A great, central location overlooking the harbour, above Belushi's bar. Bunks in small dorms sleeping 4–10 go up to £23.50 at weekends and in summer, including a basic breakfast; check out the website for reduced rates and great-value winter deals. There's free wi-fi, but no self-catering; guests get discounts on food from the bar.

Campsites

Porth Beach Porth ⓣ01637/876531, ⓦwww.porthbeach.co.uk. Located behind Porth Beach to the east of town, this site has a villagey feel, and is

Surfing in Newquay

Newquay's surfing buzz is infectious enough to tempt scores of non-surfheads to try their hand every summer. Close to the centre of town, the sheltered beaches of **Towan**, **Great Western** and **Tolcarne** are suitable for beginners with bodyboards, while further to the north **Watergate Bay** is slightly more exposed, so good for intermediates. Experts should head for **Fistral Bay** to the west of the town, which enjoys fast hollow waves, especially when the wind comes from the southwest, and is the focus for national and international championships. The beach is under the surveillance of up to ten lifeguards – conditions are most dangerous at low tide, especially mid-afternoon on the spring tide. For information on **surfing conditions** see any one of a number of websites – for example ⓦwww.a1surf.com, www.dailysurf.net or magicseaweed.com – which provide surf reports and webcam images (you can monitor conditions on Fistral Bay at ⓦwww.fistralsurfcam.com).

A range of **surfing equipment** is available to **rent** from shops and beach stalls (boards £5–15 a day, wet suits around the same), or to **buy** from such outlets as Bilbo, 6 Alma Place, off Fore St (ⓣ01637/879033, ⓦwww.tvsurfshop.co.uk), Surfers Paradise, 62 Tower Rd (ⓣ01637/877373); North Shore, 36 Fore St (ⓣ01637/850620), or Ocean Magic, 11 Cliff Rd (ⓣ01637/850071).

Newquay offers plenty of opportunities for **surf tuition**; anything from a two-and-a-half-hour session (around £25) to a week (£100–150). The British Surfing Association provides a list of approved schools, clubs and events, as well as beginners' info and weblinks on its website ⓦwww.britsurf.co.uk. They also put on courses of up to ten lessons between Easter and October at Fistral Beach (ⓣ01637/850737, ⓦwww.nationalsurfingcentre.com), and can arrange weekend specials, women's workshops and personal coaching. Local outfits include Dolphin Surf School (ⓣ01637/873707, ⓦwww.surfschool.co.uk), which runs courses year-round and also offers accommodation at *Trewinda Lodge* (see p.327); Offshore Extreme (ⓣ01637/877083, ⓦwww.offshore-extreme.co.uk), with day, weekend or week-long packages including accommodation, and Reef Surf School (ⓣ01637/879058, ⓦwww.reefsurfschool.com), open all year round and offering sessions lasting half a day (£25), a full day (£35) and two days (£55) – their three- or four-day surf packages including B&B cost £50–150 according to season. Many places offer **women-only** surf courses, and Hibiscus (ⓣ01637/879374, ⓦwww.hibiscussurfschool.co.uk) does nothing else, with half-day (£25), full-day (£35) and two-day (£64) courses, and an accommodation option. Good for **children**, Lusty Glaze Adventure Centre (ⓣ01637/872444, ⓦwww.adventure-centre.org) also specializes in other adventure sports such as coasteering and zip-wiring, For kitesurfing, land yachting, surf canoeing and paragliding, head for The Extreme Academy on Watergate Bay (ⓣ01637/860543, ⓦwww.watergatebay.co.uk).

If you can, try to arrange your visit to Newquay to coincide with one of the **surfing competitions** and events that run right through the summer – contact the tourist office (see opposite) for dates.

reached on the B3276, half a mile from the A3058 turn-off. No same-sex groups. Closed late Oct to early March.

Trevelgue Trevelgue Rd ⓣ01637/851851, ⓦwww.trevelgue.co.uk. Beyond Porth Beach, this place separates its camping, caravan and family sites from groups. There's a restaurant, a large indoor pool and nightly entertainment in summer, when surf rental is available. Minimal facilities in winter.

The town and around

Newquay's partly pedestrianized centre is a somewhat tacky parade of shops and restaurants from which lanes lead to ornamental gardens and sloping lawns on the cliff-tops. The town has plenty of family entertainment, including a steam railway, a water amusements park and the **Blue Reef Aquarium**, adjacent to the harbour at the bottom of Beach Road (daily 10am–5pm; £9; Ⓦwww.bluereefaquarium.co.uk), where Cornish coastline, Mediterranean and Caribbean seas and a coral reef are re-created in large, open-top tanks, underwater tunnels allow you close-ups of tropical fish, and there are tours, talks and various feeding sessions. In a similar but more traditional vein, **Newquay Zoo**, in Trenance Gardens off Edgcumbe Avenue (daily: April–Sept 9.30am–6pm, Oct 10am–5pm, Nov–March 10am–5pm or dusk; last admission 1hr before closing; £9.95, or £6.95 in winter; Ⓦwww.newquayzoo.co.uk), has a programme of talks highlighting its conservation programmes, as well as subtropical lakeside gardens, a maze and play areas for children. The zoo is a stop on the kiddy-size **road train**, which circulates around Newquay's main attractions hourly in summer (Easter–Oct; £4 day ticket). While you're wandering the main Fore Street, you might have a glance at the **world's longest surfboard**, displayed outside Longboard House on Alma Place, just off Fore Street: thirty-six and a half feet long, it was ridden by eleven people in honour of the total solar eclipse of August 1999.

If you feel like escaping the seaside crowds, you'll appreciate the tranquillity of **Trerice** (March–Oct Mon–Thurs, Sat & Sun 11am–5pm; £6.36, garden only £2.18; NT), three miles southeast of Newquay, reachable by road on the A392 and A3058 (by bus, #527 stops at Kestle Mill, nearly a mile distant). Little changed since it was built by Sir John Arundell in 1571, the manor house has a Dutch gabled facade and a sequence of period-furnished rooms, most impressive of which are the magnificent **Great Chamber** upstairs, and the **Great Hall** on the ground floor, both with ornate plaster barrel ceilings with pendants. The Great Hall also boasts a latticed window that preserves much of the original glass in 576 panes, and displays a rare set of fat sixteenth-century wooden skittles, or "kayles", with necks on top and bottom, similar to those used by Francis Drake when playing "bowls" on Plymouth Hoe (see p.159); visitors can participate in a game of Cornish skittles on the bowling green, or "slapcock" – a version of badminton.

Newquay's main attraction, though, is its remarkable **coastline**. While development has extended unchecked east and north up the coast, the cliffs of Towan Head have limited Newquay's growth to the west, and you don't have to walk far to leave the shops behind. You can take in some good views round this headland, up Beacon Road from Fore Street's western end, turning right at King Edward's Crescent, and passing the whitewashed **huer's hut** (not open to the public), a reminder of the town's former fishing role. Stationed here as a lookout for pilchard shoals, the huer would send the fleet docked in the port into action by his cry of "heva!" ("found!") bellowed through a three-foot-long horn.

The beaches

Sheltered by the headland and adjacent to the small harbour in the crook of the massive headland, Newquay's most central swimming spot, **Towan Beach**,

Boardmasters Festival

Newquay's **Boardmasters Festival**, touted as Europe's biggest surf, skate and music festival and attracting huge crowds, takes place over five days in early August. There are three venues: Watergate Bay, where there are four stages for the 50-odd rock, hip-hop and indie acts; Fistral Beach for surfing, skateboarding and BMX competitions and the musical Beach Sessions, and the skate park in Trenance Leisure Park. Advance tickets for the whole event cost around £90, tickets for single days and the weekend cost less, but are more expensive at the gate (if still available). Book early at Ⓣ0844/847 2517 or Ⓦwww.relentlessboardmasters.com.

▲ Fistral Beach

is a smooth sandy expanse reached from the bottom of Beach Road off Fore Street. It's bound on its eastern side by a tall crag connected to the promenade above by a quaint replica of Bristol's Clifton Suspension Bridge. A favourite with families, and with the full range of equipment-rental facilities, the beach can get unbearably crowded in high season, and you'll get more elbow room on any of the succession of firm sandy beaches which extend for seven miles to the east. Nearest are **Tolcarne**, reached by steep steps from Narrowcliff, and, past Crigga Rocks, **Lusty Glaze**, accessible from Lusty Glaze Road – both well protected from the wind by the bordering cliffs. You can reach these spots along the sandy shore at low tide, but for some of the more distant beaches, such as **Porth Beach**, with its grassy headland, or the extensive **Watergate Bay**, a glorious expanse of fine sand two and a half miles north of the centre, you can use local bus #556.

All of the above are popular with **surfers**, particularly Watergate, but the most challenging is **Fistral Bay**, to the west, which you can reach on foot past Towan Head or across the golf links, or by bus #588. Fully exposed to the Atlantic, the fierce breakers make it an ideal venue for surfing championships, but the violent rip currents are hazardous. On the other side of East Pentire Head from Fistral, **Crantock Beach** – reachable over the Gannel River by regular passenger ferry in season, by upstream footbridge or on bus #585 or #587 – is usually less packed, and has a lovely backdrop of dunes and undulating grassland. Further west, past Kelsey Head, **Holywell Bay** (bus #587) was the setting for the opening sequence of the James Bond film, *Die Another Day*. All the main beaches are lifeguarded in season, and you should heed all warnings. All except Watergate Bay, Porth and Crantock beaches merited a Marine Conservation Society recommendation in 2009, but none received a Blue Flag award.

Restaurants and cafés

Newquay is well equipped with **places to eat**, especially of the fast-food ilk; most are mediocre, but the best places are listed below. The Fore Street Deli, next to *Café Irie* at 40 Fore St, provides good-quality organic fare to **take away**, including Roskilly's ice cream, while the *Venus Café*, renowned for its wholesome takeaways, has outlets at Tolcarne Beach and on Watergate Bay.

Beach Hut Watergate Bay ⓣ01637/860877. Open from early morning to late evening, this is a trendy hangout for surfers and a good venue for a sundowner. Breakfasts, snacks and daily specials are available all year, but the restaurant, where main courses cost £10–15, is only open eves Fri & Sat Nov–Easter.

Café Irie 38 Fore St ⓣ01637/859200. This funky, lattice-windowed cottage serves all-day breakfasts, soups, veggie food, cream teas and, between July and Aug, inexpensive evening meals in the upstairs restaurant. There's usually a mellow music accompaniment, with weekly live jam sessions in summer. No credit cards. Closed Mon–Thurs Nov–Easter.

The Chy Beach Rd ⓣ01637/873415. Sleek, contemporary setting for steaks or seafood (around £12–18) upstairs, or breakfasts, sandwiches, salads, mussels and burgers (around £7.50) downstairs. There's a spacious terrace, DJs in the evenings and wi-fi access. Closed Tues–Thurs Oct–Easter.

Fifteen Cornwall Watergate Bay ⓣ01637/861000, ⓦwww.fifteencornwall.co.uk. Opened by Cockney TV chef Jamie Oliver on an inspired site overlooking the beach, this contemporary-looking place with large windows showcases the culinary talents of local trainee chefs in the form of inventively Italian-influenced dishes made with seasonal Cornish ingredients. An evening tasting menu of six courses will set you back £55, or £95 including select wines. During the day you can have breakfast (£4.40–9.30) or lunch (around £20 for mains, or a three-course set menu for £25.45). Well worth the splurge.

Kahuna Tolcarne Beach ⓣ01637/850440. The perfect hangout after a day on the beach, either for an evening drink or meal of seafood or local lamb (£10–16), with great views. You can also come here for a breakfast bap, a doorstop sandwich for lunch or a late cocktail. Booking essential in the evening (and book early for a table on the deck). Closed Nov–Easter.

New Harbour Restaurant Newquay Harbour ⓣ01637/874062. Enjoy seafood and a romantic atmosphere on the decked terrace of this harbourside eatery, where you can watch the ingredients being landed just yards away, and pick from among the lobsters scurrying around in the adjacent pools. Choose from a range of hot and cold snacks at lunchtime (under £10), grab a bite at the outdoor Crab Shack, or dine on meat and fish dishes in the evening (mains £10–15) Closed Oct–March.

Señor Dick's East St ⓣ01637/870350. Popular ranch-style theme bar and restaurant, with a full range of Mexican dishes available, for example *quesadillas* and *enchiladas* (around £10), plus salads, burgers, chargrills (£15–16) and vegetarian options, all in large portions. There's a cocktail bar upstairs. Closed daytime Sept–May.

The Source Marcus Hill ⓣ01637/875114. A converted church provides a contemplative ambience for this relaxed café, a pleasant spot for a latte or an inexpensive bite to eat, with nachos, pancakes and burgers on the menu for under £5, and there's a pool table, surf videos and internet access. Closed eves, also Wed during winter school terms.

Drinking and nightlife

Newquay's **pubs** overflow in summer, getting rowdy at night when surfers and clubbers take over, though many are still suitable for families during the day. The town has become Cornwall's biggest centre for **nightclubbing**, with busloads of party-goers converging from various parts of the region at weekends; it can get particularly boisterous on summer evenings when the town centre is filled with roaming boozy gangs. The magazine *247* has listings; most places have licences until 3am, but may stay open later in summer. Entry prices range from free to £10.

Barracuda 27–29 Cliff Rd ⓣ01637/875800, ⓦwww.barracudanewquay.com. Dance and r 'n' b anthems alternate with electro, metal and indie nights at this popular spot, and there's a great view over the beach. Occasional live bands.

The Beach 1 Beach Rd ⓣ01637/872194, ⓦwww.beachclubnewquay.co.uk. One of the hottest spots in town, open nightly in summer, when there are occasional all-nighters. With four bars on three floors, the diet is mainstream dance, retro and foam parties, with students' night on Thurs.

Berties East St ⓣ01637/870369, ⓦwww.bertiesclub.com. Newquay's largest nightclub attracts stag and hen parties and wet t-shirt competitions, with a playlist rarely straying beyond chart sounds, r 'n' b and party anthems. Open nightly in summer; Fri & Sat only in winter.

Bowgie Inn West Pentire. Brilliant views from the outdoor tables of this pub overlooking Crantock Beach. Good food available.

Fort Inn 63 Fore St. Good for families and with sea views from its ranks of outdoor tables, this pub hosts barbecues in summer and offers a range of food.

The Koola Beach Rd ⓣ01637/873415, ⓦwww.thekoola.com. On three levels, this club is stylishly done up with industrial-chic decor. When live bands aren't playing, celeb DJs spin everything from cutting-edge break beats to smooth jazzy sounds, taking in urban music and house along the way. Open daily in summer, Fri & Sat in winter.

Pure 52 Tolcarne Rd ⓣ01637/850313, ⓦwww.purenewquay.com. With four rooms and seven bars, this place gets very busy in summer, playing dance anthems, funky house, garage, cheese and chart music.

Red Lion Inn North Quay Hill ⓣ01637/872195. Large pub, popular with surfers, that hums in the evenings and is close to the harbour. There's inexpensive pub food, pizzas and skillets served lunchtime and evenings, and live music Fri & Sat.

Red Square Gover Lane ⓣ01637/878823. Bar, lounge and club with a terrace open during the day for food and, upstairs, a slightly more adventurous choice of music than you'll hear at most of Newquay's clubs, playing techno, trance, drum'n'bass, ska and hip-hop (usually free).

Sailors 11–17 Fore St ⓣ01637/872838, ⓦwww.sailorsnightclub.com. Lively pub with popular club next door for a young crowd, playing chart sounds, as well as retro, funk and house, with the occasional school disco. Expect long queues in summer. Open daily in summer, Thurs–Sat only in winter.

Walkabout The Crescent ⓣ01637/853000, ⓦwww.walkabout.eu.com. Popular, sometimes boisterous Aussie bar featuring crocodiles in hats and authentic tucker, located above Towan Beach. The huge single room is filled with TV screens tuned to different stations, there are great sea views, DJs and regular live music at weekends.

Listings

Airport Newquay Cornwall Airport is at St Mawgan, five miles northeast of town ⓣ01637/860600, ⓦwww.newquaycornwallairport.com. Air Southwest (ⓣ0870/241 8202, ⓦwww.airsouthwest.com) operates daily flights to London Gatwick, and also flies to Bristol, Glasgow, Leeds-Bradford, Manchester, Newcastle, Plymouth, Cork and Dublin; bmibaby.com (ⓣ0905/828 2828, ⓦbmibaby.com) also flies to Manchester, as well as Birmingham (late May to late Sept). Ryanair (ⓦwww.ryanair.com) has daily flights to London Stansted (not Sun mid-Oct to June); Skybus (ⓣ01736/334220, ⓦwww.ios-travel.co.uk) has regular connections with St Mary's, in the Isles of Scilly (April–Sept), and St Brieuc, Brittany (May–Sept). Jet2.com (ⓣ0871/226 1737, ⓦwww.jet2.com) flies to Belfast in summer.

Bike rental Shoreline, 7 Fore St (ⓣ01637/879165), charges £10 per day.

Car rental Europcar, Newquay Airport, St Mawgan ⓣ01637/860337, ⓦwww.europcar.co.uk; National Car Rental, 8A Quintrell Rd ⓣ01637/850750, ⓦwww.nationalcar.co.uk.

Fishing trips From May to October, half- (£20) or full-day (£35) trips can be arranged from the harbour. Contact Anchor Fishing ⓣ01637/877613 or 0796/833 4889; Atlantis ⓣ01637/878696 or 0781/101 7313, or Newquay Boatmen's Association ⓣ0777/219 6845.

Gig races Pilot gigs (simple six-oared rowing boats), relics of the days when trading schooners and ketches needed to be guided into harbour – the first to reach the vessel winning its custom – are now raced for pleasure from April to October; for details of fixtures, contact Newquay Rowing Club (ⓣ01637/876810, ⓦwww.newquayrowingclub.com).

Hospital Newquay and District Hospital, St Thomas' Rd ⓣ01637/893600, has a 24hr minor injuries unit.

Internet CyberSurf, 2 Broad St (Mon–Sat 9am–8pm, Sun noon–7pm, closes 5 or 6pm in winter; £1 per 20min), has drinks available on the outside deck; Tad & Nick's, 72 Fore St (10am–6pm, closed Wed; £3 per hour) also has drinks and snacks; tourist office (£1 per 20min).

Pharmacy Kayes, 8 East St ⓣ01637/873353 summer daily until 9pm, winter Mon–Sat until 6pm, Sun closes 4pm.

Post Office 31–33 East St, open Mon–Fri 9am–5.30, Sat 9am–12.30pm, with *bureau de change*.

Taxis A2B Taxis ⓣ01637/877777 and 10–11 Taxis ⓣ01637/871011 operate a 24hr service. Tuxi ⓣ01637/861961, ⓦwww.takeatuktuk.co.uk runs a tuk-tuk service, which you can book at *The Source* café (see p.331).

Tours Coast and Country Tours ⓣ01637/880753, ⓦwww.coastandcountrytours.co.uk operate tailor-made minibus tours anywhere in Cornwall, for example in the mining areas, on the coasts and on Bodmin Moor. Prices are around £200 for up to eight people for a full day,

Padstow

Twelve miles northeast of Newquay, **PADSTOW** almost rivals its larger neighbour in popularity, but its compact dimensions and harbour ambience lend it a very different feel. Enclosed within the estuary of the **Camel** – the only river of any size that comes out on Cornwall's northern seaboard – the town was for a long time the principal fishing port on this coast, and it still shelters a small working fleet. In recent years, the town has acquired a reputation for its **gourmet restaurants**, most famously those run by chef superstar Rick Stein, whose various outlets are scattered throughout town. Like Newquay, there are also some **first-class beaches** within a short distance on the predominantly cliffy coast, and in addition the town hosts one of Cornwall's most famous **festivals**, the Obby Oss, a costumed parade with medieval origins, taking place on May Day (see box, p.335).

Arrival and information

Padstow is linked to Newquay by bus #556, which stops right by the harbour. The town's **tourist office**, on the north side of the harbour (Easter–Sept Mon–Fri 9am–5pm, Sat & Sun 10.30am–4pm; Oct–Easter Mon–Fri 10am–4pm, Sat 10am–2pm, Sun 11am–2pm; ⓣ01841/533449, ⓦwww.padstowlive.com), offers a free booking service for local **accommodation** and has terminals available for **internet** access (£1 for 15min) – in fact the whole harbour area is a wi-fi hotspot.

For **bike rental**, you'll find Trail Bike Hire (ⓣ01841/532594; £9 per day) and Padstow Cycle Hire (ⓣ01841/533533, ⓦwww.padstowcyclehire.com; £12–14 per day) on Padstow's South Quay; see Wadebridge (p.338) for a greater choice of bikes. **Surfing tuition** is offered by Harlyn Surf School (ⓣ01841/533076, ⓦwww.harlynsurf.co.uk) at Harlyn Bay, three miles west of Padstow (see p.336).

Padstow is the start of two of the West Country's best-known long-distance paths: the seventeen-mile **Camel Trail** (see box, p.337) and the **Saints' Way**, an old pilgrims' route that extends for nearly thirty miles across the peninsula to Fowey (see p.229) – the tourist office has an itinerary.

Accommodation

There's no lack of **accommodation** in Padstow including the very stylish but expensive options at three of the dining establishments run by celebrity chef

Boat trips and the ferry to Rock

Padstow's harbour is jammed with boats advertising **cruises** and **fishing trips** in Padstow Bay (from £5 per hour), including excursions to view the seals and cormorants, and occasionally – between May and July – puffins, razorbills and guillemots, which can be seen off the shores hereabouts. Padstow Sealife Safaris (ⓣ0775/482 2404) offers two-hour **wildlife-watching** and fishing excursions (£35 and £25 respectively). The harbour is also where you can board the **regular ferry** across the estuary to **Rock** (daily from 7.50am until 4.30pm from Rock or 4.50pm from Padstow in winter, 7.30pm from Rock or 7.50pm from Padstow in high summer; not Sun late Oct to late March; £3 return, bicycles £2 subject to space) for the alluring beaches around **Daymer Bay** and **Polzeath** (see p.338). **Departures** are from the harbour's North Pier except at low water when ferries leave from near the war memorial further downstream. Between Easter and October, an evening **water taxi** takes over from 7pm till midnight (ⓣ0777/810 5297; £4 one way, £6 return).

Rick Stein (❻–❾; see Ⓦwww.rickstein.com). It's always wise to book ahead in summer, and months ahead if your visit coincides with the Obby Oss festival; the local **campsites**, too, fill up quickly.

Hotels and B&Bs

Cullinan's 4 Riverside Ⓣ01841/532383, Ⓦwww.padstow-bb.co.uk. You'll find this three-storeyed B&B right on the harbour next to the Old Custom House. The top bedroom has a prodigiously wide double bed, private bathroom and a French window leading onto a balcony, a cheaper and quieter room faces the back. No parking. No credit cards. ❹

Old Ship Mill Square Ⓣ01841/532357, Ⓦwww.oldshiphotel-padstow.co.uk. Family-run, eighteenth-century hotel close to the harbour, with antique furnishings and walls stacked with paintings. Some rooms are equipped with double showers, and all have fridges and wi-fi access. Parking is available. ❻

Pendeen House 28 Dennis Rd Ⓣ01841/532724, Ⓦwww.pendeenhousepadstow.com. With stripped floors and an appealing minimalist feel, this B&B has stunning estuary views and gorgeous, dazzling-white rooms, each with its own modern bathroom. Friendly hosts, a choice of breakfasts and wi-fi access are bonuses. ❺

Treann House 24 Dennis Rd Ⓣ01841/533855, Ⓦwww.treannhousepadstow.co.uk. A few minutes from the harbour, the elegant rooms in this wi-fi-enabled B&B are spacious, light and immaculately decorated, with amazing river views. You'll be welcomed with home-made cakes and complimentary wine, and delicious blueberry pancakes are among the choices for breakfast, which, in the Estuary Room, can be served on the balcony in fine weather. Minimum two-night stay. No credit cards. ❻

Treverbyn House Treverbyn Rd and Station Rd Ⓣ01841/532855, Ⓦwww.treverbynhouse.com. This beautifully furnished Edwardian house preserves its original character with contemporary (working) fireplaces in the spacious bedrooms. Ask for the Turret Room or Yellow Room, which have balconies. Breakfast is served in your room or on a terrace with river views. No credit cards. ❺

Campsites and hostel

Dennis Cove Camping Ⓣ01841/532349. In a quiet field along the estuary about a ten-minute walk south of town along the Camel Trail, this sheltered, well-maintained and picturesque site caters mainly for tents, though pitches are small. No shop. No credit cards. Closed Oct–Easter.

Padstow Touring Park Trerethern Ⓣ01841/532061, Ⓦwww.padstowtouringpark.co.uk. A large, open campsite, with no static caravans, situated one mile southwest of Padstow on the A389, and accessible by footpath. There's a shop, wi-fi and free showers, and buses stop outside.

Treyarnon Youth Hostel Tregonnan, Treyarnon Ⓣ0845/371 9664, Ⓔtreyarnon@yha.org.uk. Four and a half miles west of Padstow, this summer villa from the1930s is sited almost on the beach at Treyarnon Bay and offers surf packages, making it a popular surfers' stop. Dorms have up to six beds, costing from £14. It's half a mile from Constantine, which is accessible by bus (#556, also from Newquay). Open all year, but call ahead.

The town and beaches

With its medieval network of largely traffic-free lanes, which are draped for much of the year with window-boxfuls of hydrangeas, fuschias and geraniums, Padstow makes a pleasant place to wander. The focal point is, of course, the **harbour**, usually crowded with small craft and surrounded by a wide quayside. In summer, **brass-band concerts** take place here on Wednesdays at 7.30pm and on Sundays at 2.30pm and 7.30pm, and there's a choir on Thursday evenings; there's no seating – just have a listen as you wander around. Among the warehouses on South Quay, the **National Lobster Hatchery** (daily Easter–Sept 10am–7pm; Oct–Easter 10am–5pm; £3) offers a fascinating insight into the life of these lugubrious crustaceans, from tiny juveniles to hoary old giants.

Above and behind the quays, the parish church of **St Petroc** is worth looking into, standing amid the slate tombstones of mariners within a wooded churchyard on Church Lane. A large, mostly slate construction, the church is dedicated to St Petroc, a Welsh or Irish monk who landed here in the sixth century, founded a monastery on this site and eventually became Cornwall's most important saint,

The Obby Oss festival

Padstow's chief annual festival, the **Obby Oss**, is a May Day – or May 2 if May 1 is a Sunday – romp whose origin is obscure but has been variously ascribed as a welcome to summer, a rainmaker, a fertility ritual and even a strategy to ward off the French.

The celebration starts at midnight of the preceding day, when a **procession** sets off around town to the accompaniment of a special "Night Song", lasting until the early hours. Later in the morning, the "Obby Osses" – circular contraptions draped in shiny black material and hoisted onto fearsomely masked locals – make their appearance in streets bedecked with greenery. Two teams – all dressed in white with red or blue ribbons and bunches of spring flowers pinned to lapels – follow their own obby oss as it prances through the town on set routes, preceded by a club-wielding "teazer" and accompanied by a retinue of **musicians**, **singers**, **drummers** and twirling **dancers**. The strains of the May Song resound all day:

Unite and unite and let us all unite,
For Summer is a-come in today.
And whither we are going we all will unite,
In the merry morning of May.

You'll need to **book accommodation** well ahead if you wish to attend, and it's worth being there the day before to savour the excitement of preparation. If you can't make the festival, you can see an authentic oss in the town museum, or view it on the museum's website (see below).

bequeathing his name – "Petrock's Stow" – to the town. Inside there's a fine fifteenth- or sixteenth-century font with the twelve apostles, three on each side, carved from Catacleuse stone, and a Tudor-period wineglass pulpit. Look out, too, for a lively medieval bench-end to the right of the altar depicting a fox preaching to a congregation of geese. The walls are lined with monuments to the local Prideaux family, who still occupy nearby **Prideaux Place**, on Tregirls Lane, the main B3276 into Padstow (Easter & early May to early Oct Mon–Thurs & Sun 1.30–5pm, last tour at 4pm; house & grounds £7.50, grounds only £2), a superbly preserved example of an Elizabethan manor house. Inside, you'll find grand staircases and richly furnished rooms full of portraits and with fantastically ornate ceilings, while outside there are formal gardens, and a deer park affording long views over the Camel estuary. You might recognize some parts of the house, which is used extensively for location filming and has appeared in a plethora of films, such as *Twelfth Night* and *Oscar and Lucinda*.

Unless you're here on May 1, your only chance of seeing an "obby oss" (see box, above) is in the otherwise run-of-the-mill **Padstow Museum** (Easter to mid-Oct Mon–Fri 10.30am–4.30pm, Sat 10.30am–1pm; £1.50; Ⓦwww.padstowmuseum.co.uk), hidden upstairs in one large room in the Institute on Market Place. The oss dates back to the 1940s and looks a little the worse for wear, but brings to life the photos and descriptions of the revelries on the panels.

The coast on the western side of the estuary offers good **beaches**, which you can reach on bus #556, though walking is better for drinking in the wonderful coastline. About a mile out of town, the rivermouth is clogged by **Doom Bar**, a sand bar that was allegedly the curse of a mermaid who had been mortally wounded by a fisherman mistaking her for a seal. Apart from thwarting the growth of Padstow as a busy commercial port, the bar has scuppered some three hundred vessels, with great loss of life.

If you continue north of Doom Bar, then west round **Stepper Point**, you reach after about three miles the sandy and secluded **Harlyn Bay**, good for swimming and surfing. The area's best surfing beach, though, with first-class water quality, is **Constantine Bay**, a mile south of **Trevose Head**, the promontory located two miles west of Harlyn Bay. The surrounding dunes and rock pools make this one of the most appealing bays on the coast, though the tides can be treacherous and bathing hazardous near the rocks. There are other good surfing beaches in the neighbourhood too, such as adjacent **Treyarnon Bay**, but the surrounding caravan sites can make these claustrophobic in summer. You may find a bit more peace around **Porthcothan**, a long narrow beach with dramatic cliffs and an expanse of sand at low tide, a mile or so south of Treyarnon.

Three or four miles further south lies one of Cornwall's most dramatic beaches, **Bedruthan Steps**, whose jagged slate outcrops were traditionally held to be the stepping stones of a giant called Bedruthan, a legendary figure conjured into existence in the nineteenth century. You can view the grand panorama from the cliff-top path, at a point which drivers can reach on the B3276. From here steep steps lead down the sheer face to the sandy beach, though there is no access between November and February. The beach makes a great place to ramble about, but swimming is dangerous on account of the rocks and often violent waves, and you should be careful not to get trapped by the incoming tide. For the beaches on the eastern side of the Camel estuary, see p.338.

Eating and drinking

Padstow's quayside is lined with **snack bars** and **pasty shops** as well as **pubs** where you can sit outside, but foodies know the town best for its high-class restaurants, particularly those associated with chef **Rick Stein**, who has reigned in Padstow for 30 years. Stein's TV fame has spawned a range of food outlets in the town, including some healthy competition from eateries offering their own brand of culinary excellence. You'll probably have to blow some of your budget to sample them – and you should always book ahead, especially in summer and at weekends – but you'll rarely be disappointed.

Apart from his famous restaurants, Rick Stein also has a superior **fish and chip shop** on South Quay, *Stein's Fish & Chips*, where you can choose between such items as monkfish and gurnard alongside the standards of cod, haddock and plaice, either grilled or battered; specialities include battered oysters and scallops, squid and prawns. You can eat inside or buy a takeaway. If you fancy a posh picnic, Stein has a **delicatessen** next door, and a **patisserie** on Lanadwell Street (closed Sun), for bread, pastries and chocolates. Roskilly's **ice cream** is available at the harbour.

London Inn Lanadwell St. Unpretentious pub with wood panelling, nautical decorations and a friendly atmosphere. Sandwiches, fish specials and St Austell ales are available.

Margot's 11 Duke St ☎01841/533441. Intimate bistro with blue and beige decor, offering daily changing menus that include seafood, for example grilled fillet of grey mullet, or such meat dishes as breast of guinea fowl, for £12–17. There are also regular set menus (£23.50–28.50). Leave room for such luscious desserts as Eton mess. Closed Sun, Mon & lunchtime Tues.

No. 6 6 Middle St ☎01841/532093. Smart restaurant with black-and-white-tiled floor and white walls, offering top-notch modern European cuisine, with mains at around £15, for example cod with cockles and chorizo. Closed Sun eve & Mon.

Pescadou South Quay ☎01841/532359. Spacious and stylish restaurant offering a selection of steaks alongside such seafood choices as grilled scallops, sirloin steak and seared squid with rocket. Most main courses cost £13–18, and cheaper set menus are available in winter. Pub meals such as scampi for under £10 are served at the adjoining *Old Custom House*.

Rick Stein's Café 10 Middle St ⓣ01841/532700. This baby-Stein has a bright and breezy decor and lays on Mediterranean-type snacks at lunch (arrive early) and fuller meals at night, when booking is necessary. Main courses, such as lamb kofta kebabs and devilled mackerel, cost around £12, and there's a set-price three-course menu for £22. You can also come in the morning for coffee and *huevos rancheros* (tortillas with fried eggs and chilli sauce). Closed Sun eve & Mon eve in winter.

Rojano's 9 Mill Square ⓣ01841/532796. If you're sick of fish, grab a pizza (£5–11) or pasta (£7–11) here, washed down with a Belgian beer. Takeaways are available too. Closed Sun lunch Nov–March & Mon.

St Petroc's Bistro 4 New St ⓣ01841/532700. More casual than *The Seafood Restaurant*, this has a cheaper, more French-inspired version of the *Restaurant's* menu with a few more meat selections, at around £16 for main courses, plus a long wine list. You can sit in the modern, simply furnished indoors area, or dine alfresco in the courtyard or garden.

The Seafood Restaurant Riverside ⓣ01841/532700, ⓦwww.rickstein.com. One of the country's top fish restaurants, Rick Stein's flagship is classy without being snooty, with contemporary art on the walls and a bright, modern feel. Oysters and lobster feature on the menu, along with such exotic concoctions as Indonesian seafood curry. Most main courses will set you back £28–35, or you can opt for local hake and chips for £17.50; a six-course tasting menu is offered for £64, and the three-course lunch menu costs £35 (you can lunch in the rooftop Terrace Bar in summer for great harbour views). The waiting list often stretches for months ahead, though you could well strike lucky on a weekday out of season.

Shipwrights North Quay. Family-friendly St Austell's pub opposite the tourist office, offering ploughman's lunches and other snacks, or hot pies, scampi and meat dishes for £7–15. There are tables downstairs, upstairs and outside.

Wadebridge

About eight miles up the Camel River from Padstow, and reachable on frequent buses, **WADEBRIDGE** is nowadays a rather unremarkable market town, a far cry from its eighteenth-century heyday as one of Cornwall's main corn-exporting ports. The chief sign of its former stature is the impressive fifteenth-century bridge spanning the River Camel on seventeen arches, and built on a foundation, so it is claimed, of woolpacks. You're unlikely to want to spend much time here, unless you're passing through on the Camel Trail (see box, below), or you might be here to attend one of the town's major annual events. The **Wadebridge Folk Festival**, taking place over three days during the August

The Camel Trail

The Camel Trail is one of the West Country's best **cycle routes**, running a total of seventeen miles from Padstow up the River Camel as far as Poley's Bridge, a mile west of Blisland (see p.358) on the edge of Bodmin Moor. The five-and-a-quarter-mile Padstow–Wadebridge section of the trail follows an old railway line and offers glimpses of a variety of **birdlife** – especially around Pinkson Creek, habitat of terns, herons, curlews and egrets. However, this stretch can get very crowded in summer, and you may choose to join at Wadebridge – from the town centre, follow Eddystone Road (from the south side of the bridge) until you reach the trail. From **Wadebridge**, the route heads five and a half miles southeast towards Bodmin (see p.354), before turning northwards for a further six and a quarter miles to Poley's Bridge, within spitting distance of Wenfordbridge. This, the quieter end of the route, traces the winding river through tranquil woods, always within sight of the moor. The trail is also open to **walkers**, and to **horses** between Padstow and Dunmere, a mile west of Bodmin. You can pick up **guides, maps and leaflets** from the **tourist offices** at Padstow, Wadebridge and Bodmin (see p.333, p.338 & p.355).

bank holiday, features traditional music from around the region and beyond (for details, call the Wadebridge tourist office, below, or ⓣ01208/814638). You can buy tickets online at ⓦwww.wadebridgefolk.co.uk (weekend tickets £60 before Aug, then £66, or £5–18 for the individual ceilidhs and concerts). Cornwall's most important agricultural fair, the **Royal Cornwall Show** (ⓣ01208/812183, ⓦroyalcornwallshow.org) lasts three days in June and has everything from showjumping, sheepshearing and rare breeds to parachute displays.

Practicalities

Wadebridge's **bus station** is located on Southern Way, on the south side of the medieval bridge, from where there are hourly connections to Padstow (#555). The **tourist office** is inside the Kernow Harvest gift shop on Eddystone Road (Mon–Sat 9am–5pm, also July & Aug Sun 10am–4pm; ⓣ01208/816123). **Bikes** can be rented by the Camel Trail on Eddystone Road from Bike Smart (ⓣ01208/814545, ⓦwww.bikesmart.eu) and Bridge Bike Hire (ⓣ01208/813050, ⓦwww.bridgebikehire.co.uk), both open daily all year 9am–5pm. Bridge Bike Hire also operates a delivery and collection service, Go By Cycle (ⓣ01208/815715, ⓦwww.gobycycle.co.uk), covering all Cornwall and South Devon.

The town isn't the liveliest place to spend a night, and if you're looking for somewhere, it's worth venturing a couple of miles west of town on the Padstow road to St Breock, where the traditional, slate-hung *Pawton Stream* has contemporary decor and extensive gardens including a patio (ⓣ01208/814845, ⓔjon.bristow@btopenworld.com; no credit cards; ❺).

You don't need to go far to find a bite to **eat** in Wadebridge: on Eddystone Road opposite the tourist office, the modern, family-friendly *Glasshouse* café /**restaurant** (ⓣ01208/814800; closed Sun) should satisfy most appetites, serving decent pizzas (£7–10) and pastas (£8.50–12) as well as seafood, steaks and pies (£11.50–16).

Polzeath and around

Situated three miles northwest of Padstow, on the far side of the Camel estuary, **POLZEATH** is renowned for its fine, flat beach, the only one around here to achieve Blue Flag status in 2009. The slow wave is ideal for wannabe surfers – even the babies turn out in wet suits – and the sandy beach also attracts sand yachters, not to mention its fair share of rich kids whose high-spirited shenanigans regularly hit the headlines in the silly season. Surrounded by dunes, and with fine views across the estuary, **Daymer Bay**, a mile or two to the south, is a great place for sunbathing, its shallow waters popular with families. Daymer is also a big hit with the **windsurfing** crowd, and equipment is available to rent from stalls in summer.

Few people are tempted away from the sand and sea to visit the thirteenth-century church of **St Enodoc** (daily 7.30am–dusk), the burial place of the poet John Betjeman, whose holiday haunt was here, but it's an appealing spot, the building half buried in the grassy sand dunes and surrounded by a protective hedge of tamarisk. So invasive were the surrounding sands that at one time the vicar and his congregation had to enter through a hole in the roof. It's now incongruously stranded in the middle of a golf course, most easily approached from the Daymer Bay car park, where the footpath is signposted (alternatively, cross the golf course from Rock, following the white stones and keeping a weather eye open for golf balls).

Practicalities

From Padstow, Polzeath can be reached via the **Rock passenger ferry** (see box, p.333) – if you're **driving**, the journey is five times longer as it involves a detour round the Camel estuary. By **bus** it's accessible on #584 (not Sun in winter) from Wadebridge, Camelford and Port Isaac. Polzeath's volunteer-run **tourist office** is set back from the beach in Coronation Gardens (July to mid-Sept Mon–Sat 10am–2pm; no telephone); limited information about Polzeath can also be found at Ⓦwww.polzeath.co.uk. **Surf gear** can be rented on the beach, or from Ann's Cottage (Ⓣ01208/863317) or TJ's Surf Shop (Ⓣ01208/863625). Surf's Up, at 21 Trenant Close and on the beach (Ⓣ01208/862003 or 0776/012 6225, Ⓦwww.surfsupsurfschool.com), runs a range of courses and individual lessons from £25 for two hours including wet suits and boards; booking is advisable in July and August. For local surf reports, see Ⓦmagicseaweed.com.

The *Seascape Hotel* offers about the only solid-walled **accommodation** around here, beautifully sited a few yards up from Polzeath's beach (Ⓣ01208/863638, Ⓦwww.seascapehotel.co.uk; no under-12s; closed Nov–Easter; ❻). The nearest **campsites** are *Valley Caravan Park* (Ⓣ01208/862391, Ⓦwww.valleycaravanpark.co.uk; usually closed Oct–Easter), 150m from the beach, signposted up the lane behind the shop, which has a stream running through it attracting ducks and geese, and *Tristram*, on the low cliff just above the beach (Ⓣ01208/862215, Ⓦwww.polzeathcamping.co.uk; closed Nov–Feb), which is clean, well equipped and with glorious views, but pricey. Polzeath campsites, like those in Newquay, have barred same-sex groups owing to past fracas, though *Trenant Steading* (Ⓣ01208/869091; closed Oct–Easter), between Polzeath and New Polzeath, currently admits small groups. All local sites are teeming in July and August, when booking is advised.

For **refreshments** and full **meals**, seek out *The Waterfront* (Ⓣ01208/869655; Oct–Easter closed Sun eve & Mon–Wed), a cheerful eatery behind the beach, with blue-washed walls, wooden tables and a first-floor terrace, offering snacks during the day and in the evening such starters as steamed mussels (£8), and mains including monkfish and prawn Thai curry, and trio of lamb (most dishes £17–18). The down-to-earth *Galleon Café* (closed eves & Nov–Feb), right by the beach, does a brisk trade in breakfasts, baguettes, all kinds of chips and baked potatoes. A few steps up the hill from here, the *Oyster Catcher* **pub** has a panoramic terrace that fills up with families during the day, and serves steaks and pub food; it gets fairly merry at night, too, with live bands most Saturday nights.

Port Isaac and around

Heading north from Polzeath, the **coastal path** brings you through cliff-top growths of feathery tamarisk, which flower spectacularly in July and August. From the headland of **Pentire Point**, views unfold for miles over the offshore islets of **The Mouls** and **Newland**, with their populations of grey seals and puffins. Half a mile east, the scanty remains of an Iron Age fort stand on the humpy back of **Rump's Point**, from where the path descends a mile or so to **Lundy Bay**, a pleasant sandy cove surrounded by green fields. Climbing again, you pass the shafts of an old antimony mine on the way to **Doyden Point**, which is picturesquely ornamented with a nineteenth-century castle folly once used for gambling parties. A mile east of Lundy Bay, the tiny inlet of **Port Quin** has a few placid cottages but no shops, the place having been abandoned in the nineteenth century when the antimony mine at nearby Doyden failed. The land is now managed by the National Trust who have maintained a tidy appearance. At low tide, you can poke around the patches of sand and the rock pools.

A couple of miles east of Port Quin and five miles east of Polzeath (connected by #584 bus), **PORT ISAAC** is wedged in a gap in the precipitous cliff wall. Only seasonal trippers ruffle the surface of life in this quiet and cramped harbour town which remains largely dedicated to the crab and lobster trade. It makes a lovely secluded spot to hole up for a few days, with granite, slate and whitewashed cottages tumbling down steeply to a largely unspoilt seafront, where a pebble beach and rock pools are exposed by the low tide and **fishing** and sightseeing **boat trips** along the coast are offered in summer. Half a mile further east from here, **Port Gaverne** (pronounced Gayverne) makes an easy expedition: a small cove with a pebble and sand beach and sheltered bathing, where you can also grab a bite to eat in the *Port Gaverne Hotel*.

From Whit Sunday until September, Port Isaac's local choir gathers at the harbour from 8pm on Fridays to regale listeners with shanties, and there's a brass band on Thursdays. On a more elevated note, a twice-yearly **classical music festival** is held at **St Endellion**, two miles south of the village (a week at Easter and ten days in July/Aug): see Ⓦwww.endellion.org.uk for information.

Practicalities

Bus #584 links Port Isaac with Wadebridge and Camelford (not Sun in winter), stopping at the top of the village. **Parking** is limited and the lanes are narrow, so drivers should deposit their vehicles in the car park at the top (there's also parking on the beach at low tide).

Both of the village's two main **hotels** enjoy terrific views: the *Slipway Hotel*, right on the harbour, with mainly modern, clean and comfortable rooms (Ⓣ01208/880264; Ⓦwww.portisaachotel.com; ❻), and the *Old School Hotel* (Ⓣ01208/880721, Ⓦwww.theoldschoolhotel.co.uk; ❻), looking down on the port from Fore Street, with exposed beams and slate walls in its schoolroom-themed rooms; check the rooms before booking in to either place, as some can be noisy and they're somewhat over-priced. Slightly cheaper places lie at the top of the village, for example opposite the car park on the Terrace, the *Bay Hotel* (Ⓣ01208/880380, Ⓦwww.bayhotelportisaac.co.uk; ❺), which has en-suite rooms with Victorian decor and lofty views, including two with spa baths, and there's a wood-burning stove in winter. Overlooking the harbour on its south side, right on the coast path (and accessible from the steep lane running past Port Isaac Pottery), *Hathaway*, a **B&B** on Roscarrock Hill, overlooks the harbour from its front-facing rooms, all of which have en-suite or private bathrooms, and there's also a self-catering flat (Ⓣ01208/880416, Ⓦwww.cornwall-online.co.uk/hathaway; closed Nov–Easter; no credit cards; ❺).

Seafood and specifically crab are Port Isaac's specialities, found in all the local **restaurants**. Sample it in the oak-beamed dining area of the *Slipway* or at the *Old School*, which also has a decked eating area; in both, main dishes cost around £16 in the evening, and booking is recommended. *The Harbour*, 1 Middle St (Ⓣ01208/880237; closed Sun, Mon & daytime, also Tues & Wed in winter and all Dec & Jan), is both quaint and chic, with pale-coloured walls and an inventive, Modern European menu strong on seafood (mains mostly £17–22). The nearby *Golden Lion* **pub**, with bare floorboards and nautical bits and pieces, offers a range of cheaper meals, excellent crab sandwiches and Sharp's, Doom Bar and HSD beers on tap.

At **Port Gaverne**, you can dine cheaply at the bar of the *Port Gaverne Hotel* on such dishes as Walker's Special – chips topped with cheese and fresh onion rings – or more expensively at the same hotel's restaurant, which specializes in fish and has three-course menus for £27 (booking advisable at ⓣ01208/880244). Pleasantly old-fashioned rooms are also available here (❼).

Tintagel and around

Seven miles northeast of Port Isaac, the village of **TINTAGEL** is a magnet for visitors throughout the region on account of its fabled **castle**, whose scanty ruins stand on an outcrop of the nearby coast. Apart from this and a medieval manor house restored by the National Trust, the village amounts to little more than a dreary collection of bungalows, guesthouses and souvenir shops milking the area's associations with King Arthur for all they're worth. It's worth running through this gauntlet for the main attraction, but don't bother to linger.

Arrival and information

Reached along inland lanes, Tintagel is linked by **bus** #594 with Camelford, Wadebridge and Boscastle (not Sun in winter). Buses stop on Bossiney Street, at the top of the main Fore Street and right by the **tourist office** (daily: March–Oct 10am–5pm; Nov–Feb 10.30am–4pm; ⓣ01840/779084, ⓦwww.visitboscastleandtintagel.com), where you can view illuminating panels on the area's history and (naturally) the Arthur saga, and buy leaflets on local **walks** (50p–£1). There's also **internet** access here (£1 for 15min).

Accommodation

Competition among Tintagel's numerous **accommodation** choices has kept prices – and charm factor – low. The best B&Bs are a few minutes' walk east from the centre, on or around Atlantic Road. You'll also find a useful **campsite** here, the *Headland*, which offers scenic but exposed pitches and clean facilities (ⓣ01840/770239, ⓦwww.headlandcaravanpark.co.uk; closed mid-Oct to Easter). Spectacularly sited on Glebe Cliff, three-quarters of a mile south of the village at Dunderhole Point, the offices of a former slate quarry now house a **youth hostel** with great views of the coastline (ⓣ0845/371 9345, ⓔtintagel@yha.org.uk; call for winter opening; from £12); self-catering only is available, and advance booking is essential. On foot, it's a mile outside the village.

The Avalon Atlantic Rd ⓣ01840/770116, ⓦwww.tintagelbedbreakfast.co.uk. Classy B&B in the centre of the village, with Gothic-style beds and Victorian fireplaces, but contemporary decor. Some rooms are small, but all are spotless and most have amazing views. Free wi-fi. Closed late Nov to early Feb. ❺

Bosayne Atlantic Rd ⓣ01840/770514, ⓦwww.bosayne.co.uk. At the far end of the village, but facing the ocean 300m in front, this solid Victorian house has pleasant, eco-aware owners and comfortable rooms enjoying sea views, with en-suite or shared bathrooms and mini-fridges. Breakfasts are mainly organic with home-made bread and cakes. Free wi-fi, a luggage transfer service and a self-catering cottage are all available. ❹

Michael House Trelake Lane, Trecknow ⓣ01840/770592, ⓦwww.michael-house.co.uk. This vegetarian and vegan B&B with good-size rooms stands a mile south of Tintagel and a fifteen-minute walk from Trebarwith Strand. Breakfasts are a highlight, and evening meals are available on request (£14.50 or £18.50 for two or three courses). Wi-fi access. ❸

Tregenna Lodge Castle Heights ⓣ01840/770264, ⓦwww.trevennalodge.com. In a quiet cul-de-sac near the village centre, this place has rooms with coastal views, comfy beds and good bathrooms (mostly en suite). There's a guests' lounge and free wi-fi, and luggage transfer and packed lunches are offered to walkers. ❺

The castle and village

Thankfully, none of the tourist palaver lessens the impact of the forsaken ruins of **Tintagel Castle** (daily: April–Sept 10am–6pm, Oct 10am–5pm, Nov–March 10am–4pm; £4.90; EH), magnificently sited on the black, rocky littoral a short walk west of Tintagel. Although the castle makes a plausibly resonant candidate for the abode of the "Once and Future King", it was in fact a Norman stronghold occupied by the earls of Cornwall, who after sporadic spurts of rebuilding allowed it to decay, most of it having washed into the sea by the sixteenth century. Much older remains are still to be seen, however – notably the ruin of a **Celtic monastery** that occupied this promontory in the sixth century, which has become an important source of information on the setup of the country's earliest monastic houses. Digs begun in 1998 on the eastern side of the island have also revealed glass fragments dating from the sixth or seventh century and believed to originate in Malaga, as well as a 1500-year-old section of slate bearing two Latin inscriptions, one of them attributing authorship to one

King Arthur in Cornwall

The big question about **King Arthur** has always been: "Did he really exist?" If he did, it is likely that he was an amalgam of two people, a sixth-century Celtic warlord who united local tribes against the invading Anglo-Saxons, and a Cornish saint. Whatever his origins, his role was recounted and inflated by poets and troubadours, particularly in Welsh poems, the earliest of which, *Gododdin*, is thought to date from the sixth century. The basic narrative of Arthur, Queen Guinevere and the knights of Camelot was later elaborated and augmented by the twelfth-century chroniclers **Geoffrey of Monmouth**, who first popularized the notion that Tintagel was Arthur's birthplace, and **William of Malmesbury**, who further embroidered the legend that, after being mortally wounded in battle, Arthur sailed to Avalon (thought to be Glastonbury, in Somerset, where the tombs of Arthur and Guinevere were "discovered" by Benedictine monks in the twelfth century). The Arthurian legends were crystallized in **Thomas Malory's** epic, *Morte d'Arthur* (1485), further romanticized in **Tennyson's** *Idylls of the King* (1859–85) and resurrected in **T.H. White's** saga, *The Once and Future King* (1937–58).

Although there are places throughout Britain and Europe that claim some association with Arthur, not least in Brittany and Wales, it is England's West Country, and **Cornwall** in particular, that has the greatest concentration of places boasting a link, and where the spirit of Arthur is said to be embodied in the Cornish chough – a bird now virtually extinct in Cornwall. The most famous Arthurian site is **Tintagel**, where today every kind of swords-and-sorcery hogwash is peddled, while nearby **Bodmin Moor** is full of places with names like "King Arthur's Bed" and "King Arthur's Downs". Camlann, the battlefield where Arthur was mortally wounded fighting against his nephew Mordred, is thought to lie on the northern reaches of the moor at **Slaughterbridge**, near Camelford (see p.363), which itself is sometimes identified as Camelot. Nearby, at **Dozmary Pool** (see p.360), the knight Bedivere was dispatched by the dying king to return the sword Excalibur to the mysterious hand emerging from the water – though **Loe Pool** in Mount's Bay also claims this honour (see p.260). According to some, Arthur's body was transported after the battle to **Boscastle** (see opposite), from where a funeral barge carried it to Avalon.

Cornwall is also the presumed home of **King Mark**, at the centre of a separate but later interwoven cycle of myths. It was Mark who sent the knight **Tristan** (or Tristram) to Ireland to fetch his betrothed, Iseult; Mark's palace is traditionally held to have been at **Castle Dore** near Fowey (see p.231). Out beyond Land's End, the fabled, vanished country of **Lyonnesse** is also said to be the original home of Arthur, as well as being (according to **Spenser's** *Faerie Queene*) the birthplace of Tristan.

"Artognou, father of Coll's descendant"; some people have taken this as a trace of Arthur's existence, though Artognou was quite a common name at that time. The slate is currently on display in Truro's museum (see p.242).

From the village, the shortest route to the castle is along a well-trodden signposted path, a ten-minute walk; alternatively, there's a Land Rover service from the end of Fore Street (Easter–Oct, or out of season call ⓣ01840/770060; £1.50 each way). The most evocative approach to the site, though, is from **Glebe Cliff** to the west (accessed off the B3263), where the Norman parish church of **St Materiana** sits in windswept isolation; the South West Coast Path passes close by, and out of season drivers can park here before descending to the castle (there are also numerous **car parks** in the village).

Back in the village, a couple of items on Fore Street present contrasting versions of the past. The **Old Post Office** (late Feb & Nov daily 11am–4pm; mid-March to Sept daily 11am–5.30pm; £3; NT) is a rickety-roofed, slate-built manor house from the fourteenth century, now restored and furnished with local oak pieces, though the original gallery can still be seen. One room, used in the Victorian era as a post office, preserves its appearance from that time. Note the huge buttresses propping up the building, visible from the garden. Further up the street, you can dip into the world of make-believe at **King Arthur's Great Halls** (daily: June–Oct 10am–5pm; Nov–May 11am–3pm; £4.50), created in the 1930s by Frederick Thomas Glassop, a wealthy London grocer, and now owned by the masons (who still meet here). The centrepiece of this earnest re-creation of King Arthur's court is a medieval-like chamber containing a grandiose throne, a round table and much other pseudo-twaddle, including 72 Pre-Raphaelite windows depicting the deeds of the knights. Call to check winter opening at ⓣ01840/770526.

South of Tintagel, the coast is wild and unspoiled, making for some steep and strenuous **walking**, well compensated by some stupendous sandy beaches en route, such as **Trebarwith Strand**, two miles down, with its beautiful rock formations. Reached by a passage through the rocks, the beach here is only accessible at low tide, and is lifeguarded during the summer months. Between half tide and low tide, Trebarwith becomes a magnet for **surfers**, rated as one of the finest beach breaks in the country, with the high surrounding cliffs providing a natural arena.

Eating and drinking

Tintagel has little in the way of quality **restaurants**. Opposite the tourist office on Bossiney Road, *Wyldes Café* (ⓣ01840/770007; closed Sun and eves Sat & Mon; no credit cards) has the best options, ranging from breakfasts, panini and pies to the local version of Mexican *quesadilla* (£5). In the evening, seafood and other dishes cost around £10. At the bottom of Fore Street, the *Olde Malt House* serves pub snacks as well as meat and fish dishes costing £9–15 and local beers. Almost next-door, Treleaven's sells lip-smacking **ice cream** (closed Mon–Thurs in winter), while, further up Fore Street, the *Village Tea Rooms* has tempting snacks, cakes and home-made lemonade during the day (closed Nov–Easter).

Boscastle

Compressed within a narrow ravine drilled through by the Jordan and Valency rivers, the tiny port of **BOSCASTLE**, three miles east of Tintagel, presents a tidy appearance, its riverbanks lined by thatched and lime-washed cottages. Few traces now remain of the destruction wreaked in 2004, when freak weather conditions created a powerful torrent that surged through the valley, sweeping away much of the orderly riverfront. Although the destruction was immense, the houses have been meticulously repaired or rebuilt, the harbour cleared of debris and Boscastle's picturesque setting restored.

The town grew up around twin settlements – at the harbour and around **Bottreaux Castle**, built in the twelfth century on a spur above the Jordan valley but now vanished (the site is below the Methodist chapel on Fore Street) – there's a model of its presumed appearance in the tourist office. The two parts are connected today by High Street at the top of the hill, which changes its name to Fore Street, Dunn Street and Old Road on the way down. The port's heyday was during the nineteenth century, when sailing vessels had to be "hobbled" (towed) through the twisty harbour entrance by boats manned by eight oarsmen, and centred in the channel by gangs of men pulling on ropes. Horses then hauled the goods, which came from as far afield as Canada, up Boscastle's steep inclines, bringing back in return slate, manganese and china clay for export. To take in the village and its various Thomas Hardy connections (see below), you can follow a **circular walk** that traces the valley of the River Valency for three miles or so to **St Juliot**, the church restored by Hardy when he was plying his trade as a young architect (drivers will find it signposted off the B3263). It's small and nondescript – Hardy later regretted his draconian restoration – and pretty much as he left it. The rectory where he stayed lies a quarter of a mile beyond the church, and is now a comfortable B&B (see opposite). You can pick up a leaflet describing the walk from the tourist office.

If you need a break from Hardy, check out the **Museum of Witchcraft**, down by the harbour (Easter–Oct Mon–Sat 10.30am–6pm, Sun 11.30am–6pm; £3), an intelligent, comprehensive and non-gimmicky account of witchcraft through the ages, displayed in themed galleries. Look out for the "dark mirrors" – which are supposed to see into the future – and "healing poppets" (dolls) used in cursing, with pubic hair and nail clippings sewn onto them. You can even listen to a rare recording of occultist Aleister Crowley intoning his poetry and excerpts from "The Gnostic Mass". There's little else of specific interest to see around the village, though in rough weather you could walk to the end of the harbour an hour either side of low tide to see the **Devil's Bellows** in action – a blowhole that shoots water across the harbour entrance.

Thomas Hardy in Boscastle

Why go to Saint-Juliot? What's Juliot to me?
Some strange necromancy
But charmed me to fancy
That much of my life claims the spot as its key.

A Dream or No (1913)

After eight years working as an architect in London, **Thomas Hardy** came to Boscastle in 1870 to restore the church of St Juliot. It was in the course of this work that he first met **Emma Gifford**, the sister-in-law of the rector, and after return visits he eventually married his "West of Wessex girl" in 1874. A year earlier he had published his third novel *A Pair of Blue Eyes*, which opens with an account of an architect arriving in a Cornish village to restore its church, and which is full of descriptions of the country around Boscastle. Although the marriage to Emma was highly strained, her death in 1912 inspired Hardy to return to the village and to write the bittersweet love lyrics recalling happier moments in their married life, published in *Poems 1912–1913*, which have been called amongst the most moving love poems in the language. In 1916, he erected a plaque to Emma's memory in St Juliot, still visible on the wall of the north aisle.

Practicalities

Boscastle's **tourist office** is situated at the harbour (daily: March–Oct 10am–5pm; Nov–Feb 10.30am–4pm; ⓣ01840/250010, ⓦwww.visitboscastleandtintagel.com). For Thomas Hardy fans, there's only one **place to stay** in the area: the *Old Rectory*, outside the village on the road to St Juliot, signposted from the B3263 northeast of Boscastle (ⓣ01840/250225, ⓦwww.stjuliot.com; no under-12s; closed Dec to mid-Feb; ❺), where you can sleep in Hardy's or Emma's bedroom, in the Rector's Room, or in a converted stables with a separate entrance – all en suite. There's fruit from the kitchen garden and fresh eggs for breakfast, evening barbecues and extensive grounds for roaming. A good alternative stands a ten-minute uphill walk from the harbour – but with a bus stop outside – *Boscastle House*, on Tintagel Road, offering spacious and elegant rooms, impressive breakfasts and a large garden with croquet (ⓣ01840/250654, ⓦwww.boscastlehouse.com; ❺). In a fabulous position overlooking the harbour, the whitewashed *Pencarmol*, above the youth hostel, has three cottagey, comfortable rooms, all en suite, with free wi-fi (ⓣ01840/250435, ⓦwww.pencarmol.co.uk; no credit cards; ❹). Advance reservations are recommended for all the above.

The harbour also has a beautifully positioned **youth hostel** (ⓣ0845/371 9006; call for winter opening); all beds, from £14, are in dormitories, and there's a self-catering kitchen but no parking. You'll find a couple of peaceful **campsites** at *Trebyla Farm* (ⓣ01840/250308, ⓦwww.boscastlecampsite.co.uk), close to the coast path and one and a half miles from Boscastle on the B3263 towards Bude (on the #595 bus route), and *Lower Pennycrocker* (ⓣ01840/250257, ⓦwww.pennycrocker.com; closed Oct–Easter), signposted two miles out of Boscastle on the same road, near St Juliot – both quite basic but cheap, friendly and with amazing sea views.

For **eating and drinking**, choose between a good selection of lively **pubs** that provide food and music nights as well as good ales. Of these, the beamed old *Napoleon* (ⓣ01840/250204) at the top of Fore Street has tankards hanging off the ceiling and offers such diversions as shove ha'penny and live music on Friday evenings; it also houses *Boney's Bistro* for fresh seafood dishes costing around £10. Down by the harbour, the busy *Cobweb* serves fresh bar food (including vegetarian) for £5–15 and has rock bands on Saturdays. Nearby, the *Wellington Hotel* has a beer garden and the smart *Waterloo* restaurant upstairs (ⓣ01840/250202; closed Thurs), where dishes of rabbit, duck and lamb cost £14. Next to the harbour, the saggy-roofed *Harbour Light* café is a pleasant spot for a snack, and dispenses superb local organic ice cream from its outlet across the river (closed Oct–Easter).

Bude and around

There is little distinctively Cornish in the seaside town of **BUDE**, just four miles from the Devon border. Built around the mouth of the River Neet and the parallel Bude Canal, the town is nonetheless one of Cornwall's premier holiday resorts, thanks to the broad sands on either side, much beloved of surfers. Smaller and quieter than Cornwall's other resorts, the town has not been unduly spoiled by its crop of holiday homes and hotels, and the magnificent cliffy coast surrounding it preserves a wild beauty.

Arrival and information

Bude's helpful **tourist office**, in the centre of town at the Crescent car park (April & May Mon–Sat 10am–5pm, Sun 10am–1pm; June–Sept Mon–Sat 10am–5pm, Sun 10am–4pm; Oct–March Mon–Fri 10am–4pm, Sat 10am–1pm;

Activities in and around Bude

Bude has a choice of **surfing** equipment rental outlets, including Zuma Jay on Belle Vue Lane. Surfing gear can also be rented from the car park of the *Bay View Inn* in Widemouth Bay and from the beach at Crackington Haven. There are numerous surf courses offered: Raven Surf School (ⓣ01288/353693, ⓦwww.ravensurf.co.uk) has one of the best. Boogie-boarding, **kayaking** and Canadian canoeing are available for half- or full-day sessions from Atlantic Pursuits (ⓣ01288/321765, ⓦwww.atlanticpursuits.co.uk), with full instruction and equipment included. Broomhill Manor Stables in Poughill (ⓣ0789/967 6746, ⓦwww.broomhillmanor.co.uk) provides **horseriding** for all ages and abilities (not Sat), including rides along the beach, while Efford Down Riding Stables on Vicarage Road (ⓣ01288/354244, ⓦwww.efforddown.co.uk) offers **pony treks** on weekdays (plus weekends during school hols) between Easter and October. **Bikes** can be rented from North Coast Cycles at 2 Summerleaze Ave, off Downs View (ⓣ01288/352974).

ⓣ01288/354240, ⓦwww.visitbude.info), can book rooms. Advance reservations are necessary in summer and during the biggest event of the year, the **Bude Jazz Festival**, which attracts a range of stomping sounds from around the world for a week in August/September (ⓣ01288/356360, ⓦwww.budejazzfestival.co.uk). You can log on to the **internet** at the tourist office (£1 for 15min).

Accommodation

Most of Bude's **hotels** are aligned close to the beaches and charge quite high rates in summer, with significant reductions out of season. There's a cluster of cheaper **B&Bs** along Downs View and Burn View, around the golf course, which are still quite central. There are numerous **campsites** around Bude.

Hotels and B&Bs

Bay View Inn Widemouth Bay ⓣ01288/361273, ⓦwww.bayviewinn.co.uk. A good choice if you want to be near Widemouth Beach, with clean and functional rooms, most with excellent views. The bar has real ales and there's a good restaurant serving everything from burgers and pies to steaks and seafood. ❺

Elements Widemouth Bay ⓣ01288/352005, ⓦwww.elements-life.co.uk. A wonderfully sited surf hotel less than two miles south of Bude, near Upton; there are facilities for surfers, including storage and drying rooms, courses and surf breaks, as well as health and fitness rooms. Rooms have TVs, music and games consoles, and there's a good café/restaurant. ❻

Falcon Hotel Breakwater Rd ⓣ01288/352005, ⓦwww.falconhotel.com. Within sight of the tourist office, this turreted, white pile claims to be the oldest coaching house in North Cornwall. Rooms are smart, though old-fashioned, and have great views, and there's a garden, bar and restaurant. Tennyson broke his leg while staying here in 1848. ❼

Palms 17 Burn View ⓣ01288/353962, ⓦwww.palms-bude.co.uk. The best of a tidy row of terraced B&Bs near the centre and south of the golf course, with simple but comfortable rooms with en-suite bathrooms, and free parking. No credit cards. ❸

Stratton Gardens Hotel Cot Hill, Stratton ⓣ01288/352500, ⓦwww.stratton-gardens.co.uk. A mile inland from Bude, this small, whitewashed, sixteenth-century building provides all the comforts, including some four-poster beds. It also has a great restaurant. ❺

Campsites and hostel

Efford Down Vicarage Rd ⓣ01288/354244, ⓦwww.efforddown.co.uk. Just a few minutes' walk south of the tourist office, with basic facilities, and only open for four weeks in Aug–Sept.

North Shore 57 Killerton Rd ⓣ01288/354256 or 0797/014 9486, ⓦwww.northshorebude.com. Friendly backpackers' hostel not far from the beaches, with a large garden including a barbecue area, internet access and free tea and coffee. Bunkrooms have 4–6 beds and cost £16–18 in high season, and there are three double rooms with shared bathrooms (❷).

Upper Lynstone Caravan and Camping Park ⓣ01288/352017, ⓦwww.upperlynstone.co.uk. Three-quarters of a mile from the centre on the coastal road to Widemouth Bay, this family-run site is friendly and well managed, with a children's play area, but can be exposed and some pitches aren't level. No groups. Closed Nov–Easter.

Wooda Park Poughill (pronounced "Poffil") ⓣ01288/352069, ⓦwww.wooda.co.uk. Two miles north of Bude, this tidy, well-equipped site lies away from the sea but with grand views of it, and a short stroll away from a good village pub. Spacious pitches, clean facilities and wi-fi connection. Closed Nov–March.

The Town

Apart from the **sea**, Bude has little in the way of specific attractions, but it's worth setting aside some time to visit the battlemented **Bude Castle**, prominently sited at the confluence of the River Neet and Bude Canal, behind Summerleaze Beach. The "castle" dates from 1850, built by local inventor and philanthropist **Sir Goldsworthy Gurney**, apparently in order to prove that it was possible to build a house on sand – albeit on concrete rafts. Gurney himself (1793–1875) was one of a noble Cornish line of eccentric scientific geniuses, credited with inventing a steam jet, an oxyhydrogen blowpipe and a bizarre musical instrument consisting of glasses played as a piano. He's probably best known, though for improving the lighting in the House of Commons by replacing the 280 candles with three "Bude Lights" of his own invention, used for sixty years until the arrival of electricity. He adapted his light – which shone extra brightly by means of oxygen injected into the flame – for use in lighthouses by placing it in a revolving frame. Each lighthouse had its own sequence of flashes – a principle still in use today. Gurney's former home now holds the **Castle Heritage Centre and Gallery** (daily: Easter–Oct 10am–5pm; Nov–Easter 11am–4pm; last entry 1hr before closing; £3.50), whose overview of Bude's history includes figureheads retrieved from local wrecks, displays of the area's geological make-up and a section on Gurney himself. His major invention is commemorated in front of the castle by the **Bude Light**, a tall, stripy cone that comes into its own at night, when a system of fibre optics lights it and the surrounding Zodiac circle on the ground in a pattern of constellations.

The museum also holds exhibits relating to the **Bude Canal**, which was dug in 1825 to transport lime-rich sand and seaweed inland for improving North Cornwall's acid soil, and slate and granite for export. The recently restored waterway provides an excellent delightful towpath walk, with rare species of flora and fauna to look out for – pick up a leaflet at the tourist office, located adjacent to the canal.

The beaches

Of the excellent **beaches** hereabouts, the central **Summerleaze** is sandy and wide, growing to such immense proportions when the tide is out that a sea-water swimming pool has been installed near the cliffs – the best place for kids to swim as local sewage discharge makes sea-swimming dubious. Two and a half miles south of Bude, the mile-long **Widemouth Bay** (pronounced "Widmouth") is the main focus of the holiday hordes, backed by a straggle of white bungalows, though bathing can be dangerous near the rocks at low tide. Surfers congregate five miles south down the coast at **Crackington Haven**, wonderfully situated between 130m crags at the mouth of a lush valley. The cliffs on this stretch include Cornwall's highest (High Cliff, 210m/700ft) and are characterized by remarkable zigzagging strata of shale, limestone and sandstone, a mixture which erodes into detached formations, vividly contorted.

North of Bude, just beyond Summerleaze Beach, the classic breaks at acres-wide **Crooklets** have made it the scene of surfing and lifesaving demonstrations and competitions in summer. A couple of miles further on, beyond the signposted *Atlantic Hills Caravan Park*, **Sandy Mouth** is a pristine expanse of sand with rock pools beneath encircling cliffs, but it's mainly rocky at high tide. Surfers prefer the tiny sandy cove of **Duckpool**, less than a mile north, flanked by jagged reefs at low tide and dominated by the three-hundred-foot promontory of **Steeple Point**. The beach lies at the mouth of a stream that flows through the **Coombe Valley**, once the estate of the Elizabethan master mariner Sir Richard Grenville, and now managed by the National Trust.

Eating and drinking

Though not over-burdened with good **restaurants**, Bude has a couple of outstanding choices, as well as a plethora of **pubs** and fast-food joints. A mile and a half inland from Bude, the village of **Stratton** offers further good possibilities, worth striking out for.

Atlantic Diner 5–7 Belle Vue ⓣ01288/354167. A good town-centre choice, popular with shoppers and surfers alike for its burgers, steaks, curries and ice creams, with most dishes under £10. Closed Sun eve & Mon, also eves Tues–Thurs in winter. No credit cards.

Bencoolen Inn Bencoolen Rd ⓣ01288/354694. Real ales and a patio make this a good spot for a pint. You can eat Spanish in the adjoining *El Barco* restaurant (eves only), where main courses cost £12–19.

The Castle The Wharf ⓣ01288/350543. Smart, modern dining is available within Gurney's old home, either an express lunch (£12.50 for 2 courses or £15 for 3) or a less casual evening meal, when there's a short menu of seafood, steaks and curries at around £16 for mains, and a wider-ranging seven-course tasting menu for £37. Lovely views.

Coombe Barton Inn Crackington Haven ⓣ01840/230345. Chargrilled steaks, fresh fish (£8–15), a Sunday carvery (£9) and a wide range of Cornish ales are served right next to the beach, with great views.

Life's a Beach Summerleaze Beach ⓣ01288/355222. Injecting a much-needed shot of style to Bude, this place right on the sand beats all the competition for style, location and cuisine. It's a café by day, offering baguettes, bruschettas and burgers for under £7, and a romantic bistro in the evening, when fish dishes feature on the menu at around £17. Check winter opening, which is weather-dependent, and book anyway for the evening. Closed Sun eve, also winter Mon–Wed.

Tree Inn Fore St, Stratton ⓣ01288/352038. Thirteenth-century pub with a selection of ales, bar meals (including good vegetarian dishes) and fuller meals in the beamed *Galleon* restaurant, where there's a carvery on Sundays (£8.50); there's courtyard seating for fine weather. The building was used as the Royalist headquarters during the Battle of Stamford Hill in 1643 – an engagement re-enacted annually on the nearest weekend to May 16 – and was also the home of the "Cornish Giant" Anthony Payne, manservant of Lord Grenville, who commanded the king's forces at their victory.

Morwenstow

Tucked into Cornwall's northwest tip, seven miles due north of Bude and just two miles south of the Devon border, **MORWENSTOW** has an appealing end-of-the-world feel to it. Surrounded by windswept cliffs and fields, this isolated hamlet is best known for its colourful opium-smoking poet-vicar **Robert Hawker**, credited with introducing to England the custom of the **Harvest Festival** in 1843. You'll find his church of **St John the Baptist** nestling in a wooded coombe to the right of where the road through the village peters out. In the graveyard, look out for the white figurehead of the *Caledonia* which serves as a gravestone for its wrecked captain. Numbering a good proportion of smugglers, wreckers and dissenters among his parishioners, Hawker insisted on giving shipwrecked sailors a churchyard rather than a traditional beachside burial, with the result that forty mariners now repose here. If the state of decomposition of the corpse was far advanced, he would encourage his gravediggers with liberal doses of gin. Inside the church are some impressive Norman arches carved with bearded men, menacing bird-like creatures and what is reckoned to be a hippopotamus, and a wonky tub font that's the oldest of its type in the country. Below the church, Hawker's vicarage sports a diversity of chimneys in imitation of various church towers known and loved by him.

Hawker's tiny **driftwood hut** (always accessible; free; NT) complete with stable door, lies embedded in the cliffs, down steep steps, 400m along a footpath from the end of the road. Opposite the church, the *Rectory Tea Rooms* (Easter–Oct daily 11am–5pm) is a handy spot for a tea, on stone flags and high-backed settles inside, or in the garden when it's hot. Soups, quiches and other snacks sourced from the organic garden are also available. For **a hack** in the area, a range of horses and ponies are available at Gooseham Barton Stables (ⓣ01288/331204; ⓦwww.gooseham-barton.com; £13 for 30min), two miles east of Morwenstow, signposted from the A39, where you can learn to ride "Western-style". Self-catering cottages are also offered here.

The rugged coast on either side of Morwenstow makes for strenuous but exhilarating **walking**. Immediately to the north of the village, **Henna Cliff** has, at 137m/450ft, the highest sheer drop of any sea-cliff in England after Beachy Head, and affords magnificent views along the coast and beyond Lundy to Wales.

Travel details

Trains

Newquay to: Par (Mon–Sat 5–7 daily, Sun mid-June to mid-Sept 5 daily; 50min–1hr 10min).

Buses

Boscastle to: Bude (Mon–Sat 6 daily, also April–Oct Sun 4 daily; 35min); Tintagel (Mon–Sat hourly, also April–Oct Sun 4 daily; 10min).
Bude to: Boscastle (Mon–Sat 6 daily, also April–Oct Sun 4 daily; 40min); Exeter (Mon–Sat 5–6 daily, Sun 2 daily; 1hr 50min–2hr 10min); Morwenstow (Mon–Sat 3 daily; 20min).
Morwenstow to: Bude (Mon–Sat 3 daily; 20min).
Newquay to: Padstow (Mon–Sat hourly, Sun 1–5 daily; 1hr 25min); Perranporth (1–2 hourly; 20–50min); Portreath (April–Oct Sun–Fri 2 daily; 1hr–1hr 15min); St Austell (Mon–Sat hourly, Sun 5 daily; 55min); Truro (Mon–Sat 5–6 hourly, Sun 1–2 hourly; 50min–1hr 45min).
Padstow to: Bodmin (Mon–Sat hourly, Sun 6 daily; 55min); Newquay (Mon–Sat hourly, Sun 1–4 daily; 1hr 20min); Wadebridge (Mon–Sat hourly, Sun 5–6 daily; 20min).
Perranporth to: Newquay (1–2 hourly; 25–55min); St Agnes (Mon–Sat 1–2 hourly, Sun 2–4 daily; 10min).
Polzeath to: Port Isaac (Mon–Sat 5 daily, also April–Oct Sun 4 daily; 20min); Wadebridge (7 daily, also April–Oct Sun 4 daily; 25min).
Port Isaac to: Polzeath (Mon–Sat 7 daily, also April–Oct Sun 4 daily; 20min); Wadebridge (Mon–Sat 7 daily, also April–Oct Sun 4 daily; 45min).
Portreath to: Newquay (April–Oct Sun–Fri 2 daily; 1hr); Redruth (Mon–Sat hourly; 25min); St Ives (April–Oct Sun–Fri 2–4 daily; 45min).
Redruth to: Falmouth (Mon–Sat hourly, Sun 5 daily; 40min); Portreath (Mon–Sat hourly; 25min); St Agnes (Mon–Sat 6 daily; 35min); Truro (Mon–Sat 8 hourly, Sun hourly; 30–50min).
St Agnes to: Perranporth (Mon–Sat 1–2 hourly, Sun 2–4 daily; 10min); Redruth (Mon–Sat 6 daily; 35min); Truro (Mon–Sat 2 hourly, Sun 6 daily; 40min).
Tintagel to: Boscastle (Mon–Sat hourly, also April–Oct Sun 5 daily; 10min); Camelford (Mon–Sat hourly, also April–Oct Sun 4 daily; 15min).
Wadebridge to: Bodmin (Mon–Sat hourly, Sun 6 daily; 45min); Padstow (Mon–Sat hourly,

Sun 5–6 daily; 25min); Polzeath (Mon–Sat 5 daily, also April–Oct Sun 4 daily; 20min); Port Isaac (Mon–Sat 5 daily, also April–Oct Sun 4 daily; 40min).

Flights

Newquay to: Belfast (late May to early Sept 2 weekly; 1hr 10min); 4 weekly; 1hr 15min); Birmingham (late May to late Sept 4 weekly; 1hr 15min); Bristol (1–2 daily; 40min); Cork, Ireland (3–4 weekly; 1hr); Dublin, Ireland (4–7 weekly; 1hr 5min); Edinburgh (April to late Oct 2–5 weekly; 1hr 40min); Glasgow (6–7 weekly; 1hr 45min); London City (Mon–Fri & Sun 1–2 daily; 1hr 45min); London Gatwick (4 daily; 1hr 10min); London Stansted (April to late Oct 1 daily; 1hr 5min); Leeds Bradford (Mon–Fri 1 daily; 2hr 5min); Manchester (6–7 weekly; 1hr 15min); St Brieuc, France (early May to late Sept 2 weekly; 1hr 20min); St Mary's, Isles of Scilly (Mon–Sat: April–Sept 3–4 daily; Oct–March 1–2 daily; 30min).

12

Bodmin and Bodmin Moor

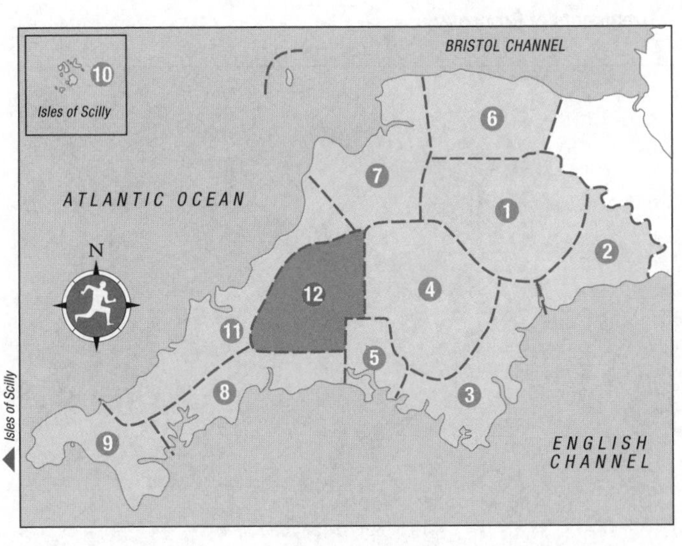

CHAPTER 12

Highlights

* **Lanhydrock** One of the country's most fascinating and complete nineteenth-century stately homes, stuffed with art and antiques, and surrounded by glorious grounds bordering the River Fowey. See p.357

* **The hike to Rough Tor and Brown Willy** A not excessively demanding walk, taking you to the highest points of the moor, with the remnants of Bronze Age settlements along the way. See p.362

* **St Neot church** This fifteenth-century church, in one of the moor's prettiest villages, has a stunning collection of stained glass. See p.364

* **Trethevy Quoit** Looming over the moor, Cornwall's most striking example of this type of prehistoric tomb. See p.365

▲ St Neot

12

Bodmin and Bodmin Moor

Just ten miles in diameter and effectively bound in by a quartet of rivers – the Fowey, Lynher, Camel and De Lank – Bodmin Moor is the smallest, mildest and most accessible of the West Country's great moors, its highest tor rising to just 1375ft from a platform of 1000ft. Though bisected by the main A30, the moor's bare, desolate appearance conveys a sense of loneliness quite out of proportion to its size, its emptiness only accentuated by the scattered relics left behind by its Bronze Age population. Like Exmoor and Dartmoor, the moor also has a small population of wild ponies, though its most celebrated animal occupant – if it exists at all – is the Beast of Bodmin (see box, p.358), whose phantom presence might add some frisson to your ramblings.

This miniature wilderness is best experienced away from the roads. Having parked your vehicle at one of the numerous parking places, you can sally forth – armed with a good map (Ordnance Survey *Explorer* OL109 takes in the whole moor at a scale of 1:25,000) – on tracks across the moorland. The highest tors lie to the west of the A30 and can easily be reached from **Bolventor** at the centre of the moor, an area steeped in both literary and Arthurian associations, not least in nearby **Dozmary Pool**. The southeastern moor holds some of Cornwall's most important prehistoric sites, including **The Hurlers** and **Trethevy Quoit**, while some of the region's finest examples of fifteenth-century church art can be seen nearby in the attractive village of **St Neot**, which makes the best base for the southern reaches of the moor. Other good bases on the perimeter include **Blisland**, on the western fringe, and **Altarnun** on the northeastern edge, while up near the Devon border, **Launceston** is an unsung off-moor town with a better choice of food and accommodation, and has plenty of historical atmosphere.

The town of **Bodmin** itself lies to the west of the moor, and, with the widest range of accommodation in the area, makes the most viable base for excursions. In addition it has some local sights worth catching, including the notorious Bodmin Jail and, just outside town, a pair of impressive country piles, most notably **Lanhydrock**, one of the West Country's grandest mansions. Along with the unexceptional town of **Liskeard**, thirteen miles to the east, Bodmin is the main **public transport** junction for the moor – both are stops on the main train route to Penzance. Bodmin is linked to St Austell on bus #529, to Liskeard on #593 (not Sun) and National Express coaches, and to Padstow and Wadebridge

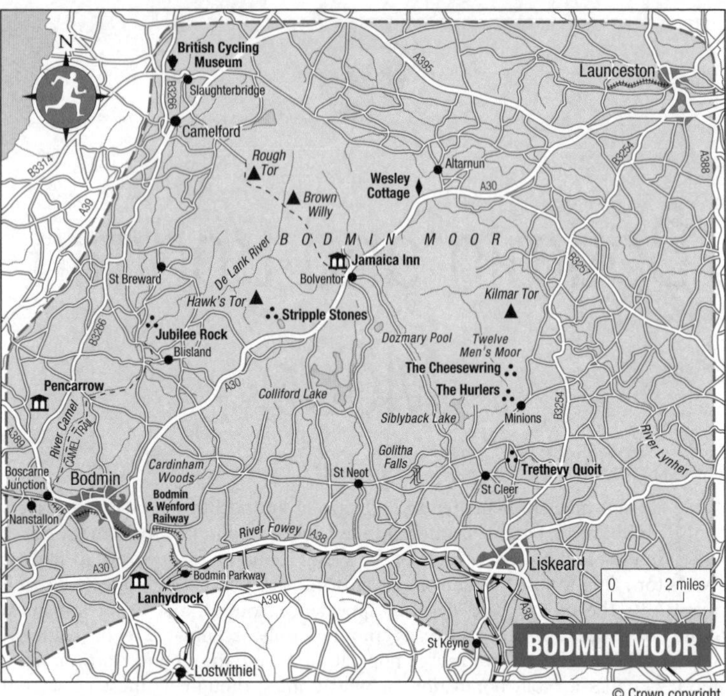

on bus #555. Liskeard is connected to Looe (see p.224) by bus #573 and by hourly branch-line trains (not Sun in winter). Bus links to smaller centres are more sporadic, however. From Launceston, Group Travel operates service #225 three times daily on weekdays to Altarnun, and Western Greyhound #510 runs to Camelford and Okehampton three times daily (once on Sun). Group Travel's bus #236 runs three or four times daily on weekdays between Liskeard and Launceston, stopping at Upton Cross, close to Minions; Western Greyhound's #574 from Liskeard (not Sun) stops at Darite and St Cleer. In addition to these services, you can reach many of the moorland villages, including Blisland and St Breward, by using **Corlink**, a dial-up minibus service that covers the Bodmin, Wadebridge and Camelford areas along predefined routes, operating Monday to Saturday between 7am and 7pm; book your journey at least one hour in advance at ⓣ0845/850 5556 (Mon–Sat 8am–5pm).

For general information on the moor, check out the **websites** ⓦwww.bobm.info, which has a range of accommodation as well as details of villages and local attractions, and ⓦwww.bodminmoor.co.uk, a very informative site with lots of background and practical tips.

Bodmin and around

The no-nonsense town of **BODMIN**, the largest of those on the moor's edge, lies two or three miles west of Bodmin Moor proper, equidistant from the north and south Cornish coasts and close to both the Fowey and Camel rivers. This central position encouraged Bodmin's growth as a trading town; it also became an important ecclesiastical centre with the establishment of a priory by Saint Petroc after he moved here from Padstow in the sixth century. Bodmin became Cornwall's county town in 1835, but sacrificed much of its administrative role by refusing land for the Great Western Railway in the 1870s, resulting in many local businesses transferring down the road to Truro.

Arrival and information

Bodmin Parkway **train station** lies three and a half miles southeast of town, with a regular bus connection (#555) to the centre. The same **bus** provides access to the town from Padstow and Wadebridge. The main **bus stop** is located on Mount Folly, close to the tourist office and the shopping area. From Penzance or Plymouth it's easiest to take National Express coaches, which call at Bodmin five times a day, stopping at Priory Road, just off Mount Folly coming from the east, or at nearby Dennison Road from the west. Bodmin's on-the-ball **tourist office** (April–Oct Mon–Sat 10am–5pm; Nov–March Mon–Fri 10am–5pm; Ⓣ01208/76616, Ⓦwww.bodminlive.com), located in Shire Hall, Mount Folly, can supply **information** on all parts of the moor, including walks, rides, transport and accommodation (which it can book for a £3 charge). You can also buy National Express tickets here. For **internet** access, head to the library on Lower Bore Street, at the end of Fore Street (Mon–Wed & Fri 9.30am–6pm, Sat 9.30am–12.30pm). **Rent bikes** from Bodmin Bikes & Cycle Hire at 3 Hamley Court, off Dennison Road (£12 per day).

Accommodation

There are some outstanding **accommodation** options in and around Bodmin, and central **camping** at the *Camping and Caravanning Club Site*, on Old Callywith Road, a fifteen-minute walk north of the centre from Castle Street, which starts behind St Petroc's Church (Ⓣ01208/73834; closed Nov–March); pitches are sheltered but some are slightly sloping.

B&Bs

Bedknobs Polgwyn, Castle St Ⓣ01208/77553, Ⓦwww.bedknobs.co.uk. Victorian villa in an acre of wooded garden with quietly luxurious accommodation in three spacious rooms, the priciest with its own en-suite spa bath and the cheapest with a separate bathroom that includes a spa bath. Friendly, eco-aware hosts and lots of extras. Free wi-fi. No under-12s. ❺

Bokiddick Farm Near Lanivet Ⓣ01208/831481, Ⓦwww.bokiddickfarm.co.uk. Five miles south of town, two miles outside Lanivet and close to the Lanhydrock estate, this large working farm boasts fantastic views from the conservatory/breakfast room. Rooms are in the farmhouse or a converted barn (worth the extra), and there's also self-catering. ❺

Priory Cottage 34 Rhind St Ⓣ01208/73064. Dating from the seventeenth century and lattice-windowed, this quiet place with two en-suite rooms is surrounded by gardens and conveniently sited near St Petroc's Church. No credit cards. ❹

Roscrea 18 St Nicholas Rd Ⓣ01208/74400, Ⓦwww.roscrea.co.uk. Central and friendly B&B with tastefully decorated Victorian rooms. Breakfasts include eggs laid in the garden, and you can request a great two-course dinner for £18.50 – a good option in Bodmin. No credit cards. ❺

The Town

Bodmin's central square, **Mount Folly**, stands at the junction of the main Fore and St Nicholas streets (B3268). Next to the tourist office here, **Bodmin Museum** (Easter–Sept Mon–Fri 10.30am–4.30pm, Sat 10.30am–2.30pm; Oct Mon–Sat 10.30am–2.30pm; free) is worth a quick whizz round for a low-key introduction to the town. The overview of local history is illustrated with features on various local worthies, and the collection includes such miscellany as a sixteenth-century granite font later used as a corn measure, the town's first ramshackle fire engine dating to the late eighteenth century, blue Cornish bardic robes from the 1980s and a stuffed chough. More theatrical is the adjacent **Courtroom Experience** (Easter–Oct Mon–Sat 11am–5pm; Nov–Easter Mon–Fri 11am–5pm; last tour at 4pm; £3.75), housed in the Georgian Shire Hall – formerly the assize court and now part-occupied by the tourist office. The hour-long tour includes a re-enactment, using film and moving waxworks, of the trial of Matthew Weeks, controversially indicted for the murder of Charlotte Dymond on Bodmin Moor in 1844, a verdict which was widely questioned at the time – visitors are invited to cast their own vote at the end of the show. You can also visit the holding cells below the courtroom, their ambience enhanced by such refinements as the rancid smell of urine.

From Mount Folly, descend Turf Road to reach Priory Road (A389), dominated by the granite hulk of **St Petroc** (April–Sept Mon–Fri 11am–3pm; at other times, ask at the rectory next door or call ⓣ01208/73867), Cornwall's largest church. Mainly fifteenth-century but with its Perpendicular windows restored in the nineteenth century, its interior reveals a typical Cornish wagon roof embellished with fine bosses and, in a glass case embedded in the south wall, an ivory casket that once held the bones of Petroc (now lost). Between the chancel and the north chapel is the **Vyvian tomb**, a powerful recumbent effigy of one of the last priors of the abbey carved from black Catacleuse stone. The most striking item here, though, is the formidable **Norman font** near the entrance, its base resting on one column and its bowl, encrusted with fearsome beasts and deeply carved with interlacing trees of life, supported by four others and topped by impassive angels.

West of the church on Berrycombe Road, on the northern outskirts of town, **Bodmin Jail** (daily 10am–dusk; £5.50) is menacingly redolent of the executions that were once guaranteed to pull the crowds, for which special trains were hired. After 1862 the hangings continued behind closed doors until the jail's closure in 1909. You can explore parts of the original eighteenth-century structure, including the condemned cell, all now considerably run-down and gloomily eerie. Pinned up on the cell walls, the stories of the inmates incarcerated for such crimes as stealing milk from a cow recount a far more telling story than the bedraggled dummies which re-enact their foul deeds. There's also an atmospheric bar/restaurant here.

The area's most prominent landmark is the **Gilbert Memorial**, a 144-foot obelisk occupying a commanding location on Bodmin Beacon, a high area of moorland south of the town centre. The monument honours Sir Walter Raleigh Gilbert (1785–1853), a descendant of Walter Raleigh, who distinguished himself as a general in the Bengal army – you'll find more about him in the town museum. The all-round views from here are stupendous.

Eating and drinking

Bodmin has a poor selection of places to **eat** though you can do a lot worse than the panini, pizzas and wholesome veggie dishes served during the day at the *Bara Café*, in the shopping precinct across from St Petroc's at 14 Honey St (closed Sun except during school summer holidays). The restaurant in Bodmin Jail (see above) makes an excellent stop for lunch, cream tea or full dinner (mains £10–15). Near the top of Fore Street, *Chapel an Gansblydhen*, a former Methodist chapel from 1840, is now a Wetherspoons **pub**, with tables outside and cheap food and beer all day. At the opposite end of the virtuous scale, the Hole in the Wall **pub** in Crockwell Street, off Fore Street, was originally a debtors' prison, the exposed fourteenth-century walls now enclosing a collection of antiquities and bric-a-brac. You can snack at lunchtime and sip Doom Bar bitter in the back-room bar, or in the courtyard in summer, and there's **live music** on alternate Saturday evenings.

Around Bodmin

There are several easy excursions you can make from Bodmin without a car. Further up from Bodmin Jail, Berrycombe Road holds a section of the **Camel Trail**, linking the town by a one-and-a-half-mile cycleway and footpath to the main route along the River Camel, a mile northwest (see box, p.337). In summer, you can also approach the Camel Trail on steam locomotives of the **Bodmin & Wenford Railway** (June–Sept 2–4 daily; sporadic services April, May, Oct & Dec; £9 return, or £11 for All Day Rover ⓣ0845/125 9678, ⓦwww.bodminandwenfordrailway.co.uk), which run to Boscarne Junction, right next to the trail, in fifteen minutes from the renovated Bodmin General station. The latter, situated a few minutes' walk south of the centre on the Lostwithiel road, formerly served trains of the Great Western Railway and now offers train buffs the chance to watch the locomotives being restored in the Engine Shed.

The same line from Bodmin General station goes in the opposite direction to Bodmin Parkway (20 minutes), for connections with main-line trains and for the footpath to Lanhydrock (see below). Halfway along this line, there's a stop at Colesloggett Halt – from here a half-mile path takes you to the nature trails and cycle tracks of **Cardinham Woods**, a mixed-forest plantation where Douglas fir is grown for the timber industry. It's a lovely spot for a ramble, with waymarked trails and other paths winding through ravines and alongside small streams that run down to the main river, Cardinham Water, where there's a small clapper bridge. Deer roam the woods, buzzards wheel overhead, and if you're lucky you may catch sight of an otter.

From Parkway train station, it's less than two miles' walk westwards along a signposted path to one of Cornwall's most absorbing country houses, **Lanhydrock** (house: March & Oct Tues–Sun 11am–5pm; April–Sept Tues–Sun 11am–5.30pm; garden: daily 10am–6pm; house & grounds £9.45; grounds only £5.30; NT) – and National Cycle Route 3 passes right outside (cyclists get discounted entry). Entered through an imposing pinnacled gatehouse, Lanhydrock was originally constructed in the seventeenth century, but was totally rebuilt after a disastrous fire in 1881. The granite exterior remains true to its original form but, apart from the north wing, containing the long picture gallery with its remarkable barrel-vaulted plaster ceiling depicting 24 Old Testament scenes, it's all High Victorian in tone. You're free to wander around the fifty rooms at will (guidebooks cost £5, or there's a leaflet that gives a brief summary for £1), where the grand style in which the local Robartes family lived is best illustrated by the quantities of equipment in the nurseries, luggage room, linen lobby and livery room. Most illuminating of all is the kitchen, built in the style of a college hall with clerestory windows, and supplemented by an unending series of dairies, sculleries, larders and pantries, with a spit large enough to roast an entire cow. The small museum in the north wing shows sundry photographs and letters relating to the family, and the thousand acres of wooded parkland bordering onto the River Fowey is worth a prolonged wander, especially in spring for the spectacular beds of magnolias, azaleas and rhododendrons. A leaflet (£1) available at the ticket desk details the choice of walks you can take.

In the opposite direction to Lanhydrock, four and a half miles north of Bodmin, the mile-long drive at **Pencarrow** (house: April–Sept Mon–Thurs & Sun 11am–5pm, last tour 3pm; gardens: March–Oct daily 9.30am–5.30pm; £8.50, gardens only £4; ⓦwww.pencarrow.co.uk) might suggest something on the same scale, but this country house has a very different, more intimate feel.

The Beast of Bodmin Moor

Of all the many myths and strange stories spawned on the moor, one of the most enduring has been that of the **Beast of Bodmin Moor**. Moorland farmers were the first to raise the issue of this phantom mauler of their livestock in the 1980s, and there have been around sixty big-cat sightings recorded in the area since then, as well as six-inch paw prints and cat droppings. Although an official investigation in 1995 could not confirm the existence of the so-called beast, some persuasive evidence emerged afterwards: a photograph taken in the St Austell area in 1997 apparently showing two creatures, one an adult female puma, possibly pregnant – or anyway looking "very fat, fit and contented" in the words of the curator of Newquay Zoo – and measuring about two and a half feet tall, the other possibly a cub; and a twenty-second video taken the following year that seemed to show a sleek, black animal about three- and- a- half feet long. These two findings prompted a systematic trawl of the moor by RAF reserve volunteers in 1999, using state-of-the-art night vision and seismic equipment, but again they failed to unearth any positive proof. All the same, farmers have continued to lose sheep to what they maintain to be a large, savage creature, and there has been ongoing pressure to persuade the government to reopen the inquiry.

The farmers do not entirely lack support within the scientific community, however. Some scientists believe the moor could well be home to a species of wild cat thought to have become extinct, though others maintain that the mysterious beasts sighted in various parts of the country are probably escaped or abandoned exotic pets. The puma is the most popular candidate, while the lynx, which would be well suited to the often cold British weather, also has a strong claim, and it is even possible that jaguars could live in the wild in the British Isles (black-coloured varieties exist). Most likely of all, however, is that any big cat on the moor would be a hybrid – the result of different species crossbreeding. Such an animal could easily survive on a diet of rabbits and other mammals and would only attack sheep or other stock in extreme desperation. To date nobody has ever been attacked by a large cat on Bodmin Moor, but if you chance to encounter one, your best bet is to walk nonchalantly by – but not before taking a precious photograph of the fabulous beast.

The Georgian building was begun by Sir John Molesworth, co-founder in 1771 of the banking house that was the forerunner of Lloyds Bank. A portrait of him by Joshua Reynolds is one of many paintings on display here. The present scions of the family have stamped their personality by jauntily placing hats on the busts of the various worthies, though the exquisite carpets and furnishings are what make the deepest impression. A guided tour gives you the lowdown on the family's history and points out such items as the piano on which Sir Arthur Sullivan, a guest here in 1882, composed much of the music for *Iolanthe*. Again, leave time to explore the beautiful wooded grounds.

Three miles northwest of Bodmin, signposted off the A389 Wadebridge road, the **Camel Valley Vineyard** (Ⓣ01208/77959, Ⓦwww.camelvalley.com) produces of some of the region's finest white wines. You can **tour** the vineyard (April–Sept Mon–Fri 2.30pm; £5; also Easter–Oct Wed 5pm plus Thurs in Aug 5pm; £7.50), ending with a tasting, or just stop to purchase a bottle or crate.

Blisland

Three miles northeast of Bodmin, **BLISLAND**, tucked into the Camel valley on the western slopes of Bodmin Moor, is mostly interesting for its Norman **church** among the Georgian and Victorian houses scattered around the village green. It has the distinction of being the only one in England dedicated to **St Protus and St Hyacinth**, brothers who were martyred in the third century. Sensitively restored at the end of the nineteenth century, the church has a seventeenth-century carved pulpit and a startlingly colourful Victorian Gothic rood screen, while overhead, the beams of the wagon roof are as wildly wonky as the columns in the nave.

You can make an easy and rewarding ramble less than half a mile north of the village to the gigantic **Jubilee Rock** on Pendrift Common, reached along a signposted and well-trodden path across the moor. The rock is inscribed with various patriotic insignia commemorating the 1809 jubilee of George III's coronation, but the view is the main attraction from this seven-hundred-foot vantage point, looking eastward over the De Lank gorge and the boulder-crowned knoll of **Hawk's Tor**, three miles away. On the shoulder of the tor stand the neolithic **Stripple Stones**, a circular platform once holding 28 standing stones, of which just four are still upright. Blisland also lies less than a mile east of the **Merry Meeting** crossroads, a point near the end of the Camel Trail (see box, p.337).

If you want to treat yourself to a luxury **stay** in Blisland, head for *Lavethan* (Ⓣ01208/850487, Ⓦwww.lavethan.com; no under-8s; ❻), a beautiful sixteenth-century manor house set in thirty-five acres of park-like fields and gardens sloping to a small river; a ten-minute walk west from the village towards St Mabyn, it has a huge open fire in the drawing room and a heated outdoor pool in summer. *Torr House* (Ⓣ01208/851601, Ⓦwww.torrhousecottages.co.uk; no credit cards; ❺), a Victorian ex-farmhouse, provides a cheaper alternative in a fine garden setting; it's a quarter-mile up the St Breward road. The best **campsite** hereabouts is the small *South Penquite*, one and a half miles north of Blisland, also on the St Breward road (Ⓣ01208/850491, Ⓦwww.southpenquite.co.uk; closed Oct to mid-May); as well as pitches, it offers four Mongolian yurts available for weekly rent (or three-night weekend stays in June, Sept and Oct), heated by a woodburner and sleeping up to six.

Back on the village green, the *Blisland Inn* is a popular place for its eight real ales on tap, fruit wine and inexpensive pub lunches or evening **meals**. It has outdoor tables, stages live music most Saturday nights and sells newspapers too.

Jamaica Inn and around

Lying at the centre of the moor, on the A30 midway between Bodmin and Launceston, **Jamaica Inn** is one of the area's chief focuses for walkers, sight-seers and coach parties alike. The inn, located just outside the unprepossessing village of **Bolventor**, was a staging-post even before the precursor of the A30 road was laid in 1769, and was described by **Daphne du Maurier** in her book of the same name as being "alone in glory, four square to the winds". The combination of its literary association and its convenient position has led to its development as a hotel and restaurant complex and to the establishment in an annexed building of a **Smuggler's Museum** (daily: April–Oct 10am–5pm, closes 6pm during school hols; Nov to early Jan & early Feb to March 11am–4pm; £3.95), an engaging exhibition documenting the history of the practice up to the present day, where you can marvel at such diverse ruses used for concealing contraband as secret pouches in corsets and hollowed-out turtles. The same building holds waxworks and sound-and-light gadgetry that replays the story of *Jamaica Inn* at the touch of a button, and a room devoted to Daphne du Maurier, displaying her Sheraton writing desk and a dish of her favourite sweets.

The inn's car park is a useful place to leave your vehicle and venture forth **on foot**, although you should notify staff if you plan to do so. A free leaflet is available at the inn detailing the three-mile walk to Brown Willy (see box, p.362), and the well-travelled route to **Dozmary Pool**, a mile south. According to Arthurian mythology, after King Arthur's death, Sir Bedivere is supposed to have hurled the king's sword, Excalibur, into this desolate pool, where it was seized by an arm raised from the depths (Loe Pool, on the Lizard, also claims the honour: see p.260). Despite its proximity to the A30, the diamond-shaped lake usually preserves an ethereal air, though it's been known to run dry in summer, dealing a bit of a blow to the legend that the pool is bottomless.

The lake is also the source of another, more obviously Cornish myth, that of John Tregeagle, a steward at Lanhydrock in the seventeenth century, whose unjust dealings with the local tenant farmers are supposed to have resulted in a curse condemning his spirit to endlessly baling out the pool with a perforated limpet shell. As if this were not enough, his ghost is said to be further tormented by a swarm of devils that pursue him as he flies across the moor in search of sanctuary; their infernal howling is claimed to be audible on windy nights.

Though it's the obvious **place to stay**, with splendid views on all sides, the completely revamped and modernized but rather over-priced *Jamaica Inn* (Ⓣ01566/86250, Ⓦwww.jamaicainn.co.uk; ❻) lacks much character, and you'd do better to press on to Altarnun (see below).

Altarnun and around

ALTARNUN, three miles northeast of Bolventor, just off the A30 at Five Lanes, is a pretty, granite-grey village snugly sheltered beneath the eastern heights of the moor, the front doors of its cottages approached by slate slabs crossing the trickle of a stream. By the picturesque packhorse bridge over the River Inney, its fifteenth-century church – dedicated to **St Nonna**, mother of David, the patron saint of Wales – has been dubbed the "cathedral of the moors" on account of its lofty west tower and spacious interior. The fine solid Norman font here was the prototype of the dozen or so "Altarnun fonts" in the area, characterized by their square shape, with geometric flowers surrounded by snakes on the four sides and fierce faces at the corners. Look out, too, for the set of 79 superb bench-ends, carved at the beginning of the sixteenth century, boldly depicting secular and sacred subjects – saints, musicians, clowns, moorland sheep and even a bagpipe player. Some of the slate memorials in the churchyard were carved by local sculptor Nevil Northey Burnard, also responsible for the effigy of John Wesley, the co-founder of Methodism, over the door of the Methodist chapel on the village's main street. A regular visitor to the neighbourhood, Wesley used to stay at **Wesley Cottage** (April–Sept Tues, Fri & Sat 10.30am–3.30pm; free; Ⓦwww.lamc.org.uk/wesleycottage), half a mile to the southwest at Trewint and now within earshot of the A30's roar, 400m away. You can visit his two small rooms in the "Prophet's Chamber" area of the house, and view a few of his letters, but there's not a lot to fire the imagination.

There's little in the way of **accommodation** in the village, though *Terra Nova*, a mile or so north at Treween (Ⓣ01566/880128, Ⓦwww.terranova-bnb.co.uk; ❺), offers a modern, self-contained studio room in a loft, with a garden and free internet access. A brief walk south of Altarnun, off the A30, the *King's Head* at Five Lanes (Ⓣ01566/86241; ❸) has beams, saggy ceilings, patchwork quilts on the beds and inexpensive **meals**.

Launceston

Unpromoted as a tourist town, **LAUNCESTON** was Cornwall's capital until 1835, and still retains much of its original architecture, overlaid with a sedate, well-to-do charm. Situated less than a mile from the Devon border, it was, until the construction of its bypass twenty years ago, literally the "Gateway to Cornwall", since all traffic entering the county here passed through the narrow twelfth-century **Southgate Arch** – the last remaining of the three original gateways to the county's only walled town.

Launceston developed around its **castle** (daily: April–June & Sept 10am–5pm; July & Aug 10am–6pm; Oct 10am–4pm; £3; EH), which still dominates the skyline from the top of a grassy mound just west of the centre, though all that now remains is the rough-hewn cylindrical keep and round curtain walls. In the thirteenth century this was the chief fortress of Richard, earl of Cornwall and brother of Henry III, but later fell into decay until repaired by the Black Prince. In a sturdy cell near the castle's north gate, **George Fox**, founder of the Society of Friends, or Quakers, was imprisoned in 1656 for "disturbing the peace" in St Ives. Launceston had earlier taken a stand against religious dissenters when St Cuthbert Mayne was hung, drawn and quartered in its main square in 1577 – the first Roman Catholic seminary priest to be executed in England.

North of the castle, Castle Street was described by John Betjeman as the finest Georgian street in Cornwall. Its red-brick buildings include **Lawrence House Museum** (April–Oct Mon–Fri 10.30am–4.30pm; free), a graceful setting for some well-displayed local exhibits, which include a reconstructed Victorian kitchen and, on the upper floor, mourning clothes and other costumes, a Victorian bier, and a collection of nineteenth-century Christmas decorations. The museum also has items relating to John Couch Adams (1819–92), co-discoverer of the planet Neptune, who was born in nearby Lidcot.

East off Castle Street on Church Street, the church of **St Mary Magdalene** is unique in England for its prolifically carved exterior walls – no mean feat, considering the unyielding qualities of granite. Completed in 1524, the church was commissioned by one Henry Trecarrel, whose coat of arms and that of his wife can be seen on the upper storey of the south porch, among a profusion of leaves, quatrefoils, pomegranates and heraldic shields. In the east wall, a recumbent figure of Mary Magdalene was the subject of a poem by local resident and one of Cornwall's most celebrated poets, **Charles Causley** (1917–2003). According to local lore, if you throw a stone over your shoulder and it lands on the effigy's back, you will receive good luck. Highlights inside the church include the fine Perpendicular pulpit painted red, black and white, and contrasting Art Nouveau carved bench-ends.

From St Thomas Road, just west of the castle, **Launceston Steam Railway** runs frequent five-mile round-trips to New Mills through the Kensey valley on the original Waterloo to Padstow line (Easter daily 11am–4.30pm; late May to late Sept Mon–Fri & Sun 11am–4.30pm; £8.25, valid all day; ⓣ01566/775665, ⓦwww.launcestonsr.co.uk). The narrow-gauge steam locomotives, built in the 1880s and 1890s, formerly worked in the slate quarries of North Wales. There are also veteran cars and motorcycles on show in the small transport museum here (free).

Practicalities

A few metres south of St Mary Magdalene, Launceston's **tourist office** (Mon–Fri 8.45am–5pm, closes 4pm Fri; ⓣ01566/772321, ⓦwww.visitlaunceston.co.uk) is located in the Market House Arcade in Market Street. For the pick of the town's **accommodation**, head for the Georgian *Eagle House Hotel*, close to the museum at 3 Castle St (Ⓣ01566/774488, Ⓦwww.eaglehousehotel.eu; ⑤), which has elaborate plaster moulding and cool, spacious rooms, or, through the Southgate Arch and close to the car park, *Glencoe Villa*, 13 Race Hill (Ⓣ01566/775819, Ⓔkeigil.robinson@virgin.net; no credit cards; ③), with

The walk to Rough Tor and Brown Willy

One of the best hikes on Bodmin Moor, and one which can be accomplished without too much difficulty, is to its two highest peaks – **Rough Tor** (400m/1311ft) and **Brown Willy** (420m/1378ft) – accessible either from Camelford or *Jamaica Inn* (see p.359). The forbidding landscape was the setting for the final climactic scenes of Daphne du Maurier's novel, *Jamaica Inn*. Though the ascents don't present particular hazards, you'll need suitable clothing and footwear, and a good map, such as OS *Explorer* OL109. Do not attempt the walks in poor visibility.

Rough (locally pronounced Row – to rhyme with "cow") **Tor** (map ref SX146808) lies about a mile south of the car park at Rough Tor Ford, which is three miles southeast of Camelford and reachable on foot or by car from Rough Tor Road, a right turn off Victoria Road at Camelford's northern end. From the bridge over the stream below the car park, walk about a mile over springy turf and a well-worn trail, past a stone monument to Charlotte Dymond (see p.356) and the three boulders of **Showery Tor** (map ref SX149813), before bearing left along the ridge to the slight elevation of **Little Rough Tor** (map ref SX138817). From here, continue in a south-easterly direction to the summit, a gentle but steady uphill trudge over the heath, as often as not accompanied by a biting wind. The sides of Rough Tor are very rocky and the last stretch is not well defined, so care is needed. The piles of flat precariously balanced rocks crowning the summit present a different aspect from every angle – an ungainly mass from the south, and a nobly proportioned mountain from the west – and were described by Daphne du Maurier as "shaped like giant furniture with monstrous chairs and twisted tables". Nearby are the ruins of a medieval chapel, and the whole area is scattered with Bronze Age remains.

Originally named Bronewhella, or "highest hill", Bodmin's loftiest peak, **Brown Willy** (map ref SX159800), is easily visible less than a mile and a half to the southeast of Rough Tor. Like the latter, Brown Willy shows various faces, its sugarloaf appearance from the north sharpening into a long, multi-peaked crest as you approach. To reach it, continue from the summit of Rough Tor in a southeasterly direction, towards a ruined building near which a bridge crosses the upper reaches of the De Lank River. From here the ascent is clearly marked, with the final stretch along a steep but well-defined track. From the summit, the highest point in Cornwall, you get a grand panorama of the rock-strewn, green-and-brown patchwork of high moorland on all sides. Both Rough Tor and Brown Willy can be climbed in a couple of hours from the car park.

Brown Willy can also be accessed **from** *Jamaica Inn* (see p.359), a three-and-a-quarter-mile walk from the car park there. Turning left out of the car park, follow the old road down the hill, and take the second turning on the left under the A30. From here, take the first turning on the right, then first left, walking along this road for 150m until you see a signed footpath on the right. Follow this path for the length of three fields until it becomes a broader track, and continue up this, bearing to the right of the buildings in front, from where a lane leads to a gate after 750m. Pass through the gate and onto the moorland, bearing right for 250m to **Tolborough Tor** (map ref SX175778), the highest point of the surrounding downs and a mile from *Jamaica Inn* as the crow flies (but more like 1.5 miles walking). From here, Brown Willy is clearly visible less than two miles to the northwest across bare moor. Walk towards it for another 250m to a gate, beyond which you should continue for another mile and a half with a wire fence on your left, crossing this over a stile and then climbing the steep slopes of the tor.

a sunny breakfast room and colour-coordinated bedrooms with private or en-suite bathrooms. North of the centre, *Rose Cottage*, off the A388 Dutson Road at 5 Lower Cleaverfield (Ⓣ01566/779292, Ⓦwww.rosecottagecornwall.co.uk; no under-12s; no credit cards; ❺) has three rooms – one a single – with wi-fi access, great views of Launceston and the Kensey valley and a good vegetarian breakfast option. The nearest **campsite** is *Chapmanswell Country Park* (Ⓣ01409/211382, Ⓦwww.chapmanswellcaravanpark.co.uk) at St Giles on the Heath, six miles north of town along the A388 (in Devon).

Launceston has a handful of good **places to eat**. On Dockacre Road, *La Bouche Creole* (closed daytime and all Sun & Mon; Ⓣ01566/779294) brings a touch of New Orleans to Cornwall, offering set-price menus (£20 for two courses, £23 for three) that might include crab and crayfish cakes and spicy seafood gumbo. Alternatively, there's *Harvey's*, a buzzing restaurant and wine bar at 13 Church St (Ⓣ01566/772558), offering a wide range of food including fish and steaks in the evening (£10–15). During the day, the *Mad Hatter's* at 28 Church St (closed Sun) is a cosy spot for sandwiches, paninis, steaks (£5–7) and numerous veggie and gluten-free options, or just a cup of tea.

Camelford and around

The northern half of Bodmin Moor is dominated by its two highest tors, both of them easily accessible from **CAMELFORD**, a small town once thought to be the site of King Arthur's Camelot. Though the town itself hardly lives up to the expectations raised by its associations or its exotic name ("Camel" is probably derived from a contraction of Cam meaning "crooked" and "hayle" meaning "estuary"), it makes a useful touring base and is easily negotiated, its one main street starting as Victoria Road at the town's northwestern end and changing its name to Market Place, Fore Street and High Street. In addition, a trio of museums provide some diversion, the most conventional of which is the **North Cornwall Museum** on the Clease (April–Sept Mon–Sat 10am–5pm; £3), at the junction of Fore and High streets, which displays a low-key collection of domestic items, tools and farming implements from the last hundred years, alongside background information on the local slate industry. In complete contrast, the **British Cycling Museum**, housed in the old train station a mile north of town on the B3266 Boscastle road (Mon–Thurs & Sun 10am–5pm; ring ahead for Fri & Sat, Ⓣ01840/212811; £4), is a cyclophile's dream, with some four hundred examples of bikes through the ages filling every inch of floor, ceiling and wall space. Among the oddities are a reverse penny farthing, a four-wheeled quadracycle and a pentacycle (one large wheel, four small), and there's a library of books and manuals on site as well. The collection may be of special interest to bikers on Route 3 on the National Cycle Way, which runs through Camelford.

The third museum lies on the River Camel a mile or so north of town at **SLAUGHTERBRIDGE**, possibly the site of King Arthur's last battle of Camlann – at which the king was mortally wounded by Mordred – though the identification of this site probably has more to do with the fact that a decisive battle between the Saxon King Egbert and the Celts was fought near here in the ninth century. Despite the tenuous connection, you'll now find the **Arthurian Centre** here (Easter to late Oct daily 10am–5pm; £3), which includes the Land of Arthur exhibition, covering Arthur-related art and poetry by means of a video and photographs, and highlights the background to the site, focusing particularly on Lord Tennyson's visit here in 1848, when he was inspired to write his Arthurian elegy *Idylls of the King*. There are also gardens with riverside walks, and a tearoom overlooking a children's play castle. The main basis of the centre, however, is the sixth-century inscribed **King Arthur's Stone**, a pleasant five-minute walk away, which supposedly marks the site of the final battle. Viewed from a platform, the funerary stone is inscribed in Latin and an ancient Celtic script which is thought to indicate the former presence of southern Irish people in North Cornwall; it was first recorded in 1602 but had lain on the banks of the Camel for a thousand years before that.

Otherwise, the area's attractions are all to do with the wilderness of the surrounding moorland, easily accessible to the southeast of Camelford. Near the **Arthurian Centre**, *Lakefield Equestrian Centre*, Lower Pendavey Farm (ⓣ01840/213279) provides **horseriding** – tuition, short rides and longer hacks from £17–20 per hour. For a good walk up to Rough Tor and Brown Willy, in the heart of the moor, see the box on p.362.

Practicalities

Camelford's **tourist office** is housed in the North Cornwall Museum (see above; same hours; ⓣ01840/212954). Accommodation options are few and far between, but there's an excellent central **B&B**, *Warmington House* on Market Place (ⓣ01840/214961, ⓦwww.warmingtonhouse.co.uk; no credit cards; ⑥), an elegant Queen Anne building with clean, airy rooms, period furnishings and modern comforts. Next door, the thirteenth-century, slate-hung *Darlington Inn* (ⓣ01840/213314; ③) has spacious en-suite rooms and a no-breakfast option. Four miles northeast of Camelford at Owls Gate, Davidstow, *Belle Tents* (ⓣ01840/261556, ⓦwww.belletentscamping.co.uk; closed late Sept to late May; ⑤) offers a novel alternative: pre-erected tents resembling stripy, mini-marquees, each sleeping two or three people and equipped with rugs, duvets and separate kitchen tents. In peak season tents are available weekly only and for groups or families. More conventional **camping** is provided at *Lakefield Caravan Park*, Lower Pendavey Farm (ⓣ01840/213279; closed Nov–March), a mile or so north of Camelford off the B3266.

The *Four Seasons* at 5 Market Place serves all-day breakfasts and other inexpensive **meals** (closed eves, also Sun mid-Sept to mid-July), while the *Mason's Arms* on Fore Street serves great pub grub, including steaks and grills (£8–16; no credit cards), and has a beer garden. Otherwise, try the *Gurkha Restaurant* at 8 Market Place, a recommended Nepalese restaurant with most dishes £7–8 (ⓣ01840/213050; closed daytime).

The southeastern moor: St Neot and around

ST NEOT, seven miles east of Bodmin and reachable from the A38 two miles south, makes a good entry point for the southeastern tracts of Bodmin Moor. As one of the moor's prettiest villages, it also strongly merits a visit in its own right, not least for the fifteenth-century **church**, overlooking the village, which contains some of the most impressive medieval stained-glass windows of any parish church in the country. The set begins with the oldest glass, at the east end of the south aisle, where the fifteenth-century **Creation Window** shows God with mathematical instruments and Seth planting in Adam's mouth the seeds from which the wood of the cross will grow. The first window in the south aisle,

Noah's Window, continues the sequence with lively scenes of the ark as a sixteenth-century sailing ship. However, the narration soon dissolves into windows portraying saints and – due to the need of sponsorship when the money ran out – patrons and local bigwigs, as well as the ordinary men and women of the village.

St Neot makes a pleasant base in the southern part of the moor, though **accommodation** options in the village are limited to the three en-suite rooms in the *London Inn*, next door to the church (Ⓣ01579/320263, Ⓦwww.ccinns.com; ❹) and, signposted 350m down a track below the village car park, *Lampen Farm* (Ⓣ01579/320284, Ⓦwww.lampenfarm.fsnet.co.uk; no credit cards; ❺), a sixteenth-century farmhouse with Victorian furnishings and large, quiet rooms. A couple of miles south of the village, close to the A38 turn-off, *Treverbyn Vean Manor* (Ⓣ01579/326105, Ⓦwww.treverbynvean.co.uk; ❻), a handsome neo-Gothic house complete with Great Hall and minstrels' gallery, offers two large rooms and can provide a quality two-course dinner for £20. Back in St Neot, the *London Inn* provides a cosy setting for Cornish ales, bar food and full **meals.**

The southern edge of Bodmin Moor is far greener and more thickly wooded than the north due to the confluence of a web of **rivers** into the Fowey, which tumble through the **Golitha Falls**, a couple of miles east of St Neot, below Draynes Bridge. One of the moor's best-known beauty spots, this is actually more a series of rapids than a waterfall, enlivened by the dippers and wagtails that flit through the surrounding beech trees. There's also an attractive woodland walk to the dam at the **Siblyback Lake** reservoir just over a mile to the northeast: follow the river up to Draynes Bridge, then walk north up a minor road until a path branches off on the right after a half-mile, leading down to the water's edge.

North of Siblyback Lake, and reachable from the B3254 Launceston road, **Twelve Men's Moor** holds some of Bodmin Moor's grandest landscapes. The quite modest elevations of **Hawk's Tor** (329m/1079ft) and the lower **Trewartha Tor** appear enormous from the north, though they are topped by **Kilmar**, highest of the hills on the moor's eastern flank (390m/1280ft). Sunrising Riding Centre at Henwood, west of the B3254 on the edge of Twelve Men's Moor, offers **riding** lessons and, for experienced riders, hacks in the area (Ⓣ01579/362895, Ⓦwww.tminternational.co.uk; £24–35 per hour).

Three miles east of Siblyback Lake, Cornwall's highest village, **MINIONS**, makes a good base for exploring these bleak areas, and also lies within easy reach of a cluster of important prehistoric remains. To get to the closest of these, follow the signposted path a few steps west of the centre of Minions, which brings you after a quarter-mile to **The Hurlers**, a wide complex of three stone circles dating from about 1500 BC. The purpose of these stark upright stones is not known, though local lore declares them to be men turned to stone for playing the Celtic game of hurling on the Sabbath. Following the path a further half-mile or so north, **Stowe's Hill** has a top-of-the-world wilderness feel and is the site of Bodmin Moor's most famous stone pile, **The Cheesewring** (map ref SX258724), a precarious pillar of balancing flat granite slabs that have been weirdly eroded by the wind to resemble a hamburger in a peaked cap. Gouged out of the hillside nearby, the disused **Cheesewring Quarry** is a centre of rock climbing.

Three miles south of Minions and less than half a mile south of the village of Darite (off the Tremar road), **Trethevy Quoit** (map ref SX259688) is another Bronze Age survivor, a chamber tomb 15ft/4.6m high and surmounted by a massive capstone. Originally enclosed in earth, the slabs have been stripped by centuries of weathering to create Cornwall's most impressive megalithic monument. Bus #574 (not Sun) from Liskeard calls at Darite and St Cleer, both of which are close to Trethevy Quoit; alternatively, it's a three-mile walk from Liskeard.

Off the southern limits of the moor, where the B3254 meets the A390 and the A38, **LISKEARD** is a useful bus and rail junction at the head of the East Looe valley, connected by a branch line with Looe, on the coast (see p.224). The town's **museum** on Pike Street (Mon–Fri 11am–4pm, Sat 11am–1.30pm; free) mainly deals with local history and industry in five rooms, and shares a building with the **tourist office** (same hours, but opens 30min earlier; ⓣ01579/349148). Otherwise, the only distraction hereabouts lies out of town at the exhibition of **Magnificent Music Machines** (Easter–Oct daily 10.30am–5pm; £6), three miles south in St Keyne (a request stop on the line to Looe, and signposted off the B3254), where an hour's enthusiastic tour brings you face-to-face with a delicate 1895 polyphon and a Wurlitzer cinema organ from 1929.

In Liskeard, you can **snack** on baguettes, soups and jacket potatoes at *The Coffee House*, Pike Street, with comfy sofas, or at *The Fat Frog*, a more colourful, child-friendly café offering all-day breakfasts and vegetarian dishes (both closed daytime & all Sun). For a full evening **meal**, continue along this street towards St Martin's Church to find the *Bay Leaf*, 27 Church St (ⓣ01579/344557; closed all Mon and lunchtime Tues–Sat), where dishes costing around £12 range from chicken creole to Moroccan lamb and poached sea bass.

Travel details

Trains

Bodmin Parkway to: Liskeard (1–2 hourly; 12min); Penzance (1–2 hourly; 1hr 25min); Plymouth (1–2 hourly; 40–50min).

Liskeard to: Bodmin Parkway (1–2 hourly; 12min); Looe (Mon–Sat hourly, Sun mid-June to mid-Sept 8 daily; 30min); Penzance (1–2 hourly; 1hr 35min); Plymouth (1–2 hourly; 30min).

Buses

Altarnun to: Launceston (Mon–Fri 3–4 daily; 45min).

Bodmin to: Liskeard (Mon–Sat hourly, Sun 1 daily; 30min); Padstow (Mon–Sat hourly, Sun 6 daily; 1hr); St Austell (Mon–Sat hourly, Sun 5 daily; 50min); Wadebridge (Mon–Sat hourly, Sun 6 daily; 30min).

Camelford to: Launceston (Mon–Sat 3 daily, Sun 1 daily; 25–35min).

Launceston to: Altarnun (Mon–Fri 3 daily; 30min); Bodmin (Mon–Sat hourly, Sun 1 daily; 30min); Camelford (Mon–Sat 3 daily, Sun 1 daily; 25–35min); Liskeard (Mon–Fri 3 daily; 40–55min); Plymouth (Mon–Sat 9 daily, Sun 3 daily; 1hr 20min).

Liskeard to: Launceston (Mon–Fri 3–4 daily; 45min–1hr); Looe (Mon–Sat hourly, Sun 5 daily; 25min); Plymouth (1–2 hourly; 50min); St Austell (5 daily; 40min); Truro (5 daily; 1hr 15min).

Contexts

Contexts

History

Remote from England's main centres of political and industrial activity, the counties of Devon and Cornwall have played a largely peripheral role in the country's history. The region has been most pre-eminent in matters related to the sea, namely fishing, smuggling and buccaneering, while inland, Devon's cloth industry and Cornwall's mines for centuries provided a solid economic base.

Prehistory

The first evidence of human settlement in the region is from around 30,000 BC – a teenager's jawbone found in Kents Cavern, Torquay – but the subsequent prehistory of the region is a succession of long blanks of which next to nothing is known. In general, however, it seems likely that England's westernmost counties shared much the same experiences as other parts of the land, the scattered tribes relying on hunting and gathering with a rudimentary social organization. In common with the rest of England, the region was settled by Neolithic tribes from mainland Europe during the fourth millennium BC, who introduced relatively advanced domestic and industrial skills. Strangely, despite the unearthing of large quantities of flints and arrowheads from Neolithic sites, relics of habitation are paltry, though Cornwall has numerous examples of "quoits", or chambered tombs set in open country with a giant slab, or capstone, for a roof. The beginnings of cereal cultivation and livestock farming are also traced to these times.

More prolific are finds associated with the **Bronze Age** peoples who began to arrive on the scene during the second millennium BC. These tribes left a contrastingly rich legacy of granite menhirs, kistvaens, stone rows, stone circles and hut circles throughout the region – more than 1200 barrows (burial mounds) have been discovered in Devon alone, of which a significant number lie on Dartmoor. In Cornwall, remains are concentrated particularly on the Isles of Scilly, the Penwith peninsula and Bodmin Moor, where The Hurlers, a complex of three circles dating from about 1500 BC, represent a fine example. Most of these sites were rifled centuries ago, and the surviving relics have yielded frustratingly little information about the life and structure of the society which occupied them.

In around 500 BC, another wave of immigrants, the **Celts**, established themselves in the region, bringing with them weapons and tools made of iron. Much given to tribal wars, the Celts constructed sturdy hill forts throughout the peninsula; the best-preserved relic from these times is the village of Chysauster in Penwith, dating from around the first century BC and occupied until long after. Good examples of the form and layout of the fields farmed in these times still exist hereabouts, notably the small, stone-hedged field systems around Zennor.

The Romans and the Dark Ages

Recorded history begins with the coming of the **Romans**, who occupied Exeter (known by them as Isca Dumnoniorum) in the first century AD but did not venture much further west. Little interested in this extremity of their empire, the Romans left few traces in Devon and Cornwall, content to establish a strong military presence at Exeter to keep an eye on the Celtic tribes which were left to their own devices further west. Although the region as a whole benefited from the *Pax Romana*, Roman ways were never greatly assimilated, as far as historians can tell, and the Roman interlude left less of an impression here than on most other areas of the country.

The accelerating disintegration of the Roman Empire towards the end of the fourth century led to the withdrawal of the legions and a rapid reversion to pre-Roman practices in the West Country. Almost immediately, incursions were begun by the **Saxons**, a Germanic people, who settled in much of the region during the sixth and seventh centuries. The invaders were at first unable – or unwilling – to subdue the Britons in the far west, however, making an unconquered enclave of Cornwall. As the last stronghold of Celtic resistance in England and the torch-bearer of Christianity, the "**Dark Ages**" here were actually a golden age during which much of the county's rich folklore originated. In this scantily recorded era, saints and mystics were said to wander the pilgrimage routes between Wales, Ireland and Brittany, and the various strands of the **Arthurian saga** were first woven together, probably based on the exploits of a Celtic chieftain resisting the Saxons. The county's isolation aided the survival of the Celtic tongue, and while **Cornish** has not been spoken as a living language since the eighteenth century, Celtic place-names are still much in evidence today.

Cornwall was not fully conquered by the Saxons until the time of Athelstan in around 926. In Devon, the local Dumnonii more readily absorbed the Saxon newcomers who, by the **eighth century**, were at least nominally Christians. Much of the work of conversion was undertaken by such individuals as St Boniface (c.680–754), born Wynfrith in Crediton, who went on to spread the faith in Devon and later among the Frisians in Germany and the Lowlands. The integration of Saxons and Celts was further strengthened by the need to confront the threat of **Danish raids** which afflicted the region, in common with the rest of the country, during the **ninth and tenth centuries**. Unlike in other parts, however, there was little Viking settlement in the West, but a constant skirmishing between invading armies and the forces of the West Saxons under Alfred the Great and his descendants. The Danes occupied Exeter for the last time in 1003, but the Anglo-Saxon state was not to last much longer, for the entire region was shortly to be absorbed into the new Norman kingdom following William the Conqueror's capture of Exeter in 1068.

The Middle Ages

The **Normans** built castles at Exeter, Totnes, Okehampton, Restormel and Launceston, which acted as nuclei for the growth of towns. This urban development was also spurred on by the **cloth trade**, Devon's principal industry at this time, as it continued to be throughout the medieval and early modern periods. Wool from the county's fertile inland pastures was processed locally or in the towns, and exported to mainland Europe from the great estuary ports of the south coast. This established both a robust rural economy and a strong mercantile class in such towns as Topsham, Totnes and Dartmouth. Exeter's primacy in Devon was assured when the diocese was transferred here from Crediton in 1050, and the great cathedral constructed soon afterwards.

In Cornwall, the indigenous Saxon manors were taken over by the Normans to form the basis of an earldom, which was granted to Edward III's son, the Black Prince, in 1337; since then, the earldom has belonged traditionally to the eldest son of the English sovereign, who acts as duke of Cornwall. On the whole, the Norman yoke was accepted here, the greater links with France and centralized economy promoting commerce and the growth of inland ports such as Truro and Fowey.

Although Cornwall played a comparatively minor part in the region's cloth trade, it had a much larger role in the region's **mining** industry. Tin had been extracted here since prehistoric times, when it was alloyed with copper – also found in the region – to make bronze. Though the Romans do not appear to have utilized the resource, the greater level of protection and organization that existed under the Normans made Cornwall Europe's biggest supplier of tin in the twelfth century. Over the next hundred years Helston, Lostwithiel, Truro and Liskeard in Cornwall, and Ashburton and Tavistock in Devon were made **Stannary towns**, according to which they were granted special privileges and placed by the Crown under the separate legal jurisdiction of the Stannary (tin mine) courts. Stannary towns were visited twice a year by officials from London who came to test the smelted tin, chipping a corner if it was approved – "coigning" it, from the French for "corner", hence the English word, *coin*.

After farming and mining, the third most important activity in Devon and Cornwall was **fishing**, and many of the ports of the southern coast in particular – such as Beer, Brixham, Polperro and Mevagissey – have retained their medieval layout. In 1272, however, the imposition of custom duties for the first time gave birth to another lucrative spin-off which existed side-by-side with fishing – **smuggling**, for which the inlets and estuaries proved ideal terrain. The activity was to carry on until well into the nineteenth century, and there are even echoes of it in the present era with shipments of drugs regularly apprehended off the peninsula's coasts.

The fifteenth and sixteenth centuries

While the region had consolidated its wealth in comparative peace during the later part of the Middle Ages, the **fifteenth and sixteenth centuries** saw Devon and Cornwall increasingly drawn into the turmoil of national events. Stirrings of **revolt** against the new centralizing Tudor state surfaced in 1497 when Thomas Flamank, a Bodmin lawyer, and Michael Joseph, a blacksmith from the Lizard area, led 15,000 Cornishmen to London to protest against high taxation. By the time the force arrived at Blackheath, they were much depleted and easily crushed by Henry VII's army. However, the rejection of the rebels' demands and the execution of their leaders ensured that resentment continued to simmer in Cornwall. This created widespread support for **Perkin Warbeck**, who landed at St Ives just three months later claiming to be Richard, Duke of York – one of the disappeared "Princes in the Tower" who had in fact probably been dispatched by Richard III in 1483. Warbeck received a rapturous welcome in Bodmin and attracted some support from local gentry who proclaimed the pretender Richard IV. Crossing the Tamar in September 1497, however, the rebels failed to take Exeter and Warbeck's army melted away when confronted by the king's forces at Taunton.

A further revolt took place in 1549 against the Act of Uniformity and its insistence on the Book of Common Prayer and the simplified service in English rather than the old Latin Mass – a particular aggravation to the non-English-speaking

Cornish. The **Prayer Book Rebellion** began in the village of Sampford Courtenay, near Okehampton, and drew support in both Devon and Cornwall, but the rebels were defeated in battle at Clyst St Mary, outside Topsham, by Lord Russell, who happened to be the principal beneficiary of dissolved monastery lands in the West Country.

As England's defence came to rely more heavily on its maritime prowess, and trade began to focus increasingly on the Atlantic, Devon assumed an important naval role. It was not just the county's geographical position that accounted for its growing significance: some of the greatest mariners of the age – Drake, Grenville and Raleigh, among others – were all Devon-born and -bred, and all were to take a leading part in the defence of the realm and the expansion of trade to the Americas. Less to their credit, all were also involved in piracy and slavery. **Francis Drake** (c.1540–96), born near Tavistock, was plundering the coast of Guinea and the Spanish Main when he was only in his twenties, becoming a popular hero on his return to Plymouth, of which he later became mayor. **Walter Raleigh** (1552–1618), born in Hayes Barton, East Devon, also indulged in piratical activities in addition to his attempts to colonize America, and represented the county in parliament. His cousin **Richard Grenville** (1542–91) commanded the fleet that carried English colonists to Roanoke Island in present-day North Carolina in 1585, and died heroically against overwhelming odds in a celebrated tussle with a Spanish treasure fleet in the Azores – his ship, the *Revenge*, was crewed by "men of Bideford in Devon". Grenville's preparations for a voyage of discovery to the South Pacific were adopted by Drake when the latter circumnavigated the world in 1577–80, the first Englishman to do so. As the home port of these and other maritime adventurers, Plymouth became the western centre of Britain's maritime power and remains a prominent base of the Royal Navy today. Devonport Dockyard here is still one of the area's biggest employers, while Appledore on the northern coast also continues its centuries-old shipbuilding activities – though on a much reduced and increasingly precarious scale.

Elsewhere on the south coast, defences were strengthened against French and Spanish raids, with fortifications erected or expanded in Dartmouth, Fowey, St Mawes, Falmouth and St Mary's, on the Isles of Scilly. The ever-present fear of Spanish invasion during the second half of the **sixteenth century** were realized in 1588 with the sailing of the **Spanish Armada**, whose approach was first announced from the Cornish coast at the Lizard, and which was eventually scuppered by Elizabeth I's fleet docked in Plymouth – the occasion of Drake's famous sang-froid when he insisted on finishing his game of bowls on Plymouth Hoe before putting to sea to fight the enemy. Far more dangerous than the Armada for Cornwall was the Spanish invasion of Brittany in 1590, which provided a convenient base for raids on Cornwall, including a devastating attack in 1595, when two separate Spanish assault parties joined forces to sack and burn the three ports of Mousehole, Newlyn and Penzance.

The Civil War

Fifty years later, the **Civil War** engulfed and divided the West Country no less than other parts of England. Although most places preferred to keep their options open and observe the course of events before rallying to either side, sentiment here was pretty squarely behind the Royalist cause – with the notable exceptions of Exeter and Plymouth, which declared both ways. Where it was necessary to come out in favour of one side over another, most people followed their religious and political beliefs. Thus, in Cornwall for example, Bevil Grenville – celebrated warrior and hero of Robert Hawker's ballad, *Song of the Western Men* – together with many others sided with the king in defence of the Anglican Church, while Lord Robartes, a Presbyterian merchant, and others who rejected absolutism, sided with parliament. The Royalist mint was established in Truro in 1642–43 and Cornwall became a major theatre of war. Battles were fought and won by the Royalists at Braddock Down and Stratton in Cornwall and at Lansdown near Bristol, where Bevil Grenville fell. There were two campaigns in 1643, and the following year Charles I defeated the earl of Essex's army at Lostwithiel. However, Royalist fortunes were reversed when the New Model Army under the command of Thomas Fairfax appeared in the West in 1645. This final brutal campaign culminated in the Royalist surrender at Tressillian, near Truro, on March 12, 1645, although St Michael's Mount, Pendennis Castle and Exeter held out until the following year.

The main legacies of this sequence of sieges and small battles – there was none on the scale of Naseby or Marston Moor – were harvest failure, starvation and the destruction of many great houses and forts, though some of the latter were simply decommissioned and converted to domestic use. The wool trade in Devon, however, was largely unscathed, and entered a hugely prosperous phase in the second half of the seventeenth century.

The eighteenth and nineteenth centuries

Tin and copper mining brought a degree of prosperity to Cornwall in the **eighteenth century**, with the introduction of beam engines in 1716 allowing ever-deeper shafts to be excavated, pumped and mined. The more extensive underground networks were largely made possible by the innovations of such engineers as Thomas Newcomen of Dartmouth (1663–1729), who constructed a steam engine for pumping water out of pits, and the Cornish scientists Humphry Davy (1778–1829), famous for his "Davy lamp", and Richard Trevithick (1771–1833), who invented a steam carriage for use in the mines. The beam engines were fuelled by coal from South Wales, helping to keep the peninsula's northern ports busy. For the miners themselves, the working conditions were both squalid and dangerous, and the circumstances of their families were equally appalling. These impoverished communities provided a fertile ground for the preaching of **John Wesley**, the co-founder of Methodism who travelled extensively in Devon and Cornwall between 1743 and 1786. His first visits met with a hostile response, but he later found a receptive audience for his pared-down version of the Christian message, and it is from this period that many of the Methodist chapels dotted around the region date.

The copper industry peaked during the 1840s, focused on the area around Redruth and Camborne, but shortly afterwards the mining industry collapsed when cheaper deposits of both copper and tin were found elsewhere in the world market. Pit closures during the nineteenth and twentieth centuries were followed by large-scale emigration from Cornwall, chiefly to Australia and South America.

On a much smaller scale, the region's extensive deposits of slate and granite continued to be quarried as they had been for centuries, while the eighteenth century also saw the beginning of the **china-clay** industry in Cornwall. The deposits were first discovered by William Cookworthy

(1705–80) of Kingsbridge in the area around Helston, and more significantly north of St Austell, where the conical white mountains of debris are still a feature of the landscape (often now coated with greenery), and where extraction remains an important industry. First used in the making of ceramics, the kaolin is now used in a wide range of products.

On the coasts, Devon's seaside towns were finding a new source of income in the tourist industry that expanded throughout the **nineteenth century**. Since the Napoleonic Wars in 1803–15 had prevented society folk from taking the fashionable Grand Tour of continental Europe, there was an increasing trend to sojourn in the comparatively mild climate of such towns as Torquay, Exmouth and Sidmouth, on the south coast, and, on the north, the villages of Lynton and Lynmouth, which were said to recall an Alpine landscape. The extension of Brunel's railway to Exeter in 1840 had the immediate result of accelerating this phenomenon, and the railway's extension over the Tamar into Cornwall in 1859, and to North Devon in 1872 brought these regions for the first time into the ambit of mass tourism. Ilfracombe became an archetypal Victorian seaside resort, while Falmouth, Newquay and St Ives in Cornwall found their full flowering in the twentieth century. Along with the tourists, the railways also brought other groups from metropolitan England: artists, who congregated first in Newlyn, at the end of the nineteenth century, and later in neighbouring St Ives (see pp.383–386).

The twentieth century and the present

Along with the steady stream of artists who were drawn to Devon and Cornwall, various writers became associated with the region in the **twentieth century**, though again these were mainly outsiders who settled in or had links with the West – D.H. Lawrence, Virginia Woolf, Henry Williamson (of *Tarka the Otter* fame), Daphne du Maurier and Agatha Christie, among others.

However, here, as elsewhere in the country, all else was overshadowed during this period by the two world wars. While **World War I** had little direct effect on the region beyond cutting a swathe through its adult male population, the south coast of Devon and Cornwall in particular suffered from both military requisition and enemy bombing during **World War II**. Although most of the West Country was designated safe from German aerial attack – and accordingly received many evacuees from London and the Midlands – Plymouth suffered the highest bombardment of any British seaport, and Exeter too was targeted in the so-called "Baedeker raids", so-called because they were directed at centres of cultural and historic interest that would have appeared in the Baedeker guidebooks of the time. The subsequent reconstruction in these two cities followed very different paths, more conservative in Exeter, bolder in Plymouth, but arguably less successful. Neither city has escaped the brutalizing of large tracts of land, and the imposition of unsympathetic shopping centres and unsightly car parks.

In the 1950s, the designation of Dartmoor and Exmoor as **national parks** was a significant indication of both the new importance of tourism to the area and the urgency of conservation for the future well-being of the region. However, the decade was also marred by tragedy when heavy rain on Exmoor in 1952 caused the River Lyn to burst its banks, resulting in the catastrophic flooding of Lynmouth and the loss of 31 lives.

The closure of most local rail lines in the 1960s had no significant impact on the region's economy as it was well compensated by the huge expansion of motor traffic, encouraged by the extension of the M5 motorway to Exeter and the building of the link road to North Devon. However, the volume of traffic, which intensifies during the peak summer months, has brought its own massive environmental problems and today remains one of the most pressing concerns for the region's well-being.

The last 35 years have seen major shifts in Devon and Cornwall related to Britain's membership of the **European Union**, with both the farming and fishing communities losing out as a result of agricultural and fisheries policies. Fishermen have also been hard hit by declining fish stocks and the imposition of quotas which have met stiff resistance. Many in both groups have turned to tourism as a source of a secondary income, though only a small fraction can benefit from this sector, and many businesses have folded for good. The choice of Devon and Cornwall as places of retirement or for second homes has also had a significant effect in pricing locals out of the area. Cornwall has qualified for European aid, and has energetically raised its profile with such projects as the opening of a branch of the **Tate Gallery** in St Ives and the creation of the **Eden Project** near St Austell, an ambitious exhibition of the planet's eco systems. Considerable investment has accompanied these schemes, though again, this can have only a limited effect on the local economy.

The biggest blow to the region in more recent times has been the **foot and mouth** epidemic, a highly infectious disease affecting livestock that swept through England in 2001. Devon farmers were hit particularly hard, but the ramifications affected every aspect of economic life, and had almost as heavy an impact in Cornwall. Although the crisis abated in time, and tourist numbers had recovered by the summer of 2002, many small farms went out of business permanently. In 2004, the region was further struck by calamity, in the form of a **flash flood** that engulfed Boscastle, in North Cornwall, though, unlike the 1952 tragedy in Lynmouth, there was no loss of life.

With farming increasingly at the mercy of the giant food retailers and the fishing industry struggling in the face of European competition, depleting fish stocks and strict fishing quotas, the region has further been hit by the global **recession** that swept through the UK – and the world – in 2008–09, leading many local businesses to go bust and unemployment figures to climb. Tourism, at least, has remained strong, with "stay-cationing" Brits pouring into the southwest peninsula to escape unfavourable foreign exchange rates, though even this sector cannot be immune to the economic vagaries of an uncertain future.

Wildlife

Devon and Cornwall are rightly famous for the beauty of their landscapes and the richness of their coastline. The peninsula on which these counties lie drives a wedge deep into the Atlantic and ensures a strong maritime influence, with the benevolent effects of the Gulf Stream giving the region's flora and fauna an almost subtropical diversity that's unmatched in the British Isles.

The sea around Devon and Cornwall is at the junction of the warm southern and cool northern water bodies, and is amongst the richest marine habitats in the world, though most people's experience of the marine environment is confined to the occasional glimpse of a dolphin or seal. More accessible is the region's **coastline**, which is generally exposed and heavily weathered on the peninsula's northern littoral and much more sheltered and indented on the southern seaboard. The long walls of sea cliffs are interspersed by bays and estuaries, whose **rivers** shelter colourful birdlife as well as the occasional otter, while their mouths are fringed by extensive areas of sand dunes. Elsewhere, on or just behind the shoreline, **reedbeds** survive in isolated patches and are an important habitat for a range of rare insects, plants and birds.

Inland, too, the geological peculiarities of the region have contributed to the peninsula's range of habitats. The upland **granite outcrops** which characterize the high moorland were created long ago by violent volcanic intrusion, which also strongly contorted the overlying strata of mudstones and limestones. These bare expanses of moorland, composed of lowland and upland heaths and blanket bog, fringed by upland oakwoods, cover Exmoor, Dartmoor and Bodmin Moor. In complete contrast, Devon and Cornwall's **agricultural heartland** has been shaped by the historic patterns of human settlement and land use. Although modern farming methods have squandered vast quantities of species-rich hedges, meadows and banks, enough have survived to preserve large numbers of thriving plants and birds – all linked in a rich mosaic of rolling countryside.

Most of the other habitats, too, have been severely degraded by human activity, particularly changes in agricultural practice, though this process is only an intensification of an influence which has moulded and influenced British wildlife throughout the human settlement of these islands. Nowadays, some of the best examples are entirely limited to nature reserves, precious but beleaguered resources about which you may gather more information from the specialist organizations detailed in the box below.

The marine environment

The **marine environment** of Devon and Cornwall constitutes one of the finest to be found around British shores. In spring and early summer especially, the coasts are bright with an abundance of **sea campion**, **kidney vetch**, **sea lavender**, orange **lichen** and green **algae**. Rarer flora to look out for include **golden samphire**, a nationally scarce plant quite common along the Cornish coastline where it grows on bare rock just above the high-water mark.

Most ubiquitous of the fauna around the coasts of Devon and Cornwall, from rugged cliff to fishing village, are the various populations of **sea birds** which, according to the season, may be nesting or wintering here, or passing through on migration. Among the many species, **fulmars** and **kittiwakes** are

Useful information sources

Cornwall Wildlife Trust ⓣ01872/273939, ⓦwww.cornwallwildlifetrust.org.uk

Dartmoor National Park Authority ⓣ01822/890414, ⓦwww.dartmoor-npa.gov.uk

Devon Wildlife Trust ⓣ01392/279244, ⓦwww.devonwildlifetrust.org

Exmoor National Park Authority ⓣ01398/323841, ⓦwww.exmoor-nationalpark.gov.uk

Marine Conservation Society ⓣ01989/566017, ⓦwww.mcsuk.org

National Trust, Devon Regional Office ⓣ01392/881691; Cornwall Regional Office ⓣ01208/265200; ⓦwww.nationaltrust.org.uk

Natural England (responsible for most National Nature Reserves), Devon Regional Office ⓣ01300/060 1110; Cornwall Regional Office ⓣ01872/245045; ⓦwww.naturalengland.org.uk

Royal Society for the Protection of Birds ⓣ01392/432691, ⓦwww.rspb.org.uk

Whale and Dolphin Conservation Society ⓣ01249/449500, ⓦwww.wdcs.org

numerous around **St Agnes Head** in Cornwall, while **razorbills** and **guillemots** are plentiful on almost all Cornish coasts. One of the most rewarding birds to look out for is the **gannet**, with long, black-tipped white wings, known for its vertical plunges into the sea as it fishes. Of the many species of gulls, most common is the **herring gull**, distinguished by its grey mantle, flesh-coloured feet and black-and-white-spotted wing tips. Chiefly a scavenger, its numbers have greatly increased in recent years as a result of expanding food supplies, which include refuse and sewage, though the birds are also known for their trick of dropping shellfish on rocks to crack them open. The richest variety of marine birds are found on the **Isles of Scilly**, including large flocks of **puffins**, which also breed on **Lundy Island**, off North Devon's coast, in April and May.

As for waterborne marine life, **grey seals** may occasionally be seen by observant coastal walkers, though they're most commonly spotted from a boat at such sites as Godrevy Island, Mousehole Rock, Falmouth Bay or, in greater numbers, the Isles of Scilly. Here, you'll encounter them hauled out onto rocks to bask in the sun or on remote beaches where females ("cows") – lighter and smaller than the males ("bulls") – often return each year to give birth. West Country seal pups are smaller than those of other UK populations, and they learn to swim earlier due to the milder conditions. You'll sometimes see seals wearing a necklace of the fishing nets with which they sometimes become entangled – one of the main hazards they face.

Dolphins and **porpoises** can also be seen off the Devon and Cornwall coasts. They live in family groups with territories covering hundreds of miles, so there are no specific places where sightings can be guaranteed – your best bet for land-based viewing would be at the far west of the peninsula, at Land's End, Sennen Cove, Cape Cornwall or Mount's Bay. The last century has seen a dramatic decline in porpoise and dolphin populations in the English Channel and southern Celtic Sea, partly due to their being a by-catch of fishing boats, but also due to the fact that fish stocks – their prey – have drastically fallen. It's now recognized that almost all the dolphins stranded on our beaches have been caught accidentally in fishing nets. Sightings of **whales**, which have also fallen prey to fishing methods, are quite rare: the best chances of seeing minke, pilot, humpbacked or even orca (or killer) whales is from **Sennen Cove**, or else from the ferry en route to the Isles of Scilly.

In summer **basking sharks** follow the warm Gulf Stream currents up Britain's west coast, allowing more than five hundred sightings in a typical year in the South West. A large cartilaginous fish – the world's second largest, at 10.5 metres – they are harmless to humans, as their huge jaws are designed to scoop up plankton, tiny plants and animals that form the basis of the ocean food chain. Less common are **leatherback turtles**, which grow to over two metres in length and also follow a migration route from their tropical breeding grounds in late summer and early autumn. They're occasionally washed up on Cornish beaches, but you're more likely to see them stuffed in local museums.

In 2001, the EU banned the notorious "wall of death" drift nets which have been responsible for countless dolphin, whale, shark and turtle deaths – to date the only statutory protection for these creatures, which are also regularly disturbed if not maimed by jet skis and private pleasure craft. If out on the waves, make sure you maintain a respectful distance – generally around a hundred metres. Any instances of harassment can be reported to the police or the Whale and Dolphin Conservation Society (see box, p.377).

Sea cliffs

Many of the long and highly scenic stretches of **cliffs** that dominate Devon and Cornwall's coastline enjoy the protection of the National Trust (see box, p.377), and can be explored along the **South West Coast Path**. Robust granite makes up most of the cliffs, though East Devon's striated and undulating red cliffs are softer sandstone, where landslips have led to the creation of thickly vegetated undercliffs. The dense scrub of **privet**, **dogwood**, **maple** and **spindle** here has encouraged the **nightingale** and the rare **dormouse**, while the close-cropped grassland at the cliff-tops is usually home to a rare community of flowers such as **wild thyme** and several species of **orchid**.

One of the best wildlife sites on the south coast is **Berry Head National Nature Reserve** near Brixham, which is home to a substantial **guillemot** colony nesting on cliff ledges, while more unusual **skuas** and **shearwaters** can be seen offshore. The area is also rich in rare plants, with over five hundred species recorded on the cliffs and surrounding scrub and limestone grassland. Many, such as **autumn squill** and the delightfully named **autumn ladies tresses** orchid, are national rarities.

The sea cliffs on the peninsula's northern coast are almost unbroken, though the fine stretch of hogback cliffs on North Devon's Exmoor coast is cut by deep wooded coombes which merge into upland moor. Here and further west, small ledges on the sheer faces provide protected habitats for many species of rare plants and nesting sites for birds such as **ravens** and the anchor-shaped **peregrine falcon**. On North Cornwall's cliffs, attempts are being made to reintroduce the **chough**, a rare, red-billed member of the crow family and the emblem of Cornwall – though virtually extinct here since 1973, the bird has recently begun to breed on the Lizard peninsula.

In West Cornwall, the **Land's End's Wildlife Discovery Centre** has nesting **razorbills**, while the **National Nature Reserve** at the Lizard headland holds a fantastic variety of wild flowers. The **serpentine** which makes up much of the Lizard peninsula is rich in magnesium, which allows rare species of plant to flourish, notably the colourful **Cornish heath** (*Erica vagans*) heather, unique to the Lizard. The magnesium also contributes to the floristically rich grasslands running up to the cliffs, harbouring plants normally found around the Mediterranean. These grassland slopes may include thirteen species of **clover**, as well as **vetch**, **ox-eye daisy**, **wild chive** and **orchid**, and are grazed by robust rare breeds such as **Soay sheep** and wild **ponies**.

Estuaries, rivers and reedbeds

Devon and Cornwall's **estuaries** hold some nationally rare species of waders and wildfowl, including the beautiful, pure-white **little egrets**. Among the most important areas for wintering wildlife are the **Tamar** complex around Plymouth, the **Hayle estuary** in Cornwall, and, most significantly, the **Exe estuary**, whose broad and shallow waters shelter around 20,000 **waders** as well as **brent geese** and **wigeon** in winter. These last two feed on **zostera**, an unusual flowering marine grass which thrives in the soft, muddy sediments adjacent to the salt marsh and also helps to stabilize the mud. The best site to watch these wintering flocks is **Dawlish Warren** at the mouth of the estuary where, just before high tide, you can usually see around twenty species. Other winter species that frequent the Exe estuary include **shelduck**, **dunlin**, **curlew**, **redshank**, the **black-** and **bar-tailed godwit**, as well as large flocks of **oystercatcher**, while one of the country's largest winter flocks of the rare and elegant **avocet** (symbol of the Royal Society for the Protection of Birds) is commonly seen higher up the estuary at **Topsham**.

The coast around Exmouth and Dawlish Warren is also a good spot for picking out a range of **sea** and **sawbilled ducks**, **grebes** and **divers**, though you'll need patience, expertise and good binoculars to identify these.

Many of the estuaries of Devon and Cornwall's southern seaboard are **rias**, or river valleys drowned long ago by a rise in sea level, with narrow, deep and well-defined channels and high levels of salinity. The **Helford** in the south of Cornwall is a delightful example of one, its winding creeks and wooded shorelines a haven for **eelgrass**. The salty water is also ideal for **cuttlefish** and **oysters**, while the rich rock pools at the estuary mouth shelter numerous **sea anemones** and **crabs**. The other important ria on the south coast is the **Kingsbridge estuary** in Devon, around which the rare **cirl bunting** has its stronghold.

The **rivers** of Devon and Cornwall, fast-flowing and varied in character, tend to run south from the high ground of the region's three moors, for example the Teign, Dart and Fowey. Along their banks, it's not difficult to spot **kingfisher**, **heron**, **dipper**, **sand martin** and **grey wagtail**, among other birds, while in the evening you may glimpse a **Daubenton's bat** skimming low over the water. These rivers are also home to the migratory **Atlantic salmon** and the resident **brown trout**, as well as many species of dragonfly and damselfly. The most important of the rivers that empty from the region's northern coast are the **De Lank** and **Camel** in Cornwall, and the **Taw** and **Torridge** in Devon, all of which are habitats of the highly secretive **otter**. The best chance of spotting these elusive mammals is on one of the guided excursions organized by the Devon or Cornwall Wildlife Trusts (see box, p.377).

Reedbeds constitute a highly scarce habitat nationally, much depleted after the drainage and reclamation of wetlands that occurred in previous centuries. However, the National Nature Reserve at **Slapton Ley**, between Dartmouth and Kingsbridge in South Devon, is one of the nation's finest freshwater reed and aquatic areas. Its main feature is the Ley itself, the largest natural lake in southwest England and separated from the sea by only a narrow shingle bar. The extensive areas of reedbed surrounding the lake shelter an abundant aquatic flora, including the rare **convergent stonewort** and the only British occurrence of the **strapwort**, while the monotonous call of **sedge** and **reed warblers** can be heard through much of the summer.

You'll also find reedbeds on the **River Exe** just upstream from Topsham on RSPB and Devon Wildlife Trust reserves, where it is possible to see **bearded tits**. Further west, **Marazion**, near Penzance in Cornwall, harbours a discreet and picturesque little RSPB reserve where the reedbeds are becoming famous for rare migrant **dragonflies** and such **butterflies** as the migrant **clouded yellow** and **painted lady**.

Sand dunes

Extending northwards from the tip of the Taw/Torridge estuary in North Devon, **Braunton Burrows** is one of the largest **sand dune** systems in Britain, nearly four miles in length and over a mile wide. Forming part of a designated International Biosphere Reserve, the dunes, which reach up to thirty metres high, are composed of wind-blown marine sand and crushed shells held loosely together by **marram** grass. These dynamic natural systems are continually – if imperceptibly – on the move, and the site's rich community of highly specialized plant and animal species has excited botanical interest since the seventeenth century. Among the 400-plus species of plants recorded here, the myriad wild flowers include **evening-scented sea-stock**, vivid patches of **biting stone crop**, deep-blue **viper's bugloss**, and the tall, lemon-coloured **evening primrose**, while throughout the summer months the ground is carpeted with an abundance of **bird's-foot trefoil** and **wild thyme**. In damper areas **yellow flag iris** and **marsh marigolds** are replaced later in summer by **marsh orchids** and **marsh helleborines**.

Other notable dune sites are at **Dawlish Warren**, in South Devon, and on the edges of the **Hayle estuary**, near St Ives in Cornwall, where **kestrels** may sometimes be seen hovering overhead.

Meadows and hedges

Unimproved neutral grassland – or **meadow** – constitutes one of the most picturesque British habitats, sheltering a wealth of colourful flowers and insects. This is particularly true of rush pasture, which occurs on poor soils. Flower-rich meadows are relatively plentiful in North Devon where they are known as **Culm grassland**, featuring a range of highly attractive and increasingly rare plants such as **devil's bit scabious**, the sublime **meadow thistle** and various **orchids** and **sedges**. Meadows are also very important for the rapidly declining **marsh fritillary butterfly**, whose remaining stronghold is in Devon, notably in Exmoor and Dartmoor National Parks; for more on these, information is best acquired from the relevant Wildlife Trusts (see box, p.377).

Small fields, woodland and thick, banked species-rich **hedgerows** are characteristic elements of the South West's meadows, harbouring a rich variety of wildlife such as the **blackbird**, **bullfinch** and **song thrush**, which nest here. The hedges – which might include **hawthorn**, **honeysuckle** and other woody plants – are also an important refuge for the predatory **aphids** that control agricultural pests. Over these fields and copses, the **buzzard** is a common sight wheeling above, one of the region's most common birds of prey.

Upland oakwood

Devon and Cornwall hold some remarkable relics of **upland oakwood**, the majority of which are to be found on Dartmoor, Exmoor and Bodmin Moor. The woods were traditionally managed for charcoal and tanbark through **coppicing** – stimulating woodland plant growth through regular cropping – but the post-World War II era has seen a dramatic decline in this form of management and some change of character as the coppice stools grow out and gradually revert to forest. On Dartmoor, **Yarner Wood** has probably existed as woodland since prehistoric times, a mixture of sessile oak, holly, rowan, beech, ash and wych elm with an under-carpet of bilberry. It's rich in woodland **butterflies**, **moths** and **wood ants**. Breeding birds include **sparrowhawk** and all three British **woodpeckers**, while **red**, **roe** and **fallow deer** may occasionally be seen. Adjoining Yarner Wood, **Trendlebere Down** is a mixture of typical upland oakwood and heath where over four hundred species of plants have been recorded. Many stands of trees on the higher ground show the multiple stems and stunted growth typical of abandoned coppice, with a dense cover of **bilberry** on the ground. On Bodmin Moor, **Golitha** is a stunning, steep-sided, tree-lined gorge formed by the River Fowey which tumbles down a waterfall and rapids, creating the humid conditions that allow **lichens** and **mosses** to thrive.

Heathland and blanket bog

The southwest peninsula's wide swathes of **lowland heath** typically comprise open ground poor in nutrients and dominated by **heathers** and **gorse**, with a scattering of scrub and trees (often Scots pine). There are excellent examples of this habitat near Exmouth in East Devon, where the pebblebed heaths of **Aylesbeare** and **Harpford Common** are managed as reserves by the RSPB and are a refuge for the nocturnal moth-eating **nightjar**, the **Dartford warbler** and the agile **hobby falcon**. To the west of the Exe estuary, **Haldon Forest** is a heavily wooded ridge interspersed with heath, where the woodland rides reveal glimpses of **high brown fritillary** and other rare species of butterfly – you can sometimes also spot the insect-eating **honey buzzard** along with the rare **goshawk** overhead.

The warm and wet nature of the climate in Cornwall's Lizard peninsula harbours outstanding examples of **maritime heath** of a type not found elsewhere in Britain. The unusual mix of maritime species creates a glorious spectacle in summer, when the ground is a blue carpet of **autumn** and **spring quill**, **rock sea lavender** and **golden samphire**, and later in the year, when the flowering purple **heathers** and golden **gorse** add a regal blaze. Maritime heathlands also range along the coasts of Penwith and North Cornwall, and on the Isles of Scilly. On the Cornish mainland, **adders** may be found basking on rocks in hot sunny weather, identifiable by their brownish colour with a lozenge pattern down the back.

In global terms, Britain holds a high proportion of **upland heath**, characterized by poor-quality soil and vegetation consisting of **heather**, **bilberry**, **crossleaved heath** and **western gorse**. The largest area of this type of terrain is to be found on **Exmoor**, where such unusual plants as **lesser twayblade** grow, while **crowberry** and **cranberry** occur at the very southern edge of their geographical range. Exmoor is the most important stronghold of the endangered **heath fritillary** in the UK, but its most famous long-term residents are its **red deer** and ponies. **Exmoor ponies**, descended from wild ponies, have a total population lower than many more recognized rare species, but they are hardy and well adapted to the tough conditions of winter on the exposed hills. A significant cause of casualties to the pony population is accidents with cars, and visitors are asked to drive carefully on the moor. In spring, lambs, too, often fall victim to speeding drivers.

Ponies are also a feature of the upland heaths of **Dartmoor**, which is characterized by granite tors that came about as a result of erosion of granite outcrops. Tors are regionally important for their **lichen** communities. You'll see the best examples at the edges of the Dartmoor plateau, rising above a patchwork of heath, bracken and valley mire, where scattered trees and shrubs may provide important nesting sites for birds such as the **raven** and the agile and rare hawk, the **merlin**.

Blanket bog is restricted to plateau areas where the wet conditions have allowed a mantle of **peat** to develop, with a high proportion of **heathers**, **cottongrasses** and **bogmosses** and very small populations of breeding **golden plover** and **dunlin**. Other typical birdlife of these moors includes the summer visitors **wheatear** and **ring ouzel**, while **peregrine falcons** occasionally nest on the sheer rock faces.

The arts

Stuck on the margins of British cultural life, Devon and Cornwall have produced few artists of great renown, though the late nineteenth and twentieth centuries saw the establishment of two of Britain's rare "art schools" linked to a particular place – namely, the Newlyn and St Ives schools, both in West Cornwall. The same factors which drew these artists' colonies – the combination of picturesque charm, rugged grandeur and the clear light – have continued to work on successive generations of artists, so that the region now has one of the largest arts and crafts communities in the country.

The eighteenth and early nineteenth centuries

Before the advent of the Newlyn and St Ives schools, Devon and Cornwall saw a relatively low level of artistic activity, though in the **eighteenth century**, each of the counties produced one nationally acclaimed figure. Of these, **Joshua Reynolds** (1723–92), born in Plympton, near Plymouth, achieved more lasting fame. After a sojourn in Italy, he found rich patrons who adored his Grand Manner and heroic style. Closely identified with formal "Academy art" (he was the first president of the Royal Academy in 1768), Reynolds advocated above all history painting, though he excelled at what he considered the inferior (but better-paid) field of portraiture.

John Opie (1761–1807), the first Cornish artist of any significance, was also highly esteemed for his portraits, though these were of a very different ilk. Something of a child prodigy, the untutored Opie was discovered by the Devon-born political satirist John Wolcot, then practising as a doctor in Truro, who in 1780 accompanied Opie to London to launch his artistic career (and simultaneously Wolcot's own as "Peter Pindar", author of a series of caustic poetical pamphlets). An instant success, the "Cornish wonder", as he came to be known, was most comfortable with his portraits of simple country folk – old people and children in particular – for which he used plenty of chiaroscuro in a style reminiscent of Caravaggio and Rembrandt. Opie was commissioned to paint seven illustrations for John Boydell's Shakespeare Gallery in 1786, the same year he exhibited his first historical work, *The Assassination of James I of Scotland*. This was followed a year later by *The Murder of Rizzio*, which secured his election as a member of the Royal Academy. Although his later work is now deemed undistinguished and repetitive, he was made a professor of painting at the Academy in 1805, and his death two years later was met with universal grief. Buried with great pomp in St Paul's Cathedral, next to Joshua Reynolds, Opie attracted the largest gathering of artists since Reynolds' own funeral, including Benjamin West, Henry Fuseli, John Flaxman and Joseph Turner.

Reynolds' and Opie's West Country successors included such figures as the marine artist, **Thomas Luny** (1757–1837), associated with Teignmouth, and the Irish-born Romantic painter **Francis Danby** (1793–1861), who settled in Exmouth in 1847 and was famous for his bombastic, apocalyptic biblical scenes but better liked for his sunsets and landscapes.

Art galleries and museums in Devon and Cornwall

The prolific output of Joshua Reynolds is well represented in stately homes throughout the country, a good number of them in Devon, such as **Hartland Abbey** and **Saltram House**. Most of the region's major public collections also hold examples of his oils, notably Exeter's **Royal Albert Memorial Museum** which, along with Truro's **Royal Cornwall Museum**, is also the place to see works by John Opie. You'll find a few paintings by Thomas Luny, among other local nineteenth-century artists, exhibited in Torquay's **Torre Abbey**.

The central role of St Ives in the region's art world was confirmed by the siting there of **Tate St Ives**, which opened in a beachside location in 1993 to showcase the works of the local school. The gallery also manages the town's **Barbara Hepworth Museum**, which showcases Barbara Hepworth's sculptures, while the **Leach Pottery** is the place to see work by Bernard Leach, Shoji Hamada and their various pupils and disciples. Contemporary work by local artists is on view at the **St Ives Society of Arts Gallery**. Some of the other current art on display in town is arresting, but much of it is uninspiring.

Most of the important works of the Newlyn School are in major collections, but a good representation is on view in Penzance's **Penlee House**. The **Exchange**, housed in an old telephone exchange in Penzance, is a significant new addition to the local arts scene, with a focus on modern art. Just up the road, the **Newlyn Art Gallery** also features contemporary art by local and other artists, while recent years have seen a thriving arts scene emerging in Falmouth, which you can experience at **Falmouth Arts Centre** and **Falmouth Art Gallery**.

Apart from these places, you'll find tiny galleries in scores of smaller towns and villages throughout Devon and Cornwall, which are often worth a glance or more. Local tourist offices can sometimes provide a list if you're seriously interested; alternatively, pick up a copy of one of the local **arts magazines** occasionally available from newsagents and tourist offices, or check the listings in the monthly magazines *Inside Cornwall* and *Cornwall Today*.

The Newlyn School

The arrival of the railway in Devon and Cornwall in the late nineteenth century generated a huge growth of interest in the region. Artists were particularly drawn to the far west of the peninsula, encouraged by the mild climate and exceptional light which, together with the strong fishing culture, recalled a corner of continental Europe. Two Birmingham artists, **Walter Langley** (1852–1922) and **Edwin Harris** (1855–1906), had already settled in Newlyn in 1882, but it was the arrival of **Stanhope Forbes** (1857–1947) two years later that really set the ball rolling for the "**Newlyn School**". Inspired by the fishing port's resemblance to villages in Brittany where he had studied, Forbes showed his fascination with the effects of the luminous light and with the life of the local fishing community in such works as *Fish Sale on Newlyn Beach* (1884). When displayed at the Royal Academy, this lively depiction of men and women trading fish on the wet sand established Forbes and the Newlyn School as the most prominent exponents of the new French-influenced styles, which contrasted with the predominantly insular and backward-looking tone of most British painting of the time. The Newlyn painters tried to immerse themselves in the life of the fishing community in order to represent it more faithfully, and their work shows great sympathy with the people of the locality, even if it is occasionally prone to sentimentality. Other prominent members of the school included **Norman Garstin** (1847–1926), an Irishman who came to Newlyn in 1886 – supposedly the most "intellectual" member of the group. His most famous work, *The Rain It Raineth Everyday* (1889), was accepted by the Royal Academy but never shown there – it's currently viewable in Penlee House, Penzance. **Henry Scott Tuke** (1858–1929), born in York but brought up in Falmouth and London, had already spent some time painting in Newlyn before he settled in Falmouth in 1885, with the stated intention to "paint the nude in open air". Unable to find suitable models locally he imported one from London, Walter Shilling, and, though his numerous depictions of nude boys aroused controversy, his work did gain some respectability and was actively encouraged by Stanhope Forbes. Truro's museum has some of his homoerotic nudes together with maritime subjects and a self-portrait.

Although most Newlyn artists shared Forbes' devotion to open-air painting, another member of the school, **Frank Bramley** (1857–1915), made his reputation with *A Hopeless Dawn* (1888), an interior scene suffused with light from different sources. Elizabeth Armstrong, later to become Stanhope Forbes' wife and better known as **Elizabeth Forbes** (1859–1912), also painted domestic scenes and portraits characterized by a directness and warmth sometimes missing in her husband's works. Her output was at one time valued more highly by the critics than that of her husband, but her career was cut short by her early death.

There was another wave of artists to Newlyn some twenty years after Forbes first arrived in the town – including **Dod Proctor** (1892–1972), then known as Doris Shaw, and **Laura Knight** (1877–1970), who became better known for her later paintings of ballet and the circus – but Newlyn's golden period had ended by the beginning of the twentieth century and interest subsequently focused on St Ives.

The St Ives School

Across the neck of the Penwith peninsula, St Ives had also previously attracted the attention of the art world, starting with a visit by Turner in 1811. With the new age of rail travel, other artists followed in his footsteps, including Whistler and Sickert in 1883–84, who left a few tiny oil studies as evidence. A trickle of English and foreign artists set up studios during the ensuing years, so that by the 1920s there were scores of artists working locally, including many amateurs alongside more established names. Among the latter were **Ben Nicholson** (1894–1982) and **Christopher Wood** (1901–30), who, on a day-trip to St Ives in 1928, were jointly responsible for discovering the work of **Alfred Wallis** (1855–1942), a retired sailor born in Devonport. Having previously worked on fishing boats both inshore and out to sea for over twenty years, Wallis later took up a variety of jobs such as dealing in marine scrap and selling ice cream, and following the death of his wife in 1925, he turned increasingly to painting. His work, often produced on scraps of driftwood, depicted primitive scenes of ships and seascapes around St Ives and the adjacent coasts. Despite the efforts of Nicholson, Wood and others to promote his work, and his subsequent rapid rise to fame as Britain's best-known naive artist, he nonetheless ended his days in a St Ives workhouse.

Wood himself produced some of his best work during his short residence in Cornwall (1929–30), while Nicholson went on to be the guiding spirit of the **St Ives School** which flourished between the late 1940s and early 1960s. He shared with the other artists of the group a preference for non-figurative work, his delicate reliefs and semi-abstract still lifes acknowledged to have had a greater influence on abstract art than any other British artist. He had settled in the town in 1939, together with his second wife **Barbara Hepworth** (1903–75), a sculptor who had abandoned figure-based art in favour of abstract geometric forms, and whose work was increasingly inspired by the rock and sea landscape of the Penwith peninsula. Nicholson left St Ives in 1958, but Hepworth spent the rest of her life in the town, eventually dying in a fire in her studio there, after which her house and garden became a museum dedicated to her work.

Probably the most influential of the group during the war years was the Russian constructivist **Naum Gabo** (1890–1977) whose spatial geometric sculptures had a profound effect on Nicholson and Hepworth as well as other members of the community. Though Gabo left for the USA in 1946, many of his ideas are reflected in the work of younger St Ives artists such as **Wilhelmina Barnes-Graham** (1912–2004), whose work is alternately abstract and figurative, and **Peter Lanyon** (1918–64), who was born in the town and lived there most of his life; such works of his as *Porthleven* (1951) mix abstract themes with allusions to the local landscape.

On the periphery of the group, **Bernard Leach** (1887–1979) arrived in St Ives from Japan in 1920, accompanied by **Shoji Hamada** (1894–1978). Together they set up the St Ives Pottery which over the next six decades remained at the centre of the studio pottery movement in Britain. Among the foremost potters who studied under Leach in St Ives were Michael Cardew and Katherine Pleydell-Bouverie.

In the late 1950s and 1960s, a third wave of St Ives artists rose to prominence, including **Brian Wynter** (1915–75), **Roger Hilton** (1911–75), **Terry Frost** (1915–2003) and **Patrick Heron** (1920–99). More recently, locally born **Bryan Pearce** (1929–2007) achieved some prominence, the vibrant colours and simple lines in his still lifes, church interiors and scenes of St Ives recalling those of Alfred Wallis.

Books

We've highlighted a selection of books below which will give you a flavour of Devon and Cornwall, past and present; books marked ★ are particularly recommended. Some of the titles may be out of print, but these are often available from Amazon (www.amazon.co.uk) or AbeBooks (www.abebooks.co.uk); otherwise try local libraries or the region's numerous secondhand bookshops, which usually stock a sizable section of local-interest books – note, however, that the same books are usually cheaper (if harder to find) in shops outside the West Country. Many of the memoirs and novels listed here are available as CDs or downloadable audiobooks.

History, memoir and background

Evelyn Atkins *We Bought an Island*. Humorous account of the purchase of Looe Island off the coast of Cornwall and the various characters encountered. *Tales from Our Cornish Island* is the sequel.

★ **John Betjeman** *Betjeman's Cornwall*. Collection of prose and poetry relating to Cornwall, with illustrations by John Piper and photos. Fans will also be interested in a DVD, *Betjeman's West Country*, a compilation of films about the region made by the poet, intercut by interviews with his family and friends.

Michael Bird *The St Ives Artists: A Biography of Time and Place*. Entertaining but meticulously researched narrative of the waves of artists who settled in St Ives from 1946. It's a fascinating tale, but should be read in conjunction with a pictorial guide to the works as it's scantily illustrated.

Anthony Burton *Richard Trevithick: The Man and his Machine*. The extraordinary story of Cornwall's greatest engineer and inventor (1771–1833), who built his first locomotive in 1801, the first of many innovations for which the world was not ready. He spent ten years wandering South America in pursuit of ever-more speculative ventures, but died penniless in England.

Marion Dell and Marion Whybrow *Virginia Woolf and Vanessa Bell: Remembering St Ives*. The two sisters of the title spent large parts of their childhood in St Ives, an experience that infused their later work, as this book absorbingly describes by means of extracts of letters, journals and Virginia's own fiction. It's beautifully illustrated too, with old photos and examples of Vanessa's paintings.

★ **Daphne du Maurier** *Vanishing Cornwall*. The book chronicles all aspects of the place where du Maurier lived for most of her life, fusing history, anecdote and travelogue in a plea for Cornwall's preservation.

F.E. Halliday *A History of Cornwall*. First published in 1959, this plainly told and readable general history covers everything from the Stone Age to the twentieth century, taking in Celtic culture, tin mining and the impact of John Wesley en route.

Patrick Hutton *I Would Not Be Forgotten: The Life and Work of Robert Stephen Hawker*. The eccentric vicar of Morwenstow in North Cornwall, Hawker (1803–75) was the author of Cornwall's anthem, "The Song of the Western Men"; this biography includes his verse alongside details of his colourful life.

Arthur Mee *Cornwall* and *Devon* (o/p). Chunky volumes from the 1930s in the *King's England* series; precious anecdotes and historical snippets set among dense text, interspersed with sepia photos.

Philip Payton *Cornwall: A History*. Learned and comprehensive history of the county, bringing the story up to the present day.

Nikolaus Pevsner and Enid Radcliffe *The Buildings of England: Cornwall*. The first of the series of Pevsner's monumental guides researched on long car journeys with his wife, this is also one of the slimmest, with few mentions of vernacular architecture or Cornwall's rich heritage of nonconformist chapels. The book needs updating and in parts rewriting to reflect recent changes and new knowledge, though it's still the best available of this ilk.

Nikolaus Pevsner and Bridget Cherry *The Buildings of England: Devon*. First published as two volumes in 1952 (*North Devon* and *South Devon*), this single fat volume has been updated and enlarged, and tells you everything you wanted to know about every building of note in the county – and plenty that you probably have no wish to know. It's comprehensive, but cumbersome and expensive.

A.L. Rowse *A Cornish Childhood*. Autobiography by the distinguished historian and scholar covering his early years in Cornwall at the beginning of the twentieth century.

Tim Smit *Eden*. Often inspiring chronicle of the trials and triumphs that went into the Eden Project; humorously narrated, if sometimes over-burdened with the nitty-gritty. In *The Lost Gardens of Heligan*, Smit has also written of his involvement with the other great project for which he is known.

C.J. Stevens *The Cornish Nightmare (D.H. Lawrence in Cornwall)* and *Lawrence at Tregerthen* (both o/p). The story of Lawrence and Frieda's Cornish sojourn during World War I, as told to the author by Stanley Hocking – "the boy" in *Kangaroo* (see below) – and others. This is everyday Lawrence seen fondly, sometimes critically and with some amusement, by the Cornish locals.

Carol Trewin *Gourmet Cornwall* and *Cornish Fishing and Seafood*. The first of these two books is an expert gastro-guide, sumptuously photographed, with well-informed background, the second takes a well-balanced look at the local fishing industry and speculates about its future; both are laced with recipes.

Mark Wallington *Travels With Boogie: 500 Mile Walkies*. Hilarious account of a low-budget hike on the South West Coast Path in the 1980s, in the company of the dog of the title. A must for anyone familiar with or attempting the coast path.

Fiction

R.D. Blackmore *Lorna Doone*. Swashbuckling Exmoor yarn of romance and inter-clan warfare during the time of the Monmouth Rebellion. Don't let the archaic language and antiquated style put you off this page-turner that was televised by the BBC in 2000.

Daphne du Maurier *Frenchman's Creek*. Named after the creek off Cornwall's Helford River, this love story with piracy is set in Cornwall during the Restoration and concerns Dona St Columb, who escapes from London to her house in Cornwall where she gets embroiled in nefarious activities, mainly to do with contraband.

Daphne du Maurier *Jamaica Inn*. A young girl goes to live with her aunt and her husband who own the stark and forbidding inn of the title (which stands today on Bodmin Moor) – a gripping yarn of smugglers.

Daphne du Maurier *Rebecca*. From the first line, "Last night I went to Manderley again… ", this tale of deception and paranoia gallops along at an unputdownable pace – "Manderley" was Menabilly, near Fowey, where du Maurier lived.

Helen Dunmore *Zennor in Darkness*. Dunmore's first novel is an imaginative re-creation of D.H. Lawrence's experience while living in West Cornwall 1915–17, seen from the perspective of a local girl who falls under his spell. With World War I as a constant background, the haunting atmosphere and erratic protagonists are skilfully depicted.

Patrick Gale *Rough Music*. A well-plotted read to accompany a holiday on a Cornish beach. Separated by thirty years, the two interwoven story lines set in a beach house in Cornwall sensitively explore gay and inter-generational relationships.

Winston Graham *Poldark* series. *Ross Poldark*, *Demelza* and *The Angry Tide* are among the ten novels set around Perranporth and St Agnes through the late 1700s and early 1800s, featuring Ross Poldark, his wife Demelza, his arch-rival George Warleggan, and a colourful supporting cast of characters – filmed for TV and extremely popular.

Thomas Hardy *A Pair of Blue Eyes*. Partly based on Hardy's own experiences as an architect in Cornwall, this tragic story of Elfride Swancourt, caught between the love of handsome, gentle Stephen Smith and the intellectually superior Henry Knight, sheds light on the struggle between the classes and sexes in the England of that time.

D.H. Lawrence *Kangaroo*. The semi-autobiographical tale follows Richard and Harriet Somers arriving in Australia from the decay of postwar Europe and incorporates a nightmare sequence recounting the Lawrences' trauma of being chased out of Cornwall.

Arthur Quiller-Couch *The Delectable Duchy*. Fowey was "Troy Town" in the works of this formidable critic, best known for his literary studies. This collection of short stories highlights different facets of social history and the Cornish psyche as it was in the late nineteenth century. See also the author's *From a Cornish Window* (o/p), if you can find it.

Derek Tangye *The Minack Chronicles*. A local hero in West Cornwall, Tangye was a former deb's delight who came to Cornwall to find the "good life", revealing all in his "shocking" tales. Minack is the Cornish flower farm where he and his wife Jeannie lived. Titles in the series include *A Drake at the Door*, *A Gull on the Roof* and *A Cat in the Window*.

Henry Williamson *Tarka the Otter*. The natural history of North Devon is a minutely detailed backcloth to this animal tale which has spawned an industry.

Virginia Woolf *To the Lighthouse*. Although the novel is set on a Hebridean island, the lighthouse of the title is Godrevy, near Hayle, where Woolf spent her summers, and the story recalls strands of her Cornish sojourns.

Guidebooks

Alf Alderson *Surfing – A Beginner's Manual.* The best guide to the ins and outs of surfing. The same author's *Surf UK* is geared towards more experienced surfers.

John Betjeman *Cornwall* and *Devon* (o/p). First published in 1933 and 1936 respectively, and revised in 1964 and 1953, these Shell Guides are now collectors' items, imbued with Betjeman's forthright views on churches and architecture in general, and still pertinent – a welcome antidote to glossy brochures.

Nick Cotton *Ordnance Survey Cycle Tours: Cornwall and Devon.* Fourteen on-road and ten off-road routes in Devon and Cornwall, including rides across Dartmoor and Exmoor. 1:50,000 *Landranger* mapping is used, and there are introductions to each route, with gradient diagrams, information on length and difficulty and notes to places of interest en route. See also Cotton's *South West Mountain Biking*, with rides on Exmoor and Dartmoor, and *More Cycling Without Traffic: Southwest*, which has around 30 leisurely, off-road rides with families in mind, avoiding hills and difficult terrain.

Nick Cotton and John Grimshaw *The Official Guide to the National Cycle Network.* Covers all the routes of the National Cycle Network so far opened in the UK. Well presented with good maps and pictures, the guide also provides info on surfaces, traffic hazards and refreshment stops, and has useful advice for families.

Max Darkins *Mountain Bike Rides in & around Exmoor & Dartmoor.* Beautifully produced guide to off-road biking in the region – not just the two moors but as far afield as Saunton and Truro – in a ring binder that can accommodate "expansion packs" (available from ⓦwww.rougharideguide.co.uk). The OS maps and directions are first-class.

Devon County Council *The Two Moors Way/Devon Coast to Coast.* Walking itinerary covering the hundred-odd miles between Plymouth and Lynmouth, incorporating the Erme–Plym trail and the Two Moors Way crossing the length of Dartmoor and Exmoor. Can be used for both directions.

John Earle *Dartmoor: Walks into History.* Mainly short and undemanding hikes on Dartmoor, each based around a place of historical significance – prehistoric sites, castles, old mining remnants, quarries and ancient trackways – with other items of interest pointed out en route.

John Gilman *Exmoor Rangers' Favourite Walks.* Thirty circular walks to get the most out of Exmoor, originally written by a former head ranger and subsequently updated by National Park staff and volunteers. The routes vary from two to eight miles.

David Norman and Vic Tucker *Where to Watch Birds in Devon and Cornwall.* An excellent introduction to birdlife and other aspects of the region, including birdwatching sites, information on access for the car-bound or disabled, and an update of recent occurrences at each site.

South West Coast Path The official National Trail Guide to the coast path in four pocket-friendly volumes, with excellent 1:25,000 Ordnance Survey maps, copious information on background and things to see, and details of circular walks en route.

Woodland Trust *Exploring Woodland: The South West of England.* One of a series of illustrated guides with maps and lots of description covering what to see, historical background and wildlife.

Travel store

Travel

Andorra The Pyrenees, Pyrenees & Andorra Map, Spain
Antigua The Caribbean
Argentina Argentina, Argentina Map, Buenos Aires, South America on a Budget
Aruba The Caribbean
Australia Australia, Australia Map, East Coast Australia, Melbourne, Sydney, Tasmania
Austria Austria, Europe on a Budget, Vienna
Bahamas The Bahamas, The Caribbean
Barbados Barbados DIR, The Caribbean
Belgium Belgium & Luxembourg, Bruges DIR, Brussels, Brussels Map, Europe on a Budget
Belize Belize, Central America on a Budget, Guatemala & Belize Map
Benin West Africa
Bolivia Bolivia, South America on a Budget
Brazil Brazil, Rio, South America on a Budget
British Virgin Islands The Caribbean
Brunei Malaysia, Singapore & Brunei [1 title], Southeast Asia on a Budget
Bulgaria Bulgaria, Europe on a Budget
Burkina Faso West Africa
Cambodia Cambodia, Southeast Asia on a Budget, Vietnam, Laos & Cambodia Map [1 Map]
Cameroon West Africa
Canada Canada, Pacific Northwest, Toronto, Toronto Map, Vancouver
Cape Verde West Africa
Cayman Islands The Caribbean
Chile Chile, Chile Map, South America on a Budget
China Beijing, China, Hong Kong & Macau, Hong Kong & Macau DIR, Shanghai
Colombia South America on a Budget
Costa Rica Central America on a Budget, Costa Rica, Costa Rica & Panama Map
Croatia Croatia, Croatia Map, Europe on a Budget
Cuba Cuba, Cuba Map, The Caribbean, Havana
Cyprus Cyprus, Cyprus Map
Czech Republic The Czech Republic, Czech & Slovak Republics, Europe on a Budget, Prague, Prague DIR, Prague Map
Denmark Copenhagen, Denmark, Europe on a Budget, Scandinavia
Dominica The Caribbean
Dominican Republic Dominican Republic, The Caribbean
Ecuador Ecuador, South America on a Budget
Egypt Egypt, Egypt Map
El Salvador Central America on a Budget
England Britain, Camping in Britain, Devon & Cornwall, Dorset, Hampshire and The Isle of Wight [1 title], England, Europe on a Budget, The Lake District, London, London DIR, London Map, London Mini Guide, Walks In London & Southeast England
Estonia The Baltic States, Europe on a Budget
Fiji Fiji
Finland Europe on a Budget, Finland, Scandinavia
France Brittany & Normandy, Corsica, Corsica Map, The Dordogne & the Lot, Europe on a Budget, France, France Map, Languedoc & Roussillon, The Loire, Paris, Paris DIR, Paris Map, Paris Mini Guide, Provence & the Côte d'Azur, The Pyrenees, Pyrenees & Andorra Map
French Guiana South America on a Budget
Gambia The Gambia, West Africa
Germany Berlin, Berlin Map, Europe on a Budget, Germany, Germany Map
Ghana West Africa
Gibraltar Spain
Greece Athens Map, Crete, Crete Map, Europe on a Budget, Greece, Greece Map, Greek Islands, Ionian Islands
Guadeloupe The Caribbean
Guatemala Central America on a Budget, Guatemala, Guatemala & Belize Map
Guinea West Africa
Guinea-Bissau West Africa
Guyana South America on a Budget
Holland see The Netherlands
Honduras Central America on a Budget
Hungary Budapest, Europe on a Budget, Hungary
Iceland Iceland, Iceland Map
India Goa, India, India Map, Kerala, Rajasthan, Delhi & Agra [1 title], South India, South India Map
Indonesia Bali & Lombok, Southeast Asia on a Budget
Ireland Dublin DIR, Dublin Map, Europe on a Budget, Ireland, Ireland Map
Israel Jerusalem
Italy Europe on a Budget, Florence DIR, Florence & Siena Map, Florence & the best of Tuscany, Italy, The Italian Lakes, Naples & the Amalfi Coast, Rome, Rome DIR, Rome Map, Sardinia, Sicily, Sicily Map, Tuscany & Umbria, Tuscany Map, Venice, Venice DIR, Venice Map
Jamaica Jamaica, The Caribbean
Japan Japan, Tokyo
Jordan Jordan
Kenya Kenya, Kenya Map
Korea Korea
Laos Laos, Southeast Asia on a Budget, Vietnam, Laos & Cambodia Map [1 Map]
Latvia The Baltic States, Europe on a Budget
Lithuania The Baltic States, Europe on a Budget
Luxembourg Belgium & Luxembourg, Europe on a Budget
Malaysia Malaysia Map, Malaysia, Singapore & Brunei [1 title], Southeast Asia on a Budget
Mali West Africa
Malta Malta & Gozo DIR
Martinique The Caribbean
Mauritania West Africa
Mexico Baja California, Baja California, Cancún & Cozumel DIR, Mexico, Mexico Map, Yucatán, Yucatán Peninsula Map
Monaco France, Provence & the Côte d'Azur
Montenegro Montenegro
Morocco Europe on a Budget, Marrakesh DIR, Marrakesh Map, Morocco, Morocco Map,
Nepal Nepal
Netherlands Amsterdam, Amsterdam DIR, Amsterdam Map, Europe on a Budget, The Netherlands
Netherlands Antilles The Caribbean
New Zealand New Zealand, New Zealand Map

DIR: Rough Guide **DIRECTIONS** for short breaks

Nicaragua Central America on a Budget
Niger West Africa
Nigeria West Africa
Norway Europe on a Budget, Norway, Scandinavia
Panama Central America on a Budget, Costa Rica & Panama Map, Panama
Paraguay South America on a Budget
Peru Peru, Peru Map, South America on a Budget
Philippines The Philippines, Southeast Asia on a Budget,
Poland Europe on a Budget, Poland
Portugal Algarve DIR, The Algarve Map, Europe on a Budget, Lisbon DIR, Lisbon Map, Madeira DIR, Portugal, Portugal Map, Spain & Portugal Map
Puerto Rico The Caribbean, Puerto Rico
Romania Europe on a Budget, Romania
Russia Europe on a Budget, Moscow, St Petersburg
St Kitts & Nevis The Caribbean
St Lucia The Caribbean
St Vincent & the Grenadines The Caribbean
Scotland Britain, Camping in Britain, Edinburgh DIR, Europe on a Budget, Scotland, Scottish Highlands & Islands
Senegal West Africa
Serbia Montenegro Europe on a Budget
Sierra Leone West Africa
Singapore Malaysia, Singapore & Brunei [1 title], Singapore, Singapore DIR, Southeast Asia on a Budget
Slovakia Czech & Slovak Republics, Europe on a Budget
Slovenia Europe on a Budget, Slovenia
South Africa Cape Town & the Garden Route, South Africa, South Africa Map
Spain Andalucía, Andalucía Map, Barcelona, Barcelona DIR, Barcelona Map, Europe on a Budget, Ibiza & Formentera DIR, Gran Canaria DIR, Madrid DIR, Lanzarote & Fuerteventura DIR Madrid Map, Mallorca & Menorca, Mallorca DIR, Mallorca Map, The Pyrenees, Pyrenees & Andorra Map, Spain, Spain & Portugal Map, Tenerife & La Gomera DIR
Sri Lanka Sri Lanka, Sri Lanka Map
Suriname South America on a Budget
Sweden Europe on a Budget, Scandinavia, Sweden
Switzerland Europe on a Budget, Switzerland
Taiwan Taiwan
Tanzania Tanzania, Zanzibar
Thailand Bangkok, Southeast Asia on a Budget, Thailand, Thailand Map, Thailand Beaches & Islands
Togo West Africa
Trinidad & Tobago The Caribbean, Trinidad & Tobago
Tunisia Tunisia, Tunisia Map
Turkey Europe on a Budget, Istanbul, Turkey, Turkey Map
Turks and Caicos Islands The Bahamas, The Caribbean
United Arab Emirates Dubai DIR, Dubai & UAE Map [1 title]
United Kingdom Britain, Devon & Cornwall, Edinburgh DIR England, Europe on a Budget, The Lake District, London, London DIR, London Map, London Mini Guide, Scotland, Scottish Highlands & Islands, Wales, Walks In London & Southeast England
United States Alaska, Boston, California, California Map, Chicago, Colorado, Florida, Florida Map, The Grand Canyon, Hawaii, Los Angeles, Los Angeles Map, Los Angeles and Southern California, Maui DIR, Miami & South Florida, New England, New England Map, New Orleans & Cajun Country, New Orleans DIR, New York City, NYC DIR, NYC Map, New York City Mini Guide, Oregon & Washington, Orlando & Walt Disney World® DIR, San Francisco, San Francisco DIR, San Francisco Map, Seattle, Southwest USA, USA, Washington DC, Yellowstone & the Grand Tetons National Park, Yosemite National Park
Uruguay South America on a Budget
US Virgin Islands The Bahamas, The Caribbean
Venezuela South America on a Budget
Vietnam Southeast Asia on a Budget, Vietnam, Vietnam, Laos & Cambodia Map [1 Map],
Wales Britain, Camping in Britain, Europe on a Budget, Wales
First-Time Series FT Africa, FT Around the World, FT Asia, FT Europe, FT Latin America
Inspirational guides Earthbound, Clean Breaks, Make the Most of Your Time on Earth, Ultimate Adventures, World Party
Travel Specials Camping in Britain, Travel with Babies & Young Children, Walks in London & SE England

ROUGH GUIDES Don't Just Travel

Computers Cloud Computing, FWD this link, The Internet, iPhone, iPods & iTunes, Macs & OS X, Website Directory
Film & TV American Independent Film, British Cult Comedy, Comedy Movies, Cult Movies, Film, Film Musicals, Film Noir, Gangster Movies, Horror Movies, Sci-Fi Movies, Westerns
Lifestyle Babies & Toddlers, Brain Training, Food, Girl Stuff, Green Living, Happiness, Men's Health, Pregnancy & Birth, Running, Saving & Selling Online, Sex, Weddings
Music The Beatles, The Best Music You've Never Heard, Blues, Bob Dylan, Book of Playlists, Classical Music, Heavy Metal, Jimi Hendrix, Led Zeppelin, Nirvana, Opera, Pink Floyd, The Rolling Stones, Soul and R&B, Velvet Underground, World Music
Popular Culture Anime, Classic Novels, Conspiracy Theories, Crime Fiction, The Da Vinci Code, Graphic Novels, Hidden Treasures, His Dark Materials, Hitchhiker's Guide to the Galaxy, The Lost Symbol, Manga, Next Big Thing, Shakespeare, True Crime, Tutankhamun, Unexplained Phenomena, Videogames
Science The Brain, Climate Change, The Earth, Energy Crisis, Evolution, Future, Genes & Cloning, The Universe, Weather

Small print and Index

A Rough Guide to Rough Guides

Published in 1982, the first Rough Guide – to Greece – was a student scheme that became a publishing phenomenon. Mark Ellingham, a recent graduate in English from Bristol University, had been travelling in Greece the previous summer and couldn't find the right guidebook. With a small group of friends he wrote his own guide, combining a highly contemporary, journalistic style with a thoroughly practical approach to travellers' needs.

The immediate success of the book spawned a series that rapidly covered dozens of destinations. And, in addition to impecunious backpackers, Rough Guides soon acquired a much broader and older readership that relished the guides' wit and inquisitiveness as much as their enthusiastic, critical approach and value-for-money ethos.

These days, Rough Guides include recommendations from shoestring to luxury and cover more than 200 destinations around the globe, including almost every country in the Americas and Europe, more than half of Africa and most of Asia and Australasia. Our ever-growing team of authors and photographers is spread all over the world, particularly in Europe, the US and Australia.

In the early 1990s, Rough Guides branched out of travel, with the publication of Rough Guides to World Music, Classical Music and the Internet. All three have become benchmark titles in their fields, spearheading the publication of a wide range of books under the Rough Guide name.

Including the travel series, Rough Guides now number more than 350 titles, covering: phrasebooks, waterproof maps, music guides from Opera to Heavy Metal, reference works as diverse as Conspiracy Theories and Shakespeare, and popular culture books from iPods to Poker. Rough Guides also produce a series of more than 120 World Music CDs in partnership with World Music Network.

Visit www.roughguides.com to see our latest publications.

Rough Guide travel images are available for commercial licensing at www.roughguidespictures.com

Rough Guide credits

Text editor: Tim Locke
Layout: Sachin Gupta
Cartography: Ashutosh Bharti
Picture editor: Sarah Cummins
Production: Rebecca Short
Proofreader: Karen Parker
Cover design: Dan May, Chloë Roberts
Photographer: Tim Draper
Editorial: Lara Kavanagh, Ruth Blackmore, Andy Turner, Keith Drew, Edward Aves, Alice Park, Lucy White, Jo Kirby, James Smart, Natasha Foges, Róisín Cameron, James Rice, Emma Traynor, Emma Gibbs, Kathryn Lane, Monica Woods, Mani Ramaswamy, Harry Wilson, Lucy Cowie, Alison Roberts, Joe Staines, Peter Buckley, Matthew Milton, Tracy Hopkins, Ruth Tidball; **Delhi** Madhavi Singh, Karen D'Souza, Lubna Shaheen
Design & Pictures: **London** Scott Stickland, Dan May, Diana Jarvis, Mark Thomas, Nicole Newman, Sarah Cummins, Emily Taylor; **Delhi** Umesh Aggarwal, Ajay Verma, Jessica Subramanian, Ankur Guha, Pradeep Thapliyal, Sachin Tanwar, Anita Singh, Nikhil Agarwal.
Production: Liz Cherry
Cartography: **London** Ed Wright, Katie Lloyd-Jones; **Delhi** Rajesh Chhibber, Rajesh Mishra, Animesh Pathak, Jasbir Sandhu, Karobi Gogoi, Alakananda Bhattacharya, Swati Handoo, Deshpal Dabas
Online: **London** Faye Hellon, Jeanette Angell, Fergus Day, Justine Bright, Clare Bryson, Aine Fearon, Adrian Low, Ezgi Celebi; **Delhi** Amit Verma, Rahul Kumar, Narender Kumar, Ravi Yadav, Debojit Borah, Rakesh Kumar, Ganesh Sharma, Shisir Basumatari
Marketing & Publicity: **London** Liz Statham, Louise Maher, Jess Carter, Vanessa Godden, Vivienne Watton, Anna Paynton, Rachel Sprackett, Laura Vipond; **New York** Katy Ball, Judi Powers; **Delhi** Ragini Govind
Reference Director: Andrew Lockett
Operations Assistant: Becky Doyle
Operations Manager: Helen Atkinson
Publishing Director (Travel): Clare Currie
Commercial Manager: Gino Magnotta
Managing Director: John Duhigg

Publishing information

This fourth edition published April 2010 by
Rough Guides Ltd,
80 Strand, London WC2R 0RL
14 Local Shopping Centre, Panchsheel Park, New Delhi 110017, India
Distributed by the Penguin Group
Penguin Books Ltd,
80 Strand, London WC2R 0RL
Penguin Group (USA)
375 Hudson Street, NY 10014, USA
Penguin Group (Australia)
250 Camberwell Road, Camberwell, Victoria 3124, Australia
Penguin Group (Canada)
195 Harry Walker Parkway N, Newmarket, ON, L3Y 7B3 Canada
Penguin Group (NZ)
67 Apollo Drive, Mairangi Bay, Auckland 1310, New Zealand
Cover concept by Peter Dyer.

Typeset in Bembo and Helvetica to an original design by Henry Iles.
Printed in Singapore

408pp includes index
A catalogue record for this book is available from the British Library
ISBN: 978-1-84836-505-6

1 3 5 7 9 8 6 4 2

Help us update

We've gone to a lot of effort to ensure that the fourth edition of **The Rough Guide to Devon and Cornwall** is accurate and up-to-date. However, things change – places get "discovered", opening hours are notoriously fickle, restaurants and rooms raise prices or lower standards. If you feel we've got it wrong or left something out, we'd like to know, and if you can remember the address, the price, the hours, the phone number, so much the better.

Please send your comments with the subject line "**Rough Guide Devon and Cornwall Update**" to ⓔmail@roughguides.com. We'll credit all contributions and send a copy of the next edition (or any other Rough Guide if you prefer) for the very best emails.

Have your questions answered and tell others about your trip at ⓦwww.roughguides.com

Acknowledgements

This book is dedicated to all UK surfers.

The current edition could not have been completed without the invaluable input of Almighty Quinn, the universal skills of the Emerald Princess, and a doughty performance by Marge. Tim Locke was an exemplary editor, full of suggestions from his own familiarity with the region, and at Rough Guides, Robert Andrews would like to thank Monica Woods and Jo Kirby for guidance and support in the face of mangled deadlines.

Readers' letters

Thanks to all the readers who have taken the time to write in with comments and suggestions (and apologies if we've inadvertently omitted or misspelt anyone's name):

Derek Britton, Ms G M Charles, Cathy Melia, Lin and Jean-Paul, James Spooner, Val Stacey, Cait Weston.

Photo credits

All photos © Rough Guides except the following:

Full page
Abbey Gardens, Tresco © Robert Harding Ltd/Alamy

Introduction
Tin mine © TTL Images/Alamy

Things not to miss
01 Aerial view of Tresco © Peter Barritt/Alamy
04 Outdoor dining © Mr Standfast/Alamy
09 Fowey © Stuart R Harrop/Photolibrary
11 Women competiting in World Pilot Gig Championships © Mike Greenslade/Alamy
13 Lanhydrock House © Paul Thompson/Photolibrary

The Sea, The Sea colour section
Par Beach © Sarah Cummins

Devon and Cornwall on a plate colour section
Mackerel on a barbecue © John Carey /Photolibrary
Camel Valley Vineyard © Ashley Cooper/Alamy
Porthminster Café © Marc Hill/Alamy
Fifteen Restaurant, Watergate Bay © West Country/Alamy

Black and whites
p.296 Bishop Rock Lighthouse © Tim Cuff/Alamy
p.306 Seals on Scilly © Stephen Bond/Alamy

Index

Map entries are in colour.

D

E

F

Q

R

S

T

V

W

Y

Z

Map symbols

maps are listed in the full index using coloured text

Chapter division boundary	Lighthouse
County boundary	Viewpoint
Motorway	Ruin/archeological site
Main road	Stately home
Minor road	Castle
Footpath	Fortress
Steps	Abbey
Pedestrianized street	Museum
Ferry route	Vineyard
Railway	Gardens
River	Tourist office
Boat	Post office
Bridge/tunnel	Internet access
Wall	Hospital
Airport	Parking
Point of interest	Church (regional maps)
Cave	Church (town maps)
Waterfall	Building
Mountain peak	Park/National Park/forest
Rocks/cliffs	Beach